robert c. beck
*WAKE FOREST UNIVERSITY*

# MOTIVATION
## Theories
## and
## Principles

**Prentice-Hall, Inc.,** Englewood Cliffs, New Jersey 07632

*Library of Congress Cataloging in Publication Data*

BECK, ROBERT CLARENCE,
  Motivation.

  Bibliography: p.
  Includes index.
  1. Motivation (Psychology) I. Title.
BF683.B35    153.8    77-11673
ISBN 0-13-603902-2

This book is dedicated to my mother,
**Lena Beck Harding,**
whose faith in education
has always been unswerving.

© 1978 by Prentice-Hall, Inc.
Englewood Cliffs, New Jersey 07632

Printed in the United States of America

10   9   8   7   6   5   4   3

Cover Design: Joel S. Beck

PRENTICE-HALL, INC., *London*
PRENTICE-HALL OF AUSTRALIA PTY. LIMITED, *Sydney*
PRENTICE-HALL OF CANADA, LTD., *Toronto*
PRENTICE-HALL OF INDIA PRIVATE LIMITED, *New Delhi*
PRENTICE-HALL OF JAPAN, INC., *Tokyo*
PRENTICE-HALL OF SOUTHEAST ASIA PTE. LTD., *Singapore*
WHITEHALL BOOKS LIMITED, *Wellington, New Zealand*

# Contents

# 3

## SPECIES SPECIFIC BEHAVIOR    44

# 4

## THE CONCEPT OF DRIVE    72

# 5

## ACTIVATION AND AROUSAL    103

# 6

## REWARDS: 1. THEORIES OF REINFORCEMENT    123

# 7

## REWARDS: 2. INCENTIVE MOTIVATION 147

# 8

## AVERSIVE STIMULATION: 1. ESCAPE LEARNING, FEAR CONDITIONING, AND FRUSTRATION 177

# 9

## AVERSIVE STIMULATION: 2. AVOIDANCE CONDITIONING AND PUNISHMENT 203

# 10

## CONSISTENCY AND CHANGE 232

## 15

### PHYSIOLOGY OF SOME CONSUMMATORY BEHAVIORS 375

## 16

### EPILOGUE 416

# Preface

My intent in this volume is to survey basic motivational concepts so they will be understandable to students regardless of the students' (or their instructors') particular orientation (e.g. physiological or social). I have tried to provide fair representations of many different areas of motivational research and to relate these to each other where possible. No one can be expert in all of these and I have depended on friends and anonymous reviews to help keep me from straying too far down interesting, but distracting or erroneous, side paths. Any remaining defects, of course, are my errors, not theirs.

It is not really possible to maintain a tight, completely logical and consistent conceptualization of motivation without sacrificing a large amount of material to the Procrustean bed of conformity. It has seemed didactically useful, as well as congenial to my own way of thinking, to intertwine human and animal research without apology for either. The experimental and illustrative details of animal and human research differ but the theoretical problems have much in common. For example, the concept of drive is supposed to be an animal problem and is often considered passe. Nevertheless, the concept appears and reappears in social-personality theories in almost axiomatic form, with little consideration of the logical and empirical dispute surrounding the concept at the animal level.

The chapter organization is a relatively straightforward progression. The earlier chapters deal relatively more with animal research, but each of these chapters has extensive data or illustrations for both humans and other animals. The later chapters, whose concepts rely greatly on verbal behavior, are obviously more restricted to humans. Chapter 15 (physiological mechanisms) is out of sequence for practical reasons. The instructor with a strong biological orientation may wish to assign it much earlier. The instructor not inclined toward this kind of detail can omit Ch. 15, but still illustrate the biological perspective through chs. 3, 4, and 5.

A book preface is also a place to pay off one's intellectual debts. My own conceptions of motivation certainly did not spring from the sea full-blown. They were molded, transformed and refined by countless teachers, colleagues, and students, as well as investigators and authors whom I have never met. There is a countable number of individuals to whom I would particularly like to express my appreciation, however. Four of these are friends and former professors to whom I owe my greatest intellectual debts: G. R. Grice, L. I. O'Kelly, O. H. Mowrer and P. T. Young (in alphabetical order.) Their very different approaches to motivation are a testimonial to the futility of conceiving motivation within any narrow framework. Perhaps none of them will like what follows, but they are not completely blameless. In addition, two colleagues from my graduate student days, D. J. Mason and J. A. Dyal, provided me stimulation and insights at a critical time.

Truly countless are the students who suffered with goodwill through earlier Xeroxed versions of the present material. With each successive draft their patience became more obvious to me.

A number of colleagues were generous in reading portions of the manuscript critically, adding ideas and support. These are Rosemarie Anderson, Liane Bidwell, Linda Dudley, Phillipe Falkenberg, Charles Richman, Kendon Smith, and Peter Weigl. Appreciation is also due Professors Irwin Badin, Ronald Baenninger, Lowell Crow, Joel Raynor and Dominic Valentino for their many helpful comments and suggestions about the manuscript. A number of anonymous reviewers also provided valuable comments.

The exhuberance, as well as expertise, of Ms. Jane Reade in typing much of the manuscript is gratefully acknowledged, as is the careful work of Steve Briggs in reading and rereading copy, checking and cataloging references, and generally being my man Friday. Martha Lentz expertly read galleys. Wake Forest University provided a Semester research leave during which time I was able to collect many of my thoughts and the Department of Psychology in the person of John Williams has arranged teaching schedules optimal for sustained effort. Appreciation is expressed to Joel S. Beck for the cover design. Finally, my wife and children were most gracious in their support of my efforts and in not burdening me with guilt for being at the office so much.

ROBERT C. BECK

chapter

# The Nature of
# Motivation Theory

On August 1, 1966, Charles Whitman, twenty-five years of age, climbed to the observation deck of the Tower Building at the University of Texas. In two hours, he killed fourteen people and wounded twenty-four others before he himself was slain by the police. The question raised for all of psychology, and especially for motivation theory, is *why?* By any common meaning of the term, Whitman was not rational, even though his actions seemed carefully planned. There were numerous interesting little twists in the accounts that followed.[1] Many people thought him a fine young man. He liked children, worked hard, and had been an Eagle Scout at the age of twelve. He was humorous and most of his friends and acquaintances seemed to regard him highly. But there were ominous undercurrents.

Although his father, a relatively uneducated and self-made man, had done well financially as a plumbing contractor, Charles went from high school into the Marine Corps rather than college. He apparently served well and went to the University of Texas as part of preparation for a Marine Corps commission. But there he ran into difficulties, including poor grades, and was dropped from the program. He continued on in architectural engineering. One of his closest friends said that Whitman was always very tense, especially before an exam. He had also beaten his wife on at least two occasions.

On Sunday night, July 31, 1966, this friend and his wife visited Whitman, who was to have a summer school exam the next day. He seemed unusually relaxed. By that time he had already slain his wife, made plans to murder his mother, and had completed preparations for moving his arsenal to the observation deck of the Texas Tower the next morning. Having a foreboding that something terrible was going to happen, he had seen a psychiatrist about a month before but had not returned for a second visit. In various notes left behind, he described a deep hatred toward his father, even though it was his mother he killed—to save her from embarrassment, he said. He also left a written request that his brain be autopsied. And, indeed, a tumor the size of a walnut was found in the amygdaloid area of his brain.

In this brief account, we see many possibilities for explaining Charles Whitman's two-hour spree. He apparently had a very high level of need for achievement, particularly to surpass his father. There was the frustration of not doing as well as he had hoped in school. There was the continued stress of overwork; he carried heavy academic loads and part-time jobs. There was his family's abiding interest in guns, which reporters saw in every room of his parents' home after the incident. Finally, there is possibly a straight biological interpretation: The tumor was located in an area well known to be implicated in aggressive behavior. Any or all of these factors,

[1] I am indebted to Dr. James Steintrager, who was on the Texas campus that day, for a detailed description of the unfolding events and for local newspaper accounts.

as well as others not considered here, might have led to the final tragic outcome. We cannot really know the answer to this particular drama, because the central character is gone. This much we do know: The answer is not simple. But it is the kind of mystery psychologists are supposed to help unravel. Its very irrationality is what seems to demand a "motivational" account.

We cannot, of course, sustain the intense macabre drama of a Charles Whitman story for the duration of a textbook, for that is not the way science progresses. We have to go into the more mundane and prosaic world of the laboratory, where progress is measured in inches, not miles. There are numerous motivational concepts of which the reader will have undoubtedly heard before: instinct, need, drive, goal, incentive, conflict, libido, will to power, frustration, and aggression. We shall have to look at many such ideas critically, becoming more and more wary of the too-easy answer or the too-quick solution. However, we may hope to gain some insight into what motivation theory has to offer and where it may fall short; which concepts are useful and which are chaff.

The very proliferation of concepts has lead some psychologists to argue that a general concept of "motivation" is too vague to be useful. B. F. Skinner, certainly one of the most noted psychologists of our time, holds such an opinion, as do other respected theoreticians. Nevertheless, the motivational idea lingers on, continually fed by the kinds of questions it is supposed to answer: Why do children steal? Why do people take drugs? Why don't kids do better in school? How can we get people more interested in their work? Why do we have wars and killings? Why do people create? No one can deny the importance of such problems or that they seem to involve motivation.

In this chapter, we first want to see what a kind of commonsense psychology has to say about behavior. Then we turn to the scientific requirements for developing theoretical concepts in psychology, ideas that can be applied with some rigor and can be tested. Two particular problems have to be faced first: the relationship between our minds and our behaviors (bodies) and the question of how free we are to do as we choose.

## A LAYMAN'S VIEW OF MOTIVATION

For the man on the street (mythical though he may be), the relationship of mind to body is probably clear. The "official doctrine" (Ryle, 1949) is that "body" is physical, material, limited in space, time, and size, and objectively observable. "Mind," on the other hand, is just the opposite of all these qualities. It is subjective, directly known only to the individual possessing it, unlimited in physical dimensions, and is, perhaps, everlasting.

This distinction is essentially the same doctrine generally accepted in Western theology to maintain the separation of "body" and "soul." It goes back to the Greek philosopher Plato, but in its more modern philosophical form it is generally attributed to the French philosopher René Descartes.

As the man on the street might view it, then, he is aware of his circumstances and his own feelings and ideas. Faced with several possible actions, he consciously and freely *wills* himself to do this or that. This brief statement, however, is based on the assumptions that Descartes was correct in his view of mind and body and that we really are free to make any choice we wish. Since psychologists generally look at both these matters quite differently, we need to examine these assumptions more closely.

## THE MIND-BODY PROBLEM

There are two general classes of opinion regarding mind and body. The *dualisms* assume that mind and body are qualitatively different. The *monisms* assume that the mind and body really are qualitatively the same.

### Dualisms

***Interactionistic Dualism.*** This is the view held by Descartes, commonly called *Cartesian dualism.* Mind and body are considered qualitatively different categories, immaterial and material, and what the body does depends on the mind. That is, there is a causal relation. Where and how do the two interact, however? Descartes ([1650] 1892) suggested the pineal gland in the brain as the point of interaction and developed a physical model based on reflected light rays to incorporate this idea. He proposed that light energy comes into the eyes and activates "spirits" that are reflected one way or another by the pineal gland, which he saw as something like a pivoting mirror. Depending on where the spirits were reflected, different movements of the body occurred. The term *reflex,* referring to an automatic movement following a particular stimulus (such as a knee jerk when the patellar tendon is struck), comes from Descartes' description of the "reflection of spirits." We would now call these "spirits" *neural impulses.* Animal behavior consisted entirely of reflexes; humans were said to have reflexes, but the human mind could will various behaviors as well.

The logical problems with such a theory seem insurmountable to scientists. If our minds and bodies really are so unlike each other, how could they conceivably interact? At a purely factual level we know, of course, that the pineal gland serves no such function as Descartes speculated. Other philosophers, as well as scientists, have therefore sometimes held to a different kind of dualism.

*Parallelistic Dualism.* Suppose we set two atomic clocks to exactly the same time, then leave them to run out their separate existences. Whenever we look at one clock we will be able to tell what the other says. The German philosopher Gottfried Wilhelm Leibnitz (Duncan, 1890) proposed such a view of mind and body. Just as one clock does not cause the other to tell a particular time, so the mind does not cause the body to do a particular thing. In either case, however, there is a high correlation between the two events in question. This view recognizes the obvious existence of mental life, as well as the body, and the correlation between experience and behavior, but does not raise the problem of how they could interact.

Parallelism may indeed sidestep the whole question of the ultimate natures of mind and body and simply make a practical distinction between them. Many people believe that the *methods* for studying mental activity (such as recording what people *say* about their experiences) are sufficiently different from the methods of studying bodily action that the mind-body distinction is worth maintaining for this reason alone. "Mental" and "bodily" events can be considered to "run in parallel" without necessarily arguing that in some ultimate, unknowable sense they are really different.

### Monisms

*Mentalistic monism.* Consider this question: How do we *know* about the existence of a world outside our own minds? The answer seems simple: We know about it through our consciousness of it, through our minds. But if our awareness is really and truly private experience, known directly only to ourselves, do we *need* to assume the existence of anything other than our minds? What proof could we offer that things exist outside our minds? After all, our dreams in all their terror or sensuousness *seem* real at the time, but we know they are not "real." Neither are hallucinations. Mentalistic monism, then, is the view that we do not *have* to postulate any external world if our only knowledge of it is our experience. This was proposed by the British philosopher Bishop George Berkeley ([1710]) 1939).

This view may sound preposterous, but another British philosopher, David Hume ([1739] 1939) proposed one even more extreme, called *solipsism.* Hume's logical extension of Berkeley is the *possibility* that there is but a single mind and that any other apparent minds are but the experience of this mind, just as apparent objects are the experience of this mind. There are no physical objects, no bodies, no other minds. The logic is unassailable. Now, someone may cry, "Why do thorns pain me unless thorns exist?" The two-part answer is straightforward. First, the existence of thorns has first to be *assumed* in order to answer the question. The assumption was *built into* the question. The solipsistic argument assumes the opposite, that such things do *not* exist. The burden of proof falls on "you" to show that they *do* exist as separate entities. Second, if the experience of pain accompanies the experience of thorns, that is just the way experiences are. "But," may come another cry, "if there is but one mind, surely it would not produce pain for itself." This is irrelevant. I do not pick and choose experiences, they just *happen*. And, finally, the objections to my argument do not exist outside my own mind. There is no "you." The mind-body problem disappears, since there is only the mind. Stepping outside the whole argument, however, the argument has a practical implication, which has to do with the nature of causality. We shall return to this later.

**Materialistic Monism.** According to the materialistic monist view, the single underlying reality is *material*. The mind represents the functioning of the brain. Let us use the analogy of a dump truck. The truck moves about, picks up and drops things, generally acting the way a dump truck should. We do not, however, talk about these *functions* of the truck *causing* the truck to behave in its ordained manner, or existing separately from the truck. From this view, the body is so constructed that one of its functions is consciousness, but this function does not in itself cause behaviors to occur.

The *neural identity theory* (e.g., Pepper, 1959) says that a single reality can be viewed in different ways, however, as we view the two sides of a coin. As Pepper (1959, p. 52) puts it, the physiologist's description of the brain and the introspectionist's report of *his* own experience are both *symbolic statements about the same thing*. There is a correlation between the two reports because they are about the same thing. The physiologist and the introspectionist are both describing the activity of the brain, but from different points of view and with different languages.

Every conscious mental event, then, has a corresponding brain event, although the converse is not true. We are not aware of the neural activities that control breathing, for example. Many neural processes involved in motivation, emotion, and memory may influence our behavior even though we are not aware of them at the time. Such "unconscious" influences, of course, were crucial in Freud's theories and the development of psychoanalysis. Neural processes of which we are aware *may* be particularly important for certain kinds of activities, such as learning, but this is an empirical question, to be resolved by research rather than by speculation.

The close identity of experience and brain function has more and more been indicated in neurophysiological research in the past few years. For example, some individual neurons in the visual brain are responsive only to lines with a particular orientation—vertical or horizontal—but not to lines of both orientations. Other neurons are responsive only to moving stimuli, not stationary ones. Such relationships are found in frogs, cats, and monkeys. It is reasonable to assume they exist in man.

Perhaps the most dramatic evidence of a mind-brain identity in man is the fact that if the two hemispheres of the brain are surgically separated there are now two independent minds where before there was one. Each half of the brain is now an independent unit and things learned in one half are unknown to the other half (e.g., Gazzaniga, 1967). Reason or logic would have never predicted that splitting the brain into two hemispheres would have produced two minds. The early philosophical arguments about mind-brain dichotomies severely underestimated the complexity of the mammalian brain, not to speak of the complexity of matter itself. Such research has yielded a rough, stick-man sort of drawing of brain function, but new data continually unfold new complexities.

One final point. By the very nature and definition of science, we must deal with observable events. For psychology, these observable events are *behaviors,* body activities ranging from filling out attitude surveys to describing drug experiences to throwing baseballs. The question is whether we need to infer something behind these behaviors that is *qualitatively* different from the nervous system. The answer would seem to be no. This is not to say that all of experience is expressed in behavior or that behavior tells us everything about a person. It simply says that, from the point of view of science, mind is a kind of logical construction inferred from behavior. Hardly anyone would question the fact of his own consciousness. The *immediate experience* of consciousness is not *public data,* open to other observers, however, and only such public data are scientifically useful. But experiences can be publicly *communicated,* and this communication itself constitutes behavior which can be used to infer consciousness.

In summary, the popular view that mind and body are different and that mind controls body is but one of several logical possibilities. The view that we hold may have important practical consequences—in the way we treat "mental" disorders, for example. But how are we to know which one is correct? The answer is that there is no way to know. It is a puzzle to meditate on.


## FREEDOM AND DETERMINISM

All of us like to feel that we are free to act as we choose. An unkept resolution is the failure of our will in keeping it. Freedom and will are among our most precious intellectual commodities, as attested by the cries of outrage against Skinner's *Beyond Freedom and Dignity* (1971). From a scientific point of view, however, such freedom poses a problem, for if we can do anything we wish at any time, then how can we predict behavior? Furthermore, if we could not predict the behavior of others, social chaos would arise. Not knowing how others would respond, we would be at a loss as to how to act toward other people. But we do manage to make pretty good guesses about other people's behavior, and society does manage to stay more or less glued together. Indeed, if someone behaves in completely unpredictable ways, do we not usually say he is "crazy"?

Society at large deals with the question of freedom inconsistently. For example, a man may be imprisoned because he chose to commit a crime. But if we assume he will always have such freedom of choice, then punishment should not deter him from future crimes. Imprisonment, or a fine, then is merely retribution, an eye for an eye. Punishment only makes sense if we expect it to determine future behavior. The argument that punishing one person sets an example for others is no different; it also assumes that the example will determine the behavior of others.

Because of such inconsistencies in the free-will argument, as well as of the impossibility of having a science of behavior without assuming determinism, determinism has been widely accepted. It is easy to understand the argument that if one science depends on determinism, then others must also. The meaning of determinism is reasonably simple: If Cause A occurs, then Effect B will follow. If I suddenly produce a loud sound behind you, you will jump. If I am hungry, I will go to the refrigerator. If I am driving down the street and the traffic signal facing me is green, I can pretty well predict that no one is going to dart into the intersection from a side street. Occasionally, of course, the prediction is wrong, but it is such relatively rare exceptions that make headlines, not the millions of times when the prediction is correct. In the laboratory, we can repeatedly do experiments with human subjects and obtain the same results under the same conditions.

Behavior, however, is affected by many conditions (variables), and to the extent that we do not know what conditions are prevailing at a given time, we will predict with greater or less accuracy. We should rightfully be unwilling to predict the behavior of a man at a party for the same reason that a physicist would balk at predicting the behavior of a handful of confetti thrown at that party. In neither case are all the conditions bearing on the outcome known.

Finding those variables that influence behavior is fundamental to any science. It is doubly difficult in psychology, however, because the variables are not only observable external events; they are also internal events not open to direct observation. The "impressions" of past experiences are obviously important, but we can never recall all our own past experiences, much less know those of other people. Ebbinghaus ([1885] 1964) invented nonsense syllables, meaningless conglomerates of letters, just so that he would have novel materials to learn and thereby neutralize the effects of past experience on learning. Similarly, we commonly use animals for research because their lives can be better controlled in the laboratory than those of humans.

What we often mean by freedom, then, is *lack of predictability* by an outside observer. Within this framework, freedom is perceived according to the locus of the determinants of behavior. If a particular behavior is mainly controlled by external events, we say it is *determined*; if the behavior is primarily controlled by internal events, we would consider it to be *free.* Interestingly, people perceive these categories differently in themselves and others. We tend to put the causes of behavior *inside other people,* but *outside ourselves* (particularly if things do not work out right).

### Hard, Soft, and Probabilistic Determinism

If we knew enough, perhaps we could predict the behavior of an individual person with mathematical precision. This is an untestable hypothesis, however, since we are never privy to such information. The precise prediction required by *hard determinism* may be correct in some ultimate sense, but only as an ideal.

A different view, called *soft determinism,* is that some behaviors are determined, while others are not. This is perhaps the worst solution to the problem because it provides no grounds for distinguishing between freedom and all the other possible reasons for inaccurate prediction. If I conduct an experiment and my prediction fails, it may be that I am simply a crude experimenter and someone else might have been successful. Soft determinism provides no rules for saying whether a failed prediction means freedom or ignorance of relevant variables that tomorrow we might understand.

We would not, then, expect to have perfect predictions of behavior, but, like insurance companies, we would predict on an actuarial basis. This is *probabilistic determinism* (e.g., Vorsteg, 1974). We could say that under given conditions there is a high probability that a person will perform in a certain way and if most people do perform that way, then we predicted successfully. We have powerful statistical techniques to help us in such probabilistic situations. Science is notoriously pragmatic—prediction with measurable error is better than no prediction at all. Probabilistic prediction is no denial of determinism; it is simply a realistic recognition of the fallibility of science and scientists.

### Electrons and Behavior

Strangely, developments in quantum physics have been taken as support for free will in humans. When electrons are fired singly at a photographic film under standard conditions, it is impossible to predict exactly where a particular electron will land. We know it will land on the film but classical Newtonian physics leads us to believe we should be able to make a more precise statement. The argument for free will is this: If physicists have found freedom at the level of electrons, surely people must be free to behave as they choose. There are two answers to this. First, the failure to predict does not necessarily imply lack of determinism, either for humans or for subatomic particles. Secondly, ignoring the fact that extrapolations from electrons to human behavior are unwarranted under any circumstances, we have found that the *pattern* produced on the film by *many* electrons *is* predictable. And, with changes in details of the experiment, it is possible to obtain a variety of equally predictable patterns. In brief, when we deal with large numbers of electrons, we find good predictability; and the very least we could say about complex organisms, including man, is that they contain very large numbers of electrons.

The question of *social* freedom or control is not the issue here. Belief in freedom does not change the laws of behavior and belief in determinism does not imply any particular social control. We cannot make behavior lawful if lawfulness does not exist and we cannot make behavior free if it is determined. The question of social control is simply a different problem than we are considering here. A *belief* in freedom, however, may determine behavior in different ways than belief in determinism. For example, political leaders who believe in determinism might exert different external controls over individuals than if they believed in freedom. Freedom of the individual from external constraints (especially from governments) has been the foundation of American government—in theory, if not always in practice. In many ways, this is salutary, for no one wants highly restrictive external controls over his behavior. (Indeed, the aversiveness of such controls may form a basis for a belief in freedom.) At the same time, we must recognize that anyone asking for improvements in education, cures for mental illness, or reduction of antisocial behavior is asking "What can we do to produce these ends?" Like it or not, these very questions assume an underlying determinism and potential understanding of the causes of behavior.

## PHILOSOPHY AND LANGUAGE OF SCIENCE

The problem we want to deal with now is this: If I try to give a scientific account of behavior (for example, Charles Whitman's), how can I accurately communicate to you what I mean? Will the words mean the same thing to you that they do to me? Will they produce an explanation that at least has the possibility of being substantiated by carefully gathered evidence? Or will my words be devoid of any meaning except that which you yourself provide?

If we simply wanted an emotional or poetic *description* of behavior or thought, we could use "poetic license" to produce the desired effect, without concern for detailed accuracy. If we wanted a chronology of events such as preceded the Whitman killings, we would have to be historically precise in our language. If we wanted to be scientifically accurate, we would have to be more mathematically and logically precise. Even the language of science, especially that of psychology, is far from perfect, however. The philosopher Charles Morris (1938) has provided us with a guide for better understanding scientific language. He calls his system *semiotic* and the two subareas of it we will deal with here are *syntactics* (the relations of different signs to each other) and *semantics* (the relations of signs to the objects to which they refer).

### Syntactics

As children, we all go through the laborious process of learning to put words together to form "good" sentences and to make grammatically correct utterances. Such correct sentences follow the *rules* of the language. Articles go before nouns, adverbs precede adjectives, and so on. These are the formal rules for manipulating *signs* (words), the way signs are related to each other. The term *syntactics* simply refers to such formal rules.

There are more precise languages than our mother tongue, logic and mathematics being the most precise of all. Each of these has very formal rules for relating signs to each other (which come at the sacrifice of poetic license). Consider the following example: $M = \Sigma X/N$. By the basic rules of arithmetic and algebra, we can manipulate these symbols in various ways. For example, $NM = \Sigma X$ or $N = \Sigma X/M$. We can move the signs around into different combinations even if the signs do not actually refer to anything. As any psychology student would recognize, the initial statement is the formula for the arithmetic mean, in which $M$ equals the mean, $\Sigma X$ is the sum of all the individual scores counted and $N$ is the number of scores.

The mathematical manipulation of the symbols in no way depends on the symbols meaning these things, however. All that has been said is that $M = \Sigma X/N$ and all that is required to manipulate the symbols as we did is to know the meanings of the equality sign, the summation sign and the division sign.

As another example, consider the syllogism:

> Blondes have more fun.
> Racquel is a blonde.
> *Therefore:* Racquel has more fun.

Now, we can determine the *validity,* but not the *truth,* of the conclusion that "Racquel has more fun" by *logically* analyzing the two premises and the conclusion. If these are in proper form, as described in any introductory logic book, the conclusion is valid, which means that the conclusion follows from the premises according to some set of rules. In order for the conclusion to be true, however, both of the premises would have to be true *in fact,* as well as being logically sound. If all blondes *do* have more fun and if there is a Racquel who *is* a blonde, then the conclusion that Racquel has more fun is both valid and true. (We will ignore the question, "more fun than whom?") We might arrive at a *true* conclusion without any logic—by a lucky guess or by knowing Racquel, for example.

The syllogism, as well as the more sophisticated forms of symbolic logic, is important because the validity of an argument can be determined in symbolic form, separately from the specific content of the argument. The content may actually obscure the argument. The name *Racquel* might produce visual imagery that would suggest the conclusion was true regardless of the logic. But to take a less illustrious example:

> Hippie freaks wear long hair and crazy clothes.
> Bobby wears long hair and crazy clothes.
> *Therefore:* Bobby is a hippie freak.

The conclusion, of course, does not follow from the premises; Bobby might be a circus clown. Because the factual details are close to emotionally charged issues, however, logical subtleties may be lost. Putting the argument into completely symbolic form, substituting the letters A, B, and C for the words "hippie freak," "wears long hair and crazy clothes," and "Bobby" would remove the emotional aspects and allow a purely syntactical conclusion. Not as exciting to do, but we might more accurately evaluate the argument:

> All A are B.
> C is a B.
> *Therefore:* C is an A.

The conclusion is clearly wrong: C might or might not be A, because there may be some Bs that are not A. Put briefly, then, syntactics is concerned with the establishment and use of agreed-on rules by which we can relate signs (symbols or words) to each other so that there is no ambiguity about what we are doing.

### Semantics

The term *semantics* refers to the conditions or rules by which we may assign a symbol to an object or event. This is a problem in definition. The simplest definition is the *ostensive,* or pointing, definition—for example, saying "That is what I mean by a *dog,*" while pointing to a dog. All definitions eventually have to appeal to sense observations. We can read from the dictionary that a "dog" is (hypothetically) "a four-legged animal that barks and is commonly used as a house pet," but we have the prior problem of knowing what is meant by "four," "legged," "animal," "barks," and so on. The individual reading the definition must have had some prior knowledge of these more *primitive terms*, based on observation, before the definition makes sense. We usually assume that everybody knows what we mean by color names, simple numbers, and so on, and go from there to build more complex definitions via language.

*Operational Definitions.* P. W. Bridgman (1927) argued that we define the *meaning* of something in terms of how we measure it. The procedures for *measuring* length are what we mean by the term *length*. "In general," he says, "we mean by any concept nothing more than a set of operations; the concept is synonymous with the corresponding set of [measurement] operations" (Bridgman, 1927, p. 5).

Bridgman examines such physical concepts as space, time, and causality in terms of their measurement. His point is that without measurement procedures such concepts are *empirically* meaningless words not related to the "real world." Length, for example, can be measured by laying down a standard rod repeatedly and counting the number of times it takes to go from one end of an object to the other. This gives us a common definition and meaning for "length." But what about situations where we want to deal with something called *length* but cannot perform this operation? What about the diameter of the sun? The distance of the stars? The diameter of an atom? The length of any object (e.g., a photon) that we might measure only when it is in high-speed motion? The Einsteinian revolution produced surprises, says Bridgman, only because we had come to believe that the measurement procedures in physics were the *only* procedures and because those procedures gave us definitions of physical concepts dependent on those measures. When we use new measurement procedures, we may be led to changes in fundamental concepts, either in physics or in psychology.

*Operationism and Psychological Concepts.* Stevens (1939) and Underwood (1957) have nicely discussed the problem for psychology. Consider intelligence. There is a saying that "intelligence is what intelligence tests measure." In a trivial sense, this remark denies any understanding of intelligence. Operationally, however, it means that intelligence is to be understood in terms of the measurement operations, and this is correct. If we define intelligence in terms of such hypothetical properties as "problem-solving ability," we do little to understand it and nothing to measure it. If we set up a series of problems, however, and measure the ability to solve them, we have taken a step in the right direction. Alfred Binet did just this. He defined mental age in terms of successfully completing various tasks. The concept of intelligence quotient: $IQ = MA/CA$, gives a *series* of operations by which to define the concept. We define mental age (MA) and chronological age (CA) and divide to get IQ.[2]

Do different operations *necessarily* define different concepts? For example, do two intelligence tests with different tasks define different concepts? Not necessarily. All we need is a set of operations for combining operations (Stevens, 1939). If we found a correlation (statistical operation) of 1.00 between two tests, we would conclude that they were measuring the same thing.

*Converging Operations.* Garner, Hake, and Eriksen (1956) pointed out that a *single* set of operations never really isolates just one concept. Rather, by a series of different operations, we *converge* on a concept. For example, if emotion-arousing stimuli have higher tachistoscopic thresholds than neutral stimuli, we might conclude that the effect of the emotional stimuli was on *perception*. Rather complicated psychological explanations have been used to account for such results. The effect, on the other hand, might be caused by *response bias.* Thus, in the so-called dirty word experiments, a college coed might hesitate to say the word *bitch* flashed at her in the psychological laboratory unless absolutely certain of what she saw (remember, these were the 1950s). Other experiments, involving other operations, pinpoint the proper concept, perception or response bias, to explain the results. Thus, Postman, Bronson, and Gropper (1953) told different groups of subjects that it was a sign of good or poor mental health to recognize such words readily. As expected, the former group was quicker to "recognize" the words and the latter group was slower than a group given no instructions. These experimental operations converge on the response bias concept rather than on a perceptual explanation. The principle of converging operations is found in many experimental designs used to isolate learning effects from motivational effects.

*A Loosening of Operationism.* An operationally defined concept is not necessarily useful (it may not relate to anything) and, conversely, a concept not fully defined may still be useful. Most theorists have backed off from the notion of highly restrictive operationism, but the problem needs to be considered at two levels: as a concept is used in research and as a concept is used in theory. In a specific experiment, for example, if we talk about "hunger" affecting some behavior, we have to define in exact operational terms what we mean by hunger (such as hours of food deprivation

---

[2]Binet himself did not use the concept of IQ. This was a later development. Binet worked out the problem of measuring mental age, on which IQ is then based (Goodenough, 1949, p. 63).

prior to the experimental test). Within a broader theoretical context, however, we might find it useful to theorize about hunger under conditions not yet operationally manipulated. We should be clear to ourselves when we are so speculating.

## SCIENTIFIC THEORY

### Nature of Scientific Theory

A scientific theory is like a model. A model airplane is not exactly like a real airplane but it contains the main features. Similarly, a scientific theory does not represent all the world but only the parts of concern to us. We can use the word *model* in a broad sense, referring to an actual physical model, or a set of diagrams, or a set of mathematical equations.

Toulmin (1953) likened a scientific theory to a map, the map being a kind of model. There is a domain of reality, such as the geographical terrain, which can be described by a map, but only imperfectly. The map also includes lines for longitude and latitude that, although useful, are not found on the terrain itself. As part of the map, they do not have to have an actual correspondence to reality to be good or useful. Furthermore, we may have an entire set of maps for the same geographic area. Every city has maps for sewer lines, power lines, water lines, streets, topography, and population density. Which one is the *real* city? None of them is the "real" city, but each is a model, or theory, for particular events. None is a perfect representation, but each is useful for its purpose. No scientific theory encompasses everything, but most are useful for some kind of events.

In a theory, observable events are summarized and "mapped" into theoretical terms. Concepts are defined in terms of particular observable events (semantics) and the theory states how the concepts are related to each other (syntactics). Predictions are made on the basis of this syntax. The rules are generally in standard mathematical or logical form. For example, in Figure 1.1, *A, B,* and *C* are theoretical concepts defined by specific experimental control procedures *a, b,* and *c*. That is, operations *a, b,* and *c* provide us with the definition of concepts *A, B,* and *C*. Concept *D*, however, is defined by the syntax of the theory: $D = (A \times B) + C$. If we know the values for *A, B,* and *C* (which are the *independent* variables in the experimental situation), then we can predict the value for *D*, which is measured as the *dependent* variable in the situation. If we hold *A* and *B* constant, systematically changing the value of *C*, the measured outcome should tell us how *C* affects the dependent variable. If the theory does not predict accurately, we will change its syntax, add new concepts, or eliminate old ones, and so on. We may have to scrap the theory if it never works right.

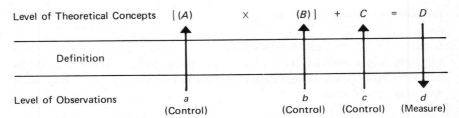

**Figure 1.1** *Relationships of observations, definitions and theoretical concepts. The concepts are syntactically related in the theory, as shown at the top. At the level of observations certain events are controlled and related by definition to the concepts in the theory. If the relevant observed events are properly controlled, then the syntax of the theory predicts a particular outcome which is observed and measured (d). See text for details.*

As a more specific example, Hull (1943) proposed that learning multiplied with motivation to determine performance. He symbolized learning as $H$ (for habit), motivation as $D$ (for drive) and performance potential as $E$ (for excitatory potential). His theoretical statement then was: Excitatory Potential = Habit × Drive, or

$$E = H \times D$$

Defining $H$ operationally in terms of number of previous learning trials, $D$ as hours of food deprivation, and $E$ as $H \times D$, we have Figure 1.2, a more specific illustration of the principles embodied in Figure 1.1.

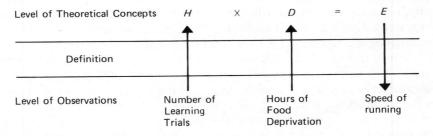

**Figure 1.2** *Relationships of observations, definitions, and theoretical concepts in Hull's (1943) theory of behavior. H and D are defined by controlling amount of learning and amount of deprivation, and E is measured by speed of running. See text for further details. The theory is discussed at length in Chapter 4.*

We can then predict a variety of experimental outcomes. For example, running speed depends on the multiplication of habit and drive. If a particular response has not been learned ($H = 0$), or if there is no drive ($D = 0$), then $E = 0$ and there would be no performance of the response in question. The multiplicative hypothesis leads to different predictions than if the syntax were, say, $H + D$ or $H - D$, or $H/D$.

Exact prediction requires exact numerical values for the concepts, but in psychological research we seldom have the required precision. Therefore, we usually deal with inequalities. We can say that two hours of food deprivation produces less drive than twenty-two hours, but we cannot say exactly how much less. Performance should be "better" (e.g., faster running to food) with twenty-two hours than with two hours of deprivation, but we cannot give exact running speeds. The sheer number of relevant variables complicates the prediction process for most behaviors.

***Cosmologies and Models.*** Theories encompassing great ranges of events were once the ideal of the sciences, but theories are typically now much more modest. The term *model* itself implies something on a small scale. In place of such comprehensive theories as Hull's, which were thought to account for all of behavior, we tend now to have theories specific to particular subareas (such as human verbal learning) or even subproblems of these (such as one-trial verbal learning). The more data there are to be accounted for, the greater the demand on a theory and hence a tendency to deal with fewer phenomena in a theory.

### Criteria for Goodness of a Theory

***Testability.*** The most important characteristic of a good theory is that it can be shown to be wrong (Popper, 1959). Its predictions are specific enough to be "risky." That is, some other outcome than the predicted outcome will *disconfirm* (or *falsify*) the theory. It is difficult to *confirm* a theory by specific experiment, because the same evidence will probably confirm more than one theory. Evidence that *disconfirms* one theory is not likely to simultaneously disconfirm a rival theory, however. A theory that cannot be falsified is not a good theory, because there is no test for it.

***Fruitfulness.*** A theory which generates research starts off a multiplier effect, so that in the long run there is more knowledge gained than from just the initial attempts to test the theory. Hull's (1943) theory generated so much research that it was itself defeated. Such built-in obsolescence is characteristic of a good falsifiable theory. As Conant (1947) has shown, however, falsification alone is not enough to overthrow a theory; another has to be there to replace it.

***Simplicity.*** If there are two explanations for an event, the simpler of the two is preferable. This principle of *parsimony* is commonly called "Occam's razor" or, in comparative psychology, "Lloyd Morgan's Canon" (do not attribute a complex mental process to an animal if a simpler one will do). The term *simplicity* may refer to the number of concepts in a theory or to the complexity of the relationships between them.

*Comprehensiveness.* The better theory is the one that explains the greater number of observations. Einstein's theory was more complicated than Newton's, but Einstein's theory also explained far more. A less comprehensive theory may be better for some situations, however. We would not use Einstein's theory to build a bridge or work out rifle trajectories.

## OBJECTIVITY, EXPLANATION, AND CAUSATION

### Objectivity: Intersubjective Reliability

We may think of *objectivity* as involving "perfect" observation, free from bias on the part of the experimenter. Less than perfect observations are "subjective" and hence "nonscientific." All observations are subject to some kind of error, however; *objective* and *subjective* are then relative terms, not absolute. We try to keep errors to a minimum by recognizing that they may occur and using techniques that tend to be relatively error free (e.g., counters or timers). We also try to measure errors which do occur, so that we will know what we are dealing with.

Amount of error can be estimated by taking repeated measurements, such as several observers observing the same events simultaneously. If such observers are in high agreement (have high intersubject reliability), then the measurement is relatively objective. With low agreement, then the measurement is relatively subjective (low intersubject reliability).

Refined instruments may often give us only small errors; almost anyone could read a thermometer and agree with anyone else's reading. It is less easy to agree on whether a child's behavior at a given time is "aggressive" or on how aggressive it is. We depend on statistics to sort out our errors of measurement from experimental effects.

### Explanation

What does it mean to "explain" an event? Turner (1967) distinguishes between explanations that are *psychologically* satisfying and those that are *logically* satisfying. The former may just be pleasing to hear, familiar, or even mystifying, and not necessarily accurate. To say that "aggression wells up in a person until it spills into behavior like water overflowing a tank" may be appealing (both Sigmund Freud and Konrad Lorenz have used such an analogy), but the appeal is based on our familiarity with water tanks and has little to do with the facts of behavior or of the nervous system.

A logical (or scientific) explanation is one in which a specific event is an instance of a more general law or theory. Such explanations may go against familiar or commonsense observations or explanations. Recall from history the opposition to the idea that balls of different weights drop at the same speed or that air has pressure. Similarly, Freud's explanation of behavior in terms of unconscious motivation went against commonsense ideas at the turn of the century.

An example of a law in psychology is the serial position effect in verbal learning. Items in the middle of a list are harder to learn than those at the beginning or end. If someone were having trouble learning the middle of a list, we would explain his difficulty as an instance of the serial learning effect. This is a "low-level" explanation, however, and we would like to have a "higher-level" explanation to account for the serial position effect itself. Such a more comprehensive theory, explaining the serial position effect as well as other facts of verbal learning, was proposed by Hull, Hovland, Ross, Hall, Perkins, and Fitch (1940). They used the broader concepts of "excitatory" and "inhibitory" response tendencies, from which many different specific facts of learning could be deduced. This theory has long since been regarded as inadequate, but this does not negate the point that it was a higher-level theory.

### Causation

Explanations often involve statements of causation. If we strike the patellar tendon and the knee jerks, we could say that the blow to the knee caused the response. Or, if we see a child start crying when a dog approaches, we might say the dog caused the child to cry. Psychologists often phrase cause-and-effect relations in terms of stimuli and responses; i.e., a stimulus causes a response.

But is the notion of physical causality required in these examples? All we have is a series of *sense impressions.* By observing that some events occur closely in time and space (plus additional criteria), we arrive at a *verbal statement of causality.* We are aware, said David Hume, of things happening together, but can we be *sure* that a particular effect had the cause we attributed to it? In the case of the child, perhaps something that we failed to observe was the "real" cause of crying. Hume concluded, and later philosophers have generally concurred, that causes are what we perceive or think them to be. Scientists do not find ultimate truths or ultimate causes. Rather, they make formal statements, called *laws,* about observed events. The causality is in the statements and the logic, not directly in the physical world.

## CONCLUSION

Because there are so many theories of motivation, we have dealt at some length with the nature of theories in general. We must be prepared to make some rough judgment about whether a particular theory meets any of the qualifications of a good theory. Most of the theories presented throughout this volume have been selected because they have proved fruitful within their particular areas of specialization. A few are included because they hold promise or are in some way novel and interesting departures from older theories, but are not necessarily well tested yet. In the next chapter, we will define the subject matter of "motivation" more precisely and try to see how it fits into the larger scheme of psychological theory.

chapter 2

# The Concept of
# Motivation

A definition of motivation cannot be given in complete isolation from other concepts. Most theories of behavior share at least two concepts: *learning* and *motivation.* Learning is generally considered to be some kind of permanent structural change in the organism, whereas motivation is generally considered to be some kind of shifting, dynamic activity within the organism. It is widely believed that the behavior of an organism reflects both learning and motivation, rather than either one in isolation from the other. The way we define learning necessarily influences our definition of motivation.

## WHAT IS LEARNED: MECHANISM VERSUS COGNITION

There have historically been two broadly opposing schools with reference to what is learned (see Bitterman, 1967).[1] One is the so-called mechanistic view, which says that organisms learn specific responses to specific stimuli. This approach falls into the classic stimulus-response (S-R) analyses of Pavlov, Watson, Thorndike, Hull, and Spence. Earlier versions (e.g., Watson (1924)) held that simply presenting the appropriate stimulus was sufficient to arouse the response associated with that stimulus. More recent versions (Hull, 1943; Spence, 1956), however, have held that the learning component ("habit," an S-R connection) has to be "energized" by the motivational component (drive). The organism is said not to engage in any behavior unless drive is greater than zero. Internal stimulation (drive) "goads" the organism into activity. The exact form and direction of the activity is determined by the stimuli associated with particular responses.

Drive theorists have maintained that motivation should be restricted to accounting for the energization of behavior, not its direction. This energy-versus-direction distinction was introduced into psychology by Woodworth (1918). He used the analogy of a car, which has a drive mechanism (motor, fuel system, etc.) and a steering mechanism. Both are required to make the car go somewhere, but they are otherwise mechanically independent. The motor provides the "dynamic" source of energy and the steering mechanism provides the direction.

A second view, generally referred to as *cognitive,* holds that what is learned is relationships between environmental events or between responses and their outcomes. The organism is said to learn *expectancies,* to gain information about the relationships of responses, things, and places, rather

---

[1] Both the forms of learning considered here are *associative* learning, it being assumed that the learning process is one of relating things to each other. This, of course, is not the totality of cognitive processes. There are even other views of learning. The Gestalt psychologists held that learning consisted of a "restructuring" or "reorganization" of the phenomenological field. Unfortunately, it was never clear how one got from this reorganization to action, since there was no theoretical mechanism for this in the theory.

than to learn only specific responses to specific stimuli. Said another way, the organism learns that "in this situation, if I do such and such, there will be a particular result." The situation in which the organism finds itself arouses a cognition (what the nonpsychologist would call a *thought*) and this cognition is the learning part of the determination of behavior. This point of view was defended most vigorously by E. C. Tolman and his students.

On the motivational side, the organism performs a particular act if it expects that the act will have an outcome with some *value*. Value is a motivational concept and something that has value is an *incentive*. This differs from a strict S-R drive theory in that *anticipation* of goals is seen both to arouse and to direct behavior. Since the idea of anticipation is crucial, the notion of *purpose* is heavily emphasized. This view does not keep such a neat distinction between motivation and learning, because anticipations must, to exist, involve prior learning.

We may clarify this distinction about what is learned as follows. Suppose a hungry rat runs to the left side of a T maze, where it finds food. Over successive trials, it comes to perform flawlessly in going left. Now, what has the animal learned? The S-R theorist would say that the animal has associated the *response* of turning left to the choice point cues and this response is motivated by hunger drive. The cognitive theorist, on the other hand, would say that the animal has learned *where* the food is and *how* to get to it. That is, the animal has learned the expectancy that if it turns left it will get food, and, if the animal is hungry, the response is motivated by the anticipation of obtaining the valued food. The left-turning response happens to be the only response in the T maze that will get the animal to the food.

Since we have two competing explanations for the same behavior, how might we determine which is correct? One way, described by Tolman (1948), involved a "sunburst" maze. After training in a maze involving 90-degree turns, rats were put into a maze in which a series of straight paths radiated from the starting point like wagon wheel spokes. The prediction was that if the animals had learned the location, rather than a specific response, they would tend to take more direct routes to the goal than the original path. There was indeed a tendency for animals to take more direct routes.

These distinctions between S-R drive theory and cognitive-incentive theory are oversimplified, particularly with reference to S-R theory. There are many variations in S-R theory, including some with sophisticated treatments of purpose, goal-directedness, and anticipations. What we have tried to impart, however, are certain differences in flavor of the methods of approaching behavior that are embodied in the S-R and cognitive interpretations. As we examine a variety of evidence and theoretical concepts throughout the book, the distinction between these two points of view, and their importance, will become clearer.

## The Question of Mechanism

The S-R notion has historically had great appeal because it seemed to make sense physiologically. The classical notion that stimuli enter the nervous system, go to the sensory parts of the brain, and then are connected to the motor parts of the brain via the association areas once seemed to provide an explanation for learning. After a career of testing this theory, however, Karl Lashley (1950) was led to the droll conclusion that learning was not possible. All he meant, of course, was that learning probably did not take place via this particular mechanism. Given our general ignorance of brain function, but our increasing appreciation for its complexity, a cognitive view of learning can be considered just as viable physiologically as an S-R view. We can assume that *all* learning is "mechanistic" in the sense that it has a physiological basis. One's preference for a *psychological* concept of learning should therefore be determined by the adequacy of that concept in explaining the facts of behavior. The physiology of learning is an important problem in its own right and physiological data influence our thinking about the concept of learning. For the moment, however, the physiological data are not adequate for making any critical decision about concepts of learning.[2]

Based on many considerations that are developed and documented throughout the remainder of this book, I lean toward the cognitive-incentive view rather than toward the S-R drive view. It is important to point this out because this preference is reflected in the definition of motivation that follows.

## THE DEFINITION OF MOTIVATION

*Motivation is broadly concerned with the contemporary determinants of choice (direction), persistence, and vigor of goal-directed behavior.* When two or more behaviors are equally possible, one is chosen and the organism persists in this behavior with more or less vigor until some anticipated goal is either achieved or some other goal becomes more dominant. The word *contemporary* is used to distinguish immediate and fluctuating causes of behavior from more enduring "structural" factors such as learning.

[2]One problem for many theorists was that the cognitive view did not seem to account for action. Whereas the S-R view inherently contains the notion that a response is elicited by a stimulus—not all S-R theorists use a drive concept—the cognitive view does not seem to have such an action-inducing element. In the words of E. R. Guthrie (1952), the animal is left "buried in thought." *The cognitive theorists, of course, have argued to the contrary and used motivation concepts (incentives) to account for particular actions.* Bolles (1972) argues that there is no more physiological basis for an S-R view as an action concept than there is for an expectancy view. Both are *postulated* for the purpose of accounting for action.

We consider the problem of the choice of behaviors to be the primary motivational question. This is because we do *not* assume that organisms, either animals or people, are inert unless stimulated or motivated. The nervous system is continually active, sometimes even quite violently when we are asleep, and we shall assume that organisms are continuously active throughout life. The motivational problem, then, is how to account for the "temporary" fluctuations in the choice of activities.

Our basic premise is that organisms *approach* goals, or engage in activities that are expected to have *desirable outcomes,* and *avoid* activities that are expected to have unpleasant or *aversive outcomes.* Our immediate task is to define what we mean by *desire* and *aversion.* Our longer-range task throughout the book is to look at situations, animal and human, in which desire and aversion are operative and to seek the *determinants* of desire and aversion. We do not just define *motivation*; we define a set of variables that are called *motivational.*

## DESIRE AND AVERSION AS INTERVENING VARIABLES

To use the concepts of desire and aversion in anything more than a purely descriptive sense, we must define them clearly. For example, just to say that "George went to the ball game because George had a desire to go to the ball game" may tell us little or nothing. If we were asked how we know that George desired to go, we might answer "Because he went." We need better definitions of our concepts than such blatantly circular answers. The *intervening variable* is psychology's best definitional approach.

### Intervening Variables: The Example of Thirst

Let us start off with a simple example to illustrate what Tolman (1938) referred to as the *defining operations* for an intervening varible. Suppose we have a pair of rats that we let run in a maze. One runs slowly to a water reward and the other runs quickly. We might believe that one is thirstier than the other but we cannot define thirst in terms of running speed because running speed is what we are trying to explain. Doing a little detective work, we find that the slow rat has had water continuously available right up to the time of running and the fast rat has been without water for a day. Since hours of water deprivation is an operation independent of running speed, we have a basis for defining thirst noncircularly. In an experiment, we would more precisely control the water deprivation prior to running.

The elements of the intervening variable are, then (1) an *antecedent condition* controlled by the experimenter (hours of deprivation) and (2) a *consequent condition* measured by the experimenter (speed of running). Keeping all other conditions constant (such as amount of prior running experience), we can define thirst on the basis of these antecedent and consequent conditions. We can diagram this as follows:

| Antecedent Condition | Intervening Variable | Consequent Condition |
| --- | --- | --- |
| Water Deprivation  ⟶ | Thirst  ⟶ | Running |

The longer the deprivation period is, the greater the thirst and the faster the running. If there were no such systematic relationship, of course, we would have no basis for talking about a variable at all. The intervening variable is a *theoretical entity,* which is not specifically related to the details of the physiology of thirst.

You may ask, however: Why bother with the intervening variable? Is it not simpler just to relate hours of deprivation to running speed? Indeed, for the illustration just given, this is a sound criticism. The story was made more complicated by the intervening variable. But if there are a number of antecedent conditions (e.g., water deprivation, salt injections, and eating dry food) and a number of consequent behaviors (e.g., preference for water over food, amount of water drunk, speed of running to water, and rate of lever pressing for water), then an intervening variable that relates all of the antecedents to all of the behaviors *does* simplify our thinking (Miller, 1959). A theoretical concept must have some generality across a number of situations or it is of no utility.

### Different Ways of Defining Intervening Variables

The example of an intervening variable just given was of one particular type: The antecedent condition was *manipulated* by the experimenter. There are a number of ways of defining intervening variables, however, corresponding to different kinds of functional relations one might obtain in research (Spence, 1944; J. S. Brown, 1961). Any of these could legitimately specify an intervening variable for us.

*1. Stimulus-Response (S-R) Relations.* We used a stimulus-response relation in the example of thirst. The experimenter controls some condition (S) and measures responses (R). The experimenter might manipulate intensity of electric shock (S), observe behavioral changes (R), and thereby define the intervening variable *pain*—or, perhaps, *fear*—which we would expect to be aversive. The S-R specification is the most potent because it is under experimenter control. Once we have done the initial defining experiment, we are reasonably confident that future manipulations of the antecedent condition alter the same variable. We can then relate this to behaviors other than that used in the defining experiment.

**2. Response-Response (R-R) Relations.** In response-response (R-R) relations, one set of responses is taken to define the intervening variable on the antecedent side and a second set of responses is taken on the consequent side. One of the best-known examples is achievement motivation. McClelland and his colleagues (McClelland, Atkinson, Clark, & Lowell, 1953) developed a content analysis procedure for scoring imaginative stories written in response to picture stimuli (such as cards on the Thematic Apperception Test). One can analyze such stories for *achievement* (e.g., in the story, a man is seen as striving for success in life, which will come if he works hard). It is assumed that these stories are *projective,* that they are indicative of something about the person who writes them. On the basis of several such stories, an individual is categorized as high or low in achievement motivation. The stories constitute $R_1$. The individuals are then compared on one or more other tasks ($R_2$) to determine if there is a relationship between the stories and the tasks. Overall, a great deal of personality theory involves defining motivational (or other) concepts in terms of two independent sets of response measures. It is more difficult to establish causal relations with R-R variables than S-R variables, because the person scoring high or low on the first measure might also differ in other dimensions that we have *not* measured.

**3. Organism-Response (O-R) Relations.** In organism-response relations, some physiological condition of the organism is related to performance. For example, the concept of *activation* (e.g., Lindsley, 1951) is defined in terms of any of a variety of physiological measures (such as brain waves, galvanic skin response, or heart rate) and is then related to performance.

To be exhaustive, one could define intervening variables in terms of any of the other logically possible relations, i.e., S-O, R-O, but that serves no particular purpose for us. The intervening variable can be defined by any two independent operations. We just have to be careful in specifying what our operations are.

### Criteria for Calling an Intervening Variable Motivational

If we have reliably defined some intervening variable, how do we decide whether it is a *motivational* intervening variable? *If a change in the level of the intervening variable leads to a change in preference, persistence, or vigor of behavior, the intervening variable is motivational.* Depending on the nature of the change, we might call the variable *desire or aversion.* In the following discussion we use the logic developed by Irwin (1971).

**Desire.** Consider the following example. We put a rat in a T maze without reward a number of times and find that it goes equally often to either side. The goal boxes are not particularly good or bad in and of themselves, and the animal is indifferent to them. The two goal boxes provide equal or *common outcomes* for either choice. Now we bait one side with food and observe that our subject soon goes regularly to that side. Because the animal prefers the food side to an otherwise identical side, we say that the food is *desirable*. If the addition of something to one side did not change the animal's preference for that side, we would say that the addition was *neutral*. A desirable outcome, then, is a particular kind of preference: It is a preference over a neutral outcome or some other desirable outcome.

It is necessary to control for nonmotivation effects, however. Suppose we had our animal running to lab chow on one side of the apparatus and then put a much more desirable food on the other side. The animal just might keep running to the chow simply because he never discovered the other food was there. We could be fooled into believing that the lab chow was preferred. This example is trivially obvious. Less obviously, a man might have a job that he continues in because he does not perceive any better alternative. To the outsider, it might seem that his present job is desirable to him.

*Aversion.* Suppose that instead of food we had added electric shock to one side of the maze and made no change in the other. The animal would now go to the nonshock side. We would then say that the shock side was *aversive,* because a previously neutral side is now preferred to it. An outcome is aversive if a neutral or less aversive outcome is preferred to it.

*A Note on Neutrality.* The concepts of desire and aversion both hinge on the idea of neutrality, or *affective zero.* This is sometimes a difficult notion to grasp because (1) it is a relative matter and (2) it changes from time to time for a particular organism. There is probably no outcome that is always neutral: A particular outcome may be desirable, neutral, or aversive, depending on circumstances. Irwin's (1971) definition of neutrality is meant to apply only to a particular organism at a particular time. That is, if there are two common outcomes, and the addition of something to one of them does not change preference, then the change was neutral. At another time or place, such a change (e.g., addition of food, water, or entertainment) might have a quite different effect. It is clearly a technically difficult problem to determine neutrality, but such methodological problems as might occur in making the actual determinations should not be considered a flaw in the *logic* of the definitions. The necessity of having a neutral point, or range, is readily seen when we consider that saying there is a *preference* for the less aversive of two alternatives is *not* the same thing as saying that the preferred alternative is *desirable.*

### Desire and Aversion as Classes of Variables

Many different operationally defined concepts might be put under the broad headings of *desire* or *aversion*. We have indicated the defining properties of desire and aversion that would apply to all concepts, but this is not to say that they are all the same concepts or subject to manipulations of the same variables. For example, sweet food, sex objects, and good music may all be desirable and may be approached, but otherwise they are hardly the same thing. Similarly, pain, fear, noxious odors, and whining children might all be aversive and avoided, but they are not otherwise the same things. Thus, even though most motivational concepts are not specifically identified as desire and aversion, as we go along we can indicate into which *class* of concepts they fall.

### The Hedonic Axiom

We can now make the following explicit: *It is assumed, as an axiom, that organisms direct their behaviors to minimize aversions and maximize desirable outcomes.* Such an axiom has been held by all hedonic theorists, from Jeremy Bentham, the English philosopher ([1789] 1939), to P. T. Young (1961), as well as Irwin. In none of the definitions we have given have we stated what the necessary conditions for desire or aversion are—just the *criteria* for saying when one has them. Whether a particular object, event, or state is desirable or aversive is *not* determined by the theory or by argument; it is determined by investigation. Simply saying that something ought to be good or bad, desirable or aversive, is not adequate.

At any given point in time, there is assumed to be an ordering of things along the dimension ranging from very aversive through neutral through very desirable, and the organism is assumed to make choices always in the direction of the arrow shown in the following diagram, the *hedonic continuum.*

$$-5 \quad -4 \quad -3 \quad -2 \quad -1 \quad ^0 \quad +1 \quad +2 \quad +3 \quad +4 \quad +5 \longrightarrow$$

| Very Aversive | Neutral | Very Desirable |

What is indifferent at one time may be aversive or desirable at another and the search for the determinants of desire and aversion provides many opportunities for research. We need to scale objects along this dimension and we need to find the factors that determine the location of objects along the dimension. Hunger, for example, influences the desirability of food, perhaps in a systematic manner that can provide a functional relation (e.g., between hours of deprivation and responsiveness to food). Intensity of stimulation can be related to avoidance behavior, and so on. Most, if not all, problems of motivation can be conceived within this framework.

It should also be pointed out that, like most analytical approaches, we have conceptually simplified the situations described by dealing with only two choices at a time. In a situation with many choices, however, one would still assume that the organism would pick the most desirable alternative. The picture is more complicated by the fact that many choices are not purely desirable or aversive, but have elements of both. Thus, *on balance* one alternative might be better than another. They could be ordered along the hedonic continuum for the net sum of their positive and negative values, but the problem is immensely complicated by such considerations.

### The Interlocking Triad

What we have described as a means of determining desire and aversion is what Irwin (1971) has termed an *interlocking triad.* The triad consists of the following related parts: (1) the organism has an expectancy that Act 1 will be followed by Outcome A, (2) an expectancy that Act 2 will be followed by Outcome B, and (3) that A is preferred over B. In such a situation, if we have some reasonable guarantee that the expectancies are equal, then choices should be determined only by the preference for A over B (whatever outcomes A and B might be in any given situation.) If there is no such guarantee of equal expectancies (that is, equal knowledge about the probable outcomes of two different behaviors), then it is not possible to determine whether the choice behavior is really based on a difference in preference between two outcomes.

### Persistence and Vigor as Motivational Indices

Having defined desire and aversion in terms of choice, we can now relate persistence and vigor to choice more precisely. We may say the following: *The more preferred (desirable) an object or state is, the greater the persistence and vigor in achieving it; conversely, the less preferred (more aversive) an object or state is, the greater the persistence and vigor in avoiding it.* To the extent that measures of vigor or persistence are correlated with preferences, they would, of course, give us the same information.

Such correlations are often less than perfect, however. For example, laboratory rats given a choice between two concentrations of sugar solution almost invariably choose the higher. But if we test them with one solution at a time and measure amount consumed, we find their intake of higher concentrations is less than of intermediate ones. Similar results are found in experimenting with animals pressing a lever for sucrose. This means that measures of persistence are influenced to some degree by different variables than are measures of preference.

On the other side of the coin, we might find that a wide range of sucrose concentrations is preferred over water 100 percent of the time. There is an obvious "ceiling effect"—100 percent is the highest score possible. One laborious strategy to determine preference among the sucrose concentrations would be a direct comparison of each of them, two by two, until we arrived at a scaled preference ordering. Some measure of persistence or vigor might show differences between them in tests with single solutions, however. The moral is simple: We may need several different measures to determine a particular kind of relationship because different methods themselves are inherently sensitive to somewhat different variables. In the present example, sweetness of solution is not the only variable that determines the results.

*Problems with Persistence and Vigor.* The term *persistence* refers to the amount of time spent at some activity or the resistance in changing from one activity to another. But, as Atkinson (1964) points out, we cannot take any single behavior in isolation from other behaviors. A child washing dishes is easily tempted away by ice cream, but it is a little harder to get him away from a favorite game. Much of motivational research, particularly at the animal level, has not been approached with such multiple-response tendencies in mind. This is perhaps largely because of the fact that arousal and persistence of behavior have generally been considered *the* important motivational problems. Therefore, single-response situations, such as running in an alleyway or pressing a lever, have been appropriate response measures. These provide little opportunity to observe shifts in activity or preference, however, because they offer little opportunity for alternative behaviors. Multiple-response situations have been discussed in elegant detail by Atkinson and Birch (1970), as well as by Dunham (1971) and Premack (1971).

Vigor of response (e.g., speed or force) is often difficult to interpret because it may be part of what is learned. For example, we soon learn that the game of pick-up-sticks is played with persistence but never with vigor.[3] Even the lowly rat learns to run fast or slow if it is selectively rewarded for running fast or slow (Logan, 1960). Differences in response vigor, therefore, are not necessarily indicative of differences in motivation unless we can be sure that they are not learned differences.

---

[3]We refer here to behavioral vigor. The degree of energy output that is not translated into overt motor activity is another problem.

## MEASUREMENT OF MOTIVES

### Scales of Measurement

Every science depends on techniques for quantifying its variables. The goal of any science is to obtain relationships that can be incorporated into theories. A relationship, however, means that different amounts of some variable (*X*) are related systematically to different amounts of another variable (*Y*). Speed of running is a function of amount of deprivation, preference for food varies with sweetness, and so on. To measure something, however, does not necessarily mean using a yardstick or putting something into a test tube. The concept of measurement is much broader than such caricatures.

***Definition of Measurement.*** Measurement is the assignment of numbers to objects by some defined rules. There are several different measurement scales, of which we shall discuss the four most common to psychology: nominal, ordinal, interval, and ratio. Let us start off with reference to a real-number line, as in Figure 2.1, which has several "scores," identified by letters. We shall refer to Figure 2.1 to illustrate the features of the four measurement scales.

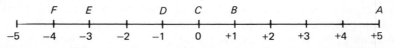

**Figure 2.1**   *Real-number line with letters representing particular scores.*

***Nominal Scale.***  The term *nominal* refers to naming, to simple identification. It has nothing *necessarily* to do with a real-number line. We can identify people as blue-eyed or brown-eyed and then code them onto a computer card as either 0 or 1. These numerals do not mean that the 1's are *quantitatively* different from the 0's (bigger, better), since we could have used any two numbers for the same coding purposes. Such codes can be very useful, however. We find them on license plates, social security cards, and football jerseys. We can count the frequencies of certain codes. For example, we might find that a different percentage of Catholics prefer artificial birth control measures than do Protestants and Jews. We can determine the statistical significance of differences in such percentages. They are all based on counts of identified, not quantified, individuals, however.

Nominal scores may represent quantification under some circumstances. For example, we could give fifty subjects in an experiment instructions intended to relax them and give another fifty no such instructions. We could then obtain the numbers of subjects who finished an experimental task in, say, ten minutes or less. The result would be a nominal score, "finish" versus "not finish." This would yield us relatively little information (actual time scores for each individual might be much better), but in some situations such a procedure is the best we can do. In reference to Figure 2.1, this would be like assigning all the letters on the negative side of the line values of 0 and all the numbers on the positive side values of 1.

There are certain things we *cannot* do with nominal scores. We cannot add, subtract, multiply, or divide any one score in relation to another. What sense would it make to record the numbers off the football jerseys of a team and then get the average value?

*Ordinal Scale.* The rule for ordinal scales is that data are simply rank ordered from top to bottom and the assigned rank is the score. In Figure 2.1, we have six scores (*A* through *F*): *A*'s score is 1, *B*'s is 2, and so on down to *F* = 6. Note that the *assigned* numbers do not correspond to the numbers on the real-number line, but they are in the same order. As long as the same order was maintained for these six scores, they would all get the same values regardless of where they fell on the number line. To illustrate further, the real-number line might represent *actual time* scores to finish a problem but we did not have a watch and therefore only got the relative scores, the rank order. The ordinal scale tells us nothing about the absolute values of the data or about the size of the differences between the scores. For example, *B* could be just slightly less than *A* or much less than *A*, but they would still have the same rank scores.

Most psychological measurement involves ordinal scores. For example, if we have rats deprived of food for two, twelve and twenty-two hours, we do not know anything about differences in hunger (as a "drive") except that it should be progressively greater. The difference between two and twelve (ten hours) may not be motivationally equivalent to that between twelve and twenty-two (also ten hours). Similarly, tests of power motivation may give us numerical scores, but we have no guarantee that equal numerical differences are equal motivational differences.

*Interval Scale.* On an interval scale, equal differences in the numbers represent equal differences in the phenomena being measured. On the Celsius scale, the difference in warmth between 30 and 40 degrees is the same as that between 40 and 50 degrees.

The interval scale has an *arbitrary* zero point, however. Thus, the "real" (absolute) zero is −273 degrees Celsius, not zero degrees Celsius. This limitation means that we can add and subtract scores, but not multiply or divide them meaningfully. For example, is 10°C twice as warm as 5°C? Emphatically no, because these particular values are entirely an artifact of where the zero point happened to be set. If we use the "true" absolute zero, then these temperatures are not 5 °C and 10 °C but are 278 ° and 283 °, hardly a half and a double. Thus, even in physics zero points can be mildly deceptive. On the real-number line in Figure 2.1 we could arbitrarily set the zero any place we wanted and the *difference* between *F* and *E* would be equal to the difference between *D* and *C* or between *C* and *B*. We would not have absolute values, however.

In psychology, we would not seriously consider that a person with an IQ score of 150 was twice as smart as one with a score of 75. To make such a statement we would have to know (1) what the absolute zero of intelligence was and (2) that equal differences in test scores represented equal differences in intelligence. Intelligence test scores are best considered only ordinal scores, although for statistical purposes we often treat them as if they were on an interval scale. Similarly, we might treat achievement motivation scores as if they were interval scores, but they probably are not.

*Ratio Scale.* A ratio scale has a true zero, as well as equal differences in scores representing equal differences in the phenomenon being measured. If the zero in Figure 2.1 were the real zero point, we would have all the lettered scores (*A* through *F*) on a ratio scale, assigned the numbers below them. Grams, seconds, and meters are all ratio scales. Ten seconds are twice 5 and 3 grams *are* twice 1.5. In Figure 2.1, we could add, subtract, multiply, or divide the scores for our six subjects with perfect impunity. The ratio scale is an ideal rarely attained in psychology, however. The procedures for obtaining such scales are complex and involve many assumptions. To be sure, we can use time or distance measures (which are ratio), but the psychological variables to which they apply may not have the necessary ratio scale properties. For such variables as anxiety level, aggression, or cognitive dissonance, we are nowhere near such sophistication in measurement.

Given the kinds of data psychologists work with, usually ordinal (sometimes interval, but rarely ratio), we can seldom make *absolute* predictions of experimental outcomes. Physical theories are based on such constants as the speed of light, and exact physical measurements can be predicted. Virtually every psychological phenomenon is so complex, is influenced by so many relevant variables, and has such a limited scale of measurement, that we can usually only predict inequalities. Thus, we can say that highly anxious individuals will perform less well in some situations than individuals low in anxiety, but not how much less well. Or we can say that strong electric shock will produce a larger galvanic skin response than weak shock. Perception is quantitatively the best developed area of psychology but even here we have no good way of quantifying a *form*. This may sound discouraging but it also provides a constant challenge to our research ingenuity.

## CONTROL AND MEASUREMENT OF HUMAN MOTIVES

*Stimulus-Defined Motivational Concepts:*
*The Experimental Approach*

In animal research, motivation is almost always controlled by experimental manipulations, such as amount of deprivation, shock level, type or amount of reward, and so on. The concepts involved are operationally defined as S-R concepts. The antecedent event for defining such a concept is an experimental manipulation (S) and the consequent behavior is the R. Many behaviors have been used; no particular behavior is necessarily uniquely related to motivation.

Human motives are also experimentally manipulated. Research on hunger and obesity has often imitated animal procedures, varying taste, environmental conditions, difficulty of obtaining food, and so on. In conditioning experiments, level of shock with galvanic skin response (GSR) conditioning and intensity of a puff of air with eyelid conditioning are common examples. Experiments in learning, psychophysics, and reaction time have used rewards and punishers effectively. The whole behavior modification movement is experimentally oriented in this fashion.

Another important type of manipulation is *instructional set*. The following three examples illustrate such sets: (1) anxiety might be aroused by telling subjects that a particular experimental task is a measure of intelligence, related to important events in their lives; (2) threat of electric shock is a powerful source of anxiety, even though shock is never delivered; and (3) in *level of aspiration* experiments, telling subjects they do well or poorly on a task (independently of their actual performance) changes the level of goal they set for themselves in subsequent experimental tasks.[4]

*Manipulation Checks*

It is usually advisable at some point, either during or after an experiment, to determine whether the experimental manipulation was effective for each subject. After an experiment, for example, we would try to find

[4]In any such experiment as these, ethical considerations demand that the experimenter "debrief" the subject at the completion of the experiment, preferably as soon as the subject is finished. Such debriefing may not tell the subject all the details of the experiment but at the very least tells him that there was subterfuge involved and that task performance was not really related to intelligence or whatever. The subject should be told as much as possible short of negating the purpose of the experiment. The American Psychological Association's *Ethical principles in the conduct of research with human participants* should be carefully consulted before undertaking research with humans (Ad hoc committee on ethical standards for psychological research, 1973).

out whether, say, threat of shock really did arouse an anxiety. Present-day subjects, college students in particular, are an increasingly suspicious lot and may not even believe what the experimenter says.[5] A particularly good way to get such information is the *funnel questionnaire*. We start with questions that give no hint about what we are looking for and finish with questions that can literally be answered yes or no. The initial question might be "What did you think was the purpose of this experiment?" and "When did you first think this?" (The subject might have heard about it from his roommate before he ever got to the laboratory.) We could then progress to such questions as "Did you feel tense or nervous about the task?" and "Did you believe what the experimenter said about the task?" At the very end, we might actually state the hypothesis of the experiment and ask the subject if he had thought that was what the experiment was about. For example, "The purpose of the instructions was to make you feel somewhat tense about the task; did this purpose ever occur to you?" Page and Sheidt (1971) suggest that such specific questions might be followed by a rating scale to indicate the subject's confidence. For example, the subject could be asked, "How confident were you about your guess as to the nature of the experiment: very much, much, some, little, or very little?" Spielberger and DeNike (1966) have discussed similar questionnaires in relation to the problem of whether subjects are aware of reinforcement contingencies in verbal operant conditioning.

We can learn a number of things from these interrogations. We might find the subjects had not understood the instructions, did not believe them, did not remember them, or perhaps did not even notice them. Such information is especially important if our experiment fails; we know where to start changing it. We might also find experimental effects, but not for the reasons intended. Thus, subjects may be only conforming in an experiment to what they thought were the experimenter's expectations. This is the problem of experimental demand.

In summary, the various possible artifacts to which all human experimental research is susceptible (Rosenthal & Rosnow, 1969) may also appear in motivational research and have to be guarded against.

### Response-Defined Motivational Concepts: The Correlational Approach

Because of both the practical and ethical problems of manipulating significant motives in people's lives, much human motivational research takes advantage of pre-existing individual differences in motives. Motive

---

[5]The story is told that a student on the University of Texas campus during Charles Whitman's reign of terror came across a body on the sidewalk and thought it was part of a social psychological experiment! This was a more reasonable guess than what was actually happening and says a lot about what students think of psychological research.

level is determined from test scores, which are then correlated with other behaviors. The antecedent event for a particular motivational concept (e.g., anxiety or achievement) is one kind of response, a test score ($R_1$), and the consequent behavior is some other performance ($R_2$). This gives us an R-R concept.

*Full-Range versus Extreme Scores.* There are two different tactical approaches to the use of antecedent response measures ($R_1$). First, we could correlate the test scores of all subjects with their scores on some other performance. This is common when the second measure is just another test score and easy to obtain. Correlating many different variables with each other allows highly sophisticated statistical analyses.

Second, we could use only subjects with extremely high and extremely low scores as our final subjects, such as the top and bottom 25 percent of a large group of individuals on an anxiety scale. This is typical when the second measure is very time consuming or expensive. The extreme groups approach *appears* to be an experiment because it has two groups and because the statistics are commonly those used in the analysis of experiments (not correlations). It is *not* really experimental, of course, because level of motivation (or any other subject characteristic) *is not controlled by the experimenter* as an independent variable and such control is the defining characteristic of an experiment. An *additional* controlled variable, such as task difficulty, could be introduced, and we would then have an experiment. It would be an experiment because of this controlled variable, however, not because of the subject differences in anxiety.

Since the R-R approach depends on measurement of individual differences, it has all the problems of psychological tests in general (i.e., reliability and validity), which we shall discuss shortly. The extreme groups strategy, however, has a peculiar problem of its own, which we shall discuss first. This is the problem of regression to the mean, or simply "the regression problem."

*Regression to the Mean.* In measurement theory, a test score is considered to consist of two components, *true score* and *error.* The true score is that part of the total test score that is a stable measure of the characteristic under consideration. The error part of the score results from miscellaneous unstable factors related to the subject and to the assessment procedure itself. These errors may fluctuate more or less randomly over time. For example, in a test of anxiety we might find that the overall score was partly a measure of anxiety but that it also varied with such situational factors as time of day, test administrator, and circumstances under which the test was taken, as well as such individual factors as inattention, lack of interest, state of health, recent past experience, or occasional random answers.

With readministration of the same test, the true score component remains constant, by definition, but the extraneous error factors might change in such a way that the total score is pushed up or down. This means, in effect, that *extremely high or low scores* on any particular administration of a test are very likely to result from error of measurement. On *retest,* those individuals with extreme scores are more likely to obtain scores closer to the mean of the group than they obtained on first testing. This statistical fact is what we mean by regression to the mean. The less reliable a test is, the greater such regression effects are. We should always check a test for reliability with some care.

Any measured performance is subject to the regression effect. Accuracy of shooting a rifle outdoors depends on skill ("true score") but also on the winds ("error"). A math problem can be thrown off by a misunderstood word. The lie of a golf ball can be improved by a lucky bounce. All of these unpredictable things would not occur the same way another time. Similarly, an individual who performs extremely well or extremely poorly on a first trial is less likely to do so the second time.

The regression effect is not just a test-retest effect either, because (1) it can work across *different* measures and (2) it "works backwards." That is, the extreme scorers on the second administration of a test are not likely to have been the most extreme on the first administration. The regression effect may have quite opposite effects on our research.

First, *the regression effect may work "against" us.* The regression effect may operate conservatively in an experiment, i.e., make it harder to obtain an experimental difference. Thus, differences in anxiety level would have to be "extra strong" to overcome the regression effect on a subsequent task.

Second, *the regression effect may work "for" us.* The regression effect may work in favor of supporting an hypothesis in two situations: test-retest and matching subjects from very different groups. First, let us consider *test-retest* conditions. Suppose that we select very highly anxious subjects on the basis of some test, administer some kind of treatment, and then test again for anxiety level. We might interpret improvement (lower scores) as evidence of therapeutic success when it is in fact only caused by the regression effect. Most students are aware of the test-retest problem, and the need for an appropriate control group with no treatment, so let us consider a more complicated example. Suppose we believed that school children with low achievement motivation would benefit from some particular intervention treatment, that an average group would not, and that a group with high achievement motivation would find the treatment detrimental. If the retest scores showed this to be happening, we would surely be impressed; but the results could also be interpreted in terms of regression. In a pointed discussion like this the need for nontreated control subjects is obvious, but, in the press of real-world data collecting, such problems are sometimes unnoticed and spurious results are even published. Solomon (1949) has described a number of controls for such situations.

Next let us consider *matched groups.* Suppose we had two populations with very different overall levels of measured achievement motivation, Group H is high and Group L is low. Suppose further that we believe training for achievement motivation will affect the two groups differently. To achieve "maximum experimental control," we decide to use matched groups, subjects from each population matched for scores on the achievement motivation test. To do this we have to pick the highest scorers from Group L and the lowest scorers from Group H. Regardless of treatment, however, Group L subjects should tend to regress down toward their population mean and those from Group H up toward *their* population mean. At the very least, we should have control groups from each population. More generally, the use of matched samples from extremely different groups is inadvisable. Random experimental groups, as well as equivalent control groups, are more appropriate.

### Reliability

Reliability is the degree to which a test *consistently* measures the same way. If a person scores high or low one time, he should do so at another time. A test consisting of nothing but "true score" would be perfectly consistent and hence perfectly reliable. The degree of reliability is usually found by correlating two sets of scores for the same test. This is called a *reliability coefficient,* and there are four general ways to get such reliability estimates.

*1. Split-half Reliability.* After a single administration, we can divide a test into halves and correlate the scores for the two halves. This measures consistency at one point in time. It tends to be higher than other reliability measures because factors that might depress or facilitate performance for an individual on one half of the test on a particular day will probably also do so on the other half.

There are many ways to split a test into two halves, using odd versus even items, for example. A statistic called *coefficient alpha* (Cronbach, 1970) gives the average correlation of all possible split halves. One should not generally compare the first half with the second half, however, because these might be differentially affected by such factors as boredom, fatigue, or insufficient time.

*2. Test-retest Reliability.* Consistency over time is determined by correlating scores from two different administrations of a test. This is most applicable when the experience of the first administration is not likely to influence scores at the second administration.

**3. Simultaneous and Delayed Alternate Forms.** If we have alternate and equivalent forms of a test (as determined by the performance of a standardizing group of subjects), we can administer these in a single session or with a delay. Simultaneous administration (i.e., one test following the other by a very short time) is equivalent to a split-half procedure. Delayed administration with alternate forms gets around such problems as subjects memorizing specific items. Furthermore, by giving half the subjects Form A first and the other half Form B first, we can determine order effects above and beyond those related to specific test items.

**4. Interjudge Reliability.** The methods just described apply best to tests with standard scoring procedures, such as the popular intelligence, aptitude, and interest tests. Standard tests for motivation are relatively rare, however. We often use a test that has only one administration and subjective scoring. Under these circumstances, reliability is estimated by having at least two judges score the tests and by obtaining a measure of agreement between the judges. This agreement can be in the form of a correlation coefficient but can also be in terms of the percentage of times the judges agreed on the presence of particular details of content in the tests.

Interjudge agreement can be spuriously high. Suppose subjects write stories about pictures, each story being scored for agressive content. We might find a high correlation between judges, indicating high reliability, but a low correlation between pairs of pictures, indicating low reliability. This could occur because some pictures elicited aggressive content and others did not. The judges could be consistent even though the test itself was not. More than one index of reliability may then be useful.

How high should a reliability coefficient be? In practice, the highest reliability coefficient we can expect is about .90. This is obtained with good tests and standardized scoring. For interjudge reliability, coefficients of about .70 are considered good. A general rule has always been that if a test is not reliable it cannot be valid either. This rule has been questioned in recent years by some workers in achievement motivation (e.g., see Atkinson & Raynor, 1974) who dispute the relevance of standard reliability concepts when applied to the fantasy-based achievement measures. We shall discuss this in Chapter Thirteen.

### Validity

Validity is the degree to which a test measures what it purports to. A test of mechanical aptitude should relate to actual performance in mechanics situations. Four kinds of validity are generally recognized: content validity, concurrent validity, predictive validity, and construct validity.

*1. Content Validity.* A valid test of a child's knowledge of the multiplication tables would be his ability to do problems from the tables he has studied. The main concern is getting a representative sample of items from the universe of items the individual is expected to know. If this is done, then the test is, by definition, valid. This approach is of little use for tests of motivation, however.

*2. Concurrent Validity.* If I give a test of "mechanical aptitude" to a group of assembly line workers and correlate it with some independent measure of their job performance (a *criterion measure*), I can determine concurrent validity. The criterion measure might be some objective measure, such as amount of waste or number of units produced, or it might be a supervisor's ratings. The reliability of the criterion, and its relevance, is as important as that of the test itself. Validity coefficients understandably run lower than reliability coefficients, typically being in the range of .40 to .70 for acceptable ones. A number of factors beyond consideration here determine acceptability.

*3. Predictive Validity.* Concurrent validity may give us a start on getting a test validated, but it may not really tell us which job *applicants* would be good workers. To find this out, we need to give the test to applicants and then put either all or a random sample in relation to the test on the job, to see how they perform. The test-criterion correlation would then give us the predictive validity. In educational or industrial settings, this is certainly our goal, predicting performance, just as in research settings.

*4. Construct Validity.* The three previous forms of test validation may simply not be applicable to measures such as personality tests, where there is no criterion. Cronbach and Meehl (1955) have argued that if we have a theory or hypothesis about how people with different levels of test performance should perform in other situations, then we could set up testable research hypotheses. If such hypotheses were confirmed, the test used to predict the outcome would have construct validity. For example, we could predict that highly anxious people should perform one way and people with low anxiety another way. If this prediction was proved correct, then we would have evidence for the construct validity of our anxiety measure. The procedures for determining concurrent or predictive validity are relatively cut and dried, but the potential for determining construct validity is limited only by the ingenuity of the investigator.

It is also possible to achieve construct validation by the multitrait-multimethod matrix procedure. Any enduring *motivational disposition* (e.g., disposition to be anxious) may be considered a *trait*. Traits may vary in degree from one person to another, but are relatively constant for one individual. Thus one person may seldom be anxious and another frequently so.[6]

Any trait, however, is measured by a method (such as test, personality scale, or self report) and a trait score at any given time is some combination of both the individual and the measurement procedure. With a *single* measurement, we cannot separate the relative contributions of these two sources. The multitrait-multimethod matrix (Campbell & Fiske, 1959) separates these two contributions and simultaneously validates the traits and their measures.

Suppose we have three traits (A, B, and C) and two methods of assessing each (X and Y). If the traits are different and the methods valid, then the following should be found: (1) the intercorrelations among A, B, and C by either method should be low (this is called discriminant validity), and (2) the correlations between the two measures of A, B, and C should each be high if the methods are valid in measuring the same traits (called *convergent validity*).

Table 2-1 gives an example. There are three traits: anxiety, aggressiveness, and need for achievement; and two methods of measurement: a test and a self-report scale. The measures of the different traits all show low intercorrelations, but the two measures of each trait correlate highly. We expect only three high correlations in this situation, out of a possible twelve. These are underlined in Table 2-1.

There is no limit on the number of traits or methods that could be used. Indeed, the more traits and methods showing discriminant and convergent validity, respectively, the more confidence we have in the traits and the methods. We cannot say how high or how low correlations should be, but they can be examined for statistical significance. As a final note, this procedure can sometimes be *approximated* in a literature search. Enough data from scattered sources may be brought together to "rough out" a matrix like that in Table 2-1. Doing this in a single research study is nice, but may be limited by time and money.

## CONCLUSION

In this chapter we developed the idea that motivational concepts are intervening variables used to explain the direction of behavior—approach or avoidance. Organisms are conceived as being continually active, the type

[6]There is considerable dispute over the value of the trait approach for personality theory. The opposing view is that any persisting tendencies an individual might show regarding aggressiveness, for example, are the result of the kinds of situations the individual finds himself in and how he has learned to handle them. We cannot here deal with this very large issue and for the sake of the method under discussion will simply assume that certain characteristics can be treated like traits. The reader is referred to Mischel (1967) for a more detailed discussion.

**Table 2-1**   *Hypothetical results for a multitrait-multimethod matrix following the example in the text.*

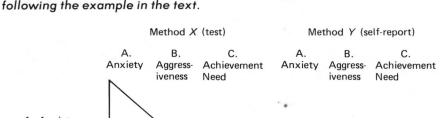

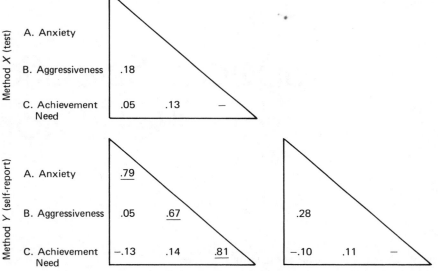

| | Method X (test) | | | Method Y (self-report) | | |
| --- | --- | --- | --- | --- | --- | --- |
| | A. Anxiety | B. Aggressiveness | C. Achievement Need | A. Anxiety | B. Aggressiveness | C. Achievement Need |
| **Method X (test)** A. Anxiety | | | | | | |
| B. Aggressiveness | .18 | | | | | |
| C. Achievement Need | .05 | .13 | — | | | |
| **Method Y (self-report)** A. Anxiety | .79 | | | | | |
| B. Aggressiveness | .05 | .67 | | .28 | | |
| C. Achievement Need | −.13 | .14 | .81 | −.10 | .11 | — |

of activity being the problem to be explained. We saw that a great many concepts can be classified within the definitional frameworks for desire and aversion as developed by Irwin (1971). This approach is broad enough to cover a wide range of phenomena but is specific enough to set motivation off from other areas of psychology. There is a continual problem, both in laboratory research and real life, of distinguishing between motivational and associative (learning) interpretations of behavior, and in subsequent chapters we shall see many instances of this dual possibility for interpretation. The key to making the distinction lies in careful operational definitions of concepts within research settings. Such definitions embody the problems of measurement and control of motivation, as well as of behavior itself.

chapter 3

# Species Specific Behavior

In addition to different overt physical characteristics, each species has behaviors that set it apart from other species. Structure and function are intimately related, of course. Thus, spiders have the capacity to construct webs and different kinds of spiders build different kinds of webs. Different kinds of birds build unique nests and sing songs peculiar to their species. Such behaviors are often called *instinctive,* usually to imply that they are not learned. One of the first psychologists to define instinct was William James (1890, p. 393), who said that it was the "faculty of acting in such a way as to produce a certain end, without foresight of that end, and without the individual's having previous education in that performance." More recently, the biologist Nikolaas Tinbergen (1951) said that an instinct is demonstrated if the following four criteria are met: (1) the behavior in question is stereotyped and constant in form; (2) the behavior is characteristic of the species; (3) the behavior appears in animals reared in isolation from each other; and (4) the behavior develops fully formed in animals prevented from practicing it.

One of Tinbergen's favorite examples of an activity seeming to meet these criteria is the mating behavior of the three-spined stickleback. This little European fish displays a highly stereotyped reproductive behavior that occurs normally in laboratory fish tanks as well as in ponds (Tinbergen, 1952). It begins with the male staking out a territory that he defends against males and females alike. Then he digs a two-inch square pit in the sand at the bottom of his territory and hauls in threadlike weeds to make a mound-shaped nest, through which he hollows out a tunnel slightly shorter than he is. At this point, he changes color from a bland gray to a bright red and bluish white and begins to court females.

When a female swollen with eggs enters the male's territory, he does a zigzag dance, swimming alternately toward and away from her. This is a kind of vacillation between attack and enticement. Eventually he leads her into the nest where, with some prodding on his part, she lays her eggs. The whole routine takes only about a minute. He then fertilizes the eggs in the water and does such caretaking tasks as fanning the water to aerate the eggs. Tinbergen believes that this behavior meets his four criteria for defining an instinct. The main question we are concerned with here is whether the concept of instinct is actually useful in explaining such behavior and what other explanations might account for such species-specific behaviors.

## THE PROBLEM OF INSTINCT

### Common Uses of the Term

The term *instinct* is loosely used in different ways, sometimes contradictory. For example, we may apply the term when a particular behavior seems to occur very commonly in a species, including man. Thus, maternal behavior may be said to be *instinctive,* since most mothers do engage in something called *maternal activities.* William James (1884) thought no woman could resist the charm of a small, naked baby. John B. Watson (1924), however, pointed out the fallacy of attributing such a universal instinct. He noted that in a hospital where they could be closely observed new mothers were very awkward with their first child and did not do all those tender, loving things that supposedly characterize the "maternal instinct."

A second way in which the term is applied is to activities which seem to occur without much forethought.[1] The prizefighter who is quick to dodge his opponent's jabs may be said to "duck instinctively," but very little imagination is necessary to see that one either learns to duck or gets out of the business. In this kind of example, the term *instinct* is used as if some people have it (the capacity to respond quickly) and some do not. Thus, it seems to be used as an account of *differences within a species* rather than as an explanation for the *universality* of a species behavior. This is just the opposite of the use described in the preceding paragraph or in Tinbergen's definition.

### Instinct as Urge versus Instinct as Behavior

Another kind of confusion arises in treating instinct as an *urge* toward some activity (thus being like a motive or emotion) as compared to referring to such specific *behaviors* as web building. James and Freud both talked more in terms of urges than of behaviors. In fact, what are usually referred to as instincts in Freudian theory (sex and aggression) come from the German word *Trieb,* which can be translated as either "instinct" or "drive." As it happened, the term *instinct* was originally used and hence picked up connotations which Freud did not necessarily intend. Freud talked about instincts as having *source, impetus, aim,* and *object.* This means that either internal or external stimulation produces "instinct" (source); that the instinct carries some degree of force (impetus) that is related to the intensity of behavior; that the person tries to reduce the tension (aim); and, finally, that this process is all ended by some object. Freud saw neither fixed behaviors nor variant objects related to instincts; both, in his view, are subject to change because of particular individual experiences. In Freud's view, these built-in urges might find their outlets in very disguised forms, because of social pressures. He saw many behaviors as being apparently irrational

---

[1] Just to speculate for fun, it may be that behaviors that are relatively more under the control of the right cerebral hemisphere may also be called *instinctive* because the right hemisphere does not communicate well verbally. The left hemisphere seems to be involved relatively more with rational, sequential thought and the right hemisphere with more "global," non-sequenced activities (e.g., see Gazzaniga, 1967; Ornstein, 1972). We are simply speculating that an activity whose origin cannot be readily verbalized may be attributed to instinct and that activities under right hemispheric control may fall into this category.

because they are stimulated by instincts that the individual cannot identify, but that can be studied and their causes determined. The concept of psychic determinism, including "unconscious" motivation, was the touchstone of Freud's theorizing.

Most serious theorists have argued that as far as behavior is concerned the term *instinct* should be limited to some very specific small segments, almost at the level of reflexes. William James, John B. Watson, William McDougall, and Sigmund Freud all believed that there were some inborn tendencies or urges, but that these are quickly overshadowed by learning. James, for example, described instinct as being without foresight of its end, but also said that once an instinctive activity occurred that there would be foresight of its end on future occasions. This foresight would either facilitate or block the expression of the instinct. James (1890, p. 395) even referred to the idea of invariable instincts as "mystical" and observed that "The minuter study of recent years has found continuity, transition, variation and mistake wherever it has looked for them, and decided that what is called an instinct is usually only a tendency to act in a way of which the *average* is pretty constant, but which need not be mathematically 'true.' "

### Origins of the Instinct Concept

Given the considerable agreement that so-called instinctive behavior is never as invariant as supposed, how did the concept gain such a foothold and how does it still maintain such a grip on popular opinion? One reason is that it keeps getting revived by people like Lorenz (1965) and Ardrey (1966), who argue, respectively, that aggression and territorial behavior in humans are instinctive. Most biologists have been skeptical of these views, but they have had great popular appeal.

A deeper running current, however, is that the instinct concept derived from theology rather than biology (Beach, 1955).[2] The line of reasoning, which would have applicability today in some circles, is as follows. Man gets to heaven or hell according to his earthly choices. If he makes the correct moral decisions, his reward is paradise; if not, his "reward" is perdition. But the whole problem is meaningless unless we assume that man is free to choose. This capacity to make choices was said to be a unique property of man's rational soul, just as an afterlife was said to be reserved to him. But without a capacity to make rational decisions, how could animals carry on the complex activities that they obviously do? It was simply postulated that animals are not rational and do not have to make decisions

---

[2]The early confusion between theology and actual animal behavior is nowhere more dramatically illustrated than in the medieval "bestiaries," or books of beasts. One story reported by White (1954) says, for example, that lion cubs are born lifeless and after three days the father lion breathes life into them just as God the Father resurrected Christ the Son after three days.

because their behavior consists of predetermined responses to particular situations. This view of theology is still widely held, as we saw in Chapter One, and might still tend to lend credence to the concept of instinct in animals.

### The Anti-Instinct Revolt

One way that Darwinian biology bridged the gap between animals and humans was by proposing that humans also have instincts. William James and William McDougall both believed that man actually had more instincts than other animals. And, while they saw these more as urges than specific behaviors, less sophisticated writers proposed human instincts running into the hundreds. By about 1920, a number of psychologists became alarmed by this proliferation, which in effect was nothing more than putting names to behaviors without further explanation. Knight Dunlap (1919) and Zing Yang Kuo (1922) were particularly strident in their attacks on the practice, arguing for the greater importance of environmental determinants on behavior.

Kuo went further in undertaking a productive program of research on so-called instinctive behaviors. He showed that all cats do not "naturally" kill rats and that such factors as familiarity are involved (1930). From his extensive investigation of the development of the embryonic chick, he also made a convincing argument (1932) that the "instinctive" pecking and swallowing of the newborn chick has its origins in embryonic movements that are "forced" in the course of morphological development. For example, after the embryonic heart starts to beat, the chick's head is moved back and forth in the egg, the mouth opens and closes, and there is some swallowing. As a result of the many attacks on it, the instinct concept fell into ill repute in American psychology in the 1920s.

### Resurgence of Interest

In 1938, Karl Lashley spoke out in favor of instinct. He gave fifteen examples of what he believed were "confirmed" instinctive behaviors, most of which involved mating or maternal activities. But as Beach (1955) pointed out, few American psychologists had ever seen *any* of the behaviors listed (responses of the sooty tern to her nest and young, for example). And Beach once more made the point that the more closely any behavior is studied, the less likely it is to be considered automatic. Gradually, however, increasing numbers of examples of species-specific behaviors, such as the mating of the stickleback, caught the attention of both psychologists and biologists, particularly after World War II. Tinbergen's (1951) and Thorpe's (1956) books on instinctive behavior were influential, as were a number of edited volumes on animal behavior.

A paper by Breland and Breland (1961) was particularly interesting to learning-oriented psychologists. Entitled "The Misbehavior of Organisms," a switch on Skinner's *Behavior of Organisms* (1938), it attracted attention in part because it was an insider's account of the difficulties of doing operant conditioning with many different species. Originally students of Skinner's, Keller and Marian Breland were so impressed by the power of operant conditioning that they started a business training animals for shows. They reported that certain behaviors simply could not be trained with some species. In one act, for example, a pig was supposed to carry a large simulated gold coin to a piggy bank. This was learned, but then, in spite of continued reward for success, the animals began dropping the coin on the ground, rooting around at it, and never got it to the bank anymore. It seemed as if the animals were trying to "root" the coin, much as they would root for food in the ground. Similarly, racoons had great difficulty in letting go of objects which they were supposed to deposit someplace else, tending to hold them in their hands and "wash" them. The Brelands referred to such problems as a drift from learned to instinctive behavior. To avoid the difficulties of this instinctive drift, they eventually built all their acts around what the animals *would* do reliably rather than try to train responses arbitrarily selected.

### Present Status of the Instinct Concept

Biologists now agree that there is partial genetic determination of behavior, but the actual term *instinct* rarely appears in the biological literature on behavior. Many major textbooks do not even have the word in their indexes (e.g., Hinde, 1970; J. L. Brown, 1975; Marler & Hamilton, 1966). Others give it a perfunctory few words, mainly to put it into historical context (e.g., Eibl-Eibesfeld, 1975). Instead, it is argued that genes establish the *potential* for species-specific behaviors and that these behaviors are *realized* under some environmental conditions, but not under others. The problem is to determine what specific mechanisms are inherited and what environmental conditions bring them into play. This kind of analysis proceeds nicely without any concept of instinct, except as it may refer generally to motivational mechanisms, which are also generally subject to systematic analysis, of course.

## THE ETHOLOGICAL APPROACH

Ethology is that part of biological science concerned with animal behavior. It has developed separately from American comparative psychology, coming largely from Europe and under the leadership of Konrad Lorenz, Nikolaas Tinbergen, and Karl von Frisch in recent years. It is usually dated back to earlier work in this century, however, especially that of Heinroth (1910) and Wallace Craig (1918). According to Tinbergen (1951), the main question of ethology is: Why does the animal behave as it does? His answer is that behavior is the joint product of environmental events and internal conditions, which is what comparative psychologists also say. The difference is that the ethologists have placed more emphasis on (1) detailed study of animal behavior in natural settings, (2) closer attention to the development of behavior, (3) genetics and the phylogenetic development of a species, and (4) studies of birds, fish, and insects, as well as mammals.

### The Ethogram

The first step in the ethological analysis of behavior is to map out the typical behavior of a species in its normal environment. Activities are observed, recorded, and counted, as are the circumstances under which they occur. This behavioral map is the ethogram. The description of the stickleback's mating behavior is an ethogram, valuable because it gives a baseline of normal behavior against which the effects of changing the organism or its surroundings can be evaluated.

### Erbkoordination

The general name given to an "instinctive" pattern of behavior is *Erbkoordination.* It is a core of more or less complex and fixed "inborn" movement forms. This fixed core is also referred to as a *fixed action pattern* (FAP). The FAP does not involve all the behavior in any such sequence as feeding or mating, but instead it generally refers to the terminal or *consummatory behavior*[3] that is the final phase of a "motivated act." An animal may engage in widely variable movements, or *appetitive behaviors,* which bring it into contact with food or a sexual partner. As the animal gets closer to the end of the sequence, the behavior is relatively more stereotyped. As an example of such stereotypy, the drinking rate of a rat licking from a water tube is relatively constant, at about six licks per second. This figure may be higher for some solutions and lower for others and as the animal slows down with fatigue or satiation, but under any normal conditions, it is never reported as low as three nor as high as ten per second; the range is small. The distinction between appetitive and consummatory behaviors is essentially the same as psychologists usually make between instrumental (or operant) and consummatory behaviors. The FAP constitutes only a small fragment of an overall sequence of motivated behavior.

---

[3] The word *consummatory* comes from the verb *to consummate,* not from "to consume." To consummate something is to complete it, not necessarily to consume it. Eating and drinking are both consumatory and consummatory acts, but sex and aggression are acts that are consummated.

The early Lorenz-Tinbergen analysis emphasized that *reaction-specific energy* (RSE) builds up in the organism much as water fills a tank. The RSE was so-called because it was considered specific to particular kinds of behavior—e.g., feeding, mating, or aggressive behaviors. A particular behavior was said not to be stimulated by external events, but *released* by them. Until a specific stimulus called a *releaser,* or *sign stimulus,* is presented to the organism, the RSE is internally blocked and is not expressed overtly. The releaser is a "key" that fits the "lock" of the *innate releasing mechanism* (IRM). When a releaser (such as the gaping mouth of a baby bird) is presented, the appropriate behavior is released (the parent putting food into the mouth).

### Hierarchical Ordering of Action

A crucial concept is that the neural centers storing the RSE are ordered in a hierarchy according to complexity. At the highest level, there are "moods," which correspond to such broad kinds of behavior as are involved in feeding, mating, sleeping, or aggression. Within each mood, there are successively "lower" levels of hierarchy corresponding to more and more specific kinds of behaviors involved in the total activity, down to the movements of specific muscle groups. Figure 3.1 (Tinbergen, 1951) shows the nature of this hierarchical structure in the specific example of stickleback mating behavior. The hierarchical concept has been given support in research described by von Holst and von St. Paul (1962), using electrodes permanently implanted in chicken brains so that behavior could be artificially stimulated. Depending on exact electrode placement, either an overall "mood" or very specific behaviors could be produced. The sleepy chicken, for example, goes through a standard ritual in preparation for sleep, including standing on one leg and putting the head under a wing. Von Holst reported that, at one electrode site, the entire mood could be stimulated, with all the behaviors in sequence and the chicken actually going to sleep. Presumably, the electrode had tapped into a fairly high position in the hierarchy. With other locations, only very specific parts of the overall behavior pattern were evoked, such as putting the head under the wing, but the other behaviors did not occur and the chicken did not sleep.

### Vacuum Reactions and Displacement

If a releasing stimulus does not occur to "unblock" the IRM, the buildup of a particular RSE may be so great that the reaction occurs anyway. This is called in German a *Leerlaufreaktion* (vacuum reaction). Continuing the hydraulic analogy, the "water tank" overflows so that an FAP occurs, such as "spontaneous" aggressive behavior or inappropriate sexual activity.

An animal may try to mate with an inanimate object or a member of another species.

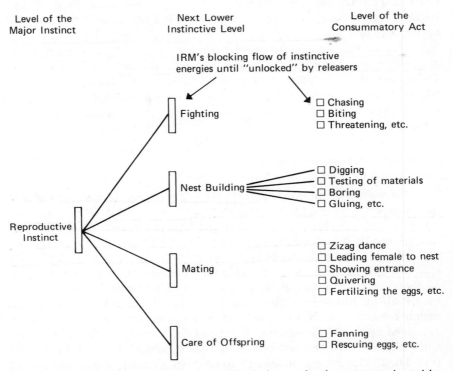

**Figure 3.1** *The reproductive instinct of the male three-spined stickle-back. The hierarchical ordering of action, with different levels of instinct indicating innate releasing mechanisms. (Modified from* The Study of Instinct *by N. Tinbergen, 1951, p. 104.)*

If two incompatible reactions are simultaneously released, as with courtship and aggressive activities, the animal cannot really complete either. Recall that the zigzag dance of the male stickleback seemed to involve alternation between attack and enticement. Under such conditions, an unexpected response may occur. For example, in the middle of courtship or fighting, a chicken may suddenly start pecking at the ground. This is called *displacement activity* and is thought to be caused by released energy from the conflicting (and blocked) RSE's "spilling over" to release other behaviors.

Both vacuum and displacement reactions, including reactions to unusual stimuli, are based on the hydraulic model. While such a model is an interesting analogy, biologists do not take it seriously as an explanation of behavior. There is no known physiological mechanism (except in a literal sense, perhaps the bladder) which has the properties of such a model. In the case of displacement, moreover, Zeigler (1964) showed how specific kinds of stimulation could determine what behaviors would occur when conflicting activities block each other. In the courtship-fighting conflict, a bird might start to preen because of the engorgement of blood close to the skin. Similarly, "vacuum" reactions do not occur completely in isolation from the environment; they are also responses to some kind of stimulation.

### Present Status of Ethological Concepts

To summarize, then, to the extent that the term *instinct* is used at all any more, it refers to some very broad notion of motivation (the "urge" concept of instinct) with only a small amount of consummatory behavior considered to be anything like invariant. The bulk of such motivated behavior is appetitive and highly variable, depending on complex interactions between the organism and its environment. The possibilities for behavior are set by certain sensorimotor organizations specific to a species.

A number of different aspects of animal behavior have particularly concerned ethologically oriented biologists and psychologists. For illustrative purposes, we shall look at just a few. These are (1) the evolution of behavior; (2) stimulus factors, including imprinting; (3) circadian rhythms; and (4) orientation and communication in bees. For more exhaustive surveys, the interested reader may consult Altman (1966), J. L. Brown (1975), Eibl-Eibesfeldt (1975), Hinde (1970), Klopfer (1974), or Marler and Hamilton (1966). Eibl-Eibesfeldt is of particular interest for his concern with the ethological study of humans and Hinde for his integration of biological and psychological concepts.

## THE EVOLUTION OF BEHAVIOR

### Darwin's Theory

The *Origin of Species* (1859) was neither the only nor even the first attempt to describe continuously evolving life, but was certainly the most influential. Based on a myriad of observations during his worldwide travels on the *Beagle,* Darwin's thesis was, briefly, as follows: There is a natural selection of organisms based on their fitness to reach maturity and reproduce themselves. Or, as Wilson (1975) more recently has put it, natural selection is the process whereby certain genetic material gains increased representation in the following generation. Such "survival of the fittest" does sometimes depend on savagery and cunning, but not always. The opossum, which exhibits neither of these characteristics in great amount, has survived for over sixty million years.

The core of Darwin's theory is that specific survival rules are not laid down in advance. Evolution is opportunistic and whatever assists survival at a given time and place is the physical or behavior character selected in a species. Some animals survive by being inconspicuous, their form and coloring providing *camouflage* that allows them to blend almost invisibly into their environment. Insects are particularly adept at this, but the spotted coat of the fawn, the stripes of the zebra, and the white fur of the polar bear are also protective. Other animals show *mimicry,* looking like different species that are more dangerous than they. For example, one species of butterfly (*Limenitis archippus*) survives in part because it looks like the Monarch butterfly, which feeds on poisonous plants and is rejected by predators such as the bluejay because it tastes bad. Many animals have *rituals* that make them appear more dangerous and threatening than they really are, such as spreading feathers, puffing up the cheeks, and so on.

Selection itself, however, depends on two other factors: *genetic variation* (which Darwin simply referred to as "natural variation") and *environmental pressure.* What Darwin recognized was that there could be no selection unless there were alternatives to be selected from and reasons for them to be selected. Unless organisms differed from their parents, and hence from each other, all the members of a species would be equally likely to perish or survive. As an example of such pressure, in England the industrial revolution led to cities that became black with coal dust and smoke. Moths that were darker could survive and multiply in the cities, where they literally blended into the walls (camouflage) and were protected, but the lighter colored moths of the same species could not. In more rural areas, however, lighter colored moths were less conspicuous and continued to survive better than the darker ones. If there had been no variation among the moths, with complete adaptation to the country living, city survival would not have been possible—this would have been an instance of over-specialization in natural selection.

Abrupt environmental changes may provide pressures that a species cannot withstand because it does not possess sufficient variability among its members. It then becomes extinct. Shifting land masses and bodies of water possibly had such effects on the dinosaur, although this particular example is controversial. Sometimes the introduction of a new species may play havoc because the new species is better adapted to survival in the environment than the established inhabitants. Thus, the placental jackrabbit was better adapted to life in Australia than the indigenous marsupials and rapidly multiplied when introduced there. The incessant movement of men into wilderness areas has caused extinction of numerous species, and endangered many others. Sometimes, however, environmental changes in the form of such geographic upheavals may give new life to a species. Many of Darwin's most important observations were made of the variations of finches among the different Galapagos Islands, of volcanic origin. The finches experienced somewhat different environmental pressures on these suddenly appearing islands and therefore developed along different lines.

### Mendel's Theory

Gregor Mendel did his work on inheritance in the middle 1880s but it was about 1900 before it became evident that this was the mechanism of Darwin's natural variation. An organism passes some of its characteristics to its offspring. The mechanism of transmission is the *genes* (Mendel himself just referred to "factors"). A particular organism has a *genotype,* the actual genes it receives from its parents, and a *phenotype,* that part of its genetic inheritance that is actually expressed in observable characteristics under appropriate environmental conditions.

Each adult individual has *pairs* of genes for a particular character. The genes may be of the same kind or they may be different. Such different forms of the same gene are called *alleles.* When reproductive cells, or *gametes,* are formed in the adult individual only one member of each gene pair goes into the gamete. In the combination of gametes from each parent, then, the offspring gets a full complement of genes but the exact combinations depend on which genes from a particular parent went into the gamete and on which adults happen to mate with each other. If one allele, which we may call A, is *dominant* over another allele, A', which is *recessive,* then an individual receiving A from one parent and A' from the other will have the phenotype of A. Suppose that A represents the allele for brown eyes and A' for blue, and that A is dominant (which it is). We may then ask what the eye color of the offspring will be on the basis of the parental phenotypes and genotypes.

Figure 3.2 shows some of the possibilities. We show here the combinations of the two phenotypes, but with different underlying genotypes. If one parent is AA, then the offspring will be brown-eyed, because, no matter what alleles the other parent brings to the situation, A will always be dominant in the combination. If both parents are AA', they will have brown eyes, but it is expected that one out of four offspring will be blue-eyed (an A'A' combination). If both parents are blue-eyed, then we know immediately what the genotype of the offspring will be; since both parents have to be A'A', there is no way for the offspring to be anything but A'A' and hence blue-eyed.

Such genetic crosses as we have described produce these particular phenotypes in the specific cases where dichotomous characters (such as eye color) are controlled by a particular gene and are unrelated to other genes. If the genes in question interact with other genes, the outcomes may be quite different. As it happened, the garden peas that Mendel studied did show such simple dominant and recessive characters. Other genetic crosses may show "blends," or combinations of the phenotypic characters of the parents. For example, in flowers a red male and a white female may produce a pink offspring. Two pinks may produce either red, white, or pink.

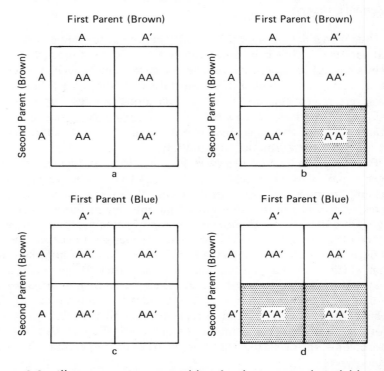

**Figure 3.2** *Illustrative genetic tables for brown-eyed and blue-eyed parents and their offspring. The margins of each table show the genotypes of the parents (A = Brown, dominant; A' = Blue, recessive.) Blue only occurs when two recessive blue genes are paired. The phenotypes of the parents are indicated in the marginal parentheses and the blue phenotype for offspring is in the stippled cells in (b) and (d). Note that the parental phenotypes are the same in (a) and (b) (both brown), but the genotypes are different, and 1 out of 4 offspring in (b) is expected to be blue-eyed. In (c) and (d) there is one blue-eyed and one brown-eyed parent, but only in (d) are there blue-eyed offspring.*

Somewhere along the way, however, there may be a genetic error. Perhaps a gene is not reproduced correctly, or is not passed on to the offspring. An offspring that does not get the normal genetic complement from each parent is a *mutant* (there is a *mutation,* or genetic change). Usually this is lethal, sometimes harmless, and only rarely advantageous. Advantageous mutations have had time in their favor, however—millions of years to occur, to be selected, and to become part of the gene pool of a species as a whole. It is through gene mutations that the necessary variability in species is maintained and on which natural selection works.

*Genetic versus Environmental Contributions to Behavior.* The problem of "nature versus nurture" or "heredity versus environment" generates heated discussions on topics such as personality, intelligence and criminal tendencies. At various times, the pendulum has swung in favor of one or another view of the relative importance of genetic or environmental factors for each of these characters. The inevitable conclusion, however, is that both factors are involved and that the problem is to determine the conditions under which one or the other is relatively more influential. We cannot judge by simple observation the extent to which a particular behavior is caused by nature or nurture. By appropriate analytic and/or experimental procedures, however, we can estimate the relative amounts of variation in behavioral or other characteristics caused by genetic and environmental factors in groups of animals. These techniques may involve experiments with selective breeding of particular individuals; comparisons of monozygotic twins (from a single egg and hence with identical genes) with dizygotic twins or other relatives; or statistical studies of behaviors in populations of individuals.

*Selective Breeding.* If we take an unselected sample of subjects from some population and measure a specific behavior, we find that there is a distribution of scores for that behavior around some average (mean) value. The amount of variation among the scores, how widely they spread, can be determined by calculation of a statistic called the *variance* (which is the square of the *standard deviation*). This population variance, $V_{pop}$, consists of two components: (1) the individual differences caused by genetics, or the genetic variance, $V_{gen}$, and (2) differences caused by environmental factors, or the environmental variance, $V_{env}$.[4] Now we take a group of subjects that are, say, very close to the group mean and selectively inbreed them. (We could inbreed subjects at the extremes of the distribution.) With each succeeding generation, we continue to inbreed those subjects closest to the group average. Over successive generations, we will find that the variance of the inbred groups gets progressively smaller until, after about twenty

[4]There is actually a third term *interaction variance,* that is a measure of the *interaction* between genetic and environmental variance. Thus, for example, genetic potential is realized one way in one environment and a different way in a different environment. In order to determine this, we would have to do selective breeding experiments in several environments. Since our purpose here is just to illustrate the general approach, we have simplified things by assuming that the interaction variance is zero.

generations, it reaches a stable value and is no longer reduced by further inbreeding. At this point, we have a *homozygous* group (i.e., all the members have virtually identical genotypes with regard to the character being bred for). There is still some variability, however, that must be caused by environmental factors.

Now, we have already said that $V_{pop} = V_{gen} + V_{env}$. In this experimental procedure, since we reduced $V_{gen}$ to zero, any remaining variability is attributable to environmental factors, and constitutes $V_{env}$. We then can determine $V_{gen}$ by the formula:

$$V_{gen} = V_{pop} - V_{env}.$$

Suppose the initial unselected population variance was 10 and the twentieth generation variance was 3. Then $V_{gen} = 10 - 3 = 7$. The final step would be to obtain a *heritability coefficient,*[5] which is calculated as $V_{gen}/V_{pop} = 7/10 = .70$. This ratio is the proportion of the unselected population variance that is caused by genetic factors. This does not say that 70 percent of the behavior of a given animal is caused by genetics and 30 percent by environmental factors, but that for the group as a whole, 70 percent of the variance among animals is genetic and 30 percent is environmental.

Many such selective breeding experiments have been done, both in laboratories and agricultural situations. The latter are generally less quantitative, but we know well that animals can be bred for certain features. Horses, cattle, chicken, turkeys, hogs, and so on, can be bred for commercially desirable characteristics. Dogs can be bred as gentle children's pets, hunters, or for sheep herding. In laboratories, fruit flies have been bred for such characteristics as phototaxis (tendency to approach a light) and mice have been bred for aggressiveness or for either high or low emotionality (fearfulness). The common laboratory rat, intentionally or not, has been bred for tameness. In one of the early studies of behavior genetics, Tryon (1940) inbred rats that quickly learned a standard maze and rats that were slow to learn the maze. Within twenty generations, he had bred virtually nonoverlapping populations of animals for the maze task.

*Twin Studies.* Identical twins are homozygous because they come from a union of the same sperm and egg. Nonidentical twins or siblings do not have the same genes because the eggs and sperms from which they come are not genetically identical. The closer the familial relationship, the more similar the genetics of two individuals, however. Using a *coefficient of concordance,* one can compare the likelihood of one identical twin having a certain characteristic if the other has it and so on through the rest of the familial relations. For example, if one member of every pair of one hundred twins has a particular characteristic and eighty of the second members have

[5]There are a number of ways to arrive at heritability coefficients. This one is illustrative.

it, the coefficient of concordance is .80. If a particular characteristic is genetically determined, then identical twins should have the highest coefficients, siblings next, and randomly paired members of the population as a whole should have the lowest. Using this approach, Kallmann (1946) found that schizophrenia seemed to have a large genetic component. The counterargument is that more closely related members of a family also have more similar environments. The answer to this lies in demonstrations that identical twins reared in very *different* environments have higher concordance ratios than nonidentical twins reared in the *same* general environment. We could also calculate a heritability coefficient from twin data. If we assume that any variation between identical twins is environmental, then we could compare this variance to the total population variance. Thus, $V_{gen} = V_{pop} - V_{twin}$ and we could go from there to calculate $V_{gen}/V_{pop}$, the heritability coefficient.

***Population Genetics.*** Selective breeding is not feasible with humans and the occurrence of particular phenotypic characteristics with twins may not be frequent enough to be enlightening about the genetic basis of a given human characteristic. Data on the frequency of particular phenotypic characters in families or other genetically close groups can give us much information, however. A variety of characteristics are thus found to be hereditary, including blood type, extra fingers, the Rh factor in blood, some forms of mental retardation, color blindness, and hemophilia (excessive bleeding). Some genes may be carried by both sexes but be sex-linked in their expression. Thus, color blindness occurs almost exclusively in males.

A particular group, because of its geographic or social isolation may contain a gene virtually unknown in other groups. For example, in the United States, sickle cells in the blood are found only among blacks and are pathological (sickle-cell anemia). In Africa, however, sickle cells are more widespread and were apparently naturally selected because they are resistant to malaria. Similarly, the Jewish population carries a recessive gene for Tay-Sachs disease (a lethal central nervous system disorder) and shows a much higher incidence than in other populations. At the same time, however, a genetic defect called phenylketonuria (PKU), which produces mental retardation, is virtually unknown among Jews. Other religious groups (e.g., the Amish and Moslems) also have particular recessive pathological genes that are uncommon in other populations. Hemophilia is caused by a recessive gene and, although occurring rarely in any broad population, is found with considerable frequency in European royal families. These families have intermarried so frequently over the years that the gene has become common enough that the probability of two recessives mating is much higher than the chance pairing in the general population.

*Eugenics.* Sir Francis Galton, one of the pioneers in the study of inherited characteristics, was concerned with the problem of *eugenics,* or the "improvement" of the human gene pool. He was particularly interested in intelligence, but we might be equally involved with any other social problem thought to result from inherited characteristics. (In Chapter Twelve, we discuss this in relation to aggression.) Even if it could be universally agreed that some particular characteristic were undesirable and shown to be genetic, however, there is little chance of eliminating it by preventing those who show the characteristic from breeding. There are several reasons for this.

First, some forms of genetic pathology (including PKU) are related to the age of the parents and therefore appear in the offspring of parents who themselves show no sign of the disorder nor of passing it on and whose earlier children may not have it. They would therefore not have been prevented from breeding. Second, a disorder might be maintained by a mutation that occurs with the same frequency in each generation. Again, there would be no way of identifying potential carriers. Finally, assume that a particular disorder is caused by a simple recessive gene that has a frequency of 1 in 100 in the population. On the basis of random mating the probability of two recessive genes in an offspring would be (1/100) (1/100) or 1 in 10,000. For every one individual who actually displayed the disorder phenotypically, there would be 99 other undetected carriers. The recessive gene would be passed on with virtually the same frequency from generation to generation regardless of whether individuals who display the disorder have offspring.

*Genetic Counseling.* On the basis of family histories, biochemical tests (including blood analyses) and even analysis of embryonic chromosomes (which can be obtained from the amniotic fluid), it is now possible to make estimates of the chances of some genetic defects occurring in offspring of particular parents. A genetic counselor, familiar with the disorder potentially involved, could give some guidance to future parents. In the case of the Rh factor, this kind of counseling has been done for a long time. According to McKusick (1969), the chances of genetically determined disorders are usually much less than parents expect. At the very least, then, such counseling may reduce anxiety and at best it may alert both parents and physicians to difficulties that can be dealt with in advance of their occurrence.

## STIMULUS CONTROL OF SPECIES-SPECIFIC BEHAVIOR

Of the many energy forms in the environment, living organisms are sensitive to only a few. An animal's sensory system operates as a filter that lets some energy forms "pass" into the animal, but not others. If an animal has a receptor mechanism for transducing a particular environmental energy into neural activity, it is sensitive to that energy. The kinds of receptors an animal has, and the kind and complexity of neural machinery for processing the sensory inputs, determine the perceptual world of a species. We may all occupy the earth, but we do not all live in the same perceptual world, because of this differential stimulus filtering. The following examples illustrate something of species differences in perception.

1. Humans can hear from about 20 herz (Hz) to 20 kilohertz (kHz; herz is the term for cycles per second) sound waves, but dogs and rats hear up to about 40 kHz and bats and porpoises into the range of 80–100 kHz.
2. Migrating birds are sensitive to the earth's magnetic fields, but humans are apparently not.
3. Bees and some birds are sensitive to polarized light, to which humans are blind.
4. Humans are sensitive to light wavelengths in the range of 400 to 700 millionths of a millimeter but are blind to infrared and ultraviolet wavelengths just on either side of the visible spectrum, as well as to radio frequencies. Many mammals seem to be color blind, but birds typically have excellent color vision.
5. Sea animals, such as sharks, do not have particularly good vision, but have highly developed smell, which is essential to them for the location of food. A variety of land animals also have excellent smell and utilize body secretions called *pheromones* to communicate with other members of the species, particularly for sexual attraction. Male butterflies can detect and locate female odors at distances up to several miles. According to Wilson (1975), such chemical communication is virtually universal among living organisms.

Such a list could go on and on, but the general point is made: There are large differences in perceptual sensitivity and we cannot make any assumptions about what nonhumans are perceiving on the basis of our own perceptions.

Given that a particular species is sensitive to a particular range of stimuli, the species then has to respond appropriately to stimulus configurations within that range. Such responding may be based on inherited neural mechanisms for responding in relatively specific ways to specific configurations and/or may depend on prior experience. We may refer to these respectively as *releasing stimulus control* and *acquired stimulus control*.

## Releasing Stimuli

Many species may be *sensitive* to a particular stimulus pattern but only some are uniquely *responsive* to them. Thus, releasing stimuli[6] depend on species-specific sensorimotor organizations for their effectiveness in addition to stimulus sensitivity per se. For example, many species are sensitive to other organisms looking at them; primates are especially aggressive in response to being stared in the eye. Rhesus monkeys bare their teeth, scream, and may attack. Male squirrel monkeys, on the other hand, make penile displays as a ritualistic response that has apparently replaced fighting. As another kind of social interaction, baby birds gape in response to particular stimuli from the parents; the gaping is, in turn, a releaser for the parents to feed the babies.

Mother love and love for mother both suffer at the hands of the ethologists, however, because it turns out that the *effective* stimuli for releasing many social behaviors are only a small fraction of the total stimulus input from another organism. We find out what the effective stimuli are by making models with varying degrees of similarity to living organisms, or parts thereof, until it is determined what *minimal* aspect of the natural stimulus will release a particular behavior. The following examples illustrate such minimal stimuli.

1. For the stickleback, a wooden model on a stick lowered into the water tank will release male sexual behavior, but all that is required of the model is that it look vaguely like the swollen belly of a female with eggs.
2. The gaping behavior of hungry baby birds can be released by a stick with a spot on it (in some cases, a ring around it) similar to the bill of the parent.
3. Male turkeys get excited by a model of a female turkey head, although a real head is better (whether or not attached to a body).
4. The squirrel monkey's penile display is released by a mirror reflection of nothing more than its own eyeball.
5. A cardboard model of a "hawk" produced fearful behavior in chickens when "flown" over the flock, but the same model "flown" in reverse (now having a long neck on the leading edge and looking more like a goose) did not. The exact interpretation

[6]The concept of releaser is still a kind of holdover from the concept of reaction specific energy that is blocked until a particular stimulus releases it. If this view of motivation is wrong, which it certainly seems to be, then we have to think of releasing stimuli in somewhat different terms. For our purposes, we shall simply view releasing stimuli as any stimuli that evoke specific response patterns, based on some prewired perceptual-motor organization. The terms *stimulate* or *arouse* would then be equivalent to *release*.

of this phenomenon is controversial, but it seems well established that such a phenomenon occurs.

6. Frogs strike out at any small, buglike objects in motion, but not if the stimuli are stationary. They respond to large, dark stimuli by escaping.

7. There are also *supernormal stimuli,* artificial stimuli that are better releasers than natural ones. Thus, gulls will take care of oversize artificial eggs in preference to their own.

Desmond Morris (1968) tried to make the argument that human female breasts and lips are sexual releasers because of their similarity to the female buttocks and genitalia. The argument was that in the course of the evolution of walking erect, women minimized the display of those sexual releasers that are obvious in the more typical bent-over primate position; therefore, new ones were evolved. As Eibl-Eibesfeldt (1975, p. 495) notes, however, "The artificially up-lifted breast of a movie star may evoke such an association, but a normal breast is as dissimilar from a buttock as lips are from the labia." Besides which, men also have lips.

*Interaction of Internal States and Releasers.* A stimulus which will release a behavior such as sexual activity at one time may not do so at another time. Responsiveness depends on internal hormonal conditions that may be present only at a particular time of the month (e.g., estrus) in cyclic fashion or at certain seasons of the year (as with ungulates). In the case of seasonal mating, sex hormone changes are initiated by the pituitary gland; the pituitary is, in turn, under the control of dark-light cycles. Sexual arousability by members of the opposite sex is therefore under the control of complex organismic and environmental interactions. Only in the human species do females seem prepared to mate at any time, and even here the common restrictions against intercourse during menstruation are based on social taboos rather than on biological factors. Human females are also more sensitive to musk odors (as in perfumes) during their childbearing years; men are sensitive to them only if injected with estrogen prior to the odor test. We shall have considerably more to say about the interaction of internal states and external stimuli in subsequent chapters.

### Acquired Stimulus Control

Beside the innate releasing mechanisms, organisms learn to use stimuli as cues. They learn that a particular food is good or bad, that a particular event is painful, or that a stimulus signals a pleasant or unpleasant situation to come. Depending on the individual circumstances of learning, the range of stimuli to which an animal responds in a particular way may be widened or narrowed. A child may learn to be afraid of all dogs or only of one special dog. But, again depending on the particular structural characteristics of a species, some things are learned more readily than others. Presumably in the course of evolution, animals have developed mechanisms for responding to stimuli which are biologically important to them. In the case of releasers, there was *phylogenetic* selection for such responsiveness. Even in the case of learning there appears to be some preprogramming so that there is a bias in *ontogenetic* selection as well; that is, there is greater ease of learning some things than others. Seligman (1970) has referred to this as "preparedness." In humans, for example, Valentine (1930) reported that it was easy for a child to learn to be afraid of caterpillars, but that children did not readily become conditioned to fear opera glasses or a bottle. As Hebb (1955) suggests, there may be a latent fear of certain things that makes it easy to condition them. Such a "latent fear" is a genetic predisposition.

Recent research on poison avoidance, important for any species, indicates for example, that in rats there is a greater readiness to associate taste stimuli with illness but that in quail there is a greater readiness to associate a visual stimulus with illness (Wilcoxin, Dragoin, Kral, 1971). Since a rat has highly developed taste and olfactory systems, as compared to its vision, and since just the reverse is true for the quail, it all makes good biological sense.

In later chapters, we will look at the role of reward and punishment in relation to learning. A particular kind of learning, *imprinting,* has been of special interest to both ethologists and psychologists, however, and so we will deal with it here.

*Imprinting.* Imprinting has been most studied, and occurs most reliably, with precocial birds (those born with down and active immediately after hatching, such as chickens and ducks). The behavior generally studied is the *following response.* The basic phenomenon is that newborn birds will follow any object that moves in front of them in the first day or so of life. There is a critical posthatching time period during which this response occurs, and once it occurs it is supposed to be permanent. Thus, mallard ducklings will follow a duck-mother model or *anything else that moves* and are imprinted on the stimulus most strongly at about sixteen hours after hatching (Hess, 1962). In the normal course of duckling events, fortunately, the most likely moving stimulus is the real mother.

*Critical Periods.* For different species, there are different critical periods, but in all cases there is considerable variability. Hinde, Thorpe, and Vince (1956) found imprinting in coots as late as six days after hatching and were able to correlate the end of the imprinting period with the onset of a *flight period.* That is, the birds would imprint until they reached an age where they became afraid of strange objects and would not follow them. There apparently is no unique physiological process involved in imprinting; it is just that after a while birds (or other animals) become afraid of novel stimuli and do not become "attached" to them. This same view of attachment behavior in mammals has been expressed by Scott (1962), and may be seen in humans. For about the first three months of life, human infants show little response to parental billing and cooing; then they begin to smile and make answering noises. At about six months of age, they suddenly become frightened by unfamiliar stimuli, including new faces. This is often to the chagrin of grandparents or friends who arouse screaming and crying when they expect laughing and smiling. Eventually, of course, most children lose their extreme fear of unfamiliar stimuli.

The approach-flight view of the critical period has been given rather nice experimental support. Moltz (1960) noted that the imprinting period could be extended for a number of days by the use of tranquilizers, which presumably delayed the onset of the flight response, and then interpreted imprinting as follows. During the "critical period" for imprinting, the animal is in a state of low "anxiety," as shown by various behavioral observations. Any stimuli present during this time become conditioned to low anxiety responses by simple association. In the future, when the organism is fearful, it approaches (follows) those stimuli previously associated with low anxiety.

*Permanence of Imprinting.* Lorenz (1955) had argued from a rather small amount of evidence that imprinting is very nearly irreversible, citing cases in which adult shell parakeets made sexual advances toward humans to whom they had been imprinted in early life. He believed this aberrant sexual behavior had been caused by imprinting when the parakeet was young and did not believe it represented instrumental conditioning, because the response had not occurred at the time of imprinting. Irreversibility of imprinting can refer either to lack of generalization of the imprinted behavior to other stimuli or a failure of the strength of the imprinted response to decline, but the evidence seems to be negative in either case. Hinde, Thorpe, and Vince (1956) found that coots would follow objects very dissimilar to the one on which they were imprinted and Fabricius (1951) found that, although he could establish a strong following response in tufted ducks, shovellers, and eiders, the following response gradually diminished beginning at about three weeks of age. The most likely explanation for the attractiveness of humans to parakeets is that they were in each other's company over a long period of time, during which a strong attachment developed. Furthermore, as Moltz (1960) suggests, what is "imprinted" may be primarily an emotional response that leads to generalized approach behavior toward a given stimulus rather than a specific response toward that stimulus. The general conclusion from research on imprinting (e.g., see Sluckin, 1965) is that it is not a unique process but is a fairly typical kind of learning that happens to occur at a particular stage in life.

## CIRCADIAN RHYTHMS

Consider the following three situations.

1. If you have been traveling in Europe for a while and fly back to New York from London, a six-hour time difference, your body will still be on London time. It takes several days to get out of the disorientation and irregular sleeping characteristic of jet lag.
2. Finches kept in alternating twelve-hour dark and light cycles are very active in the light phase, but not in the dark. If now put into constant illumination, they still show about the same twelve-hour fluctuations in activity.
3. Potatoes grown in underground containers with constant light and temperature show cyclic growth spurts with twelve-hour peaks.

Each of these illustrations is an example of a circadian ("about a day") rhythm. Such rhythms may actually be about twenty-four hours or they may be multiples thereof (e.g., six or twelve hours). Such examples can be multiplied almost indefinitely, circadian rhythms being demonstrable for almost any living thing down to unicellular organisms or single cells within complex organisms.[7] Given that such biological clocks are a pervasive phenomenon, how do they work? They are certainly related to the movement of the earth around its axis, but are they controlled internally or externally, or by some combination?

### Entrainment

Under natural conditions, the circadian period is *entrained to* (synchronized with) the period of the earth's rotation by periodic factors or cues called *Zeitgebers.* Daily fluctuations of the earth's temperature and dark-light pattern are the most obvious of these. For many apparently

[7]There has recently been popular interest in multiple rhythms in humans. Based on the month, day, and year you were born, there are said to be a number of cycles of different phase length, with "peaks" and "valleys" when all the cycles happen to be simultaneously at high or low points. We are then told to guide our lives by these cycles, to make sure that we do thus and so when they are at their peaks. This bears the same relationship to reputable work on circadian or other biological rhythms that astrology does to astronomy, i.e., no relationship at all.

cyclic activities, it may be sufficient to explain them as responses to external cues. For example, the increased activity of caged laboratory animals just before feeding time (the "caretaker effect") could be accounted for in terms of the animals learning specific daily cues related to feeding (noises, lights coming on, etc.). For many other instances, however, such an explanation is challenged by two facts, illustrated in the finch behavior. First, when the finches are put into constant illumination, they continue to show the activity rhythm characteristic of dark-light cycles. This is known as the *free running pattern* (it is "free" of the entraining stimulus). Secondly, the total period of time between cycles is not exactly twenty-four hours and is not exactly the same for all animals. They may range from twenty-three to twenty-five hours for different individuals. This indicates that the rhythm is internal, since an externally controlled period should show the earth's twenty-four hour periodicity for all animals (Aschoff, 1965).

Humans have also gone into caves or underground bunkers for several days or weeks. These environments have constant light and temperature, with no clocks or other external time cues allowed. The subjects still show circadian rhythms for such things as volume of urine secreted, as well as concentrations of sodium and potassium in urine, and body temperature. Total daily sleep time is very close to that occurring in the normal environment, but particular individuals may go on some "day" other than twenty-four hours and gradually shift completely through the regular earth-clock day.

A particularly striking form of entrainment has been described for the fruit fly *Drosophilia pseudobscura*. In its pupal stage, if the fly is kept in the dark, but exposed to light for a few seconds, it hatches either twenty-four hours later or some multiple thereof and has its activity set on the cycle entrained to the light flash. This is interesting for many reasons, not the least of which is that such behavior looks like a primitive form of learning.

### Internal versus External Control of Rhythms

As already indicated, there are two competing interpretations for circadian rhythms. The first is that there is an internal "oscillator" set for about a twenty-four hour period. There would be an obvious advantage to such built-in oscillation because the individual could maintain a circadian rhythm under adverse environmental conditions. Some animals should be quiet at some times of day for their own protection from predators, to be awake to hunt, or just to recuperate from activity. Such a natural oscillation would provide for the periodicity of biological rhythms and particular Zeitgebers could entrain the phase relationships.

The primary argument for internal clocks has been that free running patterns are the same as when Zeitgebers are present. Even more convincing, however, is evidence showing specific physiological locations for such oscillators. In a series of ingenious experiments with cockroaches by a number of investigators, and summarized by J. L. Brown (1975), it has been found that the circadian rhythm is controlled through the optic lobe of the brain, although details of the mechanism that generates the oscillation are not yet known. It has also been possible to breed fruit flies selectively for particular activity cycles, and removal of the pineal gland from house sparrows disrupts their cyclic activity. These experiments all strongly indicate that some circadian rhythms can be internally controlled, although not that *all* are necessarily controlled internally.

The alternative interpretation is that circadian rhythms follow geophysical changes. These changes may be considerably more subtle than light-dark or temperature cycles, however. Magnetic fields, barometric pressure, and change in ionization of the atmosphere may be involved. Since humans are not consciously aware of magnetic fields, for example, it has been difficult to imagine how other animals are responsive to them. But F. A. Brown (1970) showed experimentally that planaria (flatworms) could use magnetic fields to orient themselves spatially, and the same is true for rats in mazes and for migratory birds. The theory of atmospheric changes is given rather dramatic support by the fact that unusual changes in biological rhythms of experimental animals have been found to correlate with atmospheric changes of which the experimenters were unaware at the time (such as radiation storms).

### Some Practical Problems for Humans

We have already mentioned jet lag, a factor now taken into account in planning diplomatic conferences or other negotiations. Similarly, night shift workers get "out of phase" and job errors and accidents are most likely to occur at about three o'clock in the morning (Aschoff, 1965). A 180-degree phase shift in circadian rhythm can usually be accomplished in about six days, with new entraining stimuli, but if one is expected to change work shifts every week or two, there is hardly time to take advantage of the adaptation.

Men in space could, theoretically, follow any arbitrary activity cycle most convenient to their work. In fact, however, the total activity cycle can only be reduced to "days" of about eighteen hours or increased to about twenty-eight hours, and performance is best on an approximately twenty-four-hour day. American earth-orbital flights therefore use an artificial day based on central standard time (Folk, 1974). There are actual sunrises and sunsets about every ninety minutes. In the case of crews who fly jet aircraft long distances in either east or west directions, it is found that the best plan is to have a crew fly both ways in a single day, thus allowing them to keep adapted to a single time zone. There seem to be no tricks for speeding up adaptation, although there are considerable individual differences. Some people seem to adjust to a six-hour time change within a day; others make little adjustment in a week.

## ORIENTATION AND COMMUNICATION: THE DANCE OF THE BEES

We have discussed some general aspects of the stimulus control of behavior with particular reference to the differential responsiveness of different species to the same *apparent* stimuli. They are not the same stimuli, of course, since they are not responded to in the same way. There are many fascinating biological problems about how animals are able to orient themselves correctly with regard to returning home from long distances, going to a particular feeding place, or migrating seasonally over thousands of miles. We shall deal here with how bees communicate orientation to each other. This is a double-barrelled question concerning both orientation and insect communication. The discovery that bees dance is virtually synonomous with the name of Karl von Frisch (e.g., 1967, 1971) who has intensively studied these social insects for many years. J. L. Brown (1975) gives a good brief review of von Frisch's work.

The basic phenomenon is this: An experimenter puts a dish of sugar water at some distance from a beehive. Eventually it is found by a few foraging bees, who then disappear. Shortly thereafter a larger number of bees arrive at the site, apparently recruited by the foragers. We find out more precisely what happens by (1) marking bees with different colors, either to indicate different hives or individuals within a single hive, and (2) using special hives that have glass walls on one side so that the behavior of the bees inside can be directly observed.

The foraging bees use two kinds of cues to the food: odors and dancing movements. If the sugar is on a particular kind of flower (e.g., phlox) but not on a different kind which is nearby (e.g., cyclamen) the recruits carry the odor of the phlox back to the hive on their bodies and in their stomachs. On entering the hive, they regurgitate their stomach contents. Thus other bees in the hive can get the scent, which might otherwise be lost from the exterior of the body in a long flight back to the hive. The recruits then go to the source of the sugar water, the phlox, rather than to the other flowers. This process is reversed if the sugar is on the other flowers. The bee may also use a pheromone from a gland on its abdomen to mark the source. The odor of this is detectable at a distance of several meters. On the basis of the odor cues, then, the recruits know what to search for, but require more information about direction and distance.

The orientation of the food supply is given by a dance that the forager does in the hive. There are several dances (Figure 3.3). When the food supply is a short distance from the hive, the *round dance* is used. The forager bee goes in a circle. It is believed that this dance simply indicates food close to the hive and conveys no information about direction or exact distance. The recruits simply fly in all directions from the hive until the food is found. The second dance is the *waggle dance,* illustrated, along with the round dance, in Figure 3.3. The waggle dance has two characteristics that convey information. The first is the orientation of the central axis, which is in relation to the sun. If the dance is done with the central axis

**Figure 3.3**  *Dances of the bees. Round dance (left) indicates distance to food and waggle dance (right) indicates distance and direction in relation to the sun. See text for further details. (From Krogh, "The Language of the Bees." Copyright © August, 1948 by Scientific American, Inc. All rights reserved.)*

*downward,* the direction is away from the sun. If the central axis is vertical and *upward,* it means "go toward the sun." Intermediate orientations of the central axis indicate the general size of the angle away from the sun. Interestingly, while these dances are visually observable to the human experimenter, they are usually done in the hive in the dark, and hence the recruits are actually using other cues than vision. The distance is indicated by the tempo of the waggle dance, there being an orderly relationship between the speed with which the bee goes through its modified figure eight and the distance; the faster the dance, the nearer the food. The distance is apparently communicated by either sound or vibrations picked up by the recruits' antennae coming into contact with the forager. There are also some intermediate dances, one of which is called the *sickle dance,* which gives a rougher approximation to direction for an intermediate distance to food.

Just as there are species differences in spider web constructions or bird nest building, there are dancing differences in different populations of bees. These may be correlated with their flight ranges (J. L. Brown, 1975)— the smaller the overall flight range, the more the whole meaning of the dance is scaled down regarding distance. It should be noted, however, that not all of the bees in a recruited group actually do find the food. This is another instance of the fact that species-specific behaviors are not invariant. Homing pigeons also get lost. There are many other flight problems for bees, such as winds that blow them off course, obstacles, and so on. The main cue the bees use to orient with regard to the sun is probably the polarization of light from the sun. Even if the sun is not directly visible on a cloudy day, as long as there is a little blue sky the bees can orient adequately. If the sky is completely overcast, however, so that there are no direct rays from the sun, they seem to lose their directional orientation. The orienting capacity of bees, particularly with regard to the dances, has been periodically challenged but according to J. L. Brown (1975, p. 457) the original findings are apparently valid.

## CONCLUSION

The instinct concept has had a checkered history. Because it is so widely misunderstood we have tried to indicate some of the meanings and misunderstandings surrounding it and to give some indication of the direction that research in this area is taking. Biological bases for the behavior of all organisms is taken for granted but rather than depending on a vague concept of instinct most biologically-oriented researchers are concerned with the details of sensory, motor, developmental and integrative processes involved in particular behaviors in particular species. The continuity of life is recognized, but so are the variations from species to species. Behavior involves a continuous interplay between organism and environment and the message of the ethologists is that we must understand the environment as well as the organism if we are to interpret behavior meaningfully.

# The Concept of Drive

When we say that a person "has a lot of drive," we are invoking a motivational concept to account for the fact that this person "works hard," "gets a lot done," or is "energetic." Many theories at both animal and human levels have leaned heavily on such a notion. Thus, hunger may "drive" a rat to food and inconsistent beliefs may "drive" a man to change his opinions. Different as the specifics of these two situations are, the core idea is the same: rat and man are goaded by drives and are more comfortable when these are reduced. Drives, then, are generally considered to be aversive internal states and organisms act to relieve them. The apparent value of the concept is that it seems to explain such widely separated observations as those of the rat's hunger and the man's change of opinion.

Drive is generally said to account only for the arousal or vigor of behavior, not its direction. For example, we may take the simple observation that hungry animals and people work harder to get food and eat more than do ones that are not hungry. It is this vigor and persistence that drive is supposed to account for so well. Furthermore, since food and water are such fundamental biological necessities, the concept of drive should help us account for performance in obtaining them. Any shortcomings in the explanatory value of the concept at this level should give us pause in using the concept at the level of complex human behavior. Our purpose in this chapter, then, is to examine the drive concept in sufficient detail that the student can get some notion of its strengths and weaknesses.

## EVOLUTIONARY BACKGROUND

The concept of drive is thoroughly grounded in evolutionary theory. Claude Bernard (1878) recognized that land-dwelling and sea-dwelling organisms had different survival problems. The sea provides its inhabitants with nutrients and eliminates the problem of dehydration, but land animals have to seek food and water and protect their cellular structures against evaporation. Bernard argued that if the land-dwelling organism is to have the freedom of mobility necessary for survival in its *external* environment, it must be able to maintain its *internal* environment, the watery medium of its cells, in some condition roughly equivalent to that of the sea. Bernard's central theme then was that the necessary condition for a free life is constancy of the internal environment.

Walter Cannon (1939) incorporated Bernard's ideas in the concept of *homeostasis:* "The central problem in understanding the remarkable stability of our bodies . . . is knowing how the fluid matrix is preserved" (1939, pp. 287–288). Cannon summarized a wide range of evidence on this self-regulating capacity of the organism for keeping its internal matrix within narrow limits, such problems as blood sugar level, water content, blood pressure, temperature, and acid-base balance. The problem is twofold. First, there are the automatic homeostatic adjustments made by the body, such as shivering or sweating when body temperature lowers or rises. Secondly, there are behavioral adjustments, such as seeking a warmer or cooler place. In the cases of food and water shortage, the body has a limited capacity for self-regulation before new stores must be sought. Land-dwelling animals must then do something overtly active.

The relationship between biological needs and behavior was the theme of the functional school of psychology, whose keywords were *adaptation* and *adjustment.* Carr (1925), a leading proponent of this school, argued that the basic animal behavior was the *adaptive act.* When an organism needs food or water, there is a persistent internal stimulus that produces activity until the need is satisfied. From this approach, a number of concepts have emerged.

*1. Need.* Need is an excess or deficiency of some product related to survival.[1] As an intervening variable, we may define need on the antecedent side in terms of deprivation (such as food) or excess (such as carbon dioxide). On the consequent side, we would define need in terms of some health or survival criterion. One might expect that such needs should lead to activity that would restore the appropriate balance in the organism. In point of fact, however, some needs do *not* lead to any activity (some vitamin deficits or oxygen deficit, for example). Therefore, the concept of drive is introduced.

*2. Drive.* Drive is an inferred state, not directly observable. Its antecedent conditions could be the same as for need, but the consequent conditions are behavioral acts. It is drive, then, that goads the animal, that provides the persistent stimulus to behavior. One suggestion (e.g., Miller, 1951b) is that any persistent and strong stimulus can have drive properties. Therefore, a drive could be aroused without a need in the usual sense. Need and drive may be correlated, but not necessarily so. It is this lack of correlation which has led to the two different concepts.

*3. Goal.* A goal is some commodity that will reduce the drive that initiated the activity. A hungry animal consumes food, after which it is inactive with reference to hunger. The elements assumed in this sequence, then, are commonly that need leads to drive, which energizes activity, and reduction of the drive reduces activity.[2] Unfortunately, for most of its

[1]In personality theory, needs are not defined this way. For example, need for achievement is not defined in terms of a survival criterion. We shall discuss needs of the achievement variety in later chapters.

[2]There are many subsidiary questions. For example, is there only one drive, which has many behavioral manifestations, or are there many different drives, with correspondingly different behaviors? Are drives learned, and, if so, how? What about sex, where there is no apparent deficit but nevertheless highly motivated behavior?

history there has been little in the way of specification as to *how* drive
energizes behavior, or why one particular behavior rather than another
occurs under a particular drive condition. Clark Hull produced the most
systematic attempt to deal with these kinds of questions.


## HULL'S THEORY

Clark Hull has been one of the most influential of American psychologists.
His ascendence began with work in aptitude testing around the time of
World War I. From that, he turned to the study of hypnosis and his *Hypnosis
and Suggestibility* (1933b) is still considered worthy of serious study. About
1930, however, Hull also began to publish a series of papers that have
become classics in behavior theory. These culminated with his *Principles of
Behavior* (1943), which was enthusiastically received. Research related to
the *Principles* dominated the field of motivation and learning for twenty
years. Even research directly opposed to the theory used it as a baseline for
comparison.

Hull's theory purported to be the beginnings of a complete theory of
behavior, but we shall deal only with the motivational aspects here. His
concepts of drive and drive reduction have stimulated a vast amount of
research and any survey of motivation would be inadequate without discussing them. This is of more than just historical interest, however, because
drivelike motivational concepts keep reappearing in new places. While there
are many things wrong with Hull's theory, it would be shortsighted to brush
it aside as outmoded without looking at it. The kinds of problems that have
been raised point to the inherent difficulties in any drivelike theory, of
which we should be aware. At the very least, we should become hesitant
to use the term *drive* loosely.


### Drive as an Intervening Variable

Hull started off with the clear distinction between performance and
the variables that determine the direction and vigor of performance. The
two main considerations were *habit strength* (sHr), which is a statement of
the associative strength between a given stimulus and response, and *drive* (D),
the energizing component for "activating" a habit into performance. Hull
started from evolutionary considerations and, therefore, from physiology,
but in his formal theory drive was strictly an intervening variable. Drive
was an operationally defined concept in his syntactical system, not a process.
Hull clearly separated habit and drive as intervening variables, arguing
that drive per se has no directive (steering or guiding) properties. Instead, he
made the rather unusual proposal that drive energizes *all* habits, as well as
unlearned responses. Thus, if several responses were connected to the stimuli

in a given situation, drive would tend to activate them all. The response with the strongest association to these stimuli at the moment would be the one most likely to occur.

In the more precise language of the theory, drive *multiplies* habit to produce the excitatory potential for a particular response. Thus, in the case of a learned response:

$$\text{Excitatory Potential} = \text{habit} \times \text{drive}$$

or, symbolically:

$$sEr = sHr \times D \quad \text{(or more simply, } E = H \times D\text{)}$$

In relatively simple situations, where one habit is clearly stronger than others, it is predicted that the response represented by the stronger habit will be the one to occur. In a simple, straight alleyway, for example, if an animal had learned the response of running to food, it would be expected that this would be a very dominant habit and that increasing drive level, by increasing deprivation, would produce a more vigorous running response.

If a number of habits of nearly equal strength were involved, the situation would be considerably complicated because different excitatory potentials would interfere with each other. Suppose, for example, that a machine operator has a number of very similar levers to operate for different functions. These very similar stimuli would arouse competing responses. An increase in the level of drive, such as during an emergency, would actually produce greater interference and greater chance of an error.

Drive would also energize *unlearned* response tendencies if the stimuli for these responses were present and more dominant than learned response tendencies in the same situation. Thus:

$$E = sUr \times D$$

where $sUr$ is a stimulus-response relationship that does not require learning, such as a reflex. Examples of $sUr$ would include simple reflexes, but would also presumably include "spontaneous" or "random" activity.

In the formula $[E = H \times D]$, $E$, $H$, and $D$ are intervening variables. Variable $H$ is defined in terms of number of learning trials, increasing with the number of S-R associations. The variable $D$ is defined in terms of number of hours of food deprivation, strength of a noxious stimulus, or some other appropriate manipulation. The variable $E$ bears a strictly syntactical relation to $H$ and $D$ and is measured in terms of amplitude, frequency, probability, or latency of responding. We may illustrate this with a slight variation on Figure 1-2 in Chapter One. Observable events are outside the box, intervening variables are inside the box.

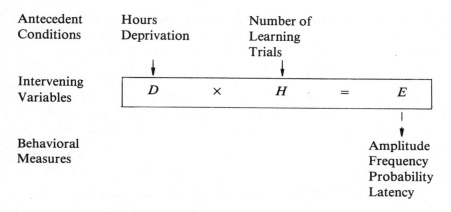

| Antecedent Conditions | Hours Deprivation | | Number of Learning Trials | | |
|---|---|---|---|---|---|

Intervening Variables

$$D \quad \times \quad H \quad = \quad E$$

Behavioral Measures

Amplitude
Frequency
Probability
Latency

If $H$ is held constant and $D$ is varied, then $E$ varies strictly with $D$ and the response measure varies only as $D$ varies. The range through which $E$ varies, of course, depends on the level at which $H$ is held constant. For example, if $H$ is arbitrarily set at 1.00 and $D$ varies from 1 to 5, then $E$ will also vary from 1 to 5, since $E = H \times D$. If $H$ is set at 3, however, with $D$ varying from 1 to 5, then $E$ will vary from 3 to 15. This is shown graphically in Figure 4-1. The main prediction of the theory here is that <u>as $H$ increases, performance curves will diverge as a function of $D$, as</u> indicated in Figure 4-1, which shows $E$ when $H = 1, 2, 3,$ or $4$ and $D = 1$ or $2$.

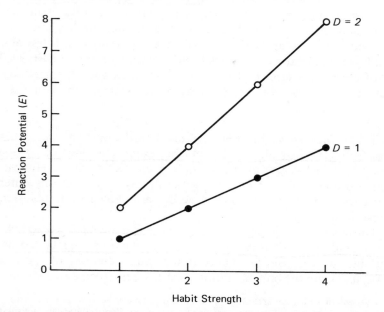

**Figure 4.1** *Habit and drive interaction in Hullian theory* ($E = H \times D$).

Such data were obtained by S. Williams (1938) and Perin (1942) in experiments in which animals were given different numbers of acquisition trials with bar pressing and then extinguished under either three or twenty-two hours of food deprivation. Other experiments have produced similar results.

*Criteria for Calling an Intervening Variable Drive.* Within Hull's theory, there are a number of theoretical concepts, and specific criteria are established for distinguishing between them. The following three are commonly used for drive.

*1. An Increase in the Level of the Variable Energizes a Wide Range of Responses.* If food deprivation energized only one response, such as eating, we could argue that deprivation simply provides a stimulus for this particular response. The concept of drive would be unnecessary because a simple associative interpretation would account for the data. If a variety of responses can be energized, however, (e.g., running, eating, and bar pressing) then a specific S-R connection is ruled out for any particular drive-producing operation and a "general" energizing variable is indicated.

*2. A Decrease in the Level of the Variable is Reinforcing.* If an animal reduces its hunger by making a response that leads to food, and thereafter makes the response more often, then the variable (hunger) may be said to be drive. Reduction of drive reinforces an association between stimulus and response. This criterion best applies to painful stimuli, because we can tell more readily that the level of a painful stimulus has been reduced. It is obvious, for example, when an animal escapes shock. It is less obvious that a hungry animal's hunger has been reduced by a food pellet weighing 1/20 of a gram because (1) the amount is so small and (2) something else about the food (taste or texture) may be rewarding rather than hunger reduction.

*3. An Increase in the Level of the Variable is Punishing.*[3] If a response is followed by increased pain, the response is less likely to occur. Therefore, pain has one of the defining properties of drive. Hunger and thirst, however, are not thus far demonstrably drives by this criterion, because their onset or increase has never been shown to be punishing in an experiment.

Unfortunately, there is no universal convention for saying whether just one or all three of the criteria just described have to be met in order for a variable to be considered motivational. Manipulations of the level of electric shock are the only operations which seem to come close to meeting

[3]Stimulation of brain areas that produce eating can also serve as rewards. In terms of drive theory, this looks as if an increase in drive were rewarding, rather than punishing. We will discuss this view in detail later.

all three. This may be caused by the fact that it is difficult to get either a rapid onset or reduction of appetitive states. It is therefore difficult to associate changes in the level of hunger or thirst with particular responses.

The *energizing* effect of drive should not be so dependent on rapid arousal or reduction, however. Drive theory should then be more testable by this criterion. Since such arbitrary responses as bar pressing are established by use of rewards like food and water, there is considerable potential confounding of drive and incentive variables. So-called random or spontaneous activity[4] is not presumably related to specific rewards, and therefore should provide a less ambiguous measure. Let us then look at some of the evidence relating deprivation to activity.

## DRIVE AND ACTIVITY

In the classic study in the area of drive and activity Dashiell (1925) found that hungry rats explored a "checkerboard" maze more than did rats that were not hungry. This was taken by a generation of psychologists to mean that drive stimulates activity and was "confirmed" by many later experiments (e.g., Richter, 1927). There are a host of problems, however, related to types of measurement, deprivation procedures, and species.

### Definition of Activity: Methods of Measurement

The term *activity* is defined operationally in terms of any of several specific measurement procedures. If the drive concept has any generality, it ought to affect all such measures in more or less the same way, and they should be correlated. Let us first see what some of the common measures have been and then look at some of the data.

1. *Checkerboard Maze.* The Dashiell (or checkerboard) maze is a latticework of pathways. The animal is released at the starting point and its particular pathway to the other end is traced by the experimenter on a piece of paper diagrammed like the maze. The number of different pathways entered from start to finish is the score.
2. *Activity Wheel.* This is the common "squirrel cage" type of wheel in which the animal can run. The animal may live in the wheel, obtaining its food and water in an adjacent cage to which it has access. A counter records each revolution of the wheel.
3. *Stabilimeter.* Sometimes called a "jiggle cage," the stabilimeter is a cage mounted on springs so that as the animal shifts its weight

---

[4]Such activity is spontaneous or random, of course, only to the extent that we cannot identify the specific preceding events.

electrical contacts open and close, counting the number of movements. The sensitivity of the switches can be set so that only the most gross movements are recorded or so that very delicate movements are recorded. Using devices called *strain gauges,* it is also possible to detect and record minute distortions of the floor of an apparatus as an animal moves around.

4. *Activity Cage.* The activity cage is commonly a standard cage with a device for recording the number of times the animal crosses the midline. The cage may be mounted on a pivot or the animal may interrupt photoelectric beams as it moves across the cage.

5. *Sound Cage.* A more recent variant of the activity cage involves a sound field inside a box. The animal's movements alter the field and each alteration is recorded electrically.

6. *Open Field.* A field, or open area, is marked off by intersecting lines and the number of lines crossed per unit time is scored. Each time all four paws cross a line, for example, a score is recorded. The open field has been particularly useful in studying "emotionality" in rodents. It is apparently stressful to these animals, particularly if the field's well lighted, and a reduction of activity is taken as an index of the degree of emotionality.

7. *Time Sampling.* The measures just described do not distinguish well between different types of activity. Time sampling does this by utilizing direct observation of the subjects by the experimenter. Bindra and Blond (1958) recorded walking, grooming, sniffing, lying, and miscellaneous behavior of the rat. The experimenter looks at an animal at the beginning of each minute, for example, and simply records the type of behavior observed. Since it is always possible that the experimenter's observations might influence the animals' behavior, the subjects are often observed through a one-way glass or under red light (invisible to the rat, which is color-blind).

Each of these seven measurement procedures defines operationally what we may mean by "activity." The question, then, is whether deprivation, pure and simple, produces an increase in any or all of them, as drive theory would predict.

### Effects of Deprivation on Activity

We have already seen evidence (Dashiell, 1925) that food deprivation leads to increased activity. This is particularly true in the running wheel. Strong, however (1957) compared the activity of animals in high- and low-sensitivity stabilimeter cages with typical running-wheel performance. He

found that in the low-sensitivity cage there was virtually *no* change in measured activity, and in the *high*-sensitivity cage there was actually a *decrease*
in activity with greater deprivation. Strong concluded that food deprivation
alters the *kinds* of activity the animal engages in rather than just increasing
activity. Such gross body movements as running increase with deprivation
but fine body movements decrease. Because the very sensitive stabilimeter
records all activity, fine and gross, more or less equally, an increase in
gross movements is more than offset by the decline in fine movements.
Strong's results do not seem to be congruent with drive theory.

*Apparatus, Species, and Deprivation Differences.* In one of the more
systematic series of studies, Campbell (1964) compared different apparatuses,
deprivation conditions, and species. The animals were never fed or watered
over their several days in the apparatus, guaranteeing that they were not
specifically rewarded for more activity. Any changes are therefore presumably caused by deprivation alone. Campbell found distinct differences
in activity at the peak of change from baseline, summarized in Figure 4-2.

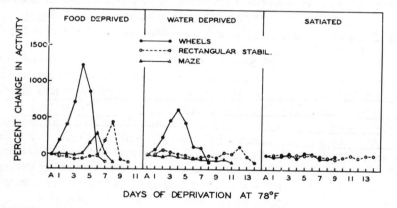

**Figure 4.2** *Percent change in activity of food-deprived, water-deprived,
and satiated rats in activity wheels, rectangular stabilimeter cages, and
an automatic Dashiel maze at 78° F. (From Campbell, 1964, p. 330.)*

For example, there is a 1200 percent increase in the activity of food-deprived
rats in wheels at four days of deprivation, but smaller changes in stabilimeters or checkerboard mazes. Water-deprived rats showed only about a
600 percent increase in the wheels and virtually none at all in the other
apparatuses.

Looking at different species, Campbell, Smith, Misanin, and Jaynes
(1966) found consistent activity changes in response to deprivation within a
given species (chicks, guinea pigs, hamsters, and rabbits), but these changes

were sometimes in *opposite directions,* depending on species, type of deprivation, and apparatus. For example, food- or water-deprived rabbits showed *less* stabilimeter activity than satiated rabbits. Hungry hamsters were more active in the wheel, but thirsty hamsters showed less activity than satiated ones. If the drive concept is to have any broad utility, it ought to have some generality across species, but it does not, even in the case of gross activity.

*Estrus and Activity.* One of the most reliable activity changes in the wheel occurs as the female rat goes through her estrus cycle. As she goes into estrus, her activity increases until the peak of the estrus period, then declines until the onset of the next cycle (e.g., Richter, 1927). Since estrus has been presumptive evidence of sex drive, the change in wheel-running activity has been considered strong evidence for drive as an energizer. Bolles (1963), however, was unable to observe any activity changes related to estrus when he used the time-sampling technique with animals in their home cages. He concluded that the wheel itself is crucial to activity during estrus. One could easily conceive of the running wheel as a means of providing relief from tension, with running therefore being rewarded. Estrus alone does not appear to be a drive that stimulates activity, however, as psychologists so long believed.

The experiments of Strong, Bolles, and Campbell—among many others (see Baumeister, Hawkins, & Cromwell, 1964)—clearly indicate that the effects of deprivation are specific to the type of measurement, deprivation, and species. This means that the conception of drive as a unitary variable, a single motivational dimension that affects all behaviors in the same way, simply is not correct. Interestingly, with the checkerboard maze Campbell (1964) found only a small activity increase with food deprivation, Bolles (1962b) found none, and Montgomery (1953) found a decrease. Thus, the experiment that stood for so long as the prototype demonstration of the effects of drive on activity (Dashiell, 1925) has not withstood replication.

*Body Weight Loss and Activity.* In spite of these kinds of inconsistencies described, there does seem to be some increment in running as a function of food deprivation. One reason for some of the inconsistencies may be that different procedures for deprivation lead to different amounts of weight loss. Several experiments with food deprivation have shown that rats begin to get more active when they reach about 15 percent body weight loss (e.g., Moskowitz, 1959). Treichler and Hall (1962) also found this for the wheel, but not the stabilimeter, using food or water deprivation, or the two combined. Bolles (1967) also reported supportive evidence, but this appears to be contradicted by Campbell (1964) who found only hungry rats more active in the stabilimeter even though thirsty rats lost as much weight. The hypothesis that in some experiments animals have simply not lost enough weight to become more active does seem to account for some of the data, but not all of it.[5]

### The Learning of "Spontaneous" Activity

Since activity is not a simple, direct response to deprivation, could it be learned? First, during early life, are animals specifically rewarded for being more active when hungry? Second, is it possible that they even learn to be more active during the course of an experiment because they are rewarded for it?

In answer to the first question, several experiments have followed up the hypothesis that hungry animals might be more active than thirsty ones because they have previously learned to scurry about looking for food when hungry. Water, on the other hand, is usually found in a fixed location. This might be a water bottle mounted on the side of a cage or, in the wild, a water hole. The animals would not have learned to hunt for water when thirsty and therefore might not show more activity when water deprived. If food were always found in a fixed location, then hungry rats might not be any more active than thirsty ones. Campbell and Cicala (1962) tested this hypothesis by rearing rats on liquid food (Metrecal) dispensed from a tube in a fixed position in the cage. Running-wheel activity still increased after food deprivation, just the same as always, indicating that the spatial location of food was not critical. Finger (1965) tested the same hypothesis and obtained similar results with weanling rats that had not yet started eating regular lab food. Both of these experiments lead to the conclusion that there can be at least *some* activity induced by food deprivation and hence lend some mild support to the drive concept.

In answer to the second question, Finger, Reid, and Weasner (1957) and Hall (1958) showed that if hungry rats were fed immediately after running in the wheel they ran more than if food were delayed for an hour after running. Other experiments (e.g., Wright, 1965) also lead to the interpretation that running can be rewarded "accidentally" by the experimenter. The evidence is clear that running is affected by reward, but there is also evidence that sometimes deprivation facilitates running without specific reward. The experiments in the previous paragraph suggest this, as do the experiments by Campbell (1964) in which the animals were never fed in the apparatus or

---

[5]An interesting theoretical variation of the weight loss interpretation is the suggestion by Collier (1964, Collier & Knarr, 1966) that thirsty rats run to reduce weight, the end point being some fixed ratio of body water to lean body weight. His idea is that if the rat is water deprived it has "too much" body weight for the amount of water available and increases its running until it has lost enough weight to recover the optimal ratio.

after running. At the same time, such increments are pretty much limited to food-deprived rats in the activity wheel. This constitutes support for the drive concept in a very restricted range of conditions, hardly of impressive generality.

### The Lowered Response Threshold Concept

We can say with some confidence that "spontaneous" activity is not reliably increased by deprivation alone. On the other hand, when appropriate *rewards* are involved, there are pretty consistent increases in responsiveness with longer deprivation. Thus, hungry rats run faster to food, thirsty rats to water, and so on. Several authors (e.g., Campbell & Sheffield, 1953; Ausubel, 1956) have therefore argued that deprivation does not directly stimulate behavior, but instead *deprivation lowers the threshold for responding to environmental stimulation.* This is not to say that organisms have lower *sensory* thresholds when deprived, but rather that they are more *ready to respond* to such stimuli as occur. Hungry or thirsty animals respond to stimuli that would be ineffective in arousing satiated animals.

Such arousing environmental stimuli might be either rewards or stimuli leading to rewards. They might also be such extraneous stimuli as miscellaneous sights and sounds. Could such extraneous stimuli instigate spontaneous activity in deprived animals? Campbell and Sheffield (1953) performed one of the first experimental tests of this hypothesis. They had rats living individually in stabilimeter cages in a constant environment; light off and exhaust fan on. For ten minutes a day, the light was turned on and the exhaust fan off—a *stimulus change.* Food-deprived animals showed increased activity during the ten-minute period, but nondeprived animals did not.

Hall (1956) further tested the lowered response threshold hypothesis, but used activity wheels rather than stabilimeters. His results indicated that both deprivation and stimulus change were important, having additive effects. Unfortunately, by its very nature the activity wheel is a major source of stimulation to the animal in the wheel. The animal can hear, see, and feel it moving. It is therefore possible that even though the experimenter does not explicitly provide the wheel-running animal with stimulation the wheel itself is a sufficient source of sensory input to arouse activity. If this were the case, then the lowered response threshold hypothesis could explain Hall's results.

This ends our discussion of activity studies. We have seen that activity is not a simple, unidimensional phenomenon. It varies with the type of measure, species, deprivation, and possibly other specific methodological details. Emphasis on the role of external stimuli as causes of activity has become more predominant in recent years (e.g., Tapp, 1969) than an explanation in terms of drive. Many behaviors are now being seen as influenced by deprivation only insofar as deprivation increases responsiveness to external stimuli. At best, we find little support for the classic drive concept in evidence from studies of deprivation and activity. There is another area of research we should look at, however, in which the drive concept can be tested independently of specific reward effects. This is the research on irrelevant drive.

## THE CONCEPT OF IRRELEVANT DRIVE

The implication of Hull's drive theory is that *any source of drive* should energize any learned or unlearned response tendency. As we have just seen, it does not appear that deprivation energizes activity in any very indiscriminate manner. The activity studies were considered important because the effects of reward could be controlled. There is another implication of Hull's theory, however, that does permit testing with such arbitrary responses as bar pressing. If any source of drive energizes any habit, then thirst should energize a habit originally learned with food deprivation and food reward. In this instance, hunger is called a *relevant* drive (relevant to the food reward) and thirst is an *irrelevant* drive (irrelevant to food reward). Hull's equation for excitatory potential is then expanded as follows:

$$E = sHr \times (D_r + D_i)$$

where
$$D_r = \text{relevant drive and}$$
$$D_i = \text{irrelevant drive}$$

The theory is not limited, of course, to hunger and thirst. Pain, fear, or any other source of drive should serve as either relevant or irrelevant drive, depending on the situation, and should multiply any habit.

The concept of irrelevant drive was originally developed by Hull (1943) to account for data (Perin, 1942) that showed that animals satiated for food made a considerable number of responses during extinction. Hull felt this could only mean that some source of drive other than hunger was present during extinction, since, according to the theory, there should be no responding without some drive. Evidence flatly contradictory to the Perin data appeared very shortly after the publication of Hull's book (e.g., Koch & Daniel, 1945; Saltzman & Koch, 1948). These data, plus those of Kimble (1951) and Horenstein (1951) all showed that resistance to extinction was virtually nil at zero hours of deprivation. Nevertheless, the problem lingered on, probably because the concept of irrelevant drive provided predictions that seemed to be tests of the general drive concept. Since the concept of irrelevant drive has not fared well, we shall note only a few of the more important studies.

### Animal Studies of Irrelevant Drive

One way to determine if irrelevant drives are effective is to combine or *summate* relevant and irrelevant drives in the very straightforward manner indicated previously $(D_r + D_i)$. Thus, if relevant drive has a value of 1.0 and irrelevant drive also has a value of 1.0, then the combined value is 2.0 and the subjects should show improved performance.

Kendler (1945) used this drive summation approach. He trained five groups of rats to lever-press for food; all rats had been deprived of food for 22 hours, also of water, for 0, 3, 6, 12, or 22 hours. The animals' lever pressing was then extinguished under the same conditions. The four groups deprived of water for 0, 3, 6, and 12 hours, showed an orderly increase in the number of extinction responses but the group deprived of water for 22 hours showed a significant decrease. Very similar results were obtained by Bolles and Morlock (1960). This reversal of performance at the highest thirst level is obviously contrary to prediction, since this group should perform best.

Danziger (1953) slightly modified the approach taken by Kendler. He trained rats to lever-press for food while deprived of food for 22 hours, but in extinction they were either hungry or thirsty, or both. The addition of the irrelevant thirst hastened extinction rather than slowing it. The evidence generally indicates that, at best, irrelevant thirst appears to be effective only at low levels in the drive summation approach to the problem (see Bolles, 1967 or 1975, for a more detailed review).

A different strategy for studying irrelevant drive is to *substitute* an irrelevant drive in testing for a relevant drive used in training. Thus, the value of the relevant training drive should be zero in testing, but it should be compensated by the irrelevant drive. Using this technique, Webb (1949) trained rats deprived of food for 23 hours to press a panel for food, then extinguished them satiated for food, but with 0, 3, 12, or 22 hours of water deprivation. A food-deprived control group was also used in extinction. The mean numbers of extinction responses for the increasingly thirsty groups were 2.8, 5.2, 5.1, and 7.2 and, for the hungry group, 14.2. The differences between the irrelevant drive (thirsty) groups were small and none gave more than about half as many responses as the food-deprived control group.

The most damaging evidence against the irrelevant drive hypothesis, however, comes from a host of consummatory studies and one behavioral study. For years, the physiology literature has contained evidence that experimental restriction of water intake leads to voluntary reduction of food intake and vice versa. Psychological thinking on the problem was finally changed, however, by Verplanck and Hayes (1953). They again showed that restriction of food or water depresses intake of the alternate substance, but they used procedures more familiar to psychologists and published in a psychological journal. Aiming their research directly at the irrelevant drive problem, they pointed out that if an animal voluntarily reduced water intake when food deprived, in some sense it was also water deprived. Therefore, water deprivation was not entirely irrelevant in a drive substitution experiment. The parallel account would hold for water deprivation followed by food deprivation. The so-called irrelevant drive, they suggested, was very relevant to the animal. Since this interrelationship between hunger and thirst is virtually always present, the hunger-thirst irrelevant drive studies have been largely discredited as meaningful tests of the general drive hypothesis.

The coup de grace to the hunger-thirst tests of the irrelevant drive hypothesis came from Grice and Davis (1957). They trained rats deprived of food for 22 hours to press a panel for food, then extinguished subgroups under four different conditions: (1) deprived of food for 22 hours; (2) satiated with both food and water; (3) deprived of water for 22 hours— the usual irrelevant drive substitution procedure; and (4) deprived of water for 22 hours, but *given water without food* just before testing. The results are shown in Table 4-1 and are quite clear. The thirsty group does no better than the satiated group and the thirsty-drink group is almost as good as the hungry group. Thus *reducing* the irrelevant drive in Group 4 led to an *increase* in responding. This was caused by a release of inhibition of eating that in turn was caused by water deprivation and is contrary to the prediction of general drive theory.

**Table 4-1** *Mean number of responses during extinction testing. (From Grice and Davis, 1957, p. 349. Copyright © 1957 by the American Psychological Association. Reprinted by permission.)*

| | |
|---|---|
| Hungry | 26.5 |
| Satiated | 13.5 |
| Thirsty | 13.0 |
| Thirsty-Drink | 22.0 |

The Grice-Davis experiment was so compelling that, as Bolles (1967, p. 274) put it, "So ended the hunger and thirst period in the history of the generalized drive concept. Although there continues to be some interest in the area of hunger and thirst and their interaction, the area no longer seems a proper place to investigate drive summation and substitution."

### Human Applications of Irrelevant Drive

Although the irrelevant drive concept has not been very useful in predicting hunger-thirst interactions with animals, it has led to some interesting data at the human level. These data may turn out to be better explained in some other manner, but the concept has nevertheless been fruitful. We shall here look briefly at three examples: anxiety, social facilitation, and aggression.

   ***Anxiety in Simple Learning Situations.*** Fear and anxiety are such important concepts in many areas of motivation that we deal with them separately in Chapters Eight, Nine, and Eleven. Here we restrict ourselves to seeing how anxiety, considered as an irrelevant drive, fits into the context of Hull-Spence theory. Spence (e.g., 1958) talked about the role of what he called an "emotionally based drive," showing how it related to performance in various laboratory learning tasks.

   The theory is as follows. If a person has two habits, $H_1$ and $H_2$, with $H_1$ being much stronger, then the higher the level of drive, the greater the difference between $E_1$ and $E_2$. ($E_1 = H_1 \times D$ and $E_2 = H_2 \times D$). This is the relationship between $H$ and $D$ illustrated in Figure 4-1. For any situation where there is a clearly dominant response, an increase in drive should facilitate the occurrence of that response.

   Consider, however, a more complicated situation, in which there are habits of similar strength. For example, suppose that $H_1$ is just slightly stronger than $H_2$, such as might occur during the early stages of learning. The resultant reaction potentials may be in strong competition because of their similarity in strength. This will be disruptive, because the reaction potential for the *weaker* habit may sometimes be stronger. (The overall theory has other concepts, such as inhibition and oscillation, which we have not dealt with, but which partially determine reaction potential. These allow for the possibility that a response with a *slightly* weaker habit strength could be the one to occur.)

   There are, then, three general situations of interest that could occur. First, a very *low* level of drive would not raise the reaction potential for either habit above the threshold for responding. Hence, there is poor performance with low drive. This is, of course, a basic statement of the theory regardless of habit strength. Second, at some *intermediate* level of drive, the slightly stronger habit would be multiplied sufficiently so that its reaction potential would generally be above the threshold for overt responding but the reaction potential for the weaker habit would not be above that threshold. This intermediate level of drive would be optimal for performance related to the stronger habit. Third, with a *high* level of drive, the reaction potentials for both habits would be above the threshold for overt responding and response competition may then occur, again producing relatively poorer performance, i.e., errors. As an example, some of us may recall that in an early stage of learning to drive a stick-shift car, when we were not thoroughly trained in all the responses, we "panicked" and pushed in the clutch pedal rather than the brake. Let us now consider two laboratory learning situations that demonstrate experimentally these principles: (1) eyelid conditioning, where there is a single dominant response, and (2) paired associate verbal learning, where there are multiple competing responses.

*1. Eyelid Conditioning.* The eyelid conditioning procedure is to present a tone or dim light as the conditioned stimulus (CS), followed by a puff of air to the cornea as the unconditioned stimulus (UCS). The eye normally blinks to the airpuff. Conditioned responses are those eyeblinks to the CS that occur before the airpuff occurs. There is then a single dominant response, the eyeblink. The literature quite consistently shows that the level of conditioning, as indicated by the percentage of trials on which a conditioned response occurs, is higher with a more intense puff of air. A variety of control conditions indicates that the higher performance is *not* just caused by a stronger level of conditioning but is also caused by a motivational effect of the stronger airpuff. The intensity of the UCS is therefore one of the antecedent conditions for the emotional drive Spence referred to and multiplies habits as the theory predicts.

Janet Taylor Spence (Taylor, 1953), however, described another way of operationalizing drive. Her procedure involved two assumptions. First, variation in drive level from one person to another is related to the level of anxiety. Second, the level of anxiety can be determined by a self-report scale of manifest symptoms of anxiety. She had clinical psychologists judge over 200 items from the Minnesota Multiphasic Personality Inventory, designating those which were indicative of chronic anxiety reactions. The final result was a twenty-eight-item scale, including such statements as the following: "I am often sick to my stomach" and "My sleep is restless and disturbed." Very high and very low scorers on the scale could then be selected and their performance compared in other situations.

The results from the University of Iowa laboratories consistently showed that subjects with high scores on the Taylor Manifest Anxiety Scale (Hi A) showed higher level of eyelid conditioning than did subjects with low scores (Lo A). Furthermore, there were additive effects between anxiety level and UCS intensity, just as general drive theory predicts. Although some investigators have not obtained the expected results with Hi A versus Lo A subjects, the Hi A subjects typically show a higher level of conditioning. One of the complications has to do with the nature of anxiety rather than the theory per se, however. Thus, for example, Ominsky and Kimble (1966) found that in a rather threatening-looking experimental situation there were conditioning differences between high- and low-anxiety subjects, but in a less threatening appearing laboratory setting there were not. The question, then, is whether anxiety is "chronic" or "situational." We will discuss this question in Chapter Eleven.

*2. Paired Associates Learning.* In paired associates learning, the subject views a series of word pairs, the first being the stimulus word, the second being the response word. The subject's task on successive trials is to give the correct response word when just the stimulus word is shown. The particular advantage of this procedure is that one can readily set up word pairs that have very strong initial associations (e.g., *dog-cat*) or very weak ones (e.g., *zov-dax*). The experimental prediction for the paired associates learning situation is that Hi A subjects should perform better on lists of high association value (i.e., where there are highly dominant responses to the stimuli) and poorer on lists with low association value. The data have been inconsistent in the latter prediction, with Hi A subjects sometimes performing better than Low A subjects under both conditions (see Bolles, 1967, or Byrne, 1974, for more detailed reviews). As Spence (1958) pointed out, however, negative results may not necessarily be related to the presumed multiplicative relationship between $H$ and $D$. Many factors determine the level of $H$, and other variables in the theory contribute to reaction potential as well as $H$ and $D$. These variables may account for the conflicting results. The theory has produced a rather impressive amount of research regardless of the details of outcomes, however, and the results are sufficiently positive to be often provocative.

*Social Facilitation.* The term *social facilitation* refers to the fact that the presence of observers influences individual behavior. This is the oldest experimental problem in social psychology, dating back to the work of Triplett in 1897. Interest in the phenomenon declined, but was revived more recently when Zajonc (1965) proposed that the effect was caused by the "audience" arousing an irrelevant drive in the "actor." As with anxiety, the prediction is that very dominant responses should be facilitated and nondominant responses should interfere with each other, producing inferior performance. Zajonc and his colleagues found this to occur with both humans and cockroaches, a real tour de force for comparative social psychology.

As one example, Zajonc and Sales (1966) established different degrees of response dominance (habit) by presenting different nonsense syllables to subjects 1, 2, 4, 8, or 16 times. The subjects then had a "subliminal perception test," in which they thought they were going to see the previous nonsense syllables, but in fact were shown only irregular lines for 1/100-second flashes. Control subjects saw the slides individually and alone, but experimental subjects saw them in the presence of an observer, a silent stranger. Previous literature (e.g., Goldiamond & Hawkins, 1958) has shown that under such conditions subjects will guess the occurrence of nonsense syllables in the same proportion as they have actually seen them previously. This can be considered a difference in habit strengths. In the Zajonc-Sales experiment, both groups did exactly this, but the experimental group guessed the more frequently presented syllables with an even higher frequency than the control group. There was thus a habit-drive interaction of the kind illustrated in Figure 4-1, and hence rather impressive support for the irrelevant drive hypothesis. Weiss and Miller (1971) have extended the theory to cover a much greater range of social facilitation phenomena.

*Aggression.* As our final illustration of the ingenuity with which the irrelevant drive hypothesis has been applied, we mention briefly some work on aggression. What is found in laboratory settings is that such arousing conditions as sexual stimuli (pornographic movies), loud sounds, and the presence of weapons all contribute to an increase in the level of aggressive responses shown by the subjects. Berkowitz (1974) has specifically said that such effects are interpretable in terms of general drive theory. We discuss this research in some detail in Chapter Twelve.

Overall, we see that the irrelevant drive hypothesis has not held up well in the animal literature in the case of hunger and thirst, but is probably more productive at the level of a kind of diffuse emotional arousal with humans. We shall later see (Chapter Thirteen, on attribution theory) that there are additional complications caused by subjects' cognitions about what is going on in a given situation. In defense of his position, however, Spence never claimed that his theorizing applied to complex human situations, for which many parameters of learning and drive were unknown and for which additional concepts of a more cognitive nature would probably be necessary.

## DRIVE STIMULUS THEORY

### Nature of Drive Stimulus Theory

We have seen that deprivation does not reliably energize responses in the way that drive theory seems to predict. Specific drive-producing operations seem to have fairly specific effects. One way around this difficulty is to postulate that specific drive-producing operations also arouse unique internal stimuli in the organism. These *drive stimuli* would then have a *directive* effect on behavior, just like any other source of stimulation. In fact, increased drive might not facilitate performance, because drive stimuli themselves arouse competing responses. Hull was, of course, well aware of this possibility. Furthermore, the rather obvious need for such a concept in Hull's theory is seen in the fact that we eat when hungry and drink when thirsty. As self-evident as they are, these facts are *not* predicted by general drive theory alone, because according to that theory the "same" drive is aroused by all the different drive-producing operations.

According to the drive stimulus concept (Hull, 1943; Spence, 1956), each drive-inducing operation, such as food or water deprivation or noxious stimulation, also produces stimuli that are qualitatively or quantitatively unique to the operation. This is shown as follows:

$$\text{Drive Operation} \underset{\large\searrow}{\overset{\large\nearrow}{}} \begin{array}{l} S_d \\[4pt] D \end{array}$$

where $S_d$ is some specific internal stimulus produced by the drive operation and $D$ is general drive. Such internal stimuli are presumed to have the same properties as external stimuli: They can be discriminated, they can serve as cues, they can be conditioned to responses, and some can arouse unconditioned responses. In Hull's theory, drive stimuli become conditioned to responses, forming a habit ($S_dH_r$). This habit is then multiplied by the drive that was produced by the same operations which produced the drive stimuli. Thus, we have:

$$\text{Drive Operation} \underset{\large\searrow}{\overset{\large\nearrow}{}} \begin{array}{l} S_dH_r \\[2pt] \times \quad = E \\[2pt] D \end{array}$$

The role of drive stimuli is illustrated more specifically in the following hypothetical example (Spence, 1951), diagrammed in Figure 4-3. A rat is trained in a T maze, alternately hungry or thirsty on successive days. Food is always in the right-hand goal box and water in the left. After sufficient training, the animal goes to the right on the first trial each day when it is hungry and to the left side each day when it is thirsty. (The first trial is critical because the animal could learn on the first trial each day where the food or water was for that day and all later responses be determined by this information.) Since the *external* stimuli remain constant, the animal's behavior is presumably guided by the *internal* drive stimuli.

Figure 4-3 also shows the explanation symbolically. The animal becomes conditioned both to turning right and to turning left on the basis of the external cues. However, the left turn response is rewarded by water only in the presence of thirst drive stimuli ($S_d$ thirst) and the right turn response is rewarded only in the presence of the hunger drive stimuli ($S_d$ hunger). The general drive is, of course, produced by either form of deprivation. Since there are more thirst drive stimuli conditioned to the left turn response on water deprivation days, the animal turns left. On food deprivation days, the hunger drive stimuli evoke the right turn response.

A number of empirical questions immediately arise, however. Can animals indeed discriminate qualitative (hunger versus thirst) or quantitative (e.g., different levels of thirst) differences in drive, as the explanation just given requires them to do? Can such differences in drive stimuli act

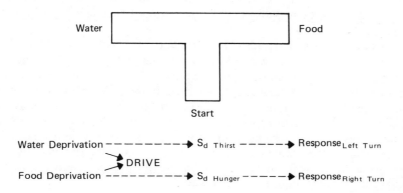

**Figure 4.3** *The drive stimulus interpretation of drive discrimination. The drive produced by water or food deprivation energizes both right and left turn responses equally. The drive stimuli provide distinctive cues ($S_d$ Thirst and $S_d$ Hunger) that, however, become conditioned to left-turning and right-turning responses respectively. Since the maze cues themselves are the same under either hunger or thirst conditions, the drive stimuli provide the only distinctive cues for which response to make.*

as cues to guide instrumental behavior? Do variations in drive stimuli lead to behavior effects that we might consider to be alternative explanations for drive?

### Can Qualitative Differences in Deprivation Be Discriminated?

Hull (1933a) was the first to try to find out if rats could learn to use hunger and thirst stimuli as cues to different responses. On alternate days, the subjects were hungry or thirsty and were required to take one path to food and the other to water, but the same goal box was used and the animals were allowed to retrace their path if they initially followed the wrong path. At five trials a day, the animals began to show better than chance performance on the *first* daily trial after about 500 trials. After 1,200 trials, the animals were at about 85 percent accuracy. This seemed to be a very difficult discrimination problem. Leeper (1935), however, made the problem simpler by using two distinctively different pathways and goal boxes for hunger and thirst days. It took his animals only about ninety trials to learn the problem. Furthermore, if they were allowed to explore the apparatus and find food and water in the goal boxes prior to actual training, it took only about twenty-five trials to learn. This number is typical for a simple discrimination problem using external stimuli as cues. It thus appears that Hull did have a particularly difficult problem, and that there are distinctive internal differences in hunger and thirst stimuli that can be readily discriminated..

Bolles and Petrinovitch (1954) thought they had made the problem even simpler. Their technique involved animals that were both hungry and thirsty, with either feeding or drinking prior to each test trial. Eating made the animals thirsty and drinking made them hungry. At one trial a day, the animals reached a criterion of nine out of ten correct responses in an average of seventeen days. Unfortunately, as Bolles (1962) later recognized, the animals may have been responding to the cues of just having drunk or just having eaten rather than now being hungry or now being thirsty. Thus, the after-stimulation from eating or drinking may have been cueing the animals rather than drive stimuli from deprivation.

Bailey (1955), in a rather neat study, got around all such problems of confounding drive stimuli and consummatory stimuli by not having the animals eat or drink in the situation at all. He trained rats to turn off a very noxious bright light by pressing one of two panels. For example, one panel was pushed when the animal was hungry, the other when it was thirsty. He trained animals on hunger versus thirst, thirst versus satiation, and hunger versus satiation. A fourth group pressed after a seventy-five minute sound. All groups learned the problems equally easily, except the seventy-five-minute sound group, which did not learn at all. Since the long-lasting hunger or thirst cues were effective but the seventy-five-minute sound was not, we may reasonably ask what the difference was. An immediate possibility is that the animals adapted to the long-lasting external stimulus so that it became a nonstimulus. There is much experimental evidence for such adaptation. On the other hand, animals probably do not adapt readily to the internal drive stimuli. In fact, such adaptation would seem intuitively to be a maladaptive way for organisms to have evolved. Need stimuli *should* persist if the organism is to offset the need state. The thrust of the literature, then, is that animals can fairly readily learn discrimination problems with qualitatively different internal stimuli as cues.

## Can Quantitative Differences in Deprivation Be Discriminated?

The literature here is much more meager. Jenkins and Hanratty (1949) found that the rat could apparently discriminate different intensities of thirst. Bolles (1962a) apparently found the same for hunger, but since he used the same procedure as the earlier Bolles and Petrinovitch study the results are open to the same criticism. Bolles (1975) has reviewed the overall drive stimulus literature in greater detail than we have done here.

The evidence seems to indicate that it is possible for animals to learn to differentiate between different deprivation conditions since they seem to use these as cues for responding. A more radical extension of the concept is that drive is not necessary even to account for such deprivation effects as are reported. Proponents of this approach believe that all so-called drive effects can be accounted for on the basis of the conditioning of external responses to deprivation-induced internal stimuli. This is the heart of Estes' (1958) theory.

### Estes' Theory

Hull and Spence used drive stimuli to supplement the concept of general drive, to account for the direction to behavior that deprivation gave. Estes throws out the concept of drive altogether. In this, as in the rest of his theorizing, Estes follows Guthrie's (1952) theory of learning, which says, in effect, that all learning consists of the association of stimuli with responses, and that all responses are directly elicited by the presentation of such conditioned stimuli. If it is true that unique drive stimuli[6] can become conditioned to specific responses, it follows from the principle of *stimulus generalization* that if these stimuli are changed after conditioning there will be a reduction in response strength.[7] Estes assumes that responses that occur when an animal is under a particular level of deprivation are conditioned to the specific set of drive stimuli present at the time. If tested under a different level of deprivation, then fewer of the set of conditioned stimuli are present, and the response is less strongly evoked. This provides the basis for the most important differential prediction between drive theory and drive stimulus theory. Both theories predict that if an animal is trained at one deprivation level, and then tested under a lower one, there will be a response decrement. When animals are tested at deprivation higher than training, however, the predictions differ. Drive theory predicts a *stronger* response because drive is higher. Estes' theory predicts a *weaker* response because the internal stimuli conditioned to the response have been changed.

---

[6]In this context it may seem incongruous to refer to "drive stimuli," since the concept of drive is specifically disavowed. The precedent for this is simply historical. Estes generally refers to his theory as an "S-R theory of drive" (1958). The point to keep in mind is that the internal stimuli he refers to are the "same" ones that drive theorists refer to.

[7]To refresh the student, the term *stimulus generalization* refers to the tendency to respond, but to a lesser degree, to stimuli that are similar but not identical to the conditioned stimulus in an experimental situation. There are a number of interpretations of the phenomenon, but for discussion here we shall think of it in terms of stimulus-sampling theory. If a subject is conditioned to respond to a stimulus, he is really responding to a *set* of stimuli that are but a part of the total stimulus situation (and are thus a stimulus sample.) If these stimuli are altered, then the set of stimuli impinging on the animal are different than the training set and the animal responds with lower probability or amplitude, or whatever the measure.

These different predictions are diagrammed in Figure 4-4, which also includes some specific numerical examples to show the derivations of the curves. To illustrate the distinction between drive and drive stimulus theory, these examples have been oversimplified, a point to which we shall return later.

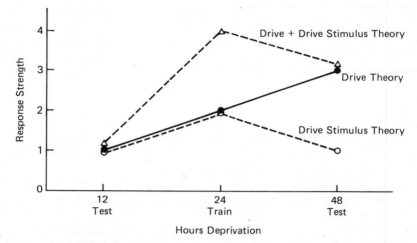

**Figure 4.4** *Predictions from drive theory and drive stimulus theory for response strengths of animals trained at 24 hours deprivation and tested at 12 and 48 hours deprivation. Both theories predict a lower response strength at 12 hours. Drive theory predicts a greater response at 48 hours (since the value of D in E = H × D is greater). Drive stimulus theory predicts a lower response strength, however, because there are fewer conditioned stimuli present at 48 hours than at 24 hours.*

What kind of evidence is there to support the prediction that a change in conditioned drive stimuli leads to lowered performance? Let us begin by first looking at an experiment where consummatory responses were conditioned to easily controllable external stimuli, which were then altered. Since external and internal stimuli are supposed to have the same properties, the predictions for external stimuli are the same as for internal. If this experiment is successful, then we can hold some hope for similar results with the invisible drive stimuli and have more faith in the drive stimulus interpretation.

### Conditioning of Consummatory Responses to External Stimuli

Fink and Patton (1953) hypothesized that if an animal learned to drink in the presence of particular external stimuli that the drinking response would be weaker if those conditions were changed. In the presence of specific

The following numerical examples show the predictions used in Figure 4-4.

1. *Drive Theory* $(E = H \times D)$

| Deprivation | Value of D | Value of H | Value of E |
|---|---|---|---|
| 12 hr | 1 | 1 | 1 |
| 24 hr | 2 | 1 | 2 |
| 48 hr | 3 | 1 | 3 |

2. *Drive Stimulus Theory.* Numbers represent only the strength of association between the set of drive stimuli and the response.

| | S-R strength (response strength) |
|---|---|
| 12 hr | 1 |
| 24 hr | 2 |
| 48 hr | 1 |

3. *Drive Theory in combination with Drive Stimulus Theory*

| | Value of D | $S_dH_r{}^a$ | Value of E |
|---|---|---|---|
| 12 hr | 1 | 1 | 1 |
| 24 hr | 2 | 2 | 4 |
| 48 hr | 3 | 1 | 3 |

$^aS_dH_r$ = the habit strength corresponding to the relationship of the drive stimuli to the response. Other stimuli in the situation would be conditioned to the response, but equally, and hence are ignored.

light, sound, and tactual cues, their rats learned over a five-day period to get water from a drinking spout, having previously drunk only from dishes. On the sixth day, various combinations of cues were changed, and drinking was found to decrease in proportion to the number of changed stimuli. This would appear to support the hypothesis that the drinking response had become conditioned to the various external stimuli and declined when they were altered. The major criticism of the study seems to be that since the test period was only five minutes long the animals could well have been responding to *stimulus change* per se (i.e., the orienting reflex, looking around, or exploring novel stimuli) quite independently of stimulus generalization decrement. What would any of us do if we entered our dining room at home one night and suddenly found new furniture, new light fixtures, new floor covering, and new wallpaper? If the animals had been given opportunity to *adapt* to the new stimulus conditions, but *not allowed to drink* during the adaptation period, they might not have shown a decrement. Beck (1964) found some support for this argument. Animals were allowed to explore the drinking apparatus, but without being allowed to drink. In the first actual drinking test, they drank significantly more than animals not previously familiarized with the apparatus. It was suggested that prior apparatus exposure allowed habituation of the orienting response, leaving the animals "free" to drink.

### Conditioning of Consummatory Responses to Internal Stimuli

Birch, Burnstein, and Clark (1958) were the first to test the specific hypothesis that consummatory responses might be conditioned to deprivation-specific internal stimuli. They maintained rats on a 22-hour food deprivation schedule for approximately five weeks. A food trough was continuously available, but the animals could only get food by depressing the trough during a set 2-hour period each day. The animals were then given extinction testing continuously over 46 hours without food. Responding was low over the first few hours, reached a peak at about 22 hours, and declined again thereafter. Since the peak of responding was at the usual eating time, the results suggested that trough responses were conditioned to the 22-hour deprivation stimuli. Stimuli from either longer or shorter deprivation periods were less conditioned to the food-getting response. This, of course, is support for the drive stimulus theory.

Brown and Belloni (1963) criticized the study by Birch, Burnstein, and Clark, however, on two major points. First, during the first 20 hours of the 46-hour test period the animals may have responded very little because they had previously learned *not* to respond during this time, having been reinforced only in the presence of specific *external* cues associated with the 2-hour eating period each day. Second, in the latter part of the test period (28 to 46 hours) responses during the test were not reinforced by food and may simply have extinguished. The net result of these two factors would be maximal responding at 22 hours. Brown and Belloni controlled for both of these possibilities by (1) training the animals with troughs in the cages *only* during the daily feeding sessions, at 22 hours deprivation; (2) housing the animals in a sound-proof room with constant light, thereby eliminating extraneous cues that might signal feeding time, and (3) giving 1-hour tests to five independent groups of animals (at 2, 12, 22, 35, and 46 hours of deprivation), thus eliminating the problem of differential extinction during the test. They found no decrement at either 35 or 46 hours, failing to support the interpretation of Birch et al. On the other hand, there was *no increment* in responding beyond 22 hours and the results did not support drive theory, either.

Monti (1971) claimed positive results for amount of feeding in an experiment similar to the two just described. On the other hand, extensive studies involving hypertonic saline injections (Wayner & Reimanis, 1958) or stomach loads (O'Kelly and Beck, 1960) have shown that after the very first injection the animals increase their intake in proportion to the amount of salt given. This result is clearly contradictory to any simple drive stimulus prediction, since the animals seem to be responding directly to the level of water need induced by the novel saline injections. The literature on drive stimulus conditioning and consummatory behavior is thus ambiguous at best, and leans in the direction of not supporting such conditioning.

### Drive Stimuli and Instrumental Behavior

The literature on "drive shifting" shows rather convincingly that animals shifted from a high-drive training condition to a low-drive test condition outperform animals both trained and tested under low drive (e.g., Barry, 1958; Campbell & Kraeling, 1954; Eisman, Theios, & Linton, 1961; Theois, 1963). This result is quite opposite a simple drive stimulus prediction. A common interpretation is that animals trained under high deprivation learn different responses than those trained under low deprivation. Campbell and Kraeling, for example, noted that their high-deprivation subjects learned to orient to the start box door and leap quickly into the runway, a response carried over to the low-deprivation condition. Animals trained and tested with low deprivation did not learn this behavior. At this point, one might suggest that drive stimulus theory is stated too simply— that such differential responses have to be taken into account. This may well be correct, but the difficulty of testing the theory markedly increases if one tries to do this.

### Physiological Manipulation of Thirst Drive Stimuli

Hatton (1965) attempted to study the drive stimulus conditioning problem by direct physiological manipulation of the need for water, hoping for more precise control. Rats were trained to press a lever for water while deprived of water for 23.5 hours, and then were tested in extinction with saline stomach loads in addition to the deprivation. The saline increases the animals' need for water and is therefore presumed to change the drive stimuli. Control subjects were given mock injections, with nothing placed into the stomach. As predicted, the saline-loaded animals gave fewer extinction responses than controls, which Hatton interpreted to mean that there was stimulus generalization decrement. Similar results have been reported by Beck and McLean (1967).

Hatton's prediction holds, however, only when there is no opportunity for the saline stimuli to be conditioned to responding. In his experiment, there was thus only a single test. Beck and Brooks (1967b) hypothesized that the depressive effect of saline loads should diminish with repeated saline testing. This prediction was not supported; the same amount of depression of water-reinforced responses was found following each of five successive stomach loads spaced at one-week intervals. Furthermore, when these same subjects were finally extinguished following saline loading, they responded exactly the same as two different control groups for whom saline stimuli could not have been conditioned to responding. These results are not in line with drive stimulus theory and cast doubt on Hatton's interpretation of his results. Direct physiological manipulation of thirst does not seem to produce any better drive stimulus conditioning to overt responses than does natural deprivation.[8]

### Combination Drive and Drive Stimulus Effects

In these comparisons of drive and drive stimulus theories we have made the overly simple assumptions of *either* drive theory *or* drive stimulus theory. In point of fact, the Hull-Spence approach has included both concepts. In drive theory, if one uses both drive and drive stimulus concepts, the predicted outcome for a test level lower than the training level is the same as we have been discussing: Responses should decline. With test levels of deprivation higher than training, however, there should be (1) *lower* response strength, due to drive stimulus change; but (2) *increased* response strength, due to a higher drive level. This leads to the prediction of an asymmetrical curve, flatter on the increasing deprivation side than on the decreasing deprivation side. Such a curve is also shown in Figure 4-4, where drive stimuli are part of the $s$ in $sHr$. One cannot readily predict whether there would be an actual decrement on the increasing deprivation side, or just a flattening, without knowing the precise values for conditioning to $S_d$ and for $D$, a task beyond our present measurement capabilities. Such an asymmetrical gradient, however, was reported by Yamaguchi (1952) for running speeds in the straight alley, and Estes (1958) summarized other similar evidence.

Estes' (1958) theory was also more complicated than we have indicated. To account for the fact that animals are generally more responsive under higher deprivation levels, he assumed that high-deprivation drive stimuli weighted more than low-deprivation stimuli. That is, even though there was stimulus generalization decrement from medium to high deprivation levels,

[8]We are still left with accounting for the load-induced depression. One possibility is that saline loads produce a nonspecific depressive effect on instrumental behavior. Grimsley (1965) found that saline injections under the skin of the back reduced activity in either a running wheel or an activity cage. Since one would not expect drive stimulus conditioning to be involved in these behaviors, the depressive effect appears to be a general one. Very concentrated saline stomach loads will also temporarily inhibit drinking or running in a straight runway (O'Kelly & Beck, 1960) or bar pressing (Beck & McLean, 1967). Running is more inhibited in a six-foot runway than in a two-foot runway, suggesting that responses that require more effort are more easily inhibited.

the conditioned deprivation stimuli were relatively more important in determining the animal's performance under high deprivation. The net effect of this was that Estes could also predict a flatter gradient on the high-deprivation side, just as Hull and Spence did. This makes differential predictions of the two theories much more complicated. Storms and Broen (1966) have analyzed these competing theories in considerable detail, concluding that, in the absence of specific numerical values to assign to drive levels and to drive stimuli, differential predictions between the two theories are almost impossible.

Any overview of the evidence, however, leads to the conclusion that the evidence for drive stimuli as the basis for "drivelike" effects on behavior is not strong. As Webb (1955, p. 296) put it: "the extensive theoretical use of the concept of drive states alone as cues is likely to be charming but unsupportable." Even Estes in his more recent writings (e.g., 1969) has suggested that incentive stimuli are important, a neglected factor in the 1958 theory, and are likely to carry much of the burden in any accounting of the facilitation of behavior. The same conclusion has been reached by drive theorists. We should recall that the primary importance of drive stimuli (for drive theorists) was in using them to account for the *direction* of behavior under conditions where external stimuli were the same but internal stimuli were varied. To the extent that another motivational concept—e.g., incentives—is able to carry the burden of accounting for direction, then drive stimuli become less necessary as explanatory devices.

### State Dependent Learning

There is one final area of research that may relate to the role of drive stimuli and therefore deserves mention here.[9] *State dependent learning is a phenomenon wherein behaviors learned under one physiological state may be performed later only in that same state, but in not others.* For example, a response learned while under the influence of some drug (e.g., alcohol) may not be recalled as well without the drug. Retention is not as good if the total stimulus complex at the time of recall is different from that at the time of original learning. Meyer (1972) has summarized a series of experiments in which electroconvulsive shock (ECS) was used to impair retention under different motivational conditions. The general results were that ECS given to food-deprived animals impaired responses previously learned when the animals were hungry, but did not impair responses learned previously by the *same* animals when they were fearful. Retention of fear-related responses were impaired following ECS under fear conditions, indicating that the phenomenon was not specific to one or the other motivational state. Meyer also showed that it was not just the most *recent* response that was

[9]We are indebted to James Summe for pointing this out.

impaired. For that matter, there was no order effect of any kind. State dependent learning experiments, of which there are not a great number at the present time, may shed more light on the drive stimulus question than the drive stimulus experiments themselves have.

## CONCLUSION

The evidence reviewed indicates that the concept of drive as a nonspecific energizer of responses does not seem to account for a great deal of behavior. Studies of activity show that any relationship between "drive" and "activity" is at best complicated, depending on type of deprivation, species differences, definitions (measurement procedures) for activity, and association of the activity with reinforcement. The irrelevant drive concept gains little experimental support, and the addition of drive-specific stimuli does not apparently add a great deal.

The relatively small amount of behavior that does seem to be interpretable in terms of general drive seems to be insufficient to account for the tenacity of goal-directed behavior, and it is this problem that is of prime interest to the motivational theorist. It is apparent that we must look at the goals toward which animals (including man) strive, in order to account for the powerful motivational effects we see around us. At the level of lower animals, it appears that the primary role of deprivation is to influence responsiveness to environmental stimulation, including goals. At the human level, deprivation probably plays a very small role, since most human goals do not appear to be related to deprivation. In later chapters, then, we turn to an examination of rewards and punishers, positive and negative stimuli toward or away from which animals and people strive. First, however, we examine activation theory, a kind of modified drive theory.

chapter 5

# Activation and Arousal

## ACTIVATION THEORY

Activation theory deals with the relationship between physiological arousal and behavior, and treats motivation and emotion as a single dimension with different degrees of "excitement." Like drive theory, arousal theory has generally been restricted to dealing with the nondirective energization of behavior. It is quite different from drive theory in several other important ways, which will be elaborated as we go along. The theory was originally proposed under the name *energy mobilization* by Elizabeth Duffy (1934) but recent versions (e.g., Duffy, 1962; Berlyne, 1960; Lindsley, 1951; Woodworth & Schlosberg, 1954; Hebb, 1955; Malmo, 1959) were mainly stimulated by the pioneering research of Moruzzi and Magoun (1949) on the *reticular activating system* (RAS). This recitation of names and variations on the theory indicates the widespread interest in the concept of activation and the range of phenomena to which it has been applied. Everything from stage fright to curiosity has been "explained" by activation theory. Because it was supposed to be a kind of physiological equivalent of (or substitute for) drive theory, and because it has been related to many of the phenomena with which we are concerned in later chapters, we introduce it here. Other physiological aspects of motivation are dealt with separately in Chapter Fifteen. (You are free to read that chapter now, however, if you prefer.)

### The Reticular Activating System

The RAS is a complex tangle of neurons in the brainstem, illustrated in Figure 5-1. It receives inputs from all sensory systems except smell and then distributes these diffusely to all parts of the cerebrum via the *ascending* RAS. Specific sensory information is lost in the RAS, but the widespread distribution of RAS output "tones up" the cortex in preparation for further input and attention to the environment. At the same time, impulses sent to motor neurons via the *descending* RAS serve to maintain muscle tonus over long periods of time.

Increased RAS activity is seen in the electroencephalogram (EEG—brainwaves recorded from various locations on the scalp) as a shift from a "resting" alpha wave pattern (8 to 12 Hz$_1$); to an "activated" beta pattern 15 for hertz, or cycles per second) to an "activated" beta pattern (15 Hz and up, lower amplitude and more irregular.) This shift in EEG pattern, illus-tualized as something like a fire alarm that gets people into action but does not really say where the fire is. To determine the direction in which to go, specific environmental information must be gained over the individual sensory channels that run more directly to specific areas of sensory cortex.

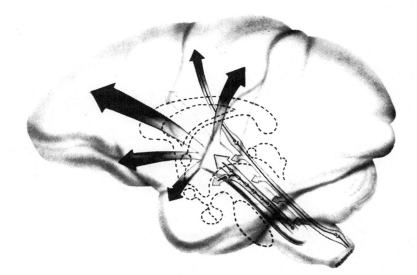

**Figure 5.1** *Schema projected upon monkey brain showing ARAS, including reticular formation in central core of lower brain stem with multisynaptic relays and its upward diffuse projections to all parts of cortex. To right a single afferent pathway with a relay in thalamus proceeds to postcentral cortex, but gives off collaterals (arrows) to reticular formation. These are respectively the unspecific and the specific sensory systems. (From H. W. Magoun, "The ascending reticular system and wakefulness." In J. F. Delafresnaye (ed.) Brain Mechanisms and Consciousness, 1954, p. 13.)*

The alpha pattern, which has a relatively high amplitude and low frequency, is said to be "synchronized." The beta pattern, of higher frequency and lower amplitude, is "desynchronized." Such desynchronization is readily seen in EEG records from the occipital cortex at the back of the head, the primary receiving area for visual input. If a normal human subject has his eyes closed, the occipital alpha pattern is very pronounced, but when he opens his eyes there is immediate desynchronization as the light input is carried through the RAS. Alpha and beta normally fluctuate as we go about our daily activities. Moruzzi and Magoun (1949) showed that direct electrical stimulation of the RAS through permanently implanted electrodes produces this same desynchronization.

Early research of the 1950s indicated that destruction of the RAS had effects opposite to those of stimulation. Severe damage of the RAS left the animal comatose, unresponsive to stimulation, with a continuous highly synchronized EEG. Electrical records showed that stimuli reached the sen-

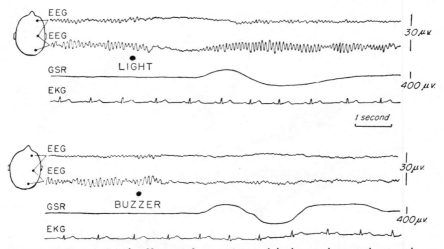

**Figure 5.2** *Arousal effects of unexpected light and sound stimuli on the electroencephalogram, (EEG), galvanic skin response (GSR), and heart rate (EKG). Electrode placements for the EEG are indicated from the top of the head. Note that the posterior electrodes show a large-amplitude, low-frequency alpha wave before the presentation of light or buzzer. This is a typical, relaxed, waking record. After the light or buzzer, there is a transition to a low-amplitude, high·frequency beta wave that is typical of a more alert or excited subject. The alpha is "blocked" by activity from the brain stem reticular system following presentation of the light and buzzer. The buzzer in this illustration was obviously a more "exciting" stimulus, since the alpha blocking lasted longer and there was a larger GSR change as well. HR is not obviously faster after stimulation, but the naked eye is not a good indicator of HR records shown in this manner. (From D. B. Lindsley "Emotions and the Electroencephalogram." In M. L. Reymert (ed.), The Second International Symposium in Feelings and Emotions, p. 241. Copyright © 1950 McGraw-Hill Book Company. Used with permission of McGraw-Hill Book Company.)*

sory cortex but that no overall desynchronization of the EEG appeared and there was no overt response to the stimulation. Energizing drugs like amphetamines increase RAS activity and alertness, which are decreased by central nervous system depressants like barbiturates. Such data supported the idea that the RAS is an important, if not completely critical, area of the brain for attention and consciousness.

### Autonomic Measures of Activation

Although EEG activity is heavily emphasized in activation theory, other measures are probably more commonly used for practical reasons. These include heart rate, blood pressure, muscle tension, respiration, galvanic skin response, and vasodilation and constriction. It is presumed that all such physiological activity should increase or decrease together under conditions of stress or relaxation, reflecting greater or lesser energy expenditure by the organism. Figure 5-2 also shows the effect of a sudden stimulus on some of these other measures. As we continue the discussion, we shall see problems that arise with regard to some of the general assertions made about both EEG activity and measures of autonomic activity.

### The Optimum Level of Arousal Hypothesis

The primary motivational proposition of activation theory (e.g., Hebb, 1955; Malmo, 1959) has been that there is an optimal level of arousal for behavior, an inverted-U function, as shown in Figure 5-3.[1] Some inter-

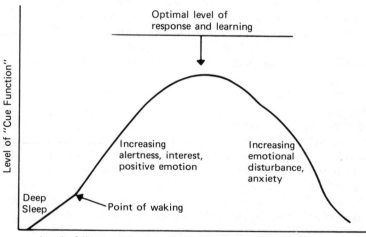

**Figure 5.3** *Relationship between level of arousal (in the ascending reticular activating system) and effectiveness of response to cues in the environment. (From Hebb, 1955, p. 250. Copyright © 1950 by the American Psychological Association. Reprinted by permission.)*

[1]This function, in even more complex form, was proposed by Yerkes and Dodson (1908). The Yerkes-Dodson law says that the optimal level of motivation for any task is lower as the task difficulty is greater. In their particular experiments, they purported to show, with different difficulty brightness discrimination problems and different levels of electric shock as punishment for errors, that the optimal level of punishment was lower as the discrimination was more difficult. A careful reading of the paper shows, however, that this is an unwarranted extrapolation from very inadequate data, and there are those who contend that the validity of the "law" has never been established. The reason for doubt is that with problems of different difficulty there are typically not equivalent levels of motivation by which to demonstrate different optimal levels. On the other hand, inversions of performance are common with increasing motivation, however defined. The inverted-U hypothesis is simply not as strong a theoretical statement as the Yerkes-Dodson law.

mediate level of RAS activity is said to be better than either lower or higher levels. It is also generally implicit that such a medium level of arousal is desirable and actively sought.

Hebb's development of this view was strongly influenced by studies of sensory isolation conducted at McGill University. The early experiments (e.g., Bexton, Heron, & Scott, 1954) indicated that after many hours of severely reduced sensory input, normal college-age subjects had difficulty in concentrating, solving simple problems, and, indeed, showed abnormalities in their ordinary perceptions. Printed lines refused to stay in place, walls bowed outward, and objects seemed to retreat as one looked away from them.

Later experiments with *stabilized retinal images* were equally dramatic (e.g., Pritchard, 1961). A tiny, high-frequency vibration of the eyes normally produces constantly changing retinal stimulation. By various mechanical means, such as mounting a miniature slide projector on a contact lens, we can have the visual stimulus vibrate right along with the eye. In effect, then, with reference to the visual pattern, the eye is not really moving. Such "stabilized" images disappear within a minute or so and it is therefore clear that stimulus change is very important for normal visual perception.[2] A great variety of experiments show similar phenomena and indicate that unchanging sensory input (as with sensory deprivation) is detrimental to the proper organization and functioning of perceptual-cognitive systems.

At the high end of the arousal scale, very intense stimulation is also detrimental. For example, it is consistently found in such highly stressful situations as fires, floods, or auto accidents that only about one person in four responds in any appropriately rational way. This same percentage has even been reported for trained soldiers under enemy fire. The child with stage fright and the overly tense athlete are less dramatic examples.

***Why Are Extremes of Arousal Detrimental?*** What makes low or high activation disruptive to behavior? Hebb (1955) argued in terms of his theory of the neural organization of behavior, positing that extreme levels of RAS activity tend to keep sequences of neural activity from running smoothly. (In the technical terms of his theory, *phase sequences* are disrupted; for details, see Hebb, 1955 or 1972.) An intermediate level of RAS activity is simply optimal for integrated neural functioning.

Actually, however, Hull's drive theory does rather well in accounting for an optimal level. The logic is that used at the end of the last chapter

---

[2]It is easy to simulate the results of this research in an ordinary classroom. Draw a somewhat fuzzy pattern (picture, letter, or word) on the blackboard using the side of a piece of chalk. Then stare at the pattern intently under reduced illumination. It will alternately disappear and reappear in whole or in part. Blinking tends to prevent disappearance and facilitates reappearance. Patterns drawn with luminous paint on black cardboard are even better at producing this effect.

in discussing irrelevant drive with humans. Thus, if there are two habits, $H_1$, and $H_2$, with $H_1$ being only slightly stronger than $H_2$, both will be equally multiplied by high drive. The resultant reaction potentials will be in strong competition because of the similar strengths, and this will tend to disrupt performance because the weaker habit may sometimes determine which response is made. If there is very low drive, the reaction potential for either habit would not be raised above the threshold for responding; hence performance is also poor with low drive. At an intermediate level of drive, however, the slightly stronger habit would be multiplied sufficiently so that its reaction potential would be above the threshold for overt responding, but the reaction potential for the competing habit would not. This intermediate level of drive would then be optimal for performance related to the stronger habit. A distinct advantage of Hull's theory is that it says something fairly specific about when a strong drive will produce inferior performance. That is, performance will be poorer when there are closely competing responses involved, but will be better if there is a single highly dominant response.

As we observed before, activation theory and drive theory both deal with an intensity dimension of motivation. But whereas drive theory assumes the lowest possible level of drive (or drive stimulus intensity) is the "ideal" state of the organism, activation theory assumes that Nirvana is at some intermediate level of stimulation. To reach this intermediate level, an organism may try either to increase or decrease stimulation, depending on which would achieve the optimal level. This, in turn, depends on the individual's momentary level of arousal. This is presented in simplified form in Table 5-1, where we see that if the momentary arousal level is low, an even lower level would be aversive but a higher level would be desirable. Conversely, if the momentary level is already high, a lower level would be

**Table 5-1**   *Desirable ( + ) and aversive ( − ) outcomes of stimulus change in terms of the optimal level of arousal hypothesis.*

|  |  | Present State of Arousal | |
| --- | --- | --- | --- |
|  |  | *Low* | *High* |
| Anticipated State of Arousal | Lower | − | + |
|  | Higher | + | − |

desirable but a higher level would be aversive. This is only an approximation, however, because such variables as duration of the present state and past history of the organism would be important. Total lack of stimulation may be desirable for a while, but not permanently. Or, one could become so adapted to an unusually high level of stimulation over a period of time that it would become a more nearly optimal level of arousal.

The fact that extremely high levels of arousal are *ever* sought is somewhat troublesome, but people do indeed jump out of airplanes and the like. Berlyne (1960) dealt with this in terms of what he called the *arousal jag*. Extremely high arousal is temporarily "good" *if* it is reduced fairly readily. A mountain climber might get a thrill from dangling briefly in space, but after a while this experience could become terrifying.

### Intermediate Stimulation as Low Arousal

Thus far, following Hebb's approach, we have said that (1) arousal level is equated with activity level in the RAS; (2) an intermediate level of such activity is optimal for functioning; and (3) an intermediate level of arousal is generally desirable to the organism.

Berlyne (1960) and Hunt (1965) voiced opposition to Hull's drive theory but nevertheless were more comfortable with something like drive and drive reduction theory than with Hebb's position. They argued that either low or high levels of *stimulation* produce strong *arousal but that intermediate levels* of stimulation produce weak arousal. In their view, then, an organism seeking moderate stimulation is really seeking minimal arousal. This is summarized in Figure 5-4, and it differs from traditional drive theory in that the minimal arousal is at some level of stimulation greater than zero.

The main virtue of any variant of an arousal theory, of course, is its capacity to handle factual detail which gives pause to traditional drive theory. Drive theory and arousal theory account equally well for stimulus-reducing behavior, but only arousal theory makes sense of stimulus-increasing behavior. Both the attraction of peace and quiet, on the one hand, and the excitement of crowds, contests, and fast cars, on the other, are equally well accounted for by arousal theory.

### Arousal Theory and Animal Appetitive Behavior

If arousal theory is to be a viable alternative to drive theory, then it should make predictions for appetitive situations where the bulk of animal research on "drive" has been conducted. Two specific predictions are particularly important. First, physiological measures of arousal should increase with deprivation as well as decrease with satiation. Second, there should be an inverted-U function for performance and deprivation. Such an inversion does not, of course, include the trivial case where an animal is so weakened by deprivation that it cannot perform. The evidence supporting these two predictions is somewhat short of compelling.

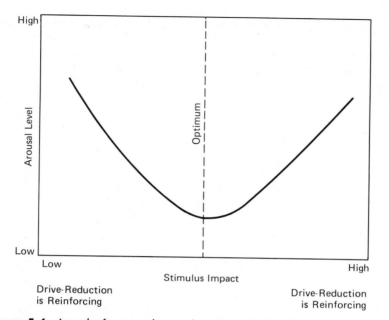

High

Arousal Level

Low

Optimum

Low                                              High

Stimulus Impact

Drive-Reduction
is Reinforcing

Drive-Reduction
is Reinforcing

**Figure 5.4**  *Level of arousal as a function of stimulus impact. Stimulus impact refers to the effectiveness of stimuli as arousers, dependent on qualitative differences among stimuli (such as meaning or complexity) as well as quantitative differences (such as intensity.) Situations with a medium level of stimulus impact for a particular individual are "optimal" in terms of producing low arousal level. This represents the view that low or high stimulus impact leads to high arousal and the organism works to return to the lowest level of arousal. See text for further discussion.*

***EEG and Deprivation.*** Either water deprivation or saline injections produce EEG activation at both cortical and subcortical levels of the rat brain (Steiner, 1962). After drinking, there is a more synchronized pattern. Similarly, injections of glucose into food-deprived rats produce a shift from desynchronized to a more synchronized EEG pattern (Hockman, 1964). These experiments found that EEG activity varied with deprivation, as the theory predicts, but the literature here is woefully thin.

***Heart Rate and Appetitive Behavior.*** Although there are problems in using heart rate as an index of arousal, it nevertheless has frequently been used so. One of the earliest and most exciting experiments (Belanger & Feldman, 1962) found that heart rate increased steadily with hours of water deprivation (presumably reflecting activation), but that in the same test periods lever pressing was an inverted-U function (see Figure 5-5). This is just as predicted by the theory. Mathieu (1973), however, has found that specific training procedures overcome the decrement at high deprivation levels, a finding that casts doubt on the arousal interpretation of the Belanger and Feldman data. Within their own data, too, there was the problem that functions obtained with sequentially *increasing* deprivation periods fit the theory, but those obtained with *decreasing* periods did not.

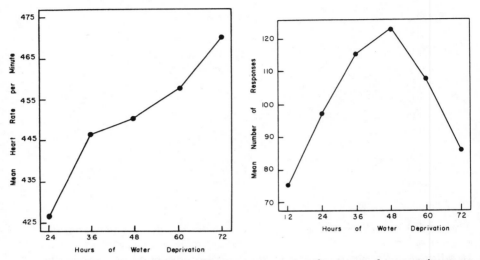

**Figure 5.5** *Heart rate and bar pressing as a function of water deprivation. (From Belanger & Feldman, 1962, p. 222-223. Copyright © 1962 by the American Psychological Association. Reprinted by permission.)*

In general, heart rate data are inconsistent in a way that should lead us to be suspicious of a simple unidimensional arousal theory. Heart rate has been reported to increase with water deprivation up to 96 hours (Ashida, 1968, 1969); to show no change at all (Eisman, 1966); or to show a decrease (O'Kelly, Hatton, Tucker, & Westall, 1965). A number of uncontrolled variables might account for these variations, the animals' activity levels being especially important. In their original paper, for example, Belanger and Feldman suggested that the linear relation between heart rate and deprivation might hold only for animals actively pressing levers. Had their animals been relatively inactive (as in the O'Kelly, Hatton, Tucker, & Westall experiment), heart rates might not have increased with deprivation. Experiments in which the amount of an instrumental activity necessary to obtain water has been experimentally manipulated have shown inconsistent correlations between the instrumental activity and heart rate (e.g., Hahn, Stern, & McDonald, 1962; Hahn, Stern, & Fehr, 1964; Ducharme, 1966).

If gross body movement is measured, however, instead of instrumental responses, it is consistently found that activity and heart rate are highly correlated. This has been termed *cardiac-somatic coupling* by Obrist and his colleagues (e.g., Obrist, 1976). Recently, Elliott (1975) and Brillhart

(1975) have independently reported average correlations of about + .75 between gross body movement and heart rates for individual animals over successive time segments of single lever-pressing test periods. In both experiments, activity was measured in terms of the distortion of the floor (electronically amplified) as the animals moved about. Since Elliott used water deprivation and reward and Brillhart used food deprivation and sucrose rewards, there appears to be some generality to the results. This generality is considerably extended by the fact that similar correlations are found in aversive conditioning (CER) situations with either rats or dogs (e.g., Roberts, 1974). Furthermore, animals trained to be immobile to avoid shock show a lower heart rate than controls and, when trained to be active to avoid shock, show a higher rate than controls (Goesling, Gomes, Lavond, & Carreira, 1976).

Correlations between lever-pressing rate and heart rate are much less consistent (Brillhart, 1975), apparently depending on individual styles of responding. Some animals press the lever with a slight touch of the paw and little or no movement otherwise. This results in negligible correlations between their heart rates and lever pressing. Correlations between activity and lever pressing are equally small. Other animals almost literally pounce on the lever with their whole bodies, in which cases there are high positive correlations between lever pressing and heart rate, because the animals are working so hard for each response. To the extent that heart rate is correlated with deprivation or incentive parameters, it seems to be because the animals are more active under some conditions than others.

Several experiments have also reported that thirsty rats show accelerated heart rates to a tone previously paired with water, as well as to water itself (Goldstein, Stern, & Routhenberg, 1966; Goldstein, Beideman, & Stern, 1970; Goldstein, Stern, & Sturmfels, 1969). Satiated rats showed no acceleration under either condition. It is possible, however, that the conditioned stimuli aroused body movement in deprived animals (but not satiated), and this accounts for the heart rate acceleration. There was no measure of activity in these experiments.

The heart rate data, then, indicate a general flaw in arousal theory—namely, how can we index physiological arousal independently of behavior? As we have seen, heart rate is hardly the place to look, because heart rate seems to depend on behavior. Furthermore, the whole concept assumes that multiple measures of arousal should be correlated. Correlations among various measures tend to be quite low, however, on the order of .20 or less (Lacey, 1962).

### Multidimensional Arousal Theories

In the previous section, we dealt with arousal as a single dimension whose presumed neural substrate was the RAS. We saw that a commonly used measure (heart rate) is probably not an accurate index of arousal. We shall now see that the RAS itself is a dubious basis for arousal theory. The early experiments suggested that the RAS was a critical area for EEG arousal as well as behavioral arousal, but we know that the RAS is not indispensable, nor is its destruction the only way to produce a comatose animal.

First, RAS destruction produces only temporary somnolence. If the animal survives the operation for a week or so, it recovers a normal sleep-waking pattern and is responsive to external stimulation (Lindsley, Schreiner, Knowles & Magoun, 1950). Second, if destruction is done in several stages, with postoperative recovery time allowed between, even the temporary comatose state is forestalled (Adametz, 1959). Third, if the RAS is removed by suction rather than by electrolytic lesions, there is no disturbance of sleep-waking cycles. Finally, massive lesions of sensory pathways, but sparing the RAS, produce many of the same behavior effects as do RAS lesions (Sprague, Chambers, & Stellar, 1961). Present evidence indicates that the posterior hypothalamus is possibly more crucial than the RAS in sleeping and waking because RAS lesions that spare the posterior hypothalamus do not eliminate behavioral arousal. However, lesions restricted to the posterior hypothalamus do eliminate behavioral arousal. This suggests that there is more than one system for arousal.

*Routtenberg's Two-Arousal-System Theory.* On the basis of the large amount of evidence showing dissociations (lack of correlations) between RAS activity, EEG, and behavioral arousal, Routtenberg proposed that there are two different arousal systems (see Routtenberg, 1968, for further details of the evidence). The first (Arousal System I) is the brainstem RAS system. The second (Arousal System II) is in the limbic system.

According to Routtenberg's theory, the RAS system is primary for producing neocortical desynchronization, but the limbic arousal system can perform this function if the RAS system is damaged. Many apparent inconsistencies in the effects of brainstem lesions can be understood in terms of whether one or both systems were damaged at the same time. Selective damage to one system or the other produces lesser impairment and apparent recovery of function, but simultaneous massive destruction of both areas does produce permanent deficit.

Following what should be a well-worn path for us by now, Routtenberg suggested that the RAS system is predominantly concerned with drive, or the neuronal organization for responding, and the limbic system predominantly with reward. Response occurrence is more likely if the RAS system is active, and perhaps mild RAS excitation is in itself rewarding. The limbic arousal system, on the other hand, is most important for reward effects, increasing the likelihood that a particular response will occur again.

*Lacey's Situational Stereotypy* Lacey (e.g., 1962) distinguished among behavior arousal, EEG arousal and autonomic arousal (heart rate, galvanic skin response [GSR], etc.). Although the different kinds of arousal may vary together under some circumstances, there are frequent dissociations among them. For example, in either cats or dogs, the drug atropine produces EEG wave forms similar to those found in sleep, in spite of the fact that the animals are behaviorally alert and responsive. Conversely, other drugs (e.g., physostigmine, chlorpromazine) may produce an "alert" cortex but a behaviorally drowsy animal.

Lacey holds to a view he calls *situational stereotypy*. He argues that activation processes do not represent a single dimension of arousal, or even a dual one, but rather that there are multiple arousal processes. Which ones are aroused depend on the goal of the behavior as well as its intensity. In other words, different processes have different roles to play in different behaviors and situations. One particular pattern of arousal may be characteristic of one individual in one particular situation (that is, it is stereotyped for him), but a different pattern would characterize other individuals or situations. Different persons would have different patterns partly because they perceive the same situation differently. There would thus be no expected correlation among arousal measures except for the same individual in the same circumstances at different times.

*Lacey's Attention-Rejection Model of Cardiac Function.* John and Beatrice Lacey (e.g., 1970) have for a number of years been developing a model of cardiac function that is inconsistent with the generalized arousal hypothesis. One must first recognize that the autonomic nervous system is not just an effector system; it is also a sensory system. About one-third of the nerve fibers in the autonomic system provide feedback function that has intrigued the Laceys. Their general view is that cardiac acceleration, which produces increased pressure on baroreceptors in the carotid sinus and aortic arch, provides *inhibitory* stimulation to the brain via a brainstem pathway that is close to (but not part of) the classic RAS. Increased pressure on these receptors produces a shift from low-voltage fast activity to higher-voltage slow activity. Such a mechanism was identified by Bonvallet and Allen (1963), who used both electrical stimulation and ablation techniques. The Laceys then say "The temporary hypertension and tachycardia [increased heart rate] observable in acute emotional states and in 'aroused' behaviors of all sorts may not be the direct index of so-called arousal or activation they are so often considered to be. Instead, they may be a sign of the attempt of the organism instrumentally to constrain stimulating circumstances" (1970, p. 209). In their view, then, cardiac acceleration is neither an autonomic index of arousal, nor just a correlate of behavioral activity; rather, it is a physiological *coping mechanism* by which the organism can actually increase or reduce activation.

The Laceys then proceed to the converse proposition, that cardiac *deceleration* makes the organism *more* receptive to external stimulation. First of all, in aversive conditioning the conditioned heart rate response is an initial *decrease* in heart rate, not an increase, as we might expect. The same is true of muscle action potentials. (The GSR response is an initial increase, however.) There would seem to be some adaptive significance in this; becoming more quiet should better prepare the organism to be receptive and responsive to the upcoming unconditioned stimulus. The same kind of heart rate pattern holds for the presentation of a ready signal in a reaction time experiment, as shown by work in the Laceys' laboratory as well as by Obrist's work. If the ready signal is presented ten seconds before the "imperative signal" (the one the subject is supposed to respond to), there is an initial cardiac acceleration, followed by an even larger deceleration prior to the imperative signal. If the ready signal is presented just four seconds in advance, however, the initial acceleration disappears but the deceleration remains. If the imperative signal is omitted on some trials, the deceleration is even more pronounced and continues for a while as the human subject "works on the problem" (Lacey & Lacey, 1970).

In another test of their hypothesis, Lacey, Kagan, Lacey, and Moss (1963) had subjects do a number of different tasks requiring (1) close attention to external stimulation; (2) mental problems that presumably would be disturbed by external stimulation; and (3) combination problems. The GSR simply increased in a nondifferential fashion to all tasks, but the heart discriminated among them. When problem solving requiring internal cognitive activity was called for, there was an *increase* in heart rate. On tasks where the subject was to respond to external stimuli, there was a *decrease* in heart rate. In a combined task, requiring the subject to discover rules about the presentation of external stimuli, there was an indifferent change, as if the heart were in conflict about what to do. Lacey also cites experiments by Israel (e.g., Israel, 1969) relating to "cognitive styles." Some individuals seem to take in large parts of the environment rather diffusely (levelers) and others to respond closely to specific parts (sharpeners). It was predicted that the sharpeners (very attentive to environmental details) would show greater cardiac deceleration in preparation for their typical attentiveness to the external environment, as opposed to the levelers who are presumably less attentive. When sharpeners and levelers were defined, in terms of standard perceptual tasks, the heart rate changes indeed were in the appropriate directions. Overall, then, while the Laceys' theory has not gone without challenge, it has nevertheless generated interesting data related to such a range of topics as classical conditioning and personality differences in perception.

## SLEEP AND AROUSAL

### REM (Paradoxical) and NREM Sleep

Hebb's diagram (Figure 5-3) shows sleep as a low level of EEG arousal. This generally corresponds to the idea that sleep might be a passive process resulting from reduced sensory input. Sleep is a very active process, however, with at least two describable states, "normal" (NREM) and "paradoxical" (REM).[3]

As the individual goes to sleep, there is a progressive change in EEG activity, illustrated in Figure 5-6. The amplitude of alpha waves decreases, then the record becomes relatively flat and irregular, possibly interspersed with *theta* waves (4 to 8 Hz) in some parts of the brain. In very deep sleep, *delta* waves (1 to 3 Hz) are prominent. Respiration is deep and regular, heart rate is slow and regular, the eyes are relatively still, and there is some muscle tension. This is *nonrapid eye movement* (NREM) sleep.

Then, after about ninety minutes, something striking occurs. The EEG becomes very active, showing the beta waves of an alert waking person. There is pronounced movement of the eyes, breathing becomes shallow and irregular, heart rate is faster and more irregular, and in males there is penile erection. This is *rapid eye movement* (REM) or paradoxical sleep. Over the course of a night, REM and NREM sleep fluctuate, with REM periods becoming gradually longer, culminating with a REM period of about ninety minutes in early morning. About 20 to 25 percent of a night's sleep is REM.

Figure 5-7 shows various physiological measurements during NREM and REM sleep. REM sleep was first described by Kleitman and his students (Aserinsky & Kleitman, 1953; Dement & Kleitman, 1957). Jouvet and Michel (1958), working with cats, coined the phrase *paradoxical sleep* because there was so much violent internal activity in sleeping animals during this phase of sleep. Also paradoxically, it is harder to awaken a subject from REM sleep than from NREM sleep, even though the brain appears alert.

### REM Sleep and Dreams

The most exciting discovery for most psychologists, however, was that individuals awakened from REM sleep almost always reported dreams, whereas when awakened from NREM sleep they almost never did. The REM dreams are the strange dreams we often recall with puzzlement.

---

[3]Dement (1973) argues that the value of this particular distinction may have passed. For our purposes, however, it is still useful because it describes certain features of sleep that are of concern here.

EXCITED

RELAXED

DROWSY

ASLEEP

DEEP SLEEP

COMA

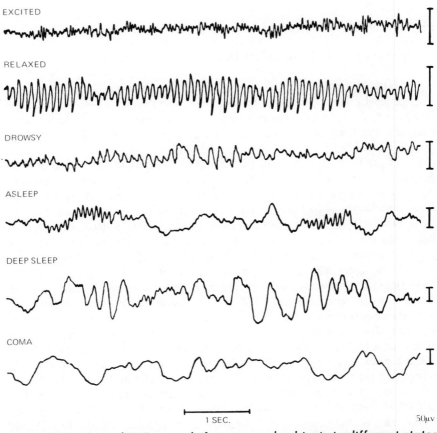

1 SEC.

50μν

**Figure 5.6** *Typical EEG records from normal subjects in different states of arousal and from a comatose subject (From Penfield and Jasper, 1954, p. 188.)*

Since there is amnesia for most dreams, we typically remember the REM dreams that occur in early morning just before waking. Some people claim never to dream but research has yet to uncover such a person; everyone in sleep experiments reports dreaming at least some times when awakened from REM sleep.

It is also found that individuals awakened from NREM sleep report mental activity, but it is typically a kind of unemotional "thinking." They may even report not having been asleep, that they were just lying there awake, but the EEG and other recordings belie this. One might expect that nightmares would come during REM sleep but they actually occur during NREM sleep, as do sleep walking and sleep talking (see Webb, 1968, 1973, for discussion).

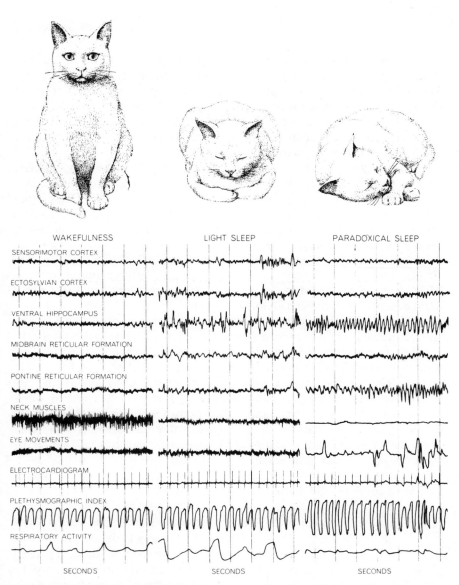

WAKEFULNESS      LIGHT SLEEP      PARADOXICAL SLEEP

SENSORIMOTOR CORTEX

ECTOSYLVIAN CORTEX

VENTRAL HIPPOCAMPUS

MIDBRAIN RETICULAR FORMATION

PONTINE RETICULAR FORMATION

NECK MUSCLES

EYE MOVEMENTS

ELECTROCARDIOGRAM

PLETHYSMOGRAPHIC INDEX

RESPIRATORY ACTIVITY

SECONDS      SECONDS      SECONDS

**Figure 5.7** *Characteristic rhythms associated with deep sleep in a cat (group of traces at right) are so much like those of wakefulness (left group) and so different from those of light sleep (middle group) that Jouvet has applied the term "paradoxical" to deep sleep. Normal cats spend about two-thirds of the time sleeping. They usually begin each sleep period with 25 minutes of light sleep, followed by six or seven minutes of paradoxical sleep. In the latter state they are hard to wake and their muscles are relaxed. (From Jouvet, "The states of sleep," p. 63.*

At first it was believed that during REM periods the individual was "following" the activities in his dreams with his eyes, just as he might follow the same activities while waking. For example, one subject reported watching a ping-pong game while showing rapid eye movements. This seems now not to be the case, however, because most dreams do not really have this back-and-forth element and because the eye movements themselves are not typical of a waking person.

In another early report, Dement (1960) deprived subjects of REM sleep by waking them whenever the recordings of their EEG and eye movements indicated they were going into REM sleep. His results indicated that the subjects developed some neurotic characteristics as a result, e.g., anxiety and irritability. This was quickly repudiated by Dement himself, however, because neither he nor others could reproduce his results. Furthermore, by use of drugs it is possible to selectively eliminate REM sleep while leaving NREM intact. Either humans or animals get along well for months without REM sleep, as compared to Dement's original report that just a few nights REM deprivation produced abnormal effects.

The selective deprivation procedure does, however, produce an important phenomenon. Over several successive nights of REM deprivation, the individual goes more quickly into REM sleep and, when allowed to sleep without interruption, spends relatively more time in REM sleep for a night or two. There seems to be a kind of accumulated REM deficit that the person (or animal) tries to make up, just as someone deprived of water drinks more. This same "rebound" effect is also reported for NREM sleep following selective NREM deficit. It appears then that there is some kind of "need" for both REM and NREM sleep, although lack of one or the other does not appear to be lethal.

### Universality of REM Sleep

Virtually all animals with brains more complicated than reptiles show NREM and REM sleep. (So, yes, your dog probably *is* dreaming when he yips in his sleep.) In adult humans, it is virtually constant at about 22 percent of total sleep time. Surely anything this constant and universal must be important. But for what? Since human infants spend as much as twenty hours a day sleeping and about 50 percent of this is REM sleep, it is possible that this heightened brain activity is important for the proper development and organization of the brain. In adults, REM sleep might be the brain's own way of countering sensory deprivation—it is self-exciting. This would, of course, fit nicely with Hebb's view were it not for the fact that the absence of REM sleep does not seem to be particularly harmful. William Dement (1973), one of the world's foremost authorities on the subject, simply says we do not know what REM sleep is good for.

### Jouvet's Theory of Sleep

There have been many theories of sleep proposed over the years (see Kleitman, 1963, or Van de Castle, 1971, for reviews). These range from sleep perceived as the result of reduced sensory input to sleep perceived as a build-up of some kind of toxic substance that produces sleep until the substance is cleared out by sleeping. None of the theories has garnered much research support. Jouvet (1967) has proposed an apparently more durable theory, however, by which he is able to account for both normal and paradoxical sleep in terms of activity in different parts of the brainstem. In the *raphe nuclei* of the brainstem RAS, there is a high concentration of *serotonin* (5-hydroxytryptamine, or 5-HT). In a different brainstem area, the *locus coeruleus*, there is a relatively high concentration of *noradrenaline*. Jouvet found that anything that potentiated the activity of serotonin in the raphe nuclei increased normal sleep, but decreased paradoxical sleep. Conversely, increased noradrenaline in the locus coeruleus produced an activated EEG pattern, but inhibited overt muscle movement. Lesions in these areas have opposite effects, i.e., raphe lesions produce sleepless cats and locus coeruleus lesions produce dreamless cats. Jouvet's theory, then, is that at the onset of sleep there is a predominance of raphe nuclei activity, then an increase in locus coeruleus activity, the two alternating over the period of a night's sleep.

Dement (1973) suggests that a simple two-stage sleep theory may not be entirely accurate and that the events that define REM sleep may not even be unique to sleep. There is some evidence that similar patterns occur during the day, during waking. Whatever the final outcome of this story, however, it is agreed that sleep is a very active time for the brain and in no sense represents just a low level of arousal.

### General Sleep Deprivation

Where else does sleep, or lack thereof, fit into the motivational picture? Dement was once asked on a nationally televised talk show why we need to sleep. His immediate answer was that we *don't* need to sleep—it's just that we get sleepy! When the laughter died he went on to explain that we do not require sleep for survival in the same way that we require food, water or air. We do not die, in other words. However, there are rather dependable effects of unusually long sleep deprivation, e.g., three or four days. First, we tend to fall asleep under unusual conditions, sitting up or even leaning against a wall. We have a strong preference for sleeping over other activities. Second, we may develop such physical symptoms as loss of appetite, gastrointestinal upset, muscle twitches, miscellaneous little pains, and a feeling of great effort to do rather small physical tasks. Psychologically, we may have difficulty concentrating or performing simple problems, and we may become anxious and paranoid. There is evidence that a build-up of lactic acid, a by-product of muscle metabolism, can produce both the physiological and psychological symptoms of anxiety (Pitts, 1969). These symptoms may disappear quickly after even one good night's sleep.

Obviously, there are times, as during the excitement of traveling, or before Christmas or a birthday, when we do not get to sleep easily. But sooner or later we must "recover" some of our lost sleep. This recovery— sleeping longer than usual—is in itself evidence for some kind of chemical build-up in the body, probably neurochemical, that is dissipated by sleep. Thus far, however, there is no known specific substance that accumulates. We can still ask the question: Why do we need to sleep?

## CONCLUSION

Arousal theory accounts for a number of different kinds of facts that were especially troublesome to drive theory. Particularly, it accounts for the apparent tendencies of organisms to do things that increase rather than decrease excitement. At the same time, it is clear that arousal is *not* a single dimension with sleep on one end of a continuum and great excitement on the other. This is shown by the facts that different measures of arousal do not correlate well with each other and by the fact that sleep itself consists of at least two very different states. In REM sleep, the organism is just as active physiologically as during alert waking periods, as far as the brain, autonomic nervous system, and viscera are concerned. At the same time, however, arousal theory has led to somewhat greater unification of behavioral and physiological data than drive theory did. The fact that arousal theory is not as simple as it once seemed is because it generated sufficient research to lay bare the difficulties. As we shall see in later chapters, there are some situations in which arousal theory still seems the most useful explanation.

chapter 6

# Rewards: 1. Theories of Reinforcement

Rewards are behavioral outcomes that are desirable and worked for. Such response-contingent outcomes are sometimes called *reinforcers,* because they increase the probability of those responses that produce them. The concept of reinforcement has been important in two contexts in recent years. First, in Skinner's operant conditioning approach the basic concept is reinforcement. This concept tends to have an engineering orientation, concerned with the question of how reinforcers function under different conditions of presentation. Such an analysis is important but is the topic of many volumes on operant conditioning and behavior modification, so we shall not dwell on it here.

Second, the *theory* of reinforcement has attracted attention. In particular, Hull's (1943) theory has generated considerable interest and research on the questions of whether drive reduction or some other mechanism is the basis of reinforcement and whether reinforcement is necessary for learning. These questions are mainly relevant to an S-R theory of response selection, i.e., an explanation of how a particular response gets "hooked" to a particular stimulus. Much of this kind of research is best understood in the specific context of the theoretical questions being addressed in a particular experiment. In this chapter, we look at rewards within the framework of reinforcement theory and response selection; in the next chapter, we will look at rewards in the framework of incentives to be approached regardless of responses involved.

Empirically, there has been little dispute that reinforcers can "strengthen" behavior, in the sense that a behavior is made more likely to occur in certain circumstances. This is especially true with lower animals. At the same time, reinforcers do not always act as expected, as we saw in the "misbehavior of organisms" encountered by the Brelands (this book, Chapter Three). We shall also see that reinforcers may actually inhibit the behaviors they are supposed to facilitate.

## THE CONCEPT OF REINFORCEMENT

### Empirical versus Theoretical Statements about Reinforcers

*The Law of Effect.* The phrase "law of effect" comes from E. L. Thorndike (1932) and means that the effect of a behavior (its consequences) determines whether that behavior will occur again. The phrase is still widely used but now could equally well be called the "law of reinforcement."

*Empirical versus Theoretical Law of Effect.* The *empirical* law of effect says only that reinforcers are effective in changing behavior. We may study how delay, amount, quality, or scheduling of reinforcers affect behavior without questioning the mechanism(s) underlying them. A *theoretical* law of effect is a statement of theory about how reinforcers function.

Some theoreticians consider that the mechanism of reinforcement is drive reduction; others believe it is the active response occurrence. Still others believe that the capacity to reinforce is inherent in the nature of stimuli.

*Learning and Reinforcement.* What does a reinforcer reinforce? Thorndike and Hull both said that a reinforcer strengthens the association between a response and the preceding stimuli. (Skinner emphatically does *not* hold to an S-R theory of reinforcement, in spite of the fact that this is widely attributed to him.) The S-R interpretation of learning says that reinforcement is necessary for response selection. A *weak* law of effect specifies only that reinforcement is sufficient for learning, without detailing what the requirements of a reinforcer are. A *strong* law of effect says that a particular characteristic of reinforcers, such as drive reduction, is necessary for response selection.

### Is the Concept of Reinforcement Circular?

Postman (1947) argued that the concept of reinforcement is circular, that a reinforcer is known only by its effects on behavior. Meehl (1950) agreed that it *would* be circular *if* a particular reinforcer applied only to a *single* response in a *single* situation. If, however, a stimulus (e.g., food) is reinforcing in one situation and then also "improves" performance in other situations, there is no circularity. Meehl argued that, by definition, *all* reinforcers are *transituational,* reinforcing in more than one situation and for more than one response. Reinforcement is thus a response-defined (R-R) concept and is no more or less circular than any other response-defined concept.

### Types of Reinforcement Theories

Given that the organism in a typical situation involving reinforcement is *"motivated"* and makes a *response* and that some *stimulus* (the reinforcer) is contingent on that response, there have been three general classifications of reinforcement theories: response, motivational, and stimulus. There is evidence for each kind of theory, suggesting they may all be partly correct or may have a common element.

## RESPONSE INTERPRETATIONS OF REINFORCEMENT

### Empirical Laws for Reinforcers: Functional Analysis

As Meehl (1950) pointed out, most psychologists use some stimuli as reinforcers with great confidence that they are not being circular—food, for example. This confidence is based on years of laboratory experience. Skinner holds this empirical view of reinforcement, saying only that if a response is followed by a reinforcer, the response is more likely to occur. Skinner has even been content to be circular, which has some practical utility at the human level, where it is often difficult to say what will be an effective reinforcer for a given person in a given situation. A *functional analysis,* in operant conditioning terms, seeks to determine what stimulus is reinforcing for a particular person and then to use it. When trying to train a retarded child to use the toilet, the question of whether the definition of reinforcement is circular must surely be academic.

*The Premack Principle.* Some measure of order has been brought into the use of empirical reinforcers by Premack (1959, 1961, 1965) who stated his thesis as follows (1959, p. 220): "Any Response A will reinforce any other Response B, if and only if the independent rate of A is greater than that of B." For example, if a rat licks at a water tube at a higher rate than it presses the bar, then licking can reinforce bar pressing. This example is so obvious it may appear trivial and, furthermore, we are tempted to ask: is the reinforcer not the water, rather than the licking? Let us take a less obvious example from Premack. He determined that, under specified conditions, the probability of running in an activity wheel could be either higher or lower than of drinking. He then showed that if running were the more likely response, the animals would drink more if drinking were followed by running. As a third example, school children had their choice of operating a candy machine or a pinball machine. According to his most frequent choice each child was designated as either an "eater" or a "manipulator." Premack then found that for the eaters, getting candy reinforced playing the pinball machine and for the manipulators, playing the pinball machine reinforced getting more candy.

As a corollary of Premack's principle, a *stimulus* may be used as a reinforcer *if* the stimulus controls some Response, A, that occurs at a higher rate than some other Response, B. In this view, a stimulus such as food or water is important only because it controls such a high-rate response as eating or drinking.

An advantage of Premack's approach is that it may be possible to determine what responses are likely to occur without knowing what stimuli control these responses. It is hard to specify the stimuli controlling running in an activity wheel, but it is easy to measure the response rate.[1]

Even if not applicable to all situations, Premack's analysis has been very influential among applied workers in behavior modification and has provided a different way to look at the problem of reinforcement. It follows

---

[1]Actually, Premack considers duration of responding a better index of probability than rate, since a low-probability response might occur at a very high rate during the infrequent times it occurs at all.

from his analysis, for example, that the sequencing of events during the daily classroom routine in elementary school can be arranged to considerable advantage. This is especially true if it is possible to determine and take advantage of individual differences in the children. "Unpopular" activities can be put earlier, followed by progressively higher-probability activities, each reinforcing the previous. Dollar (1972) has an interesting discussion of this approach.

### The Elicitation Hypothesis

Denny and Adelman (1955, p. 290) postulated that "the essential condition for the strengthening of one response tendency over and above another response tendency is the consistent elicitation of the response in question." The theory applies either to classical or instrumental conditioning. In classical conditioning, by definition, the unconditioned stimulus (UCS) is one that reliably elicits the unconditioned response. A neutral stimulus just preceding the UCS thereby becomes a conditioned stimulus (CS) to arouse the response. In instrumental conditioning, food reliably elicits eating. Eating reinforces running to the feeder after some cue. Running to the feeder on presentation of the food cue reinforces bar pressing, and so on. The reinforcing events in this sequence are said not to be the stimuli (food or the cue to food presentation) but the responses that are elicited by these stimuli. The primary weakness of the theory seems to be that stimuli can be reinforcing when no reliable responses are elicited by them. And behavior in extinction (bar pressing, for example) may continue even after the animal has stopped running to the food hopper when the cue for food (which is no longer being presented) is presented.

### Sheffield's Consummatory Response Theory

Sheffield (1966, p. 102) says "The most general statement of the overall mechanism [of his theory] is that the animal is forced to follow courses of action that maximize conditioned arousal of the consummatory response." A consummatory response, such as eating, is said to be conditioned to preceding stimuli by simple association. Eating may be conditioned to maze stimuli, for example. When these conditioned stimuli are presented but are not followed by food, the conditioned consummatory response is partially aroused but frustrated, because there is nothing to eat. This frustration is excitatory and facilitates such behavior as running down the runway to a goal box where food is found and eating can occur. The critical reinforcing event is this final consummatory response. Sheffield's theory and several experiments are mainly set in opposition to drive reduction theory.

Sheffield, Wulff, and Backer (1951) showed that male rats will learn responses reinforced by copulation without ejaculation. They argue that the reinforcement was the consummatory response (copulation) rather than drive reduction (ejaculation). Their interpretation is sensible in comparison with drive reduction theory but is less convincing if we consider sexual stimulation reinforcing in itself. Sheffield and Roby (1950) found that saccharin, a nonnutritive substance and therefore not need-reducing, is consistently consumed in greater quantity than water. They accounted for this in terms of saccharin eliciting the consummatory response more strongly than water does. Again, this interpretation is weaker if we believe that the taste of the saccharin is the reinforcing event.

An important implication of Sheffield's hypothesis is that more vigorous consummatory responses should produce more vigorous instrumental responses. Sheffield and Roby (1950) found a correlation between amount of saccharin consumed and speed of running to saccharin reinforcement. Kraeling (1961), however, found that rats ran faster to higher concentration sugar solutions even when drinking rates were the same for all concentrations. Other experiments have also failed to find a correlation between instrumental and consummatory responding. The conclusion is that the reinforcement is caused by the taste, not by the consummatory response. The taste is presumed to arouse some neural activity that is reinforcing.

### The Glickman-Schiff Theory

Both the elicitation and consummatory response theories require that the appropriate behaviors actually *occur* in order for there to be a reinforcing effect. Glickman and Schiff (1967, p. 85), on the other hand, proposed that "the activation of the underlying neural systems is considered the sufficient condition for reinforcement." That is, if the neural activity underlying a particular response is aroused by some stimulus, even though the actual overt response itself does not occur, this would be a sufficient reinforcer. For example, arousal of the neural activity underlying feeding would reinforce a prior behavior even though eating itself did not occur.

One of the most important lines of evidence for the theory is from studies of electrical stimulation of the brain. For many animals, the stimulation of certain areas of the brain with weak electric current is the most powerful reinforcing stimulus known (see Chapter Fifteen). Stimulation of these same locations also elicits feeding behavior if food is available. By implication, excitation of the neural system for eating is reinforcing for other responses, such as lever pressing. Eating itself does not have to occur in order for the electrical stimulation in the feeding areas of the brain to be reinforcing. A rather interesting related argument, developed by Kendon

Smith (1974), suggests that, in humans, *imagined* rewards (which are assumed to involve some of the same neural systems as real rewards) are effective reinforcers for certain kinds of associations. It is well known that humans imitate behaviors they have seen rewarded in others, as if this "vicarious reinforcement" were somehow rewarding. Bandura and Walters (1963) have discussed such imitation and modeling in detail.

## MOTIVATIONAL INTERPRETATIONS OF REINFORCEMENT

### Drive Reduction Theory

The best-known theoretical law of effect is that drive reduction is the necessary condition of reinforcement (Hull, 1943). This relates reinforcement directly to drive, because drive has to exist before there can be drive reduction. It is important, however, to distinguish between *need* reduction and *drive stimulus* reduction. The word *need,* in a biological sense, refers to a deficit or excess in the organism. The word *drive* refers to some hypothetical energizing state. Need and drive are not perfectly correlated, however, since all needs do not instigate behavior. With oxygen deficit, for example, there is no particular discomfort and no escape behavior by which we could index the presence of a drive (it is carbon dioxide excess that produces these effects). Miller (1951a, 1959) has handled this problem by arguing that (some) need states have stimulus properties. If strong enough, need stimuli or any other stimuli have drive properties (for example, energize responses).

To demonstrate the distinction between need reduction and drive-stimulus reduction, Miller and Kessen (1952) showed that milk drunk by a hungry rat was a better reinforcer in a T-maze than was the same amount of milk tubed directly into the animal's stomach. Tubed milk, however, was more reinforcing than tubed saline solution. Presumably there would be the same amount of *need* reduction from the milk regardless of its route to the stomach. Miller and Kessen therefore suggested that the consumed milk both reduced drive stimuli (consumption itself somewhat reduces drive stimuli) *and* reduced need, whereas tubed milk *only* reduced need.

Such analytical experiments as Miller and Kessen's are important, because the simple observation that food reinforces hungry animals and water reinforces thirsty ones does not necessarily support drive reduction theory. Other properties of the food (e.g., palatability) may be the basis of reinforcement. The trick is to separate these different possibilities, often by rather ingenious experimental procedures, so that they may be examined individually.

### Evidence Supporting Drive Reduction

***1. Pain Reduction.*** Hull considered all reinforcement to be drive reduction but based his main examples on pain reduction, in particular from offset of electric shock. Shock is relatively easy to control and its termination, like that of a toothache, is a powerful reinforcer. Because there is no observable incentive corresponding to food or water, it is often considered a "pure" case of drive reduction (but see Chapter Eight, on escape learning). Termination of almost any intense stimulus is demonstrably reinforcing, and escape from cold water, bright light, loud noises, cold air, and heat have all been cited as support for drive reduction.

***2. Fear Reduction.*** The problem of acquired drives will be examined later, but we need here to look at "fear" sufficiently to relate it to the present problem. The classic experiment is by Miller (1948).[2] Rats shocked in one compartment of an apparatus escaped into another. The apparatus is shown in Figure 6-1. After this training, the escape route was blocked and no more shock was given. A wheel was made available to the animal, as indicated in Figure 6-1. When the animal turned the wheel, the door was lowered and the animal ran to the "safe" side of the apparatus. After wheel turning had been learned, the wheel was made inoperative and pressing a lever in the apparatus was now reinforced by allowing the animal to escape to the safe side. Wheel turning extinguished and lever pressing increased. The conclusion was that fear reduction, provided by escape into the safe compartment, was the reinforcer for these new instrumental responses. Unfortunately, we do not know in any *direct* way that drive was reduced; we only know that the animal escaped and that this was reinforcing. Perhaps the stimuli associated with the shock were just unpleasant (bad odors are unpleasant and avoided, but not necessarily fear arousing). We must recall that a single operation does not serve to define a concept uniquely, however. It takes many experiments to *converge* on a particular explanation, and Miller and his colleagues have performed many experiments converging on an interpretation of fear reduction. For example, Davis and Miller (1963) found that previously shocked rats pressed bars more than nonshocked controls pressed for intravenous injections of sodium amytal, a nervous system depressant. The argument was that the sodium amytal reinforced the shocked animals by reducing their fear but did not reinforce the controls because they were not fearful in the first place.

***3. Reward by Fistula.*** The effects of taste, texture, odor, appearance, and temperature of foods have to be eliminated in order to evaluate a drive-reduction interpretation of food as a reinforcer. By inserting a plastic

---

[2]This is one of those experiments that every psychology student should know.

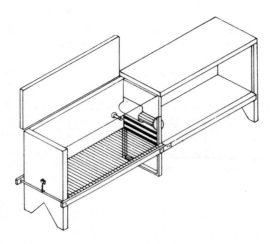

**Figure 6.1** *Acquired drive apparatus. The left compartment is painted white, the right one black. A shock may be administered through the grid that is the floor of the white compartment. When the animal is placed on the grid that is pivoted at the inside end, it moves down slightly making a contact that starts an electric timer. When the animal performs the correct response, turning the wheel or pressing the bar as the case may be, he stops the clock and actuates a solenoid that allows the door, painted with horizontal black and white stripes, to drop. The experimenter can also cause the door to drop by pressing a button. The dimensions of each compartment are 18 × 6 × 8½ inches. (From Miller, 1948, p. 90. Copyright © 1948 by the American Psychological Association. Reprinted by permission.)*

tube (a fistula) directly into the stomach or bloodstream so that nutritive material bypasses the mouth, we can eliminate these characteristics. The head receptors are not sensitive to the taste of such fistula-delivered fluids, e.g., rats do not avoid tubed quinine, even at concentrations far higher than those rejected by animals drinking normally. There is some evidence that the cool temperature of such nutrients may be important for reinforcement, however. This raises questions even about fistula feeding as a "pure" case of drive reduction because something about the temperature change may be reinforcing (Holman, 1969; Mendelson & Chillag, 1970). At any rate, besides the work from Miller's laboratory, A.N. Epstein and Teitelbaum (1962) found that animals could properly regulate their appropriate amount of food and water intake by pressing a lever that controlled injections of food and water directly into their own stomachs. Furthermore, the animals compensated accurately for dilution of nutrients by injecting more. Sterritt and

Smith (1965) also found that newborn chicks with stomach tubes could learn various responses with food-injection reinforcement. Since the chicks had never eaten before, the chance that food in the stomach might have some learned reinforcing property was greatly reduced.

### Evidence Against Drive Reduction

It may be that drive reduction is a *sufficient* condition for reinforcement, but it may well not be the *only* such condition. The main evidence against a monolithic drive reduction theory comes from research showing that excitatory stimuli are also reinforcing. The remainder of the evidence in this section, as well as that in the next, is negative for drive reduction theory.

*The Pain-Fear Paradox.* We can consider fear a response, because it can be conditioned to new stimuli. We then have the paradox (Mowrer, 1960a) that *pain reinforces the learning of fear but seems to punish other responses.* Furthermore, the drive reduction theorist would have to say that it is the *end* of pain that reinforces the fear learning. The paradox is resolved, however, by showing that pain onset, not pain termination, is what reinforces fear learning. Mowrer and Aiken (1954) and Mowrer and Solomon (1954) found that a stimulus paired with shock onset is, in fact, more aversive than one paired with shock offset.

Miller (1951a) had argued, however, that there might be an initial burst of pain following shock onset and a rapid diminution immediately thereafter as (1) the animal partly adapts to the pain and/or (2) possibly makes skeletal responses that reduce the pain. It is well known that some nerve fibers fire rapidly at the onset of a stimulus and quickly slow down if the stimulus is continued. Davitz (1955) tested Miller's hypothesis by confining rats in a cage so small they could not escape from the shock by moving, and paired the CS with a very slow (25-second) increase in shock level. The slow increment should alleviate the quick on-off burst of neural firing. This group showed greater fear conditioning, as measured by the suppressive effect of the CS on activity, than did a group in which the CS accompanied the abrupt termination of the shock. A common solution to the pain-fear paradox has been a two-factor theory. One version of this (Mowrer, 1947) is that fear (an autonomic response) is conditioned to stimuli associated with drive increase, and that instrumental (skeletal) responses are reinforced by drive reduction. Two-factor theory is further discussed under avoidance learning (Chapter Nine).

*Brown's Defense of Drive Reduction.* J. S. Brown (1955) eloquently defended drive reduction theory against the onslaught of experiments indicating that increased excitation was reinforcing. He said that *"an increase in stimulation, even when relatively intense, need not always be categorized as an increase in drive"* (1955, pp. 171-172). He then applied his argument to four cases.

1. If the organism has been exposed to progressively stronger stimuli that have been followed by drive reduction, the stimuli may not produce a drive effect. Miller (1960) did demonstrate that animals would run across a strongly electrified grid to get food if the current were built up gradually, over many trials. Animals given the full current on first exposure to shock, however, ran hesitantly, if at all.
2. Stimuli that have drive properties may lose them because the stimuli take on secondary reinforcing properties. Loud buzzers are noxious to rats, but if paired with food the buzzer is approached rather than avoided.
3. There is some sensory adaptation even with pain.
4. Competing stimuli may reduce the drive properties of the painful stimulus in question. Most of us have observed that if we are distracted by something else we do not notice pain as much. Loud sound has therefore been used by dentists to reduce the perceived pain of drilling.

Brown's arguments undeniably have some validity, but not enough to save drive reduction theory as *the* theory of reinforcement.

### Arousal (Activation) Theory

We shall simply put activation theory into context here. If arousal is high, a reduction is said to be sought, but at low levels of arousal a higher level is sought. The theory can thus be treated as a kind of two-factor theory: the optimal level of arousal may sometimes be attained by decrement and sometimes by increment.

Arousal theory can also be treated strictly as a drive or tension reduction theory. Berlyne (1960) and Hunt (1965) both considered that departures from an optimal level of stimulation produce arousal. When the organism strives for its optimal level of stimulation it is, in effect, striving for arousal reduction only. The difference between this version of arousal theory and drive reduction theory is that the optimal level of stimulation is greater than zero. Since there are no reliable operations for specifying arousal level at a given time for a given individual, we cannot typically tell whether an increase or decrease is being sought.

## STIMULUS INTERPRETATIONS OF REINFORCEMENT

Some stimulus theories of reinforcement are similar to motivational inter-pretations in that they postulate stimuli are effective reinforcers because they are *arousing,* or exciting. Other stimulus theories, however, are rela-tively nonmotivational, postulating only that *information* provided by stimuli is reinforcing.

### Hedonic (Positive Arousal) Reinforcers

*Sweet Substances.* For many years, P. T. Young (e.g., 1959) and his students used as experimental subjects rats not under any known dietary deficiency. The animals were always fed ample amounts of a well-balanced diet and were never deprived of food or water. Repeatedly it was found that such animals preferred more sweet to less sweet substances.[3] They would learn to make preferential responses, such as a specific turn in a maze, to obtain a sweeter reward. Taste factors, not drive reduction, seem to account for this.

Drive reduction theorists have generally raised two criticisms of the hedonic interpretation of preferences for sweets. First, they suggest that sugar solutions may in fact be drive reducing. This, however, requires the gratuitous assumption that such nondeprived animals as Young used were under some amount of unspecified drive. Second, the sweet taste of sugar may have been previously associated with drive reduction, particularly during nursing, when the animals received lactose in their mothers' milk, and this may account for the sweet preference shown by the adult animals. These two criticisms are apparently negated by research involving non-nutritive sweet substances such as saccharin and by experiments showing taste preferences in early infancy.

*Nonnutritive Substances.* Sheffield and Roby (1950) have argued that if sweet saccharin is reinforcing because of prior association with hunger reduction, then it should be possible to extinguish the preference for it with repeated exposure. Over many weeks of testing, however, their animals continued a high intake of saccharin solutions. Many experiments have found saccharin preferences under a great range of test conditions. Evidence that even saccharin may be drive reducing was reported by Miller (1957),

---

[3]Whenever we talk about such taste qualities as *sweet* and *bitter* with reference to lower animals it may be assumed that we are talking about how substances taste to humans. There is never any guarantee that they taste the same to other animals. Species differences in response to sugars are well known: rats, dogs and humans accept sugars eagerly, but many animals are indifferent to them, including cats.

who found that animals that had just previously drunk saccharin pressed bars less for saccharin reinforcement than did control animals. An alternative explanation is that the animals had temporarily adapted to the taste of saccharin so that it was a less reinforcing taste stimulus. Valenstein, Kakolewski, and Cox (1967) also showed that a combination of saccharin and glucose is consumed in amazing quantity by the rat on its first exposure to such a solution, much more than would be predicted on the basis of any drive reduction interpretation.

*Preference of Infants.* Foods associated with "well-being" become preferred and foods associated with illness are avoided (Rozin & Kalat, 1971). Galef and his associates (e.g., Galef & Henderson, 1972) reported that weanling rats show food preferences similar to their mothers'. This appears to be based on social factors (learning to go with their mothers to eat) and on an experience with the mother's milk. Galef suggests that the mother's diet is reflected in the taste of her milk and that the infant thus learns a preference for certain substances while nursing. A learned reinforcement explanation may thus account for some of the taste preference data, but this hardly seems the entire explanation.

Jacobs (1964a) found that rats would accept (lick, swallow) sugar solutions placed on the lips almost immediately after birth. Conversely, they rejected (withdrew from) bitter solutions. Furthermore, they showed a greater acceptance of sugar solutions that were much sweeter than the lactose content of rat milk. If the sweet preference were learned by association with milk sugar, we would expect, on the basis of stimulus generalization, that either less or more concentrated sucrose would have been less preferred. Warren and Pfaffmann (1958) tried to change guinea pigs' aversion to sucrose octa-acetate, a bitter solution, by putting it into their drinking water starting two days after birth. At the end of twenty-one days of this treatment, the animals still did not prefer the solution to plain water, although they did show a lesser aversion than control animals. By three months of age, however, their preferences were indistinguishable from nontreated animals. It is apparently very difficult to overcome an inherent taste aversion by simple exposure to the nonpreferred taste. Other experiments have shown genetic differences in taste preference. Ramirez and Fuller (1976) found 71 percent, 78 percent, and 83 percent genetic contributions for water, saccharin, and sucrose consumption in mice. In humans, there is a well-known genetic factor in the ability to detect the chemical phenothio-carbamide (PTC). Some people are completely taste blind to it, whereas others find it bitter. We would conclude there are genetically determined taste preferences that can, however, be changed to some degree by experience.

### Sex Studies

The male rat mounts and copulates with the female several times before it ejaculates. Sheffield, Wulff, and Backer (1951) suggested that ejaculation is the part of the sequence that would be considered drive reducing; the rest of the sequence would be drive arousing. Since their rats learned an instrumental response for the reinforcement of copulation without ejaculation, a reinforcer that was not drive reducing was demonstrated. This would hardly surprise anyone but the most dedicated drive reduction theorist.

### Brain Stimulation

Electrical self-stimulation of the brain as a positive reinforcer has been mentioned already and is discussed in detail in Chapter Fifteen. Suffice it here to say that it seems unlikely, if drive reduction were the mechanism of reinforcement, that non-deprived animals would work so hard for such stimulation. The stimulation seems to produce excitement, not a reduction thereof.

### Stimulus Change and Information

Harry Harlow (1953, p. 24) said: "It is my belief that the theory which describes learning as dependent upon drive reduction is false, that internal drive as such is a variable of little importance to learning, and that this small importance steadily decreases as we investigate learning problems of progressive complexity." He then went on to point out that he usually fed his monkeys *before* the experimental session; the monkeys stored food in their cheek pouches and then proceeded to swallow a little food after every response they made, whether the response was right or wrong. But the animals learned the correct responses. "It would seem," said Harlow (p. 26), "that the Lord was simply unaware of drive reduction learning theory when He created, or permitted the gradual evolution of, the rhesus monkey." In general, Harlow makes the point (p. 25) that external stimuli are more important sources of motivation than are internal drive states and suggests the argument, which we have already noted, that "the main role of the primary drive seems to be one of altering the threshold for precurrent responses."

Monkeys will work for hours on puzzle-type problems without deprivation or external reinforcement; they will work inside a dark box at a task that will open a window permitting them to see out of the box; and they are very active in exploring their environments. Montgomery and his associates showed that even rats would choose the arm of a T-maze that led to an explorable checkerboard-type maze, and that food deprivation actually reduced the exploratory behavior of the rat (Montgomery, 1953), although the evidence on this is conflicting. Much research shows that when no specific external reinforcement is given, rats in a T-maze will alternate the goal box to which they choose to go on successive trials. That is, they tend *not* to go to the goal box they entered on the previous trial. How are such results to be accounted for? Let us consider two information-type hypotheses: stimulus change and stimulus predictiveness.

*1. Stimulus Complexity and Change.* A number of authors (e.g., Berlyne, 1960; Dember, 1960, 1965; Dember & Earl, 1957; Fiske & Maddi, 1961a) have proposed variations on the theme that exposure to complex, changing stimuli is reinforcing (and, motivationally, that such stimuli have incentive properties). We will take the theory of Dember and Earl (1957) as a core idea. They proposed that there is an optimal level of stimulus complexity which is reinforcing for each organism and that organisms vary in the level of complexity which is optimal. The greater the complexity of an object or event, the more information it contains.[4] Different organisms (between or within species) have different "ideal" levels of complexity that they find attracting, as measured by preferences. It is argued, furthermore, that organisms tend to respond to stimuli which are just a little more complex than the ideal. When these *pacers* have become "mastered" (i.e., familiarized, appropriate responses to them learned), the organism tends to show a preference for yet more complex stimuli. Once an individual's complexity level is determined, any change in preference will be in the direction of greater complexity, not lesser. The concept of "growth"—capacity to deal with progressively more complex situations—is thus built into the theory. Levels of complexity which are too *low* are avoided, but so are levels of complexity which are too *high*.

Two experiments described by Dember (1965) illustrate the theory. The first involves *alternation behavior*. Rats tend to alternate between goal alleys on successive trials in a T-maze if not reinforced in one of the goal boxes (and, in fact, in the early trials of discrimination learning, they also alternate when they *are* reinforced). Thus, if a rat went to the left goal box on Trial 1, it would have a greater than chance tendency to go to the right goal box on Trial 2, and so on. Two primary theories have been postulated to account for this phenomenon, *response inhibition* and *stimulus satiation*. The first theory says that the animal tends not to repeat the same response; the second says that the animal tends not to go to the same stimulus. Both theories account equally well for simple alternation, so a more critical test is necessary.

---

[4]In the mathematical theory of information, if the environment is simple or highly redundant, there is little information. Information is defined in terms of uncertainty reduced; in very simple situations, there is little uncertainty to *be* reduced. If the environment is more complex, there is less redundancy and more information.

One such test, consistently producing reliable results, is the following. The animals are run in a maze in which the left goal arm is white and the right is black. Assume that on the first trial the animals run to the *right* and choose the *black* goal arm. Now the animals are run with the black on the left and the white on the right. According to the response inhibition theory, the animals should go to the left (since they went to the right on the first trial). According to the stimulus satiation theory, they should go to the right (repeating the response), because that is where the alternative stimulus is. The research shows that animals are *not* alternating with regard to responses. The earlier experiments indicated that they were alternating to goal box brightness, but it now appears (Douglas, 1966) that they are alternating with regard to absolute direction (e.g., east versus west) rather than brightness. It is still stimulus alternation rather than response alternation, however.

The second experiment involves *human preference for complexity in poetry.* Kammann (1964), as described by Dember, used an objective procedure for determining the degree of complexity of a number of poems. Fifteen poems were pre-selected to cover a wide range of complexity. He found that (1) poems of intermediate complexity were most preferred, and (2) subjects' preferences for the poems were correlated with their abilities to accurately fill in omitted words. In other words, the subjects' "ideals," as indicated by ability to work with the poems, were related to preference in the manner suggested by the theory.

**2. Stimulus Predictive Value.** Bower, McLean, and Meacham (1966) asked whether information about speed of delivery of reinforcement would be rewarding even if the information did not influence delivery time. Pigeons were allowed to peck at either of two white disks (keys), taking their choice and being reinforced equally on each key, regardless of the choice. One key, however, changed color to green when food followed shortly, and to red if there were a delay, but the other key changed to yellow regardless of delay. With more than 200 free-choice trials, there was over 90 percent preference for pecking at the key which predicted the amount of delay. The subjects preferred to know when a reward was to be delivered, even when it made no difference in the outcome. Such responses are traditionally known as "observing responses" (e.g., Wyckoff, 1952; Prokasy, 1956), a term referring to the fact that animals will learn responses which seem to do no more than let them know what is going on.

## SECONDARY REINFORCEMENT

Because such "basic drives" as hunger and thirst do not dominate us most of the time, the corresponding reinforcers are not very effective most of the time. The concept of secondary (acquired, conditioned) reinforcers was devised to fill the gap. We may define a secondary reinforcer as a formerly neutral stimulus which, through association with a primary reinforcer, comes to serve some of the same functions as the primary reinforcer.

### Functions of Secondary Reinforcers

Four different functions are commonly ascribed to secondary reinforcers (see Wike, 1966; Hendry, 1969; Mowrer, 1960a, 1960b, for book-length discussions).

*1. Acquisition of New Responses.* Saltzman (1949) trained rats to run down an alleyway to a black goal box (white for some subjects) with food in it. The empty goal box was then put on one arm of a U-maze and, over a series of test trials, the animals ran more often to this side than to the opposite side, where there was a neutral goal box.

*2. Maintenance of Behavior During Extinction.* Bugelski (1938) trained hungry rats to press a lever that produced a clicking sound and a food pellet. In extinction, half the animals continued to get the clicking sound when they pressed the lever, but the other half did not. The "click" group made significantly more responses in extinction, which was interpreted to mean that the click was reinforcing lever pressing during extinction.

*3. Mediation of Delay of Reinforcement.* In well-controlled laboratory experiments, if there is much delay between response and reinforcement the response is not reliably learned. In a particularly dramatic experiment, Grice (1948) trained rats on a nonspatial brightness discrimination problem. With a delay of ten seconds between response and reinforcement some animals failed to learn after as many as 1400 trials. In a second part of the experiment, some animals had goal boxes which were the same color as the positive and negative cues. Under this condition there was much better learning, interpreted to mean that these color cues became secondary reinforcers, mediating the delay between choice responses and reinforcement.

*4. Establishing and Maintaining Schedules of Reinforcement.* In the typical operant conditioning procedure, a pigeon is trained to peck a key on a particular schedule of reinforcement, with a particular color light as a cue. For example, the bird might be trained on a *variable-interval* schedule (responses at the end of variable intervals of time are reinforced) when a red light is on. This produces a constant rate of responding. The bird might then be trained on a *fixed-interval* schedule, with a green light on. On the fixed-interval schedule, pecking is reinforced at the end of a fixed time period. The typical performance is a gradually increasing response rate, peaking just before the reinforcer is given. Instead of being reinforced with food, the bird is reinforced by a light change from green to red. The bird can then obtain food on the variable-interval schedule. The red light, however, is the secondary reinforcer for learning the fixed-interval schedule.

It might be argued that the responding on the fixed-interval schedule has simply been given delayed food reward, because the animal now obtains food on the variable-interval schedule. This argument is weakened by the fact that several schedules in sequence can be learned in this manner, but with food reward only in the final schedule. This procedure may be potent, however, as demonstrable with single animals, because in this continual recycling through the sequence of schedules, the animal does always end up with food reward. There is thus continual reconditioning of the various light cues which are the secondary reinforcers (Wike, 1966).

### Variables Influencing the Strength of Secondary Reinforcement

The "strength" of a secondary reinforcer (its capacity to reinforce) is a function of a number of variables, most of which are similar if not identical to those that influence classical conditioning. Wike (1966) has discussed these in detail, and we shall summarize them briefly. The strength of a secondary reinforcer depends on (1) number of pairings with the primary reinforcer (Miles, 1956); (2) amount of primary reinforcement (e.g., Greene, 1953; D'Amato, 1955); (3) time delay between the primary and secondary reinforcers (Jenkins, 1950; Bersh, 1951); and (4) probability of pairing with a primary reinforcer. In addition, (5) secondary reinforcers are more effective with high deprivation levels at the time of test (J. L. Brown, 1956) and operate weakly, at best, with satiated rats (Wike & Casey, 1954). And, (6) secondary reinforcers extinguish if not paired again with primary reinforcers, but with frequent reconditioning a secondary reinforcer may retain its strength almost indefinitely (Wike, 1966). Finally, (7) partial reinforcement procedures, both in pairing the secondary reinforcer with the primary and in presenting the secondary reinforcer after the instrumental response, increase greatly the "durability" of secondary reinforcers. Zimmerman (1957, 1959) obtained literally thousands of responses from his animals when he used such partial reinforcement techniques, as compared with the more typical number of experimental responses, which is in the hundreds (at best) with rats. Zimmerman likened this highly persistent behavior to Allport's (1937) concept of *functional autonomy of motives*. Allport's idea was that organisms (people in particular) can come to be motivated by factors that are very enduring and that outlast the original reasons for carrying on some activity.

### Theories of Secondary Reinforcement

Theories of secondary reinforcement can also be classified as stimulus, response, or motivational, with the additional complication that learning is necessarily involved in establishing the secondary reinforcer.

*Stimulus Theories.* Hull (1943) saw secondary reinforcers as condi-tioned stimuli—that is, as neutral stimuli paired with primary reinforcers. Keller and Schoenfeld (1950), however, argued that a secondary reinforcer had first to be established as a *discriminative stimulus* through differential reinforcement of responding. Thus, if responding is followed by reinforce-ment during or after a particular stimulus, but not otherwise, the stimulus becomes discriminative. A number of experiments have indeed indicated that simple pairing of a stimulus with a reinforcer is not enough to establish a secondary reinforcer (Schoenfeld, Antonitis, & Bersh, 1950; Egger & Miller, 1962). Dinsmoor (1950) showed that if a discriminative stimulus was extinguished prior to testing it as a secondary reinforcer, it was a much weaker secondary reinforcer.

The most popular contemporary interpretation of secondary reinforce-ment is that the reinforcer is an informative stimulus. Egger and Miller (1962, 1963)[5] showed that a stimulus which provided *reliable* and *unique* in-formation about the coming presentation of food was a good secondary reinforcer. A *redundant* stimulus, coming immediately after another stimulus had already signaled food, was not a good reinforcer; it gave the animals no information. If the first stimulus sometimes signaled food and some-times did not, then the "redundant" stimulus was no longer redundant and was a good reinforcer.

*Response Theories.* Elicitation theory says that a secondary rein-forcer is just another stimulus that elicits a response. Food is reinforc-ing because it reliably elicits eating and a click is reinforcing if it elicits going to the food magazine. The theory makes no distinction between primary and secondary reinforcers; either is assumed effective only so long as it elicits responding. Bugelski (1956) says that in extinction the click of the food hopper is not a reinforcer, in the sense of being a reward, but is part of a stimulus pattern that evokes a response. Denny and Adelman (1955)

[5]An earlier experiment by Wyckoff (1952) is generally credited with being the first study of this type of problem, but it was not cast in terms of information theory. The Bower, McLean, and Meacham (1966) experiment is also in the information framework.

make the same interpretation, and even Hull (1943) recognized it as a distinct possibility.

*Motivational Theories.* The most obvious motivational interpretation is *drive reduction.* A secondary reinforcer cannot reduce *need* in any meaningful way, such as making an animal less hungry (Wickens & Miles, 1954), but it might produce *drive stimulus reduction* through previous pairing with drive reduction. Mowrer (1960b) proposed that every primary drive has a conditionable emotional component which he called *fear.* A hungry animal has hunger-fear, and a thirsty animal has thirst-fear. A stimulus continually associated with food and hunger reduction could then reduce hunger-fear in anticipation of actual hunger reduction. Such anticipatory fear reduction *is* positive secondary reinforcement for Mowrer. Since Mowrer used the language of secondary reinforcement, we have included him here, but in his emphasis on anticipatory changes he was an incentive theorist, and we will discuss him as such in more detail in the next chapter.

According to drive reduction theory, a stimulus preceding shock termination should also become a positive secondary reinforcer. (This is predicted by many theories but is more crucial to drive reduction.) There is, however, little evidence that such a secondary reinforcer can be established, and there are no *replicated* experiments showing such an effect (Beck, 1961; LoLordo, 1969; Siegel & Milby, 1969).

It does appear possible, however, to establish a secondary reinforcer by having a stimulus signal a *shock-free period of time,* an information property. One phase of this research is to show that such a "safety signal" reduces fear. The second phase is to show that the signal is reinforcing. Rescorla and LoLordo (1965) trained dogs to shuttle back and forth between two grid-floored compartments to avoid shock. A "danger" signal was then paired with shock onset in another apparatus but a second stimulus (safety signal) was not followed by shock. On return to the shuttle situation, the subjects (dogs) shuttled *more rapidly* when the danger signal was turned on and *less rapidly* when the safety signal was on. Since these signals had not previously been paired with any specific behavior, the interpretation was that the danger signal made the animals more fearful and the safety signal made them less fearful.

Moscovitch and LoLordo (1968) and Rescorla (1969) then showed that if such an animal could push either of two panels with its nose, responses increased only to the panel that turned on the safety signal. The safety signal selectively reinforced one response and did not increase the level of indiscriminate responding.

Why has the Rescorla-LoLordo procedure been effective in establishing a positive reinforcer and other shock procedures not? Denny (1971) distinguishes between *relief,* which occurs immediately after shock offset, and *relaxation,* which does not start until 15 to 30 seconds after shock offset and is not complete for perhaps 90 seconds. Denny considers a stimulus paired with relaxation to be a secondary reinforcer, whereas a stimulus paired with relief is not. Most experimenters have tried to pair a stimulus very closely with shock termination, assuming that a closer association with shock offset would be more effective. They were probably then working under a strong handicap, but the Rescorla-LoLordo research met the conditions for pairing a stimulus with relaxation.

### Interpretations of Secondary Reinforcement As an Artifact

Various authors have proposed that secondary reinforcement is really an artifact of experimental operations. There are obvious increments in behavior, but it has been suggested that something besides reinforcement accounts for them.

*Stimulus Artifact.* According to the discrimination hypothesis (Bitterman, Fedderson, & Tyler, 1953), when the animal learns to press a lever for food, the response comes under the control of a number of different stimuli. Two of these are the food and the click that precedes the food. In extinction, eliminating the food takes away one controlling stimulus and eliminating the food and the click takes away two controlling stimuli. The click then just appears to be reinforcing because the response decrement is not as rapid when the click is presented.

*Response Artifact.* Wyckoff, Sidowski, and Chambliss (1958) suggested that secondary reinforcement might be an artifact of *generalized response facilitation.* They showed that a buzzer paired with water facilitated lever pressing whether or not the buzzer was actually contingent on responding (a control group got the buzzer as often as the experimental group, but not following lever pressing). This led the authors to suggest that the buzzer was not reinforcing the response but was simply facilitating many different responses, of which lever pressing happened to be one. Crowder and his colleagues (Crowder, Gay, Bright, & Lee, 1959; Crowder, Gay, Fleming, & Hurst, 1959; Crowder, Gill, Hodge, Nash, 1959; Crowder, Morris, & McDaniel, 1959) seem to have consistently obtained about twice as many responses from the "reinforced" animals as from yoked controls. Response facilitation may then account for some of the secondary reinforcement effect but certainly not for all of it.

*Motivational Artifact.* The procedures used to *test* for secondary reinforcement are identical to those used to *produce* nonreward frustration (Lott, 1967). Such frustration is usually considered a drive-like aversive

motivational state (see Chapter Eight). One could then argue that the
"secondary reinforcing" stimulus is just a "teaser" which arouses frustration
so that the animal responds more vigorously. (Note that this is similar to
Sheffield's interpretation of the effect of conditioned consummatory responses on instrumental behavior.) Such vigorous responding is typical of
animals just beginning extinction. The similarity of secondary reinforcement and frustration procedures has hardly gone unnoticed (Amsel, 1968),
but there has been no good way to deal with it *in reinforcement terms*.
Furthermore, many phenomena seem to defy a frustration interpretation.
For example, why would an animal learn a new response to get an aversive
(frustrating) stimulus? According to the frustration interpretation, secondary reinforcing stimuli ought to be avoided, not sought. The frustration
interpretation works best for extinction situations, because it is there that
the energizing effects of nonreward are most apparent.

## INTERACTION OF EXTRINSIC REWARDS
## WITH INTRINSIC MOTIVATION

In the field of industrial psychology, a distinction is commonly made
between intrinsic motivation and extrinsic rewards. The term *intrinsic motivation* refers to factors that make certain activities rewarding in and of
themselves. This would include such things as games, puzzles, artistic or
other creative endeavors, and so on. Almost anything could potentially be
intrinsically motivating for some individuals. The term *extrinsic rewards*
refers generally to the kinds of reinforcement situations we have considered in this chapter. That is, a person makes a response and is reinforced
for it by some external agent. This is the standard approach of operant
conditioning and behavior modification. It has often been said (Notz, 1975)
that the two forms of motivation should be additive. Thus, to maximize
productivity in a work situation, it would seem reasonable that if (1) a person were doing a job that was interesting to him, and (2) were paid well for
it, then (3) he should work harder. This may not in fact occur, however.
(See Deci, 1975, for a book-length discussion of this area.)

In some experimental situations, it has been clearly demonstrated that
providing external reinforcement for an already interesting task may actually
*decrease* the performance of that task. The ideal paradigm is to (1) pretest
subjects on their level of performance at a task in order to determine those
for whom the task is intrinsically motivating; (2) give external reinforcers
for performance of the task; and (3) posttest the subjects to see what effect
the treatment had. There are, of course, necessary controls for simple
pretest-posttest changes independent of treatment, amount of time spent at
the task during the treatment, and so on. There is not a great deal of

research, but that available consistently shows that external reinforcers such as money actually do produce a decrement in later frequency of performance of the behavior.

For example, in a study of nursery school children, Anderson, Manoo-gian, and Reznick (1976) compared the effects of money, a "good player" award, and verbal praise as external reinforcers. Both money and the good player award produced a pretest-to-posttest decrement in the amount of time spent drawing pictures with different-color magic markers, but verbal praise produced an increase. This experiment was particularly well conducted and controlled, and the results are in line with those from previous research (Notz, 1975; Deci, 1975). Other tasks, such as working puzzles of varying degrees of intrinsic interest, have also supported the hypothesis with adults (e.g., Calder & Staw, 1975).

How are such results to be accounted for? First, this line of research was stimulated by the suggestion of de Charms (1968) that there should be an *interaction* of intrinsic motivation and external rewards, not just an additive effect. This interaction, he believed, would be based on the subject's perception of whether he was the controlling agent or at the mercy of outside agents in achieving rewards. If the individual sees himself as the causal factor for desirable outcomes, then the behavior producing those outcomes is intrinsically motivating and desirable. The individual will then continue to do those things over which he has some control. On the other hand, if the individual sees his rewards as being dependent on someone else, the activities necessary to get those rewards will be less intrinsically motivating. A person may continue to work at his job because he needs the money to live, but not find the work intrinsically motivating.

From this line of argument, then, de Charms derived two counter-intuitive predictions. First, he predicted that the introduction of extrinsic rewards would decrease intrinsic motivation, because the individual would perceive that the locus of control is changed from internal to external. Second, a withdrawal or reduction in extrinsic rewards would increase intrinsic motivation, because the perceived locus of control would change from external to internal. We have already seen some evidence supporting the first proposition, and Notz (1975) adduces two experiments done in other contexts as support for the second. The actual amount of research on the problem thus far is small and some of it not highly convincing, but there is enough evidence to take the hypotheses seriously. The problem is certainly important enough to devote some considerable effort to finding the conditions under which such undermining of intrinsic motivation may occur. Whether or not de Charms' theoretical analysis is correct, he seems to have hit on an important phenomenon. We can hardly help but be in-trigued by any phenomenon that shows that rewards (and—see Chapter Nine—punishes) can work just the opposite of the way they are sup-posed to.

A proper analysis of the problem will take a great deal of theoretical effort and much research, however, for it will have to account for the results obtained in innumerable studies of behavior modification. There are obviously many experimental variables that would be involved, such as type and scheduling of external reinforcers, type of intrinsic motivation, and so on. A reconceptualization of the intrinsic-extrinsic distinction might also be required. We do not, for example, find the distinction, as made earlier, to be a terribly compelling one theoretically. Such questions can only be raised, however, by an idea that was fertile in the first place.

## CONCLUSION

It is probably impossible to fit all the evidence on reinforcement into a single coherent theory, partly because reinforcement may not be the best concept to work with in the first place. An incentive concept is probably more fruitful, as discussed in the next chapter. Nevertheless, we can make some relevant summarizing remarks, related to the notion of the importance of responding. Since there is evidence for each kind of reinforcement theory—stimulus, response, and motivational—they presumably have something in common. But what?

An important key could be the Glickman-Schiff theory. If a reinforcer arouses a neural response system, then we could argue that response theories are correct because neural response systems have been aroused. At the same time, however, stimulus theories could be correct if we postulate that reinforcing stimuli are ones that arouse neural response systems, even if overt responses are not aroused. A response system is probably more strongly aroused if the response occurs (electrical stimulation of the brain aside, because that is a nonnormal physiological precedure), but stimuli which only weakly arouse response systems could still be reinforcing. Secondary reinforcing stimuli might be in this class of relatively weak stimuli.

If we furthermore postulate that arousal of *autonomic* response systems, as well as skeletal, can be reinforcing, then we could incorporate drive (or arousal) increments and decrements as reinforcing events. If a stimulus arouses fear, then that stimulus would be a reinforcing stimulus. Similarly, a stimulus arousing a "positive" excitement would be reinforcing. Such a conception forces us back to a very old, but important question: What do we mean by stimuli and responses when we talk about the internal machinery of the body? The body, especially the brain, is one continuing *process* from which we have arbitrarily selected certain aspects to refer to as *stimuli* and *responses*. With humans there are complex interactions between extrinsic reinforcers and intrinsic motivation.

chapter 7

# Rewards: 2. Incentive Motivation

## THE CONCEPT OF INCENTIVE

In the last chapter, we examined the idea that rewards "work backward" to "strengthen" responses in some sense. Now we develop the idea that the anticipation of rewards is the effective determinant of behavior. Incentives, like drives, are often said to energize behavior, but are described as "pulling" rather than "pushing." Future incentives, of course, are not really pulling; it is their anticipation at the moment that is effective.

Conceptually, drives also differ from incentives (Bolles, 1967) in that

1. "Primary" drives are considered biologically inevitable consequences of circumstances; hunger follows food deprivation, and the like. Incentive motivation is not inevitable in this way; it is learned through experience with rewards (e.g., we learn about good steak dinners.)
2. Drives are cyclic, fluctuating inevitably with deprivation levels, hormone conditions, and so on. Incentive motivation can be aroused whenever the appropriate stimulus conditions are present.
3. Incentive motivation is increasingly being considered an associative learning phenomenon rather than an "energetic" phenomenon.

### Why the Incentive Concept Was Developed

Most of us probably believe that our anticipations of rewards (or punishers) influence our behavior. Such introspections have frequently not been taken seriously in behavior theory, however, and such nonintrospective accounts as drive and drive reduction were developed. Laboratory evidence pointing to an incentive interpretation has been accumulating for over a half century, however, and this evidence is being taken very seriously. The following kinds of phenomena seem amenable to incentive interpretations, but not to drive or S-R learning interpretations.

*1. Amount of Reward and Reward Shifts.* Performance varies with amount of reward (see Black, 1969, for review), which might mean greater learning with larger reward. This interpretation (or a drive interpretation) does not seem to account for the fact that when incentives are shifted from large to small, or vice versa, performance changes more rapidly than we would expect from either changes in drive or changes in response learning.

The classic incentive shift study is by Crespi (1942). Rats received either 1, 4, 16, 64, or 256 small food pellets at the end of a straight runway. The more pellets received, the faster the animals ran, and, when shifted to a different number of pellets, their running speeds changed appropriately. Figure 7-1 shows illustrative data from Crespi's experiment. The improvement of the group shifted from 1 to 16 pellets was faster than the original "learning" rate of the 16-pellet group. Assuming that a new postshift *habit* should develop at the same rate as the preshift response, the results indicate a change in incentive motivation. The animals knew the response; the motivation to perform it changed.

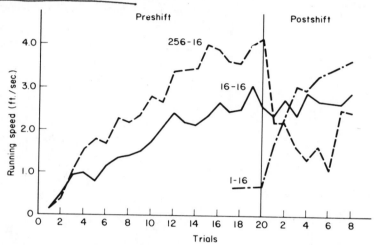

**Figure 7.1** *Speed of running in a long runway as a function of amount of reinforcement. For the first 19 trials, different groups were given 1, 16, or 256 pellets of food (acquisition data for the 1-pellet group are not presented); from trial 20 on, subjects all were given 16 pellets. (From Robert C. Bolles,* Theory of Motivation *(after Crespi, 1942). Harper & Row, 1967, p. 335.)*

Crespi later suggested that the animals developed different amounts of anticipatory tension, or excitement, which he called *eagerness*. "Eagerness," he said (1944, p. 352), "is related to learning only in the sense that the animal must find out how much incentive he is obtaining before he exhibits a corresponding amount of eagerness." Zeaman (1949) replicated Crespi's results in another well-known experiment.

**2. Quality of Reward.** Simmons (1924) reported better maze performance by rats rewarded with bread and milk than those rewarded with sunflower seeds. Generally, the more preferred a substance is, the better a reward it is. Guttman (1953, 1954) recognized that amount of reward was typically confounded with amount of consummatory activity or amount of time spent consuming. (Both of these variables influence reward value

[Wolfe & Kaplon, 1941; Logan, 1960]). Guttman therefore manipulated amount of reward by varying the concentrations of sucrose or glucose solutions. Rate of lever pressing increased regularly with concentrations of either sugar, as shown in Figure 7-2. We would now consider that different concentrations represent different *qualities* of reward rather than amounts, since taste seems to be the critical factor, but the incentive interpretation remains the same. Collier (e.g., Collier & Myers, 1961; Collier, 1962) has studied both sucrose and saccharin in detail. Lever pressing for sucrose in-

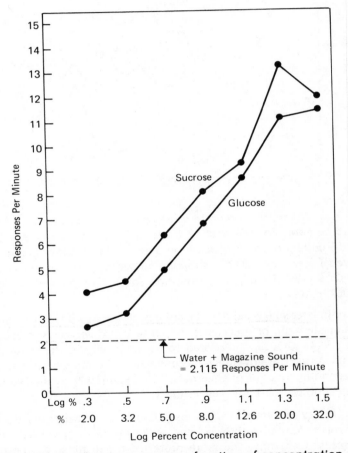

**Figure 7.2** *Rate of bar pressing as a function of concentration of rein-forcing agent. (From Guttman, 1954, p. 359. Copyright © 1954 by the American Psychological Association. Reprinted by permission.)*

creases linearly with the logarithm of concentration up to 64 percent if the rewards are small and widely spaced in time (e.g., .05 ml and three minutes apart for the rat). With large or closely spaced rewards, there is an inversion of response rate at higher concentrations, because of postingestional variables. Responding for saccharin increases up to about 0.5 percent and then declines as the solutions become more bitter to human taste (and, apparently, to rats as well.)

**3. Incentive Contrast Effects.** By the term *contrast effects,* we mean that if two different incentives are presented in sequence (or alternating) animals will perform differently for each than if either were the only one presented. To illustrate, Collier and Marx (1959) trained three independent groups of animals to obtain either 4, 11.3 or 32 percent solutions from a dipper, on cue. All animals than pressed a lever for 11.3 percent. The animals shifted *down* to 11.3 percent performed more poorly than the animals maintained at 11.3 percent and the animals shifted *up* to 11.3 percent performed better. There were thus both positive and negative contrast effects. More recently, Flaherty and his colleagues (e.g., Flaherty & Avdzej, 1976; Flaherty & Largen, 1975) have also obtained contrast effects with both consummatory (number of licks) and instrumental (running speed) measures of performance, using 4 percent and 32 percent sucrose.

Negative contrast effects have been commonly obtained, but positive contrast effects have been reported less frequently. One possibility for this is that a "large" reward group might be responding so near the upper limit of performance that a group shifted up to that level could not possibly exceed it (a ceiling effect). Collier and Marx (1959) avoided this difficulty by testing with a response different from that used in training. Shanab and Biller (1972) and Mellgren (1972) also obtained a positive contrast effect using delay of reward, so that the control animals at a high level of reward would not be responding at their highest level of performance. Contrast effects generally support incentive theory, because they are presumably due to contexts in which incentives are obtained, rather than to different drive levels or different response learning. There are a number of complications in this research, however, both in methodology and interpretation. Dunham (1968), Mackintosh (1974), and McHose and Moore (1976) have reviewed the literature from different points of view.

**4. Amount of Deprivation.** Incentive theorists uniformly argue that deprivation enhances incentives. Food is more rewarding for a hungry animal because food deprivation enhances the incentive quality of food, and so on. Furthermore, preference for food of a particular flavor is increased if it has been consumed under long food deprivation (Revusky, 1967), with similar results for fluids and water deprivation (Revusky, 1968). There are also cross-deprivation effects. Thirsty rats developed no preference for 8 percent sucrose solution over water in a choice situation like a T maze, whereas hungry animals developed a 100 percent preference (Beck & Bidwell, 1974). Preferences were changed simply by reversing the deprivation conditions. J. Cohen and Oöstendorp (1976) did find a sucrose preference with water-deprived animals in a discrimination-learning situation, but P. Cohen and Tokeida (1972) found a preference *reversal* (water preferred 100 percent to sucrose) under high water deprivation (in this experiment the animals only got one drop of water at each choice). Many experiments have shown that food deprivation heightens already existing sucrose preferences of nondeprived animals (e.g., Collier & Myers, 1961; Beck & Ellis, 1966).

   **5. Latent Learning and Latent Extinction.** Tolman and Honzik (1930) rewarded some of their animals in a maze, but not others. Only the food-rewarded animals achieved a low-error performance. When the nonrewarded animals were shifted to reward, however, their performance quickly improved to the level of the continuously rewarded subjects. The results are shown in Figure 7-3. The authors argued that the shifted animals had *learned* the maze pathways without reward, but were not motivated to perform efficiently until they expected food. There are many such *latent learning* experiments (Thistlethwaite, 1951).

   In the typical *latent extinction* experiment, two groups of animals are trained in a straight runway with food reward. One group is then placed in the goal box a number of times without food; the other is not. In the normal extinction that follows, the placement group runs slower and extinguishes faster than the nonplacement group. Since drive was not changed, and the animals did not actually perform the response of running during latent extinction, the results are interpreted as an incentive effect caused by changed expectancies.

   These lines of research converge on the idea that incentives are the most important motivational determinants of performance, although they themselves are influenced by experience and internal states of the organism. How, then, do we theoretically account for incentive effects? We shall examine theories that assume incentive motivation develops out of responses and theories that consider incentive motivation as a central nervous system process.

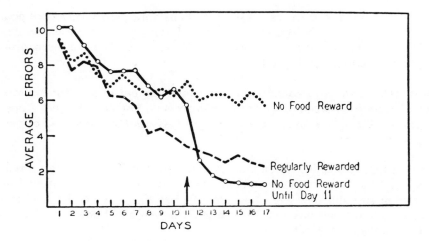

**Figure 7.3** *Evidence for latent learning in the maze. With no food reward, there is some reduction in errors, but not as great a reduction as with regular food reward. Despite the higher error scores prior to the intro- duction of food, the group rewarded only from the 11th trial immediately begins to do as well as the group that had been regularly rewarded. The interpretation is that some learning went on within the first 10 trials, which did not show in performance until the food incentive activated it. (After Tolman and Honzik, published in 1930 by The Regents of the Uni- versity of California; reprinted by permission of the University of Cali- fornia Press.)*

### RESPONSE THEORIES FOR INCENTIVE MOTIVATION

#### Hull-Spence: The Anticipatory Goal Response ($r_g$)

On the basis of the Crespi data, Hull added an incentive concept (called *K*, in honor of Kenneth Spence) to his system (1952), proposing that it multiplied *H* and *D*, giving the formula: $E = H \times D \times K$. The ante- cedent conditions for manipulating the strength of *K* were said to be the amount, quality, and delay of reinforcement. R. W. Black (1965) suggested that *K* might also be a function of deprivation.

Spence (1956) suggested that *K* itself might be *derived* from the *frac- tional anticipatory goal response*, a concept developed by Hull (1931) to provide an account of purpose and expectation in S-R rather than mentalistic terms. The details of the establishment of the anticipatory fractional goal response are given in Box 7-1, a series of successively more elaborated diagrams modified from Hull's paper. We may describe the mechanism as follows, corresponding to Box 7-1.

**Box 7-1.** *Detailed Description of the Development of the Anticipatory Goal Response Mechanism. (Modified from Hull, 1931, pp. 489-496. Copyright © 1931 by the American Psychological Association. Reprinted by permission.)*

To make the illustration more graphic, assume that we have a rat running down a straight runway and that the different parts of the runway have different stimulus characteristics, identified as $S_1$, $S_2$, $S_3$, and $S_g$. $S_1$ corresponds to the start box and $S_g$ to the goal box. Assume the animal is hungry and running to the food reward.

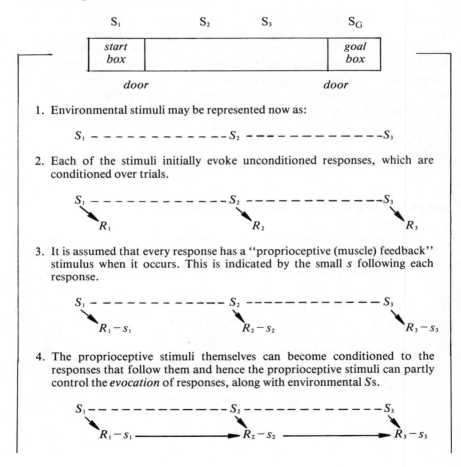

1. Environmental stimuli may be represented now as:

$S_1$ $-----------$ $S_2$ $-------------$ $S_3$

2. Each of the stimuli initially evoke unconditioned responses, which are conditioned over trials.

$S_1$ $------------$ $S_2$ $-------------$ $S_3$
$R_1$ $R_2$ $R_3$

3. It is assumed that every response has a "proprioceptive (muscle) feedback" stimulus when it occurs. This is indicated by the small $s$ following each response.

$S_1$ $------------$ $S_2$ $-----------$ $S_3$
$R_1 - s_1$ $R_2 - s_2$ $R_3 - s_3$

4. The proprioceptive stimuli themselves can become conditioned to the responses that follow them and hence the proprioceptive stimuli can partly control the *evocation* of responses, along with environmental $S$s.

$S_1$ $-----------$ $S_2$ $-----------$ $S_3$
$R_1 - s_1$ $\longrightarrow$ $R_2 - s_2$ $\longrightarrow$ $R_3 - s_3$

Each response is now under multiple stimulus control, from the environmental stimuli and from the proprioceptive feedback from the previous response.

5. Since the animal is hungry, we also assume that a drive stimulus, $s_d$, is continuously present and that it also becomes conditioned to the various responses. Three sources of stimulation now control the various responses, but $R$s occur in the proper sequence because both the environmental and proprioceptive stimuli occur in sequence.

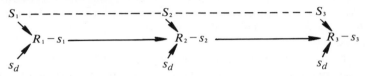

6. At this point in the diagram, we introduce a crucial element: the goal response itself. (It has been present all along, of course, as far as the animal was concerned. It is just that now we explicitly introduce it to the diagram.) When the animal eats the food, he makes the overt goal response ($R_G$). At the same time, there is a covert or *fractional goal response* ($r_g$) which occurs along with eating but which can also occur without actual eating. This $r_g$ is also conditionable. Furthermore, like other responses, it has its own stimulus feedback ($s_g$).

We momentarily abbreviate the diagram to show this part of the sequence:

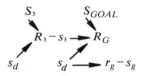

7. $R_g$ is conditioned directly to $s_d$ and to $S_G$ (the goal box stimuli) since both of these are present when it occurs. $r_g$ is somewhat less strongly conditioned to $S_1$, $S_2$, and $S_3$ by two means, (1) delay of reinforcement and (2) stimulus generalization, the earlier stimuli having characteristics something like the later stimuli.

Since $r_g$ is aroused early in the sequence, $s_g$ is also aroused and can become conditioned to the overt responses, just as was $s_d$. We finally have the following diagram, which shows the overt responses being evoked by environmental stimuli ($S$s), feedback stimuli from responses ($s$s) drive stimuli ($s_d$s) and feedback stimuli from anticipatory goal responses ($s_g$s).

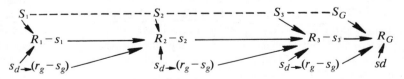

To the extent that $r_g$ is strongly aroused by the food (or other appropriate incentive, then $s_g$ will be strongly aroused and will play a relatively bigger role in the evocation of responses.

When the animal is given food after responding, it eats. Eating is the goal response ($R_G$) and, of course, only occurs when there is food. At the same time, however, there are *fractional* goal responses, such as small chewing or licking movements or salivation, which can occur even without food. These fractional responses ($r_g$s) are considered conditionable. In a maze, for example, the environmental stimuli preceding the goal response could become conditioned stimuli for the fractional goal response(s). Similarly, internal stimuli present when the animal eats could also be conditioned to $r_g$s. After some number of experiences, such internal and external stimuli at the start of the maze could arouse these $r_g$s so that the $r_g$s are *anticipatory.*

These $r_g$s become motivational by virtue of the fact that they have *stimulus consequences* ($s_g$s) and these $s_g$s become conditioned to responses leading to the goal. We then have the sequence

$$S \longrightarrow (r_g - s_g) \longrightarrow R$$

where $S$ and $R$ are external stimuli and overt responses

The stronger that $r_g$s are conditioned to internal and external stimuli, then the stronger the effect of $s_g$s on behavior. For Spence (1956), the $r_g - s_g$ mechanism accounted for incentive motivation.[1]

There is some ambiguity in this account of how the $r_g - s_g$ mechanism might work, however. First, $s_g$ might facilitate responding because it is an *intense stimulus* and therefore has a drivelike property. This could quite readily account for situations where response vigor is measured, as in the Crespi experiment. Secondly, however, $s_g$ might facilitate responding because it is just another stimulus conditioned to overt responses. This is Hull's original interpretation: $r_g - s_g$ simply *mediates* between external stimuli and responses. The stimulus intensity interpretation is motivational; the mediation interpretation is associative. A third alternative is that both might be correct.

There is little evidence that incentives are arousing except that they produce vigorous and persistent behavior. Since this is what we want to explain, we need independent evidence for an energizing effect. The lack of such positive evidence led Trapold and Overmier (1972) and Bolles and Moot (1972) to argue that incentive effects probably are mediational rather than arousing. Considerable evidence indicates that heart rate is highly correlated with activity and therefore is probably not a good independent measure of arousal (Brillhart, Osberg, & Beck, 1975; Elliott, 1975; Meinrath & Beck, 1977) in instrumental situations. Meinrath and Beck, however, found that when animals were not required to work for sucrose, their heart

---

[1]It also accounted for secondary reinforcement. Stimuli paired with reward could arouse $r_g - s_g$ and thereby maintain responding.

rates increased when they were drinking even though their body movements decreased. This suggests there may be some arousal associated with a positive incentive, but this arousal effect is rather fragile and masked in situations where there is activity required. At least, a positive incentive arousal effect seems possible.

### Applications of $r_g$ Theory to Incentive Phenomena

*Incentive Shifts.* In the Crespi-type experiments, the shift to large reward produces a larger $r_g$. Since $r_g$ was previously conditioned to environmental stimuli, a sudden shift in $r_g$ could account for the behavioral change. A simple stimulus intensity interpretation would suffice for such changes in vigor.

*Latent Learning.* Incentive motivation does not develop in nonrewarded animals because there is no $R_G$ (eating) and hence no $r_g$. When food is introduced, however, $r_g$ occurs and is rapidly conditioned to the various maze stimuli. Hull's (1933) earlier account of the elimination of maze errors as an $r_g$ phenomenon applies equally well to the latent learning problem. He argued that $r_g$ is most strongly conditioned to responses that get the animal to the reward faster. Since errors slow the animal down, they are less strongly conditioned, because the delay of reward is greater for errors than for correct responses.

*Latent Extinction.* The $r_g$ is initially conditioned to goal box stimuli but during the nonrewarded goal box placement $r_g$ partly extinguishes because it is aroused but is not followed by food. In regular extinction, which follows, the animals stop running sooner because part of the stimulation for running ($r_g - s_g$) has already been partially extinguished.

*Quality of Reward.* A more preferred reward arouses a strong $R_G$ and hence a stronger $r_g - s_g$. Therefore, the animal responds more vigorously for a "better" reward.

### Criticisms of $r_g$ Theory

Anticipatory goal response theory had a seductive appeal for S-R theorists because it accounted for incentive motivation while still leaning heavily on overt responses for the development of $r_g$. The major criticisms of the theory hinge on the lack of evidence that any overt "fractional goal responses" actually are conditioned to environmental cues.

First, if the theory is correct, then the vigor of the consummatory response should be correlated with the vigor of the preceding instrumental responses. Running speed is correlated with sucrose concentration, but not with drinking rate in the goal box (Kraeling, 1961). Kling (1956) found a positive relation between drinking rate and running speed, but neither amount of reward nor duration of exposure to it predicted running speed. R. W. Black (1969) and Robbins (1969) both noted the overall low correlation between consummatory and instrumental behaviors in the literature.

Secondly, $r_g$s should become conditioned to start box cues, clearly necessary if the theory is to account for faster starting speeds. Animals do start faster with various conditions of reward, but Sheffield (1966) reports, for example, that he has never seen any kind of responses act as $r_g$ theory says they should. His own research was concerned with the conditioning of salivary responses in the dog, the kind of response that $r_g$ was supposed to be.

Finally, Spence (1956) used $r_g$ theory to account for incentive motivation because behavior seemed to change more rapidly with incentive shifts than either drive or S-R learning would account for. Since $r_g$ itself is conditioned, however, we still have the learning problem, and in addition must argue that $r_g$ is conditioned faster than other responses. This is inconsistent within Hull-Spence theory, however, because $r_g$ *was* supposed to be conditioned like other, observable, responses. There may indeed be very rapid incentive conditioning; the galvanic skin response can be conditioned in one trial, for example. If one postulates that incentive learning involves expectancies rather than slowly developing S-R connections, the dilemma is avoided. It has always been argued that expectancies can be learned immediately.

In conclusion, then, $r_g$ theory has been ingeniously applied but seems inadequate because of (1) little evidence that peripheral anticipatory responses either occur or function as the theory says, and (2) the inconsistency in the treatment of learning. We are again pushed back to the central nervous system and some kind of cognition (expectancy) for incentive theory. Within the broader context of Hull's theory, however, the formula $E = H \times D \times K$ does not absolutely depend on the $r_g$ concept. The theory simply requires that there be an incentive effect.

### Drive and Incentive: Multiplicative or Additive?

One point over which Hull and Spence differed about the role of drive and incentive was whether they were interchangeable. In Hull's multiplicative theory, they are not; if either $H$, $D$, or $K$ is zero, the behavior represented by $H$ would not occur. To Spence, however, it appeared that $D$ and $K$ were somewhat interchangeable, and he proposed that the proper formulation should be $E = H \times (D + K)$. While generally treated as a special problem within the theory, the data and arguments merit more attention, because they are applicable to the whole problem of deprivation-incentive interactions, not just "drive" and "incentive," as conceived in Hull-Spence theory.

The substantive nature of the argument is this. Hull's multiplicative formula says that a fixed difference in $K$ will have a larger effect with a high value of $D$ than with a low value of $D$. Assume that $H$ has a constant value of 1 (all subjects have learned some behavior to equal levels of proficiency), and that $D$ and $K$ can each take on values of either 1 or 2. By Hull's multiplicative formula, the products given in Figure 7-4(a)—values of $E$ on the ordinate—are the values of $E$ that can result. If $D$ is 1, the difference between $E$ for the two levels of $K$ is $2 - 1 = 1$, but if $D$ is 2, the difference is $4 - 2 = 2$. There is thus an *interaction* between $D$ and $K$, indicated by the fact that the two lines are not parallel. Experimental results conforming to this general picture are said to support Hull's position.

Spence's $D + K$ formula says there is no interaction, however, that the variables are simply additive. In Figure 7-4(b), the same values of $H$, $D$, and $K$ were used, but $D$ and $K$ were added rather than multiplied. The

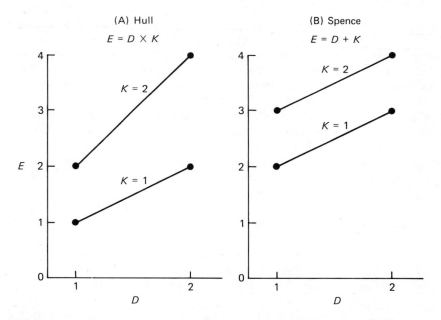

**Figure 7.4** *Values of reaction potential (E) when either (a) E = H ×
D × K with H = 1 and D = 1 or 2 and K = 1 or 2; and (b) when E = H ×
(D + K) and H, D, and K take on the same values as in (a).*

slopes of the two lines are the same; the *difference* in the magnitude of $E$ is the same for both values of $K$, regardless of the value of $D$. Such parallel (noninteractive) functions are taken as support for Spence's position. There are certain logical problems in formulating the problem just this way, favoring Spence (Evans, 1967), because the statistical requirements for demonstrating an interaction are more stringent than those for showing noninteractive results. R. W. Black (1965) argued for Spence's position and Dyal (1967) and Evans (1967) criticized Black.

The actual evidence tends to be as follows. Where two values of food deprivation (both greater than zero) and two different amounts of food are combined, the results have supported Spence (e.g., Reynolds & Pavlik, 1960). Similar results have been obtained in the present author's laboratory when two different levels of food deprivation have been combined with different concentrations of sucrose reinforcement (e.g., Lawler, 1970; Ellis, 1968).

If, however, one of the deprivation levels is zero, an interactive relationship is obtained for hunger and food (e.g., Seward, Shea, & Elkind, 1958), for hunger and sucrose (Beck & Ellis, 1966; Collier & Myers, 1961), and for thirst and water reward (Kintsch, 1962). In the larger view, interactions seem to be more typical. Dramatic interactions are found between different kinds of deprivation and reward. For example, reports of the lack of sucrose preference by thirsty rats engaged in instrumental tasks are as consistent in the literature (Beck, 1963; and many subsequent reports) as is the preference for higher concentrations of sucrose by hungry rats. Under some conditions, these trends may be reversed (e.g., J. Cohen & Oöstendorp, 1976; Mook, 1974; Beck, Nash, Viernstein & Gordon, 1972), but that does not belie the fact that the kind of deprivation makes a very large difference in the animal's responsiveness to this or that incentive. There has been no final resolution of the problem of how deprivation and incentives relate to each other that accounts for all the data, but, as this author reads the literature, it appears that interactions are more common than not.

### Mowrer's Revised Two-Factor Theory

Mowrer (1960a, 1960b) also has a peripheral incentive theory, but rather than building it around fractional consummatory responses, he based it on fractional *emotional* responses. The core of his theory is that "fear" is a fractional and conditionable component of all "primary drive" states. Behavior is then controlled by anticipatory increases or decreases in the conditioned fear response.

Mowrer started out following Hull, but in 1947 departed from a strict drive and drive reduction position. He argued that classical conditioning (stimulus substitution) is learned by simple contiguity of CS and UCS. Instrumental learning (response substitution) was said to be learned with drive reduction reinforcement. This was Mowrer's original two-factor theory and was particularly applicable to avoidance learning, as we shall see in Chapter Nine. Rescorla and Solomon (1967) have provided an excellent history of the logic and development of two-factor theories. Mowrer was anticipated by Skinner (1938) and Schlosberg (1937), among others.

In 1960 Mowrer completely revised his theory so that (1) it was no longer a two-factor theory in the sense of distinguishing between classical and instrumental conditioning, and (2) it was basically an incentive theory. He uses the term *secondary reinforcement,* as we noted in Chapter Six, but says that secondary reinforcers produce anticipatory emotional changes and do not strengthen S-R connections. He thus has an incentive concept.

In Mowrer's revised theory, all learning is by contiguity and the "two factors" referred to are drive increment and drive decrement. "Primary" drive may be produced by many procedures, all of which have in common that they also produce a conditionable component of any drive, i.e., fear. In specific instances, we can speak of *thirst fear, hunger fear,* or *pain fear.* For general discussion, we can simply use the term *drive* to mean the unconditioned state aroused by an antecedent motivational condition and the term *fear* to refer to the conditionable emotional component of any such unconditioned state.

Stimuli associated with primary drive increments arouse fear in anticipation of the actual drive state and stimuli associated with primary drive decrement produce *hope,* which is the anticipatory reduction of fear. The basic postulate of the system is that organisms work to decrease fear. All "positively rewarding" events are thus really fear reducing.

***Habit not an S-R Relationship.*** Instead of arguing that reinforcement strengthens a stimulus-response (S-R) relationship, Mowrer argues that behavior is controlled by the *emotional feedback* when a response is made. For example, a hungry animal runs down an alleyway to food. The food is said to reduce both the hunger drive and hunger fear, and stimuli preceding the reduction of these can produce anticipatory fear reduction. These stimuli are both apparatus cues and proprioceptive stimuli from running. The experienced animal runs to the goal box when hungry because proprioceptive stimuli, as well as goal box cues, produce anticipatory fear reduction. The same analysis would be made for thirsty animals running to water or shocked animals running to safety. The role of the primary drive is simply to produce a fear, which can then be conditioned and fed back to the organism on the basis of its behavior. The production of fear decrement by responses previously associated with drive reduction *is* habit. For Mowrer, habit is not an S-R bond but rather is the association between response-produced stimuli and the emotional feedback conditioned to them.

Mowrer developed a special taxonomy for the different "secondary reinforcing" conditions. A stimulus associated with the onset of drive is a "danger" signal and arouses "fear"; a stimulus preceding drive reduction becomes a "safety signal" and produces "hope." The offset of a danger signal produces "relief" and the offset of a safety signal (if the drive is not otherwise reduced) produces "disappointment."

Mowrer hypothesized some ten different sources of incremental and decremental "reinforcement," involving both "independent" (environmental) and "response-correlated" (proprioceptive feedback) stimuli. The distinction between these is nicely made with active and passive avoidance learning. In passive avoidance, the animal is punished if it *makes* a response. The feedback stimuli associated with the response become fear arousing and whenever the animal starts to make the punished response the fear is increased, decreasing only when the animal inhibits the response. The animal is thus "rewarded" by fear reduction when it inhibits the response and continues to show this inhibition—hence, passive avoidance. In active avoidance, the animal is punished if it *fails* to respond by some appropriate behavior. In this case, the fear-arousing cues are generally external (such as a buzzer) rather than proprioceptive and are eliminated by the active performance of the response.

*Critique of Mowrer's System.* Mowrer's system is ingenious in many ways, particularly in trying to get rid of the notion that learning involves S-R relations. His particular solution, in terms of emotional feedback, runs into a set of problems, however, that seem almost as insurmountable as the ones he was trying to solve.

First, what gets a response started? The feedback mechanism can presumably operate only after a response has been made. Such an elicitation mechanism is built into S-R theory, but was never really solved by Mowrer.

Second, many responses, particularly such highly skilled motor behaviors as playing a musical instrument, seem much too rapid and accurate to be controlled by the relatively slow feedback from emotional responses. Miller (1963) has been particularly critical of the theory on both the points mentioned. Slower behaviors, such as the initial stages of avoidance learning, might involve such feedback, however.

Third, the theory assumes that every primary drive state has an aversive conditionable component, but there is in fact a long and persistent history of failure to find such "drive conditioning." Those studies that have reported positive results have never withstood replication (see Cravens & Renner, 1970, for a review of the literature), although one recent report appears to be the exception (Enscore, Monk, Kozub, & Blick, 1976). Seligman and his colleagues (Seligman, Ives, Ames, & Mineka, 1970; Seligman, Mineka, & Fillit, 1971) thought they had produced drive conditioning with artificially induced thirst, but the result turned out to be an artifact of the procedure.

Fourth, while it was assumed that stimuli associated with drive reduction became positive secondary reinforcers (incentives), this in fact has never been clearly demonstrated, as observed in Chapter Six.

Fifth, the theory says that removal of a fear-arousing cue is reinforcing. While we can debate the exact interpretation of this phenomenon, it does seem to be well established (e.g., Miller's 1948 experiment and many similar ones that have followed).

Sixth, stimuli associated with the offset of a "hope" signal should be punishing. There is some evidence for this in operant conditioning research, with pigeons especially, showing that removal of a discriminative stimulus for reinforcement is avoided (Leitenberg, 1965).

Seventh, in order for Mowrer's system to work, there has to be proprioceptive feedback to which emotional changes are conditioned. There is evidence, however, that monkeys with the nerves carrying feedback stimuli from their limbs severed, jump and climb about with the abandon of normal animals—presumably an impossibility if Mowrer's theory were correct (Taub & Berman, 1968). Such results argue against an emotional feedback control for the guidance of all responses and in favor of a more central programming of behavior.

In summary, then, Mowrer's system is ingenious and has stimulated considerable comment and research. As a theory of behavior for some aversive situations, it has been one of the most complete available. Its shortcomings, however, are severe enough that we cannot consider it definitive, particularly in its emphasis on emotional feedback as the controller of the direction of behavior.

## CENTRAL STATE THEORIES FOR INCENTIVE MOTIVATION

For both Spence and Mowrer, we saw problems in arguing that incentive motivation grows out of peripheral responses, whether skeletal or autonomic. The result has been an increasing return to central state theories of incentive motivation. Here it is assumed that incentive motivation is a primary process and not a derived one. That is, either positive or negative incentive motivation is a process *directly aroused* by stimuli. Some stimuli produce unconditioned arousal of positive or negative states, and stimuli associated with these evoke anticipatory arousal or expectancy of these states. Such theories agree that skeletal responses are learned by simple frequency of occurrence, or contiguity with environmental events (i.e., reinforcement is not necessary for learning), and that incentives provide the motivation for selection among available responses. There is no such neat distinction between learning and motivation as Hull had hoped to maintain. In this section, we shall go on to discuss the theories of Tolman, Logan, and Young, and the central motive state theories of Morgan and Bindra.

### Edward Chace Tolman

For many years, E. C. Tolman, of the University of California at Berkeley, and his followers were the primary antagonists to the Hull-Spence groups at Yale and Iowa. Because of the active controversy, differences between the two theories were often emphasized, to the exclusion of their similarities. Tolman and Hull were both thorough-going behaviorists and their theoretical concepts were anchored in observable events. In fact, it was Tolman (1938) who introduced the concept of the intervening variable to psychology. From this common methodological background, however, came a diversity of concepts. The adequacy or superiority of concepts is to be determined by objective test, however, and such "surplus meanings" as are attached to terms such as "cognitive" and "mechanistic" are unfortunate, because they are not really relevant to the usefulness of the concepts. Nevertheless, the concepts were different in the two schools.

First, Tolman (1932, 1938) was concerned with what he called "molar behavior," not with specific responses. Thus, if an animal turns to the right in a maze, then "turning right" is the response, not any specific set of muscle group contractions. In this way of defining behavior, he was indeed very much like Skinner, for whom a lever press is a lever press, no matter how consummated. Thus, Tolman was a behaviorist but not an S-R theorist.

Second, Tolman was concerned with what he called "purposive behavior." So, of course, was Hull, but Tolman viewed it in what seems a more commonsense way than Hull. Tolman's theory involved both learning and motivational concepts, but these were called "expectancies" and "demands." An expectancy was the anticipation held by an organism that under a given set of circumstances a particular behavior would lead to a particular outcome. As compared to the S-R approach of Hull, Tolman had an $S_1 R_1 - S_2$ theory. This is, of course, virtually the same notion embodied in the situation-act-outcome expectancies defined by Irwin (1971), as discussed in Chapter Two. For Tolman, the $S$s were environmental events and the behavior was how a person or animal got from one to the other. An expectancy was that one would get from here to there (that one thing would follow another) with a certain degree of probability if one performed a certain action. In line with this way of thinking, then, Tolman's usual response measure was probabilistic, such as the percentage of correct turns in a maze.

The "demand" was related to the outcome. We might expect that if we do a certain thing there will then be a certain outcome, but not actually engage in that behavior unless there is a demand for that outcome. For example, I may know that if I go to the refrigerator there will be a piece of chicken there, but if I have no demand for food at the moment I will not go to the refrigerator. Demands are determined by both internal and external events, and the details of the demand for any particular outcome have to be worked out individually. There are also demands against some outcomes, i.e., unpleasant ones.

### Cognition in Tolman's Theorizing

Tolman was a "cognitive" theorist, who considered that expectancies were central processes not necessarily involving the occurrence of any particular responses. What distinguished him from the "mentalistic" approach of some earlier psychologists was his insistence on working with observable events and inferring expectancies and demands on the basis of these observations. Since his usual subject was the laboratory rat, this was, in fact, absolutely necessary for him. He showed that it was possible to discuss purpose, foresight, and expectation using objective events as the primary data rather than introspections. Purpose, foresight, and expectation were intervening variables.

*Cognitive Maps.* In one of his later papers, "Cognitive Maps in Rats and Men" (1948), Tolman described kinds of research that he felt were critical to his arguments favoring a cognitive rather than an S-R approach. As a general methaphor, he likened the brain to a map room—the organism has "cognitive maps" of the environment in its head by which it directs itself around the environment. This was in contrast to the S-R analogy of the brain as a telephone switchboard, where there is automatic switching from incoming (sensory) lines to outgoing (motor) lines. But Tolman's language should not be confused with his experiments. He and his followers showed it clearly possible to do experiments with nonverbal species from which we can infer complex organizing and information-processing capabilities.

As a theorist, Tolman was generally less systematic than Hull and did little in the way of attempting to quantify his theory. He had two reasons for this. First, he admittedly did not have the right temperament for such quantification, even though his original training was as an engineer at MIT. More importantly, however, he believed that detailed quantification was premature and would be so specific to particular experimental situations that it would not generalize to other situations anyway. The most detailed attempt to systematize his work was by MacCorquodale and Meehl (1954). Tolman (1959) did offer a final attempt at systematizing his own thinking, however, and we shall use that work as the basis of our discussion here. We shall oversimplify, just as we did with Hull, so that we may catch the flavor of his thinking important to us here, but we shall bypass those details that do not immediately concern us.

### Tolman's Systematic Theory (1959)

Consider the following modified formula from Tolman (1959, p. 134; we do not use his symbolism and do not present the entire formula):

$$\text{Performance Tendency} = f(\text{drive stimulation, expectancy, incentive valence})$$

Each of these terms has an apparent equivalent in Hull's theory, although there are obvious dissimilarities.

***Performance Tendency.*** Performance tendency is an intervening variable equivalent to excitatory potential; its magnitude determines the occurrence of a particular response. It is a function of the three other intervening variables indicated, as well as others not shown. Tolman does not state the specific syntax (i.e., whether they multiply or whatever), but simply indicates that some function relates them. The nature of the relationship would depend on situational details. The performance tendency is the strength of the tendency for the expectancy $S_1R_1-S_2$ to be expressed in behavior, just as *sEr* in Hull's theory is the tendency for *sHr* to be expressed in behavior.

***Drive Stimulation.*** The term *drive stimulation* refers to internal or external stimulation, which Tolman believed was necessary for behavior to become activated. In a famous comment, Guthrie (1952, p. 143) suggested that Tolman's rats should have been "buried in thought" because Guthrie saw no way in Tolman's theory that cognition would lead to action. Here we see in Tolman's theory a definite activation principle, but it is an expectancy that is activated, not a habit or highly specific response. Quite differently from Hull, however, Tolman argued that specific types of drive stimulation (hunger, thirst, sexual arousal) caused certain goal stimuli ($S_2s$) to have positive or negative valences and hence lead to performances that would be related to these goals. In other words, specific drive stimuli are only related to specific goal objects and there is no "general" activation function. Tolman says very specifically that drive stimulations lower the thresholds for responding to particular stimuli.

***Expectancies.*** Tolman distinguished two kinds of expectancies: $S_1R_1-S_2$ and $S_1-S_2$, but generally believed that the former was the more important case. Expectancies increase in strength, he said, as a function of frequency, recency, and distribution of occurrence. It is important to note, however, that this increase *can* be sudden. Sometimes expectancies might build only gradually, especially if the outcomes are delayed.

Tolman also believed that incentive value (i.e., positive or negative value of $S_2$) plays a role in the acquisition of expectancies, but certainly not in the sense of drive reduction theory. He suggested (1959, p. 128) that the influence of "effect" might be particularly important in $S_1 - S_2$ expectancies, such as when a stimulus predicts the occurrence of shock.

A concept closely related to expectancy is *means-end-readiness* (or *belief*). By this Tolman means that there can be learned dispositions for certain types of $S_1R_1-S_2$ or $S_1-S_2$ sequences so that when a particular $S_1$ is presented, there is "released" an expectancy that a particular $R_1$ will lead to a particular $S_2$. These means-end-readinesses are purely *cognitive* dispositions. Expectancies and means-end-readinesses are virtually identical but Tolman wished to retain the distinction on the grounds that "the means-end readiness [belief] is an enduring disposition, whereas the expectancy is a specific then-and-there activation . . . of this disposition (1959, p. 113)." What this says, for example, is that I can have a very general *belief* that with certain temperature and cloud conditions it is likely to snow, but only if these conditions actually prevail at a given time will I *expect* it to snow.

*Incentive Valence.* In some sense, a particular environmental event, $S_2$, has an objective *value.* For example, if I sample a particularly tasty food, it will have a high positive value for me at that time. In the future, I expect that this food will also have a high value and this expected value is the *valence* of the food. As a motivational intervening variable, then, valences (equivalent to $K$ in Hull's theory) are learned on the basis of experience with objects of particular values. The combination of drive stimulation and valence is what we earlier referred to as *demand,* a term that Tolman did not use in his 1959 paper but that was prominent in earlier writings and that rather nicely catches the spirit of his view of motivation.

### Evidence for Tolman's System

Tolman (1959) himself very briefly indicated what he thought was evidence for his theory; he saw evidence in its favor throughout all experiments on instrumental learning, wherever done. And, indeed, we tend to agree with him. The problem is not a lack of specific evidence, but rather that his approach simply looks at everything differently from Hull's. Many of the problems that arose for Hull-Spence theory seem to dissipate within the scope of Tolman's approach. Part of the reason for this may indeed be its "looseness," but the danger of "tightening up" a theory too much is that we may become too specific in the wrong places and go down a blind alley. Many people believe that drive reduction theory was such a blind alley. Tolman himself saw limits to his theory. Since his own research was limited to rats, he did not see much relevance to motor skills learning or higher mental processes in human beings. He did "modestly" believe, however, that his approach was more likely to be fruitful for the latter problem. The increasing emphasis on cognition, organization of stimulus materials in verbal learning, and so on seem to bear him out in this belief.

### Logan

Frank Logan was originally trained in the Hull-Spence tradition and tends toward the kind of quantification and organization of intervening variables typical of that tradition. He assumes (1968) that each quantitative value of reward has a particular *incentive value* when the organism is exposed to it—the larger the reward, the greater the incentive value. Over successive experiences, *incentive motivation* increases with particular rewards, up to a maximal value as great as the incentive values. His concepts of incentive value and motivation are clearly like Tolman's value and valence. If there are several different rewards associated with a particular situation, the net incentive motivation is based on an average of the different reward values. That is, the incentive motivation will be somewhere between that which would occur if the organism were exposed only to the highest or only to the lowest incentive. If there are both positive and negative incentive values in a particular situation, they combine algebraically to produce a net positive (approach) or net negative (avoidance) incentive motivation.

Incentive motivation takes time (and trials) to develop and, accordingly, if reward values are changed it takes time for incentive motivation to follow this change, either increasing or decreasing. The rapidity of the motivational change is partly a function of the direction of the change. For example, if an animal is trained to escape from strong shock, it continues to escape rapidly for a while if the shock is reduced. There is a more immediate change if the shock level is increased. Similarly, there is a slower decrement in approach motivation if a reward is decreased than there is an increment if reward is increased. Either people or animals may persist in responding for some time (perhaps thousands of responses) after rewards have ceased. This would seem to be biologically adaptive; the chances of survival are increased if we "keep trying" for a while, even without reward.

In his research, Logan has used a choice situation wherein by definition if the rat chooses Alley A over Alley B, the reward in A has the greater incentive value (Logan, 1960, 1968). To equalize experience with the two alleys, the animal is forced to the nonpreferred side as necessary to equalize experience with the outcomes of the two choices. An especially interesting result with this procedure is that with 100 percent reward on one side and fifty percent on the other side of the choice apparatus during acquisition, there is a continued strong preference for the 100 percent side throughout extinction (Logan, 1968). This is just the opposite of the usual partial reinforcement effect found with single-response (nonchoice) procedures and independent groups of animals, and provides considerable difficulty for most theories of extinction.

Logan has also studied "decision making" in rats. For example, how much does one have to increase the amount of a long-delayed reward to make it equally preferred to a smaller reward with a short delay? A long delay produces lower incentive motivation than a short delay. He has determined such "indifference functions" with some precision (e.g., 1965). Of all the incentive theorists, Logan has done the most in attempting to quantify incentive motivation and its relationship to behavior.

### Young's Hedonic Theory

Paul Thomas Young has long held to an hedonic theory of motivation (e.g., 1961, 1966, 1968). The major criticism of hedonic theories in the past has concerned their apparent introspective nature, based, as it were, on feelings of "goodness" and "badness." Affective processes can be inferred from objective data, however, and even Premack (1971), formerly a devout Skinnerian, has "caught up with common sense" (his own words) and moved in this direction. Young's theory is in many ways similar to Irwin's (1971) theory, which we have used as a model throughout this volume.

*Affective Arousal.* Young assumes that incentive objects produce *primary affective arousals* (for Tolman and Logan, incentive values). These primary affective arousals come to control behavior because stimuli repeatedly associated with them come to elicit *conditioned affective arousals* (Tolman's valences and Logan's incentive motivation). Motives, says Young, are "acquired determinations" that regulate the pattern of action and arouse or activate behavior, determining both its direction and intensity. The strength of a motive depends on the intensity of the original affective process.

Young defines affective processes in terms of their valence (positive or negative), intensity, and duration. He assumes that if animals develop approach behavior in a particular situation the underlying process is positive, and if they develop avoidance the process is negative. The *development of approach or avoidance* is particularly important because the mere occurrence of these behaviors might be indicative of unconditioned approach or avoidance responses in lower animals or habitual behavior in higher animals. An experiment by Young and Chaplin (1945) illustrates how a habit can obscure other processes. They first showed in a taste preference apparatus that need-free rats developed a consistent preference for sucrose over casein (a not too palatable form of protein). They then made the animals protein deficient by removing it from their diet, but the animals continued to choose the sucrose (which they did not need) over the casein (which they did need). When they moved the animals to a different kind of choice apparatus, however, the animals developed a preference for casein over sucrose. That these results were due to a combination of need and habit factors, rather than to apparatus differences, was shown by the fact that animals made protein deficient *before any testing* developed a casein preference in *either* apparatus.

*Hedonic Continuum.* Affective processes differ in degree as well as kind and are ordered from maximal negative to maximal positive. This is diagrammatically represented by Young with the same hedonic continuum used by Irwin (see Figure 2-1, this book). Young has also scaled preferences for various foodstuffs. The general rule for behavior is that "neurobehavioral patterns are organized that minimize negative affectivity (distress) and maximize positive affectivity (delight)" (Young, 1961, p. 153).

*Palatability, Appetite, and Food Preference.* Young's own research has been primarily on food preferences. Food intake is determined by many factors, the foremost of which are palatability and appetite. The term *palatability* refers to the hedonic properties of foodstuffs that depend on taste, aroma, texture, temperature, and other *sensory* properties of food. If an animal is need free, but shows a taste preference, this preference would be due entirely to differences in palatability. The term *appetite* refers to such internal determinants as deprivation, illness, or pregnancy. Palatability and appetite are not two kinds of hedonic process, but two different sources (external and internal) of determinants of affective process.

Young also assumes an algebraic summation of positive and negative incentives and has worked with a variety of taste combinations. For example, suppose one uses 4 percent sucrose as a standard comparison stimulus; how much more sucrose does one have to add to different concentrations of quinine (bitter) solutions to make them *equally palatable* to the 4 percent sucrose? The outcome of this experiment would give us an *isohedonic curve.* Young and his students have worked out a variety of such curves for combinations of sweet, salty, sour, and bitter taste stimuli (e.g., see Young, 1968).

### The Solomon-Corbit Opponent Process Theory

Hedonic theories generally assume that particular environmental events arouse certain internal states in the same way, i.e., either positive or negative. The effects of experience are usually assumed to be caused by conditioning such processes to other stimuli, in an associative manner. The Solomon-Corbit (1974) theory of opponent processes postulates a *nonassociative effect of experience on hedonic processes.*

Consider this illustration. A woman discovers a lump in her breast and is immediately fearful of cancer. She makes an appointment with her doctor but frets about it anxiously until he reports the tumor is benign. Her strong anxiety is then replaced by great elation. An opposite example would be the sudden loss of something or someone that has brought us great pleasure; we are then depressed. The crux of the opponent-process theory, then, is this: *every affective state, whether pleasurable or aversive, tends to arouse the opponent state.* Extreme fear arouses the opponent process, which is pleasurable, and when the source of the fear is removed the pleasurable process becomes dominant and lingers on for a while.[2] At any given time, the affective state of the individual is the algebraic sum of the two processes. The process directly aroused by a stimulus situation is *dominant* while the situation lasts, but the opponent process becomes dominant when the situation changes.

The initial process aroused is called an *A-state,* whether positive or negative, joy or terror. The opponent process, which is aroused by the A-state and not directly by the situation, is called the *B-state.* The person who does something very frightening, such as jumping out of an airplane, initially has a fearful A-state aroused and the joyful B-state automatically follows. The A-state is dominant until the person lands safely on the ground, the danger is over, and then the joyful B-state is very strong for a while.

The degree to which the B-state is aroused depends on (1) the magnitude of the A-state, B increasing with A, and (2) the number of times the A-state has occurred, B again increasing with A. With successive A-state arousals the effectiveness of the A-state stimulus *decreases* because the A-state effect is being diminished by the opponent B-state. Over a period of time, then, a stronger arousal of the A-state is necessary just to get the same degree of pleasure from the positive A-state that was initially obtained. Figures 7-5 and 7-6 illustrate the temporal course of events with the A and B states as a function of the number of times the A-state has occurred.

*Addictions.* Addictions are a good illustration of the theory. A person takes heroin, which produces a highly euphoric effect (the A-state). This is pleasurable, but also strongly arouses the aversive B-state. Over successive drug experiences, the opponent process is more strongly aroused, offsetting the euphoric effect of the drug so that larger doses are required to produce the original euphoric effect. Moreover, when the drug wears off, the B-state is so unpleasant (withdrawal symptoms) that the individual takes the drug to get rid of the B-state. He is then considered addicted. Eventually, if the A-state is not aroused for a long period, the B-state automatically becomes weaker; the withdrawal symptoms subside. Until this happens, however, the individual without the drug is in a very unpleasant affective state. Viewed

[2]This theory follows the opponent-process theory of color vision, which has recently been expanded as a general property of neural function by Hurvich and Jameson (1974).

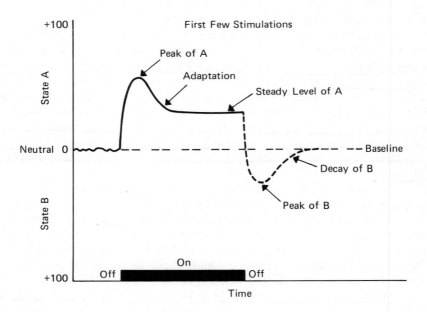

**Figure 7.5**   *The manifest temporal dynamics generated by the opponent process system during the first few stimulations. (The five features of the affective response are labeled.) The curves are the algebraic summation of the opponent processes. Note the high level of A relative to B. (Solomon and Corbit, 1974, p. 128. Copyright © 1974 by the American Psychological Association. Reprinted by permission.)*

very broadly, addictions are "common events"; most of us are addicted to something—husbands, wives, lovers, and children. Many people are addicted to drugs, including alcohol and nicotine. Not *all* events are addictive, of course. Some situations may arouse A-states only weakly or not at all.

The opponent process theory is like drive theory in that it is postulated that individuals work to reduce an aversive state, whether it be an A-state or a B-state. Although B-states are "slaves" to their A-states, either can be conditioned to contiguous stimuli, once aroused. For example, in the case of addiction, stimuli associated with the aversive B-state (including needle, syringe, situation in which the drug is taken) might either (1) arouse an A-state, which, being very weak, would be less than the slave B-state that follows, or (2) might arouse a conditioned B-state directly. In either event,

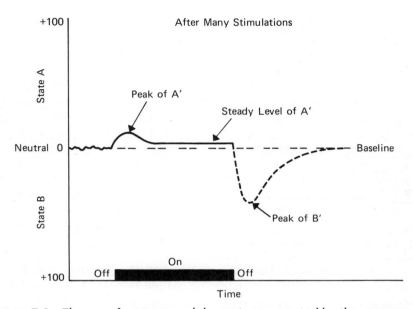

**Figure 7.6** *The manifest temporal dynamics generated by the opponent process system after many repeated stimulations. (The major features of the modified patterns are labeled.) Compared to the curves in Figure 7.5, note the low level of A, and the relatively high level of B.*

the individual would then perhaps try to reduce the B-state by taking the drug. This suggests some difficulties in treating drug addiction: B-states can be aroused by many events, and the arousal leads back to taking the drug.

Most of the evidence for the theory at the moment is adduced from prior research or observation, rather than from direct test of the theory. The approach is novel within the field of motivation, however, and exceptionally interesting both theoretically and practically. We shall refer to it several times in various contexts.

### Central Motive State

Morgan (1943, 1959) proposed that a variety of circumstances lead to a central nervous system change that he called the *central motive state* (CMS). The CMS has the following properties: It persists for some time without outside sensory support; it predisposes the organism to react in certain ways to some stimuli, but not others; and it may directly cause certain responses to be emitted. Morgan intended the CMS to apply to drive states, such as hunger and thirst. Its theoretical importance at the time Morgan developed it was that it departed from the prevailing views that such drive states are aroused by peripheral events, hunger by stomach contractions, thirst by a dry mouth, and so on. Voluminous research in the last twenty years has shown the importance of the central nervous system for such motive states (e.g., see Chapter Fifteen).

Bindra (e.g., 1968, 1969) has further elaborated the CMS concept, saying that the CMS is generated by the interactions of "neural representations of organismic state and incentive object" (1969, p. 12). A "reinforcing" stimulus does not produce any specific response selection, but arouses a motivational state that influences *many* subsequent behaviors. The supporting arguments are the same as we have already seen for incentive theories: Response occurrence can be changed without the "reinforcing" stimulus directly following the response in question. The CMS alters the value of incentive objects and changes the likelihood of appropriate approach and consummatory responses. Stimuli associated with incentives control approach responses, but not consummatory responses (e.g., food controls eating responses, not stimuli paired with food).

An experiment by Bindra and Palfai (1967) illustrates the theory. Thirsty rats had the click of a metronome paired with water while they were confined in a small cage where locomotor activity was impossible. The animals were then divided into three groups (low, medium, and high water deprivation) and, in a larger cage, the activities of perambulation (locomotion), sitting, and grooming were recorded before, while, and after the metronome was turned on. Perambulation was generally higher under medium or high deprivation, but presence of the metronome, the conditioned stimulus signalling water, further increased perambulation only under medium or high deprivation. The results are similar to those reported by Sheffield and Campbell (1954), discussed in Chapter Four, and Bindra's theory has many similarities to their lowered response threshold theory of drive. Bindra's theory deals with the question of how animals select certain responses at some times and not at others only to the extent of saying that animals approach some stimuli and avoid others. It does not deal with how particular arbitrary responses, such as bar pressing, are selected.

### Incentive Stimuli as Predictive Stimuli

In Chapter Six we presented evidence that a secondary reinforcer is a stimulus that reliably informs the individual about some important forthcoming event. It is also reasonable to think of incentive stimuli in the same way: They predict the occurrence of good or bad events. Considering them as predictive stimuli, we might then expect that they would readily *transfer* their predictive properties to new situations without requiring specific learning in the new situations. Predictive relations might develop in classical conditioning (noncontingent) situations or instrumental conditioning (contingent) situations. The term *contingent* refers to whether the predicted outcome is contingent on the animal's behavior. The terminology of *contingent* versus *noncontingent* is better, however, because there can be elements of either in classical or instrumental conditioning situations. The animals in classical conditioning might make "unauthorized" responses that are followed by food or shock, and maze cues inevitably precede food in the goal box, for example.

### Positive and Negative Predictive Relationships.

An obvious classification for such predictions is according to whether the predicted outcomes are positive (desirable) or negative (aversive.) Let us say that an S + is a stimulus that predicts the occurrence of an event, whether positive or negative, and an S − predicts the nonoccurrence of such events. We then have the following possibilities:

1. S + for a positive event (e.g., food) predicts a *desirable* outcome.
2. S − for a positive event (e.g., no food) predicts an *aversive* outcome.
3. S + for a negative event (e.g., shock) predicts an *aversive* outcome.
4. S − for a negative event (e.g., no shock) predicts a *desirable* outcome.

We can briefly illustrate these with some research. In Chapter Six, we noted that if dogs were trained in a shuttle box to avoid shock, that a stimulus paired with shock in a different situation (S + ) then facilitated the shuttling. Conversely, a stimulus paired with no shock (S − ) slowed down the rate of shuttling. Second, Bolles, Grossen, Hargrave, and Duncan (1970) paired a stimulus with food (S + ) or non food (S − ) in one situation, independently of the animals' behavior. Then, in another situation, a runway, they presented the previously learned stimuli in the start box. The S + (predicting food) facilitated running and the S − (predicting no food) impaired running when presented during extinction in the runway. Other experiments with lever pressing have shown a facilitative effect of S + on the acquisition of a response (e.g., Trapold & Winokur, 1967).

There are many possibilities for such transfer experiments, depending on (1) whether outcomes are positive or negative; (2) whether S + or S − are used; (3) whether initial training is contingent or noncontingent; and (4) whether the transfer tests are contingent or noncontingent. As a brief approximation, we can say the following about the evidence (Bolles and Moot, 1972): If the transfer is from one appetitive situation to another, or from one shock situation to another, the predictive relations seem to work rather well. If the transfer is from shock to food situations, or from food to shock situations, the theory works less well (with the exception that an S + for shock inhibits performance in many different situations). Bolles and Moot (1972) can be consulted for many details and problems.

## CONCLUSION

Incentive motivation has become an increasingly important concept in the last twenty-five years. It is not new, of course: Tolman's expectancy-incentive approach to behavior theory ran almost perfectly parallel in time with the development of Hull's drive-habit theory. As we have seen, however, incentive concepts account well for phenomena which drive theory does not account for at all and which are difficult for reinforcement theory. The many different incentive theories, and their frequent shortcomings, should not obscure the importance of incentive theory generally. The question is not whether there should be incentive theory, but rather: what form should incentive theory take? Contemporary theorists generally lean toward interpreting incentive motivation as a central brain process, with internal states altering responsiveness to incentive stimuli. Whatever its final form, however, incentive theory seems destined to play a major role in accounting for behavior, and we shall find it reappearing frequently in subsequent chapters.

chapter 8

# Aversive Stimulation: 1. Escape Learning, Fear Conditioning and Frustration

## INSTRUMENTAL ESCAPE LEARNING

The term *instrumental escape learning* refers to any situation in which responses are reinforced by a reduction of aversive stimulation. Responses may literally be those of running away, but any response having the same net effect would be similarly classified. Electric shock has been the most commonly used aversive stimulus in laboratory research, but cold water, loud noises, and bright lights are also effective and familiar to most of us.

In spite of the convenience of escape learning procedures (they do not require deprivation, and one subject can be run many trials in a single session without "satiation"), there is much less research than with positive reinforcers. Possibly, this is because, except for drive theory, there has been relatively little theorizing specific to escape situations. It may also be because we have often assumed that the laws for escape would be like those for appetitive situations. If thirst could be turned on as fast as electric shock the two might be equivalent, as D'Amato (1970) has said.[1] The main reason for believing this, however, is faith in drive theory; it is hardly a foregone conclusion. Let us first look at some fundamental escape learning data and then consider some alternative interpretations.

### Some Variables Affecting Escape

*Amount of Reinforcement.* Campbell and Kraeling (1953) placed animals in a straight alley to escape from either 200, 300, or 400 volts of grid shock. Early in training, the animals ran faster from the higher shock levels, but the groups converged to a maximal speed by fifteen trials. Amount of reinforcement and number of trials were thus somewhat interchangeable. Campbell and Kraeling also found that running speeds depended on the relative amount of shock reduction in the goal box. A drop from 100 to 0 volts was more reinforcing than a drop from 200 to 100, which was better than 400 to 300. This is an approximation to Weber's law: reinforcing capacity depends on the *percentage* drop, not just the absolute voltage decrement. Campbell and Masterton (1969) have discussed the psychophysics of reinforcement in detail. Since running speeds depend on anticipated goal box shock level as well as on alley shock level, there appears to be an incentive effect.

Woods, Davidson, and Peters (1964) obtained similar results with rats swimming to escape from cold water. "Drive" was manipulated by varying

---

[1]In Guthrie's (1952) learning theory, there is no difference between appetitive and aversive situations except insofar as they produce different responses to be conditioned to preceding stimuli. The same would hold for Tolman's expectancy learning theory. Mowrer (1960a) equated the two on the grounds that every appetitive drive has an aversive (fear) component.

temperature in a "runway" tank and "reinforcement magnitude" was manipulated by varying temperature in the "goal" tank. Goal tank temperature was much more important in determining escape speed than was runway tank temperature, which added generality to the Campbell-Kraeling result.

Stavely (1966) studied speed of lever pressing to turn off shock, using all combinations of five shock levels and six durations of shock offset. Duration of offset is another way of varying amount of reinforcement. Intensity and duration were both significant and longer durations were even more effective at higher shock levels.

***Delay of Reinforcement.*** Fowler and Trapold (1962) ran rats from a 250-volt runway to a goal box where shock termination was delayed between zero and 16 seconds for different groups. Running speed was slower with longer delays (Figure 8-1). Bell, Noah, and Davis (1965) found that long delays were less detrimental with higher shock levels. Presumably, the termination of strong shock is more rewarding and counteracts the delay somewhat. Tarpy (1969) found that animals could also discriminate better among short delays than among long delays, as indicated in preferential responses for shorter delays.

***Incentive Shifts.*** Bower, Fowler, and Trapold (1959) ran animals from a 250-volt alleyway to a goal box where shocks of 200, 150, or 50 volts were continued for twenty seconds after the animal entered. As expected, the

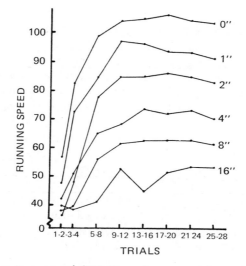

**Figure 8.1** *Running speed (100/time in seconds) as a function of the delay (in seconds) of shock termination in the goal box. (From Fowler and Trapold, 1962, p. 465. Copyright © 1962 by the American Psychological Association. Reprinted by permission.)*

animals escaped faster with greater shock reduction. More importantly, however, when the goal box shock was shifted up or down, running speeds rapidly changed appropriately for the new goal box levels. The results are shown in Figure 8-2. The authors suggest that this seems obviously like a Crespi effect. Woods (1967) reported similar results when runway tank temperatures were increased or lowered.

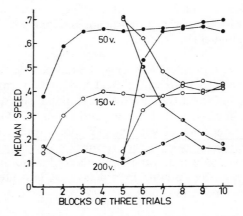

**Figure 8.2** Group median speed (1/time in seconds) as a function of goal-shock voltage. (From Bower, Fowler, and Trapold, 1959, p. 483. Copyright © 1959 by the American Psychological Association. Reprinted by permission.)

*Adaptation Level Effects.* If stimuli of different intensities are presented to the same subject, the subject tends to develop a neutral point, or adaptation level, which is an average of the stimuli. Since the point of neutrality depends on what stimuli are used, subjects respond to the same stimuli differently in different contexts. The same stimulus might be subjectively intense among weak stimuli or subjectively weak among strong stimuli.

Contrast effects in motivation have been attributed to such contexts (e.g., Bevan, 1968). In an aversive situation, an animal trained to escape low shock, then shifted to higher shock, should "overshoot." That is, it should run faster than animals initially trained at the higher level because they have *adapted* to the higher level. Conversely, a subject adapted to a high level should undershoot when shifted down. Bower, Fowler, and Trapold (1959) did not find either effect with shifts in shock level, as can be seen in Figure 8-2, and Woods (1967) obtained similar results with escape from cold water.

Quinsey (1970) reviews many instances in which testing at a high level of aversive stimulation has been enhanced by prior training at a lower level.

None of these involved instrumental escape, however, and Franchina (1969) reports escape data contrary to the adaptation level theory. Adamson, Henke, and O'Donovan (1969) did find that barely perceptible .004 and .008 milliampere preshocks facilitated later avoidance learning at higher shock levels. Overall, the evidence of adaptation level effects for aversive situations with animals is meager. About the best we can conclude is that animals do shift suddenly when shock levels are changed, as they do in the appetitive incentive shift experiments.

### Theories for Escape Learning

**Drive Theory.** Drive and drive reduction theory seem to explain escape phenomena very well. An intense stimulus produces drive; the more intense the stimulus, the harder the animal strives to escape it. Successful escape is reinforced by drive reduction. This explanation is probably inadequate, however. Thus, in the studies just reviewed, subjects not only responded to the level of runway shock (or cold water), but also to the anticipated level in the goal box. Furthermore, they shifted performance suddenly when goal box stimuli were changed. It is possible that incentive concepts alone can handle escape learning data. It might then be possible to account for appetitive approach and aversive escape behaviors in terms of common incentive principles, as assumed in the definition of motivation given in Chapter Two.

**Incentive Theory.** Both Mowrer (1960a) and Denny (1971) provide concepts for explaining escape learning in incentive terms: hope and relaxation, respectively. Both argue that when a painful stimulus ends there is an internal change conditionable to preceding stimuli. We shall simply denote this conditioned change as *anticipatory relaxation.* When the animal escapes from aversive stimuli, it also learns anticipatory relaxation. For example, a shocked rat finds its way to a shock-free goal box. The "goal response" is relaxation and the conditioned component is anticipatory relaxation. This anticipatory relaxation is strongest near the goal box but also occurs at the start. The animal then makes responses which increasingly maximize relaxation and finally lead to the end of its pain. The animal might make a variety of specific responses to get to the goal box, but always tends to move in the direction of the incentive.

What then is the role of shock intensity? Just as deprivation increases the incentive value of food, intense stimulation should increase the amount of anticipatory relaxation. The stronger the shock level, the greater the anticipated relaxation. Without shock, there should be no anticipated relaxation, so "poor" performance would result. Incomplete shock reduction would also lead to less anticipatory relaxation and poorer performance.

Increases or decreases in either alley shock or goal shock change the amount of anticipated relaxation, with appropriate behavior changes following. We have already noted experimental results corresponding to just these predictions. One exception to the statement just made is when pain has previously been experienced in a situation and there is conditioned arousal (fear). Anticipatory relaxation would therefore still occur, and the subject would continue to escape until the fear extinguished.

This formulation is different from Mowrer's in that it involves anticipatory relaxation only for aversive situations. Mowrer (1960a) also assumed there was anticipatory fear reduction in appetitive situations, i.e., anticipation of "hunger fear" or "thirst fear" reduction. We have assumed that positive outcomes, not just fear reduction, are anticipated for such situations. We differ from Denny, and agree with Mowrer, however, in believing that specific responses are not associated with specific stimuli. Denny argued that the relaxation response reinforces specific S-R connections. We would simply argue that anticipatory relaxation is an incentive and say that response learning involves some other principle.

In summary, there is an adequate theoretical and empirical base to account for escape learning in incentive terms, just as we found it fruitful to account for approach behavior in incentive terms. The organism (rat or man) learns to anticipate that certain behaviors have preferable outcomes. In one case, the outcome is desirable (i.e., obtaining a preferred food). In the other case, the outcome is preferable to continued existence in an unfriendly environment.

## CONDITIONED AVERSION: FEAR

In 1920 Watson and Rayner reported their classic experiment with Little Albert. Albert was an emotionally stable eleven-month-old child whose mother worked in the hospital where the experiment was conducted. Albert was initially exposed to a series of objects, including a white rat, a rabbit, a dog, a monkey, masks with and without hair, cotton wool, and so on. "Manipulation was the most usual reaction called out. At no time did this infant ever show fear in any situation" (Watson and Rayner, 1920, p. 2).

Albert was then shown a white rat and a steel bar behind him was struck with a hammer. The rat was the conditioned stimulus (CS) and the loud noise the unconditioned stimulus (UCS). After seven trials, spread over several days, "The instant the rat was shown the baby began to cry. Almost instantly he turned sharply to the left, fell over on left side, raised himself on all fours, and began to crawl away" (p. 5). Five days later Albert was again tested for fear responses. He not only was fearful of the rat but also of the rabbit, the dog, a seal-fur coat, and a Santa Claus mask. A fear response had been conditioned and generalized to other stimuli.

Watson saw the implications of this experiment for clinical work and pointed out that the results demonstrated that not *all* anxiety was related to sex, as Freud was saying at the time. Watson said, "The Freudians twenty years from now, unless their hypotheses change, when they come to analyze Albert's fear of a seal-skin coat—assuming he comes to analysis at that age—will probably tease from him a recital of a dream upon which their analysis will show that Albert at three years of age attempted to play with the pubic hair of the mother and was scolded violently for it" (1920, p. 14). Watson, of course, did not assume any such permanent effect on Albert.

Shortly thereafter M. C. Jones (1924) studied the elimination of children's preexisting (not experimentally induced) fears. Describing her most effective technique, she said: "By the method of direct conditioning, we associated the fear object with a craving object and replaced the fear by a positive response" (1924, p. 390). In contemporary terms, this would be called *counterconditioning*.

In these two experiments, the foundations of contemporary behavior therapy could have well been laid. One might have expected an outpouring of further research of this type. Instead, the Freudians held the day and it remained for Mowrer (1939), fifteen years later, to focus on the problem of aversive conditioning and neurosis in a way that was to have real impact on psychology.[2]

In his paper, "A Stimulus-Response Analysis of Anxiety and Its Role as a Reinforcing Agent" (1939, p. 554-555) Mowrer said:

> Freud . . . posited that *all* anxiety (fear) reactions are probably learned; his hypothesis when recast in stimulus-response terminology runs as follows. A so-called traumatic ("painful") stimulus (arising either from external injury, of whatever kind, or from severe organic need) impinges upon the organism and produces a more or less violent defence (striving) reaction. Furthermore, such a stimulus-response sequence is usually preceded or accompanied by originally "indifferent" stimuli which, however, after one or more temporally contiguous associations with the traumatic stimulus, begin to be perceived as "danger signals," i.e., acquire the capacity to elicit an "anxiety" reaction. . . . In short, *anxiety (fear) is the conditioned form of the pain reaction,* which has the highly useful function of motivating and reinforcing behavior that tends to avoid or prevent the occurrence of the pain-producing (unconditioned) stimulus.

---

[2]It is interesting to speculate why Watson and Rayner, although always quoted, seemed to have had such little influence at the time. Apparently, psychology was not yet ready for the clinic and psychiatry (including psychoanalysis) was not yet ready for Watson and classical conditioning. Watson would appear to have been too far ahead of his time. Clinical psychology as a field did not develop until World War II, at a time when the Yale group (including Hull, Mowrer, Spence, Miller, Sears, Dollard, Doob, and others) was at the peak of its collective activity. Many publications emanating from this group brought the clinic to the laboratory and vice versa. For the first time, there was a concerted attempt to analyze scientifically the problems of clinical psychology and to relate the great Freudian insights to laboratory phenomena and psychological theory.

Mowrer's analysis was the foundation for a generation of laboratory work on fear conditioning, acquired drives, and avoidance learning. Mowrer, along with Neal Miller and others, represented a new way of thinking that was developing in the United States. That is, they believed that analogues for human anxiety and neurotic behavior could be developed in the laboratory, studied, and the knowledge gained thereby applied back to clinical problems. This belief was not entirely new, of course. Most of us are familiar with the fact that Pavlov had studied experimental neurosis in dogs, and was interested in psychiatry, but this approach really did not catch on in this country until the Yale group took hold of it. Then it became "obvious" that we needed experimental procedures for producing animal equivalents of human conflicts, frustration, anxiety, and even, more recently, love and affection.

### Definition of Fear

From our brief historical introduction, we can draw a conceptual definition of fear. *Fear is an aversive state of the organism aroused by stimuli that signal a future aversive event.* Thus, the white rat produced fear in Albert because it signalled the coming of the aversive noise. Similarly, a buzzer which signals a coming electric shock arouses fear. Fear may accompany a specific unpleasant event (such as pain or loud noise), but it is the state aroused in anticipation of such events that is our main concern. We may start off, then, with two questions. First, how do we measure fear? Second, how do we condition it?

***Measures of Fear.*** We may index fear through three types of measures: physiological response, verbal report, and nonverbal behavior. First, physiological responses might initially seem to be the best and most direct measures of fear. And, in fact, a considerable amount of classical conditioning with humans has employed GSR, heart rate, blood volume change, and the like. The sole use of such measures, however, would assume that fear and autonomic responses are equivalent, conditioned at the same rate and by the same laws. We have already seen, in our discussion of activation (Chapter Five), however, that the correlations among different physiological measures tends to be low and that such measures tend to change in similar ways in both pleasurable and aversive situations. Therefore, physiological responses are not completely adequate.

Second, verbal reports are a prime source of information about anxiety in the clinic but are seldom used as a dependent variable in the laboratory. For reasons dating back to Watsonian arguments for objectivity, verbal reports have often been considered too subjective and too sensitive to non-conditioning variables to be valid measures of conditioning. Staats, Staats, and Crawford (1962) showed, however, that a word paired with shock would come to arouse a GSR and at the same time was rated "bad" on the semantic differential—a rating scale commonly related to attitudes. The author and his associates (Beck & Brooks, 1967a; Sutterer & Beck, 1970; Bobbitt & Beck, 1971) have found the semantic differential to be a sensitive measure of evaluative changes of stimuli paired with shock. Rating scales have been widely used for self-report in personality research and the Taylor Manifest Anxiety Scale has been used to define fear in conditioning situations. The point here, however, is that there seems to have been relatively little work on fear conditioning in which verbal report measures have been the dependent variable.

Third, nonverbal behavior can be used to define fear. McAllister and McAllister (1971) have argued that since fear is not equivalent to a single physiological measure, the behavior of the whole animal must be studied and fear inferred from this behavior. For example, in Watson and Rayner's (1920) study, Albert's crying and attempts to escape were behaviors from which fear was inferred. Fear is thus an intervening variable which has a particular kind of learning (i.e., aversive conditioning) as the antecedent condition and some kind of behavior as the consequent condition. We can, of course, use physiological responses or verbal behavior as consequent conditions, with the recognition that they are not perfectly valid. Following the Hull-Spence tradition, the McAllisters consider fear a drive that can energize, reinforce, or punish responses. We shall examine some of the evidence related to this later. Within the approach taken in this text as a whole, however, we may consider fear as an intervening variable that is aversive and that has cue properties, without necessarily considering it a drive.

### What is Required for Fear Learning?

If fear is an intervening variable which we may treat as a classically conditioned response, then it should be subject to the same laws of conditioning as other responses; that is, it should show acquisition, extinction, and generalization. There is a very large literature showing that these phenomena can be reliably produced, but, since the details are more properly the subject matter of learning theory, we shall not go into them extensively here. We do need to consider what the necessary conditions for fear learning are, however.

***Are Skeletal Responses Necessary?*** It appears that overt skeletal responses to either the CS or the UCS are not necessary for learning, even though necessary to demonstrate behaviorally that conditioning has occurred. Animals paralyzed by curare are unable to move during conditioning and therefore show no skeletal responses to the UCS (usually electric shock). They do show appropriate "fearful" responses to the CS immediately on testing after the drug wears off, however. There is a long history of research on the problem of what is learned, generally leading to the conclusion indicated. Bolles (1972) and Bitterman (1967) offer interesting discussions of the problem.

*The CS-UCS Interval.* There is some limit to the length of the interval between the presentation of the CS and UCS in which conditioning can occur. The *optimal* interval depends on many factors, however, including species differences and the particular response in question (Gormezano & Moore, 1969). For example, such short-latency responses as the eyeblink—a defensive reaction to a puff of air to the eye—have short optimum CS-UCS intervals (about .5 second, with humans.) Autonomic responses have longer latencies of arousal and correspondingly longer optimal CS-UCS intervals. For the GSR, the optimal interval is between two and five seconds. Fear conditioning as indexed by the overt behavior of the whole animal can be conditioned with intervals at least as long as thirty seconds (Davitz, Mason, Mowrer, & Viek, 1957). The issue of CS-UCS intervals has been thrown into consternation by the poison avoidance research showing that a particular taste can become aversive if followed several *hours* later by a poison which produces illness. What this all means is that there is no such thing as *the* optimal CS-UCS interval for all situations and that for a particular kind of CS and UCS such an interval has to be determined empirically. The whole problem is further complicated in humans because of their verbal capacity. Thus, the child who steals a cookie may be *told* that he is being spanked for this reason several hours later and may therefore associate the behavior with the spanking. If not told, on the other hand, the child would associate the spanking with some other event more close in time to the spanking.

*CS-UCS Pairing versus CS-UCS Contingency.* In our prior discussions of secondary reinforcement and positive incentives, we noted that a simple CS-UCS pairing provides relatively little information to the organism and is not an optimal condition for learning. Rescorla (1967) argues that there must be a *contingency* relation (or correlation) between CS and UCS so that a CS reliably signals a UCS and no-CS signals no-UCS. If there is such a relationship, there is *excitatory* conditioning, which is to say that the CS signals whatever it is the UCS does. If the contingency is reversed, so that a CS signals the absence of the UCS and no-CS means that UCS is coming, then there is *inhibitory* conditioning. That is, the CS inhibits the response which an excitatory CS would arouse. The contingency between CS and UCS may only be probabilistic, the correlation between the two events could be less than perfect, and there still be some conditioning.

A particularly important implication of the contingency theory has to do with the appropriate controls for ensuring that changes are actually caused by conditioning. A control in which the CS is presented every trial but is *explicitly unpaired* with the UCS (such as putting it in the middle of the intertrial interval) is not considered appropriate because it would produce inhibitory conditioning. That is, it would signal no-UCS. Rescorla suggests that a *truly random* control is appropriate. This procedure has a potential CS coming on in a random time relation to the UCS from one trial to the next so that there would be no contingency and it would not reliably predict either the occurrence or the nonoccurrence of the UCS. Rescorla's hypothesis has provoked considerable interest, along with evidence both pro and con. We shall find the idea useful, however, and return to it in a number of different contexts.

### Fear as a Cue

Since we have discussed fear as a conditioned response, let us consider it further in those terms. Fear has been called a *cue-producing response* (e.g., Miller, 1951b). It is like a response because it can be evoked and conditioned. It is like a cue in that it can become the signal to make some overt response, or responses can become conditioned to it. In this capacity, as a mediator between external stimuli and responses, it is also called a *mediating response:*

$$S \longrightarrow (r_{fear} - s_{fear}) \longrightarrow R$$

where $S$ and $R$ are the overt stimuli and responses and $s$ and $r$ are the internal stimuli and responses. In many situations, if not all, the effects of fear can be interpreted in terms of its cue properties, without recourse to concepts of either drive or aversion.

The mediating role of fear is well illustrated in an experiment by May (1948). The experiment was conducted in three phases:

*Phase 1.* Rats were trained to jump a hurdle to escape shock.
*Phase 2.* A tone was paired with shock while the animals were in the apparatus but blocked off from making the escape response.
*Phase 3.* With the situation again as in original training, the tone was presented *without shock* and the animals made the original escape response.

The interpretation of this experiment, with fear as a conditioned cue-producing response for the overt hurdling response, is shown in Figure 8-3.

Because we commonly observe painful situations that produce apparently strong emotion, it is easy to think of fear as a strong drive. This should not blind us to the continued possibility that fear can be a cue, and perhaps no more than that. The conceptual problem here is exactly the same as with

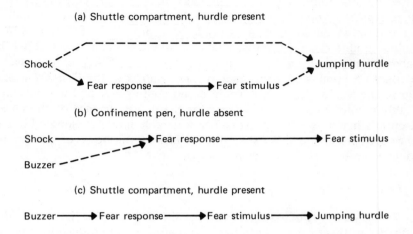

(a) Shuttle compartment, hurdle present

(b) Confinement pen, hurdle absent

(c) Shuttle compartment, hurdle present

**Figure 8.3** *Diagram of May's (1948) experiment. (From Miller, 1950, p. 440.)*

the anticipatory goal response, where we saw that the $r_g - s_g$ mechanism could be conceived as a motivational mechanism (stimulus intensity) or as a cueing mechanism.

### Fear as an Acquired Drive

Now that we have seen that fear can operate as a cue, a fact that could be interpreted in cognitive, or informational, terms, let us examine the arguments and some of the evidence related to treating fear as a drive. Does fear seem to meet the criteria for a drive in experimental tests?

*Fear Reduction as Reinforcement.* Miller's (1948) experiment (discussed on p. 130), is the standard reference experiment. To recapitulate, Miller put rats into the left side of the two-compartment box shown in Figure 6-1; each animal was shocked before being allowed to escape to the other side. The animals were then locked in the left compartment, without shock, but could open the escape door by turning a wheel. The learning of the wheel-turning response (and later a lever pressing response) was presumably reinforced by the reduction of fear when the animals escaped from the shock compartment.

Brown and Jacobs (1949) suggested, however, that Miller's animals may have been frustrated during testing when they were not allowed to make the previously learned escape response. Wheel turning might then have been reinforced by frustration reduction, rather than by fear reduction. To test this hypothesis, they shocked animals in one side of their apparatus *without* permitting the animals to escape from shock. Their animals also learned to escape to the other side when given the opportunity, however, so they concluded that fear reduction, not frustration reduction, was the reinforcer.

Many experiments have elaborated on this phenomenon. Kalish (1954) and Goldstein (1962) showed that the speed of learning to escape from the fear-arousing compartment increased with both number and intensity of shocks during the fear-conditioning phase of the experiment. Conversely, if following shocks, the animals were put in the shock side (without shock) a number of times before they were allowed to escape, the animals escaped more slowly. This is usually interpreted to mean that the fear response was partially extinguished during the confinement trials. It is also possible that during their forced retention the animals may have learned responses incompatible with escaping. Page (1955) supported this idea by showing that animals given such forced retention were *slower* to reenter the shock side to get food than were animals extinguished normally. He interpreted this result to mean that fear was not actually extinguished during forced retention, but rather that the animals had learned to do something which interfered with escape behavior. If their fear had actually been reduced, they should not have been more reluctant to go back into the shock compartment than animals extinguished normally.[3]

By and large, however, the main difficulty with the fear reduction interpretation for the Miller-type experiments is that one neither controls nor measures fear reduction in any direct manner. One could simply argue, as Schoenfeld (1950) has, that the shock environment has become a conditioned aversive stimulus and that the animal is escaping these aversive stimuli. This sounds similar to an acquired drive explanation, but the notion of aversive stimulation does not necessarily carry all the connotations of the drive concept.

***Fear as an Energizer.*** Brown, Kalish, and Farber (1951) proposed that if fear is an acquired drive it should energize all responses, reflexive or

---

[3]Page's results are compatible with more recent experiments showing that animals given inescapable shocks prior to avoidance conditioning are slower to learn the avoidance response, presumably because they have learned some kind of response that competes with the avoidance response. This is discussed in Chapter Nine, under the topic of learned helplessness.

conditioned. The advantage of a reflex response is that since it is not learned it ought to be inherently less variable and less sensitive to the learning variables that influence other responses. They first paired a tone with foot shock. Their subjects (rats) were then tested for magnitude of the startle response—a reflex response common to all mammals—by firing a cap pistol. Startle magnitude was measured by mounting the test cage so that when the animal made a startle response the bounce of the cage was recorded on a pen writer. For the experimental subjects, the pistol was fired on some trials when the CS (tone) was on, the subjects presumably being more fearful at this time. It was expected that as conditioning progressed there would be greater fear to the tone and hence a greater startle. Control subjects were repeatedly tested for startle, but not conditioned. The results are shown in Figure 8-4. The magnitude of startle did increase with number of conditioning trials and decreased during extinction (tone not followed by shock). The control animals showed no regular change over test trials. Meryman (1952, described in Brown, 1961, p. 152-154) replicated these results and found the startle response even more amplified if the subjects

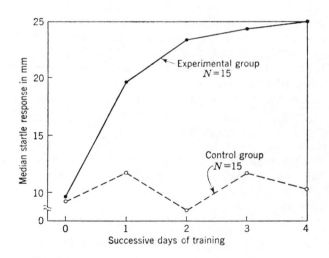

**Figure 8.4**  *Median amplitude of startle responses of fearful and non-fearful rats to a loud, sharp sound. The upper curve shows that experimental animals presumed to be fearful jumped more and more vigorously to the sound as the number of fear-conditioning trials increased. The responses of control (nonfearful) subjects, however, did not change progressively or significantly during the same period. (From Brown, Kalish, and Farber, 1951, p. 321. Copyright © 1951 by the American Psychological Association. Reprinted by permission.)*

were also hungry. This provides considerable support for the drive concept, because an irrelevant drive is summated with the fear.

The drive interpretation was challenged by Kurtz and Siegal (1966). Suppose, they said, that when the animal has its feet shocked it learns to tense up when the tone comes on, perhaps preparing to jump off the grid when the shock comes. This would facilitate the startle response, which is also a kind of "jumpy" response. They tested this idea by shocking some animals through the skin of the back and others through the feet. The results were clear. The foot-shocked group gave the same kinds of results as in the Brown-Kalish-Farber experiment but the back-shocked group showed a *smaller* amount of startle than a control group. The interpretation is that the back-shocked animals learned, perhaps, to "flatten out" on the floor when the tone came on, to "get away" from the shock, and this anticipatory behavior interfered with the startle response. Kurtz and Siegal concluded that the tone paired with foot shock did not facilitate startle by arousing a fear drive; rather, it was a cue for a preparatory response which facilitated the startle response. If a different preparatory response was learned, as in the case of back shock, there was no facilitory effect of the CS on the startle response. We cannot conclude from this experiment that there is *no* element of general drive involved, but we can conclude that the kind of behavior called forth by the CS (or the mediating fear response) certainly has a strong influence on the results.

***Fear as a Punisher.*** Stimuli previously paired with pain clearly can suppress ongoing behavior. Because punishment is such a broad topic, however, we consider it in detail in Chapter Nine. Suffice it here to note that there are a number of possible interpretations of the punishing effects of painful stimuli, all of which are even more complicated when we talk about the punishing effects of conditioned stimuli. A widespread belief is that pain evokes escape behavior that competes with the response preceding the pain. The competing behavior is reinforced by escape from the punishment. A drive concept is not necessary to this interpretation, unless one argues solely by definition that any stimulus which suppresses a response is a drive-producing stimulus. The whole punishment picture is complicated by the fact that under certain circumstances a supposedly punishing stimulus actually *increases* the occurrence of the "punished" behavior.

In summary, just as we saw in the case of "primary drives," the concept of fear as a drive does not fare as well as a drive theorist might hope when it is applied to the problem of "learned drives." The observed effects can often be accounted for directly in learning terms (as in the experiments of May and of Kurtz and Siegal). Such an interpretation simply says that specific responses are learned to specific stimuli under conditions in which it *appears* that they are being energized by a drive. In other instances, we can treat fear as an aversive state of the organism which is gotten rid of, but which does not have all the properties that drives are supposed to have.

### Some Human Applications

We began by noting Watson's experiment with Little Albert and the translation of Freudian concepts into S-R terms, with anxiety as an intervening variable. As a further illustration of the usefulness of this approach, Brown (1961) has described how miserliness, or "desire for money," could be interpreted in terms of anxiety and anxiety reduction. We could—partly, at least—account for working for money in terms of its secondary reinforcing properties: it can be traded for something else. J.S. Brown, however, deals with the case in which the individual works for, or hoards, money beyond the amount he spends or needs. Presumably money should lose some of its secondary reinforcing properties under such circumstances.

Brown suggests that at some point in life the stimulus of *not having money* becomes a conditioned stimulus for fear. The child may hear the parents argue about not having money, expressing anxiety over where money for food and rent is going to come from, and so on. The arguments and fears expressed by the parents may be considered unconditioned stimuli for fear on the part of the child, and such words as "We have no money," and other stimuli indicating lack of money, become conditioned stimuli for arousing this fear. The child or young adult may then learn that *this fear is reduced by getting and having money.* Therefore, whenever the cues for not having money are presented the adult does what he has learned as the means of reducing this fear (eliminating the cues): He gets money. This kind of fear, and a conspicuous consumption which serves to hold down the anxiety cues of poverty, has been described poignantly by the great American playwright Moss Hart in his autobiography *Act One.*

This sequence of events is diagrammed in Figure 8-5.[4]

Other kinds of compulsions may have the same or similar bases. Nymphomania is frequently interpreted in this fashion: Not being loved may serve as an anxiety-arousing cue which is temporarily removed by the sex act. From a clinical point of view, this interpretation does help account for a wide variety of behaviors that otherwise seem to have no common explanation.

### Other Sources of Fear

Thus far we have talked as if intense or pain-producing stimuli were the only sources of fear. As Hebb (1946) has pointed out in some detail,

[4]Again, anxiety reduction is certainly not the only reinforcement for making money beyond one's needs. As a character in a movie about financial sleight-of-hand said, "It's the game that's important; money is just the way you keep score." This gets us into the question of such forms of motivation as the achievement motive, which is taken up later.

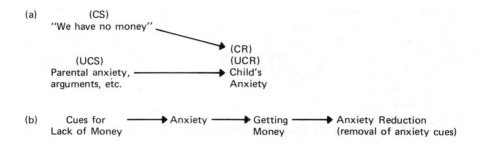

**Figure 8.5** *Illustration of how learned anxiety may become a cue and drive for getting money.*

this is not the case. A very common phobia, for example, is fear of snakes. Jones and Jones (1928) reported that young city children, who had never encountered snakes in the wild, did not have a fear of snakes, but that a large percentage of adults reared in the city did have this fear. Hebb concludes that snake phobia is the result of maturation and does not require specific learning for its occurrence.

Not only are snake phobias common in adults, but they also are a common theme in visions produced by hallucinogenic drugs throughout the world. A speculative possibility is that fear of snakes is a kind of species-specific defense reaction left over from a period of evolutionary development when it was adaptive to avoid snakes without having to be bitten first to learn the reaction. Hebb (1946) notes that even in 1930, Valentine had pointed out that some stimuli (e.g., caterpillars) were conditioned very easily, but others (e.g., bottles) were conditioned only with great difficulty. This suggests inherent differences in the emotionality aroused by these stimuli and may also relate to certain species-specific reactions in avoidance learning.

Hebb argues that "psychologically" there is little in common among the many events that arouse fear. For example, loud noises arouse fear, and so does darkness. Williams and his associates (e.g., J. E. Williams & Morland, 1976) have repeatedly found that both adults and children have more positive evaluations of light colors, objects, or persons than of dark colors, objects, or persons. This finding seems to hold worldwide and across many ethnic and racial groups. One of Williams' hypotheses, based on the universality of the phenomenon and the fact that it occurs at as early an age as it has been possible to study it, is that it is based on fear of the dark, which is either innate or learned at a very early age. Williams and Morland have then gone on to relate fear of the dark to racial discrimination.

*Fear of the Unfamiliar.* Something that every parent knows is that at about three months of age the infant begins to make positive responses to people, smiling and cooing. But at six months, there is a rapid turnabout; the child may show a strong negative reaction (crying and withdrawing) to strangers. This reaction, says Hebb (1946), is based on experience, but not the kind of associative learning we usually think of in terms of classical conditioning. Instead, the child becomes familiar with certain people and when an unfamiliar face appears, the child is afraid. Similar effects are found with chimpanzees.

*Hebb's Classification of Fears.* Hebb classified specific fears as follows. First, he categorizes fears due to "conflict." The term *conflict* is intentionally used rather loosely and includes fears induced by pain, loud noise, dead or mutilated bodies, and strange persons or animals. Pain and loud noise, which seem not to depend on any particular previous experience, seem to constitute a special subclass. Fears of snakes or small mammals (like rats) may fall into this category.

Second, Hebb categorizes fears due to sensory deficit. These include loss of support, darkness, and solitude—all of which have in common "an absence of customary stimulation." Chimpanzees avoid social isolation, just as humans normally do. This, in fact, may be one of the more aversive conditions for higher primates (see the discussion of "time out" as a punisher in Chapter Nine). Hebb suggests that this is the result of familiarity and adaptation to having others around. He further suggests that in some cultures fear of darkness and isolation might not be found if it were not the norm for individuals to spend time together in the light. As noted, Williams has not yet found evidence for such a culture.

Third, Hebb categorizes constitutional disturbances and maturation. People affected by the nutrition-deficit disease pellagra show psychotic fears that disappear on treatment with nicotinic acid. The individual may recall the fears that he had while sick and be at a loss to give any reason for them. The disease, says Hebb, produces a nervous system function different from the normal cerebral activity of the healthy adult.

Children sometimes go through "spells" of having fears of this or that, which they "grow out of." These are difficult to explain and may simply represent temporary neural disorganization due to maturational changes. Many children have nightmares but few carry them into adulthood.

The implication of this discussion is that a wide variety of potential unconditioned stimuli can produce fear. To look at Brown's example of miserliness from a different point of view, suppose that the child associated lack of money with *solitude* because the parents were out working. In this case, lack of money might become a conditioned stimulus for the fear associated with being alone and the individual might then collect money as a means of reducing this fear. In the extreme case, he might become wealthy enough to pay people to stay around him. The net result would be similar to Brown's analysis, but the source of the anxiety is different. Or, in the case of the nymphomaniac, perhaps for some reason there might be an especially strong fear of being alone which is reduced by frequent sexual activity. In any event, it is possible that fear could operate as a cue or negative incentive based on a number of sources of arousal other than just association with intense or painful stimuli.

## FRUSTRATION

### Frustration as an Intervening Variable

The following story was related to me by a student. A friend of his was going to the airport to meet his wife before she left on a flight, but he was delayed and just missed the departing plane. He thereupon beat in the hood of his car. This exemplifies what we commonly mean by frustration: if an anticipated desirable outcome is not attained, we may say that frustration has occurred and this in turn has some observable effect on behavior. Frustration itself is usually considered an aversive state.

To define frustration operationally, we must have *blocking of a goal-directed activity* as the antecedent condition and some behavioral event as the consequence. Frustration would then be inferred from the antecedent and consequent conditions, like any other intervening variable. Failing to reach the airport in time was the antecedent condition for the man in the story, and beating in his car was the consequence. A verbal report like "I feel frustrated" may or may not be a valid indicator of frustration. The person saying this may really be saying only that he is presently unhappy, without reference to some unachieved goal.

**Antecedent Conditions for Frustration.** Two agents for blocking goal-directed responses, and hence, antecedent events for frustration are *barriers* and *deficiencies.* Barriers may be external physical objects or internal states. For example, a locked door, a deep ravine, or a great distance are external physical barriers. An internal barrier might be the anticipation of punishment.

A deficiency is a lack of the necessary ability to attain a goal. For example, a door handle may be jammed and I am simply not strong enough to turn it. Or, I may want a particular job that requires training or skill that I do not have. The distinction between barriers and deficiencies is not always clear, however. For example, the jammed door handle is a barrier only because of my deficiency; it might be easily overcome by someone stronger or cleverer.

A third kind of frustrating event is the reduction or absence of an anticipated reward. Nonreward frustration has been a major research topic, and we shall discuss it in some detail later.

### Responses to Frustration

Historically, a number of different kinds of "specific" response categories have been taken to be indicative of frustration. These include aggressive behaviors, fixations (rigid, unchanging behaviors), regression (reversion to more childlike modes of responding), more vigorous behaviors, escape, avoidance, and emotional responses (e.g., crying). Lawson (1965) and Yates (1962) have discussed the literature related to these in some detail. Much of the effort toward finding specific "frustration responses" was the result of the frustration-aggression hypothesis (aggression is produced by frustration) and attempts to prove or disprove it. The clarity of hindsight shows the futility of this effort. The responses to frustration are likely to be as variable as responses to any other aversive condition. Brown and Farber (1951) took the lead in moving away from such specific responses, simply treating thwarting of goal responses as an antecedent condition for general drive.

Some authors have questioned the usefulness of the frustration concept at all (e.g., Lawson, 1965) and most contemporary motivation books rarely discuss the topic except in the context of the frustration-aggression hypothesis and nonreward frustration. This is a bit unfortunate. First, even though psychologists may question the value of the concept, frustration is commonly used by nonpsychologists to explain behavior. As with instinct, it is worthwhile to discuss the topic, if just for the sake of seeing the problems involved. Secondly, however, it *is* a useful motivational concept. It gives us a set of conditions under which aversions are found which are *not* related to otherwise noxious events. That is, frustration is an aversive motivational variable which grows out of positive expectations.

### Associative Interpretation of Frustration Effects

Frustration situations may have stimulus (cue, associative) properties as well as motivational. I have a television set in its declining years that shows a lot of snow on the screen. The temporary cure is to hit it and, if necessary, to keep hitting it until the screen clears. This is usually successful, but how would a stranger coming on the scene interpret my behavior? He might conclude that the set's malfunction produced strong frustration, which energized a vigorous aggressive response from me. In fact, however, I hit the set because the snowy screen is a cue for me to make a response that

I anticipate will be rewarded by the screen clearing. This is a strictly associative interpretation not requiring any motivational concept other than the goal (incentive) of a clear screen. It is indeed possible that frustration might produce "anger" and aggressive behaviors, but more vigorous behavior in an apparently thwarting situation does not always require a motivational interpretation beyond that of desire for some goal. In this example, the "frustration situation" itself contained the cues for the behaviors involved.

The internal state aroused by the frustration situation may also be aversive and may have cue properties. Thus, if I feel a certain way following frustrating circumstances, this feeling may serve as a cue to behave in a particular way. It may "warn me" to control my temper, for example, and not do anything rash (such as beating in a car hood). I might learn such controls and carry them into situations in which I have never been before, but the internal cues are the same. We can illustrate these effects experimentally with the research related to nonreward frustration theory.

### Nonreward Frustration

A good many years ago, an investigator named Tinklepaugh (1928) was training a monkey with standard monkey rewards, raisins and grapes, which the animal came to expect. Tinklepaugh then substituted a piece of lettuce for the expected reward, and this obviously upset the animal. This demonstration has three important elements. First, the monkey had to learn to *expect* a particular reward. Second, the monkey got something *less attractive* than he expected. Thirdly, change in reward was *disturbing*, or aversive. Presumably Tinklepaugh's monkey felt something like a student who gets a C when he has been expecting an A. The antecedent condition for *nonreward frustration* is no reward at all when one expects it.

Nonreward frustration has been used to explain extinction, the depression effect following the shift from a large to a small incentive, the partial reinforcement effect, and discrimination learning. Nonreward frustration theory (Amsel, 1958, 1962) is an outgrowth of Hull-Spence theory and is considered by many to be the last serious stronghold of drive theory.

**Amsel's Theory.** We will assume that nonreward frustration is aversive and that situations in which it occurs also become aversive and will tend to be escaped or avoided. Amsel considers frustration to have both drive and cue properties. As a drive, frustration should energize responses; an increase is punishing, and a decrease rewarding. As a cue, it may evoke responses by itself.

**Energizing Effect of Nonreward Frustration.** Amsel and his associates have used a device called a *double runway*, two separate runways strung together so that the goal box for the first is also the start box for the second. Rats are trained to run in the first runway to get food in the first goal box; then, when the door is opened, they run to get food in the second goal box. The question posed is this: Once the animals have learned the required performances, what will happen to running speed in the second runway if food is omitted in the first goal box? Frustration theory predicts the animals will run faster because the nonreward will arouse a drive (frustration) which will energize running in the second runway. And they do indeed run faster. The increase in running speed following nonreward is called the *frustration effect* (Amsel & Roussel, 1952). The faster running is not caused by the fact that the animals were not fed and hence were hungrier. Wagner (1963) ran control subjects never rewarded in the first goal box and this group ran slower in the second runway than the frustrated group. Roussel (1952) also showed that the frustration effect develops if the animals are rewarded in the first goal box on only half their trials from the start of training. The effect therefore does not require 100 percent reinforcement in initial training.

How does nonreward frustration develop? Amsel proposed that the anticipatory goal response ($r_g - s_g$) was conditioned[5] and, as $r_g - s_g$ was becoming stronger, there was frustration when reward was omitted. This produced greater drive and hence faster running. The $r_g - s_g$ mechanism, of course, is the Hullian equivalent of expectancy.

**Frustrative Nonreward and Extinction.** When an animal has come to expect reward in the goal box, there is frustration when the reward is not found there. The goal box itself then becomes aversive and the animal stops running to it, i.e., the animal extinguishes.

If some animals were trained with large rewards and some with small, which should extinguish faster? If large rewards produce greater incentive motivation, we might predict that the large-reward animals would be harder to extinguish. According to frustration theory, however, there would be greater frustration if a large reward is omitted and faster extinction should occur, and indeed this is what happens.

In similar fashion, when animals are shifted from a large to a small reward, they often fall below the performance of animals consistently given a small reward. The downshift produces frustration and some aversion to the goal box. Running speed then drops sharply, below that of animals continuously on small reward. The animals continue to run, however, because they are rewarded and their performance eventually comes back up to the level of the control animals.

---

[5]Amsel used the symbol $r_r$ to indicate anticipatory reward and $r_p$ to indicate anticipatory punishment. The symbol $r_g$ is a more general one that covers both cases. For our purposes, $r_g$ is sufficient and we will not burden the student with more symbolism than necessary.

*Partial Reinforcement Effects.* Animals usually show slower extinction after partial reinforcement than after 100 percent reinforcement (i.e., reward on every trial). This phenomenon, the *partial reinforcement extinction effect* (PREE) is a continuing mystery story. The problem is how a response rewarded only part of the time can be "stronger" (more resistant to extinction) than if rewarded all the time. There is no dearth of explanations; it is just that none is completely adequate to the data. We deal with it here mainly in terms of frustration theory and evidence that raises problems for frustration theory. Detailed accounts can be found in textbooks on learning and in several *Psychological Bulletin* reviews, the most recent of which is Robbins (1971).

According to frustration theory, when an animal has been rewarded on every trial, the shift from acquisition to extinction produces a very large nonreward frustration effect. The animal stops running to the goal box because it has become aversive. The interpretation for partially reinforced animals is more complicated. Nonreward in training produces frustration, of which the conditionable ancitipatory component is $r_f - s_f$. This is strictly analogous to $r_g - s_g$, which is to say that (1) it is a fractional component of the full frustration effect that occurs when the animal experiences nonreward and (2) it can become conditioned to various cues. The early trial effect of frustration is that the animal anticipates frustration in the goal box, and hence runs more slowly than a continuously reinforced animal. Frustration gradually develops over trials because the anticipation of reward $(r_g - s_g)$ has to develop first. The animal has conflict between anticipatory approach responses $(r_g - s_g)$ and anticipatory avoidance responses $(r_f - s_f)$, and hence runs more slowly than the animal for which only positive anticipation $(r_g - s_g)$ has developed. In early training trials, partially reinforced animals do run slower (Wagner, 1963).

As $r_f - s_f$ occurs more frequently over successive trials, however, $s_f$ becomes one of the stimuli to which running is conditioned. Eventually, instead of arousing conflicting responses, $r_f - s_f$ *facilitates* the rewarded response. At the same time, frustration drive also facilitates running. The partially reinforced animal is therefore conditioned to run in the presence of frustration stimuli and continues to run longer in extinction. Amsel's explanation was a remarkable tour de force for Hull-Spence theory.

Any theory worth its salt generates enough research, however, that it produces problems for itself. In this case, the problem is in assuming that $r_g - s_g$ has to develop slowly before frustration can occur. It was therefore embarrassing to the theory when the PREE was obtained with as few as six acquisition trials (and later reduced to two, one not reinforced and one reinforced.) The principal antagonist to the theory at this point was Garvin McCain (1966). Obviously, if the PREE can be obtained in fewer trials than it presumably takes for $r_g - s_g$ (and, hence, for $r_f - s_f$) to be conditioned to running, then Amsel's position is less tenable. The theoretical road then divided two ways. One path was toward an explanation in terms of a very rapidly developing frustration effect. The other was toward a nonmotivational interpretation.

*Frustration and the Small-Trial PREE.* Daly (1974) has nicely reviewed the literature on this problem. Her own work has shown that the goal box in which nonreward frustration occurs is in fact aversive. Her procedure has been to train animals to run in a straight alley to a goal box which is also the start box for a hurdle-jump escape apparatus. The general prediction is that the animals should find the frustrating goal box cues aversive and escape from them. The measure of frustration is the speed of jumping the hurdle from the goal box into the escape box. The data show, for example, that animals given 100 percent reward in acquisition leap out of the goal box faster in extinction than animals given partial reinforcement. Similarly, animals escape faster after large rewards than small ones, and faster after high-concentration sucrose rewards than low-concentration ones.

A further interesting variation follows from the fact that frustration theory says nothing about instrumental responses being necessary for a frustration effect. Its only requirement is that the expectation of reward be aroused, but not followed by reward. Therefore, we should find frustration effects simply by having animals consume food in a particular environment, then seeing how fast they escape if food is no longer presented. Using just this procedure, Daly showed that direct goal box placements with food in the box produced a large frustration effect when food was omitted. The animals showed increasingly faster escapes when placed in the empty goal box. Control animals having equivalent placements without food always left the box more slowly than the frustrated animals. Daly also showed that animals would learn to press a lever to escape from such frustrating circumstances, indicating some generality of escape responses.

Given this background, Brooks (1969) argued that an analysis of the small-trials PREE could more profitably focus on the aversiveness of the goal box for continuously reinforced animals than on the conditioning of frustration in partially reinforced animals. The real place to emphasize a frustration explanation for the small-trials PREE might be in extinction itself, rather than in acquisition. Brooks also used Daly's direct placement technique. One group of animals had six direct placements with food, and a second group had food on three of six trials. Half of each group got a large reward (30-second access to wet mash) and half got a small reward (one 45-mg food pellet). The results were that the 100 percent large reward group escaped faster than any of the other three groups, which were all equal to a control group never receiving placements with food. It seems clear that with large rewards one can obtain a frustration effect in extinction after only a very small number of trials, and that this could account for the small-trials PREE. The same explanation would also account for the regular PREE.

Lest the frustration theorists become too complacent, however, there are other phenomena to tax their ingenuity. We shall mention but two. First, if animals are run one trial a day, some being reinforced every day and others only half the days, there is still a PREE in extinction. This is a little difficult to interpret in terms of frustration theory, because it would seem that frustration would not carry over from the goal box one day to the start box the next, and would not be conditioned.

The second problem is even more awkward. If animals are trained in an apparatus like a T-maze, with 50 percent reinforcement on one side and 100 percent reinforcement on the other side, they eventually choose the 100 percent side almost every time. The animals are forced to go to each side equally often by closing the door to the preferred side as necessary. In extinction, the animals still choose the 100 percent side for many, many trials (Logan, 1968). This runs directly contrary to the results obtained with separate groups of animals in the straight runway. It would appear that the only way to interpret this "reverse PREE" in terms of frustration would be to say that frustration made the 50 percent side aversive during training and that it continued to be more aversive in extinction. This is just the opposite of the use of the usual frustration interpretation, however, and hence is not a consistent way to use the theory.

### Nonmotivational Theories for "Frustrative" Nonreward

Because of the difficulties faced by frustration theory in accounting for various partial reinforcement effects, Capaldi (1967) proposed a strictly associative theory. Very briefly, Capaldi's argument is that, following the presentation of a reward, there is a *stimulus aftereffect* of that reward ($S^R$) at the beginning of the next trial. This aftereffect may be considered a memory. On trials when there is no reward given, there is a different stimulus aftereffect ($S^n$). According to the theory, then, when the animal is put into the start box it remembers what happened following the last time it was in the start box, and this memory (either $S^R$ or $S^n$) is conditioned to the running response on that trial *if the response is rewarded*. The exact predictions would then depend on the patterning of reward and nonreward trials. In the case of the simple PREE, however, since $S^n$ is conditioned to running on many trials, the animal is slower to extinguish, because this conditioned stimulus is present during extinction. With the 100 percent reinforced animal, however, the aftereffect was always $S^R$, and $S^n$ was never conditioned during training. Therefore, when $S^R$ is replaced by $S^n$, there is rapid extinction. Capaldi's theory thus accounts for the PREE without recourse to frustration.

Staddon (1974) accounts for the nonreward frustration effect in the double runway in terms of inhibition. In many situations (e.g., lever pressing by rats or key pecking by pigeons), the subjects show a *postreinforcement pause*—ceasing to respond for a while after reward. Staddon's argument is that in the double runway the animal shows a postreinforcement pause after reward in the first goal box, slowing down its performance in the second runway. If reward is omitted in the first runway, there is no postreinforcement pause; the animal runs rapidly and gives the appearance of being energized by nonreward frustration. Staddon supports this hypothesis with a number of rather ingenious experiments.

### CONCLUSION

Unconditioned aversive stimulation, fear, and frustration have long been considered strongholds of drive theory because they seem to involve energization of responses and drive reduction reinforcement. Many of the phenomena indicative of positive incentive motivation (e.g., sudden changes in behavior with changes in level of reward) are also obtained in aversive situations, however. This strongly indicates that incentive interpretations are applicable to aversive situations. Anticipatory relaxation is a useful incentive concept for aversive situations. Appetitive and aversive situations thus can be interpreted along similar lines, but using incentive concepts rather than drive. Many data in aversive situations can also be interpreted in learning terms, such as when fear is said to serve as a mediating stimulus rather than as a "motivational" stimulus. This, too, is similar to theoretical concepts used in appetitive situations.

# chapter 9

# Aversive Stimulation: 2. Avoidance and Punishment

## AVOIDANCE CONDITIONING

### The Phenomenon

Suppose we put a rat into a grid floor apparatus and sound a buzzer. The rat may or may not noticeably respond. Five seconds later we electrify the grid. The response is immediate and violent. The rat may jump about, back up, and perhaps urinate or defecate. After awhile, say in fifteen to thirty seconds, it crosses the midline of the box to the other side. Buzzer and shock cease.

During a rest period of a minute or so, the animal sits rather immobile, but with some tension apparent. The buzzer sounds again. This time the animal is clearly responsive. It may freeze, look "warily" about, or shift around "uncomfortably." When the shock comes five seconds later, the animal responds vigorously and crosses to the nonshock side of the box more quickly than it did the first time. The animal becomes very proficient at *escaping* the shock and is, to the eye of the observer, less agitated at the presentation of either buzzer or shock.

Finally, after perhaps thirty-five trials, something new happens. When the buzzer sounds, the animal crosses to the safe side *before* the shock comes on. It has made its first *avoidance* response. An increasing percentage of avoidance responses are made until the animal performs almost perfectly and even, perhaps, nonchalantly. Between trials, the animal may explore the apparatus instead of just sitting frozen in a corner; it casually crosses the midline when the buzzer sounds. We now have an animal well trained on a *two-way active avoidance*.

Two important elements seem to be involved in this situation: The animal learns to become afraid when the buzzer sounds, and the animal learns to run to the other side of the box before the shock. These events have been quantified in a number of experiments. Hoffman and Fleshler (1962), for example, taught rats to push a *panel* to get food and to press a *lever* to turn off shock. Both procedures were then run concurrently, but a one-minute tone preceded the shock, during which time a lever press would keep the shock from being delivered. The measure of fear was inhibition of food getting during the tone. The results were that (1) food getting was depressed during the tone before the animals learned to avoid, which indicates that fear was learned before avoidance; (2) food getting was inhibited more on avoidance trials than nonavoidance trials, suggesting that avoidance is more likely if fear is greater; and (3) food getting generally declined (just more so during the tone) early in avoidance training, but increased again after avoidance was learned. The animals were apparently more relaxed after they learned to avoid. This experiment quantitatively supports our verbal description, as well as indicating that fear is an important element of avoidance.

Active avoidance is not always as neat as thus pictured. The rate of acquisition and final level of performance depend on the time interval between signal and shock; whether or not the CS ends when the avoidance response is made; the type of response required; shock intensity; age and sex of the animals; species; intensity of CS and UCS; the qualitative characteristics of the CS (e.g., light versus tone); and the location of the CS (animals run away from the CS sooner than they will run toward it.) There is also sometimes an "avoidance decrement," wherein performance gets worse if training is continued after the response has been well learned.

Leaving aside most of these detailed considerations (for these, see Bolles, 1967; Beecroft, 1967; Brush, 1971; Campbell & Church, 1969), the classic question has always been: *What keeps the animal avoiding?* Fear seems to be involved, but if the animal successfully avoids getting shocked, shouldn't it become less afraid? And if it is less afraid, shouldn't it stop avoiding? Yet, for example, if the shock has been strong enough, dogs may avoid almost indefinitely (Solomon & Wynne, 1954).

### Interpretations of Active Avoidance

The most popular interpretation has been two-process learning theory: a combination of classical conditioning of fear to the CS and instrumental conditioning of the escape and/or avoidance behavior (Skinner, 1938; Mowrer, 1960a, Rescorla & Solomon, 1967). A two-process theory seems to be demanded because single-process theories do not seem to be able to handle the data. Let us see why.

***Avoidance as Classical Conditioning.*** The classical aversive conditioning situation (classical "defense conditioning") had been used quite early by Bechterev (1913) and in the early 1900s was popular in this country. It was not uncommon to pair a CS with a shock to the finger of a human subject, using finger withdrawal as the conditioned response. This was exactly analogous to the leg flexion response used with dogs getting shock to the paw. It was observed, however, that dogs might learn the response better if the shock were *omitted* following the response. This would appear to be exactly opposite to expectations from conditioning theory, since the response ought to be stronger if the CS is continually reinforced by the UCS.

Brogden, Lipman, and Culler (1938) showed that simple classical conditioning could not account for avoidance. Using guinea pigs in a revolving cage, they presented a buzzer as CS to two groups. For the classical conditioning group, the buzzer was invariably followed by shock, which generally evoked running behavior. The avoidance conditioning group received shock only if it did *not* run when the buzzer sounded. Performance by the "classical" group reached a peak of about 50 percent responses to the CS after fourteen days of training whereas the avoidance group reached 100 percent in eight days. The results are shown in Figure 9-1.

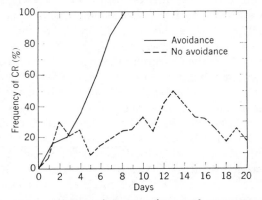

**Figure 9.1** *Learning curves showing the performance of animals for whom the response to the CS was not followed by shock (avoidance) and those for whom the CS was always followed by shock (no avoidance). These results show that avoidance learning is not just classical conditioning. (From Brogden, W. J., Culler, H. and Lipman, E. A. "The role of incentive in conditioning and learning." American Journal of Psychology, 1938, 51, p. 110. Reprinted by permission of The University of Illinois Press.)*

Sheffield (1948), also reflecting on the inferior performance of classically conditioned animals in this situation, observed that shock sometimes came on while the animals were already moving and caused the animals to *stop moving.* With the classical conditioning procedure, performance is then poorer because the shock makes the animals move on some trials and inhibits them on others. At best, the animal is in conflict about what it ought to do when the CS comes on.

Finally, Mowrer and Lamoreaux (1946) showed that animals could learn one response to escape shock and a quite different response to avoid shock. Since the avoidance response is not necessarily the same as the unconditioned response to shock, the classical conditioning interpretation is effectively killed.

***Avoidance as Instrumental Conditioning.*** The difficulty with a simple instrumental conditioning explanation for avoidance is readily seen: If the animal is not shocked, what is the reinforcement for running? It certainly is not shock reduction. If it is some other kind of reinforcement, where does that reinforcement come from? If fear reduction is the reinforcement, we have to postulate fear learning as well as instrumental response learning. This again leaves us with the two-process interpretation.

**Two-Process Interpretation of Avoidance.** According to two-process theory, the animal first learns to become afraid of the buzzer through classical conditioning (buzzer paired with shock). At the same time, the animal learns to escape from shock, with shock reduction as reinforcement. The animal next transfers the running response from the shock stimulus to the fear stimulus. This transfer occurs because the shock aroused both fear and pain in earlier training, and the fear also became a stimulus for running. The animal is reinforced on successful avoidance trials because the fear-arousing buzzer is turned off when the avoidance response is made. The fear in this case functions both as a drive and as a cue, and fear reduction is the reinforcer.

This formulation raises many questions. For example, does avoidance learning really require fear and fear reduction? Is the termination of the CS reinforcing, or is it avoidance of the UCS? Is the CS necessary at all? If fear is involved, does it function as a cue, a drive, or both?

### The Role of Fear in Avoidance Conditioning

**A Physiological Consideration: Sympathectomy.** One way to manipulate fear is to cut that part of the nervous system considered most important for fear, the sympathetic portion of the autonomic nervous system (Solomon & Wynne, 1950). If this is done prior to avoidance training, there is poorer acquisition of the avoidance response. This would indicate that the sympathetic nervous system (and by inference, fear) is important. On the other hand, if the cuts are made after the animal has already learned the response, there is no drop in performance level. The sympathetic system then seems important for the acquisition but not for the maintenance of avoidance responses once learned. After the behavior is well learned, the CS may only be a cue to make the response. What, then, reinforces the response during successful avoidance?

Solomon and Wynne (1954) proposed the concept of *anxiety conservation* to account for the fact that successful avoidances might be made for hundreds of consecutive trials, as when very high shock levels are used with dogs. According to this concept, just a little bit of fear is aroused by the CS, and the avoidance response is made so quickly that the fear does not have time to come forth completely and hence is not rapidly extinguished. The avoidance response actually helps to keep the fear aroused by the CS from extinguishing.

**Fear as Pavlovian Conditioned Excitation.** A highly productive attack on the role of fear in avoidance has been a revival of the concepts of

Pavlovian conditioned inhibition and excitation (Rescorla & Solomon, 1967). A CS signalling the onset of shock will increase the rate of avoidance responses even though it has never been specifically paired with these responses. The CS presumably increases fear. Conversely, a signal that indicates that no shock is forthcoming inhibits fear and reduces the rate of avoidance responding.

*Curare Experiments.* Another approach is to do fear conditioning when no overt response is possible and then to see if this fear will facilitate avoidance responding. A dog is trained with a light as the CS in a standard two-way shuttle situation. Then, under curare (a drug supposed to completely paralyze the skeletal muscles, but not affect sensory inputs) the dog is given differential classical conditioning. One tone (CS+) precedes shock, and a second tone (CS−) precedes nonshock. The animal, of course, makes no responses to either of the tones or the shock. When the dog recovers from the curare, it is tested for avoidance, but the tones are used as CSs instead of the light. The animals make avoidance responses to CS+, just as they did to the light in original avoidance training, but they do not respond to CS− (A. H. Black, Carlson, & Solomon, 1962; Solomon & Turner, 1962; Leaf, 1964). Since the avoidance response had never been directly paired with CS+, the reasonable conclusion is that fear conditioned to CS+ is serving as a mediator to arouse the avoidance response.

*The Kamin Effect.* Kamin (1957) reported the surprising result that performance of an incompletely learned avoidance response was poorer one hour after training than 24 hours after training. The subjects (rats) were given twenty-five trials of avoidance training and then six different subgroups received twenty-five retraining trials at 0, .5, 1, 6, or 24 hours or nineteen days later. Figure 9-2 shows the outcome. Avoidance responses during retraining decreased between 0 and 1 hour delay, then increased thereafter. This effect has been observed many times and the obvious question is "Why?" Simple forgetting would not account for poor performance at 1 hour, because performance improves later without further training.

Brush, Myer, and Palmer (1963) suggested there might be a "parasympathetic overreaction" following the strong sympathetic nervous system responses during conditioning. This overreaction, coming closely after training, would interfere with the sympathetic activity necessary for avoidance. Brush (1971) suggested that fear aroused during the avoidance trials would involve release of adrenalcorticotrophic hormone (ACTH), which stimulates the adrenal cortex to release adrenaline. By a negative feedback mechanism, the adrenaline temporarily inhibits further release of ACTH by the pituitary gland. As the adrenaline-produced inhibition wears off, there would again be a greater release of ACTH, and the animal would

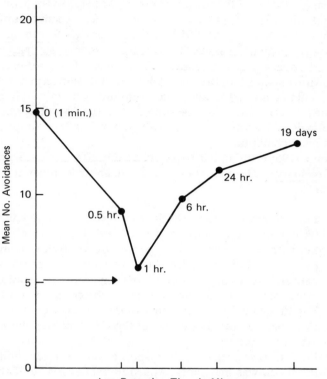

**Figure 9.2** *Mean number of avoidances during relearning as a function of retention interval. Retention interval is plotted on a log scale. The arrow from the ordinate represents the grand mean number of avoidances during original learning. (From Kamin, 1957, p. 458. Copyright © 1957 by the American Psychological Association. Reprinted by permission.)*

respond better in the avoidance situation. This would result in the kind of data shown in Figure 9-2. The argument is supported by the fact that if a number of shocks are given just prior to testing at the 1-hour delay, performance is as good as at earlier or later periods. This could be due to the extra shocks overriding the pituitary inhibition. Other interpretations are also discussed by Brush (1971).

### What is the Role of the CS in Avoidance?

***Role of CS Termination.*** As Bolles (1967) points out, the major emphasis on the CS in avoidance has *not* been its cue function but has been the presumed reinforcement that occurs when the CS terminates. Some theorists argue that the CS arouses fear (e.g., Miller, 1951b; Mowrer, 1947; 1960a) and others that the CS is just a conditioned aversive stimulus (e.g., Dinsmoor, 1954; Schoenfeld, 1950). In either case, CS termination often depends on the animal's making the avoidance response, so that CS termination at least appears to be reinforcing. There has, of course, been evidence for this. Mowrer and Lamoreaux (1946) showed that terminating the CS when the animal made the avoidance response was more effective than having the CS terminate either before or after the response. On the other hand, animals did learn under the two nonoptimal conditions, and this also requires explanation.

Kamin (1956) attempted to separate the effects of CS termination and US avoidance. He used four groups of animals under the following conditions.

1. For a *Normal* subject, avoidance was followed immediately by CS termination, and no shock was delivered for that trial.
2. For a *Terminate-CS* subject, a response was followed immediately by termination of the CS, but five seconds later the shock was delivered to whatever side of the apparatus the subject was in. The shock was terminated when the subject ran to the other side.
3. For an *Avoid-US* subject, an avoidance response caused the shock to be omitted for that trial, but the CS continued until 5 seconds after the response.
4. For a *Classical* subject, the response had no effect on the CS, and the shock was inevitably applied to whatever side of the box the subject was in. The shock was always terminated by the subject's running to the other side.

The results are summarized in Figure 9-3. Very clearly the Normal group was superior to the other three and the Classical group was inferior. The Terminate-CS and Avoid-US groups were virtually identical. Kamin then raises two questions: (1) Why don't the Terminate-CS rats make as many conditioned responses as the Normals? and (2) Why do the Avoid-US rats make more responses than the Classicals? The first question is answered fairly simply. The Terminate-CS rats are always punished for making the avoidance response. For example, if the animal responds in the first three seconds of the five-second CS-UCS interval, it will inevitably get shocked two seconds later. It is not difficult to see that this might tend to depress avoidance responding.

The answer to the second question, Kamin suggests, is that the Avoid-US rats *do* have a *delayed* termination of the CS. If a rat responded to the CS within three seconds, the termination of the five-second CS would follow only two seconds later. With such a short delay, CS termination

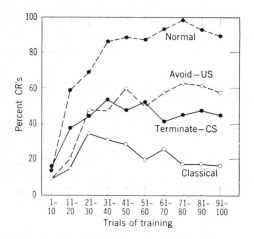

**Figure 9.3** *Data indicating that both the termination of the CS and avoidance of the UCS are important for avoidance learning. (From Kamin 1956, p. 422. Copyright © 1956 by the American Psychological Association. Reprinted by permission.)*

could still reinforce learning. In summary, the Kamin experiment suggests that CS termination is important, but other factors are involved.

*The Avoidance CS as a Discriminative Stimulus.* Herrnstein (1969) argued that neither an explicit external CS like a buzzer nor a response-feedback CS is necessary for avoidance learning. He said it is sufficient that there just be a reduction in the overall frequency of shock and that the only relevant function of the CS is that it be a cue for successful responding. Just as in appetitive operant conditioning a discriminative stimulus is said to *set the occasion* for reinforcement, in avoidance situations the CS does the same. It is not fear aroused by CS onset, nor fear reduction by its termination that is crucial. The crucial factor is that the instrumental response reduces the total amount of shock and that responding is *only* reinforced in the presence of the CS. The difficulty with two-factor theory, suggests Herrnstein, is that it has become irrefutable. There is no situation for which it cannot hypothesize after the fact that there was some internal or external stimulus which served as a CS to arouse fear.

*Nondiscriminated Avoidance.* Can there be avoidance learning without a CS? The answer is yes, if we are referring to external stimuli as CSs. Sidman (1966) summarizes much of the literature involving the avoidance procedure that bears his name. The Sidman procedure is used in free-operant situations, as follows. By means of automatic equipment, an animal is given a series of strong shocks, but they are too brief to be escaped (e.g., .5 second). The shocks are programmed according to two different time schedules, but no outside stimulus warns the animal that shock is coming.

If the animal does not press the lever the shocks will automatically occur at intervals of, say, 20 seconds. This interval is called the *shock-shock interval* (SS interval). Whenever the animal presses the lever, however, the shock is *postponed* for a fixed amount of time, say 20 seconds again. This is called the *response-shock interval* (RS interval). If the animal presses the lever at least once every 20 seconds, it can postpone the shocks indefinitely The SS and RS intervals can be set at any values the experimenter desires. If the RS interval is much longer than the SS interval, the animal responds frequently, but if the RS interval is much *shorter* than the SS interval, animals respond less often.

If the SS and RS intervals are the same length, response acquisition is highly variable from one animal to the next. Figure 9-4 shows the perform- ance of one "typical" learner and one "fast" learner. Note that these sessions are 8 and 6 *hours* long, respectively, and each blip represents a shock. Even the fast learner gets many more shocks than is typical for the shuttle box situations (see Meyer, Cho, & Wesemann, 1960, for comment).

We might expect that a subject would learn to wait out almost all his 20 seconds and then make an efficient, well-timed press to postpone the shock for another 20 seconds. The time between responses is more nearly random, however, being less than 10 seconds as often as more than 10 seconds. An animal will learn to "pile up" responses toward the end of the RS interval with special training, however. Thus, if shock is only postponed when the animal waits until the last 10 seconds of a 60-second RS interval to respond, it will wait out the interval. Or, if the animal is initially trained with an external cue signalling the shock, it will learn to wait. It will also then respond more near the end of the interval if the cue is omitted.

Animals in the Sidman situation seem to do whatever is required to reduce the *density* of the shock (total amount of shock per unit time). Thus, if the RS interval is only about half the length of the SS interval, or less, the animal responds only infrequently. It gets less shock by just sitting there than by responding. Obviously, if the animal pressed the lever often enough, it could avoid shock completely with a short RS interval, but there seems to be some kind of playoff between the amount of work the animal will do and the shock it will take.

Since there is no external CS in the Sidman situation, the role of the CS in avoidance is questioned. Sidman (1962) suggests that the reinforcing event in avoidance is the reduction in shock density, and the CS provides no reinforcement. Anger (1963), however, proposed that the CS for making

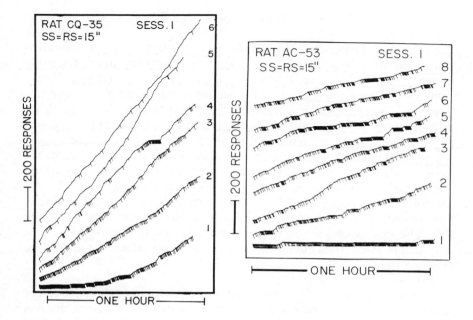

**Figure 9.4** *Cumulative records for two rats in their first sessions of Sidman avoidance learning, about six and eight hours long respectively. To condense the figures the records have been cut into segments of approximately one hour each, and are numbered in temporal order. The oblique "pips" on the record indicate shocks. Rat CQ-35 learned more rapidly than did AC-53, but CQ-35 had a few minutes in the fourth hour when it got a large number of shocks. (From Sidman, 1966, p. 451 and 453.)*

a response is some internal "stimulus trace" from the previous avoidance response. Thus the animal is never shocked immediately after responding. As time passes, however, the trace changes, and this changed trace becomes a CS for responding. Mowrer (1960a) made virtually the same interpretation, but talked about the "trace" as being fear. Fear builds up between responses, stimulates responses, and then reinforces responses by its reduction when they occur. A variety of evidence (e.g., the Rescorla-LoLordo- research) suggests that fear is involved in the Sidman situation. Occasional "free" shocks (independent of responding or the RS and SS intervals) also increase the Sidman avoidance rate. If these speculations have any validity, we may then question whether the Sidman situation involves any new *principles* beyond those involved for the typical shuttle box avoidance with a CS. And this was Herrnstein's objection to two-process theory: It is "saved" in the Sidman situation by postulating some unseen, internal CS to arouse fear.

### Some Alternative Accounts of Avoidance Learning

*Denny's Relaxation Hypothesis.* Denny (1971) applied elicitation theory and the relaxation response to avoidance behavior in the following manner. A UCS, such as shock, or a CS previously paired with shock, comes to elicit an internal state that we can equate with fear. Once this "agitated" state is present, the removal or omission of either the shock or a CS results in relief and relaxation. The response which reinforces avoidance behavior, then, is the relaxation response that occurs in the "safe" period following the removal of the aversive stimuli. Denny's hypothesis rather neatly handles some data that are embarrassing to two-process theory. For example, avoidance conditioning can be learned with a trace CS, a CS which terminates *before* the shock occurs or the avoidance response is made. Fear reduction reinforcement from CS termination could hardly explain this. The explanation is simple for Denny, however, because his critical reinforcing event (relaxation) always occurs long after the avoidance response anyway.

*Species-Specific Defense Reactions (SSDRs).* Bolles (1970, 1971) has recently taken a different perspective on the avoidance problem, arguing that there are important species-specific differences to be taken into account.[1] Each species, he argues, has its own species-specific defense reactions (SSDRs). For some animals, the normal SSDR is to freeze (e.g., the opossum). For others, it is to run; for yet others, it is to become very aggressive. The rat does all three of these things at one time or another. Bolles then says (1970, p. 33), "What keeps animals alive in the wild is that they have very effective *innate* defense reactions which occur when they encounter any kind of new or sudden stimulus. . . . It is not necessary that the stimulus even be paired with shock, or pain, or some other unconditioned stimulus. The mouse does not scamper away from the owl because it has learned to escape the painful claws of the enemy; it scampers away from anything happening in its environment." The mouse mind would indeed boggle at the thought of what would happen to mice if it took every mouse forty trials to learn how to avoid getting caught by an owl.

Bolles argues, then, that shock avoidance is more important than CS termination if the required response is the animal's normal SSDR. Because the animal will normally make this response to the shock anyway, the response is readily conditioned to other stimuli. If the response is not an SSDR, but is arbitrarily selected by the experimenter, then learning is much slower. Thus, in the case of one-way avoidance learning, where the animal is always running away from the shock source, learning can occur in just

---

[1] Even among rats, there are dramatic differences between wild and domesticated animals. In particular, the wild rat is much more "neophobic"—fearful of novel stimuli (Richter, 1957; Barnett, 1958).

one trial. If the arbitrary response of lever pressing is required, then learning is much slower. Bolles has even argued that animals do not really learn to avoid at all with lever pressing, but instead learn to hover over the lever, and when the CS occurs they give a kind of reflexive response that "accidentally" moves the lever. Other investigators have demonstrated that lever pressing is a learnable avoidance response, however. Giulian and Schmaltz (1973), for example, had rats lever press to obtain food, so it was a familiar response to them. The animals then readily learned to press the lever as an avoidance response.

In the case of arbitrary response requirements (including two-way avoidance, in which the animal has to return to the place where it has just been shocked), Bolles argues that CS termination takes on more importance. But what does it do? One possibility is that it serves as a feedback signal to inform the animal that it has actually made the correct response. If a signal entirely different from CS termination is arbitrarily paired with the avoidance response, learning is better than if no signal at all is presented (see Bolles, 1970, p. 41). Another possibility is that CS termination may become a secondary reinforcer, having frequently been paired with shock termination during escape learning prior to the onset of avoidance responses. Schoenfeld (1950) made virtually the same argument, suggesting that the proprioceptive stimuli from the avoidance response become secondary reinforcers by virtue of having been paired with shock termination. The animal continues to make the avoidance response because it is continually reinforced by the secondary reinforcing proprioceptive stimuli.

***Generality of Laws of Learning.*** Solomon and Brush (1956) pointed out that electric shock was almost the only UCS used in avoidance experiments and questioned whether different aversive stimuli might breed their own unique kinds of anticipatory reaction patterns. In other words, is avoidance learning as we usually study it in the laboratory a special kind of phenomenon? Psychologists have commonly argued that the virtue of using arbitrarily chosen stimuli and responses for learning experiments is that the results ought to be of more generality. Seligman (1970) proposes the opposite—that such laws may themselves be peculiar to arbitrary events. He outlines a series of learning experiments which run contrary to the notion that all stimuli or responses are equally associable.

Seligman's integrating concept is *preparedness.* Some stimuli are more "associable" in classical conditioning than are others, as indicated by the rapidity of conditioning, and some responses are more readily associated with some stimuli. Seligman sees preparedness as a continuum, with "prepared" at one extreme, "unprepared" in the middle, and "contraprepared" at the other extreme. One example of preparedness is SSDRs. An example of contrapreparedness would be the difficulty in getting a cat to lick itself as an avoidance response; this is just not a normal response to an aversive stimulus. We can speculate whether equivalent results in aversive conditioning or avoidance experiments would be obtained with shock, bad odors, cold air, or boredom. All of these are demonstrably aversive, but it is doubtful they would function the same way in avoidance situations. At least, it is not demonstrated that they do.

*Cognitive Interpretations of Avoidance.* Seligman and Johnston (1973) have proposed a cognitive theory of avoidance learning based on Irwin's (1971) theory of intentional behavior. The main points are as follows. At the peak of avoidance learning, the animal has acquired two expectancies: (1) If it responds in a given time after CS onset, it will *not* get shocked; and (2) if it does not respond within this given time, it *will* get shocked. The animal has a preference for no shock over shock and therefore makes the avoidance response. As long as the animal's expectancies are confirmed, it will continue to avoid. If the expectancies are not confirmed, it will stop avoiding. Since fear is also seen as a nonpreferred state, the animal will engage in behaviors that are expected to lead to nonfear.

A cognitive analysis of avoidance was also made by Osgood (1950) over twenty-five years ago, based on Tolman's theory. Osgood said the buzzer becomes a sign of shock, so that the animals do whatever is required to avoid shock. A problem for cognitive theories of this kind is why avoidance should ever decline. (Note that this is the opposite of the problem for reinforcement theories, which have to account for what keeps avoidance going.) Unless it actually fails to make the avoidance response, the animal has no way of finding out that shock will not follow the buzzer. Osgood simply assumed that the *demand* against shock declines with successful avoidance and the animal will sometimes fail to respond in time. When the animal does this, either (1) it will get shocked, its expectation of shock will be reconfirmed, and it will start avoiding again; or (2) it will not get shocked, in the case of extinction. A new expectation of nonshock will be established, then avoidance will cease.

### PASSIVE AVOIDANCE (PUNISHMENT)[2]

Punishment takes such varied guises as physical pain or its threat, social sanctions, isolation, and withdrawal of privileges. All of these are supposed to suppress "undesirable" behavior. Events that are supposed to be punishing are often ineffective, however. Supposed punishment sometimes increases the very behavior it is supposed to eliminate and sometimes suppresses behaviors indiscriminately. Neither of these is presumably what the punishing agent intends. When does punishment do what is intended?

[2]For excellent reviews, see Church (1963), Solomon (1964), Campbell and Church (1969), Fowler (1971), Azrin and Holz (1966), Mowrer (1960a), and Dunham (1971).

### Definition of Punishment

*Stimulus Definition.* We may define punishment as _the delivery of an aversive stimulus to an organism following the occurrence of some response._ The organism is expected to suppress the response as a means of avoiding punishment, hence Mowrer's (1960a) designation of punishment as *passive avoidance.* The animal avoids getting punished by not doing something. We need to know, however, whether the punishing stimulus is in fact aversive, by showing that it is escaped or avoided in some unrelated situation. Electric shock produces both escape and avoidance and is an effective punisher in the laboratory. Other aversive stimuli, such as loud noises and bright lights, are not so effective in suppressing behavior. In animal research, however, there is little research with stimuli other than shock.

*Response Definition.* Punishment may be defined as _delivery of a stimulus that suppresses behavior preceding it, whether or not the stimulus is shown to be aversive._ This does not predict for us what stimuli will be punishers but has considerable practical utility. A response definition also helps us when a fixed stimulus suppresses one response but not another response: We simply say it was punishing in the one case but not the other. We would certainly be interested in why such selective suppression occurred, however. Such factors as amount of prior learning or the incentive to make the punished response would be relevant.

Such considerations show that it is not really simple to define a punishing stimulus, but hereafter, for the sake of clarity, we will assume a response definition unless otherwise indicated.[3]

### Suppressive Effects of Punishment

*Permanence of Suppression.* Any parent may well have noted that punishment may inhibit some behaviors only very temporarily. Initially, Thorndike (1913) argued that a response which was followed by an annoying (aversive) state of affairs was "stamped out," i.e., the punished response was permanently disconnected from the stimuli that aroused it. Thorndike (1932) later replaced this argument with the *alternative response*

---

[3]There is a World War II story to the effect that a noncooperative Trappist monk in occupied territory was "punished" by putting him into solitary confinement. This was, unknown to his captors, his ideal social condition. There are other kinds of complications. If a hungry animal eats to satiation, the food has suppressed eating. Is food then punishing? The answer would appear to be an obvious no, but experiments described by Hoebel (1969) make a qualified yes not unreasonable. Hoebel found that brain stimulation that was positively reinforcing for hungry animals was aversive to satiated ones. Maybe food *does* become aversive after a certain point, and this is what stops eating in the face of an unlimited food supply. Such extreme cases as stomach ache or nausea are certainly instances of this.

assumption. This is the idea that a punished response is less likely to occur because it has been replaced, at least for a while, by some other response that is more likely to occur. Since the punished response is not considered to have become "disconnected," it could well occur again. All contemporary explanations of punishment, says Dunham (1971), are variations of the alternative response theme. Under what conditions, then, is punishment more or less permanent?

*The Skinner-Estes Experiments.* One of the earliest reports of punishment of free-operant behavior in the laboratory was by Skinner (1938), who slapped the rat's paw when it touched the lever.[4] The slapped animals stopped responding for a while but did not actually extinguish any more rapidly than nonslapped animals. From this Skinner concluded that punishment was not really effective in the long run. This was followed by the more systematic experiments of Estes and Skinner (1941), again showing only a temporary suppression of bar pressing punished by electric shock. Much research now shows very enduring suppressive effects, but there are a number of important variables.

*Response-Contingent versus Stimulus-Contingent Punishment.* The term *response-contingent punishment* refers to the immediate presentation of an aversive stimulus following a response. The term *stimulus-contingent punishment,* more commonly called the *conditioned emotional response* (CER) *procedure,* refers to the presentation of an aversive stimulus following some specified signal rather than some specified response. (The CER is not technically punishment, then, but is included with punishment for obvious reasons.) Under either condition, in Estes' (1944) experiment rats showed equal suppression, suggesting that the mechanism for the two procedures was the same—a generalized emotional response which competes with lever pressing.

Hunt and Brady (1955), however, found important differences between the two procedures. After their rats were bar pressing well on a schedule of food reinforcement, some were unavoidably shocked following a clicking sound (CER procedure), but others were shocked only when they bar pressed during the clicking. Lever pressing *during* the clicking was almost completely suppressed in both groups, but the actual behaviors of the animals were very different. First, CER animals bar pressed less than response contingent animals when the clicker was *not* on, showing a generalized behavioral suppression. Second, CER animals showed overt signs of emo-

---

[4]There have been earlier experimental uses of punishment, going back at least to the beginning of this century (e.g., Yerkes and Dodson, 1908), with many intervening experiments before Skinner. These experiments were mainly discrete trial experiments, however, rather than free operant. The 1930s ushered in a new era of punishment research, dominated by the alternative response hypothesis and using operant conditioning techniques widely.

tionality during the clicking; they were less active and defecated frequently (which the other group never did). Third, the response contingent animals often made abortive attempts at bar pressing while the clicker was going, but the CER group did not. Finally, over ten extinction days with the clicker and no shock (the animals still getting food reinforcement), the CER animals showed very little recovery of bar pressing during the clicker, but the response group did. It was concluded that the CER procedure suppresses virtually all behaviors except "fear" responses to the CS, but the response contingent procedure eliminates only the specific punished response.

Church (1969) showed a greater suppression by response contingent shock than by noncontingent shock. Three groups of rats learned to bar press for food. One group then received a response contingent shock on an average of every two minutes, a second group received noncontingent shock equally often, and a third group was not shocked at all. The results are shown in Figure 9-5. The response measure, a *suppression ratio,* is calculated

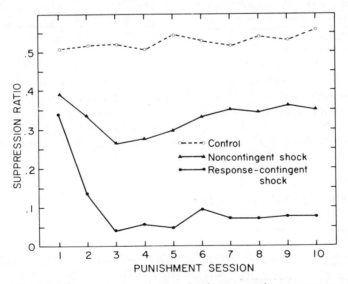

**Figure 9.5**  *Mean suppression ratio of subjects with response contingent shock (punishment) and noncontingent shock, and of an unpunished control group. (From Church, 1969, p. 134.)*

so that .50 means no suppression and .00 is complete suppression. The response contingent group is clearly more suppressed than either of the others. Azrin (1956) found greater response contingent suppression with key pecking by pigeons and Myer (1966) found it with mouse killing by rats. Shock consistently delivered even as much as 30 seconds after attacking a mouse was more suppressive than a shock given 1.5 seconds after a mouse was presented but regardless of whether the rat attacked. Lichtenstein (1950) reported similar results for feeding behavior of dogs.

### Two-Factor Theory of Punishment

Mowrer (1960a) argued that both active and passive avoidance could be explained by the fear mechanism. The distinction between the two, he said, is in *what* stimuli are conditioned to the primary aversive stimulus. In active avoidance, fear is conditioned to an *external* CS. In passive avoidance, *internal* (response-produced) stimuli are conditioned to the primary aversive stimulus. When the animal starts to make a previously punished response, the proprioceptive stimuli from the incipient response arouse fear, and the animal reduces the fear by making a different response. The alternative response is reinforced by termination of the fear-arousing proprioceptive stimuli from the incipient punished response. In the case of the CER procedure, *any* response the animal makes is liable to be followed by shock, and there is the potential for much greater generalized suppression of responses. The animal is in effect helpless to do anything that will prevent shock or remove the CS.

There is now considerable neurophysiological evidence to suggest that the differences between active and passive avoidance are more profound than just variations in the locus of the CS. For example, some brain lesions interfere with active avoidance and not passive, whereas other lesions have just the opposite effect. This evidence has been reviewed by Olton (1973). Mowrer's analysis is still cogent, however, and may well be at least partly correct.

## STIMULUS FACTORS IN PUNISHMENT

### Delay of Punishment

As with rewards, the longer the delay between response and punishment, the less effective it is. Camp, Raymond, and Church (1967) trained rats to lever press for food, and in punishment tests different groups had delays of punishment ranging from 0 to 30 seconds. The results are shown in Figure 9-6. A noncontingent punishment group responded less than a nonpunished control, but even more than the group with a 30-second delay.

Myer and Ricci (1968) studied goldfish, measuring the *threshold* voltages necessary to produce suppression at different delays. The results are of special interest because they showed measurable suppression threshold increments over short delays (0 to 20 seconds) whereas the usual delay procedure with fixed levels of shock is generally insensitive among short delays (Myer, 1971).

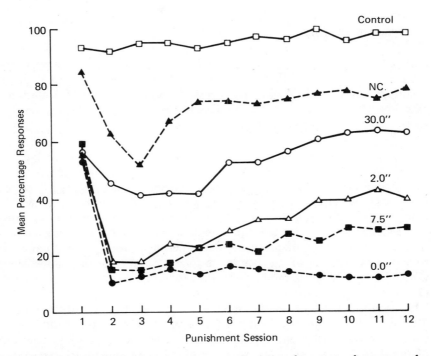

**Figure 9.6** *Mean percentage of responses as a function of sessions for groups with .0, 2.0, 7.5, and 30.0 seconds delay of punishment, noncontingent shock, and unpunished control group. (Failure to press the lever within 10 seconds of stimulus onset was defined as nonresponse.) (From Camp, Raymond, and Church, 1967, p. 121. Copyright © 1967 by the American Psychological Association. Reprinted by permission.)*

Response contingent punishment, then, is more effective than either delayed punishment or noncontingent punishment. Among humans, what is *meant* to be response contingent punishment often ends up being either noncontingent or stimulus contingent. For example, instead of punishing the child immediately for some indiscretion, the mother may wait until the father comes home to have him punish the child. In this case, the punishment is stimulus contingent, the father being the CS. The result may be generalized fear of (and hostility toward) the father, but little real suppression of the undesired behavior. Some children may become reluctant to do anything potentially punishable. Punishment should be clearly associated with the undesirable behavior. With older children or adults, this may be accomplished over long delays by verbal mediation, e.g., discussing the behavior to be punished. Even adults may not be as strongly influenced by such delayed punishment, however.

### Stimulus Intensity

The more intense the aversive stimulus, the greater its suppressive effect (Azrin & Holz, 1966). If the punishing stimulus is intense enough, the suppression may be well-nigh irreversible. Masserman (1943) found that cats which had received strong punishment for eating completely refused to eat thereafter in the experimental chamber.

### Adaptation to the Punishing Stimulus

Miller (1960) found that if animals were gradually adapted to shock the suppressive effect was considerably weakened. Furthermore, this weakening was not due to simple sensory adaptation, because animals exposed to the same shock outside the experimental apparatus did not show adaptation effects within the apparatus. In one experiment, four groups of animals were trained to run down an alleyway to food. Group 1 was then immediately shifted to 400-volt shock punishment when food in the goal box was touched. Group 2 had shock gradually increasing to 400 volts. Group 3 had gradually increasing shock in a distinctive apparatus outside the alley, fifteen minutes after each day's running. Group 4 had a shock of 400 volts suddenly introduced after thirty-eight days of training. The results are summarized in Figure 9-7. Group 2 subjects, with gradually increasing shock, ran more slowly as shock intensity increased but did not show the dramatic drop found with the other three groups. Group 2 subjects may not have been as disrupted, because they were the only ones with opportunity for learning something to do about the shock (see later section on learned helplessness).

### Punishment as a Discriminative Stimulus

A punishing stimulus ought to have some of the properties of stimuli in general, one of which is to serve as a cue. It is then conceivable that animals would actually respond *more* when punished if the punishment signalled a coming reward. Holz and Azrin (1961) found precisely this. They trained pigeons to peck steadily at a disc for food. The birds were given some daily sessions with both food and punishment (shock) and some sessions with neither. Since pecking was only reinforced when there was punishment, the punishment could become a discriminative stimulus. The animals responded more during punishment sessions, but this result is ambiguous because that is also when they were fed. In extinction, however, when there was no food, the animals also responded more if they were punished. Punishment can thus facilitate the very behavior it is supposed to suppress, as with a man who only knows he is doing a good job if people complain to him about it.

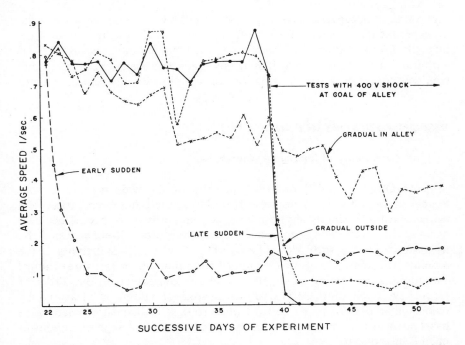

**Figure 9.7** *How speed of approach in a conflict situation is affected by following treatments: Early Sudden group given 400-Volt test shocks at goal after 21 days of approach training; Late Sudden group given similar test shocks after 38 days of approach training; Gradual in Alley group habituated to series of increasingly strong shocks at goal before test shocks; Gradual Outside group habituated to similar series of shocks in distinctive box outside of alley. Each point is average of the two trials given each day, but on the day shock is suddenly introduced producing a sharp drop, each trial is plotted separately. (From Miller, 1960, p. 144. Copyright © 1960 by the American Psychological Association. Reprinted by permission.)*

### A Secondary Reinforcing Function of Punishment

If punishment precedes food, the punishment could become a secondary reinforcer. Muenzinger (1934) found that the rat's performance in a T-maze was *facilitated* by mild shock as much when the shock followed correct (food-rewarded) responses as when it followed incorrect responses. Muenzinger suggested that the shock alerted the animal to pay more attention to the two alleys. In a later experiment, Muenzinger and Fletcher (1937) forced the animals to pay attention by requiring them to jump a gap in the floor between the arm and goal box of the maze. This also facilitated performance, supporting Muenzinger's attention hypothesis. Fowler (1971) reports a series of experiments on shock for correct responses and concludes that with difficult discriminations such shock may facilitate learning because it is an additional cue to the animal that it has made the correct response. This would be equivalent to an information concept of secondary reinforcement.

## RESPONSE FACTORS IN PUNISHMENT

### The Availability of Response Alternatives

As Dunham (1971) observes, in spite of the wide acceptance and appeal of the alternative response hypothesis, there has been little direct evidence for it. It simply has been inferred that punished responses declined because they were being replaced by other responses. Dunham tested the hypothesis directly with Mongolian gerbils. Given the opportunity, these animals will spend a high proportion of their time doing just three things: shredding paper, eating food pellets, and drinking water, in that order of frequency. Each of these is easily measured (shredding is measured by recording amount of paper pulled from a roll). It is then easy to determine baseline measures for each response and see how these change when punishment is introduced.

Dunham suggests two "behavioral rules" for predicting what the animal will do if shock is introduced. First, the response most closely associated with shock will decrease below its normal baseline (the punishment effect). Second, the response most frequently associated with the absence of shock will increase above its baseline (avoidance). Dunham then showed that punishment does suppress the punished response (any one of the three), but that only one of the other two alternatives increased above baseline. He took this as evidence for Rule 2: The response that increased was an avoidance response.[5]

### Nature of the Response Elicited

The unconditioned response elicited by the punishing stimulus is very important. If the animal is punished when running, the unconditioned response may be to stop. If it is punished when not running, the animal may run. In specific instances, the punishment may facilitate the ongoing response because the response evoked by punishment is similar to the ongoing response.

Different shock intensities evoke different kinds of responses. The rat's response to low-level shock is predominantly a *flinch* reaction. At

---

[5]Also involved was a "grid-biting" response, peculiar to situations where animals are shocked through a grid floor. We have omitted this in discussing Dunham's research.

higher levels, there is an increasing proportion of *jump* reactions; with further increases, *prancing* and *running* around are dominant. Shock intensity can thus be an important variable because different responses are evoked at different intensities. The exact role of a given response would be determined by the specifics of the experimental situation.

Gwinn (1949) found that animals in a circular maze ran faster if given inescapable shock at various points in the maze. Fowler (1963) found a bimodal distribution of running times for animals punished at the entrance to the goal box at the end of a straight runway. As shock level increased, fast-running animals ran faster, and slow-running animals ran slower. Fowler and Miller (1963) then showed that animals that had their *hind paws* shocked just as they entered the goal box (thereby facilitating forward movement) ran *faster* with high shock levels. Animals that had their *forepaws* shocked ran *slower*. Thus, it was not shock per se which determined running speed, but the response elicited by the shock.

The elicited responses are also important in determining the alternative to the punished response because the elicited responses may be more or less easily reinforced by escape from punishment. It is no accident that Mowrer and Lamareaux (1946) used running and jumping from the grid as escape and avoidance responses in their classic demonstration that the unconditioned response to shock is not necessarily the avoidance response. Either running or jumping is likely to occur and is readily reinforced.

## FURTHER PUNISHMENT PHENOMENA

### Self-Punitive Behavior: Masochism in Rats and Humans

Mowrer (1947) described what has been termed *vicious cycle behavior*. People will persistently do things that result in their own punishment (e.g., brag about themselves, insult friends, etc.). Mowrer's interpretation was that the behavior was prompted by anxiety and was temporarily reinforced by anxiety reduction. A person anxious about his self-esteem, for example, might brag about himself and temporarily reduce his anxiety. Others, however, disliking his behavior, would "put him down" even more, further increasing his anxiety and leading to further bragging.[6]

Masochism in rats is studied by shocking them just before they enter a goal box, terminating the shock as they enter. The rat is punished for approaching the goal box but is then immediately reinforced by shock termination and food. In extinction, without food, the animals run faster and longer if still shocked. The term *masochism* is applied because the animals persistently engage in self-punitive behavior when it is no longer appropriate.

[6]The goal of contemporary behavior therapy would be to help the individual break out of this vicious cycle by reinforcing him for other behaviors that do not lead to further anxiety.

J. S. Brown (1969) identified some seventeen variables related to vicious cycle behavior, conditions that tend to convert otherwise punishing events into behavior facilitation. These variables are such things as the punisher being a discriminative stimulus; the general level of motivation of the animals; shock intensity; kind of responses evoked; amount of prior approach learning; and so on. Brown concludes that Mowrer's interpretation is still the best. Fear is conditioned to environmental cues when shock is presented during training. Fear of the starting box provides motivation for running. Running is reinforced by shock and fear reduction in the goal box, but at the same time fear is kept high by the repeated shocks the animal receives. The vicious cycle continues.

### Learned Helplessness

It is a common observation that some people are at a loss to do anything in a new situation, appearing helpless and anxious. What kind of history might produce such an unwillingness to act? Mowrer and Viek (1948) described what they called *fear from a sense of helplessness*. In their experiment, a tone preceded an inevitable shock. The experimental animals could turn off the shock by jumping from the grid. Yoked-control animals received the same shocks and tones but had no control over the shock. The responses of the control group were then shown to be more suppressed when the tone was used as a punishing stimulus than were those of the experimental animals. Mowrer and Viek's argument was that an uncontrollable punishing stimulus arouses more fear than a controllable one.

More recently, Overmier and Seligman (1967) and Seligman and Maier (1967) found that prior exposure to inescapable shocks greatly interfered with later escape and avoidance learning. Dogs were first shocked while in a harness, with no escape possible. In the shuttle box, later, the dogs would just sit and take the shocks, not even learning to escape, much less avoid. Figure 9-8 shows the escape latencies for inescapably shocked and for completely naive animals. Two-thirds of eighty-two dogs given inescapable shock did not learn escape responses in the shuttle box, as compared to only 6 percent of experimentally naive animals. Maier et al. reject, on both logical and empirical grounds, a number of alternative interpretations (e.g., adaptation to shock, extreme sensitization to shock, competing responses, and emotional exhaustion), in favor of the *learned helplessness hypothesis.*

This hypothesis says that when the animal is given inescapable shocks it learns that no response can alleviate the shock. The animal then goes into the avoidance situation having learned that responding is useless and does not even attempt to escape shock. The subject's lack of control over shock while in the harness is the determinant of helplessness, not the shock per se. Seligman and Maier (1967) demonstrated this by showing that animals that

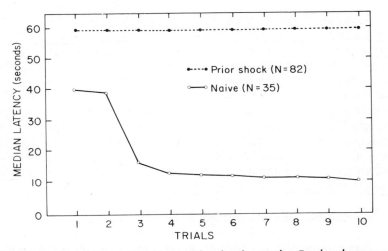

**Figure 9.8** *The effects of inescapable shocks in the Pavlov harness on escape responding in the shuttle box. This figure shows that there is rapid escape learning by 35 naive dogs that received no shocks in the harness. In contrast, the median for 82 dogs that received inescapable shocks in the harness, prior to escape training in the shuttle box, shows failure to escape shock. The arbitrary failure criterion was 50 seconds a shock (a latency of 60 seconds after onset of the S+). (From Maier, Seligman, and Solomon, 1969, p. 321.)*

could turn off shock while in the harness and animals that were not shocked in the harness were successful at escaping in the shuttle box. Only animals given prior inescapable shocks failed to learn escape.

*Immunization Against Helplessness.* Learned helplessness with dogs is such a close analogue to many human situations that it is worthwhile to spell out the implications a little further. Many authors have talked about the "helplessness" and "resignation" of the poor, minority groups, neurotics, and school children. A common element among these groups, most of whom we would not consider "sick," is that many of the members of each group have received relatively few rewards during their lives and hence do not anticipate much in the way of incentives. Consequently, they may fail to respond at times when they could be effective had they not learned to "not respond." One could potentially deal with such problems by giving *success training.* Such training is in part, at least, one of the goals of operant conditioning approaches to therapy: to reinforce the individual for doing things he did not previously do, to "shape" his behavior. This same kind of problem comes up in Chapter Thirteen, where we discuss achievement motivation.

***Stress and Sudden Death.*** Richter (1957) reported that he could produce a rapid death in wild rats simply by holding them immobile in his hand (a procedure not recommended for novice experimenters). The effect was ameliorated if he allowed them to escape from his hand a number of times before immobilizing them. Similarly, rats previously allowed to escape from a water tank swam for hours without drowning, whereas their naive counterparts drowned within minutes. Similar processes seemed to operate in World War II German concentration camps. Some new prisoners, who apparently could be identified by "oldtimers" almost immediately upon arrival at the camp, seemed to have no "hope" and survived only a short time. Others could make it for years (Bettelheim, 1960). Something about "hope," based on prior learning, seems to be important.

### Time Out from Positive Reinforcement as Punishment

A punishment widely used by parents and teachers is time out (TO) from positive reinforcement. Telling a child "Go sit in the corner," "You can't go to the movies," or "Go to bed," and solitary confinement are all examples. Within the behavior modification framework derived from operant conditioning, the use of TO is recommended rather than corporal punishment. This preference seems to be based partly on the belief that corporal punishment is ineffective (which we have already seen is not necessarily correct) and partly on ethical grounds (especially in school situations).[7]

Much of the theoretical analysis of TO is more concerned with how it operates than with its effectiveness. Two reviews have focused on the question of TO as an aversive event (Coughlin, 1972; Leitenberg, 1965). A typical experimental procedure is as follows. Pigeons are reinforced for pecking one disk, but periodically the whole apparatus is turned off for a while (TO) unless the pigeon pecks a second key with some regularity. The animals do peck regularly on the second key, as if avoiding the TO the way they might avoid shock. This interpretation is confounded, however, by the fact that if TO is avoided there is a greater total amount of positive reinforcement, and this might account for the pigeon's pecking the second key.

To determine if TO is an aversive event, we must turn to such procedures as those which show that shock is an aversive event, such as punishment, the CER procedure, or escape learning. Coughlin (1972) concludes

---

[7]The ethics are not really all that clear, however. For example, if a child misbehaved and was not allowed to go on the annual class picnic as a result, it is not hard to conceive of this as a much more "cruel" punishment than a swat or two on the bottom. Furthermore, one can argue that much of the effect of corporal punishment is in its information value rather than pain per se. Children happily take a lot of banging around in the spirit of play, but let a slap on the wrist become punishment and the tears flow. The slap tells the child something, but probably does not hurt. We are not advocating extreme use of corporal punishment, just pointing out that if used judiciously it may not be as bad as reputed.

that the evidence from these kinds of procedures, taken as a whole, does indicate that TO is aversive except in the CER situation. However, TO may not be a very powerful aversive event. For example, Baer (1962) reduced the incidence of thumbsucking in children by stopping a cartoon movie they were watching whenever the thumb entered the mouth. When the cartoon was over, however, the amount of thumbsucking immediately shot up to its previous level. In such a situation, it may also be that the movie serves as a discriminative stimulus to tell the child when he will be punished. If the movie is over, there can be no further TO.

## HUMAN APPLICATIONS OF PUNISHMENT

### The Azrin-Holz Rules for Punishment

On the basis of the kinds of evidence we have discussed, as well as considerably more literature, it is possible to make some specific statements about the effective use of punishment (Azrin & Holz, 1966; R. J. Johnson, 1972). The following is an abridgment of the "Azrin-Holz rules."

1. *No "unauthorized" escape from the punishing stimulus should be permitted.* If the child has been set off by himself for misbehaving, he should be allowed back if he is quiet, not if he throws a tantrum.
2. *The undesirable behavior should be consistently punished.* Hopefully, every occurrence of the response to be suppressed should be punished and certainly never rewarded.
3. *Punishment should be delivered as quickly as possible after the undesired behavior occurs.*
4. *Extended periods of punishment should be avoided.* Extended punishment, e.g., time out from activities, may result in greater opportunity for unauthorized "escape" or the possibility of rewards occurring during the punishment. A child may find activities that are much more rewarding than the punishment is punishing.
5. *The punishing stimulus should not be associated with a rewarding one.* Such punishment may come to signal reward and the punished behavior may increase.
6. *The motivation to make the punished response should be reduced as much as possible.* If an overly talkative child in a classroom is removed to a different part of the room, away from his best friends, there may be less motivation to talk.
7. *There should be no positive reinforcement of the punished response.*
8. *An alternative to the punished response should be made available.* It is more difficult to suppress an undesired response if there is no alternative to that response. A child may become less of a nuisance on a rainy day if given something fun to do.

9. *If there is no feasible alternative response in the present situation, then the individual could have access to reinforcement in some other situation.* It may be most profitable, for example, to simply put a child into a different classroom where there is less motivation to make a punished response and hence greater opportunity for rewarding other responses.

### Potential Problems in the Use of Punishment

*1. Making Sure That the Punishment is Really Punishing.* Punishment is supposed to reduce the frequency of some undesirable behavior. If it does not, there are several possible reasons, including (1) poor delivery time and (2) counteracting positive reinforcers for the punished behavior. It is also possible, however, that the method of punishment is not really punishing to the particular individual in the particular situation. A slight word of discouragement may stop one child from some activity but be totally ineffective with another. One may have to work at finding what is punishing for a particular individual. What the person delivering the "punishment" thinks ought to be a punishing stimulus may not in fact be so.

*2. Generalizing Beyond the Immediate Punishing Situation.* A teacher in one classroom might be able to control the undesirable behavior of a child, but in another classroom that child may still do all the things he is not supposed to do. In the second classroom, the teacher may not punish the behavior and his friends may reward it (e.g., "acting the fool," talking, etc.). Children or adults can learn to discriminate between those situations in which a particular behavior is punished and those in which it is rewarded.

*3. Side Effects of Punishment.* Punishment may produce excessive emotionality or escape behavior. Carefully controlled response contingent punishment is both more effective and less disturbing than "stimulus contingent punishment." A good effect is that punishment may suppress undesirable behavior long enough for desirable behavior to occur and be rewarded. If a child spends all his time in class fooling around or talking, he has no time to do other things that are rewarded.

As an extreme example, Lovaas and Simmons (1969), working with self-mutilating mentally retarded children, found that electric shocks delivered whenever the child started to mutilate himself reduced the occurrence of mutilation and increased the occurrence of other (quickly rewarded) nonmutilative behavior. Furthermore, the precisely delivered shocks did not produce fear of the experimenter, nor did the children try to escape or avoid him. Self-mutilation (where children may literally bite hunks of flesh from their own bodies) is one of the few cases where the use of electric shock as a punisher clearly has benefits that offset potential emotional or behavioral risks. *We should strongly emphasize, however, that electric shock is not to be recommended as punishment.* First, the social sanctions against the use of powerful stimuli are generally reasonable. Secondly, in the hands of someone who does not really understand electricity *there is a clear physical danger.* The standard safeguards used in research are not known to everyone who might think of using shock. The neophyte behavior modifier should be warned of the danger of misused shock.

*4. Social Disruption.* Crying or other emotional outbursts following punishment may be so generally disruptive that the punishment is self-defeating; the effect can be worse than the behavior that prompted the punishment. The punishment might also arouse escape behavior on the part of the child so that, instead of suppressing behavior such as too much talking so that the child will read, the child may leave or not come back to school, or may sulk. Again, punishment has to be used with sensitivity and care, details that cannot be spelled out in advance for every situation.

In summary, there are a number of potential limitations on the use of punishment. We should also keep in mind that punishment is only one way to reduce undesirable behavior: Arranging situations so the undesirable behavior cannot readily occur, not rewarding it, and rewarding alternative behaviors are all useful approaches to the problem. In particular, we should be on the lookout for the unnoticed sources of reward for such behaviors and try to eliminate them.

## CONCLUSION

The notion that avoidance and punishment are opposite sides of the same coin, the former involving reinforcement for responding and the latter for not responding, does not seem to hold. Avoidance and punishment are affected by a myriad of variables, involving both the nature of the stimuli and the responses required. Fear does seem to be involved in avoidance learning, but the role of fear is no longer clearcut, and more cognitive interpretations now seem plausible—especially for long-term successful avoidance. Punishment can be a powerful deterrent to behavior but there are additional considerations. For example, if the punished behavior is inadvertently rewarded or if the punishment serves as a signal for reward, the "punished" behavior may actually increase in frequency. The effective use of punishment involves a fairly sophisticated understanding of many such factors.

chapter 10

# Consistency and Change

There are two seemingly opposed views of inconsistency and change as motivational variables. The first is that inconsistency is aversive, and consistency is desirable. The second is that monotony (consistency) is aversive, and stimulus change is desirable. These views, of course, are not necessarily entirely opposite and to some extent may represent different points on some dimension, as suggested by activation theory. For example, either extreme inconsistency or extreme monotony may be aversive, but some intermediate degree of inconsistency may be tolerable and even sought.

Either consistency or inconsistency is in the eye of the beholder. One person may readily detect in unfolding events a pattern that completely escapes someone else. Our concern, then, is with consistency as perceived by an individual. This is commonly called *cognitive consistency* and involves beliefs and thoughts as well as perception. (Perception, indeed, depends on our prior experience and beliefs.) As a general preliminary statement, we may say that inconsistency, or incongruity, exists when an event is perceived to be different from expectation. For example, a dog with wings would be incongruous only to a child who had already become familiarized with dogs of the normal variety. The present chapter is divided into two parts. In the first half, we consider theories and evidence related to the positive aspects of consistency. In the second half, we do the same for the positive aspects of stimulus variation and change.

## INCONGRUITY MODELS FOR MOTIVATION

### A Biological Model: Sokolov

A Russian physiologist, E. N. Sokolov (1960), proposed a theory of attention based on the fact that sensory inputs which normally arouse attention may *habituate* if presented frequently. For example, with repeated auditory stimulation by a tone of unvarying pitch, loudness, and duration, the response in the EEG declines. We have all experienced situations in which normally attention-getting stimuli, such as the noise of a large city, are unnoticed after a while. A sudden change in sound, even a silence, however, may immediately command our attention. Similarly, experimental subjects show an aroused EEG if just the pitch of the habituating tone is slightly changed.

At some level of the nervous system, there must be processing of such "unnoticed" stimulus inputs, however. Otherwise, we could not be strongly aroused by minor changes or cessation of stimulation. Sokolov's theory says that repetitious inputs are stored in the nervous system, and new inputs are each *compared* with the stored input. If input and storage are the same (and carrying no biologically important information), then attention is not aroused. If an input signal is suddenly different from those previously stored, however, there is arousal of the EEG and of behavior, as well as other physiological activity (see Figure 5-2). We also noted in Chapter Eight that strong fear can occur when something different from expectation occurs. Pavlov called such behavioral arousal the "orienting reflex." We "perk up" at a novel stimulus and are more prepared to cope with a threatening situation if necessary. Sokolov's theory and related evidence are important in the context of consistency and change because they demonstrate that incongruity produces arousal and indicate the conditions under which arousal occurs.

### An Individual Model: TOTE

G. A. Miller, Galanter, and Pribram (1960) applied the incongruity notion to events ranging from neurological to social. Their basic unit for analysis was the TOTE unit. TOTE is the acronym for TEST-OPERATE-TEST-EXIT. For example, suppose we want a nail hammered into a board and have some kind of *plan* of what we want. We look at the nail (TEST) and see that it is *not* in the board. There is thus an incongruity between our plan and our *image* of how things are. We hit the nail with a hammer (OPERATE) and then look again (TEST) to see if the nail and board are congruous with our plan. If our plan and the nail in the board coincide closely enough, the incongruity is gone and we turn to something else (EXIT). Incongruity is thus a motivating force to keep us at the task until the incongruity is sufficiently diminished.

TOTE units are hierarchical. For example, a building contractor has as one large TOTE unit the completion of an entire house. Along the way, however, there are numerous smaller TOTE units that require completion, e.g., laying the foundation, carpentry, plumbing, and so on. Each of these in turn has smaller TOTE units. In an overall plan, the completion of one TOTE unit leads into the start of the next. The importance of this theory was less in generating direct experiments than in casting many psychological problems into a more cognitive frame of reference. The background of the authors (psycholinguist, experimental psychologist, and neurophysiologist) guaranteed that many problems and alternatives would be considered in the development of the model.

### A Social Perception Model: Heider

Suppose I like you and you like me, but we are in strong disagreement about a political candidate. We are in what Heider (1958) called a *state of imbalance.* If we agreed on the merits of the candidate, we would be in a state of *balance.* Imbalance is considered aversive, and we would therefore do something to reduce the imbalance. When "equilibrium" is restored, we are "satisfied." Imbalance is therefore like drive: Its presence initiates action and its reduction reinforces that action. There are a variety of cognitive or behavioral things one might do to reduce imbalance. For example, you might change your mind about the candidate, or about me, or about both of us. Or, you might avoid me until after the election. Imbalance is also perceived through the eyes of a particular individual and the problem is of social *perception,* not social conflict.

A simple state of perceived interpersonal imbalance can occur with two persons. If Frank likes Jane and Jane likes Frank, they both have a positive relation toward each other. If the affective sign of the relation is the same for both individuals (either positive or negative), the situation is balanced, and there is no "strain" to change it. A particularly interesting two-person case is where there is unrequited love; i.e., one person has a strong positive sentiment for the other, but the second is neutral or negative toward the first. It is here that we may see rapidly changing love-hate relationships. The individual whose positive sentiment is not returned may quickly come to be very negative toward the second party, thus bringing the relationship back into balance. Since the problem is perceptual, there may be interesting "distortions." For example, Frank may like Jane and perceive that she does *not* like him, when in fact she does. Frank's perception of the situation, not the "real" state of affairs, determines the imbalance.

The more general case, however, to which most researchers have directed their attention is like our initial illustration. It involves a person (A), another person (B), and an entity (X), which may, for example, be an object, a third person, an idea, or an event. We have three possible pairs of relationships within an *ABX triad:* (1) AB, where A holds some affect toward B; (2) AX, where A holds some affect toward X; and (3) BX, where B holds some affect toward X.[1] A is the person whom by definition, we are concerned with at a particular time; i.e., it is A's perception of the relationships we are examining. Each of these three relationships can be positive or negative, and the general rule is that a triad is balanced if the algebraic product of the three is positive and imbalanced if the product is negative. This rule gives four balanced and four imbalanced triads, summarized in Table 10-1. Figure 10-1 illustrates two balanced and two imbalanced triads involving you (A), me (B), and the President of the United States.

---

[1]Heider also talks about *unit relations,* as well as affective relations. The affective relations are *sentiments,* the unit relations refer to the way things "go together" (e.g., through similarity or other perceptual or logical relations). Because of space limitations and our primary concern with motivation we discuss here only the sentiment relations. We are also using the ABX symbolism popularized by Theodore Newcomb rather than the symbolism used by Heider.

**Table 10-1.** *Balanced and Imbalanced Relationships With All Combinations of Positive and Negative AB, AX, and BX Relationships.*

| | Balanced | | | | Imbalanced | | |
|---|---|---|---|---|---|---|---|
| | AB | AX | BX | | AB | AX | BX |
| 1. | + | + | + | 5. | − | − | − |
| 2. | + | − | − | 6. | − | + | + |
| 3. | − | − | + | 7. | + | + | − |
| 4. | − | + | − | 8. | + | − | + |

Let us put Relationship 3 (balanced) and Relationship 6 (imbalanced) from Figure 10-1 into verbal form. In 3, you are A and have negative affect toward both me (B) and the President (X), and since I like the President, the triad is balanced from the point of view of the focal person (i.e., A, which is you). If we shifted the diagram around so that I was the focal person,

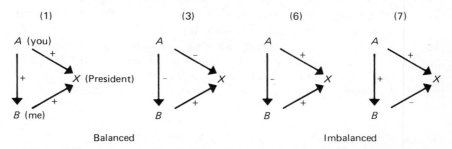

**Figure 10.1** *Balanced triads (1 and 3) and imbalanced triads (6 and 7). See text and Table 10-1 for details.*

the situation might or might not remain balanced, depending on whether my attitudes toward you were positive or negative. In Relationship 6, you have a negative attitude toward me, but we are both positive toward the President. By definition, this represents an imbalanced situation. In any real situation the valence *sign* (+ or −) and *intensity* of affect would be determined by many factors (e.g., you might like some of the President's policies, but not others), and the degree of imbalance would in turn depend on these intensities as well as on signs. A mild imbalance would not produce much effort toward reducing the imbalance. We also assume that X is of interest or relevance to both A and B before there could be any imbalance. If neither A nor B was concerned about X one way or another, there would be no triad.

Although imbalance is generally considered undesirable, we can readily see, from the point of view of activation theory, for example, that some imbalance (like some frustration) may often be sought. Up to a point, we may enjoy political arguments with our friends.

Newcomb (1968) proposes that balanced relations 1 and 2 in Table 10-1, are in fact different from 3 and 4. Considerable research evidence cited by Newcomb indicates that although 1 and 2 are desirable, 3, 4, 5, and 6 are all mildly undesirable, and 7 and 8 are the most undesirable. Newcomb, therefore, prefers to consider 1 and 2 *balanced* (pleasant), 3, 4, 5, and 6 *nonbalanced* (i.e., relatively neutral), and 7 and 8 *imbalanced* (unpleasant). The reason for this may be that negative relations are unpleasant, even though they may be balanced. Two people who do not like each other form a balanced situation, but neither one may enjoy the situation. The evidence cited by Newcomb is not always consistent, but does point up the fact that the logical relations (i.e., algebraic products) defining balance and imbalance do not necessarily coincide with the individual's perception of the situation or the affect he experiences.

### A Cognitive Model: Festinger's Cognitive Dissonance Theory

Although Heider's theory is generally accepted as the father of consistency theories, the most influential has been Festinger's (1957) theory of cognitive dissonance. This theory has probably spawned more research than any theory in social psychology in the last quarter century. It has expanded to encompass problems involving such classic motivational areas as hunger, thirst, and pain, and has even been applied to animal research.

Dissonance is said to occur when two beliefs are incongruent, or if "the obverse of one element would follow from the other." (Festinger, 1957, p. 13). That is, there is cognitive dissonance if two beliefs lead to contradictory conclusions. Being obese and continuing to eat rich food is dissonant with knowing that one's health is endangered by overeating. Similarly, continuing to smoke is dissonant with knowledge that it may lead to lung cancer. Cognitive dissonance, like imbalance, is considered a noxious state whose reduction is rewarding.

There are many possible ways of reducing dissonance but all involve a change in our cognitions. We might add a new cognition ("the lung cancer research has produced ambiguous results") or alter existing ones ("cancer really isn't all that dangerous"). Note that it is the cognitions (beliefs) which are important, not whether the beliefs are in fact accurate. We might seek more information to try to reduce our dissonance, such as reading further on the problem of lung cancer. This could lead to the apocryphal outcome that "I read so much about lung cancer and smoking that I gave up reading." Facetious, perhaps, but not an entirely unreal possibility. At the extreme, we might even give up cigarettes or rich foods.

Dissonance, however, would not be the only factor determining whether we stopped smoking or started dieting. Dissonance theory is not *all*-encompassing and was never intended to be. Other desires and aversions might override dissonance. We might even engage in dissonance-*producing* activities; group pressure, for example, might force an adolescent into doing something very dissonant with his beliefs about himself.

Let us now look at three kinds of dissonance experiments: (1) attitude change in a free-choice situation, (2) attitude change in a forced-compliance situation, and (3) dissonance and "primary drives." One of the strongest points of the theory, Festinger has repeatedly argued, is that its predictions are often not obvious, frequently being just the opposite of what an incentive theory would predict.

### Attitude Change in the Free-Choice Situation

By *attitude,* we mean only a positive or negative evaluation of some person, object, or thing. By *attitude change,* we mean a change in either the sign (from positive to negative, or vice versa) or intensity (e.g., weak positive to strong positive).

If we have a choice among attractive alternatives, we face conflict because we stand to lose one alternative if we choose the other. If I choose to buy a particular automobile, there may be dissonance because (1) I have committed myself to a particular purchase, but (2) some other car may be of better quality or a better deal. The more important the decision or the more attractive the alternative, the greater the dissonance aroused by the decision.

How would I then reduce my dissonance? I might change my mind and choose another alternative, but this would throw me back into the same conflict as before. More likely, I might perceive the chosen alternative as *more attractive* and the unchosen alternative as *less attractive.* Such changes in attractiveness ("spreading the alternatives") are perhaps the most common method of dissonance reduction in the free-choice situation (Insko & Schopler, 1972). This is illustrated in an experiment by Brehm (1956), who had subjects rate the desirability of a number of items (e.g., portable radio, desk lamp) for "consumer reactions." The subjects were then offered whichever single item they would like to have. After the choice, they rated the items again. The chosen items were now rated higher and the rejected items lower. Brock (1963) replicated these findings with additional controls.

An interesting question is whether the spreading occurs before or after the decision is made. In the former case ("predecisional dissonance"), the spreading would serve to help resolve the conflict so that a decision could be made. This would not represent cognitive dissonance in quite the same way as postdecisional changes in attractiveness, however. There is some research on the problem, but the issue is not resolved (Insko & Schopler, 1972).

Another procedure for facilitating postdecisional spreading might be seeking information to support the decision. Having purchased my automobile, I might keep a watchful eye on the newspaper ads for evidence that

I really did get a good deal. On the other hand, I might also avoid doing so, to reduce the possibility of finding out I made a bad deal. Unfortunately, the theory does not tell us which is more likely to occur and the research evidence for such postdecisional selective exposure to information is not strong.

### Attitude Change and Forced-Compliance

One of the best-known dissonance experiments, often used as the prototype experiment for explaining and describing the phenomenon, is by Festinger and Carlsmith (1959). Their experiment involved *forced compliance* and *insufficient justification.* The situation was so structured that the subjects found it difficult not to do what the experimenter asked (forced compliance), but at the same time had little apparent reason for doing so (insufficient justification). The subjects were initially run through a very tedious and boring task requiring them to turn pegs in holes. On completing the task, the subjects were asked if they would help persuade other persons to be subjects. This persuasion would involve telling the potential subjects that the task was interesting, etc. The only other person was, in fact, a research assistant.

Half the real subjects were told they would receive a $20 retainer for their services, and the rest that they would receive $1. All subjects agreed to serve (indicating the power of the forced-compliance aspect). The critical measure of dissonance reduction was how the subjects evaluated the task after they had tried to persuade the assistant. It was independently ascertained that the task really was boring and the main assumption of the experiment was that making positive statements about the task would be discrepant with one's private evaluation. Since the subjects were in effect forced to make these discrepant statements, dissonance could only be reduced by having a *more positive evaluation* of the task. Receiving $20 should produce little dissonance, because $20 is "adequate justification" for making the discrepant statements. Therefore, the subjects receiving $1 should show the most positive evaluation of the task. This is, in fact, how the experiment turned out. As Festinger has commonly described the situation, "You come to love what you suffer for."

As another example of such a forced-compliance experiment, A.R. Cohen, Brehm, and Fleming (1958) asked college students to write an essay supporting a view opposite to their own personal opinion on a matter of current interest at the time. Some students were given very minimal reasons for engaging in the discrepant activity, but others were given many good reasons (such as helping the experimenter get his Ph.D.). Again, subjects with minimal justification changed more favorably toward the view they had supported than did subjects with greater justification.

### Dissonance and "primary drives"

Will a person committing himself to something painful be less pained if he has little overt justification for the commitment? Zimbardo (1966) gave subjects in a "verbal learning" experiment electric shocks of a relatively high intensity. Half the subjects were then given the explicit choice of terminating the experiment or continuing. All continued. Of these, half received considerable justification for doing so (low dissonance), and half had minimal justification (high dissonance). All received the same intensity of shock in the second part of the experiment. The group without a choice was a control for continuing in the experiment without justification; half the no-choice subjects got the same level shock in the second half as the first half (Hi-Hi), and half got a lower level (Hi-Mod). The most interesting measure was the change in galvanic skin response from before to after making the decision to continue. The results are summarized in Figure 10-2.

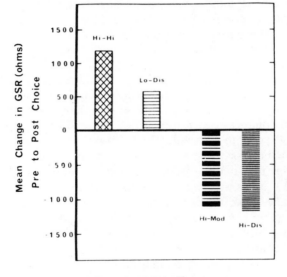

**Experimental Groups**

**Figure 10.2** *GSR changes for four experimental groups. Hi-Hi received a high level of shock in both phases of the experiment and the Hi-Mod group had a reduction in shock level. Neither had a choice of continuing in the experiment. The Lo-Dis group had much verbal justification for continuing and the Hi-Dis group had little justification. (From Zimbardo, 1966, p. 910.)*

The Hi-Hi control group showed an increase in GSR and the Hi-Mod group showed a decrease. The low-dissonance group also showed higher GSR. The GSR of the high-dissonance group, however, dropped as much as that of the Hi-Mod control group. If we can believe the GSR, it appears that the shocks actually were less painful for subjects who made a commitment with minimal justification. We thus see an element of martyrdom: Commitment to a cause with little external justification may actually reduce the pain and suffering the martyr undergoes.

Mansson (quoted by Zimbardo, 1966, p. 918) posed a somewhat different question: "What happens when a thirsty person knows that he cannot drink for a longer period of time?" The subjects were made thirsty by having them eat saltine crackers with either peanut butter or a mixture of catsup, tabasco, and horseradish. They were then asked to commit themselves to going without water. The extreme levels of dissonance were to go without water for twenty four hours with minimal justification (high dissonance) or four hours with much justification (low dissonance). Just prior to the anticipated deprivation period, the subjects were allowed to drink water and the amount was, unknown to them, measured. High and low dissonance groups drank averages of about 128 and 155 ml respectively (estimated from Zimbardo, 1966, Figure 8, p. 918). Brehm (1962) reports similar results for hunger and for thirst.

The implication of these studies is that if one has committed oneself to deprivation or pain with a small amount of justification, then the degree of hunger, thirst, or pain is less. We may question whether there is a change in *need,* because that would call for more physiological detail than these experiments have provided, but certainly the hypotheses under test are intriguing and indicative of important cognitive factors in such basic motivational problem areas as hunger, thirst, and pain. In similar fashion, we might speculate that commitment to the priesthood and celibacy may actually reduce sexual motivation.

### Criticisms of Dissonance Theory

Chapanis and Chapanis (1964) criticized the dissonance research to that date. They argued, first, that the experimental procedures for producing dissonance are so complex that it is impossible to tell whether it is really dissonance being manipulated. An example cited is a love-what-you-suffer-for experiment by Aronson and Mills (1959). College women volunteered to participate in a series of discussions on the psychology of sex and were then informed they would have to pass an "embarrassment test" before they could join an already existing group. In the severe embarrassment condition, the subjects had to read aloud in the presence of a male experimenter vivid descriptions of sexual activity and a list of vulgar sex words. Another group read some mild sexual material. All subjects then listened to a tape recording of a supposedly real session, a boring discussion of animals. The subjects then rated the discussion and their own interest in future participation. The severe embarrassment group was more favorable on both counts. The authors' interpretation was that the discrepancy between the severity of initiation and the boring discussion produced dissonance. This dissonance was reduced by coming to believe the group really was interesting and attractive.

To be confident of this explanation, however, Chapanis and Chapanis (1964) suggest that we would have to be sure that the subjects felt no relief when they found the group discussion banal instead of embarrassing, that success in passing the difficult embarrassment test did not alter the subjects' evaluations of the task (e.g., there might have been "desensitization"), and that the sexual material was not actually titillating and evoked anticipation of more of the same, regardless of the taped discussion. In brief, the experiment does not exclude the possibility that there was some relief or pleasure rather than dissonance. Gerard and Matthewson (1966) later suggested that if the severe initiation really were unpleasant, then just by contrast the taped conversation might sound more pleasant than it did to the mild initiation group.

In their own experiment, Gerard and Matthewson tried to rule out everything but a dissonance interpretation of experiments of the Aronson and Mills type. College females had to take a screening test to get into a group discussion involving college student mores. Part of the test consisted of three electric shocks. All subjects went through the same "screening" except that some subjects had strong shocks and others had very weak ones. The subjects then listened to a supposed tape of a group discussion on cheating, which was, in the authors' words, "utterly worthless," hardly provoking desire to join. The main result was that the "initiate" subjects getting strong shock consistently rated the taped discussion more favorably than those subjects getting weak shocks, just as dissonance theory predicts. Interestingly, both experimental groups gave lower ratings if first told they had passed the test.[2] Control subjects who went through the same procedure, but not in anticipation of joining any group, gave the discussion *lower* ratings if they received strong shock than if they received weak shock. This experiment, taking into account the criticisms raised by the Aronson-Mills experiment, lends considerable support to the dissonance hypothesis. It also points up the value of strong criticism; in this case, the criticism led to even better support for the theory.

Chapanis and Chapanis' (1964, p. 20) most important suggestion, however, was that "The magic appeal of Festinger's theory arises from its extreme simplicity in both formulation and application." Such simplicity is deceptive because it may conceal a large number of uncontrolled variables, as illustrated with the Aronson and Mills experiment. Indeed, the statement that dissonance occurs when two beliefs are contradictory is in itself am-

---

[2]This is reminiscent of Groucho Marx' famous comment: "I wouldn't join any club that would have me as a member."

biguous, as Festinger himself pointed out. Thus dissonance may arise from logical inconsistency, cultural mores, or past experience. It is, in fact, not always clear just what the theory predicts. Nevertheless, the theory has been productive, ingenious, and stimulating.

### Is Dissonance Actually Arousing?

If dissonance is arousing in any more than a purely cognitive sense, then it would be important to have evidence for this independently of just the behavioral outcomes of the dissonance experiments. Kiesler and Pallak (1976) reached the justifiably modest conclusion that dissonance is not demonstrated to be arousing, but "rather that manipulations typically used in dissonance experiments are arousing" (p. 1023). They report evidence that high-dissonance manipulations produce similar behavioral effects (e.g., impairment of performance in situations where there is strong response competition) as do other arousal manipulations (e.g., strong shock or high anxiety). They also cite the research of Brehm and Zimbardo, discussed earlier in this chapter, as evidence of physiological effects of arousal. However, if anything, the high-dissonance manipulations in those experiments *reduced* the level of hunger, thirst, and pain. The Kiesler-Pallak interpretation would then have to be that the dissonance operations produced so much arousal that the subjects reduced their arousal to below that of low-dissonance subjects. Since the only evidence for this is that the "high-dissonance" subjects had lower hunger levels, etc., the argument is weak. Whether dissonance produces physiological arousal is at best an open question.

### Alternatives to Festinger's Theory

***Aronson's Expectancy Interpretation.*** Aronson (1968) suggests that dissonance does not occur with just any contradiction, but is specific to a violation of expectancies. Walking in the rain and not getting wet would create dissonance because walking in the rain arouses the expectancy of getting wet. In the Aronson and Mills experiment, the severity of initiation presumably aroused the expectancy of something really worthwhile, but when this was not confirmed the subjects experienced dissonance.

Aronson also suggests that dissonance is especially likely to occur in relation to one's self-concept. In discussing the Festinger-Carlsmith experiment, for example, Aronson suggests that the dissonance was *not* just the result of telling someone the task was interesting when in fact it was boring. Rather, the dissonance resulted from the subjects' violation of their self-concept. When he lies for $1, the individual is doing something out of line with his concept of how he ought to behave. Aronson concludes that the strongest dissonance effects have been obtained in experiments where the self-concept was clearly involved.

***Bem's Self-Perception Theory.*** Aronson's theory still considered dissonance as a drive, but Bem's (1967, 1970) theory was a major change. Bem proposed to account for all the cognitive dissonance research with an essentially Skinnerian approach. Rather than argue that subjects in dissonance research perform as they do because inconsistent cognitions are aversive, Bem proposed that the individual views his *own* behavior and the situation *just as he would view the behavior of another person in the same situation*. Let us look again at the Festinger-Carlsmith experiment. Suppose we could invisibly observe a college student offered $20 to lie to someone and then see him do it. We also see another student tell the same lie for a mere $1. What might we conclude? One reasonable interpretation would be that "For $20 the subject doesn't *have* to believe in what he's doing, but if he's doing it for a crummy dollar maybe he does believe it." Bem's interpretation is that the subject may look at his own behavior and draw the same conclusion.

Bem (1967) conducted what he called an "interpersonal replication" of the Festinger-Carlsmith experiment (as well as several others.) The subjects simply listened to tape-recorded descriptions of the Festinger-Carlsmith experiment (without hearing the actual results) and then rated the experimental task as they thought the subjects would. There were three different conditions, with independent groups of subjects: the $1 inducement, the $20 inducement, and a control group with no inducement. The subjects then rated the task on a scale from $-5$ (very dull) to $+5$ (very interesting). Table 10-2 gives Bem's comparison of the ratings in the original experiment and in

**Table 10-2** *Comparison of Bem's and the Festinger-Carlsmith results: (From Bem, 1967, p. 189. Copyright © 1967 by the American Psychological Association. Reprinted by permission.) Attitude ratings and interpersonal estimates of attitude ratings toward the task for each condition.*

| Study | Experimental condition | | |
|---|---|---|---|
| | Control | $1 compensation | $20 compensation |
| Festinger-Carlsmith | −0.45 | +1.35 | −0.05 |
| Interpersonal replication | −1.56 | +0.52 | −1.96 |

his replication. The absolute numerical values in the two experiments are different, but the trend of results is the same: The $1 group is more positive than either of the other groups in each experiment. S.C. Jones (1966) compared actual subjects' attitudes toward the boring task with outside observers' judgments of the subjects' attitudes in a single experiment and found results similar to Bem's. Bem (1965) also used the same kind of simulation procedure to restudy an experiment by Brehm and Cohen (1962). In the original experiment, students who were paid a small amount of money ($1 or 50¢) to write an essay opposed to their own viewpoint (with regard to police handling of a riot) came to judge the police more favorably than did students paid either a large amount ($10 or $5) or nothing at all. Students who simply read different written descriptions of the experimental situation (including amounts of money paid for writing the essay) rated the police the same as the original subjects had.

Bem (1970) develops, with many experimental and "real-life" illustrations, the argument that our behavior determines our attitudes, rather than the other way around. For example, factory workers who become shop stewards suddenly shift their attitudes to a more prolabor position, while workers who are promoted to foreman shift suddenly in a promanagement direction. The proposition that we come to like (or believe) what we see ourselves do sounds intuitively backward, because we have all been brought up with the reverse notion, namely, that our feelings determine our behavior. Note, however, that this belief is essentially the Cartesian dualistic interpretation of the mind-body relation discussed in Chapter One. That is, mind (attitudes, beliefs, etc.) causes behavior. Bem's position is that circumstances dictate behaviors, and that we infer our mental state, at least in part, from these circumstances and behaviors.

Bem's self-perception theory is one form of a larger category of theory called *attribution theory,* which we shall discuss in detail in Chapter Thirteen. At present, the attribution theorists appear to be in ascendence, and cognitive dissonance research and interpretations are relatively less popular. This is undoubtedly due in part to the fact that Festinger himself as a matter of personal preference shifted his research from social psychology and dissonance-related topics to the study of basic perceptual processes. Overall, however, cognitive dissonance theory is still an excellent account of many phenomena and has been very fruitful.

## STRIVING FOR CHANGE

Striving for consistency is considered an important motivational concept in many different contexts. So, however, is the search for variety, novelty, inconsistency, and discrepancy.

### The Biological Importance of Change

**Early Sensory Deprivation.** Restricted sensory input in infancy has been experimentally shown to produce deficits in the sensory modality that was restricted (Reisen, 1961; Forgus & Melamed, 1976). For example, animals reared in sensory isolation take longer to learn discrimination problems involving the restricted modality. Reisen has also shown that a complete lack of visual input results in the degeneration of the visual apparatus of chimpanzees. His animals, reared in the dark from birth, actually became blind. It has since been customary to prevent such degeneration by giving visually isolated animals limited daily exposure to unpatterned light, through light-diffusing goggles. With this procedure, however, there are still deficits in visual perception. The importance of patterned stimulus input is thus reaffirmed.

Held (1965) reported that if kittens were allowed unrestricted vision, but restricted movement, they were poorer at visual-motor coordination tasks than were active kittens. The same general finding has been reported in short-term experiments with humans. Adults adjust more readily to a visually displaced image if they are allowed to actively explore. It is now widely believed that the "adaptation" which occurs in vision distorted by prisms that reverse the world or turn it upside down is muscular, not visual, adaptation. It eventually "feels right" to respond to a reversed or inverted world (e.g., Harris, 1965).

Besides perceptual deficits, there are intellectual deficits. Bennett, Diamond, Krech, and Rosenzweig (1964) and their colleagues have shown that rats reared in enriched environments, with much activity and stimulation, develop a thicker and heavier neocortex and have greater output of the neurotransmitter, acetylcholine, than do rats maintained under impoverished stimulus conditions. The "enriched" rats are also better problem solvers as adults. There is some evidence that the deficits of the animals raised under impoverished conditions can be offset by "compensatory training." A large body of research with animals also shows that stimulation in infancy is important for the development of emotional stability. We shall deal with this problem in some detail in the next chapter, under the topic of stress. At this point, it is useful to note that just about everything people consider of personal importance is influenced by early experience, as Freud long ago claimed. The *details* of the Freudian hypothesis are frequently not supported by the evidence, however. Harlow's work with primates (e.g., 1971) is classic, emphasizing the role of early stimulation and play on later emotional relationships with other animals, but not supporting the details of Freudian theory.

One does not carry out early deprivation experiments with human infants, but periodically children are found who have been kept in isolation their entire lives. Almost invariably the newspaper accounts of such children indicate severe mental and social retardation. In one case, two children in a family of five children were kept in a bedroom because the family presumed that it could not have rented the house with five children. These two children were well cared for, had the companionship of each other and their siblings, had a television set, and so on, but were never allowed outside.

When found, as young adolescents, they were considerably retarded in growth and, as might be expected, very immature socially.

*Short-term Sensory Deprivation with Adults.*   Growing out of interest in the problem of "brainwashing," research on sensory isolation in adults was undertaken at McGill University in the late 1940s. The first report of this (Bexton, Heron, & Scott, 1954) indicated bizarre changes. The subjects, McGill University students paid well to participate, were kept in a barren room with as little sensory stimulation as possible. They were fed regularly and could go to the bathroom but were not allowed any form of recreation or stimulus change that might have been stimulating. The subjects began to crave almost any variation in their monotonous environment, including taped presentations of old stock market reports. After several days in isolation, there was impairment of ability to concentrate, difficulty with visual perception (particularly with regard to reading), and in some cases even hallucinations. It was not darkness that produced such changes, but invariant stimulation. All the effects initially reported have not been found in subsequent investigations and some are found with isolation of only a few hours. Some appear to be accountable as experimenter demand effects (Orne & Scheibe, 1964). Nevertheless, the large literature on the subject indicates there are reliable impairments from such sensory deprivation procedures. These effects of monotony are usually interpreted as the result of decreased activity in the reticular activating system (RAS). The rest of the brain, then, does not function normally because of the restricted RAS inputs to it. The nervous system may have its own needs (for stimulation and activity), just as other parts of the body need nutrients (Nissen, 1951).

The phenomena resulting from stabilized retinal images (mentioned in Chapter Five) should also be reiterated here. Recall that if complex visual images are presented to the eye in such a way that they vibrate right along with the eye, they quickly disappear. Similar results can be obtained in a homogenous visual environment (a "ganzfield"). For example, if the eyes are covered with halved Ping-Pong balls, and these hemispheres are flooded with colored light, the color quickly fades. It returns suddenly, however, or is prevented from fading if a hairline shadow is cast across the otherwise homogenous field. The normal vibration of the eyes back and forth across this line produces sufficient visual change to maintain the color. Blinking also causes either colors or forms to reappear.

Many kinds of evidence, then, support the idea of a biological necessity for more or less continual change in stimulation. Without such variation, normal neural function is not maintained, and perceptual and thought processes are impaired. If stimulus change is this necessary, it is reasonable to believe that in the course of evolution stimulus change would have become desirable in its own right, just as food, water, and sex are desirable under appropriate conditions.

### Motivation Inherent in Information Processing

J. McV. Hunt (e.g., 1963) used the phrase "motivation inherent in information processing" to refer to the motivational properties of both dissonance *reduction* and dissonance *production*. His integrating concept was an activation theory. He argued that either too much or too little incongruity produces arousal (departure from an optimum level of stimulation) and the organism then does things that would *reduce* the arousal level. Organisms may work either to reduce or increase incongruity to some optimal level for them.

Empirically, there is no doubt that stimulus incongruity (or increased stimulus complexity, which we shall here consider equivalent) is actively sought at both human and subhuman levels. Many species will orient toward and approach incongruities of various kinds, including perceptual (Berlyne, 1960). Even very young infants have definite preferences for watching patterns of mild complexity. They prefer to look at a striped pattern rather than a plain gray patch, but they also prefer the stripes to an even more complex visual pattern (Fantz, 1961). As they grow older, they prefer progressively more complex patterns. From Hunt's (1963) point of view, such preference is related to the capacity of the child at a particular time to process the information available. If the stimulus is *too complex* to be processed, it is aversive (the cognitive dissonance side of the coin), but if it is *too simple* (or familiar) it is "boring" and therefore also aversive.

This is similar to the Dember and Earl (1957) argument that different individuals have different levels of complexity that are "ideal" to them, i.e., can readily be coped with. Slightly more complex stimuli than these ("pacer stimuli") are attractive, however. Once the more complex stimuli are "mastered," they become less attention-getting, in the sense of Sokolov's theory, and the individual is then "attracted to" even more complex stimuli. This line of reasoning forms a basis for Maslow's (1955) distinction between *deficit motivation* and *growth motivation*. Deficit motivation is related to such homeostatic imbalances as hunger and thirst, or to such psychological deficits as a "need" to be with other people. Growth motivation involves the "personal development" of the organism through its interactions with the environment. Growth motivation is intrinsic to the behaviors involved and not just the reward following the behaviors. We have already noted (Chapter Six) that extrinsic rewards may actually *reduce* the tendency to engage in activities which were previously done for their own sake.

### Theories for "Rewards That Do Not Reduce Tissue Needs"

Eisenberger (1972) has summarized the several theories that have been proposed to account for the fact that organisms produce stimulus complexity. We shall in part follow his outline here.

*Stimulus Satiation.*   A number of theorists have proposed that (1) the longer an organism is exposed to a stimulus, the less responsive it is to that stimulus, and (2) the longer the interval between exposures, the greater the responsiveness (e.g., Walker, 1969). Considerable evidence from several species supports these hypotheses. Spontaneous alternation (e.g., between arms of a T maze) is caused by animals alternating between the stimuli, as opposed to just making different responses. This tendency to alternate is so strong that it may even interfere with performance on a discrimination problem because the animal tends to alternate rather than go where the reward is. (Richman, Gardner, Montgomery, and Benewicz, 1970).

Animals do not always seek more novel stimulation, however. At least, they are sometimes hesitant in doing so. Montgomery (1955) suggested that novel stimuli may simultaneously arouse approach (curiosity) and avoidance (fear) tendencies. This conflict theory is not easily amenable to direct test, because it requires the demonstration that a novel stimulus actually does arouse both tendencies, when all we have to observe is the resultant behavior. Berlyne (1960) proposed that in such a situation the organism would be aroused (which would be aversive) and would approach the novel stimulus to become familiar with it and therefore be less aroused. It is not clear why the animal would not just simply go away.

*Boredom Drive.*   The postulation of additional drives, such as exploration, curiosity, or manipulation, has been resisted by many theorists, because such a practice seemed to raise the ghost of the old instinct theories. Where, they ask, will the proliferation of drives stop? Even the most parsimonious theorists have felt the need to postulate some new concept to account for the otherwise intractable exploratory data, however. Myers and Miller (1954) suggested that monotonous stimulation produces a boredom drive which is reduced by exposure to new stimulation. They found that rats would learn to press a lever to get out of one compartment into another for only the reward of getting to the other side (perhaps thus answering the question of why a chicken crosses the road). Liddell (1944) noted that the sheep in his experiments seemed perfectly happy to learn a maze with no particular reward at the end; they just seemed to enjoy running the maze. A large amount of research from Harry Harlow's primate laboratory (e.g., Butler & Harlow, 1954) showed that monkeys would play with puzzles endlessly and perform instrumental tasks for the sake of getting to look out of a box. The more interesting the view (i.e., the more going on), the greater the amount of lever pressing. Fox (1962) found that pressing a lever to turn on a light in a dark compartment was preceded by a shift from a resting to an activated EEG pattern in the monkey, as if a drive were building up.

Fowler (1965) argued for the boredom drive, but also for the idea that change in stimulation was an incentive variable—the greater the change, the greater the incentive. Manipulating boredom drive (amount of time in a start box) and incentive (amount of difference between start box and goal box brightness) independently, he found the two did combine to affect speed of running to the goal box. This, of course, is the familiar $E = f(H, D, K)$ of Hull-Spence theory. A complete Hull-Spence analysis would suggest that any source of drive should facilitate responding for stimulus change. The data are neither plentiful, nor highly consistent, but Davis (1958), for example, found that the irrelevant drive of hunger increased the amount of lever pressing to turn on a light in a dark apparatus.

*Activation Theory.* Fiske and Maddi (1961b) also argued that organisms seek intermediate levels of overall stimulation. The "impact" of a stimulus (its arousing effect on the reticular activating system) could vary not only with the intensity but also with the meaningfulness and variability of the stimulus. Impact would also vary with the internal state of the organism, such as where in the sleep-wakefulness cycle it was. Such stimulus factors were also considered somewhat interchangeable. For example, a complex, highly meaningful stimulus could have great impact, even though it did not change very much. Berlyne (1960) earlier viewed activation theory as a variant of drive reduction theory, but more recently (1967, 1969) has argued that some increases in activation may be inherently rewarding if the organism is not already very highly aroused.

*Adaptation Level Theory.* The idea that organisms adapt to stimuli so that the average of these stimuli becomes neutral holds with regard to their "affect-arousing" properties as well as to their "sensory" properties. McClelland et al. (1953) suggested that small departures from this neutral point, the adaptation level (AL), are hedonically positive and large departures are hedonically negative. Thus, if a person performs some act and the outcome is slightly different than he expected (i.e., is different from his AL for previous outcomes), pleasure would be experienced. There are certain obvious difficulties with this as a completely comprehensive theory, because it predicts that an outcome *worse* than expected could be pleasurable. Also, there are many stimuli (e.g., taste) that are inherently good (see Chapter Fifteen). McClelland et al. attempted to deal with such exceptions, although not very convincingly.

In what appears to be the only direct, rigorous, *and* successful test of this extension of AL theory, Haber (1958) had humans put their hands into a container of water until the water felt neutral, neither warm nor cool. The two hands were then put into separate containers of water, each different from the adapting temperature, and the subject indicated his preference for one of the two test temperatures. Within a certain range of adapting temperatures, test temperatures that departed slightly from adaptation were judged pleasant (more preferred), and those further from the adaptation temperatures were less pleasant (less preferred). With a very warm adapting temperature, however, an even higher temperature was not pleasant. There are thus limits to the AL interpretation even for this simple situation. Furthermore, animal experiments involving other stimulus dimensions have not provided much support for the AL interpretation. For example, McCall (1966) found that rats adapted to particular light intensities came to respond only for decrements in intensity, not increments. According to AL theory, they should have responded for either.

Eisenberger (1972) put a previous theory by Glanzer (1958) into terms of adaptation to "information flow." Eisenberger suggested that if the present rate of information processing is above or below that to which the organism is accustomed (an AL) then the organism will work to bring the rate of processing back toward the accustomed rate. This use of AL theory, of course, is *opposite* to that of McClelland et al., who assumed that small discrepancies would be attractive.

From these theories and evidence, we see that there are many well-known and authenticated examples of organisms striving for increased stimulus intensity or complexity, but there are still considerable theoretical problems in accounting for these phenomena. One or more of these theories may account after the fact for a phenomenon which drive and drive reduction cannot interpret, but it is often hard to spell out experimental predictions.

### Creative Thinking, Humor, and Aesthetics

In a brief space, we cannot do justice to the topics under this heading. Nevertheless, these topics have certain elements in common that we can discuss and thereby provide some perspective.

*Creative Thinking.* Psychologists commonly distinguish between *convergent* and *divergent* thinking. Convergent thinking is the focusing of thought toward some fixed problem solution. The diagnosis of the ailment of the old family car would involve convergent thinking on the part of the mechanic. He must zero in on a specific problem and its specific solution in order to make the car run. Divergent thinking (also called *productive* or *creative* thinking), on the other hand, is the search for many solutions to a problem, one or more of which may be optimal. Thus, if a problem were stated: "How can we make the car run?" there would be convergent thinking on the problem. If, however, the question were phrased "How can I get from home to work?" there are many possible divergent lines of thought and admissible solutions. Practicality aside, one *could* hitch a skateboard to a horse as a means of transportation. The two different kinds of questions approach the problem differently.

Creative thinking is generally considered a multidimensional process (e.g., Johnson, 1972). In Guilford's analysis, these dimensions are (1) *problem sensitivity*—dissatisfaction with things as they are now; (2) *verbal fluency*—having many different ideas; (3) *flexibility*—the capacity to shift quickly to a new problem approach when an old one fails; and (4) *originality*. Originality is sometimes taken as equivalent to creative thinking, but is better limited to the notion of the production of novel solutions to problems. Originality is frequently defined as "bringing together two or more previously unrelated elements in order to serve some purpose" (e.g., Mednick, 1962). Most people would prefer dropping the restrictive clause "to serve some purpose," but this clause also closes the door to purely random or schizophrenic kinds of novel association.

To be truly original in any field, one must first know the basics of the field and understand what is commonplace, and then strike out into the unknown. Great art, literature, and science have not been divorced from the more commonplace, but rather have grown beyond it. The histories of great new scientific ideas, for example, consistently show that such ideas were had by people completely immersed in their problems. It is sometimes informative, and certainly fun, to pick out those instances where some great discovery was "accidental," but even in these cases there had to be someone who recognized that there *was* something new and important happening (as with Sir Alexander Fleming and the discovery of penicillin).

The importance of originality for us here is that it is a form of variation seeking. By its very definition, originality involves incongruities, i.e., putting together previously unrelated elements, including the application of an old idea to a new situation. Personality research shows that creative people actively seek discrepancies and enjoy incongruities (Fiske & Maddi, 1961b). They also like to see them resolved, however.

**Humor.** Humor often involves incongruities. Creative problem solving is often fun because we arrive at unexpected solutions. The image of someone riding a skateboard hitched to a horse can hardly be taken any way except humorously. The so-called Polish joke[3] involves such incongruities as:

> *Q:* "How many Polacks does it take to change
> a lightbulb?"
> *A:* "Three: One to hold the bulb and two to
> turn him around."

We are even eager to pay for the privilege of exposure to variety and incongruity. (Note that the term "Variety Show" means just that, a se-

---

[3]All the Polish jokes I know were told to me by Leon Lorenc, Lorraine Yasinski, and Walter Zultowski, three graduate students of remarkably good humor.

quence of different acts.) It is no accident that Johnny Carson earns a million dollars a year, or that Bob Hope is (reputedly) worth *several hundred million* dollars. The rapid-fire lines of the stand-up comedian are a veritable gold mine. The usual stand-up comedy routine is one where the topics of humor shift quickly, with virtually no transition. Very few comedians actually sustain a single topic for very long (an outstanding exception being Bill Cosby).

The so-called comeback line also involves an unexpected twist. When Woodrow Wilson was governor of New Jersey he reportedly received a phone call from a politician who wanted to be appointed replacement for a just-deceased United States Senator. "That's perfectly agreeable with me," said Wilson, "if it's agreeable to the undertaker." We are all pleased when we can make such a comeback. Humor is, of course, a complex subject, and any explanation for all forms of humor depends on more than incongruity. Jack Benny, for example, was most famous (and funny) doing things that he was fully expected to do, such as his quizzical expression and saying "Well!" He was funny *because of* his predictability. Nonetheless, incongruity must be considered an important component of verbal humor, and demonstrably has a strong positive attraction.

*Aesthetics* The nature of beauty, as found in any sensory modality (visual art, music, or more recently, tactual art) is a demanding topic and our cursory treatment here is intentionally limited to a single aspect. Great art or music or writing is ultimately determined by its longevity, which is due in part to the technical skill of the artist or composer or writer and in part to the degree to which the art in question has "universal" appeal. That is, great aesthetic works seem to "speak" to many people, to carry messages that are attracting to many people over many years. The quality of concern here, however, is that on repeated exposure to the same work observers or listeners see or hear different things from what they saw or heard before. That is, people keep finding "new things" in a great work.

Put in psychological terms, great aesthetic works carry a great deal of information, more than is processed in a single viewing or listening, and as different information is detected from one time to another there is stimulus variation. In brief, the second time we hear a great piece of music we are actually hearing something different from the first time we listened, and the third time there is something different from the second, and so on. A prime example of music that is *not* aesthetically great is the bulk of contemporary popular music, which has the status of "golden oldy" within a month of its appearance and is forgotten in two. This can be contrasted with the persistent durability of much of the Beatles' music, which still sells millions of records annually from recordings made ten or more years ago. As great art is measured in time, it is premature to judge the Beatles', but the contrast of their music with that of lesser lights hopefully makes the point in terms which are immediately understandable. For particularly insightful discussion of aesthetics and psychology, Berlyne (1960, 1971) and Platt (1961) are recommended.

## CONCLUSION

The two main sections of this chapter provide the horns of a small dilemma. Inconsistencies perceived in ourselves or the environment may produce an aversive state which we strive to reduce, as we may also try to reduce the overall level of stimulation (arousal) to ourselves. At the same time too much consistency (too little change) may also be aversive; stimulus change has both biological and psychological value. Consistency and change then are motivational variables which seem to have contradictory effects. There is no ready resolution for this problem, but activation theory (in spite of its problems, as we saw in Chapter Five) and the concept of an optimal level of arousal is a useful way to approach the problem. In any event, consistency and change are important motivational factors quite apart from such biological needs as hunger, thirst, fear, pain, or sex.

# chapter 11

# Conflict, Stress, Anxiety, and Coping

## CONFLICT

Hamlet's indecisiveness formed the heart of one of the great literary expressions of conflict. He could not decide what to do, therefore did nothing. In the language of the psychologist, he was caught between "incompatible response tendencies." Virtually all behavior involves conflict, because there are always choices. Some choices are so easily made that there seems to be no conflict, but others are very difficult. The choice of jobs often involves considerable agonizing. Conflicts may often be aversive because they involve frustration; a goal cannot be achieved because of the conflict.

Conflict has long been considered a basic problem in neurotic behavior. In Freudian theory, conflicts between the *id* (biological "drives" such as sex and aggression) and the *superego* (socialization) are particularly important. It is the function of the *ego* to serve as an intermediary between these opposing forces and to resolve the conflict (i.e., make a choice). We shall not go into the clinical aspects of conflict in detail (see Janis, Mahl, Kagan, & Holt, 1969, for a more thorough discussion of the psychoanalytic approach) but should note that clinical problems have provided much impetus for experimental research. For almost forty years, conflict research has been dominated by Neal Miller and his associates, all trying to relate animal studies to real clinical situations.

Another approach to conflict involves economic decision making in a more formal mathematical sense. This is essentially expectancy-incentive theory, as compared to Miller's S-R theoretical approach. Decision theory is also a forebearer of the major theories of achievement motivation (see Chapter Thirteen). We shall deal here only with Miller's theory and with an alternative to it proposed by Brendan Maher.

### Miller's Theory

Miller and his associates (e.g., Dollard & Miller, 1941; Miller, 1959) have progressively developed the theory of conflict. Miller (1959) begins with six assumptions:

1. The closer an organism is to a positive goal, the stronger the motivation to approach that goal. This is called an *approach gradient* (in Hull's theory, it was called a *goal gradient* and played an important role in much of Hull's theorizing).
2. The closer an organism is to an aversive goal, the stronger the motivation to escape or avoid the goal. This is called an *avoidance gradient*.
3. The avoidance gradient is *steeper* than the approach gradient. It drops off more rapidly as the organism is further from the goal.

4. The level of either approach or avoidance gradients can be raised or lowered by appropriate manipulations of approach and avoidance motivation (such as changes in degree of hunger or level of fearfulness).

5. Below the asymptote of learning, an increase in the number of reinforced trials will increase the strength of the response tendency that is reinforced (either approach or avoidance).

6. When two incompatible responses are in conflict, the one with the stronger motivation (approach or avoidance) will occur.

The strength of approach or avoidance is a function of both learning and motivation, as indicated by the postulates. Miller equates approach and avoidance motives with approach and avoidance response tendencies, so that his concepts are more like Hull's excitatory potentials than just motivational concepts. The first question is whether there is evidence to support the postulates.

***Brown's Experiment.*** Judson Brown (1948) tested the first three assumptions. He tethered rats to a calibrated spring with a harness so he could record the strength of the rats' pull toward or away from a goal. Some animals were trained to run down an alleyway to food, then were stopped by the tether either "near" (30 cm) or "far" (170 cm) from the goal. They pulled harder when they were in the "near" position. Other animals were shocked (but not fed) at the end of the runway. They pulled away from the shock area harder when in the near position. Furthermore, the slope of the escape gradient was steeper between the two points than was that of the approach gradient. The results are shown in Figure 11.1 (a)

The results are as predicted, but we should note that the gradients are not necessarily linear. With only two points on each curve, it is not possible to estimate anything but a linear function. The only real requirement of the theory, however, is that the gradients cross.

In Figure 11.1(b) we see the results of testing the animals under strong versus weak avoidance. The overall gradient is lower with weak avoidance. Other animals, tested at forty-six hours of deprivation, showed stronger approach than animals deprived for one hour. They were tested, however, only at the near distance.

Kaufman and Miller (1949) supported the fifth assumption by showing that with more approach training trials the animals were more likely to go to the goal after having been shocked there.

Why is there a difference in the slope of approach and avoidance gradients? Miller (1959) suggested that hunger, which contributes to the approach motivation, is constant throughout the length of the alleyway. Incentive motivation is stronger as the animal is closer to the goal, but some stability is maintained by the internal deprivation cues. With avoidance,

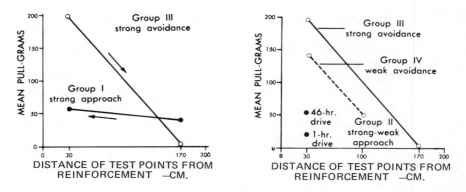

**Figure 11.1** *(a) The approach gradient represents the mean force exerted by 46-hour motivated rats when restrained at two points in the alley. The avoidance gradient reveals the force exerted by rats in their efforts to avoid a region where strong shock has been given. Although the experimental points in this figure and in (b) have been joined by straight lines, no assumption is intended with respect to the linearity of the gradients.*
*(b) This section illustrates the effect of reduced shock and reduced hunger upon the strengths of the avoidance and approach responses, respectively. (From Brown 1948, p. 457 and 459. Copyright © 1948 by the American Psychological Association. Reprinted by permission.)*

however, external cues are relatively more important; the goal box is more avoidance arousing than the start box. The farther the animal is from the source of the shock, the weaker the fear.

Miller's explanation is appealing, but raises questions. For example, it predicts that a stimulus generalization gradient under strong fear would be steeper than one obtained under weak fear. The evidence does not support this: Generalization gradients under strong fear are usually flatter (Kalish, 1969). Highly anxious people do not seem to discriminate as well among more and less fear-arousing situations as do less anxious individuals, and heart rate change with a strong shock UCS shows a flatter generalization gradient than with weak shock. Sometimes there are steeper generalization gradients under high hunger than under low. Hearst (1969) has found approach and avoidance gradients with a variety of slopes, depending on such details as number of test trials. Motivation is, then, a relevant variable in determining approach (or generalization) gradients, but not the only one.

***Types of Conflict.*** Psychologists generally distinguish four kinds of conflict, diagrammed in Figure 11.2, in terms of Miller's gradient theory.

*1. Approach-Approach.* Approach-approach conflict involves two discrete positive alternatives, A and B. As the organism moves toward A the tendency to approach A is even stronger and the tendency to approach B is less. Therefore the conflict is easily resolved. Aesop's fable of the jackass that starved to death between two bales of hay is charming but unlikely. What appears to be an approach-approach conflict may have avoidance elements, however. This produces the fourth kind of conflict we shall discuss.

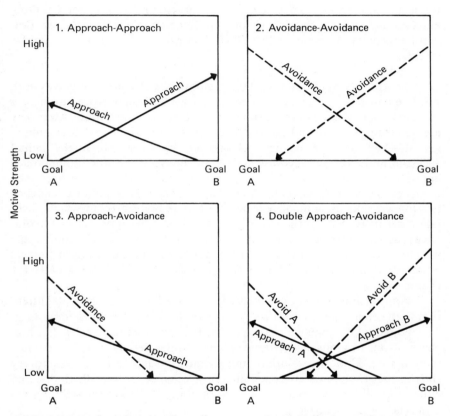

**Figure 11.2** *Four kinds of conflict in terms of Miller's gradient theory. See text for details.*

*2. Avoidance-Avoidance.* Avoidance-avoidance conflict involves two aversive goals. If the organism moves away from one it necessarily moves toward the other, then is forced back toward the first, and so on. Such conflict gives rise to sayings such as "between the devil and the deep blue sea." If the organism has to stay in the situation, it should eventually become more or less immobile at the point of minimal aversive stimulation, where the two gradients intersect. This is commonly seen when an animal (e.g., rat) is shocked at either end of a runway and settles down in the middle.

Given the opportunity to get out of such an entirely aversive situation, to "leave the field" in Kurt Lewin's terms, the organism will do so. This may involve simply running away. Human amnesias are often considered to have this same dynamic (i.e., motivational) etiology, however. A person is in such an intolerable situation that there is no escape except through an extreme psychological change, escape by forgetting (we are not counting amnesia due to brain injury, of course). Some people follow the less dramatic expedient of sleeping a lot. The ultimate device for leaving the field is suicide.

*3. Approach-Avoidance.* Approach-avoidance conflict involves both positive and negative features. The typical experimental procedure here is to train hungry animals first to run down a straight alley to food. After they are well trained to run and eat, the food container is wired so that an animal gets shocked when he touches the food. On later trials, then, the animal vacillates in the runway, because he is simultaneously motivated to approach and avoid the same goal. At some distance from the goal, the approach tendency is stronger, but as the goal is approached the avoidance tendency is stronger, and the animal reverses itself. The point around which vacillation occurs is the "conflict zone," the area where the approach and avoidance gradients intersect. Such vacillating behavior is also seen in adolescents who are attracted to members of the opposite sex but are afraid of ridicule or rebuff if they attempt to approach too closely (to ask for a date, for example).

Approach-avoidance conflicts have received more experimental attention than other types of conflict because they seem to be more important. The individual is "bound" to the goal by the approach tendencies, but prevented from reaching it by the avoidance tendencies. Usually, of course, there is some kind of resolution, and we must assume at least a temporary shift in the strength of approach and/or avoidance, so that the individual either goes all the way to the goal or so far away that the approach motivation is no longer effective.

*4. Double Approach-Avoidance.* Double approach-avoidance conflict involves two goals, each having approach and avoidance characteristics. This is in fact common, because the choice of one goal usually results in the loss of another, and this loss is a negative aspect of the chosen object. For example, you might have the choice of buying a large, prestigious car that is expensive to maintain or a small car that is cheaper but also less prestigious. To gain the good features of one car, you inevitably lose those of the other. This type of conflict, perhaps better called *multiple approach-avoidance,* because the alternatives may be more than two, is more typical of real-life situations but is also more difficult to analyze experimentally.

### *Extensions of the Theory: Stimulus Similarity and Displacement.*
Approach and avoidance gradients can be along the dimension of *spatial* distance from the goal, as we have been discussing, but they can also be along a dimension of *psychological distance,* definable in terms of the degree of similarity to the goal situation. If a person were in a situation similar, but not identical, to a previous conflict situation, what might he do? According to Miller's third postulate, the avoidance gradient is steeper than the approach gradient. In the similar situation, then, avoidance should decline more than approach, and the person should be relatively more likely to approach the goal.

Miller and Kraeling (1952) tested this possibility by first establishing an approach-avoidance conflict with rats in a white alleyway. The animals first learned to run to food, then were shocked at the goal. There were three test groups: (1) tested in the white training alley, (2) tested in a "dissimilar" narrower, gray alley, and (3) tested in a very different, even narrower, black alley. Effects of alley color and width per se were controlled. Of the animals tested in the white alley, 23 percent reached the goal, as compared to 37 percent of those in the gray alley and 70 percent in the black alley. The prediction of weaker avoidance in the generalized alleys was thus confirmed.

Murray and Berkun (1955) advanced this line of reasoning further, suggesting that the concept of *displacement* in Freudian theory could be translated into conflict theory. They argued that if an impulse arouses too much anxiety to be admitted into consciousness or to be expressed directly then a conflict exists. This could be resolved in any of several ways. For example, a man may hate his father but cannot admit this to himself and therefore dreams of killing a policeman. Why can such hostility be expressed in dreams but not openly?

The answer is found in stimulus similarity. The policeman is similar to the father (an authority figure), but not identical. Anxiety about hostility toward the father is strong, but if avoidance drops off more rapidly than approach then it is reasonable to deduce that the individual would approach the "generalized" father (the policeman in the dream) more readily than the real father.

In their experiment, Murray and Berkun (1955) studied both spatial distance from the goal and stimulus similarity. Rats were given the usual conflict training, first with food, then with shock at the goal. Tests were then conducted in the training runway, but the animals could go through newly opened holes in the wall to an adjacent runway dissimilar to the training runway. From the second runway, they could move into an even more dissimilar third runway. As predicted, the animals tended to approach the goal part way in the training alley, then to shift over to the next alley and approach closer, then to move into the third alley and approach the goal closer yet. As the animals approached the goal in the training alley, avoidance motivation increased until they sought escape into the less fearful adjacent alley. Avoidance motivation was then weaker until they moved closer to the goal, at which time avoidance motivation increased, so they escaped into the third alley.

After the animals reached the goal in the generalized alleys, they would go all the way to the goal in the original alley. This suggested the kind of effect we hope for in psychotherapy: Fear extinguished to the generalized alleyway when an animal was not shocked at the goal, much like a discussion of anxiety arousing problems might reduce anxiety when a client is not punished by the therapist. In the original alley, then, the animals could approach the goal less fearfully, just as a client might approach his or her problems less fearfully outside the therapeutic situation.

Elder, Noblin, and Maher (1961) suggested, however, that it was not the dissimilarity of the displacement alleys that was important, but their distance from the original alley. They repeated the experiment with several arrangements of alley color and closeness, and found that distance was the critical variable. This does not deny the validity of the displacement hypothesis but does raise questions about what generalization gradients (i.e., similarity versus spatial) are involved.

***A Separate Conflict-Induced Drive?*** Miller (1959) suggested that conflict might produce drives above and beyond those involved in establishing the conflict in the first place. If conflict involves frustration, then we certainly expect the aversive aspects of nonreward frustration to result in conflict situations. In Pavlov's laboratory, "neurotic" behavior was observed in dogs when a food-reinforced discrimination problem was made so difficult that the animals were in strong conflict about which stimuli to choose. Freud also argued that conflicts get "channelled" into anxiety and that the individual then responds with anxiety-reducing defense mechanisms. Experimentally, Miller's suggestion is also in line with the demonstrations of aversive effects of frustrative nonreward that we noted earlier. Maher (1966) and Geen (1976) have discussed the disruptive effects of conflict in some detail.

### Maher's Theory

The only serious alternative to Miller's theory of intersecting gradients is that of Brendan Maher (e.g., see Maher, 1966, Geen, 1976). Maher's theory grows out of a simple observation reported in several experiments. In an approach-avoidance conflict in a straight alley, one can estimate where the conflict zone is and hence approximately where the approach and avoidance gradients should be crossing. If an animal is put into the apparatus on the goal side of the conflict zone, it should, of course, run *away* from the goal because the avoidance tendency should be stronger there. In practice, however, animals often run *toward* the goal.

Maher's theory, then, presumes that approach-avoidance conflict is *not* the result of intersecting gradients. Rather, the approach and avoidance gradients increase *in parallel,* with the approach gradient always higher. As they increase, however, the *perceived* difference between the gradients is progressively smaller, until the animal finally cannot gauge the difference in their strengths. The zone of conflict is where approach and avoidance are perceptually indistinguishable in strength.[1] This accounts for the fact that the animals sometimes approach the goal when placed in the apparatus near it.

A second challenge to Miller's theory by Maher concerns the avoidance gradient as a function of distance from the *goal.* Maher argues that it is not closeness to the shock that produces increased avoidance closer to the goal. Rather, he suggests the animals use the feedback stimuli from their own approach responses as the avoidance cues. Suppose an animal has previously run three feet from the start box to the conflict zone, where it vacillates at a distance of, say, one foot from the goal box. What would happen if we put the animal in a much longer runway? According to Miller's theory (says Maher), it should run to within a foot of the goal, but according to Maher's theory it should run three feet from the start box and show vacillation. At this distance, the animal will have produced the same avoidance-arousing feedback stimuli as in training. There is evidence that animals may run such a fixed distance under these conditions (Maher, 1966). Experimentally, however, it is difficult to arrange a situation with altered response feedback stimuli without also changing external stimuli. This makes discriminating tests of the theories difficult. Maher's theory is intriguing, but will need more research support before it displaces Miller's theory.

## STRESS

### The General Adaptation Syndrome

The term *stress* has subsumed much of the subject matter of frustration, conflict, anxiety, and the like. Hans Selye, a Canadian endocrinologist, crystallized thinking about stress through his concept of the *general adapta-*

---

[1]This is another application of Weber's law. As the absolute value of a stimulus increases, a larger difference in stimulus values is required to be noticed.

*tion syndrome* (GAS), which he considered to be common to many different stress situations (Selye, 1956). The GAS is characterized by three states, with identifiable physiological reactions. When an organism is subjected to a stressor such as fatigue, disease, injury, or extreme environmental stimulation, the body first shows an *alarm reaction.* This involves a shock effect, such as a sudden drop in blood sugar level, followed quickly by a compensatory countershock response, such as recovery of blood sugar level. Other typical changes are in blood pressure, heart rate, and release of adrenal hormones. Different stressors have unique effects, but the GAS is common to all of them. Thus, if a person is already being stressed from one source, he is less resistant to a new stressor of an entirely different kind. We are, for example, more prone to illness when fatigued.

In the second stage, the *stage of resistance,* the body uses its resources to return its physiology to a normal course. This requires much work, however, and if stress continues long enough there comes the third stage, the *stage of exhaustion,* which may lead to death. The stage of exhaustion is characterized quite commonly by enlargement of the adrenal glands, shrivelling of the thymus and lymph glands (which are necessary to fight disease) and gastrointestinal ulcers. Psychological and physiological sources of stress can combine. Thus, mice living in crowded conditions (psychological stress) are less resistant to parasitic growth (physiological stress). The stress concept gives psychologists and physiologists a common conceptual framework for many problems, but the concept is not always well defined.

### Definitions of Stress

**Stimulus Definition.** We could try to define those circumstances that are stressful, but the same ones are not stressful for all individuals. A painful stimulus for one person may be almost unnoticed by another.

**Response Definition.** Selye (1956, p. 55) said that "Stress is a state manifested by a syndrome." This snydrome, or pattern of symptoms, includes enlargement of adrenals and so on. Unfortunately, this statement does not allow us to *predict* what situations will produce stress symptoms. Through experience, some things are well known to be stressors (e.g., surgical anesthesia, pain, cold, and blood loss), but others are not so readily identifiable.

**Interaction Definition.** McGrath (1970, p. 17) argues that stress involves an organism-environment interaction: "Stress occurs where there is substantial *imbalance* between the environmental demand and the response capability of the focal organism." The "imbalance" depends on whether the individual subjectively perceives he can handle the demand and on whether failure to do so is important. These considerations are mainly important for psychological stressors. Furthermore, the organism can be "underloaded" (too little demand) as well as overloaded. As with activation theory, there is an optimal stimulus load, and deviations in either direction are "stressing." Selye (1974) has recently conceded that stress is not only a part of life, but in some degree is a *desirable* part of life.

### Stress Is Not Unidimensional

It is generally agreed by many investigators that stress is not just a single dimension, ranging from low to high (Appley & Trumbull, 1967). The arguments are the same as with activation theory, i.e., there are low inter-correlations between the various physiological measures of stress. Lacey has applied his concept of situational stereotypy to stress as well as arousal. Indeed, it is not clear that stress and arousal are different concepts except for the common physiological outcomes supposedly resulting from stress.

### Stress Not Limited to Unpleasant Circumstances

We usually associate stress with unpleasant situations, but it may also occur with enjoyable circumstances. An interesting job may eventually be as stressful as prolonged anxiety. Getting married is one of the more stressful possible events in our lives. The phrase "litigator's heart" refers to the stress placed on trial lawyers and there is a distinction between "Type A" and "Type B" people (Friedman & Rosenman, 1974). The former are always trying to use their time more efficiently, do not easily relax, and are said to have more heart attacks. The latter are more relaxed, less efficient and ambitious, and less prone to heart attacks.

We may relate "pleasurable" stress (which is here different from "mild" stress) to the Solomon-Corbit (1975) opponent process theory. According to this theory, whenever a pleasurable event occurs the physiological characteristics of aversive events are also aroused. These are normally masked by the pleasurable aspects of the situation, but are nonetheless occurring. Indeed, television warnings about the dangers of high blood pressure commonly tell us that we may actually feel better with high blood pressure. Behind the experienced pleasure, however, the opponent-process may be building to an unpleasant peak and may eventually result in the GAS.

### Origins of Individual Difference in Stress Tolerance

Not everyone succumbs to the same environmental events or in the same way. Some people thrive on activities that wear away others. One person has a heart attack, while another has ulcers. The two major sources of differential responses to stress are genetics and past experience.

*Genetics.* We shall not discuss genetics in detail (see Chapter Three) except to note that we can breed animals of very different temperaments. Among breeds of dogs are those that are very unresponsive to stimulation (e.g., retrievers) and those that are typically excitable (e.g., Pekingese). In the laboratory, mice that are either highly emotional or unemotional have been genetically differentiated.

*Experience.* We can divide early experiences into *prenatal* and *postnatal.* Anything after conception may be considered an environmental effect. Early postnatal experiences have been emphasized by psychoanalysts from early Freud on. Their method of retrospection (i.e., having the client recall early experiences) does not provide a very reliable base of evidence, but a number of important observations have been made repeatedly over the years. For example, infants in orphanages had a high incidence of health problems, including a high mortality rate, which did not seem to be related directly to hygiene. That is, they were well cared for. What they seemed to lack was individual attention.

*Levine's Research.* Levine (e.g., 1960) tested the Freudian hypothesis that early infantile trauma would produce greater emotionality in adult rats. In the first ten days of life, infant rats were either (1) left alone in the nest with their mothers; (2) taken from the nest and handled for ten minutes a day, or (3) subjected to intermittent electric shock for ten minutes daily. It was predicted that the shocked ("trauma") group would be the most anxious as adults and the group kept with the mother would be the least anxious. The animals were then all reared normally. At eighty days of age, they were tested individually in an open field situation and scored for amount of locomotor activity and frequency of urination and defecation.

Contrary to all expectations, the animals left entirely with their mothers were the most emotional (least active and most defecation and urination). The shocked and handled groups were equally less emotional. Levine argued that the *stimulation* provided by either handling or shock was ultimately beneficial for emotional stability and further argued that the handling (a procedure commonly used to "gentle" animals for experimental use) was as stressful as shock. He likened the experience of handling to Gulliver's fright at being picked up by the giants in Brobdingnag. It may also be like carnival rides, external glass elevators, and parents tossing their children into the air. Recent evidence indicates that in the Levine-type experiment it may be the body cooling which occurs when the hairless infant is removed from the nest that is critical, not the shock or handling per se. This is just a different stressor, however, which does little violence to the overall interpretation.

*Critical Periods for Handling.* There is a critical period for the Levine effect. For the rat, this is between the second and tenth days of life. Animals were tested for reduction of ascorbic acid in the adrenal glands, a sign of adrenal activity, following cold stress at fourteen days of age. Handling on Days 2 to 5 was almost as effective in improving adrenal efficiency (more acid released) as was handling from Days 2 to 13. Handling only on Days 10 to 13 had no effect, and on Days 6 to 9 an intermediate effect.

*Other Behavior Measures.* Escape and avoidance are also sensitive to early handling. Escape from shock is faster with animals that have not been handled but avoidance learning is quicker with the handled ones. The interpretation is that the animals that have not been handled are more emotional and hence more ready to escape from aversive situations. Avoidance learning is more "delicate," however, since it involves carefully timed responses to a cue. Handled animals also release adrenal corticosteroids into the blood more quickly, and when a stress stimulus is removed the animals return to normal levels more quickly. Such a quick arousal and quick "relaxation" are important in avoidance learning. Handled animals, then, show efficient stress responses when appropriate and a quick decline when no longer appropriate, whereas animals that have not been handled are sluggish either to start or to stop.

**Social Psychology of Rat Stress: Interactions of Genetics and Experience.** Even in some selective breeding experiments there may be questions about environmental effects. Genotypically identical animals may behave differently under different prenatal or postnatal conditions. Levine's procedure is so reliable, however, that it can be used to produce genetically equivalent groups of rodents high or low in emotion for use in further research. We can thus vary emotionality through either experience or genes and study their interactions.

*Cross-Rearing Experiments.* Denenberg (1963) established emotional and unemotional rat mothers through differential early handling. He then cross-reared their offspring. The children of emotional mothers were fostered either by emotional or unemotional mothers, as were the children of unemotional mothers. As adults, the offspring of emotional mothers reared by other emotional mothers were the most emotional (in the open field tests), and the offspring of unemotional mothers reared by other unemotional mothers were the least so. The other two combinations fell between. There is thus some "therapeutic" effect of being reared by an unemotional mother but just the opposite when reared by an emotional mother.

Furthermore, there is also an effect of the children on the mothers. The offspring of an unemotional mother have a calming effect on an emotional foster mother, and emotional children "upset" a unemotional foster mother. For further discussion of this research, see Gray (1971).

We thus have a combination of prenatal and postnatal factors at work to determine the offspring's emotionality. Something happens to the infant in utero that increases its emotionality. One possibility is that adrenal hormones from the mother may sensitize the embryo by passing through the placenta. The infant rat would then be more "fearful" at birth, but not for genetic reasons. This idea is supported by the fact that periodically shocking an otherwise untreated pregnant female also results in more emotional offspring. The shock could well produce a release of hormones which would affect the offspring.

*Reciprocal Cross Experiments.* We can also breed female rats that are genetically high in emotion with males that are genetically low in emotion, and vice versa. In both cases, all infants should be getting the same complement of "high and low emotional genes," but some of the infants are carried and cared for by an emotional mother, others by a unemotional mother. The results of such research, with various controls for postnatal experience, show that infants carried by emotional mothers are themselves later more emotional (Broadhurst, 1960). We can conclude that genetic, prenatal, and early postnatal factors all contribute to the emotionality expressed in the behavior of the adult rodent.

### Emotional Conditioning

**Classical Conditioning.** There is little question that classical conditioning is an important factor in emotionality, as discussed previously in Chapter Eight (fear conditioning). Such physiological responses as the GSR, heart rate, and arbitrary avoidance responses, which are presumed to reflect underlying fear conditioning, have been studied in detail. Russian psychologists (e.g., see Bykov, 1957; Razran, 1961) have studied a great variety of conditioned and unconditioned stimuli and responses. Of particular interest, they have used *interoceptive* stimuli (which tell us about our internal states) and responses of internal organs (such as the kidney or pancreas), as well as the more traditional salivary and gastrointestinal responses. According to this literature, virtually any stimulus can be used as the CS for some response and any response (muscular or glandular) can be conditioned to some CS. This considerably increases the potential for particular organs to break down under stress in some individuals but not others.

**Instrumental Conditioning of Autonomic Responses.** Psychologists long assumed, with little evidence, that responses under the control of the autonomic nervous system could not be conditioned by rewarding or punishing their occurrence. Two-factor theories of learning (e.g., Skinner, 1938; Mowrer, 1947; see Rescorla & Solomon, 1967, for an excellent historical review) have commonly been built around the idea that classical conditioning was limited to autonomic responses (including fear) and that instrumental conditioning was limited to skeletal responses. The initial reports of instrumental conditioning of the GSR in the early 1960s were thus received with considerable surprise and have led to considerable rethinking about conditioning.

There are several interpretive possibilities for any apparent instrumental autonomic conditioning (A. H. Black, 1971). First, of course, it may really occur; some specific responses, such as change in heart rate or GSR, may really be instrumentally conditioned. Second, skeletal movements may occur that produce *unconditioned* changes in autonomic activity. It may be these skeletal movements which are conditioned rather than, say, heart rate, but heart rate increases with increased movement. Third, there may be unintentional classical conditioning in instrumental situations. Some stimulus may precede the reinforcer in such a manner that the animal associates the two (as a CS and a UCS) independently of the instrumental response involved. For example, in a maze, the goal box stimuli always precede the reinforcer. The experimenter may not be aware of such stimuli, even though the animal is. Finally, even without overt skeletal activity, there may be conditioning of "central movement processes." That is, the brain activities controlling skeletal movements might also affect autonomic activities. It is difficult to tease apart these alternatives, and it may be virtually impossible to do so with human subjects. With such alternative interpretations in mind, however, let us look at some of the research.

*Instrumental Autonomic Conditioning With Humans.* If GSR is recorded from a quietly sitting person, there are "random" increases and decreases. Kimmel and Hill (1960) suggested that such "emitted" responses could be increased in frequency by reinforcement. They first tried to do this by presenting subjects pleasant odors when a certain minimal increase in GSR magnitude occurred. Conversely, they tried to punish responses with bad odors. The results were negative, but odors are hard to control, so Kimmel turned to using a light flash (in a dark room) as a reinforcer. Fowler and Kimmel (1962) found that reinforced GSR's did occur more frequently than in a control group, but both groups were actually declining in frequency over the test session. Since subjects in such situations usually require some time to relax, Kimmel and Kimmel (1963) allowed more time for adaptation to the situation, during which spontaneous GSR's could decline to a lower level. Reinforced subjects did then show an increase in GSR frequency, while control subjects continued to decline. Thus, there did appear to be real autonomic conditioning.

We can, however, see the possibility that subjects were making skeletal movements (or even thinking exciting thoughts) that were reinforced, and these movements or thoughts might have increased the GSR frequency. Some experiments have shown a correlation between muscle action potentials and GSR's in such conditioning situations, and other experimenters have been unable to obtain conditioning at all (Katkin, 1971). Experimenters then turned to the use of curare, a paralytic agent used on blowgun darts by Central American Indians. One experiment (Birk, Crider, Shapiro, & Tursky, 1966) actually used curare with a human subject and showed an increase in GSR with reinforcement. Unfortunately, there was no control condition. The bulk of such research, of course, has been done with animals.

*Instrumental Autonomic Conditioning With Animals.* The most impressive results on instrumental autonomic conditioning have come from Neal Miller's laboratory. Di Cara and Miller (1968) trained separate groups of rats to either increase or decrease their heart rates to avoid shock while paralyzed by curare. Simultaneous recording of muscle activity indicated no overt or covert movements. Since both acceleration and deceleration could be conditioned, the results are not due to a simple increase in autonomic reactivity, either.

To show further that there is not just a generalized change in autonomic reactivity, Miller and Banuazizi (1968) conditioned heart rate and intestinal contractions independently. Instead of shock avoidance, they used electrical stimulation of the brain as reward. The rewarded response increased, but the other one (no matter which) did not. Di Cara and Miller (1968) also showed that curarized animals could be differentially conditioned to dilate or constrict the blood vessels in one ear but not the other. This would seem to require such a "fine tuning" of any central movement process that this interpretation would seem to be no simpler than that of direct conditioning of the different target organs. A. H. Black (1971) also cites a number of experiments in which there was initial conditioning under curare, then testing when the animals were recovered. There was no relationship between skeletal movements and responses of the heart—acceleration or deceleration—to the CS. If conditioned heart rate changes in either direction were accompanied by equal amounts of movement, it would appear that there was indeed heart rate conditioning independent of movement.

The primary flaw in this line of research has been an inability to reproduce many of the results, either in Miller's own laboratory or in others. Some investigators (e.g., Brenner, Eissenberg, & Middaugh, 1974; Roberts, Lacroix, & Wright, 1974) have been unable to obtain instrumental heart rate conditioning with hundreds of animals. Many problems have appeared, including the fact that the original procedures used by Miller and Di Cara to respirate their paralyzed animals produce hyperventilation and sudden changes in heart rate. Miller and Dworkin (1974) have postulated everything from impure drugs to laboratory demons to account for the early results. With regard to heart rate, then, it is not clear just what the role of instrumental conditioning is. It is, of course, harder to account for the differential conditioning of vascular changes in the two ears or between the heart and gastrointestinal tract in terms of hyperventilation or impure drugs.

### Stress and Crowding

Animal populations periodically increase and decrease, a fluctuation sometimes thought to be due to changing availability of food. Experimental animals in restricted living areas, however, stabilize at population numbers that are much smaller than the area can support. The most popular interpretation of population stability (e.g., Wynne-Edwards, 1962) appears to be that crowding is stressful. Stress increases adrenal hormone output, which in turn suppresses pituitary activity. The pituitary gland, in turn, does not release the hormones that stimulate various sexual and infant caretaking activities. The reproductive and survival rate then goes down until the crowding is reduced and stress is relieved, at which time the population increases again. Among humans, other social factors are important. Thus, although crowding is great in such cities as Tokyo or Hong Kong, a tightly knit social order seems to reduce the stress of crowding, and the reproductive rate does not drop precipitously.

### Decision Making, Stress, and Ulcers

Folklore has it that the conflict of making decisions takes its toll through the stomach, if not the Type A heart. In one experiment, Brady (1958) kept pairs of rhesus monkeys simultaneously in restraining chairs for six hours a day, during which time they received periodic shocks on a Sidman avoidance schedule. One monkey, the "executive," in each pair, could control the shocks by pressing a lever. The other, a yoked-control, got exactly the same shocks as the executive but could do nothing to prevent them. In a matter of days, the executive monkeys developed severe ulcers, whereas the controls did not. It was suggested that the continuous decisions ("To press or not to press") produced the ulcers. The apparent analogy with the human business executive lent considerable credence to this interpretation.

Other research does not support Brady's conclusions, however. Jay Weiss noted that Brady had *selected* as executive monkeys those that had learned most readily to respond on the Sidman avoidance schedule and may have therefore inadvertently selected animals that were more ulcer prone in the first place. Weiss and his associates (e.g., Weiss, 1972) have used yoked-control procedures with rats and repeatedly found just the opposite of Brady's results, namely that animals which control the situation are *less* prone to ulcers. Weiss suggests that being in an *uncontrollable* threatening situation is more stressful, a conclusion we might have predicted from many previous research examples (e.g., learned helplessness). To carry the business executive analogy further, being *near* the top of the managerial heap with threats and conflicts, but at the mercy of someone else's decisions, may be the ulcer-producing condition.

Control is apparently an important variable in anxiety and stress. Mowrer and Viek (1948) showed that animals that could not control an aversive situation were more fearful than those that could. They dubbed this "fear from a sense of helplessness," closely related to "learned help-lessness" (see Chapter Nine). Another reliable pair of findings is that people or animals (1) prefer signalled to unsignalled shock (e.g., Badia, McBane, Suter, & Lewis, 1966), and (2) prefer immediate to delayed shock. Uncertainty and delay are situations where there is no control, and this is apparently more aversive than just the shock.

### Aggression, Defeat, and Ulcers

Weiss, Pohorecky, Salman, and Gruenthal (1976) have recently found that rats allowed to fight when given tail shock do not ulcerate as much as animals not allowed to fight. This seems to support another bit of folklore, namely that it is "bad" to keep in our hostility. This statement, however, is too broad because, for example, the guilt and anxiety following expression of hostility might be worse than "keeping it in." The results achieved by Weiss et al. are most interesting, however, and suggest that at least under some circumstances it may be worthwhile to "release our hostility."

It is also better, when fighting, to be a winner than a loser. The physi-ology of defeat is the physiology of stress. Animals that lose fights or are at the bottom of dominance hierarchies show more physiological stress than do the winners or animals at the top of the hierarchy (e.g., see Scott, 1971).

### Symptom Specificity

Psychiatrists have long pondered why some individuals show one kind of stress disorder (e.g., ulcers), while others show different ones (e.g., asthma). The phrase "organ language" has been used quite literally to refer to the possibility that we express our emotions and thoughts (presumably repressed and unconscious) through certain body organs. Psychoanalytic theory had it that the selection was symbolic. From the preceding discussions, how-ever, we can see possible accounts more mundane than unconscious sym-bolism.

First, there may be genetic differences in susceptibility to certain dis-orders. Thus, under conditions of nonspecific stress one organ may be the "first to go" for one individual but not for another. Second, there may be specific conditioning, classical or instrumental (e.g., of gastric activity). Third, there may indeed be a kind of symbolic selection. For example, we might tense certain muscles related to activities of concern to us, e.g., muscles of the hand. Continual muscle tension leads to various aches and pains, including migraine headaches and breathing problems. Hence, the very flexibility in learning that helps us survive may also get us right back into trouble because we can learn to become emotional under conditions which are not life-threatening. Stress mechanisms which evolved hundreds of thousands of years ago as adaptations for survival when life was endangered may be inappropriate for most contemporary life.

## ANXIETY

Rollo May (1950) said that proving that anxiety is a widespread problem is like carrying coals to Newcastle. Many people have written about an "age of anxiety," each arguing that their own historical period was the most anxiety producing of all. Since we know the anxieties of our own times, we are ready to believe that ours indeed may be the worst. There is little hard evidence, however, that the man on the street now is more anxious about nuclear war or loss of identity than previous generations have been about war, famine, pestilence, and disease. That does not, however, decrease the importance of the problem of anxiety in our time.

### A Philosophical Predecessor: Kierkegaard

Many contemporary psychologists, philosophers, and theologians consider the Danish philosopher Sören Kierkegaard (1813–1855) as the most prominent forebear of contemporary thought about anxiety. Kierkegaard argued (see May, 1950) that man has the potential to be many different things, and these possibilities are his freedom. But at the same time, his confrontation with freedom is his source of anxiety. Indeed, the more creative a person is, the more likely he is to be anxious because he has more possibilities and is dealing more with the unknown. Anxiety involves inner conflict, which necessarily follows from man's alternatives. Anxiety is healthy if one moves through it to reach a higher level of personal development, but is unhealthy if one is "shut in" by it.

### Some Variations in Psychological Thought

Psychologists from Freud on have differed in their ideas about the origin and nature of anxiety. At various times Freud considered anxiety to result from repressed sexual impulses, or from conflict between such basic drives as sex and hostility and socialization. He distinguished between *ob-*

*jective anxiety* (what we would normally call fear) and *neurotic anxiety.* Objective anxiety is related to a specific object, whereas neurotic anxiety is not, and, furthermore neurotic anxiety is characterized by being disproportionate to the actual threat, involving repression and conflict, and involving defense mechanisms.

Anxiety, then, is not a terribly well-defined and well-understood concept, partly because it is approached from many directions, e.g., clinically, behaviorally, and physiologically. Furthermore, while we may think we can differentiate fear and anxiety conceptually, it is very difficult to distinguish them operationally. Many psychologists have used the terms *fear* and *anxiety* interchangeably, and more recently have thrown *stress* and *arousal* into the same pot.

Epstein (e.g., 1967) has tried to be somewhat more explicit. He considers that *arousal* is a component of all motivation and stimulation, that fear is an avoidance motive *directed* toward a specific object, and that anxiety is undirected arousal following perception of danger. He also sees fear and anxiety as qualitatively different. He suggests that anxiety is aroused when we cannot cope with threat, either because the source of the threat is not recognized or because a recognized threat is beyond our ability to cope. A soldier may be aware of the source of mortar shells dropping around him but is anxious, as well as afraid, because he cannot do anything about it. In such a situation, fear and anxiety are *additive.* Anxiety is also aroused by uncertainty about threatening situations, as we previously saw with regard to stress. We are less competent to cope with things we are uncertain about.

### Trait versus State Anxiety

The distinction between anxiety as a personality trait (A-trait) and as a temporary, situationally determined state (A-state) has been a major focus of research in recent years. Such measures as the Taylor Scale of Manifest Anxiety (MAS—see Taylor, 1953) were first thought to be measuring *chronic* anxiety levels but subjects who score high on the MAS are apparently more anxious only in stressful situations than subjects who score low. Measures of trait anxiety may then reflect only the tendency of some people to react anxiously (A-state) in a greater number of situations. This indeed is what the MAS taps, i.e., the individual indicates different kinds of situations in which he shows symptoms of anxiety.

Spielberger (1966) then considers trait anxiety as a *disposition* to respond in a certain way under certain circumstances. State anxiety, however, is *not* a dispositional concept. The term *A-state* refers to what is going on at the moment, the anxiety level of the individual in a particular place at a particular time.

### The S-R Inventory of Anxiousness and the Trait Concept. Endler,

Hunt, and Rosenstein (1962) and Endler and Hunt (1966) have also argued that anxiety is situation specific. They devised an S-R Inventory of Anxiousness to get at such situational versus personal factors. The inventory consists of eleven different situations (e.g., starting on a long auto trip, going to meet a new date, and crawling along a ledge high on a mountain side) and fourteen different kinds of responses for each of these (e.g., heart beats faster, get an uneasy feeling, emotion disrupts action, and mouth gets dry). Each of the fourteen "anxious" responses is rated on a 5-point scale (e.g., heart beats faster: "Not at all" [1] to "Much Faster" [5]). Scores on the total scale correlate about .40 with the Taylor Scale and the Mandler-Sarason Test Anxiety Questionnaire, and reliability is good. At the extremes, people might report being highly anxious on every response in every situation or not very anxious in every situation. In fact, however, whether a person rates a response high or low depends on the person, the situation, and the response being rated. There is relatively little tendency for different persons to rate themselves consistently high or low in anxiety across all situations and responses (Endler & Hunt, 1966).

*Some Therapeutic Implications.* If anxiety is specific to situations and responses, then treatments may have to be equally specific. This has been the approach taken in recent years by behavior therapists working in learning theory traditions. The classic psychoanalytic approach has been that specific fears and neurotic behaviors are the result of deep-seated problems originating in early childhood, which are supposed to produce a kind of diffuse anxiety, and that the specific neurotic fears and behaviors are responses (symptoms) to this underlying problem. Therapy is therefore said to be effective on any permanent basis only if you get at the underlying causes of the anxiety. Specific treatments of symptoms are said to be ineffective because new symptoms will just replace the old ones if the underlying cause is not treated. This is very much a medical approach.

The behavior therapy approach, on the other hand, is that specific fears and problem behaviors *are* the problem of the individual and that through re-education (e.g., extinction of fear, or learning new ways of behaving) the individual will be helped. There has been considerable heated debate over these positions. There is, however, little firm evidence to support the psychoanalytic assumptions, and these assumptions—long considered facts—are being relentlessly challenged.

## COPING

### Nature of Coping

The term *coping* refers to any way we may try to control stress or anxiety in ourselves. Psychologists have mainly talked about the Freudian *defense mechanisms* (such as repression, projection, reaction formation, projection, and denial) whose function is to reduce anxiety. Other mechanisms, cognitive and behavioral, can also be used to reduce stress and anxiety, however. Since the Freudian mechanisms are detailed in introductory texts and texts on abnormal psychology, we shall not discuss them further here. Rather, we shall examine some different approaches to thinking about coping that have developed in the last few years.

### Cognitive Factors in Coping

Contemporary theories of emotion all involve the idea that *appraisal* of the situation is a partial determinant of the experienced emotion. If two people are in a sinking boat, one may appraise the situation as dangerous (he cannot swim and believes the water to be deep) but the other appraises the situation as safe (he knows the water is only three feet deep). One way to cope with dangerous situations is to change our appraisals of them. Throwing out the anchor would indicate the depth of the water and lead to reappraisal of the danger.[2]

Psychotherapeutic technique is often aimed at helping individuals reappraise their life situations. For example, if the client becomes very angry at the therapist for no "objective" reason, he may be treating the therapist as he would someone else important in his life (this is known in psychoanalysis as *transference*). The therapist tries to interpret this to the client, to help him reappraise his situation and to understand that his life situation has perhaps changed, and that he need not react to other people as he may have once reacted toward, say, his father.

Richard Lazarus (1975, p. 557) argues that "We cannot hope to understand the emotions unless we also take into account the coping activities that affect them." Our example of the sinking boat illustrates this. Lazarus distinguishes two kinds of "emotion-regulatory" or coping processes. One is *direct action,* an attempt to directly escape or avoid the emotion-arousing situation. A student anticipating a tough exam might hit the books hard in preparation. The second Lazarus calls *palliation,* which is essentially symptom relief after one is already in an emotional situation. Tranquilizers, liquor, relaxation therapy, and defense mechanisms are palliatives. Lazarus also emphasizes that the symptom-oriented approach is not inferior to direct action, because it is often the only action left.

---

[2]Kurt Koffka (1935), the famous Gestalt psychologist, distinguished between the geographic (objective) environment and the behavioral (perceived) environment. The importance of the distinction was illustrated in the following German legend. A man arrived at an inn after travelling considerable distance through a blinding snowstorm. The innkeeper asked him if he knew that he had just ridden across Lake Constance, whereupon the traveller dropped dead. The traveller was at ease until he discovered that his perception of his situation was very different from reality, and presumably became intensely emotional at the discovery of the discrepancy.

*Lazarus' Research On Cognitive Appraisal.* Lazarus (e.g., 1968) has experimentally studied the effects of different cognitions on emotional arousal. For all subjects, GSR was continuously recorded before and during observation of a movie showing a primitive puberty rite. This rite (subcision) consists of making several cuts on the underside of the initiate's penis. The movie uniformly produces emotional reactions in the viewers. Lazarus' question was whether different kinds of cognitive reappraisals would reduce the emotional reactivity of different kinds of subjects. In one experiment, college students and relatively uneducated middle-management businessmen were subjects. Three different soundtracks accompanied the otherwise silent film: (1) no soundtrack; (2) a narrator saying that the operation was not really painful or unpleasant, and that the young man looked forward to it; and (3) a narrator saying the scene was just an interesting bit of anthropological data. The first narration involved the defense mechanism of "denial," and the second involved "intellectualization." Lazarus predicted that the college students would cope better (have lower GSR) by intellectualizing along with the soundtrack and that the businessmen would show less stress with the denial narration. The results were as predicted: The two groups showed a significant reduction of the GSR only with their particular narrations, not with the silent film or the alternative narration. Other research also showed that just presenting different introductions to the film is about as effective as the continuing narrations.

Lazarus' research has been seminal in showing that different cognitive appraisals actually can reduce physiological responsiveness, and also that these are specific to different people. We may presume they are even much more specific than Lazarus' research attempted to show.

### Studies of Extreme Stress and Coping

The typical laboratory experiment on stress or anxiety in humans may be a pale reflection of extreme clinical anxiety. In the cases of sports parachuting and major surgery, however, the stress is real, and at the same time there is opportunity for close observation. There is also an element of experimental control insofar as measures can be taken at scheduled times before and after the traumatic events because, unlike most real-life emergency situations, the experimenter can arrange to be there. It is also possible to manipulate experimental variables at different times in relation to the stressful event.

*Parachuting.* What happens emotionally the first time a person steps out of an airplane into empty air? What happens as experience in doing this is gained? Most people are so frightened that they never do it again. Istel (1961) studied 2,800 men who had volunteered for sports parachuting.

After one jump, only 15 percent returned, and only a small fraction of these lasted beyond two or three jumps. There is considerable objective anxiety here, of course, because the situation is in fact life threatening—particularly if one performs ineptly.

In a study of novice parachutists (first jumps), S. Epstein and Fenz (1965) studied the GSR's to verbal stimuli of different degrees of relevance to parachuting. On the day of the jump, the GSR was progressively greater for words of low, medium, and high relevance to jumping (e.g., *sky, aircraft,* and *ripcord,* respectively). The same kind of generalization gradient was found two weeks before and on the day before the jump, but was much more pronounced on the day of the jump. Such neutral words as *paper* or *music* produced smaller reactions, but "anxiety" words like *killed* or *hurt* also evoked very large GSR's. A nonparachuting control group did not show these effects. On the day of the jump, some individuals gave "bizarre" responses to the verbal stimuli—for example, responding with the words *jump master* to the word *chair.*

With continued jumping, there is a change in the pattern of self-reported fear in relation to closeness to jump time. Experienced jumpers report the most fear on the morning of the jump, then a steady decrease as jump time approaches. There is no increase in fear until the chute opens and the jumper lands on the ground. This suggests that the jumpers had learned to control their fear until after the jump. Inexperienced jumpers show a build-up of fear to the time they are given the ready signal to jump, and show a decline thereafter. These differences are shown in Figure 11.3.

The biggest problem for the novice is conquering his own fear. S. Epstein (1967) suggests three ways he may do this: (1) avoiding perceiving, thinking about, or doing anything that would arouse fear; (2) doing things to distract oneself; and (3) emphasizing to oneself the positive aspects of jumping. These combine in different ways to produce such defenses as activating selective perception, inhibiting anxiety-producing responses, making incompatible responses, or denying that there is anything to be afraid of. Evidence for the operation of such inhibitory mechanisms is shown by the fact that strong anxiety may occur after the individual is already safe and "lets down" his defenses. Anxiety apparently does not just decline or dissipate with experience—it is inhibited by active cognitive controls, only to return later.

Novice jumpers may "overdefend" in the sense that they appear perfectly calm and in control of themselves, but when their defenses fail there is overwhelming anxiety, including such physiological reactions as vomiting, fainting, and so on. Overcontrol was also illustrated by a jumper whose main chute did not open and who so casually counted to ten before pulling the cord for the reserve chute that it barely had time to open (S. Epstein, 1967). A different aspect of control was indicated by an experienced jumper

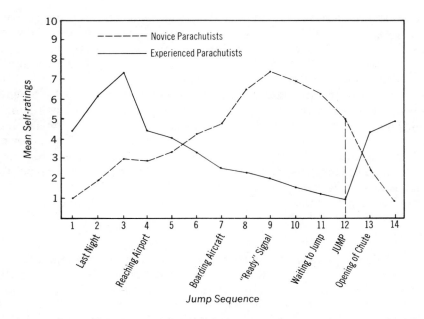

**Figure 11.3** *Fear levels of novice and experienced parachutists as they approach the jump. (From Fenz & Epstein, 1967, p. 34.)*

who fell asleep in the plane during the ascent to a high jump altitude. On awakening, he felt anxious and unprepared and did not enjoy the jump (S. Epstein, 1967). Apparently, falling asleep changed his normal routine for inhibiting fear. As Epstein phrases it, then, "The experienced parachutists developed a control system characterized by early warning signals at low levels of anxiety, as contrasted with the later signals and drastic defenses against high levels of anxiety used by novices" (1967, p. 19).

***Surgery.*** Janis (summarized in Janis, Mahl, Kagan, & Holt, 1969) studied the recovery of surgical patients in relation to their anxiety levels before surgery. The operations were dangerous and painful, such as removal of part of a lung or stomach. The patients were intensively interviewed and these data were supplemented by various hospital records, nurses' reports, and so on. It was found that patients moderately anxious prior to operation showed better recovery than patients either high or low in anxiety before surgery. Those who were initially calm became more upset than those who had been "part-time worriers beforehand." Janis believes that a moderate amount of worry induced patients to think about what was going to happen so that they were ready to cope with pain or mild setbacks during recovery. They were also receptive to the reassurances of their doctors and nurses and could reassure themselves. The most important difference between slightly and moderately anxious patients appeared to be that those who were moderately fearful obtained more information about their operations and what to expect. Egbert, Battit, Welch, and Bartlett (1964) systematically varied the amount of preoperative information given to patients, the least amount being the standard information given by the hospital. Patients given a description of postoperative pain, assurances that it was normal, told how to relax, and assured that they would be given medication if necessary, subsequently required only half as much pain medication and went home an average of 2.7 days sooner than patients given the standard information. Janis considers the "work of worrying" is important in preparing individuals for stressful events and helping them tolerate such events. The information gained is used in the cognitive control of anxiety and stress.

### Biofeedback

The term *biofeedback* refers to feedback information about any biological process. Recent interest has been centered on the electronic amplification of processes that are normally difficult to observe directly. We can tell with our eyes open or closed whether our arm is up or down because we have visual and muscle and joint receptors to inform us about the position and movement of our limbs. It is much more difficult, if not impossible, to recognize subtle differences in skin temperature, skin resistance, blood pressure, heart rate, muscle tension, or EEG. Biofeedback instruments are amplifiers specialized to convert such physiological signals into readily identifiable visual or auditory stimuli that tell us what is happening. For example, a light may come on only when our brain is producing alpha waves or a tone may change pitch upward and downward as muscle tension increases or decreases.[3]

The therapeutic logic behind the use of biofeedback most commonly is that high levels of physiological activity are associated with tension (beta waves in the EEG, low skin resistance, high blood pressure and heart rate, and tense muscles). Biofeedback techniques can help us to learn what it feels like to relax or to have other specific physiological changes. For example, there is often a gradual increase in muscle tension so that we do not notice it occurring; then suddenly we have headaches, muscle aches, tics, or we grind our teeth. For a good account of the effects of muscle tension, see Malmo (1975). From electrodes placed on the appropriate muscles, we can see on the feedback instrument when there is an increase or

---

[3]Unfortunately for the novice, there are a number of such amplification systems on the market that are probably very inaccurate. A potential buyer is urged to find somebody who knows something about electronic equipment and biological amplification before spending much money. As a rule of thumb, a good biofeedback instrument will be at least as expensive as the highest-quality stereo amplifier.

decrease in tension, and (hopefully) can thereby learn to discriminate tension from relaxation and be able to control tension.

The whole biofeedback approach is, of course, closely related to instrumental conditioning, autonomic or skeletal. The best of the biofeedback research each year is now collected annually in a volume called *Biofeedback & Self-Control* (e.g., Barber, Di Cara, Kamiya, Miller, Shapiro, & Stoyva, 1976) and there is a journal called *Biofeedback and Self-Regulation.* Suffice it here to say that sometimes biofeedback techniques work very well, clinically or experimentally, and sometimes they do not. It is, for example, very difficult to obtain a reduction of heart rate or blood pressure of clinically significant magnitude that will persist outside the laboratory setting. R. Lazarus (1975) has argued that somatic processes cannot be understood without consideration of individual people's coping styles, which in turn are influenced by many social and psychological factors.

### Altered States of Consciousness

Almost any circumstances very different from our normal environmental stimulation can produce an altered state of consciousness (ASC), which is defined at best only as a kind of awareness that we do not ordinarily experience (Ornstein, 1972; 1973; Tart, 1969). Such circumstances may include meditation, drugs, hypnosis, relaxation exercises, sensory isolation, excitement, music, and so on. There are a number of fairly common *characteristics* of ASC's, however. These include (1) change in emotional expression—we may become more happy or sad, calm or excited; (2) change in the meaning or significance of events—small things may suddenly become important or great things trivial; and (3) feelings of rejuvenation—when the experience is over, there is a common report of relaxation and "rejuvenation." A fourth characteristic is an inability to *describe* such experiences very well.

From time immemorial, shamans ("witch doctors") have used consciousness-altering procedures as a means of healing. Their techniques have included music and dancing, as well as hallucinogenic drugs (such as mescaline). There have been some authors who could capably describe their drug experiences (e.g., Castaneda, 1968; Huxley, 1954). The hallucinogenic experiences may be interpreted as religious experiences, and the healing properties related to some kind of "spirit."

Altered states are often believed to be avenues for gaining new knowledge, not normally attainable through sensory channels. This is described by such phrases as "cosmic consciousness" and "oneness with the universe." Modern shamans prescribe tranquilizers, valium being the most prescribed drug in the world. Opium and marijuana derivatives are, worldwide, among the most popular nonprescribed drugs, usually illegal. Cocaine is widely used in some parts of the world, including South America, where it is used by Indians. Such drugs often serve the useful therapeutic function of helping people who eke out a precarious existence to keep going. They are used for survival, not entertainment, as an aid to deal with reality, rather than to escape from it. In any event, ASC's, whether produced by drugs or other techniques, are often used as a way to cope with reality. There is always, of course, a kind of thrill-seeking segment of any population who take drugs, meditate, or what have you for the sake of "The Experience."

### Meditation

There are many different forms of meditation (Ornstein, 1972), but the most popular in the United States is an offspring of Zen Buddhism called transcendental meditation (TM), or the "Science of Creative Intelligence." Its primary guru (teacher) is Maharishi Mahesh Yogi, first brought to international prominence by the Beatles. Under the guidance of a trained teacher, the initiate is given a mantra, a particular word or phrase that is said repeatedly. A specific mantra is said to be given to a particular individual on the grounds that not all mantras are suitable for all people. Since the mantras are not publicly released and each individual is supposed to keep his own mantra secret, the claim is hard to validate. On the basis of other meditative techniques, we would expect a mantra to be a word or syllable like "Om," which has a soft, rolling sound to it.

Two twenty-minute periods of meditation a day are supposed to make one healthier, happier, more loving, more energetic, and better able to use one's mind creatively. Many devotees are satisfied that this has happened to them. The argument is made that through meditation our minds "naturally move to a field of greater happiness," and in the process we tap "infinite depths" of creativity. It is also claimed that most of us only use 5 to 10 percent of our mental capacity, and that through meditation we can approach 100 percent.[4]

It is also said that TM is better than other methods because it is based on the "natural tendencies of the mind." (Several generations of psychologists would dearly love to know just what the natural tendencies of the mind *are*.)

---

[4]This same kind of claim is made by the advocates of many different techniques and is often preceded by statements that "Psychologists say" we only use 10 percent of our mind or intelligence, etc. Well, psychologists do not say this, and in fact it is patent nonsense. First, there is no measure of information processing or intelligence by which we could make such a quantitative statement. Second, it is a logically inconsistent statement. If a given individual has never used 100 percent of his capacity, how can we say that he is using only 10 percent, since we do not know what 10 percent would be? Undoubtedly, we could all be somewhat more efficient with our time and perhaps think a little more clearly (perhaps even much more clearly), but any quantum jumps in intellectual capacity are more likely to come from different concepts or strategies for learning and problem solving rather than from any mechanical meditative technique.

It can be taught in just a few hours, and can be done any time or place thereafter. The exaggerated claims for TM stretch one's credulity to the limit, but the technique unquestionably does have value for some individuals, perhaps because they believe in it strongly. On the other hand, there are also claims of psychological harm (A. Lazarus, 1976).

The TM movement also makes exaggerated claims to scientific validation (World Plan Executive Council, 1975). Evidence is claimed that TM decreases reaction time, improves problem-solving ability, leads to a more self-actualized personality, better grades, reduced drug use, and greater emotional stability—among other things. As of the present date (February, 1977) the author has been unable to obtain reports of some of the claimed evidence.[5] Existing published work, however, is clearly permeated by two major research flaws: subject selection and lack of control for deep relaxation produced by any method other than TM.

*Subject Selection.* The majority of research to which the present author has access either has had no control subjects at all, simply comparing meditators with some normative population statistic, or has compared meditators with some presumably equivalent group of nonmeditators. Since the meditators have selected themselves into meditation in the first place and the nonmeditators have not, it is not known what other differences between the groups there are. It is well known that volunteer and nonvolunteer subjects for psychological research differ in personality characteristics. One reasonable hypothesis is that it takes a somewhat better-adjusted person to go into meditation in the first place, someone willing to try something different and not afraid of ridicule. This alone could account for most of the data on personality variables. Indeed, Beck (1977) found that introductory psychology students who would "definitely volunteer" to be subjects in TM research were on the average "better adjusted" on fourteen of seventeen scales on the Adjective Check List, where clear predictions could be made, than were students who "definitely would not."

*Relaxation.* The most widely quoted evidence that TM is a kind of "superrelaxation," even better than sleep, comes from a report by Wallace and Benson (1972). In this experiment, *which had no control group,* all subjects had several physiological measures taken immediately before, during, and after twenty minutes of meditation by experienced meditators. During meditation, oxygen consumption, blood lactate, skin conductance, and respiration rate decreased. The amplitude of alpha waves increased, and there was no change in blood pressure. The low level of blood lactate was taken as a prime indicator of the meditators' relaxed state. Benson

[5] Recently (April, 1977) I have seen a prepublication collection of research which I was told was not yet ready for general distribution.

(1975) has since disavowed that such effects are peculiar to TM, arguing that the *relaxation response* can be obtained under many different conditions. Michaels, Huber, and McCann (1976) found that plasma levels of epinephrine, norepinephrine, and lactate were the same in both meditation and resting states. Pagano, Rose, Stivers, and Warrenburg (1976) found that their experienced TM subjects spent about 40 percent of their meditation time sleeping, as indexed by EEG activity. Our existing knowledge, then, does not show that TM produces a clearly different physiological state than other methods of achieving relaxation. Meditation may be an especially effective way for some individuals to achieve relaxation, however, and the technique is thus worthwhile for them. No one doubts that relaxation has merit.

## CONCLUSION

Conflict, stress and anxiety are complexly related to genetics, early experience and adult learning. In recent years we have come to realize that anxiety is not just a trait that a person "carries around" with him, but also depends on the situation and even the kind of "anxiety response" that is studied. Specific physiological responses to stressful situations can apparently be learned via the mechanism of rewarding their occurrence, as well as through the more traditional classical aversive conditioning techniques. Instrumental conditioning itself is a complex process, however, involving individual perceptions and interpretations of rewards and the conditions under which they are obtained. If there is a cognitive restructuring of a stressful situation (a new or different interpretation of the situation) stress responses can also be altered. The experimental psychology of motivation has not dealt extensively with such restructuring but the role of cognitive processes in coping with stress is more generally recognized now and should generate more research. Recently (for American psychology), there has also been considerable interest in reducing stress by somewhat more direct methods, such as relaxation, biofeedback, and meditation. Each of these approaches recognizes the importance of self-control as compared to control by some outside agent.

chapter 12

# Aggression

## WHAT IS AGGRESSION?

### The Problem of Defining Aggression

The biggest problem in studying aggression is to define the subject matter. When we see what has been called *aggression,* we are amazed at the diversity, ranging from attack and killing to stories told about pictures. What makes some behaviors aggressive and others not? In Table 12-1 are summarized a set of examples (see Kaufmann, 1970, or Johnson, 1972, for similar lists). Before reading further, you may wish to check which of these *you* think is aggressive behavior and compare notes with someone else to see whether they agree with you. The problems quickly become obvious.

Looking at the list, we can see that whether an act is aggressive depends on our definition. For example, a definition including all *actual harm* would include Item 1 (Boy Scout) and Item 3 (flower pot) as well as Item 21 (hired killer). If both actual harm and *intent to harm* are necessary to define aggression, we eliminate Items 1 and 3, among others. If *intent alone* is sufficient, even though the act may have failed, as in Item 2 (assassin misses target), then we have yet another set of aggressive behaviors. If we exclude food-getting behavior (Item 4) or an act committed under someone else's orders (Item 6), the picture changes again. These matters are not easily agreed on, which leads to the conclusion that no single circumstance can satisfactorily characterize everything that might be considered aggressive. Aggression is no more a unitary process than drive is.

### Multiprocess Views of Aggression

Biologists generally talk about *agonistic* behaviors rather than aggression. These are any kind of attack, fighting, escape, or avoidance behaviors. Three common types are *predatory behavior, attack behavior,* and *defensive fighting.*

**Table 12-1**  *Behaviors that might be considered aggressive.*

1. A Boy Scout helping an old lady across the street accidentally trips her and she sprains her ankle.
2. An assassin attempts to kill a presidential candidate but his shot misses.
3. A housewife knocks a flower pot off a fifth story window ledge and it hits a passerby.
4. A farmer kills a chicken for dinner.
5. In a debate, one person belittles another's qualifications.
6. A soldier presses a button that fires a nuclear missile and kills thousands of people he cannot even see.
7. A policeman trying to break up a riot hits a rioter in the head with a club and knocks him unconscious.

8. A cat stalks, catches, tosses around, and eventually kills a mouse.
9. A wife accuses her husband of having an affair and he retorts that after living with her anyone would have an affair.
10. A frightened boy, caught in the act of stealing and trying to escape, shoots his discoverer.
11. One child takes a toy away from another, making him cry.
12. A man unable to get into his locked car kicks in the side of the door.
13. A man pays 25¢ to beat an old car with an iron bar, which he does vigorously.
14. A football player blocks another player from behind (clipping) and breaks his leg.
15. A businessman hires a professional killer to "take care of" a business rival.
16. A woman carefully plots how she will kill her husband, then does so.
17. Two students get into a drunken brawl and one hits the other with a beer bottle.
18. A businessman works vigorously to improve his business and drive out the competition.
19. On the Rorschach inkblot test, a hospitalized mental patient is scored as being highly aggressive, although he has never actually harmed anyone.
20. A young boy talks a lot about how he is going to beat up others, but never does it.
21. A hired killer successfully completes his job.

Predatory behavior is seldom considered aggressive because it is not between members of the same species and is usually unemotional, such as the quiet stalking behavior of the cat. Attack behavior between cats, on the other hand, involves a lot of noise, back arching, and hair fluffing. Defensive fighting also has a desperate and highly emotional quality.

Moyer (e.g., 1971) distinguishes eight forms of aggression, differentiated by specific behaviors and by what Moyer believes are different physiological bases. These are (1) predatory, (2) intermale, (3) fear induced, (4) irritable (e.g., pain) induced, (5) territorial defense, (6) maternal, (7) sex related, and (8) instrumental. The last involves harm-doing behaviors rewarded by something other than the aggressive behavior itself. Moyer believes that each form of aggression in lower animals has a different brain circuitry, but that the circuits may overlap—as they obviously must, if they result in common behaviors. At any given time, more than one circuit may be active, such as with intermale and territorial defense. With people, however, Moyer believes there is no good evidence for differences in brain circuitry for different kinds of aggressive behavior. Man's refined capacity for learning and using symbols provides an indefinitely wide range of possibilities for arousing aggressive behavior through the same circuitry.

Differences between animal and human aggression come up repeatedly. Those strongly influenced by the occurrence of widespread killing among animals (e.g., Lorenz, 1966) believe aggression is a universal characteristic in certain circumstances. If enough aggressive energy "builds up," then aggressive behavior may even erupt spontaneously and inappropriately. Aggressive energy could be reduced, says Lorenz, by vicarious release through the observation of such violent action as displayed on television or in sports events. There are, on the other hand, those who believe that this view is fundamentally wrong, and that the observation of aggressive events *increases* violent behavior. The practical aspects of this problem make it warrant considerable discussion, for the two views have just the opposite suggestions to make about the control of aggression. The cathartic view says that either real or vicarious ("harmless") aggression will reduce real aggressive activities; the social learning view says that it will increase aggression. We shall return to this issue after viewing more evidence and theory. Because of the difficulties of dealing with animal and human aggression in the same framework, we shall treat these separately.

## ANIMAL AGGRESSION

### Antecedent Conditions for the Arousal of Aggression

Most of us have probably experienced irritability accompanying pain. In the laboratory, we can arouse fighting behavior by application of a variety of aversive ("irritating") stimuli (Vernon, 1969). A young mouse, for example, tries to bite anything that pinches its tail. Similarly, when a monkey in a restraining chair is struck on the tail, it will bite a ball held in front of its head.

Hutchinson (1972) has summarized many such antecedents of animal aggression. These can be classified as (1) an increase of intense, noxious, or painful stimuli; or (2) the decrease or offset of pleasant, beneficial, or rewarding stimuli. Specifically, the *delivery* of physical blows, tail shock, intense heat, noxious brain stimulation, air blasts, foot shock, loud noise, and aversive conditioned stimuli lead to attacks on conspecifics, rubber hoses, toy animals, contraspecifics, response panels, and tennis balls.

Likewise, the *withdrawal* of food, morphine, mobility, rewarding brain stimulation, money, and conditioned stimuli for rewarding events also lead to many of the same attack behaviors. The range of species studied includes barn wasps, boa constrictors, snapping turtles, alligators, o-possums, foxes, ferrets, pigeons, rats, monkeys, and humans. As a rule, attack increases with stimulus intensity, duration, and closeness in time of multiple aversive stimulations and is weaker with repetitive weak stimulations or more frequent stimulations.

*Shock-Elicited Aggression.* The most widely used procedure for obtaining unconditioned aggression is to deliver foot shock to a pair of rats placed together in a grid-floor box. The shocks are presented for a half-second at repeated intervals. The initial response is to attempt escape, but the animals quickly begin to assume a stereotyped position, standing on the back paws and biting at each other when the shock is turned on. This phenomenon was first described by O'Kelly and Steckle (1939) but the bulk of research has been done by Azrin and his associates. Ulrich and Azrin (1962) for example, reported that fighting increased in proportion to shock frequency and intensity. Also, if two different species are tested together, the probabilities of fighting are not equal. A guinea pig comes out on the short end if paired with a rat, perhaps because of the greater physical dexterity of the rat. The size of the box is also important. In a .25-square-foot space there is almost 100 percent fighting between two rats, but when the area is increased to 2.25 or 4.0 square feet, shock-induced fighting is almost zero.

**Conditioning of Reflexive Fighting.** If fighting can be elicited by shock virtually 100 percent of the time, then we appear to have a good unconditioned stimulus and unconditioned response and should expect classical conditioning to a neutral stimulus. Vernon and Ulrich (1966) paired an auditory CS with foot shock in eighteen pairs of rats. Each pair showed some conditioned fighting, but the percentage of conditioned responses did not rise above about 50 percent even after hundreds of trials. Reflexive fighting in the rat, then, is not readily conditionable.

The highly pugnacious Siamese fighting fish (*Betta splendens*), however, do show reliable conditioning of an aggressive display. Thompson and Sturm (1965) capitalized on the fact that these fish show aggressive displays to their own mirror image. The CS was a colored light, followed by presentation of the mirror, the UCS. The fish came to show their aggressive display to the light alone. Conditioned reflexive fighting (the display, at least) is therefore obtainable, but with species differences in efficiency of conditioning.

**Punishment of Shock-Induced Aggression.** If pain produces aggressive behavior, can we reduce such behavior by punishing it? Nature may have built a clever biological trap here, for the very punishment that should decrease a response may serve to facilitate it by arousing further unconditioned aggression. Ulrich and Craine (1964) found that if rats were given continuous shock (presumably punishing) as long as they fought, they fought more. Similarly, punishment of reflexive biting by monkeys leads to more biting and hence more punishment, and so on. Reflexive aggressive responses may be inhibited by punishment under specific conditions, but these are not yet clearly identified within the paradigm of pain-elicited aggression. Obviously, however, other kinds of aggressive responses (not pain-elicited) can be inhibited by punishment.

**Proximity to Other Animals.** Marler (1976) argues that proximity is one of the most important antecedents for aggression. Crowding results in more fighting, with either birds or mammals. The closeness of a same-sex conspecific is especially important. Male chaffinches start fights with other males at greater distances than with females. But if the females have their breasts dyed red like males, the females are also attacked at greater distances. In the course of evolution, there may have been selection for greater fighting with same-sex conspecifics because they are the strongest competitors for resources.

***Dominance, Rituals, and Peaceful Coexistence.*** Many animals develop dominance hierarchies, usually with one male at the top who gets first chance at food and his choice of females. Positions in the hierarchy are sometimes determined by actual fighting, sometimes by *ritual* fighting—aggressive displays such as spreading out feathers, baring teeth, or making noise. High rank may also be attained "by cunning or even by accident if the critical encounters with opponents occur at a time when something else in their recent past predisposes them to be subordinate to whomever they meet" (Marler, 1976, p. 239). One can be born into a high-status position, even among monkeys, if one's mother is of high status. A hierarchy remains stable until some animal is challenged for its place.

Actual fighting also may be reduced by establishment of territories. Some species fight at territorial boundaries, but others tend not to. Shrews, for example, "give a chirp of alarm, turn tail, and run" when they meet at the common boundary of their territories (Marler, 1976, p. 240).

It has been claimed that Homo sapiens is the only vertebrate species that consistently kills off its own members, but the intraspecies violence of other animals may be underestimated. Schaller (1972) documented the death of fifty three lion cubs over a four-year observation period in the Serengeti plain of East Africa. Eleven were by attack from another lion. The greatest cause, however, was the refusal of the lioness to share food with her cubs or her abandoning of them. Konrad Lorenz in his book, *King Solomon's Ring* (1952), describes the unrelenting attacks of doves—long symbols of peace—on wounded members of their own species, literally pecking them to death.

The apparent "quietness" of ritualized aggression, dominance hierarchies, and territorial control have been said to be nature's way of preserving life. This apparent calm may mask the destruction of uncountable numbers of animals forced to live in marginal habitats, however. Ritualized aggression still favors the victor. The loser has second chance at the food, cannot move into a more fertile territory, and is less likely to mate and reproduce. In evolution it matters not how you play the game, but whether you win or lose.

***Inhibition to Aggression.*** Animals can do many things to avoid aggressive encounters, some of which are under social control. These include

1. *Keeping one's distance from the antagonist.*
2. *Arousing a noncompetitive response,* such as making a sexual display so the antagonist is distracted.
3. *Avoiding provocation of others,* including not fighting back.
4. *Producing rapid familiarity.* This includes making one's own smell, taste, sight, and sound as familiar as possible to the other animals with whom one must remain in close contact. Animals are less likely to attack "friends" than "strangers." Animals sprayed with deodorants, for example, are attacked by normally friendly members of their living group.
5. *Diverting attack elsewhere.* A victim might attack a third animal and have his own attacker then become an aggressive partner. Such coalitions are found among both human and nonhuman primates. Lorenz has repeatedly claimed that defeated wolves inhibit further aggression by baring their throats to their victors. Other authors (e.g., Scott, 1958) strongly dispute this claim, however.

### Animal Instrumental Aggression

Hutchinson (1972) also discusses what he calls *subsequent-stimulus* causes of aggression, i.e., rewarding events: This is instrumental aggression. Rewards include the delivery of target contact (i.e., being allowed to aggress against some particular target[1]), food, and rewarding brain stimulation. The removal of conspecific attack, tail shock, or attack from some other species is also rewarding.

Opposite relations then hold for rewarding or punishing events, depending on whether the stimulus is delivered or removed before or after attack. Delivery of a noxious stimulus elicits attack, and its removal following attack is rewarding. Conversely, removal of a rewarding stimulus elicits attack, and presentation of a rewarding stimulus after attack is rewarding. This classification follows operant conditioning taxonomy for positive and negative reinforcers and punishers.

---

[1]This is slightly awkward in this context because it says that the opportunity to attack is in itself reinforcing and therefore fuzzes the line normally drawn for instrumental aggression (that the reward be unrelated to the aggression per se). We shall discuss the question of the reward value of aggression later.

## HUMAN AGGRESSION

### The Problem of Intent in Human Aggression

We ignored the question of intent in the discussion of animal aggression because intent is often nebulous, at best, and has little meaning with animals. It is widely accepted in definitions of human aggression, however. One common such definition is: *Aggressive behaviors are those that are intended to do physical or psychological damage to someone.* Let us clarify this definition.

First, there is intent to harm. Often difficult to determine, this is the crux of many court proceedings. Did the defendant, with malice aforethought, intend to kill his victim? How can we determine this? Francis Irwin opens his book, *Intentional Behavior and Motivation* (1971), by describing an episode from "Bullivant and the Lambs" by Ivy Compton-Burnett (1949). The father of two young boys walks by the place in the garden where they are building a hutch, speaks with them, then continues walking on a path toward a footbridge over a deep ravine. The bridge had been so weakened the previous night by a storm that it could not support a man's weight but the damage was not immediately visible. Fortunately, a warning sign had been posted at the bridge. The father concludes, however, that his sons wanted him to die because they (in the context of the story) knew of the danger but did not tell him. Irwin analyzes this episode in terms of his criteria for intentional behavior, the interlocking triad which we discussed in Chapter Two. The father realized that (1) the sons expected he would *not* be hurt if they told him about the dangerous bridge, of which they were obviously aware; (2) they expected he *would* be hurt if they did not tell him; and (3) since they did not tell him, they preferred (2) over (1)—his being hurt to his not being hurt. Intent is inferred from the choice of one act over another when the expected outcome of each is known. In the list given at the beginning of this chapter (Table 12-1), we assume the Boy Scout does not expect that helping the old lady will harm her, so the act was neither intentional nor aggressive. The man who employs an assassin, on the other hand, intends harm, even though not directly by his own hand. His act is therefore aggressive.

The distinction between physical and psychological harm is straightforward. We may harm someone by hitting them or by damaging their self-esteem. In daily life, we make "cutting" remarks, verbal barbs as ruthless as metal ones.

Many kinds of "aggression" research do not meet these definitional criteria, however. In fact, no definition lacks for criticism. Tedeschi, Smith, and Brown (1974, p. 540) argue then that "the critics are reluctant to give up the label *aggression,* and so they continue to search for the 'appropriate' conditions under which it may be used." Tedeschi et al. challenge the definitional value of intent, at least in laboratory research, because laboratory studies almost never establish aggressive intent in their subjects and frequently involve elaborate cover stories to seduce the subjects into harmdoing behaviors. The laboratory subject has intentions, but these are more directed toward carrying out the experimenter's wishes than toward hurting someone. This should be kept in mind while reading the pages to follow.

## STIMULUS-AROUSED HUMAN AGGRESSION

### The Frustration-Aggression Hypothesis

The first modern statement that frustration produces aggression was made by Freud, but a group of Yale psychologists (Dollard, Doob, Miller, Mowrer, & Sears, 1939) first developed it into a testable theory. The original postulate was that frustration always leads to aggression and aggression is always caused by frustration. This was quickly softened to say that frustration sometimes leads to aggression and is just one of the causes of aggression (Miller, 1941). Frustration is no longer considered the primary cause of aggressive behavior, but many of the concepts are still widely used informally, if not in systematic theories. In clinical psychology, it is sometimes a good hunch to look for frustration when an individual is strongly aggressive in his or her behavior.

*Definitions.* Dollard et al. used the following example as a basis for defining their concepts. Four-year-old James hears the ice-cream truck bell and says he wants an ice-cream cone. We assume he will eat it if he gets it. An *instigator* is the antecedent condition for some response. The bell instigated James to say he wanted a cone. An instigator might also be internal, such as feeling hungry. In a particular situation, there may be several instigators of varying strengths; the strongest will determine behavior. A *goal-response* is some behavior (such as eating the ice cream) that terminates a behavioral sequence by reducing the strength to instigation.

Interference with a goal response produces *frustration.* If a goal-oriented act is prevented from occurring, we have a frustration situation. Had James' mother told him no, this would constitute frustration. *Aggression* is a reaction to frustration, and is a goal response intended to hurt someone. *Frustration serves as instigation to an aggressive response, and aggression reduces the instigation to be aggressive.* If the aggressive behavior itself is prevented from occurring, this is further frustration and hence further instigation to aggression. Such instigation depends on strength of instigation of goal responses, degree of frustration, and number of prior frustrations.

*Inhibition of Aggressive Behavior.* Obviously, not all frustrations lead to overt aggressive acts. We are less likely to be aggressive if we expect to be punished for it. Few arrested motorists jeer at policemen and few students rail at their professors. Instigation to aggression and anticipation of punishment produce conflict. Dollard et al. suggest an algebraic summation between these incompatible approach and avoidance response tendencies just as with other conflicts. A sufficiently frustrated employee may be aggressive toward his employer.

*Direct and Indirect Aggression.* Aggressive acts may be directed at someone or something other than the frustrating agent. It was postulated that we will respond most aggressively to the perceived cause of frustration but, according to the principle of stimulus generalization, will respond somewhat less strongly to similar agents. Because inhibition of aggression increases frustration and hence instigates aggressive tendencies more strongly, indirect aggression should become more likely. Such indirect, or *displaced,* aggression may be a change in either the *object* or the *form* of the aggressive behavior. The man who comes home from a hard day at the office and yells at his family exemplifies a change in object. Verbal behavior, sometimes in the form of cutting jokes, may be a change in form. In highly totalitarian states, it is apparently common to make jokes about the government, but only very privately. If all other objects are potentially too threatening, a person might aggress against himself, e.g., by hitting his hand against a wall.

*Catharsis.* The occurrence of an aggressive act is assumed to reduce further instigation to aggression. This is called *catharsis,* which means "cleansing." Large inflatable dolls and sponge rubber bats have been sold with the express claim that it is good for the child (or adult) to release his aggression (catharsis) harmlessly via these objects. Presumably an increase in one form of aggression is supposed to be accompanied by a decrease in other forms because of the cathartic effect. If the frustrated child beats on the doll, he should beat less on his little sister (assuming she provides no further instigation).

*Criticisms of the Hypothesis.* The first major criticism was the obvious fact that it is not always correct. Aggression has other causes and frustration has other effects. A second major difficulty is that it requires two unseen processes: frustration and tendency to aggression, but without independent operations for defining each. If aggressive behavior occurs, we have to speculate that there was frustration. As we saw in our earlier discussion of frustration (Chapter Eight), frustrating conditions may just arouse an aversive state, without any behavioral effects specific to frustration per se. Whether aggression occurs depends on specific circumstances. For example, people respond more aggressively if the source of the frustration is perceived as arbitrary than if it is justified. In any event, the frustration-aggression hypothesis was useful, but has now faded into history as a theory of major impact.

### Impulsive Aggression

Leonard Berkowitz (e.g., see 1970 or 1974, for recent reviews) has maintained that environmental situations often evoke attack behaviors that occur "impulsively," and perhaps independently of prior reinforcement. Most homicides, for example, are not premeditated, but are spontaneous and passionate, often arising from disagreements about relatively trivial matters. The threat of capital punishment is of little effect in such instances, because in the rage of the moment the consequences of killing simply are not anticipated.

Impulsive aggression may occur in conjunction with instrumental aggression. A soldier on duty may fire at an approaching stranger as self-protection, but at the same time he may be emotionally aroused and therefore fire indiscriminately at any moving thing. Berkowitz argues that impulsive aggression is aroused by both internal and external stimuli, especially the latter. Furthermore, lest one think that drive theory is entirely passé, Berkowitz (1974) specifically states that the emotional arousal that energizes impulsive aggressive acts may be considered equivalent to general drive.

***The Weapons Effect.*** Suppose you are to be an experimental subject. On arrival at the laboratory, you are told that another subject was supposed to come when you did, but has not appeared. The experimenter then "finds" a substitute, actually a confederate. You are told that the experiment is a study of physiological reactions to stress produced by mild electric shocks. You and your "partner" are to evaluate each other's performance by giving one another electric shocks. Only one shock means a good rating and ten shocks a poor one. The task is to list in five minutes ideas a publicity agent might use to increase product sales. The two of you then go to separate rooms. You get the "evaluative" shocks first, seven of them, not a good rating of your performance. In your experimental room, there is a telegraph key for delivering the shocks as well as a rifle and a pistol left by a "previous experimenter." You deliver your partner six shocks as your evaluation of his task performance. Your particular experimental condition was designed to (1) anger you by giving you a fairly large number of shocks, and (2) provide aggression-inducing cues (guns on the table). Both of these are expected to make you more aggressive so that you will deliver more shocks than you would under less angering or different cue conditions (Berkowitz & LePage, 1967).

The entire experiment had six main conditions and an additional control. Half the subjects received one shock and half received seven shocks. For a third of the subjects, there were no objects on the table; for another third, there were weapons on the table, but not associated with anybody; for the final third, there were weapons and an explanation that these were left over from an experiment by the person who is now your "partner." The extra control group got seven shocks, but there were two badminton racquets on the table rather than guns. The mean number of shocks given in each condition is summarized in Table 12-2.

We see that subjects getting seven shocks gave their supposed tormenters more shocks than those getting one shock. Furthermore, among the seven-shock groups, the "no-object" and the "badminton-racquet" groups were the same, but the weapons groups were higher. Berkowitz and LePage (1967) argue that, first, a high number of shocks produces instigation to impulsive aggression in the real subject. Second, the weapons are cues for further arousing aggression (or at least for reducing inhibition to aggression; these two possibilities are difficult to untangle).

Berkowitz speaks of this cue property in terms of classically conditioned aggressive responses. He is vague about *what specific responses* are conditioned, but we assume the responses must be emotional. The argument is then that, because of prior association with anger, weapons become conditioned stimuli for arousing anger. This anger is (1) a *cue* for making particular responses, and (2) a *drive* that intensifies responses elicited by the situation. This analysis is the same as the drive theory analysis of fear: Both fear and anger are seen as conditionable responses which have cue and drive properties. In the Berkowitz and LePage (1967) experiment, you (as a subject) had specific external stimuli to arouse your anger (seven shocks) and conditioned stimuli (guns) that further aroused you emotionally. These joint sources of arousal facilitated shocking the other subject.

We must assume here that it is the arousal effect of the weapons which is critical, for we can hardly believe that the subjects have previously learned

**Table 12-2**  *Mean number of shocks given in each condition. (From Berkowitz & Le Page, 1967 p. 205)*

|                      | Number of shocks received by the subject | |
| -------------------- | :---: | :---: |
| *Condition*          | *1*   | *7*   |
| Associated Weapons   | 2.60  | 6.07  |
| Unassociated Weapons | 2.20  | 5.67  |
| No object            | 3.07  | 4.67  |
| Badminton Rackets[a] | —     | 4.60  |

[a]There was no one-shock group with badminton rackets.

to press a telegraph key to the cues of anger or guns. In other situations, however, anger may be a direct cue for some particular response. If I have previously learned to fire a gun while angry, sight of the weapon might be a conditioned stimulus to anger, and the anger might be a cue for firing the weapon. Diagrammatically:

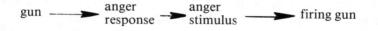

gun ⟶ anger response ⟶ anger stimulus ⟶ firing gun

Anger is a mediating response, like fear. Indeed, if I learn to fire a gun while fearful, the sight of a gun may become a cue for fear and the fear a stimulus for firing the gun. Other situational stimuli are also important determinants of whether the gun will or will not be fired, of course.

*Target Characteristics.* Berkowitz and his associates have also manipulated perceived characteristics of the person (target) to be shocked. The procedure is basically the same as described—the subject is angered by the accomplice and then shocks him. If a prize-fight film is shown to the subjects and the confederate (target) is later identified as a college boxer, he gets more shocks than if he is identified as a speech major. He also gets more shocks following the fight movie than after an exciting, but non-aggressive, track-race film (Berkowitz, 1965).

To define this effect more closely, Berkowitz and Geen (1966) showed the fight movie (a scene in which Kirk Douglas is brutally beaten), then introduced the confederate as "Kirk Anderson" (closely identifying him with the film). The confederate gets more shocks than if introduced as "Bob Anderson." Several experiments generally support the hypothesis that there is more aggressiveness aroused by a stimulus specifically associated with the violent scene. Identification of the confederate with the names of the men in the track movie did not produce any differential aggression, indicating that just seeing an exciting film did not account for the results obtained with the fight scene.

*General Versus Emotional Arousal.* Berkowitz argues that generalized *arousal* (like irrelevant drive) can facilitate aggressive behavior, although not necessarily as much as fight movies or electric shocks. Subjects frustrated when working a jigsaw puzzle shocked a confederate more than did control subjects (Geen & Berkowitz, 1967). A loud noise after seeing the prize-fight scene also made the subjects more aggressive (Geen & O'Neal, 1969). Tannenbaum and Zillman (1975) found that a brief sex film led to more punishment of an antagonistic partner than did a control condition. While such results suggest an irrelevant drive effect, perhaps subjects just do not discriminate well what their source of internal arousal is. Being cued to the aggressive situation, they may have believed that their arousal was aggressive and responded accordingly.[2] Later in this chapter, we shall also discuss some relationships between sex hormones and aggression.

*Justified Aggression.* If you inadvertently drive very far in the wrong direction on a one-way street, almost certainly someone will tell you vigorously about your indiscretion. It is as if they were waiting for somebody they could *justifiably* "jump on." In several studies, Berkowitz and his associates (summarized in Berkowitz, 1970) manipulated degree of justification for Kirk Douglas being beaten up in the prize-fight scene. Some subjects were told that Douglas deserved to be beaten and others that the beating was unfair. In the justified aggression condition, subjects shocked the confederate more than in the unjustified aggression condition.

*Is the Weapons Effect an Artifact?* The weapons effect, as just described and analyzed, is dramatic and certainly bears on the problems of gun control and the "contagion of violence." In some sense violence *is* contagious, whether due to a weakening of inhibitions or to a direct stimulation of violence by observation of others. At the laboratory level, however, there is some dispute about the weapons effect. It has been replicated by Fraczek and Macaulay (1971) and by Frodi (1973), but not in two other laboratories.

Buss, Booker, and Buss (1972) reported in five experiments that neither firing guns nor the presence of guns enhanced shocking a confederate. Page and Sheidt (1971) not only failed to reproduce the weapons effect, but found evidence that it is an artifact of an experimental situation that "demands" that the subject be aggressive. Given that guns are present, that the subject has been shocked, and that the subject is supposed to shock someone, it would appear—argue Page and Scheidt—that the subject does what he thinks is expected of him, he acts more "violently." The word *act* is used advisedly—the subject may literally be putting on a little act for the experimenter. One must determine as precisely as possible what the subjects were aware of during the experiment and what they thought they should do. We cannot accept everything subjects say at face value, but neither can we assume that what they say is completely irrelevant to what they do. Page and Sheidt report their subjects in the seven-shock condition were no more angry than subjects in the one-shock condition. It would then seem that the demand interpretation would account for what has been one of the most reliable of findings in the Berkowitz research.

Berkowitz (1974) counters that it is not just the presence of weapons that is important, but also how they are perceived and interpreted by the

---

[2]This is a "failure of attribution" interpretation discussed in detail in Chapter Thirteen. People often seem to use external cues to determine how they feel.

subjects. If a subject thinks a gun is terrible and frightening, it might arouse more anxiety than aggression and hence lead to inhibition of aggressiveness and fewer shocks being delivered. Certainly, no one would argue that meaning is not important. The question is, Why should the meaning have been so different in successful experiments than in those that failed to show the weapons effect? More evidence bearing directly on the problem is obviously needed.

*Victims May Provoke Attack.* The victim of an attack (perhaps even in the Berkowitz research) is often the stimulus for attack. Wolfgang (1957) found that a fourth of almost 600 homicides were provoked by the victim. Most murders are committed by people who know the victim well, the victim is often a relative, and the homicide is likely to have been preceded by an argument. Two individuals may engage in mutually antagonistic behavior with subsequent escalations that are not reversible. One of the best ways to avoid being attacked is not to provoke attack.

Toch (1970) found, from interviews with police and prison inmates and from police records, that about 40 percent of the time a violent sequence was initiated when an arresting officer notified a person of his arrest and was treated contemptuously. In some 27 percent of the cases, violence already existed that police action tended to inflame rather than dampen. The violence at the 1968 Democratic Party convention in Chicago certainly was not diminished by police action, nor was that at Kent State. On the other hand, the demonstrators seemed to be more taken with what they considered their legal (and moral?) rights than with any insight into the effects that they were producing. One can certainly argue that it was unconscionable to have National Guard troops with live ammunition on the Kent State campus. But surely one can also argue that the treatment of these troops by the rioters was hardly becoming to the troops' status as *mandatory* participants.

## INSTRUMENTAL HUMAN AGGRESSION

Instrumental aggression is harmful behavior rewarded by some event not itself directly related to aggression. The prize fighter may fight for money, not because he wants to hurt his opponent. Instrumental aggression is thus distinguished from impulsive aggression, which has the characteristic of being more directly aroused by antecedent events and being more "emotional." The question, again, is of intent. If I intend to make five dollars and have to hit somebody to get the money, this is different than if I intend to hit someone because I want to hurt them.

Laboratory and social examples of instrumental aggression are readily available. Animals on an electric grid will attack each other if rewarded for doing so by having the shock turned off. Johnson (1972) notes that in 1969 there were more than 6.5 times as many property crimes as crimes against persons, and many of the latter were incidental to obtaining money. Geen and Pigg (1970) followed the basic Berkowitz-LePage procedure and found that subjects praised for administering shocks delivered more shocks than those not praised. In this instance, any experimenter demand effect supports the hypothesis. Assuming the subjects really believed they were shocking someone, they did it more often because the experimenter's praise told them what he wanted them to do. Loew (1967) also found that subjects rewarded for making hostile remarks tended to be more punitive later and Lovaas (1961) found that children rewarded for making hostile remarks were later more likely to select aggressive toys to play with.

### Obedient Aggression

In our lifetimes, many major atrocities have been committed: the Nazi attempts to exterminate the Jews; the terror of the Stalinist regime in Russia; Japanese atrocities in World War II; civil strife in Ireland, Israel, Pakistan, and Chile; and the My Lai massacre by Americans in Viet Nam. There is no discrimination according to race, creed, or national origin among those who commit such crimes. The problem is that of responsibility. In postwar Germany, for example, it was very difficult to determine who was guilty of the murder of millions of Jews. A common argument for all such situations is that the "little guys" who pull the triggers are the scapegoats for the "big guys" who give the orders.

Stanley Milgram (1974) took the problem into the laboratory. How far will a normal person go, he asked, in following repugnant orders? His procedure was to have a naive experimental subject shock a victim (a trained confederate of the experimenter, of course). The fake shock apparatus had thirty clearly marked levels, ranging from 15 to 450 volts, and such verbal descriptions as "Slight Shock" (15 to 60 volts), "Danger: Severe Shock" (375 to 420 volts), and "XXX" (435 to 450 volts). Each subject had a sample shock to further convince him of the authenticity of the situation. The subject's task then was to administer a progressively higher shock to the stooge each time he made an error in a supposed verbal learning task. The "learner" was previously instructed to be wrong about 75 percent of the time so the shock level could be increased to the maximum. The subject was told to continue with the task and increase the shock each time an error was made until the learner got it right. The learner, meanwhile, went through a set routine of complaint to indicate how painful the shock was after it reached 300 volts. He pounded on the wall and finally failed to respond at all. The subjects looked to the experimenter for guidance but were told to continue and to treat a failure to respond the same as an error. There were four different degrees of insistence, depending on the subject's reluctance to do so. The primary measure was how many of the forty subjects continued to the maximum shock level. Such subjects were termed "obedient."

Prior to the experiment, the most pessimistic of Milgram's students and colleagues, given a description of the experiment, estimated that only 3 percent of the subjects would continue to the highest level. In fact, no subject stopped below 300 volts and twenty six of forty went the limit to 450 volts. Many subjects were obviously emotional about the situation, but nevertheless continued. The subjects gave a mean rating of 13.4 on a 14-point scale for how painful they thought the last few shocks had been. These results are astonishing in their suggestion of how easy it is to get one human to hurt another.[3] The subjects, furthermore, were not just jaded college students, used to carrying out experimenter instructions in research. They came from all walks of life and ranged in age from twenty to fifty years. They thought they were to participate in an experiment on learning and memory conducted at Yale University.

In subsequent experiments (e.g., see Milgram, 1974, for a book-length review), performance was generally the same if the same conditions were repeated. Other variables are important, however. For example, the closer the degree of contact between a subject and learner (e.g., remote, hearing the learner's voice, being in the same room, touching), the less likely the subject is to give the strongest shock. Sheridan and King (1972) used an authentic "learner," a puppy. The indicated shock levels were exaggerated, but sufficient to evoke negative responses from the puppy. Most subjects, male and female alike, shocked the puppy all the way to the end of the scale.

The most serious counterinterpretation, again, is experimenter demand. Orne and Holland (1968) suggested that Milgram's subjects may have been aware of what they were expected to do. O'Leary, Willis, & Tomich (1969) read subjects the method section of an "experimental proposal" for the Milgram experiment, clearly stating the shocks were not real. Subjects were then told to role play as if they believed that shocks were actually being delivered. The results were virtually the same as Milgram's, supporting the experimental demand interpretation. Strangely, however, the subjects also showed the same signs of tension as Milgram's subjects, as if they really thought the learners were being shocked. The validity of Milgram's specific results can only be determined by appropriate research, but there is no argument about the existence of the social phenomenon with which Milgram has been concerned.

[3]Over the years since this research was first reported and subsequent follow-up experiments done, there has been an interesting public reaction. Outrage is expressed not because of the ease with which subjects were induced to hurt someone, but because the experiments were done at all. The experiments themselves were considered "dehumanizing" to the subjects and this was said to outweigh the worth of the results.

### Preference for Aggression in the Laboratory?

We started off with the notion that intent was important, but in the laboratory research thus far discussed, *intent was not demonstrated*. The subjects were put into situations where they essentially *had* to shock someone. The number and intensity of shocks could vary, but there was no option *not* to shock. In either the Berkowitz-LePage or Milgram paradigms, then, it is possible that subjects, Milgram's particularly, were showing a preference for the lesser of two evils. They were avoiding a negative response from the experimenter rather than shocking somebody because they intended to hurt them.

### Social Learning and the Modeling of Aggression

Social learning theory, compared to "traditional" learning theory, lays great emphasis on *imitation* and *modeling,* what Bandura (1969) has called "no-trial learning." A child sees an adult doing something ("modeling") and copies the same behavior ("imitation"). Modeling and imitation are particularly important problems when we consider the time spent viewing television. The role of television as an instigator or reducer of aggressive behaviors is a lively and controversial topic and not easily settled. Individuals have imitated television plots very closely. For example, a hoax following the story line of a television program was perpetrated on an airline. A bomb was said to be planted on an airliner and was set to go off at an altitude less than 5,000 feet. The airliner was then rerouted to Denver, Colorado, which has an airport above 5,000 feet, so that it could land. Other, even more violent instances, have been reported.

Bandura, Ross, and Ross (1963b) compared aggressive behaviors of nursery school children after observing aggressive behavior by live adults, a film of adults, or a film of cartoon characters (adults dressed in cat costumes). A control group was not shown the aggressive sequence. The groups were further subdivided according to whether the models were of the same or of different sex from the child. The main aggressive behavior was hitting a three-foot-tall "Bobo" doll (an inflated vinyl doll that stands back up when knocked down). The model sat on the doll, hit it with his fist, or a mallet, or threw it up in the air and kicked it about the room. The model also said such things as "Sock him in the nose" or "Hit him down." Such specific responses made by the model were intended to be ones that could clearly be identified as imitative on the part of the child. The children were then (individually) mildly frustrated by being allowed to play a little while with an attractive toy and then told they could not play with it any more, but could instead play with some toys in a different room. These included the Bobo doll. In each five seconds of a twenty-minute test period, the child was scored for aggressive responses, a total of 240 possible scores. The response categories were imitative aggression, partially imitative aggression, mallet aggression, sitting on the doll, nonimitative aggression, and aggressive gun play (a gun was among the toys in the test room). The results are summarized in Table 12-3.

**Table 12-3** *Mean aggression scores for subgroups of experimental and control subjects. (From Bandura, Ross, & Ross, 1963b, p. 6. Copyright © 1963b by the American Psychological Association. Reprinted by permission.)*

| Response category | Experimental groups | | | | | |
| | Real-life aggressive | | Human film—aggressive | | | |
| | F Model | M Model | F Model | M Model | Cartoon film— aggressive | Control group |
| --- | --- | --- | --- | --- | --- | --- |
| Total aggression | | | | | | |
| Girls | 65.8 | 57.3 | 87.0 | 79.5 | 80.9 | 36.4 |
| Boys | 76.8 | 131.8 | 114.5 | 85.0 | 117.2 | 72.2 |
| Imitative aggression | | | | | | |
| Girls | 19.2 | 9.2 | 10.0 | 8.0 | 7.8 | 1.8 |
| Boys | 18.4 | 38.4 | 34.3 | 13.3 | 16.2 | 3.9 |
| Mallet aggression | | | | | | |
| Girls | 17.2 | 18.7 | 49.2 | 19.5 | 36.8 | 13.1 |
| Boys | 15.5 | 28.8 | 20.5 | 16.3 | 12.5 | 13.5 |
| Sits on Bobo Doll[a] | | | | | | |
| Girls | 10.4 | 5.6 | 10.3 | 4.5 | 15.3 | 3.3 |
| Boys | 1.3 | 0.7 | 7.7 | 0.0 | 5.6 | 0.6 |
| Nonimitative aggression | | | | | | |
| Girls | 27.6 | 24.9 | 24.0 | 34.3 | 27.5 | 17.8 |
| Boys | 35.5 | 48.6 | 46.8 | 31.8 | 71.8 | 40.4 |
| Aggressive gun play | | | | | | |
| Girls | 1.8 | 4.5 | 3.8 | 17.6 | 8.8 | 3.7 |
| Boys | 7.3 | 15.9 | 12.8 | 23.7 | 16.6 | 14.3 |

[a]This response category was not included in the total aggression score.

What we see in Table 12-3 is that (1) all the aggressive-model groups were more aggressive than the control group; (2) boys were generally more aggressive than girls; and (3) sex of the model was important. Girls were more aggressive following observation of female aggressive models and boys were more aggressive with male models. Furthermore, whether the models were live or on film, real people or cartoon characters, did not offset amount of aggressive behavior.

In another experiment, Bandura, Ross, and Ross (1963a) showed filmed aggressive behavior being rewarded or punished. Control subjects were exposed to active, but nonaggressive models or to no models at all. Children who saw the aggressive model rewarded were *more* aggressive in the test period than control subjects and those observing the aggressive model punished showed *less* imitation. After the experiment, the children evaluated the behavior of the models and selected the characters they preferred. The children correctly identified the models as "good" or "bad," but also preferred the aggressive model when he succeeded, but not if he failed. The children were frank in their reasoning: The aggressive, rewarded model was preferred because he got what he wanted. It is important to note that in these studies there was a delay between the children's observation of violence and testing, because this indicates that aggressive behavior may be facilitated at some indefinite time after the observation of violence.

The children in these experiments were not particularly aberrant, either. Actually, they came from the Stanford University Nursery School. This disputes the argument that observation of violence would only affect already-"sick" minds.

### Aggression and Coercive Power

Tedeschi, Smith, and Brown (1974) view what is called *human aggression* as just another way people try to get what they want. When other methods fail, people make threats of punishment that are sometimes backed up by violence. Tedeschi and his colleagues then raise the interesting point that perhaps it is more important to determine conditions under which society *says* that a particular behavior is aggressive. Socially justified acts are not considered aggressive; unjustified ones are. Nothing in responses per se makes them unambiguously aggressive, so researchers make their own judgments about what to define as aggressive. This leads to some diversity. A *conceptual* definition of aggression (e.g., intent to do harm) may find agreement, but the *operational* definitions (what will be called *aggressive* in a particular experiment) may not. The scientist's labeling of a behavior as aggressive sometimes involves limited assumptions about the causes of behavior, ignoring *negative reciprocity* and *equity*.

Negative reciprocity is a social norm that gives a person the "right" to retaliate for harm done to him. Equity is the social norm that says you can only retaliate in equal kind or amount. An eye for an eye, but no more. An experiment by Kane, Doerge, and Tedeschi (1973) illustrates the point. Subjects read descriptions of four conditions in an alleged experiment. In the narrative, Person A evaluated Person B's essay on some topic by administering one or seven shocks. Person B then evaluated Person A's essay by returning either two or six shocks. The question was: How will the readers perceive the aggressiveness of Persons A and B under the various conditions? Person A was considered more aggressive when he initially gave seven shocks than if he gave one shock. No surprise. Person B was rated aggressive if he gave back six shocks for one. But if B had received seven shocks he was rated equally *nonaggressive* whether he gave back two or six shocks. In other words, Person B was considered aggressive only if he gave back more shocks than he originally got, if he was not being equitable. If this indeed represents a cultural norm for aggressiveness, then the subjects in the Berkowitz and LePage experiment, and others following the same procedure, are not aggressive in giving back six shocks for seven. Tedeschi, Smith, and Brown suggest that experimenters have ignored the social meaning of the different numbers of shocks.

The principles of negative reciprocity and equity have considerable social import, for if a person can somehow change the *meaning* of his action it may be judged as nonaggressive by others. For example, in 1939 German troops dressed as Polish soldiers "attacked" various German installations along the Polish-German border. Hitler then "justified" the invasion of Poland as a countermeasure to Polish attacks. This technique has been used throughout history. A number of experiments cited by Tedeschi, Smith, and Brown support the generalization that *justified* harmful actions do not suffer retaliation, whereas arbitrary and unjustified actions do. Most of us learn early to try to avoid the impression that our aggressive acts are arbitrary or unjustified. We try to make our actions look necessary or defensive so they will be *labeled* nonaggressive (Bandura & Walters, 1963).

## CONTROL OF AGGRESSION

### Lorenz' Ethological Approach Versus the Social Learning Approach

Konrad Lorenz has written extensively on aggression (e.g., 1965). Generally he has considered aggression to be instinctive and, following the water-tank (hydraulic) model, considers that reaction-specific aggressive energy wells up inside the individual and can erupt into behavior spontaneously. Some animals, he has argued, have developed inhibitions to aggression so that intraspecies fighting does not lead a species to destroy itself. We have already noted a number of such factors, including avoiding an antagonist, arousing noncompetitive responses in the antagonist, not provoking extreme arousal, producing familiarity, and diverting attack elsewhere. With both Lorenz' model and the frustration-aggression hypothesis, however, the notion of catharsis is important and we should look at it further.

*Catharsis.* According to the Lorenzian view, without inhibitions to aggression, but with instinctive aggressive energy building up, men will engage in intraspecies aggression on a massive scale. The solution would then seem to be the provision of alternative outlets for aggression so that aggressive energy does not build up too much. Such displacement activities as athletic events would presumably be cathartic, by reducing aggressive energy and hence the likelihood of serious aggressive activity.

The alternative view, however, is that aggressive behavior is rewarded in many situations and that successful aggression is more likely to recur, rather than less likely. If either of these views were entirely correct, to act on the opposite presupposition could indeed be disastrous. There is the possibility that both views may be partly correct, depending on particular circumstances. One hesitates to argue in favor of the cathartic view in the face of such events as a soccer championship game at which the fans get into a fight and, as happened in Peru in 1964, 300 people were killed and 500 injured.

As far as the hydraulic model is concerned, as we noted in Chapter Three, the model is not taken seriously by physiologists. Energy can be stored in the body but takes the form of body fat or glycogen stored in the liver and is not "aggressive" energy. Scott (1971) has made a detailed comparison of what he calls the "psychophysiological" and hydraulic theories of aggression. We may summarize some of his more important points as follows.

1. Anger and fear are aroused by external stimuli, not by some aggression-specific energy that builds spontaneously.
2. Emotional processes intensify reactions to such external stimuli.
3. Internal arousal eventually dies out in the absence of further stimulation, not accumulating indefinitely, as the hydraulic model says.
4. Aggressive behavior can be increased or decreased by reward or punishment, a point not spoken to in hydraulic theory.
5. Catharsis is only effective if internal arousal has been produced by external stimulation; whereas hydraulic theory states that displacement and catharsis are always effective.

***Reducing Internal Arousal By Nonaggressive Behaviors.*** Given that the stimuli for aggressive behavior are present and assuming that catharsis (reduction of arousal) can occur, is aggressive behavior the only means of achieving catharsis? By measuring blood pressure, Hokanson (e.g., 1970) and his colleagues have found that with males aggressive responses were followed by rapid drops in blood pressure (catharsis) to their normal levels. "Friendly" counterresponses were followed by a slower drop. Females, on the other hand, showed a more rapid decrease when they made friendly responses to another person's (experimenter's) aggressive behavior. This is not an entirely sex-linked difference, however. Sosa (1968) selected prison inmates with records of being overtly violent or of being passive and found results similar to those reported for males versus females. Hokanson, then, feels that the tension-reducing effects of a particular counterresponse are learned, and that any behavior has the potential for being "cathartic." "Any response which serves to terminate, reduce, or avoid noxious stimulation from others will acquire cathartic-like properties" (Hokanson, 1970, p. 80–81). This is essentially an escape-avoidance model, in which the noxious stimulus is aggression from others.

### Television Violence and Behavior

The catharsis view holds that observing violence on television should reduce real violence; the social learning view holds just the opposite. There does not seem to be much evidence to support the catharsis view. At a rather gross observational level, it does not appear that increased television viewing has reduced the crime rate. Furthermore, the experiments by Bandura and his colleagues, as well as by others, indicate that children indeed do imitate what they have seen done by others. That this is not just an isolated laboratory phenomenon is shown by the fact that people have actually done hideous things they copied from television. In Boston, for example, a young woman had gasoline thrown on her and was set on fire by a group of boys who said they got the idea from a television program in which the same thing had been done. The television industry has argued that its influence is not terribly great when it comes to violence, but it does not deny its influence when it sells advertising time in which famous athletes speak the virtues of a man's cologne.

It is very difficult to get really good and unambiguous data about the effects of television-viewing habits on violence. Broad survey studies simply are not informative enough over a period of time, and it is virtually impossible to gain effective control over television viewing for experimental purposes, except in fairly limited and perhaps artificial settings, from which it is difficult to generalize. We shall refer to two studies, which arrive at somewhat different conclusions and which represent two different methodologies: correlational and experimental.

Eron, Lefkowitz, Huesmann, and Walder (1972) reviewed data relating aggressive behavior to television-viewing habits of 427 children over a ten-year period. In Grade 3, the original group of 875 children (all those in the town) were judged by their peers as to how aggressive they were. At the same time, data on other potential variables related to aggression, including each child's preferences in television viewing, were collected from the parents. Each mother was asked the child's three favorite programs and these were given violence ratings on the basis of independent ratings of all television programs mentioned.

For convenience, the ten-year follow-up data are referred to as Grade 13. At this time, there were three measures of aggressiveness (peer ratings, subjects' self-reports, and a personality test). Other data, including favorite programs, were also collected by self-reports. It is important to note that all the Grade 13 measures were obtained independently of the Grade 3 measures. The results for the boys are shown in Figure 12.1, a set of intercorrelations among the relevant measures.

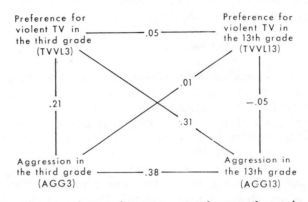

**Figure 12.1**  *The correlations between a preference for violent television and peer-rated aggression for 211 boys over a 10-year lag. (From Eron, Lefkowitz, Huesmann, and Walder, 1972, p. 257. Copyright (c) 1972 by the American Psychological Association. Reprinted by permission.)*

There was a low but significant correlation between preference for violent television and aggressive behavior in Grade 3 ($r = .21$) and an even higher correlation between aggressive behavior in Grades 3 and 13 ($r = .38$). We usually say that we cannot draw causal inferences from correlational data, but if done properly it is reasonable to do so. In this case, there was a correlation of .31 between Grade 3 television preference and Grade 13 aggressive behavior. No other correlations were statistically different from zero. Since Grade 3 television preference was correlated with Grade 13 behavior, but Grade 3 aggressive behavior was *not* correlated with Grade 13 television preference, we have reasonable grounds for the following conclusion: Watching violent television programs is a causative factor in aggressive behavior, but not the other way around. The correlation between television viewing and aggressive behavior at Grade 3 is ambiguous with respect to the direction of causality, but the correlations over time are not. Television viewing habits are obviously not the only factors involved, and the correlations are not tremendously high, but it is remarkable that there are any significant correlations at all over a ten-year period.

Taken in conjunction with other evidence cited by the authors, it seems that television viewing does have an effect on behavior. Notably, there were sex differences in this study, as there have been in so many others. There were no significant correlations for girls. There may be many reasons for this, not the least of which is the relative lack of violent females on television to serve as models for little girls. This has begun to change somewhat, with women playing violent roles in police stories now, and in a few years we might expect more similar results with boys and girls.

The second major study to which we refer is by Feshbach and Singer (1971). This was a field study involving the experimental control of television viewing in institutional settings and private boarding schools. Experimental subjects were allowed to watch violent programs and control subjects watched nonviolent programs over a period of six weeks. The primary measures of aggression were supervisors' ratings of fighting, teasing, breaking rules, and so on. At the end of the six weeks, the institution boys watching violent television were *less* aggressive than those who watched nonviolent programs. This would seem to support the catharsis point of view, but there are serious qualifications to this conclusion.

First, the results held only in the institutional settings, not the boarding schools. This questions the generality of the results at the very least. Second, the institution boys watching nonviolent television were *initially* more aggressive than were the boys watching violent television. When this factor is taken into account, the difference between the two groups dissipates. Moreover, attempts to replicate the Feshback-Singer experiment have been unsuccessful. For more details and criticisms, see Bandura (1973).

The conclusion reached by most authors seems to be that (1) modeling of violence increases the occurrence of violence in laboratory studies; (2) television programs show a tremendous amount of violence; and (3) watching violent television is related to subsequent aggressive behaviors. While not absolutely clear cut, this seems to be a sufficiently strong chain of evidence to warrant consideration of control over television viewing. This is a matter that parents will have to take into their own hands, however, rather than expecting any very strong response on the part of the industry.

## BIOLOGICAL FACTORS IN THE CONTROL OF AGGRESSION.

### Brain Mechanisms

Recall from Chapter One that a postmortem examination of Charles Whitman's brain showed a tumor in his amygdala. This is part of the limbic system, a phylogenetically very old part of the brain. The limbic system is important for motivational-emotional functions related to basic biological needs, i.e., feeding, fighting, fleeing, and procreation. Outlined in Figure 12.2, the limbic system includes a number of areas, including the hypothalamus, amygdala, and hippocampus. The system is like a circular track with

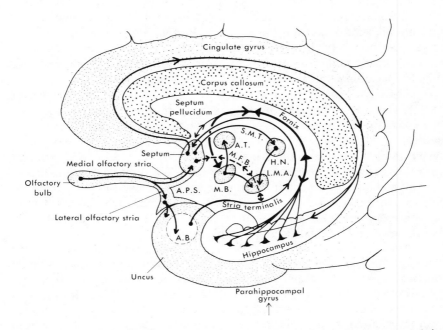

**Figure 12.2** *Schematic representation of some of the connections of the limbic system. Arrows indicate direction of conduction, and some strutures carry fibers conducting in different directions. S.M.T., stria medullaris thalami; H.N., Habenular nucleus; A.T., anterior thalamic nucleus (its projection to the cingulate cortex is omitted); M.F.B., medial forebrain bundle; L.M.A., limbic midbrain area; M.B., mamillary body; A.P.S., anterior perforated substance; A.B., amygdaloid body. (Gardner, E. Fundamentals of neurology (6th Ed.). Philadelphia: Saunders, 1975, p. 392.)*

connections in and out to other areas. It is also called the Papez circuit, after the neurologist who first outlined the theory of its functions (Papez, 1937). Kluver and Bucy (1937) removed the temporal lobes of rhesus monkeys, consisting primarily of the hippocampus and amygdala. The animals became excessively oral (taking anything into their mouths), hypersexual, very passive, and seemed not to remember things well. With the development of refined electrode stimulation and ablation techniques, as well as more information about the anatomy of the brain, it is found that the amygdala, septum, and hypothalamus are particularly important for aggression. Other areas are obviously important: A directed attack requires both the sensory and motor apparatus needed to direct an attack.

Nevertheless, the limbic areas seem more *uniquely* related to attack. The amygdala and septum seem to *modulate* the activity of the hypothalamus

(Thompson, 1975). It is possible to get aggressive behaviors in animals with the amygdala destroyed and the hypothalamus intact. The reverse is not true, however. Some areas of the amygdala are excitatory for attack, and others are inhibitory. The septum appears to be only inhibitory. Septal stimulation is calming, and septal lesions consistently produce ferocious, attacking animals, as do lesions of the ventromedial nuclei of the hypothalamus.

***Brain Mechanisms and Social Behavior.*** Rosvold, Mirsky, and Pribram (1954) removed the amygdala from the most dominant rhesus monkey in a colony of eight animals. When put back into the group, he plunged to the bottom of the hierarchy. It was later shown in another experiment (see Pribram, 1962) that this involved the loss of some capacity other than just aggressiveness. If an operated monkey was first placed postoperatively into a cage with easily dominated juveniles, and hence had opportunity to "relearn" the skill necessary to be dominant (or, perhaps, was rewarded for it), the operated monkey did not lose his place at the top of his original dominance hierarchy.

Delgado (1963) put an electrode into the caudate nucleus of the dominant monkey in a colony. A lever that turned on electrical stimulation to this monkey's brain was then put in the cage. Other monkeys in the group learned to press the lever to ward off attack from the dominant animal. This was shown dramatically, as well as humorously, when the least dominant member of the group stared the dominant one straight in the eyes (but only while pressing the lever!) and was not attacked by him. A direct stare normally arouses a violent response from a rhesus monkey.

***Psychosurgery.*** The term *psychosurgery* refers to brain operations intended to change the patient's behavior or feelings. Frontal lobotomy, an operation appropriately vilified in Ken Kesey's book, *One Flew Over the Cuckoo's Nest* (1962), is the separation of the frontal lobes of the brain from the rest of the brain. We might assume that in real life there was considerable careful laboratory and/or clinical surgical support to warrant the use of the technique. There was no such support when the technique was undertaken, nor is there any now. In 1935 an American researcher named Jacobsen reported at an international meeting that if the prefontal cortex of monkeys was removed they became gentle (Jacobsen, 1935). He also reported the animals had difficulty in solving problems involving short-term memory. Within two years, a Portuguese neurosurgeon named Moniz had performed a large number of such operations on human patients, and in the United States a pair of neurosurgeons named Freeman and Watts did the same. It is estimated that some 20,000 patients around the world were subjected to varying degrees of frontal lobotomies between 1936 and 1951 (Grossman, 1967b, p. 547).

Furthermore, the early reports of the effectiveness of lobotomy, particularly for reducing irrational fears, anxiety, and obsessional behavior were overstated. The use of drugs has now obviated the demand for such surgery, and psychosurgery is restricted to more limited neural structures. We bring up the question here mainly because of ethical considerations that can be stated simply: Do we know enough about the causes of aggressive behaviors to do irreversible brain damage that may have severe side effects? (This problem is different from the use of such surgery for the reduction of otherwise intractable pain in, say, terminal cancer patients). The only ethical grounds for such a procedure would be an affirmative answer to this question, that we could indeed say with confidence that the cause of some antisocial behavior was due to "malfunction" of a specific part of the brain. We have already seen that there are many factors (such as learning, frustration, and pain) that are determinants of aggressive, antisocial behaviors, and these are *not* neatly pinpointed in the brain.

Some patients, however, do have uncontrollable rages, often related to epileptic seizures that *can* be traced to a particular abnormality in the brain. Scar tissue, for example, is a common focal point of origin for the onset of a seizure. One technique is to implant many electrodes in the brain to locate the source of the seizure. The offending area can then be destroyed by very small localized lesions made through the same electrode that detected the abnormality. This does not produce the gross impairments that accompany lobotomy. Electrodes can also be implanted so that when a patient "feels a rage coming on" he can stimulate his own brain and head off the "attack." The problems related to psychosurgery and the control of aggression are discussed in Mark and Ervin's *Violence and the Brain* (1970) and Valenstein's *Brain Control: A Critical Examination of Brain Stimulation and Psychosurgery* (1973).

### Genetics

At one level, it is obvious that aggression is related to genetics: Predatory animals are more aggressive than prey animals. We can breed vicious watchdogs or children's pet dogs, aggressive or passive mice.

Recently, however, there has been considerable interest in a particular chromosome abnormality. As a result of their parents' mating, humans normally end up with either a pair of X (female) sex chromosomes or one X and one Y (male) chromosome. The individual with XX chromosomes becomes a female, and the individual with XY chromosomes becomes a male. Occasionally there are genetic errors. In *Klinefelter's syndrome,* an identifiable male with many feminine characteristics has an extra X chromosome and is therefore XXY. He tends to be tall and thin, has exaggerated breast development, is often mentally retarded, and is incapable of reproducing.

Of more interest here, however, is the case where there is an extra Y chromosome, so that the individual is XYY. Some initial reports indicated an unusually high number of XYY individuals in prison, and the hypothesis quickly developed that this "supermale" was genetically more aggressive. One recent introductory psychology textbook (McConnell, 1974) went so far as to suggest that genetic counseling might be indicated and that in fifty years or so we might know how to get rid of the extra Y chromosome. The behavioral problem, incidentally, is said to be not so much that the individual is aggressive in a destructive sense, but rather is unable to control his impulses. Thus, he seeks immediate gratification of his desires, and this *sometimes* leads to violence if he is interfered with.

The preponderance of available information, however, leads to only one consistent finding: The XYY individual is taller than average. (Other physical abnormalities have also been reported.) This conclusion was reached in a report published by the National Institutes of Health in 1970 and in separate literature reviews in the *Psychological Bulletin* (Owen, 1972) and in *Science* (Witkin et al., 1976). Owen says: "No consistent personality or behavior constellation has been successfully predicted from the XYY complement" (p. 209). Witkin et al. conclude that "No evidence has been found that men with either of these sex chromosome complements (XXY or XYY) are especially aggressive" (p. 554). They do not appear to be contributing particularly to society's problem with aggressive crimes, and therefore identifying them would not reduce the crime problem. Collectively, these reviews are based on literally hundreds of reports. The problem is that "What began as a reasonable hypothesis—but immediately failed to gain statistical support—was accepted uncritically by an apparently alarming number of practitioners" (Owen, 1972, p. 210).

There are numerous problems in researching this area. One is that it is not always as easy as one might think to clearly identify XYY chromosomes. Secondly, the base rate of occurrence of XYY in the general population is not well known, and in some reports subjects were selected for inclusion just because they were tall and antisocial. The only sure way to determine the relationship between XYY and behavior is to start off with a completely random selection of infants, determine their chromosomes on the basis of some established standard, then follow them through life, hoping that knowledge of their chromosomes does not influence judgments or treatment of them. We could then see if there is any unusually high incidence of antisocial behavior. Present evidence, however, does not appear to warrant any special *behavioral* consideration of XYY individuals, and arbitrary labeling of the XYY child as potentially antisocial is inconsistent with any principle of being innocent until proven guilty.

## Sex Differences, Hormones, and Aggression

Males tend to be more active and aggressive than females, beginning in play in relatively early life. With humans, this may represent socialization more than genetic differences. In other species, the effect does appear to be genetic. Harlow (e.g., 1971) has repeatedly pointed out that young male rhesus monkeys are more active and violent in their play than are females, and this difference is exaggerated with age.

At birth, all mammalian brains appear to be "female," dominated by the hormones estrogen and progesterone. Much behavior of males at early ages is like that of females. Generally, the most critical experiments on sex hormones use the technique of castration and hormone replacement therapy. A castrated male (as with a gelding horse or a steer) is much less violent and much less dominant in its group than is an uncastrated animal. Injections of testosterone, however, restore the aggressive behaviors. We also saw a hint of a hormone effect in the experiments showing that seeing a short sex movie increases the subsequent amount of shock given to another person in an experiment. This may be a general arousal, but it may also be more intimately related to the sex-aggression relationship. Many normally peaceful wild male animals become violent during mating season, when their sex hormones are at the highest level, then become relatively placid again when the mating season is over. The female sex hormones, estrogen and progesterone, on the other hand, tend to inhibit aggressive behaviors. In males, such hormones provide a kind of "chemical castration," which has the obvious advantage of being reversible (Moyer, 1971).

There is also reported a disproportionate incidence of irritability and antisocial behavior of human females during premenstrual and menstrual periods. Dalton (1961) found, for example, that 49 percent of all violence by imprisoned women was committed during these eight days of the month. There are several possible reasons for such irritability (Moyer, 1971). First, it may result directly from lower progesterone levels. Irritability can be reduced by administration of progesterone and is normally lower in women taking oral contraceptives (which contain progesterone or similar agents). Second, a more indirect effect may be an increased level of aldosterone, an adrenal hormone important for water and salt regulation in the body. This may increase neural excitability. Thirdly, hypoglycemia is well known to increase irritability and is more pronounced during menstruation. A high-protein diet tends to be therapeutic. Moyer (1971) suggests that hypoglycemia may be a more important factor in matrimonial relations, threats, and cruelty to children than is commonly recognized. Finally, social factors may be involved: Women may learn they are expected to be irritable during menstruation.

What this all means is that in addition to such factors as frustration, irritation, anger, arousal, imitation, instrumental reward, and social norms, there are also biological factors influencing violent behavior. These involve aberrations of the brain as well as variations in hormones, blood sugar level, and so on. The control of violence is truly an interdisciplinary problem. Charles Whitman had a brain tumor, but someone else with the same tumor might not have acted the same way or someone without a tumor might have done what he did.

## CONCLUSION

Aggression refers to a wide variety of behaviors which occur under a wide variety of conditions. With humans, the common defining element is generally considered to be intent to harm someone else, but such intent is often difficult to demonstrate. In many laboratory studies, intent is not demonstrated at all. The range of factors influencing aggressive behaviors includes frustration, irritation, anger, arousal, imitation, instrumental reward, and social norms, as well as such biological factors as hormones, blood sugar level, and brain damage. The study of violence, and its control, is truly an interdisciplinary problem.

chapter 13

# Achievement Motivation, Attribution, and Power

## ACHIEVEMENT MOTIVATION

An enduring practical question is how to get people to achieve more. We will consider whether there is a need for achievement that varies from person to person and that, under proper circumstances, might be learned.

### Definition of the Need for Achievement (n Ach)

We must first of all define achievement *motivation* independently of achievement *behavior*. Murray (1938, pp. 80–81) defined need for achievement as a desire or tendency "to overcome obstacles, to exercise power, to strive to do something difficult as well and as quickly as possible." In his personality theory, n Ach was one of twenty manifest psychological needs (as distinct from such biological needs as hunger). Murray also devised the Thematic Apperception Test (TAT) as a means of studying personality and needs. This test consists of a series of pictures about which the individual tells a story supposed to answer the questions: (1) What led up to the scene being depicted? (2) What is now happening in the scene? (3) How do the characters feel? and (4) What will be the outcome? The relatively ambiguous pictures are supposed to evoke themes which will be characteristically different for different individuals.

Various scoring schemes applied to the stories are intended to detect themes considered indicative of the personality and needs of the individual telling the story. For example, one card shows a boy with a violin lying on a table in front of him while he looks into space. If a story is about a boy working hard to become a world-renowned violinist, the interpretation would be different from a story about a boy who is supposed to be practicing but who wants to be outside playing with his friends. The former story would be more indicative of achievement and the latter of affiliation. In the n Ach research, there are usually four pictures, with a time limit of five minutes for telling each story. The original fantasy-scoring technique was described by McClelland et al. (1953), with others described in Atkinson (1958). A more direct test procedure might seem better but thus far no one has devised any technique with better construct validity than the fantasy measures of n Ach.

Need for achievement can presumably be *aroused,* but n Ach is not directly controlled in the way that hunger or thirst is. The procedures usually involve the selection of subjects who display different levels of n Ach in their fantasy stories and who are then tested in achievement situations. Such tasks as simple arithmetic problems are done more rapidly by individuals with a high level of n Ach (McClelland, 1955). The obvious questions are What produces higher n Ach? and Why does it lead to better performance?

## McClelland's Theory

McClelland et al. (1953) offered a hedonic interpretation of n Ach. They proposed that cues previously associated with hedonically positive events produce a partial rearousal of the positive affect originally experienced. The individual partly experiences as well as anticipates a pleasurable outcome. If prior achievement situations have led to positive affect, the individual would be more likely to engage in achievement behaviors. Conversely, if a person were punished for failing, a fear of failure could develop and there would be a motive to avoid failure.

Men with high n Ach tend to come from families in which achievement striving is emphasized, and young adults with high n Ach often report that their parents were not particularly warm individuals, who emphasized achievement rather than affiliation. The theory simply says, then, that under appropriate conditions people will do what they have been rewarded for doing. If a competitive situation is a cue for rewarded achievement striving, then in competitive situations the individual will work harder.

## The Achieving Society

McClelland's interests broadened from laboratory tasks to social problems, and he tried to determine if n Ach was related to the rise and fall of cultures (McClelland, 1961). This was related to Max Weber's thesis in *The Protestant Ethic and the Spirit of Capitalism* ([1904] 1930) that the Protestant revolution had infused a more vigorous spirit into both workers and entrepreneurs. What a society teaches its children about being independent was related to Protestantism on the one hand and social growth on the other. One advantage of the n Ach scoring system is that it can be applied to any written material, including old newspapers, books, or public records.

The Protestant Reformation was a liberation movement, a break from the authoritarianism of the Catholic church that led to a greater social, as well as ecclesiastical, freedom. Freedom also carries with it, however, a greater stress on individual responsibility and independence. Protestant individuals and countries should therefore show greater n Ach than Catholic individuals and countries. And, indeed, just as it had earlier been shown that boys separated from their fathers and forced to be more independent evidenced higher n Ach, so it was shown that Protestant families stressed independence earlier than Irish or Italian Catholic families of the same socioeconomic levels (McClelland, Rindlisbacher, & de Charms, 1955). Protestant children score higher on n Ach tests and Protestant countries are more advanced economically. The latter was shown by comparing such measures of economic development as per capita use of electricity and amount of shipping. Children's books have also been scored for achievement themes and related to economic growth. Between 1800 and 1850, for example, de Charms and Moeller (1962) found first an increase and then a decrease in number of patents per 100,000 people in the United States. This was closely paralleled by a rise and fall in achievement imagery in the children's books, with a correlation of .79 between the two measures.

Individuals in "entrepreneurial" occupations should also have high n Ach scores. Occupation may have affected achievement scores rather than vice versa, but a longitudinal study avoids this ambiguity. McClelland (1965) found that 83 percent of those Wesleyan graduates in entrepreneurial occupations fourteen years after graduation had scored high on n Ach when they were students, whereas only 21 percent of those in nonentrepreneurial occupations had high scores. Individuals with high n Ach are also more independent and less concerned with the feelings of others. McClelland came to view the "managerial type" in business as being a medium risk taker, wanting immediate feedback for his behavior, and working harder under conditions of achievement arousal. He is not happy unless he is continually rewarded with success.

### Atkinson's Theory

John Atkinson (e.g., 1964) has considerably refined achievement theory. First, he put the theory into the framework of expectancy-value theory, following the orientations of Tolman and Kurt Lewin. Secondly, he emphasized the role of conflict, especially between n Ach and fear of failure.

**The Tendency to Success ($T_s$).** In Atkinson's theory the tendency to engage in achievement-oriented behaviors (tendency to success, or $T_s$) is a multiplicative function of (1) the *motivation* for success ($M_s$), which is the same as n Ach; (2) the *probability* of success ($P_s$); and (3) the *incentive value* of success ($I_s$). As a special assumption of the theory, it is postulated that $I_s$ is $1 - P_s$. That is, if the probability of success is very low, then the incentive value of success is very high, and vice versa. Other incentives are related to achievement but, other things equal, the incentive value of success is important. The formula reads:

$$T_S = M_S \times P_S \times I_S$$

where    $T_S$ = tendency to achieve success
         $M_S$ = motive to success (n Ach)
         $P_S$ = perceived probability of
             success
         $I_S$ = incentive value of success,
             or $1 - P_S$

If any of the components is zero, then there will be no tendency to strive for success in a particular situation. The formula is like the Hullian formula in being multiplicative and there is a crude analogy between concepts. Thus, $M_s$ is something like drive in that it is internal, $P_s$ is a learning component corresponding roughly to habit, and $I_s$ corresponds roughly to $K$.

There are obviously important differences from Hull, however, particularly with regard to $P_s$ and $I_s$. To illustrate, a reliable finding on high n Ach people is that they are *medium risk takers*. Given a choice of activities involving various probabilities of success, they tend to choose those that have a medium level of $P_s$. The Atkinson model accounts for this as follows. Since $P_s$ can range from 0 to 1, $I_s$ can range from 1 to 0 because $I_s = 1 - P_s$. The maximum possible value of $P \times (1 - P)$ is obtained with $P = .50$. If $P = .90$, $1 - P = .10$, and the product is .09. Similarly, if $P = .10$ and $1 - P = .90$, the product is .09. But if $P = .50$, the product is .25. Table 13-1 shows some worked examples of $T_s$ for various values of $M_s$ and $P_s$ and Figure 13-1 graphically illustrates the same thing.

**Table 13-1**  Calculations of $T_s$ and $T_{af}$ for five different difficulty level tasks and different values of $M_s$ and $M_{af}$.

| Task | $P_s$ | $I_s$ | $T_s = M_s \times P_s \times I_s$ when | | | $P_f$ | $I_{-f}$ | $T_{af} = M_{af} \times P_f \times I_{-f}$ when | | |
|---|---|---|---|---|---|---|---|---|---|---|
| | | | $M_s = 1$ | $M_s = 3$ | $M_s = 8$ | | | $M_{af} = 1$ | $M_{af} = 3$ | $M_{af} = 8$ |
| A | .90 | .10 | .09 | .27 | .72 | .10 | $-.90$ | $-.09$ | $-.27$ | $-.72$ |
| B | .70 | .30 | .21 | .63 | 1.68 | .30 | $-.70$ | $-.21$ | $-.63$ | $-1.68$ |
| C | .50 | .50 | .25 | .75 | 2.00 | .50 | $-.50$ | $-.25$ | $-.75$ | $-2.00$ |
| D | .30 | .70 | .21 | .63 | 1.68 | .70 | $-.30$ | $-.21$ | $-.63$ | $-1.68$ |
| E | .10 | .90 | .09 | .27 | .72 | .90 | $-.10$ | $-.09$ | $-.27$ | $-.72$ |

For any value of $M_s$ except zero, $T_s$ is maximal at $P_s = .50$. With low values of $M_s$, the curve, as shown in Figure 13.1, is very shallow, but with increasing values of $M_s$, the curve is progressively steeper. With higher values of $M_s$, there is a greater tendency to choose tasks with a medium chance of success than either very easy or very difficult tasks. Part of the incentive value of a task lies in the potential attainment of risky success, some feeling of accomplishment that we may take to be pleasurable. For high n Ach ($M_s$) individuals, there is a strong desire to succeed, but success does not mean much if the job is too easy. Conversely, if the task is very difficult it has a high incentive value but little chance of succeeding and hence little chance of getting any feeling of accomplishment.

As one test of the theory, Atkinson (1958) told female subjects they were to compete for a prize of either \$1.25 or \$2.50. Four probabilities of winning were stated: 1/20, 1/3, 1/2, and 3/4. One task was to draw X's inside small circles for twenty minutes. The high-reward group performed better than the low-reward group, but performance declined for both when $P_s$ increased from 1/2 to 3/4, confirming the theoretical prediction.

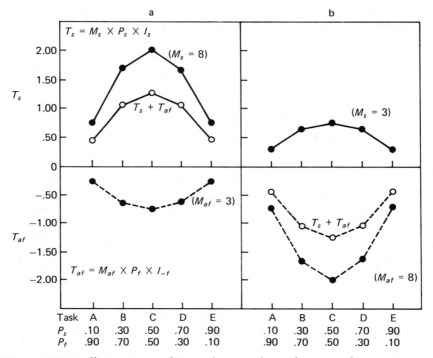

**Figure 13.1** *Illustrations of $T_s$ and $T_{af}$ and resultant tendencies to approach or avoid when $M_s = 3$ or 8 and when $M_{af} = 3$ or 8. In (a), the tendency to success is greater than the tendency to avoid failure, therefore, the resultant tendency, the algebraic summation of $T_s$ and $T_{af}$ is positive. In (b) the situation is just reversed, with the resultant tendency being negative. Note also that $T_s$ is a steeper function in (a) ($M_s = 8$) than in (b) ($M_s = 3$). This indicates why high n Ach individuals are medium-risk takers; medium probabilities of success produce much higher relative values of $T_s$ when $M_s$ is high.*

**The Tendency to Avoid Failure ($T_{af}$).** Besides the "satisfaction" or "pride" that comes from success, there is "shame" from failure (tendency to avoid failure, or $T_{af}$). This negative affect presumably depends on one's previous experience with failure, whether one was punished or ridiculed. A multiplicative formula is also used to determine the strength of the tendency to avoid failure. The components are (1) the *motive to avoid failure* $(M_{af})$, the fear of failure, commonly measured by a test anxiety questionnaire; (2) the *probability of failure* $(P_f)$, which for any given task is $1 - P_s$; and (3) the *negative incentive value of failure* $(I_{-f})$ is $- (1 - P_f)$, which is the same as $-P_s$. If the probability of failure is .90, then $I_{-f}$ is $-(1 - .90) = -.10$. Since $P_s$ for this example is $1 - .90 = .10$, then $I_{-f} = -P_s = -.10$. The tendency to avoid failure is thus given by the formula:

$$T_{af} = M_{af} \times P_f \times I_{-f}$$

where $T_{af}$ = the tendency to avoid failure
$M_{af}$ = motive to avoid failure
$P_f$ = probability of failure = $1 - P_s$
$I_{-f}$ = negative incentive value of failure = $-P_s$

Table 13-1 and Figure 13.1 also show worked examples and a graphic illustration of the use of the formula. The formula says that if there is any motivation to avoid failure, there will be some tendency to avoid tasks that could potentially lead to failure. Furthermore, the maximum value of $T_{af}$ will also occur with medium-probability tasks. The logic is the same as with $T_s$. The maximum value of $P_f \times I_{-f}$ occurs when $P_f = .50$, but the product is a negative value. The tendency to avoid failure will be the strongest for tasks having a medium expectancy of failure—just the opposite of what is predicted for the individual with high n Ach. In everyday language, the person afraid of failing may choose a task which is so easy that he cannot fail or one which is so difficult that there is no shame in failing. A task of medium difficulty is too easy to fail and the shame too great, therefore it is avoided.

**The Combination of $T_s$ and $T_{af}$.** The values of $I_s$, $P_f$ and $I_{-f}$ are all determined once we know the value of $P_s$. What differentiates $T_s$ and $T_{af}$, then, are the relative strengths of $M_s$ and $M_{af}$. The resolution of the conflict between $T_s$ and $T_{af}$ is then represented as follows:

$$T_s + T_{af} = (M_s \times P_s \times I_s) + (M_{af} \times P_f \times I_{-f})$$

Since $I_s$ is positive and $I_{-f}$ is negative, the summation can be positive $(T_s > T_{af})$, zero or negative $(T_s < T_{af})$. In effect, then, if $M_s > M_{af}$, the individual should choose medium-probability tasks, etc. but if $M_{af} > M_s$, the person should tend to avoid medium-probability tasks, etc. The theory then resolves into being the same as any other conflict theory. (An addition to the formula, omitted here, is that there are other incentives besides $I_s$ and $I_f$). Atkinson's theory, with its special assumptions about positive and negative incentives for achievement, makes interesting and unique predictions, however. We shall illustrate these with task preference and level of aspiration.

*Task Preference.* McClelland (1958) showed that high n Ach children preferred to toss a ring at a peg (the ringtoss game) from a medium distance, as compared to low n Ach children, who tended more to choose either near or far distances. Atkinson and Litwin (1960) then divided subjects into four groups of all combinations of high and low n Ach and high and low anxiety. They predicted that High $M_s$, Low $M_{af}$ subjects would show the strongest tendency to choose medium distances in the ringtoss game and that High $M_{af}$, Low $M_s$ subjects would avoid the middle range. The other two groups should fall between. The predictions were somewhat confirmed, as shown in Figure 13.2. The High $M_{af}$, Low $M_s$ group tended to choose a middle range, but their preferences were spread across a wider range of distances than any other group.

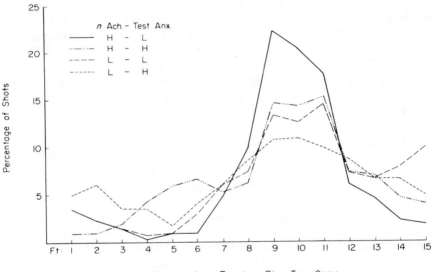

Distance from Target in Ring Toss Game

**Figure 13.2** *Percentage of shots taken from each distance by college men in a ringtoss game. Graph is smoothed according to the method of running averages, for S's classified as High or Low simultaneously in n Ach and test anxiety, H-L (N = 13), H-H (N = 10), L-L (N = 9), L-H (N = 13). (From Atkinson and Litwin, 1960, p. 55.)*

*Level of Aspiration.* Suppose a High $M_s$ person chooses a task perceived to be of medium difficulty. By experimental prearrangement, he then either succeeds or fails. What difficulty level should he subsequently choose? One of the commonest results of such *level of aspiration* research is that people tend to change their goals realistically on the basis of experience (e.g., Lewin, Dembo, Festinger, & Sears, 1944). After failure, the goal is lowered; after success, it is raised. Atkinson's explanation is that after easy success, a person would perceive $P_s$ as higher than previously expected. Therefore, he sets the next goal higher because that would bring $P_s$ closer to .50. Conversely, if he failed he would assume that $P_s$ was lower than he had expected and hence choose a simpler task to bring $P_s$ up more nearly to .50. These are *typical shifts* in level of aspiration research.

There are sometimes peculiar *atypical shifts,* however. Some individuals *raise* their goals after failure and *lower* them after success. According to the theory, if $M_{af} > M_s$, then the individual should *avoid* medium-difficulty tasks. Now suppose a High $M_{af}$ subject is told he has a task where $P_s = .50$ and fails at it. He may then believe that $P_s$ was *lower* than he initially thought, e.g., .35. An easier task would put him closer to $P_s = .50$, which should be negative for him. He may therefore select a *more difficult task* (e.g., where $P_s = .25$) than the one he failed at. Conversely, if successful at a task he believes to be $P_s = .50$, the subject may think the task was easier than he had believed, e.g., $P_s = .65$. Therefore, he would choose an even easier task next because he wants to keep away from the $P_s = .50$ task. Moulton (1965) actually got such results, for High $M_{af}$, Low $M_s$ individuals, as well as showing that High $M_s$, Low $M_{af}$ subjects and $M_s = M_{af}$ subjects made typical shifts more frequently. This is rather remarkable support for the theory.

### The Female Motive to Avoid Success

For women, TAT achievement scores do not predict performance on achievement tasks, and most achievement research has therefore been with males. Perhaps the type of pictures used in the tests, as well as the definition of achievement, is inappropriate for females. Since Horner (1968), however, it has been speculated that some females have a *motive to avoid success* (MAS). Some authors consider this to be equivalent to fear of failure, whereas others see it as a conflict between social stereotypes for female behavior and the behavior required for achievement. It is generally men or boys, not women or girls, who are rewarded for being successfully competitive.

It is important to recognize that there are very demonstrable stereotypes for men and women, and both sexes ascribe to these about equally. J.E. Williams and Bennett (1975) found on the 300-word Adjective Check List (Gough & Heilbrun, 1965) that both sexes agreed at least 75 percent of the time on thirty-three adjectives checked for males and thirty for females. Men were seen as more ambitious, assertive, confident, dominant, independent, logical, rational, steady, and unemotional, while women were seen as more affectionate, charming, emotional, fickle, frivolous, highly-strung, nagging, rattlebrained, sentimental, talkative, and weak. As judged by a clinical psychologist, these stereotypes are pathological, but presumably represent how men and women actually *think* of each other. (We presume most people are not really like the stereotypes.) People do not describe themselves like the stereotypes. Deviations from the stereotypes for one's own sex may engender some anxiety, however.

Patty (1976) found that MAS-present women saw themselves as less affectionate, more critical of themselves, having low self-esteem, and more controlled by external events. They also described themselves as being more ambivalent in their professional and interpersonal goals than did women without MAS. The MAS-present women were career oriented, but aspired to traditional female occupations, and their mothers were in more traditional occupations. The MAS-absent women, on the other hand, had mothers more likely to be employed in occupations atypical for females and hence had a nonconforming role model. The MAS-present female, then, may have conflict between career aspirations and negative consequences of achievement (e.g., being perceived as unfeminine and not getting a husband). The female without MAS may have rejected the stereotypic view and hence has no conflict about achievement, or does not have goals that conflict with the female stereotype.

Laboratory research is consistent in showing performance differences between MAS-present and MAS-absent women. In tasks which are noncompetitive, "feminine," or described as "easy," the MAS-present female performs as well or better than her MAS-absent counterpart. In tasks that are competitive, "masculine," or said to be "difficult," however, the MAS-present women do conspicuously worse, and MAS-absent women do better (Horner, 1968; Makosky, 1972; Patty & Safford, 1976). One interpretation is that the MAS-present women are in conflict about success in competitive situations and their performance therefore suffers. MAS-absent females, however, are challenged to do better and have no ambivalence about doing so.

Thus far there is no generally agreed-on integration of the motive to avoid success into achievement theory. There are some marked similarities between MAS-present females and fear-of-failure males, however, including impaired performance under achievement-arousing conditions (e.g., competition). Jackaway and Teevan (1976) have recently described a revised fear-of-failure scoring scheme that seems to work for both males and females and that may provide the integration into the theory. There has been an explosion of research in this area, and considerable theorizing can be expected to accompany it.

### Problems in Achievement Theory and Research

Measures of n Ach relate to many different behaviors, but certain questions need to be raised before we can be confident of the interpretations for this. First, what is the reliability and validity of n Ach measures? Second, does the literature support the concept of n Ach and related theory as well as generally implied? Third, is n Ach a unitary variable or can it be broken down into more situation-specific or task-specific components. Fourth, is n Ach actually a *motivational* variable at all?

***Reliability and Validity of Fantasy Measures of n Ach.*** Entwisle (1972), in a careful review of the literature, found that simple dichotomous scoring of fantasy material (i.e., either presence or absence of n Ach in a story) correlates .70 to .90 with the scores obtained using the more complicated standard scoring schemes. Since this is in the range of good test reliability, it indicates that the complex schemes are providing little more information than the dichotomous. Using just "1" or "0" to indicate presence or absence of n Ach in each of four stories is then just a four-item test. If the complicated scoring procedures were properly done in this research (which Atkinson [1974] doubts), they are providing the equivalent of only a four-item test.

With so little information from these tests, then, it is not surprising that reliability estimates are low, between .30 and .40 at best (Entwisle, 1972). Interjudge agreement is high, but this is irrelevant to the extent that different pictures evoke unrelated story material. The reliability estimates are even lower for females than for males, which alone would account for the failure to obtain significant relations with other variables when females are used as subjects.

If reliability is .40, then we could expect little in the way of validity and can wonder how differences between high and low n Ach performances are ever found. The overall strategy in the literature seems to have been that if one can demonstrate significant relationships between n Ach scores and other performances there is construct validity, and if there is validity there must be prior reliability. Atkinson (1974) has argued that traditional approaches to reliability may not be appropriate. Test-retest correlations may be low but if test scores are split at the median into high and low groups, the same individuals tend to be in the high and low groups on retest. This is sufficient for construct validity, since the standard procedure is to use median splits (or even more extreme groups) for comparing groups on other tasks.

***Does the Achievement Literature Show Consistent Results?*** Klinger (1966) divided the n Ach research into (1) studies involving relatively long-term behavior patterns, measured by such things as course grades, and (2) brief measures of performance, such as addition problems that are often administered at or near the same time as the test itself is given. Overall, he found about as many experiments with statistically nonsignificant results as with significant results.

For long-term measures, Klinger's analysis indicated that two primary variables accounted for the differences in significance. First, female subjects generally do not show significant differences. Second, for high school age or younger subjects, the relation of n Ach to behavior was usually significant, but with college-age subjects it was less likely to be significant.

With short-term tasks, the measure of n Ach was important. The French Test of Insight (another commonly used n Ach measure—see Atkinson, 1958) frequently gave positive results, whereas either the TAT or the Iowa Picture Interpretation Test gave more nonsignificant results. Klinger wryly observes that "The overall pattern of results can only be described as puzzling" (1966, p. 298). Even a close reading of some of the research with positive results frequently leaves one with a little less confidence in n Ach than when one started. One possible explanation for the inconsistencies is that n Ach is a complex variable, not a unitary dimension that is tapped by any single measure.

***Is n Ach a Unitary Variable?*** Jackson, Ahmed, and Heapy (1976), by logical analysis, postulated six distinct dimensions for achievement motivation: (1) status with experts; (2) acquisitiveness; (3) achievement via independence; (4) status with peers; (5) competitiveness; and (6) concern for excellence. They then devised five different methods for measuring each of the six different dimensions. The six dimensions and five methods resulted in thirty scales. The intercorrelations of the various measures quite nicely fit the criteria for validation by the multitrait-multimethod procedure. That is, there were low intercorrelations among different dimensions by any of the methods, but the five methods had high intercorrelations for each of the six different dimensions. This gives strong evidence that there are *at least* six achievement dimensions. The procedures allowed for no more possibilities than this.

It may thus be inadequate to say that an individual is at the "*X* percentile" in achievement motivation. We would need a *profile* of the individual, representing his location on each of the six dimensions (assuming these are *the* dimensions). We should then like to determine the conditions (situations, tasks, etc.) under which one dimension is more or less important than another. A person might be more concerned with doing his job well (concern for excellence) than with doing it independently (achievement via independence).

***Is n Ach a Motivational Variable?*** The general assumption, dating back to McClelland et al. (1953) is that the TAT measures a *motivational disposition,* the degree to which an individual will show a particular motivational *state* under the appropriate circumstances. The motive, to use Klinger's (1966, 1975) phrase, must be "engaged" before it is effective. For Atkinson's theory, this engagement is indicated by the multiplicative formula ($T_S = M_S \times P_S \times I_S$). The tendency to engage in achievement-oriented behaviors does not occur unless $M_S$ is aroused. There are good arguments for contesting the view that n Ach is a motive at all, however.

*Achievement Motive and Verbal Productivity.* Entwisle (1972) found that the number of words written per TAT story (verbal productivity) by ninth-graders correlated more highly with school grades (about .35) than did the actual n Ach scores (about .25). She concludes that such modest relationships as were found between motive scores and school performance both reflected verbal productivity, and remarks that "Fantasy-based measures of achievement motivation appear to have little or no independent predictive validity for school performance" (p. 389). Entwisle believes there may be many aspects of achievement-related motivation rather than a single "need for achievement." It is also possible that n Ach, however defined, may not be a motive.

*n Ach as a Mediator.* In Atkinson's formula, $M_S$ is treated as a causal factor, because the value of $T_S$ is zero if $M_S$ is zero. Klinger (1966) argued that TAT measures of n Ach reflect situational factors more than they do motivational factors and that n Ach is not necessarily a cause of performance in a motivational sense. The relationship between n Ach and performance may instead be correlational. Subjects who demonstate high achievement *imagery* in their TAT stores and high achievement *performance* in other situations may come from environments that "have been relatively rich in achievement cues, in the vocabularly, ideas, and strategies of achievement" (Klinger, 1966, p. 303). Achievement imagery (which may be related to verbal productivity) and achievement performance are both due to this "achievement arousal." This hypothesis is illustrated as follows:

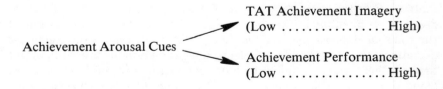

A motivational factor does not have to be postulated as a causal factor according to this hypothesis: Imagery and achievement are just correlated.

Another possibility, apparently more favored by Klinger, is that there may be an achievement motive, but that the *cue* value of achievement imagery has been neglected. We can illustrate this possibility as follows:

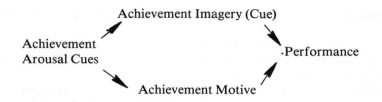

Achievement fantasy as a cue and achievement motivation both contribute to achievement performance. This looks remarkably like the Hullian formulation for the joint roles of drive and drive stimuli as determinants of performance, as discussed in Chapter Four. In Hull's theory, the antecedent conditions for drive (drive arousal operations) also arouse drive stimuli. Thus:

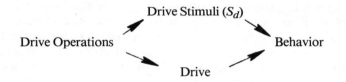

Achievement imagery sounds more complex than drive stimuli, but perhaps this is because we have impoverished ideas about drive stimuli. McClelland and Atkinson (1948) themselves showed that there was greater food imagery in food-deprived than nondeprived subjects, and studies of starvation in humans have shown the same thing. Perhaps even the lowly rat has his fantasies of crackers and cheese. At any rate, achievement theory has become more cognitive.

## ATTRIBUTION THEORY

On any Sunday afternoon in autumn, we can watch the world's finest football players on television. We see a running back plow through the line and say, "He really goes all out." Or, if a tackle is missed, we might say, "Oh, he didn't try hard enough." Or, on a wet field a running back tries to turn a corner and his feet slip out from underneath him, and we say "What bad luck." In each instance, we have observed a behavior and attributed a cause to it. The first two attributions involved characteristics of the players and were *dispositional.* The third was external, or *situational.* The players themselves might attribute different causes to the same behaviors, however. Thus, the defensive back missing a tackle might say to himself, "What tough luck, my feet slipped." The "actor" doesn't necessarily make the same attributions as the "observer."

Attribution theory has evolved from the attempt to deal with many problems in social psychology and personality theory and has not developed into a formal theory in the sense of Hull or Atkinson. For consistency here and with earlier chapters, we shall discuss attribution in terms of expectancy theory, not entirely dissimilar to Rotter's (1954) approach. We shall examine four questions: (1) *What* do we mean by attribution? (2) *Why* do we make attributions? (3) *How* do we make attributions? and (4) How is the theory *applicable* to motivational-emotional problems?

### What Do We Mean By Attribution?

Let us start with a simple example. George notices that he occasionally feels particularly happy and gradually realizes that this occurs when he is around Helen. He decides that his feelings are related to Helen, which is to say that he attributes his feelings to the presence of Helen. *An attribution, then, is an inference about causes.* We infer causes for events that we observe, including our own behavior and feelings. We all look for explanations of events by seeking consistencies in the world. Intention, desire, ability, and so on are *inferred dispositions* by which we explain our own behavior or that of others. George perceived a consistency between Helen's presence and his own feeling happy and thereby inferred that Helen was the cause.

*Attributions and Expectancies.* Let us now relate attributions to expectancies. An expectancy is a belief that one thing *will* follow from another; an attribution is a belief that one thing *has* followed from another. Expectancies and attributions are both inferences about dependent relationships between events and behavior, events and feelings, and so on. Both refer to similar correlational relationships but, depending on our time frame, we refer either to expectancies or attributions. Thus, George could *expect* that if Helen were present he would feel good; or, if he felt good in Helen's presence, he could *attribute* the cause to her. The argument then is that expectancies and attributions are *operationally identical.*

Following Bolles (1972) and Tolman (1959), we can distinguish two kinds of expectancies. First, there are SS expectancies—correlations between stimulus events. These correspond generally to our notions of classical conditioning, whereby the CS informs us that the UCS is coming (e.g., Rescorla, 1967, and prior discussions in Chapters Seven and Eight). An SS expectancy can develop regardless of our behavior. We can read a newspaper and expect that if it does not rain soon there will be higher wheat prices next year.

Second, there are RS expectancies, correlations between our behavior and environmental outcomes by which we infer that our behavior has a causal effect on the environment. Such RS expectancies correspond to the usual notions of instrumental conditioning. The rat learns that if he presses the lever, he will get food. The salesman expects that if he makes so many calls, he will make a certain number of sales. This could be learned by direct experience or vicariously.

We can also expand the notion of expectancies to combinations of internal and external events. If I go out on the tennis court feeling particularly refreshed and energetic, I may expect that I will do well. I use my feelings as a predictor of performance. In the case of George, an external stimulus (Helen) was used as the predictor of an internal state (his feeling good).

The outcomes for expectancies may be positive, neutral, or negative and the predictor events (e.g., stimuli) might in themselves be positive, neutral, or negative, independently of the nature of the outcome. Pain can signal coming reward. Similarly, if we are suffering an upset stomach we may be able to readily attribute it to an earlier pleasant event (eating something good to excess).

***Quantification of Expectancies and Attributions.*** Using the language of correlation, we shall say that expectancies can vary from $-1.00$ to $+1.00$. We may expect that Event B will *not* follow Event A (negative correlation), that they are unrelated (zero correlation) or that Event B *will* follow Event A (positive correlation). The strength of our expectation or belief is indicated by the size of the correlation. We may interchangeably use the notion of *dependent probability,* which has the same absolute range of numbers as correlation (0 to 1.00). To say that the probability of Event B following Event A is .50 is equivalent to saying that there is a positive but not perfect correlation between the two events.[1] Expectancies are generally *subjective probabilities,* however, since we seldom have the precise quantification to make an objective probability statement about everyday events.

The more often an expectancy is *confirmed,* by having an expected event actually happen, the stronger the expectancy becomes—with an upper limit of 1.00. Conversely, if an expected outcome does not occur, there is disconfirmation, and the expectancy becomes weaker. A long string of disconfirmations leads to a negative correlation, the expectancy that Event B will not follow Event A.

### Why Do We Make Attributions?

Kelley (1967, p. 193) suggests that attribution theory "describes processes that operate *as if* the individual were motivated to obtain a cognitive mastery of the causal structures of his environment." This is in general

[1]The value .50 does not mean precisely the same thing in correlation and dependent probability, but for our purposes the same principle is illustrated, and the generalization from correlation to dependent probability is worthwhile.

agreement with the view that gaining knowledge about the environment and its causal structures is rewarding, i.e., that the development of expectancies is "rewarding." There are two forms of such reward. We may feel tense when we do not know what to expect, and learning what to expect is tension reducing (i.e., the situation is less aversive). Or, the developing of expectancies may be rewarding just because it is pleasurable to gain information about events. Either of these possibilities may be correct at one time or another.

### How Do We Make Attributions?

The cause of a unique event, one that occurs for one person at one time, is usually ambiguous because we cannot derive a correlation from a unique event; a set of events is necessary. One event consistently related to some other event provides a basis for inferring a cause with some reliability. If George was with Helen only once and was particularly happy, he would be less likely to attribute his happiness to Helen than if the same thing happened several times. He would have to eliminate the possibility that other events occurring when he was with Helen were not the cause. Perhaps they were at a good movie or perhaps George had just passed a big exam and was flooded with relief when he picked up Helen. After considering, and eliminating, a number of such possibilities, he might decide that indeed he was in love with her. In most everyday events, we cannot do these things in an experimental sense (e.g., going to the same movie with several different girls), but we may do it indirectly by comparing past experiences with the present experience. We may, unfortunately, "jump to a hasty conclusion."

If two events are consistently related over several occurrences, we can reasonably attribute a cause. We can illustrate this somewhat quantitatively in Table 13-2, where it seems pretty clear that George's feelings are related to Helen's presence. If we had real frequencies in the table, we could actually calculate a correlation coefficient.

**Table 13-2**   *Percentage of Occurrences of George Feeling Happy When Helen Was Present and When She Was Absent.*

|                     |      | Helen   |         |
|---------------------|------|---------|---------|
|                     |      | *Present* | *Absent* |
| George feeling happy | *Yes* | 50%     | 5%      |
|                     | *No* | 50%     | 95%     |

Although we have dealt with correlations between just two variables, it is also possible to correlate *several* variables with a particular event, a procedure called *multiple correlation.* A particular outcome need never necessarily have only a single cause, and a major problem in laboratory research or real life is finding the most likely cause for some event at a particular time. Correlation is not the best index of causation, but it is usually all we have.[2]

Although discovering the correlation between events may be motivational in the sense of being rewarding, the resulting attribution may then serve only as *knowledge* by which we guide our behavior. The attribution itself may not motivate us to do things. This is a provisional statement which may need to be changed, but it seems generally in line with opinion in the field. Bem (1972) has discussed this problem in some detail. We shall therefore assume that attributions are informational cues and proceed to look at applications of the theory.

### Locus of Control

Several times we have referred to learned helplessness, the idea that organisms without control over events seem to "give up" and not do anything in situations where they could actually be effective. Turned around, we can relate this to such concepts as mastery, power, and competence. Alfred Adler, once a follower of Freud, broke away from the master because he (Adler) believed that striving for personal control over one's own destiny was the most important motivation. A person without such a feeling of control had an "inferiority complex" and might then "overcompensate" in his attempts to gain a feeling of control or mastery. De Charms (1968) described this in terms of "origins" and "pawns." Some individuals feel they originate their own activities and are responsible for their own rewards and punishments. Others feel that, like chess pawns, they have little freedom of movement and that such freedom as they do have is at the service of more powerful outside forces. It should be emphasized that these are subjective feelings, individual interpretations of reality. For most of us, the feeling of power, or personal control, is probably situational; in some situations, we feel competent because we know what to do and can do it successfully, but in other situations we feel more helpless.

***Rotter's I-E Scale.*** An important research tool in this area is Rotter's (1966) Internal-External (I-E) Scale. This measures the extent to which a person believes that events are under his or her own control (internal locus)

---

[2]Kelley (1967) has used the statistical technique called *analysis of variance* as the basis of his model of the attribution process. Analysis of variance is used for analyzing results of experiments in which several variables are manipulated simultaneously. We assume that the fundamentals of correlation are more familiar to most students and are therefore easier to follow. Since the correlational procedures can generally be translated into analysis of variance terms anyway, there is no real loss as far as logic is concerned.

as opposed to external control (external locus). Each item consists of a pair of statements representing opposite beliefs about locus of control, the subject indicating which one he believes. For example:

Item 15.  a. In my case, getting what I want has little or nothing to with luck.
          b. Many times we might just as well decide what to do by flipping a coin.
Item 25.  a. Many times I feel I have little influence over the things that happen to me.
          b. It is impossible for me to believe that chance or luck plays an important role in my life.

The total score is the number of external control items with which the subject agrees (e.g., "b" in Item 15 and "a" in Item 25). Reliability coefficients are about .70 for internal consistency and slightly less for test-retest (Rotter, 1966). The I-E Scale correlates well with other measures of locus of control, but not with such variables as intelligence or social desirability. The scale therefore shows discriminant validity. Its construct validity is shown in the many studies in which it has predicted other performances.

Rotter uses the term *internal* to refer to what we previously called an *RS expectancy.* The I-E Scale, then, measures "generalized expectancies," i.e., the extent to which an individual generally perceives that his own behavior determines his rewards and punishments. This should be distinguished from an SS expectancy, in which the *first S is internal.* We may attribute emotions to internal events (internal stimuli), and this is quite different from the RS expectancies involved in the locus-of-control research.

Most I-E research has assumed a single locus of control dimension, low external to high external. Collins (1974), however, found four different dimensions in Rotter's scale, named as follows, with sample items in parentheses: (1) *The difficult-easy world* ("Studying is really useless"); (2) *The just-unjust world* ("People's misfortunes result from the mistakes they make"); (3) *The predictable-unpredictable world* ("There really is no such thing as luck"); and (4) *The politically responsive-unresponsive world* ("With enough effort, we can wipe out political corruption"). The opposites of the same items would represent the other extreme of each dimension.

Collins also observes that "internal" and "external" are not necessarily mirror images. For example, "luck" and "skill" are not opposite ends of the same dimension. On Rotter's scale, the beliefs that the world is difficult, unjust, random, and politically unresponsive *appear* equivalent because they all fall at the external end of the scale. In Collins' analysis, however, they are relatively uncorrelated and seem intuitively to be of different origin.

### Some Representative Locus of Control Research

*Perceived Choice and Internal Control.* Harvey and Harris (1975) argued that we perceive we have choice and internal control when (1) we make a decision among positive options rather than negative, and (2) when the options are very similar. That is, we feel greater control when we are not *coerced* (by negative options) and not *overwhelmed* (by a single very powerful positive option).[3] Their research confirmed their predictions except that all choices among negative options were seen as externally controlled, regardless of their similarity.

*I-E and n Ach.* High n Ach people attribute their own performance more to internal than external factors (Weiner & Kukla, 1970). Presumably, they have strong RS expectancies because their previous behavior has been rewarded. A generalized RS expectancy may then serve as a cue for the high n Ach individual to (1) tell stories with greater achievement imagery; (2) respond more positively to I-E scale items involving internal control; (3) show higher achievement performances; and (4) have high perceived freedom. Schematically:

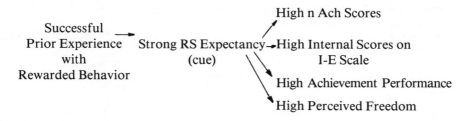

*Group Differences in I-E.* Lower- and middle-class black Americans are more external than white Americans at the same socioeconomic levels. Also, in a triethnic community, whites were the least external, then Spanish-Americans, then Indians (Lefcourt, 1966). Schizophrenics are more external than normal subjects (Cromwell, Rosenthal, Shakow, & Kahn, 1961). Such comparative group data consistently point to the conclusion that individuals in positions of minimal power are highest in externality. We would predict this because we should expect them to have low expectancies that their behavior is effective.

[3]This argument is virtually identical to the main points of Skinner's *Beyond Freedom and Dignity* (1971). Skinner argued that freedom involves lack of aversive controls and that dignity involves lack of obvious positive reinforcers.

*Individual Differences in I-E.* Lefcourt (1966) concludes that locus of control is a useful predictor of learning performance *if* the materials to be learned are relevant to the individual's goal striving. If the individual is *not interested* in particular material, it does not make much difference whether he is high or low in externality. High external individuals also conform more to group pressures than do low externals.

Liverant and Scodel (1960) found that low external subjects chose bets of intermediate probabilities more often than high external subjects, and the lows tended generally to be more cautious in their betting. This is the same pattern of risk preference characteristic of high n Ach individuals, who are also high internal. Strategies for "maintaining control" and for "achieving" are very similar.

### Success and Failure Attributions

Chance and skill are not the only attributions related to success and failure. Weiner (1972, 1974) has distinguished the two additional attributes of personal effort and task difficulty. He categorizes the four attributions according to locus (internal, external) and stability (stable, unstable), as shown in Table 13-3.

**Table 13-3** *Attributes Defined By Combinations of Internal and External Sources and Stability Over Time.*

|  |  | Locus of control | |
|  |  | *Internal* | *External* |
| --- | --- | --- | --- |
| Stability | *Stable* | Ability | Task Difficulty |
|  | *Unstable* | Effort | Luck |

Each of these four attributions has specific antecedent conditions, roughly as follows.

1. *Ability.* Repeated success or failure in the past, particularly in conjunction with social norms that may be important in defining what success or failure is.
2. *Task Difficulty.* Judged by social norms and objective task characteristics. Weiner believes that social norms, indicating how well other people do on a particular task, are the best cues for attributing ease or difficulty to the task.
3. *Effort.* Time spent on a task, degree of muscular tension in doing the task.
4. *Luck.* Lack of apparent control over an outcome; success, or failure at the task not correlated with the personal characteristics of the individual performing the task.

Ability and task difficulty are stable across time, whereas effort and luck fluctuate.

*Some Sample Research On Success, Failure, and Attribution.* First we discuss research related to *task difficulty* and *internal versus external attribution.* Weiner and Kukla (1970, Exp. 6) gave subjects hypothetical information about success or failure outcomes. With each outcome, they also gave normative information about the percentage of individuals supposedly successful (99, 95, 90, 70, 50, 30, 10, 5, and 1 percent). The results were that if the task was supposedly *easy,* then success was given low internal attribution; it does not take much on the part of the individual to succeed at an easy task. Failure on an easy task, however, was given high internal attribution (e.g., lack of trying). When the task was supposedly *difficult,* the situation reversed: Success was attributed to internal characteristics (such as trying hard and ability), but failure was attributed more to external factors (i.e., the difficulty of the task).

Subjects may not use normative information when attributing causes for behaviors, however. Nisbett and Borgida (1975) presented normative information about the occurrences of a particular behavior, "typical" level of shocks taken in a hypothetical experiment. Whether a particular behavior was said to be typical or extreme did not affect subjects' judgments of whether the behavior was typical when applied to a particular individual. Furthermore, subjects considered a particular behavior typical for a whole group even though it was specifically based on only two case descriptions, which were carefully noted as being extremely rare. One explanation is that normative information is abstract and remote, but information about only one or two people is concrete and vivid. Since Weiner and Kukla found that normative information made a large difference in success/failure attributions, it appears that the effect of normative information depends on the situation in which it is presented.

Second, we discuss research related to *ability inference* and *order effect.* Jones, Rock, Shaver, Goethals, and Ward (1968) had real subjects observe the performance of a stooge in a multiple-choice problem-solving task. For thirty successive trials, success-failure feedback was given after each trial. There were three different conditions, each involving fifteen "successes" by the stooge but differing in whether there were more successes near the beginning of the sequence, at the end, or evenly distributed throughout the thirty trials. The result was that the real subjects judged the stooges as more intelligent and more likely to be successful with future problems if success was more frequent at the beginning, and least likely to be successful if they started off slowly. Presumably the early trials establish an expectancy that is difficult to break, perhaps because the subjects tend to stop paying attention once they develop an expectancy. The subjects also recall the number of correct solutions for the stooges in the decreasing-success group as being greater than they really were and recall those of the increasing-success group as less than they really were (i.e., over fifteen and under fifteen, respectively). Using a similar situation, Langer and Roth (1975) had subjects judge both themselves and other subjects. They again found a primacy effect in judgment of skill level, and subject's self-ratings of skill were higher than ratings of others! They suggested that there are higher skill ratings when subjects are more ego involved in the situation, as when rating themselves. One might then predict that friends would also be rated higher than strangers.

### Some Complications of Success-Failure Attributions

Weiner's four-cell scheme for attributions was based on Heider's (1958) analysis, which was logical rather than empirical, but Weiner (e.g., 1974) readily concedes there may be more than four attributions. Falbo and Beck (1977) took a strictly empirical approach to the problem. They had 226 college students list all the reasons they could for success or failure in a number of occupations, resulting in 2,495 explanations. Only those reasons (and their obvious synonyms) given by at least six subjects were retained for further analysis. "Luck" did not pass even this initial screening.

The final product was a twenty-item scale for success and a different twenty-item scale for failure attributions. The scales were not mirror images of each other, however. "Ability" and "lack of ability" appeared as explanations for success and failure, but success was also attributed to such things as friendliness, enjoyment of work, interest, self-satisfaction, and leadership. The mirror images of these were not found in the "fail scale." The fail scale had conflict of interest, lack of communication, poor working conditions, and poor health. But no one attributed success to good health, for example.

The moral of this exercise is that there are a great many attributions. Some attributions are uniquely related to particular individuals and situations, but others cut across many situations (e.g., ability). The attributions used by the "man on the street" are not necessarily those provided by research psychologists.

## THE ATTRIBUTION OF EMOTION: DO WE FEEL WHAT WE THINK?

In a classic demonstration, Mowrer (1938) showed that if GSR-conditioned human subjects had the shock electrode removed prior to extinction, they extinguished instantly. In terms of attribution theory, the subjects presumably learned that the CS *plus* the shock electrode was dangerous, but that the CS *without* the shock electrode was safe. Hence they did not respond to the CS after the electrode was removed. It is this kind of problem to which we address ourselves here. But first a little background about the theory of emotion.

### James-Lange Theory and Cannon.

Early in the history of scientific psychology, emotion was considered a state of mind, or experience, along with perceiving and thinking. In 1884, however, William James proposed that *emotion is the perception of bodily changes during various activities.* In particular, he emphasized the sympathetic nervous system and the visceral responses that it innervates. The immediate importance of James' argument was that (1) it made emotion dependent on an identifiable physiological function, and (2) it was testable. About the same time, a Swedish physiologist named Lange independently proposed a similar theory, but emphasized changes in the vascular system rather than in the viscera. The theory has since been known as the James-Lange theory.[4]

It followed from James' theory that each emotional experience had its own unique physiological counterpart; otherwise, emotions would be indistinguishable. This has been referred to as the *identity theory of emotion;* there is a one-to-one relation between experienced emotion and physiology. In one sense, this is axiomatic. If two events are discriminated, there is something different in the brain about the two events. At another level, however, the theory had problems because James was referring mostly to *peripheral* physiological differences, activity of the organs innervated by the autonomic nervous system.

The inevitable attack on the theory came from Walter Cannon (1927), who proposed what he considered five telling arguments against James: (1) separating the viscera from the nervous system does not change emotional behavior; (2) the same visceral changes occur in different emotional states as well as in such nonemotional states as violent activity; (3) the viscera are relatively insensitive structures; (4) visceral changes occur too slowly (a matter of seconds) to be the source of sudden emotional changes; and (5) artificial induction of the visceral changes typical of strong emotions does not produce these same strong emotions.

Cannon's alternative proposal was a *central* neural theory. He suggested that neural impulses flowing into the thalamus (not at that time clearly

---

[4]This is not to say that earlier suggestions relating physiology to temperament had not been made. For example, Galen had related a sanguine temperament to blood flow, a phlegmatic one to phlegm, melancholia to black bile, and choleric to yellow bile. It was not until James and Lange, however, that the idea was put into a form that was both taken seriously and that led to experimental tests. Titchener (1914) pointed out that James had actually taken his entire argument from an earlier theorist named Henle.

distinguished from the hypothalamus) were experienced as emotion as they were routed "upstream" to the cortex and slightly later produced visceral changes as they were routed "downstream" to the autonomic nervous system and viscera. This contrasts with James' view that such impulses first excited the viscera and feedback from the viscera to the cortex was experienced as emotion.

Cannon's own arguments have since been criticized. In some of the experiments he cited, it is not clear that all the connections between viscera and nervous system had actually been severed. Furthermore, these experiments were with animals, usually dogs. But James had said that emotional *experience* was produced by feedback from the viscera, not necessarily emotional *behavior*. This made the relevance of the animal research questionable. It also made some investigators throw up their hands and cry that James' theory was untestable. Since our primary concern is not James' theory per se, we shall not pursue this line of argument further. However, Cannon's statement that artificial induction of emotion (by injection of adrenalin) does *not* produce emotional experience has led to fruitful research within the attribution theory framework.

Marañon (1924, cited in Schachter & Singer, 1962; also Cantril & Hunt, 1932; Landis & Hunt, 1932) reported that subjects injected with adrenalin generally described physical symptoms (nervousness, rapid pulse, and the like), but only 29 percent of the subjects reported an *emotional* experience. According to Schachter and Singer, "Of these the great majority described their feelings in a fashion that Marañon labelled 'cold' or 'as if' emotions; that is, they made statements such as 'I feel *as if* I were awaiting a great happiness' " (p. 380). Marañon indicated, however, that if the subjects had some emotional *stimulus* presented after the injection they responded more emotionally to the stimulus than without the injection.

### Cognitive-Arousal Theory

These observations led Schachter and Singer (1962) to propose that perceived emotion is a *joint* function of an internal state of arousal and an appropriate cognition with which to *label* that state (see also Mandler, 1962, or Mandler, 1975). The cognition is an attribution. If either the arousal or the cognition is absent, a particular emotion is not experienced. They tested this by giving subjects injections of adrenalin and then putting them into situations calculated to produce different labeling of internal states.

**The Schachter-Singer Experiment.** The subjects were initially told that the experiment concerned the effect of a new vitamin compound ("Suproxin") on vision. The drug in fact was epinephrine (adrenalin),[5] which produces many symptoms of sympathetic nervous system arousal, including increases in blood pressure, heart rate, skin conductance, respiration, and muscle tremor. The subjects' cognitions were manipulated by (1) telling them different things about the effects of the drug, and (2) by putting them in different kinds of situations.

The *informed* group was told there would be transitory side effects of the drug, the actual symptoms being described. The *ignorant* group was told nothing about the drug effects, and hence the physiological changes would not necessarily be attributed to the injection. The *misinformed* group was told that such things as numbing of the feet or itching might occur, not really effects of epinephrine. This was a control for experimenter demand. A *placebo* group simply got saline injections, with no information otherwise. Half the subjects in the various groups were subjected to one of two different situations, intended to arouse *euphoria* or *anger,* respectively.

In the euphoria groups, subjects were asked to wait a few minutes in another room with another subject, until the drug had time to take effect. The "other subject" was the experimenter's stooge. During the twenty-minute waiting period, the stooge did such frivolous things as flying a paper airplane and shooting paper-wad basketballs into a trash can. As much as possible he tried to engage the real subject in these same activities, but all the while following a carefully prearranged script.

In the anger condition, the subject and stooge were asked to fill out a five-page questionnaire. Starting innocently with cover sheet information, the questions grew progressively more irksome and personal, culminating with "With how many men (other than your father) has your mother had extramarital relationships? (4 and under __: 5-9 __: 10 and over__."

The subjects then filled out various self-reports having to do with both physiological symptoms and mood. There were 5-point scales (0 to 4) for degree of happiness and for anger. The actual data presented by the authors are the mean *differences* between anger and euphoria scales. A subject's score was obtained by subtracting his score on the anger scale from his score on the happiness scale. "Happy" subjects should have positive scores and "angry" subjects negative scores. Table 13-4 summarizes the relevant data.

There are several noticeable aspects of these data. First, under the euphoria conditions, the informed group was significantly below the ignorant group. The standard interpretation is that the informed group, having

---

[5]It is doubtful that this procedure would pass the American Psychological Association's present standards for ethics in research or those established by the National Institutes of Health.

**Table 13-4** *Summary of Happiness and Anger Ratings of All Groups in the Schachter-Singer (1962) Experiment. A High Number Means More Happy or More Angry. From Schachter & Singer, 1962, pp. 390-392. Copyright © 1962 by the American Psychological Association. Reprinted by Permission.)*

| Condition | N | Self-report scales | Significant differences |
|-----------|---|--------------------|--------------------------|
|           |   | *Euphoria*         |                          |
| Epi Inf[a] | 25 | 0.98 | Epi Inf was significantly |
| Epi Ign | 25 | 1.78 | below the Epi Ign or Epi Mis. |
| Epi Mis[b] | 25 | 1.90 | The Placebo group was *not* significantly |
| Placebo | 26 | 1.61 | different from *any* other group. |
|           |   | *Anger*            |                          |
| Epi Inf | 22 | 1.91 | The only significant difference is |
| Epi Ign | 23 | 1.39 | between the Epi Inf and Epi Ign. |
| Placebo | 23 | 1.63 | Neither differ from the Placebo group. |

[a]Epi Inf—epinephrine, informed;
Epi Ign—epinephrine, ignorant;
Epi Mis—epinephrine, misinformed.
[b]There was no Epi Mis group under the anger conditions.

been told of the "side effects" of the injection, attribute their internal arousal to the injection itself. Consequently, they do not label their arousal as happiness. The ignorant subjects, on the other hand, do not know of the drug effects and search for the cause of their arousal when asked. Since the obvious cause is the preceding euphoria situation, they label their arousal as happiness. Note that the placebo group is just about as euphoric as the ignorant group. The euphoric situation by itself, then, may produce as much arousal as the injection. At any rate, the results are ambiguous.

The results for the "angry" subjects are even harder to interpret. They should have *negative* scores, but the average scores were *positive* for all groups; they were all more happy than angry. The authors suggest that the subjects, students in the experiment for course credit, were not about to endanger their grade by getting angry at the experimenter. Perhaps, perhaps not. The ignorant group did report less happiness than the informed group, which is at least in the right direction, since the hypothesis says that the informed subjects should attribute their internal states to the injection and therefore be less angry than the ignorant group. Again, however, the placebo group falls between the two epinephrine groups. The authors noted that the results with the placebo condition made it impossible "to evaluate unequivocally the effects of the state of physiological arousal and indeed raises questions about our entire theoretical structure" (Schachter & Singer, 1962, p. 393). The authors were, thus, initially modest about the import of their research—a level of humility that was suppressed in later writing about the same experiment.

Other research along the same lines produced similar results. Schachter and Wheeler (1962) injected subjects with epinephrine, chlorpromazine, or saline prior to having them observe a slapstick movie. The subjects were directly observed for various signs of amusement. Chlorpromazine, an antipsychotic tranquilizer, is antagonistic to epinephrine and is therefore expected to produce effects opposite those of epinephrine. Observers' ratings of the subjects' behavior during the movie (neutral, smiling, laughing, violent laughing) showed the predicted order of the groups on an overall "amusement index." That is, the epinephrine group was most amused and the chlorpromazine group the least. Again, however, there was no difference between epinephrine and placebo groups, both being higher than the chlorpromazine. The main result, then, is that a potent tranquilizer reduces humor responses, rather mild support for the hypothesis.

A number of experiments conceptually similar to the Schachter-Singer research, but without drugs, have also supported their cognitive arousal theory, however. Cantor, Zillman, and Bryant (1975) studied the effect of prior physical exercise on self-reports of sexual arousal from erotic films. They first determined that one minute of pedaling a stationary exercise bicycle produced a sharp increase in heart rate and blood pressure as well as self-report of high excitation. After five minutes, there was still physiological arousal, but no self-report excitation. After nine minutes, physiological and self-report measures of excitation were both back to normal.

The degree of reported sexual arousal to segments of an erotic film (*Naked Under Leather*) was then studied in a separate experiment. Different groups of subjects rated arousal on a 100-point scale, at zero, five, or nine minutes after exercise. These results were: (1) when there was both high physical excitation and perceived excitation, the mean rating was 28; (2) when there was residual physical excitation but no perception of it, the mean was 52; (3) when both physical excitation and perception had subsided, the rating was back down to 28. The attribution interpretation is that immediately after exercise, there was a low rating because the subjects could attribute their arousal to the exercise. After five minutes, they did not perceive the residual excitation from exercise, so it was attributed to the movie. After nine minutes, both residual excitation and perceived excitation were back to baseline, so the subjects attributed their arousal (presumably accurately) to just the movie. The results seem clear and avoid the massive problems of deception and drugs found with the Schachter studies.

If we incorrectly attribute some effect to the wrong cause we are making a *misattribution*. In the Cantor et al. experiment, the subjects misattributed the cause of their excitation to the movie when it was partly due to exercise. Storms and Nisbett (1970) reported a different misattribution:

Insomniacs went to sleep faster if they believed that a placebo pill was actually an arousing drug. This has been called the "reverse placebo effect." Presumably, the subjects thought the drug was keeping them awake and hence they relaxed and went to sleep! Other insomniacs, told the placebo was a sedative, took *longer* to go to sleep. Presumably they believed that if they were still awake after taking a sedative they must be very upset, and this made them more wakeful than ever.

This research is both theoretically and practically important because the results are contrary to the usual placebo effect (i.e., if we thought we had an arousing pill, the *suggestion* should make us more wakeful). The data seem to give promise of a therapeutic breakthrough for a major medical complaint. Unfortunately, Kellog and Baron (1975) were unable to replicate the results and Bootzin, Herman, and Nicassio (1976) obtained results in line with placebo-suggestion expectations. As it stands, then, the reverse placebo effect for insomnia is a doubtful phenomenon.

### Valins' Cognitive Theory

To understand Valins' (1966, 1970) theory, it is helpful to review quickly the previous theories of emotion.

1. *James-Lange.* Emotion *is* the perception of physiological changes. Specific visceral changes and accurate perceptions thereof are presumed.
2. *Cannon.* Sensory inputs are processed and emotion is directly experienced without requiring autonomic arousal.
3. *Schachter-Singer.* Emotion requires both cognition and physiological arousal. Emotional differentiation is provided by different cognitions; arousal is undifferentiated.

Valins then proposed that *the perception of physiological change is the sufficient condition for experienced emotion, whether or not the perception is veridical (accurate).* This differs from James (who said there must be autonomic nervous system [ANS] activity), from Cannon (who said that perception of physiological change was not necessary for emotion), and from Schachter and Singer (who said that both cognition-perception and arousal are necessary). The heart of Valins' theory is seen in his experimental technique of giving subjects *false* information about their internal state; what they think is perception of physiological change is nonveridical.

Valins (1966) gave male subjects false heart rate feedback during the presentation of individual slides of seminude females (from *Playboy* centerfolds). Members of three groups of twenty subjects had microphones taped to their chests. In the first group, the subjects heard sounds that they had previously been told were their heart beats. Ten slides were presented for fifteen seconds. During five slides, the subjects heard an initial increase, then return to normal, of their "heart rate" but heard no change with the other five. The particular slides paired with the bogus changes varied from subject to subject. The second group was treated the same except that during five of the slides their "heart rates" initially *decreased* and then returned to normal. In the third group, the subjects were told that the sounds were extraneous. They actually heard the same sounds given to the subjects in the first two groups, again paired with half the slides. After seeing all the slides twice, the subjects rated them individually for attractiveness on a 100-point scale and selected five, which were then taken back, as remuneration for their time. Several weeks later they rated the slides again under the guise of entirely different research with a different experimenter.

The results seemed clear. In either the cardiac acceleration or deceleration conditions, the slides associated with cardiac change showed higher mean attractiveness ratings than those not associated with the change. In the miscellaneous sound group, there was a slight reversal of this trend. Twenty-nine of the forty subjects in the first two groups chose three or more of the "reinforced" slides, whereas only six of twenty subjects in the extraneous sound" group chose three or more of those paired with sound changes. The preferences still held in the follow-up a month later. Barefoot and Straub (1971) reported similar results.

One curious aspect of the results was that some subjects who gave high ratings to slides later said the ratings were not based on any immediately noticeable differences in attractiveness. Valins postulated that when they heard the fake cardiac changes they searched the slides for characteristics of the pictures (e.g., parts of the anatomy) that might have caused the cardiac changes and then justified the changes as due to these "attractive" features. In a later experiment, Stern, Botto, and Herrick (1972) instructed some subjects to pay close attention to the "extraneous sounds" and found that these subjects rated the slides as high in attractiveness as did subjects who thought the sounds were heart beats. Thus, the selective attention hypothesis does seem plausible.

We may also ask, however, whether Valins' subjects *really* had heart rate changes, possibly induced by the bogus feedback. If this were the case, then his results would be ambiguous support for his theory. Valins did not record real heart rate, but Goldstein, Fink, and Mettee (1972) did. Attractiveness ratings were greater with accelerated bogus heart rate, but real heart rate also increased. The slide preferences might then have been due to perception of real autonomic changes. Goldstein, Fink, and Mettee showed some of their male subjects slides of male nudes, intended to be repulsive because of homosexual connotations. Here, bogus heart rate was not related to "offensiveness" ratings of the slides, but real heart rate was. This suggests that real physiological changes may be more important than the bogus ones. Stern, Botto, and Herrick (1972) obtained results similar to Goldstein, Fink, and Mettee (1972). Hirschman (1975) also monitored GSR while subjects viewed slides of accident victims. Bogus heart rate changes produced more unpleasant ratings of slides, but there were also increased reports of feelings of discomfort, as well as GSR changes. In sum, then, it appears that real physiological changes may be involved in the effects obtained with false information about body states.

Harris and Katkin (1975) suggest that his whole line of research is confounded by use of different indices of emotion. Thus, Valins considered the *slide ratings* as an index of emotion, whereas Hirschman used *self-report of feelings.* Harris and Katkin suggest that it might be profitable to consider two forms of emotion: primary and secondary. The former includes both autonomic arousal and subjective perception, whereas the latter just includes perception of arousal, which may be nonveridical.

What Harris and Katkin call *secondary emotion,* however, may involve what other people call "experimenter demand." To illustate this, in a series of relatively mundane experiments, the author and his colleagues (Beck, 1971; Beck & Davis, 1974; Beck & Osberg, 1977) simulated some classical aversive conditioning paradigms by associating a light with an innocuous tone. The subjects were instructed to pretend that the tone was a very unpleasant electric shock, and the experiment was then conducted as if there actually was shock. The result was that subjects evaluated the light on a "good-bad" scale exactly the same as subjects who actually received shocks. Such evaluations seem to be what Harris and Katkin mean by secondary emotion.

Beck and Gibson (1977) then simulated the original Valins experiment, using a paper-and-pencil procedure. Subjects were given a written description of the experiment but no pictures. The ten slides were represented by numbered blank squares, with the appropriate words (e.g., "heart speeds up" or "heart stays same") beside five of them. Subjects then rated the "slides" as they thought they would had they actually been in such an experiment and "picked out" the five they thought they would like to keep. The attractiveness ratings were virtually identical to Valins', as were the numbers of subjects selecting three or more of the "reinforced" slides to keep. Furthermore, half the subjects were females, instructed to pretend they were males. There were no sex differences whatsoever. Since these results were obtained without slides and with subjects of both sexes, the questions of real heart rate change and of selective attention are irrelevant. The phenomenon appears to be entirely cognitive. This may mean that emotion can be considered entirely cognitive. It may also mean that once the subjects saw what the experiment was about they knew how they should perform and did so, in which case the results may have little to say about emotion at all. Gibson (1977) has also replicated the Barefoot and Straub results with both real slides and a paper-pencil simulation. In brief, Valins' experiment and others like it may not have dealt with emotion except insofar as subjects know that heart rate changes are supposed to be related to emotion. The whole problem of attribution and emotion is still very much an open issue, both for theory and further research.

## POWER

We all know that people have "power" over others, that they can influence or direct the lives of others as well as themselves. Some individuals, on the other hand, are relatively "powerless," exerting little control over the course of events. Following Winter (1973), we shall be concerned with such *social power*. Winter defines social power as *"the ability or capacity of one person to produce some intended effect on the behavior or emotions of another person"* (Winter, 1973, p. 5).

### Dimensions of Power-Related Concepts

Winter proposes three dimensions by which we can bring order into the numerous power concepts in the literature. The first is *legitimacy* or *morality,* which is an evaluation notion. Thus, for example, power through domination, force or conquering, exploitation, etc. is "immoral" whereas power gained through "maneuvering," inspiration, leadership, or helping is moral. The second dimension is that of the *resistance* of the person over whom power is to be gained. There may be great or little resistance. There is a kind of "tyranny of the weak," by which individuals (such as babies or the stereotyped "southern belle") gain power over other individuals. The third dimension is the status of the *strength* of the individual trying to gain power. Relatively weak individuals may gain strong influence through "moral persuasion." For example, in the 1970s the Russian author Alexander Solzenitsyn gained great influence through his writing, some of which he did while a political prisoner. An interesting contrast in power styles is that of Mahatma Gandhi and Indira Gandhi.[6] The former was very legitimate, played on his weakness, frequently gained his points through fasting, and was highly moral. The latter, as Prime Minister of India, used great force, suppression of civil liberties (such as freedom of speech and writing), and incarceration of her opponents to maintain control until she was finally voted from office.

### Power and Situations

A recurrent theme in history is the question of whether "great men" change the course of history through their influence or whether powerful people happen to be in the right place at the right time. If the time is ripe for

[6]Unrelated to each other.

revolution, whoever steps in may simply be leading the inevitable. Evidence for a situational theory is a little more clear in science and technology, where "simultaneity of invention" is not uncommon. Thus, Alexander Bell and Thomas Edison were locked into a great court battle over who should have the patent rights to the telephone, both having "invented" it about the same time. Bell won the battle (probably one of the few Edison ever lost) and is now popularly perceived as the *sole* inventor. It seems clear, however, that if *neither* Bell nor Edison had done it, someone else would have. Power struggles at national levels are seldom carried out quite this way, however, and "credit" is harder to determine in a political process. Thus, a president may fight against a congressional action but if it turns out well take credit for it when time comes for reelection.

As Winter points out, a great deal of research on leadership characteristics leaves one with the conclusion that there are no common traits among leaders except that they have power over some group. This led to the idea that leaders were individuals who could effectively lead their groups in achieving whatever it was the groups wanted at a particular time. An important question is whether the leader actually does this or whether he or she is *perceived* as doing it. There is evidence that leaders are not necessarily more sensitive to the needs of their groups, but manage to swing the groups' views around to their own, or manage to see in what direction the group is headed and then convince the group to do what it was already going to do. This is a *power strategy,* and the individual strongly motivated to gain power may indeed learn it at an early age (it is used by children as well as adults).

### Measurement of Power: Winter's System

Winter's scoring system for measuring power utilizes the same general test administration procedure as that for measuring n Ach. His revised (1973) scoring procedure concerns the following three major categories of power imagery: (1) strong vigorous actions that express power, (2) actions that arouse strong affect in others; and (3) explicit concern about reputation or position (1973, p. 73). There are also further subcategories. Winter's earlier scoring system correlated about .32 and .39 with the scoring systems of Veroff (1957) and Uleman (1972). His revised system correlates about .45 with those systems and .51 and .77 in separate studies with his own earlier system. The reliability coefficients in various studies range from .17 to .75, with a median of about .45. This is in the same range as the reliability of fantasy measures of n Ach, and, as previously noted, certainly puts a limit on the possible validity of the test. Winter gives many reasons for low test-retest reliability (including reactiveness to the first administration). All his arguments may be correct, but they still do not demonstrate high reliability.

The validity of need for power (n Power) is estimated from its ability to make predictions; that is, one uses construct validity rather than concurrent or predictive validity in the standard psychometric sense.

### Hope of Power Versus Fear of Power

Just as achievement motivation can be broken down into approach and avoidance components, tendency to success and tendency to avoid failure, n Power has been subdivided into "hope of power" and "fear of power." One reason for this distinction was that early studies in power showed that in situations where the power motive should be expected to be aroused, and in individuals for whom a power motive should be strong (campus political candidates), there was an inverse relation. That is, the subjects under aroused conditions showed lower n Power scores than under nonaroused conditions. This suggested the possibility of a kind of defensiveness in relation to power. We certainly do not expect that all individuals desire power, even those in a position to achieve it. Some individuals may dislike power and avoid it because of the responsibility it may entail or, indeed, because they do not like trying to control other people's lives. In any event, the categories of approach toward or avoidance of power are intuitively reasonable, as well as being supported by some data. The question then is whether the distinction made on a test can predict other differences in performance in reasonable ways.

### The Power Motive and Behavior

Winter (1973) also provides various data relating power motive scores to other behaviors. He found, for example, that students who were (or had been) officers in university organizations had significantly higher scores for n Power than those who had not. In fact, students who held a variety of "power positions," such as residence counselors, members of a presidential search committee, or staff positions on university publications also tended to have higher than average power scores. In athletics, varsity letter winners in directly competitive sports (man against man, as in football or basketball) had higher power scores than letter winners in sports not having direct contact (such as track).

Another intriguing set of findings was based on the power scores of students who said they were interested in particular kinds of careers, or had already made such career choices at some time after n Power scores were obtained. The results are pretty consistent: the careers selected by those with the highest power scores were teaching, psychology, clergy, business, and international diplomacy. Scores below average were associated with government and politics, medicine, law, creative arts, and architecture.

Winter speculates on reasons for this pattern, but we shall leave it here for the reader (especially if he or she is planning to continue in psychology) to speculate on explanations. The clue perhaps lies in the kinds of things people in these professions actually do, or what test subjects think is done, on a day to day basis.

### Machiavellianism

Richard Christie and his colleagues (see Christie & Geis, 1970) took a different approach to the measurement of power need, based upon the writing of Niccoló Machiavelli, 16th century Florentine author of *The Prince* and *The Discourses.* The very name Machiavelli implies deceit and opportunism and as an adjective is typically perjorative. Christie (Christie & Geis, 1970, p. 3) abstracted the following characteristics of the successful manipulator in the Machiavellian sense:

1. A relative lack of affect in interpersonal relationships;
2. A lack of concern with conventional morality;
3. A lack of gross psychopathology (very reality-oriented); and
4. Low ideological commitment.

Starting from such considerations, Christie and his colleagues developed and refined the *Mach Scales,* containing such items as "A white lie is a good thing" and "If one is morally right, compromise is out of the question." Agreement with the former item and disagreement with the latter would both contribute to the Mach score. The final scale (Mach V) contained forced-choice items, which had the advantage of not being sensitive to social desirability of responses; i.e., the Mach scores are not correlated with what subjects think are socially desirable responses. An interesting question then is: If a person is highly Machiavellian, will he/she be so deceptive as to *not* get a high score on the scale, thereby rendering the scale useless? The answer to this, Christie points out, is that scale scores do correlate with behavior in predictable ways.

***Correlations of Mach Scores with Other Behaviors.*** First of all, Mach scores do *not* correlate with intelligence, authoritarianism, political preferences, need for achievement, or anxiety. This is only to say that the Mach scale is not just a new measure of some other well-defined personality characteristic.

We shall here list a few of the results reported in Christie and Geis (1970).

1. Mach scores correlate .71 with success in interpersonal bargaining in a laboratory game called the "Con Game." When game

conditions were somewhat ambiguous, the high Mach subjects did even better.

2. In the Con Game, which involves the forming of coalitions among players, the high Machs are more dominant and decisive, are opportunistic, and seem less responsive to personal or ethical concerns of others. They tend to approach the task in a more rational and less personal-social manner than do the low Machs.

3. In a coalition formation game involving real money (the experimenter's), the high Machs won overwhelmingly and never failed to be a member of a winning coalition.

4. In a variation of the Prisoner's Dilemma game, a popular 2-person laboratory game in which cooperation usually pays off in the long run, high Machs became more cooperative when the game was played for real money. Cooperative behavior in this case is a realistic way to win, not socially motivated.

5. In a bargaining game involving problems of the kind involved in working out governmental legislation, there was no difference between high and low Machs when emotionally neutral issues were involved. High Machs were significantly better when emotionally-charged issues were involved, however. This supports the argument that high Machs have a competitive bargaining advantage over low Machs because the high Machs are not distracted by ego-involving issues.

6. High Mach subjects are more accurate at estimating the Mach scores of other individuals than are the low Machs. In particular, high Machs more accurately judge others as having higher Mach scores than do low Machs.

7. In a situation involving cheating in an experiment (at a team member's suggestion) low Mach individuals showed greater attitude change effects to support their behavior when there was minimal justification for cheating, as predicted by cognitive dissonance theory. High Machs did not conform to this pattern, however, and showed greater attitude change when there was strong justification for their behavior.

This very abbreviated survey of research on Machiavellianism generally indicates that high Mach individuals are more cool and task-oriented than their low Mach counterparts and their tactics are designed to achieve success. They test the limits of a situation more, initiate control, and exploit resources in loosely structured situations but are more perfunctory (or even apathetic) in situations which are highly structured and which cannot therefore be manipulated by them. Low Mach individuals are more socially oriented, concerned with others, and distractable. In unstructured situations they may not function as well because of distraction by irrelevant concerns, but work well within structured systems. Christie and Geis (1970, p. 351) have presented a more detailed model of differences between low and high Mach individuals.

There are, of course, many more aspects to power than we have attempted to deal with here. What we have done is to present two different ways of measuring power orientation and some research indicating that these measures predict behavior. As with other forms of motivation, the measurement process is a necessary first step for research and theory.

## CONCLUSION

During the last quarter-century of active research on achievement motivation there have been progressive refinement of the concepts, greater formalization of the theory, and an increased scope of phenomena covered by the theory. At the same time serious questions have been raised about the meaning of fantasy measures of achievement motivation, including whether a motive is being measured or just verbal behavior correlated with other achievement performance. This is the old question of associative vs. motivational interpretations. Attribution theory, as related to achievement, has been concerned with such cognitive factors as perceived locus of control and achievement performance. Many theorists have also used attribution theory as a partial account, at least, of emotion, attempting to demonstrate that experience of different emotions depends on knowledge of the situation in which emotion occurs as well as internal states of arousal. Attribution theory still awaits a formal theoretical analysis which will permit an evaluation of its adequacy over the entire range of phenomena to which it is presently being applied.

chapter 14

# Interpersonal Attraction

## SOME DISTINCTIONS: AFFILIATION, LIKING, AND LOVING

Why do people get together, and what happens when they do? Some of the most important incentive objects for us are other people, but what is it about other people that makes them attractive to us? Why do we choose to be with people at some times but not other times? Why are particular people more attractive to us than others? In this chapter, we shall apply many different principles discussed previously to the specific problem of interpersonal attraction.

*Affiliation.* We may want to be with someone for many different reasons, which do not necessarily involve a particular liking for them. Stranded on a desert island, we might be happy with practically anybody's company. The term *affiliation* refers just to associating with others, apart from the question of liking them or loving them.

*Liking.* We may prefer to be with some particular people because they have personal characteristics that provide us some pleasure. They may be interesting, fulfill some of our needs, or we are just "comfortable" with them. Rubin (1973, p. 26) says that "there are as many kinds of liking as there are reasons for choosing other people," but he reduces this to two dimensions of liking: *affection* and *respect.* Affection is based on interpersonal relations, and respect is based on admirable qualities, such as skills or performance in difficult situations.

*Loving.* Love, of course, is the most difficult of these three concepts to define unambiguously. Rubin (1973) defines love conceptually in terms of three elements: *attachment* (strong desire to be in another's presence, to make physical contact, etc.); *caring* (concern for the satisfaction and security of another); and *intimacy* (the capacity of two people to communicate easily and confidentially, verbally and nonverbally). The translation of these ideas into *operational definitions* of love usable for research purposes is difficult, however, and not readily done to everyone's satisfaction.

In specific real-life situations, observers may easily confuse affiliation, liking, and loving. Here we shall separate the research on these topics into three discrete sections so that we can more readily see how they differ.

### AFFILIATION

#### Measurement of Need for Affiliation

Boyatzis (1973) has reviewed the literature on measurement of affiliation. Like need for achievement, need for affiliation has been measured in terms of stories told about pictures. The first step was to show that certain conditions could arouse the need for affiliation (n Aff), as measured by TAT scoring. The second step was to conduct research to determine the construct validity of n Aff by showing differential performance of high and low n Aff people in other situations.

Shipley and Veroff (1952) defined n Aff in terms of a need for security. In a group of fraternity members, n Aff was aroused by having them rate each other on fifteen different adjectives. A control group rated food preferences. Following these experiences, the two groups wrote TAT stories which were compared on various characteristics thought to be related to n Aff. Statements demonstrating "concern about separation" were considered especially important. The experimental group gave significantly more statements indicating n Aff. Atkinson, Heyns, and Veroff (1954) used a similar arousal technique but for TAT scoring purposes defined n Aff in terms of seeking social acceptance, a more positive view than the "fear of separation" approach taken by Shipley and Veroff. Again, significant differences between aroused and nonaroused subjects were found.

Boyatzis (1973) considers a major theoretical issue to be whether there are indeed two different kinds of n Aff, namely "hope of affiliation" (approach) and "fear of rejection" (avoidance). The theoretical similarity to the distinction between hope of success and fear of failure is obvious. Boyatzis' conclusion is that the TAT scoring procedures do *not* distinguish between these two dimensions, although the distinction makes intuitive sense. Another projective test, the French Test of Insight (French, 1958), may distinguish between them better, but the issue is unsettled.

Boyatzis does not refer to reliability of n Aff scoring, but a number of studies do show construct validity. Atkinson and Walker (1956) found that high n Aff subjects were more accurate at picking out a face from among four briefly exposed pattern stimuli than were low n Aff subjects. Berlew (1961) compared high and low n Aff subjects on their ability to describe other people as the people described themselves. The high n Aff people were more accurate. McKeachie, Lin, Milholland, and Issacson (1966) reported that high n Aff students got better grades in courses taught by teachers judged to be warm and considerate. Finally, de Charms (1957) found that high n Aff individuals performed better in cooperatively structured groups than in competitively structured groups.

There seems to be a curvilinear relationship between n Aff and performance. Boyatzis (1973) interprets a number of studies as indicating, for example, that persons with moderate levels of n Aff are more effective managers, because those with low n Aff are unconcerned with interpersonal relationships, but those with high n Aff are so overly concerned that their concern interferes with effective performance. Fantasy measures of n Aff (which, like achievement, are as good as any) seem to be measuring something, but a fear of separation seems to be more strongly tapped than a positive motive to be with others (Boyatzis, 1973).

### Determinants of Affiliation

*Fear and Anxiety.* There is considerable evidence that when people are fearful they prefer to be with others. Presumably, other people are anxiety reducing. Even with rats it is found that in an apparatus where they have previously been shocked the animals are less fearful (are more active) if there is another animal present. Furthermore, they are more active yet if the other animal itself has not previously been shocked (Davitz & Mason, 1955). Epley (1974) suggests three ways by which the presence of others may reduce responses to aversive stimuli (or conditioned aversive stimuli). First, the other person may serve as a "calm" model for the anxious person to imitate. Second, the companion may do something to distract the subject. Third, the mere physical presence of another might be fear reducing, even though the other person does nothing.

Some of the best-known human research on this topic is by Schachter (1959). Schachter's subjects were threatened with either strong or weak electric shock, and then were given the choice of waiting alone or with other subjects. The strong-shock subjects had a greater preference for waiting with others. It was not demonstrated, however, that being with others was actually anxiety reducing. Other investigators (e.g., Wrightsman, 1960) *have* found self-reports of lower anxiety from subjects waiting with other subjects in a threatening situation. Several experiments done in the Hull-Spence framework have predicted that the presence of others should reduce drive (anxiety) and thereby facilitate performance on complex tasks and impair performance on simple tasks. The results have been ambiguous (Epley, 1974). We may also recall that Zajonc (1965) argued that the presence of others should increase drive, not decrease it. Harrison (1976) concludes that people may not desire to affiliate in anxiety-arousing experimental situations if such affiliation would lower their self-esteem, e.g., if they have to do something embarrassing in front of others.

*Others as Sources of Assistance, Stimulation, Information, or Self-Evaluation.*

*1. Assistance.* Often we can only achieve our goals with the assistance of others and may therefore affiliate with others because of this instrumental requirement. It does not follow that others are always helpful, but there are sufficient instances where we need others that affiliative behavior may be rewarded and maintained.

*2. Stimulation.* In Chapter Ten, we discussed the need for stimulus variation. What, in fact, is more variable, more full of surprises, more stimulating than other people? "Interesting" people attract friends or followers more readily than "dull" people. There appears to be an optimal level of stimulation here also; i.e., a given person may be too stimulating for some people, too dull for others, and "just right" for somebody else. Sales (1971) found subjects with a high need for stimulation more actively involving themselves in group discussions, as well as showing preferences for more complex stimuli and seeking things to do when left alone.

*3. Information.* Association with others may be sought because they provide information, or reduce uncertainty for us. Gaining information about the environment is rewarding (see Chapters Five and Ten).

*4. Self-Evaluation.* We all need to evaluate ourselves, our opinions, our abilities, and our work from time to time. One way to do this is by comparison with other people, i.e., *social comparison* (Festinger, 1954). According to Festinger's theory, we should tend to make such social comparisons, which require some degree of affiliation, when we are uncertain about ourselves. We also tend to seek such normative information to judge ourselves from someone who is similar to ourself (e.g., in age, background, interests, and experience) rather than someone who is very dissimilar. Mills and Mintz (1972) found that subjects given caffein with an incorrect explanation of its effects chose more often to affiliate with other subjects than did subjects not given caffein or subjects correctly told of its arousing effects. Presumably, the uncertainty of the source of arousal prompted the misinformed subjects to search for the cause of their arousal by associating with other subjects in the same situation whom they believed could help them evaluate their own condition.

**Freedom from Internal Constraints.** Groups often have a restraining effect on individual members; but they may also have just the opposite effect, "releasing" the individual. Nude encounter groups and lynch mobs have in common that both support kinds of behavior that are not often socially acceptable elsewhere. If an individual at a particular time is seeking freedom from internal constraints (or even the constraints of his own particular social group), he or she may choose to affiliate with others even in so innocuous a situation as a party. The individual may become relatively anonymous and without responsibility, which may temporarily be desirable. Such *deindividuation* may be perceived as bad under more permanent conditions, however, as a permanent characteristic of life. One of the cries against the large cities is indeed the degree to which people are "lost" as individuals. Zimbardo (1970) suggests that after such "freedom" from internal constraints, people may find it more pleasurable to be "reindividualized," to seek recognition from others, and so on.

## ATTRACTION

We now turn to the question of what causes one person to be attracted to another *particular* person. As compared to affiliation, where liking is not necessarily involved, we now consider some determinants of liking.

### Determinants of Attraction

***Proximity (Propinquity).*** We are more likely to be attracted to and be friends with people who are physically close to us (e.g., the boy and girl next door). In dormitory living situations, individuals who live next to each other are more likely to become friends, even though initially thrown together on a chance basis (e.g., Priest & Sawyer, 1967; Segal, 1974; Newcomb, 1961). In the Segal study, a high correlation (.90) was found between liking a person and how close that person's name was alphabetically to the name of the rater. This rather remarkable result was due to the fact that the participants had been assigned rooms and roommates in alphabetical order and therefore were living either in the same or adjacent rooms to people with similar last names.

***Familiarity.*** The effects of proximity are partly explained by the fact that the closer two individuals are, the more familiar with each other they become. We tend to like persons or objects, or even words, more if we have simply been exposed to them frequently (Zajonc, 1968). Zajonc showed many illustrations of this *mere exposure* effect. For example, subjects gave evaluative ratings of fake Chinese characters and nonsense syllables after 0, 1, 2, 5, 10, and 25 exposures. The "goodness" ratings increased regularly with increased exposure.

Zajonc's results run contrary to the old aphorism that "familiarity breeds contempt," and indeed we can all certainly think of people we liked less after we knew them better. This indicates that there are other variables involved besides mere exposure. Indeed, Burgess and Sales (1971) replicated Zajonc's results with subjects who felt positive about the overall experimental context, but not with those subjects who did not like the experimental situation. It is impossible, of course, to do an experiment without a context and experimenters try to keep their subjects happy, if possible. The discrepancies in this area of research are still unresolved (Schneider, 1976). The underlying issue is important, however: When *does* exposure increase liking? It could be awkward, to say the least, to throw people together under the assumption that they would inevitably like each other after mere exposure. A fairly obvious factor would be the behavior of the person one is thrown together with; i.e., if his or her behavior were agreeable, exposure would have good effects. If disagreeable, there would not be good effects.

*Similarity.* It is said that opposites attract, but this physical principle of magnetism receives mixed support from research on interpersonal attraction. People who are similar are more likely to get together. Similarity can be constituted in many ways, however, including similarity of attitudes, personality, and physical characteristics.

*1. Attitudes.* Don Byrne and his associates have done much of the work on attitudinal similarity and attraction. The procedure for many studies involves three steps: subjects (1) fill out an attitude survey; (2) make judgments of a hypothetical other person, based partly on information about the other person's attitudes; and (3) then indicate degree of liking for the other person. The greater the proportion of attitude statements on which there is agreement, the greater the liking for the other person (Byrne & Nelson, 1965). In this paradigm, however, the *only* information available is attitudinal, and it is clearly possible that other information might counteract the attitude similarity (e.g., sex, political or religious affiliation, or education). According to Schneider (1976), the attitudinal effects are not strong, even though significant, in more real-life situations. The purpose of laboratory research, however, is precisely to separate out variables that are weaker, or masked, in less well-controlled situations.

*2. Personality.* According to a *need complementarity hypothesis,* we might expect that opposites would attract because they would help fulfill the deficiencies of each other. This Yin-Yang theory has been proposed to account for marital choices (e.g., Winch, 1958), but the actual data offer little support. Thus, both dominant and submissive subjects prefer dominant others (Palmer & Byrne, 1970) and introverts and extroverts both prefer extroverts (Hendrick & Brown, 1971). In terms of stimulus change or arousal theory, we might expect that some degree of both similarity and difference would produce the most enduring relationships. Too much difference might be overly arousing and too much similarity might be too little arousing.

*3. Physical Characteristics.* People tend to choose others with similar physical characteristics, e.g., height and weight (Berscheid & Walster, 1969). This *matching principle* also seems to hold for personal attractiveness, but perhaps for complex reasons. Thus, a boy might *prefer* an exceptionally attractive girl, but, being of medium attractiveness himself, might believe that the chances of her reciprocating his interest are very low. He might even be rebuffed. The optimal expectation, then, might be to choose a girl of medium attractiveness, where there is a higher probability of a successful relationship.

## THEORIES OF INTERPERSONAL ATTRACTION

### Social Comparison and Self-Evaluation

In his theory of social comparison, Festinger (1954) argued that people have a drive to evaluate themselves and, to the extent that objective means of evaluation are not available, they will use other people as "social yardsticks." Thus, a boy may know objectively how fast he can run a hundred yards, but cannot tell how well he plays basketball except by direct comparison of his performance with those of other players, or from "expert" judgment by someone else. Applied to interpersonal attraction, then, the theory says that one reason people may associate with each other is to obtain self-evaluations. It is often useful to have our opinions validated (or challenged) by comparison with the opinions of others. Some people are more eager to do this than others, however.

### Cognitive Dissonance

Cognitive dissonance theory predicts that how we treat someone should affect our liking of them. If we behave in an unusually cruel way toward a neutral stranger, discrepant with the way we usually think of ourselves as behaving, we should experience dissonance and change our attitude toward the stranger. Specifically, we should come to have negative attitudes toward people to whom we have "done wrong." Conversely, we should come to have more positive attitudes toward people to whom we have been kind.

**Justification for Harm Doing.** There are various possibilities for reducing dissonance produced by harming a stranger: derogating him, minimizing the suffering produced, denying responsibility for the suffering, or arguing that the victim deserved to suffer (Berscheid & Walster, 1969, p. 15). Davis and Jones (1960) argued that cruelty would produce dissonance since most people think of themselves as kind, and the dissonance would be even greater if the subject felt he had considerable choice in doing or not doing the cruel act. Jones and Davis' subjects were induced to give another person a cruel personality evaluation. Half the subjects were led to "volunteer" and half were "forced" to read these negative evaluations to the other person (an assistant). The subjects in the "volunteer" (high dissonance) condition rated the derogated person lower on various measures of attraction than did subjects "forced" to read the description. Half the subjects in each condition also knew in advance that after reading the evaluations they could tell the subject that the evaluation had actually been prepared by the experimenter. With this anticipation of withdrawing their criticism, the dissonance effect disappeared.

Glass (1964) proposed that individuals with higher self-esteem should be more derogating in this kind of situation because there would be greater discrepancy between their self-concept and their unkind behavior. Self-esteem was manipulated by giving subjects either "good" or "bad" bogus feedback from a "personality" test. The high self-esteem subjects under conditions of "choice" of harming another person (by administering electric shocks for "errors" in a learning experiment) derogated the subjects afterwards, but low self-esteem subjects did not. When the subjects were "forced" to "harm" the victim, however, there was no derogation by either high or low self-esteem subjects, presumably because there was no dissonance. Paradoxically, then, the nicer we think we are, the more we must put down somebody else if we think we have chosen to hurt them.

Brock and Buss (1962, 1964) also found that high dissonance subjects tended to minimize the discomfort of shock administered to others, also reported by Lerner and Matthews (1967) and Lerner and Simmons (1966). Harm Doers will, however, attempt to compensate their victims if the situation permits (Berscheid & Walster, 1969, p. 20). This provides a ray of hope for humanity seldom offered in the dissonance research. At least some of us, sometimes, will try to make amends for our transgressions. The amends apparently have to be proportional to the crime, however. Thus, Berscheid and Walster (1969) found in a field study that if such compensation were either too little or too great there was still a dissonance effect and derogation.

***Justification for Benefaction.*** There is some experimental evidence that people may come to like those they have benefited (e.g., Schopler & Compere, 1971), but it is not as strong as the derogation effects (Berscheid & Walster, 1969). Bem's self-perception theory would perhaps predict positive attitudes in such a situation even more strongly than dissonance theory. That is, self-perception theory would predict an individual would perceive "If I acted so generously toward so-and-so, then I must really like him."

### Social Exchange Theory

The language of social exchange theory is modeled after that of the marketplace: Associating with others involves benefits and costs. The theory is basically a standard form of conflict theory, with anticipated rewards (benefits) and punishments (costs) applied to interpersonal relations. Positive attraction occurs when the benefits outweigh the costs and avoidance occurs when the costs are greater than the benefits. Net approach or avoidance of particular others depends on the algebraic summation of positive and negative outcomes of social interactions with others. Thus, the positive affect provided by another person may more than offset the demands of that person on our time, energy, or other resources.

As the name implies, exchange theory deals with mutually rewarding behaviors between people. For example, a male and a female may each have socially desirable qualities that they can "trade off" to each other. A male seen with a highly attractive female is rewarded by being judged more favorably than a male accompanied by an unattractive female. (In an experiment, the female was the same person, sometimes made up to look unattractive.) At the same time, attractive females are more likely to date or marry men of higher social status than they themselves are. Especially potent "attractiveness" variables of men are money, status, and power. A physically less attractive man can bring these commodities to the interpersonal bargaining table and come off rather well. Intellect, wit, and charm are also worth something. Political power seems to be a universal bargaining commodity, but the "groupies" who follow rock groups and professional athletes attest to other kinds of stature that can be traded for an attractive companion and sexual favors. At some point, the cost of maintaining a particular interpersonal relationship may be too high (e.g., in terms of emotional stress, money, or time), and it may no longer be worthwhile to maintain the relationship. That is, the costs outrun the benefits.

Since it is a reinforcement theory, exchange theory can make predictions based on a variety of phenomena studied with hunger, thirst, and other motive systems. For example, social approval should be a more effective reward for someone who has been deprived of approval. Or, approval should be a more durable reward if doled out on a partial reinforcement schedule. There is, indeed, experimental evidence for such deprivation and scheduling effects of approval (Rubin, 1973, Chapter 4). If approval is given for every act of a person, it may lose its value because it is indiscriminate, or it may even be perceived as insincere and ingratiating.

A problem for exchange theory—which, like any other reinforcement theory, is a selfish view of Homo sapiens—is how to deal with altruistic behavior, the "selfless" giving of one's time and energies to others. There are two ways out of this dilemma. One is to say that exchange theory is wrong, that people do things for other reasons than anticipation of positive benefits. The other alternative is to say the rewards are there, but not obvious. The rewards for noble self-sacrifice may be internal, such as a "feeling of self-satisfaction." We may smile at the aphorism "Virtue is its own reward" since it usually seems to be applied inappropriately. But "virtuous" behavior may in fact be intrinsically rewarding because of the self-satisfaction it provides. Such a notion of an "invisible reward" may be used loosely and circularly in situations where we simply assume that there must have been a reward because something happened. In Chapters Six and Seven, however, we saw that some responses may be inherently rewarding, or acquire rewarding properties through association with other rewards.

The role of guilt or other pressures we might feel about *not* behaving "altruistically" are also not to be underestimated. The "Give-your-fair-share" approach to charity fund raising is based on an arbitrary norm for donations that is then used to produce guilt for those who do not "live up" to the norm. Pledge cards with your name already typed on them prevent anonymity and are unsubtle attempts to "guarantee" altruism. Altruistic behaviors may then be maintained by subtle rewards or reduction of guilt or anxiety. For those who hold to other views of moral behavior, social exchange theory (or reinforcement theory generally) will seem empty. Like other large issues, however, an explanation of altruistic behavior satisfactory to everyone is not easily arrived at.

## LIKING AND LOVING

### The Measurement of Liking and Loving

At the beginning of this chapter, we distinguished between liking (based on affection and respect) and loving (attachment, caring, and intimacy). These conceptual distinctions have been incorporated into two operational measures by Rubin (1970). On Rubin's scales, each of thirteen items is rated on a nine-point scale, from "Not at all true; disagree completely" (1) to "Definitely true; agree completely" (9). The "love scale" has such statements as "I feel that I can confide in_____about virtually anything" and "If I were lonely, my first thought would be to seek _____out." The "liking scale" has such items as "I think that _____is usually well adjusted" and "I have great confidence in _____'s good judgment." As expected, there is some correlation between the scales (.56 for females and .36 for males), but the two scales apparently are not measuring exactly the same thing. The internal consistency of the scales is high (better than .80 for either males or females on either scale, using Cronbach's coefficient alpha) but test-retest reliability data are not reported.

The validity of the scales is shown in several ways. For example, the correlation between the love scale score and simply saying that you are in love with somebody is .61 for women and .50 for men. Furthermore, loving and liking for one's romantic partner (in a study of 158 dating college students) were higher than for same-sex friends, by both males and females. Liking for partners and friends were more similar than loving for partners and friends. Perhaps the major importance of Rubin's scales is that they may promote more research into the topics of liking and loving, just as the development of anxiety scales has done for anxiety.

### Determinants of the Choice of a Romantic Partner

*Physical Attraction.* While physical appearance, of either males or females, has always been assumed to be of importance in attracting others, experimental research in this area is relatively new. Walster, Aronson, Abrahams, and Rottman (1966) arranged a "computer dance" for freshmen at the University of Minnesota. The actual pair assignment was random, however (except that women were all assigned taller men). At intermission, the subjects rated their partners on various characteristics, including physical attractiveness. At the original sign-up time, four experimenters also rated the subjects to give an "objective" rating of attractiveness. In a follow-up several months later, the experimenters checked to see if there had been further dates. About 10 percent of the least attractive females were later asked for dates by their partners at the dance, but about a third of the most attractive were asked. These values are not overwhelming, but attractiveness was still the best predictor. The judge's ratings of attractiveness were not in high agreement either, however, (i.e., low interjudge reliability), which would tend to reduce the accuracy of predictions based on the attractiveness variable.

Physical attractiveness is a multidimensional variable, facial features being more important to some individuals, body characteristics to others, and so on. This inevitably leads to considerable individual differences in what is considered attractive. In fact, in the Walster et al. study, the attraction rating made by a single male subject of his date was a better predictor of later dating than was the combined rating of the judges. To each his own.

There are a number of possible reasons for the relationship between attraction and liking. One is simple sexual arousal. This may be a poor basis for marriage if it is the only source of attraction, but it nevertheless occurs. Fortunately, perhaps, attractiveness seems to be a relatively more important variable for dating than for marrying (Stroebe, Insko, Thompson, & Layton, 1971). A second reason that attraction is important is that males with attractive dates believe they will be judged more positively by others, and, in fact, they are (Sigall & Landy, 1973). Finally, attractive individuals are not only liked more; they are also perceived more positively on other characteristics. This is commonly known in attitude research as the "halo effect." Even unattractive children are perceived as more likely to transgress and their transgressions are judged more severely than those of attractive children. If attractiveness partly determines how children are perceived (and responded to), then attractiveness may be an important variable in the development of self-confidence and social behavior. Attractive people may therefore really be somewhat better adjusted, as a result of the way they are treated. The tribulations of being *too* attractive have also received at least anecdotal attention. For example, the too attractive male or female may have everything run so smoothly that they may not have opportunity to learn how to cope with situations where attractiveness does not pave the way.

Because of its immediate obviousness, as compared to such sterling qualities as intellect, wit, and loyalty, physical attraction may be relatively more important for first impressions than it is after longer contact. The physically attractive person, then, may use this factor most effectively in situations, occupational or otherwise, where there is only brief contact (e.g., sales or advertising). Attractiveness may become a relatively less important factor in such long-term associations as marriage or occupations requiring considerable interpersonal contact (Berscheid & Walster, 1974b).

*Playing Hard to Get.* Young women are often told they should play hard to get because they will then be more desirable, and there are various reasons why we would expect this to be so (Harrison, 1976). First, according to cognitive dissonance theory, "We come to love what we have to suffer (or work) for." Second, it is readily inferred that if someone is hard to get, there must be more than meets the eye (a kind of "just world" hypothesis, i.e., people get what they deserve). Third, there is frustration and arousal. This may in itself have a certain amount of attraction, as well as relating to an arousal-attribution theory of romantic love (to be discussed shortly). A number of experiments in which females were either easy or hard to get (including one with a bona fide prostitute) have failed to confirm the hypothesis, but there may be extenuating circumstances. A female who is "easy to get" may also be "hard to get rid of," or, a female hard to get may possibly produce humiliation. There is some evidence that a female easy for you to get (if you are a male), but hard for others to get, is nearly ideal.

*Social Influences.* Proximity, familiarity, and similarity are individual determinants of attraction, but they also relate to social influences. There is the so-called social filter, established by cultural groups, parents, and so on, through which a prospective romantic partner has to pass before there is serious involvement. Love may blind us to all but our beloved, but society goes a long way in determining who our beloved will be. The simple fact is that people tend to marry others of the same race, religion, social class, and education. (Interracial marriages in some states were long forbidden by law, but even without this restriction are rare.) Proximity, familiarity, and similarity are, of course, facilitated by such social variables.

Some *social structures* are almost exclusively designed for such filtering, e.g., the debutante ball and campus fraternities and sororities. There is never any question which are the most prestigious of these on a campus and it is a faux pas to become seriously involved with someone at a lower echelon. When a boundary is crossed, there is often social exchange; e.g., the boy from the inferior fraternity may be an outstanding athlete.

*Parental Influences.* Parents generally believe they know what is best for their children and may try to influence the choice of romantic partners, especially when it comes to marriage. Given appropriate resources, this can be done indirectly, such as sending a daughter off to the "right" school. It may also backfire and produce the "Romeo and Juliet effect." The more the parents try to separate the couple, the more the couple becomes involved. Such interference might produce more positive attraction for several reasons. First, by making their daughter more effortful to get, the parents may produce cognitive dissonance on the part of her potential boy friend, which he may reduce by making her appear more desirable than she really is. Secondly, self-perception theory would also account for the effect: "If I have to over-come this great an obstacle, I must really love her." And the positive arousal of mild frustration may make her more attractive.

*Peer Group Influences.* Without doubt, peer groups—individuals of like age, background, and interests—exert considerable pressure on their members. This group often dictates the kind of person, or even specific individuals, whom it is appropriate to date or marry. Through its power to give or deny approval, the peer group can limit the choices of acceptable romantic partners. Like any other behavior, choosing a romantic partner is an instrumental behavior associated with many different potential rewards and punishments. The peer group may control these rewards and punishments more than the potential romantic partner does.

### A Theory of Passionate Love: The Cognitive Arousal Model

Rubin (1973) describes what he calls the "Ovid-Horwicz" phenomenon. In his *Ars Amatoria* (*The Art of Love*), a first-century how-to-do-it manual for romantic conquest, the Roman poet Ovid gave all sorts of helpful hints, involving grooming and behavior. The one of interest here, however, is the suggestion that a good time to arouse passion in a woman was while watching gladiators fight in the arena. In modern times, a football game might suffice. A nineteenth-century German psychologist named Adolph Horwicz proposed that any strong emotional arousal could facilitate love. The Ovid-Horwicz effect, until recently, was limited to empirical observation; it seemed to work. We now have a theory to account for it, and can even make further predictions. This is Schachter's cognitive arousal theory, or any of the variations on it (e.g., Mandler, 1962), and has been discussed by Rubin (1973), Walster (1971), and Patterson (1976).

The theory says that emotional arousal is diffuse until labeled by the individual. The label given to the arousal depends on the circumstances, the cognitions the subject has about what is going on. Applied to passionate love, then, the individual may be aroused for many reasons, but if the circumstances are right (e.g., the presence of an attentive member of the opposite sex), the interpretation may that the arousal is due to love. There is an interesting cultural difference—the "double standard"—related to this. An aroused male can openly admit sexual arousal and engage in premarital sex. A female is not supposed to do this, but if she is "in love" (and especially if marriage is expected to follow soon anyway) it becomes more acceptable for her to engage in sex (Berschied & Walster, 1974a).

The theory also explains the sometimes rapid alternation between hate and love: The arousal process is the same, but the labeling is different. The theory suggests why frustration may heighten attraction: Frustration produces internal arousal, which, because of the circumstances, is interpreted as love. The hard-to-get girl produces frustration, which is labeled as love. Sexual arousal itself is readily interpreted as passionate because there are usually specific physiological cues, but other sources of arousal (such as mild fear, frustration, excitement of an athletic contest, or exercise) may readily be labeled as love if a particular person happens along at the right time. Even rejection by someone, or discovering that the object of one's romantic inclinations has another partner, may produce an emotional arousal that is interpreted as being even stronger love than existed before. Some people are "turned on" by a certain amount of "danger" in love making (e.g., doing it in locations where they might be caught or observed). This is a rather difficult phenomenon to account for theoretically, but the cognitive arousal theory seems to handle it rather well.

The cognitive arousal theory may or may not distinguish accurately between liking (based on rewards we receive or anticipate from someone else, or admiration we may have for them) and passionate love. At the moment, however, it is about the *only* theory of love that seems to account for the many circumstances that facilitate passion.[1] Right or wrong, the theory proposes enough research ideas either to disprove the theory or to lead to a more adequate and refined theory.

## HUMAN SEXUALITY

Much of the early psychology of motivation, beginning with the work of Freud, was a psychology of sex and anxiety. Research devoted to anxiety has since raced far ahead of that devoted to sex. One reason for this, expressed by J. S. Brown (1961), is that sex has not fit well into behavior theory, whereas anxiety and fear have. Cofer and Appley (1964), however, used basic research on sex as a motivational model. They proposed two mecha-

---

[1]MacLean (1949) argued that the spatial proximity of many different motivational areas in the brain, particularly in the limbic system, might lead to some kind of "spill over" from one motivational condition to another.

nisms: the *activation invigoration mechanism* (AIM) and the *sensitization invigoration mechanism* (SIM). The argument, an incentive theory, was that some external stimuli can invigorate behavior by themselves (AIM), whereas others require further sensitization of the organism by internal states (SIM). Thus, some foods are highly palatable almost all of the time (AIM) but others gain their attractiveness when the organism has been deprived of food (SIM). Similarly, some sexual objects produce sexual arousal most of the time (AIM), whereas others require additional sensitization of the organism, such as by sex hormones (SIM).

As a general topic, sex involves evolution and genetics, as well as sexual behavior, reproductive systems, and taking care of the young. All these topics are interrelated in complex ways. The bulk of our knowledge of reproductive activities has come from basic animal research (animal husbandry being an important economic stimulant to such research). Such research is well surveyed elsewhere (e.g., Bermant & Davidson, 1974), and we shall limit ourselves to some of the motivational aspects, determinants, and characteristics of the human sexual response. For further detail, consult Freud ([1920] 1935), McCary (1967), Pierson and D'Antonio (1974), McCary and Copeland (1976), and Masters and Johnson (1966, 1970).

### Sexual Attraction

Like interpersonal attraction generally, sexual attraction is the result of many stimulus factors. Among animals, birds especially, there are complex courtship rituals, and males of a species are usually characterized by more flamboyant plumage and coloration than are the females. Pure physical attractiveness of members of the opposite sex may produce sexual arousal among humans as well. The individual differences in what people consider sexually attractive are notable, however. Different anatomical parts, movements, gestures, speech, and so on are more arousing to some members of the opposite sex than to others.

There are certain fairly clear cultural determinants of sexual attractiveness. The female bosom is emphasized in Western European-American culture more so than in many others. Such cultural, or individual, differences are presumably learned. Freud argued that emphasis on the breast was the result of a fixation during the oral stage of psychosexual development (in the first year or so of life.) Other specific attractiveness characteristics could be determined by the features of the opposite sex parent, related to the Oedipus complex in Freudian theory. According to the myth that forms the basis of Sophocles' dramatic trilogy, Oedipus unknowingly killed his father and lived incestuously with his mother. Freud believed that the myth represented a universal truth, that all sons are sexually attracted to their mothers and compete with their fathers for their mothers' favors. Inadvertently or not, popular songs have also expressed the myth (e.g., ''I want a girl just like the girl that married dear old Dad"). The physical characteristics of the mother (or father) may become attractive through "mere exposure" and/or association with other rewards rather than representing a universal characteristic, however. The Oedipus theme may then have some truth to it as far as sexual attraction is concerned, but for somewhat different reasons than Freud envisioned.

It may also be possible that individual differences in attractiveness within a species are due to something besides learning. Beach (1969) found that male beagle dogs had reliable, but different, preferences for particular females. Females also had different preferences among males; some would not accept the amorous advances of a particular male, but others would. Certainly, familiarity or secondary reinforcement kinds of interpretations might be given for such beagle behavior, but an oedipal interpretation would hardly be given.

There is also a powerful element of stimulus variation in sexual attraction, known in animal research as the "Coolidge effect." This name derives from a visit of then President Coolidge to a chicken farm where it was pointed out that one rooster could service an entire flock of chickens. Considerable laboratory evidence shows that if an animal is allowed to engage in coitus to some level of satiation (the criterion might be so many minutes without further sexual responsiveness of a given male to a given female), the introduction of a new female will produce a sudden resumption of sexual activity by the male.

Such stimulus variation is not well documented *experimentally* with humans, but clinical evidence and survey research, as well as casual observation, leave no doubt that the phenomenon is prevalent. The boredom which may come with years of marriage is well known, and it is often recommended that couples make a concerted effort to introduce novelty into their sexual activity. This may involve different behaviors, change of location, and so on. Given the general positive motivational value of stimulus change, it is hardly surprising that this is an important variable in sex. Although in the past this has been applied mainly to males, there is no reason to believe that it does not apply equally well to females, except that "philandering" has traditionally been considered a male characteristic, or prerogative (the "double standard").

### The Human Sexual Response

The universal appeal of love has been a mainstay of poets, authors, and songwriters, but not until this century has a scientific study of sex been undertaken. The first great strides in the collection of normative data came with the Kinsey reports of sexual behavior in the human male (Kinsey, Pomeroy, & Martin, 1948) and female (Kinsey, Pomeroy, Martin, & Gebhard, 1953). Based on interviews with thousands of people of all ages, these reports publicly documented things that were "known all along" to some people and came as a shock to others. The high incidence of homosexual encounters and of oral-genital sex was particularly suprising. There were many who believed that the Kinsey reports were based on nonrepresentative samples (e.g., "only those women that would consent to be interviewed"), but subsequent surveys have more than substantiated the Kinsey findings.

The most dramatic breakthrough in human sexual research, however, was made by Masters and Johnson (1966). Using direct observation and color cinematography of both autosexual and heterosexual behavior, as well as extensive physiological recordings, they arrived at some general characteristics of both male and female sexual responses. Their pioneering work legitimatized this field of investigation and opened it up for further serious research.

***Phases of Sexual Response.*** Masters and Johnson divided the sexual response of both males and females into four phases, characterized by general body reaction as well as reactions of sex organs. Not all of the following occur with every individual, or some responses may be so brief that they are not noticeable by direct observation.

*1. Excitement Phase.* Sexual excitement may be produced by many different stimuli, ranging from self-induced fantasy, to observation of pictures or other erotic materials, to direct physical contact. The excitement phase may be prolonged or shortened, depending on a variety of physical and social factors. Nipple erection occurs in some males, but more commonly occurs in females. There is sometimes a "sex-tension flush," a reddening of the skin on the chest, then the head. In females, this flush may (in later phases) spread to the lower abdomen, thighs, and lower back. In males, there is penile erection, which can occur (or reverse) in a matter of seconds, as well as testicular elevation from tightening of the scrotum. In females, there is vaginal lubrication, thickening of the vaginal walls, and expansion of the inner two-thirds of the vaginal barrel. Breast size may begin to increase.

*2. Plateau Phase.* If sexual stimulation is maintained, there is more intense arousal, an increased frequency of sex-tension flush, general muscular tension, spasmodic movements of wrists and ankles, hyperventilation, and increased heart rate (100–160/minute). Female breast size may increase as much as 20 to 25 percent above prestimulation baseline. There is further vaginal expansion, as well as other changes in female sex-accessory glands. There is as much as a two-fold increase in the circumference of the corona of the penis, sometimes a change to a purplish color, further testicular elevation, and a mucoid emission from the Cowper's gland (serving to deacidify the interior of the penis, to make a more hospitable environment for the sperm passing through, as well as to lubricate it).

*3. Orgasmic Phase.* In the orgasmic phase, there are specific muscle contractions, related to pelvic thrusting as well as abdominal and facial muscles. In males, there is contraction of the various accessory organs necessary for ejaculation (vas deferens, seminal vesicles, ejaculatory duct, and prostate gland), as well as contractions of the penile urethra and of the external rectal sphincter. The female shows corresponding contractions of the uterus and other portions of the now highly vasocongested genital area, and of the external rectal and urethral sphincters. The orgasmic phase, of course, is the time of greatest excitement, when sexual climax is reached by one or both partners. The actual climax—the expulsion of the semen by males, and vaginal contraction by females—takes only a few seconds and, once started, is no longer under voluntary control.

*4. Resolution Phase.* Following climax, there is often a sweating reaction, in about one-third of both males and females, which is unrelated to actual physical exertion. There is also hyperventilation and high heart rate, which may in large part be due to the amount of physical exertion. With males there is a "refractory period," with reduced pelvic vasoconstriction and penile erection (which is also due to the reduced amount of blood in the penis). The male cannot then be readily rearoused until there has been a reduction of sexual tension to a low level. The duration of the refractory period varies considerably from one individual to another. Females, clearly showing the greater durability of their half of the species, can maintain a continuously high level of sexual tension, with no refractory period. During one bout of intercourse, a male has one climax, but during this time a female may "come" repeatedly. There are such record female performances as sixty climaxes in an hour. As in everything else, there are considerable individual differences.

The Masters and Johnson type of research has been criticized on the grounds that it deals only with the mechanics of the sexual act, that it ignores love and affection. Such criticisms border on the absurd, simply because there is only so much that any researcher can do. Obviously, there are other aspects of sexual (or affectional) relations than physiology, and there are other researchers to study them. More importantly, however, by careful study of the mechanics of the sexual act, it has been possible, in conjunction with increasing refinement of behavior therapy techniques, to develop effective therapy for sexual dysfunctions such as frigidity, impotence, and premature ejaculation. Such problems are taken lightly, or considered "merely mechanical," only by people who do not have them.

*Some Sexual Myths and Fallacies*

Considerable research shows the following myths about sex are *not true*. For more detailed discussion, see McCary and Copeland (1976).

*1. Simultaneous Orgasms are Better Than Separate Ones.* This is entirely a matter of personal preference, and if it works out better for two people to have their orgasms at different times, there is no problem if both are satisfied.

*2. It is Dangerous to Have Intercourse During Menstruation.* This may be aesthetically unpleasant for some individuals, but not dangerous in a medical sense.

*3. Athletic Performance is Diminished by Intercourse the Night Before.* Staying up half the night may impair athletic performance, but intercourse per se does not. There are highly exaggerated ideas about the amount of energy required for intercourse. Some individuals expend more energy than others, but the actual exertion is about the same as a brisk walk around the block.

*4. Sexual Satisfaction, Either Male or Female, is Related to Penis Size.* The most sensitive sexual area of the body for the female is the clitoris, which is located at the very mouth of the vagina. For the male, the most sensitive area of the penis is the glans (head). Insertion of the penis beyond the clitoris may make it easier for sperm to reach the eggs, but does not necessarily increase pleasure, especially of the female.

*5. Sexual Intercourse Should Be Avoided During Pregnancy.* With the later stages of pregnancy, there are obvious difficulties due to the female's size, but with commonsense precaution there is no particular problem as long as there is no pain for her, the fetal membrane is intact, and there is no spotting or bleeding. As soon as surgical incisions have healed after giving birth, coitus can be resumed.

*6. Alcohol is a Sexual Stimulant.* Sorry, there are no known sexual stimulants, or aphrodisiacs. Alcohol or other substances may reduce inhibitions or increase confidence, but that is about all. Alcohol is a central nervous system depressant and in any great quantity is more likely to impair sexual performance, of males especially.

*7. Menopause or Hysterectomy Ends a Woman's Sex Life.* Many women, or men for that matter, maintain active sex lives until well after age sixty, with cases documented into the eighties. There may be some slowing down related to hormone changes in either sex but impotence is far more psychological than physiological.

**8. *Masturbation Causes Insanity, Pimples, and Other Disorders.*** Not true; sexual arousal and climax are the same regardless of the means to achieve them. Individuals with skin disorders may have more trouble finding a sexual partner and resort to masturbation more frequently, but this is just the reverse of the cause-effect relation given by the myth. Psychotic individuals may also be less inhibited about masturbating; but again the cause-effect relation is reversed. In point of fact, virtually all males and most females masturbate at some time in their lives with no ill effects, and there is good evidence that there is often greater female satisfaction from masturbation than from intercourse. It is also often recommended in self-help books that women may profitably use masturbation as a means of learning how to reach sexual climax and enjoy heterosexual relations more.

**9. *There Are Two Kinds of Female Climax, Vaginal and Clitoral, and Vaginal is Better.*** This seems to be a male myth. The Masters and Johnson research clearly shows only one kind of climax, and, compared to the clitoris, the vagina is relatively insensitive. The female may enjoy a large penis and deep thrusting for other reasons, but not because there is a qualitatively different kind of orgasm.

**10. *The Average Physician is Well Trained and Emotionally Capable of Dealing with His Patient's Sexual Problems.*** Although extremely unfortunate, because the physician is the person most people would normally turn to for advice in the case of, say, impotence (thinking it to be a medical problem), the typical training of physicians includes almost nothing about sexuality. Surveys of senior medical students, even in recent years, and of practicing physicians, show that large percentages of them subscribe to one or more of the myths given above and even wish to avoid the topic of sexual behavior. Some medical schools now have courses in sex counseling but this is not very prevalent.

## CONCLUSION

The positive or negative incentive values of other persons is now one of the major research topics in social psychology. Most of the principles thus far used to account for interpersonal attraction have been taken over from other areas of psychology and applied to the attraction problem. This is indicated by the fact that in this chapter we have seen nothing in the way of principles not already encountered in previous chapters. This may indeed be considered healthy insofar as it puts the problem of interpersonal attraction into the mainstream of psychology rather than isolating it as a problem for one little corner of the field. Research on sexual attraction and love, as well as other aspects of human sexuality, have gained respectability and should be of considerable educational and therapeutic value in the not-too-distant future.

# chapter 15

# Physiology of Some Consummatory Behaviors

## BACKGROUND

We can divide physiological approaches to motivation into two categories: broad theories and specific system theories. By broad theories, we mean those which attempt to account for many different manifestations of behavior by common physiological principles, mostly neurological. We have already looked at two of these: activation and central motive state. At more modest levels are theories concerned with such specific systems as feeding, drinking, reward and punishment, sex, taste, and temperature regulation. It is some of these that concern us here.

Physiological, behavioral and cognitive theories of motivation do not always overlap because they do not share the same concepts and are not always concerned with the same phenomena. In recent years, however, there has been a healthy trend toward examining such problems as hunger and obesity from several points of view. Thus, obesity is seen as a problem of hunger mechanisms, emotion, and cognitive-social determinants. It no longer seems profitable to examine these problems in isolation from such a multitude of determinants.

In the 1930s, Walter Cannon (e.g., 1934) argued for a peripheral theory of motivation. He said that the stimuli to hunger and eating were contractions of the stomach, and that thirst and drinking resulted from a dry mouth. There was available even by that time evidence contrary to his theory. For example, several experiments had shown that animals without stomachs still ate normal amounts of food, as do human patients who have had their stomachs removed because of injury or disease. Similarly, at least one case of a man without salivary glands had been reported and this individual drank no more total fluid than anybody else (however, he did tend to wet his mouth more often).

Other investigators argued for a more central basis for motivation. For example, Karl Lashley (1938) said that mechanisms controlling instinctive behaviors were in the brain, and Frank Beach (1942) argued that a central mechanism maintained excitability for sexual behavior. In spite of the contrary evidence and counterarguments, the peripheral approach held sway for a long time, just because there was no central theory with enough support to replace it. Let us look at the central motive state again, and then look at some specific systems.

## CENTRAL MOTIVE STATE

### Morgan

Morgan (1943) proposed the general concept of a central motive state (CMS), later elaborated in more detail (Morgan, 1959). A CMS was said to be a hypothetical system of centers and pathways concerned with a particular kind of motivation, defined in terms of the kinds of things to which an organism is responsive. For example, if an animal is responsive to water, the central motive state at the moment of the response would be "thirst." Morgan attributed three properties to a CMS. First, once set off, a CMS persists for some time without further excitation—it is self-maintaining. The initial excitation might come from peripheral sense receptors or internal events, including hormones. Second, a CMS predisposes the organism to act in a certain way to particular stimuli (e.g., to approach them) but not to others. A sexually aroused animal is more responsive to a prospective mate than to food. Third, the CMS may also directly emit certain behavior patterns. Morgan believed that general locomotor activity accompanying deprivation was of this nature. We have noted (Chapter Four) that the relation between deprivation and activity is more complicated than this concept suggests, but Morgan was going by the evidence available at the time. Such specific forms of behavior as a female rat in heat making sexual movements might also occur as a direct response to the CMS.

Morgan held that humoral factors (hormones) were probably more important than external stimuli in arousing and maintaining CMS's. The primary evidence at the time was derived from sexual behavior, but recent research extends this to hunger and thirst. One good reason for positing the importance of humoral events is that a hormone circulating in the blood could maintain a state of excitability over a long time in a straightforward and understandable way. Reverberating neural circuits (i.e., self-reexciting neural activities) have often been proposed as an explanation for such maintained excitation, but are troublesome because they are seldom actually seen.

Morgan also suggested several ways in which a CMS could be turned off. These included elimination of the stimulus or humoral factor initially giving rise to the CMS, inhibitory receptor stimulation (such as the inhibitory effect of a sweet taste on hunger), and, finally, the behavior resulting from the CMS might reduce the very CMS that aroused the behavior in the first place. There is evidence for all three such factors in various systems, as we shall see.

Morgan did not see the CMS as a formal physiological theory of motivation, partly because he believed that behavior theorists would first have to provide an adequate theory into which a central theory of motivation would fit. He was pessimistic about this at the time. The main impact of Morgan's discussions seems to have been to orient investigators more toward looking at the brain as a source of motivation, rather than providing specifically testable hypotheses that could be derived from the theory.

### Stellar

Eliot Stellar (1954) was more specific in proposing a central mechanism for motivation. He suggested that motivated behavior was the result of arousal of excitatory centers in the hypothalamus. The activity of these various centers was in turn a function of (1) inhibitory centers that depress the excitatory centers; (2) sensory stimuli; (3) humoral factors representing the internal environment; and, finally, (4) cortical and thalamic centers that can produce either excitatory or inhibitory effects on the hypothalamus. Again, there is a certain "correctness" to Stellar's theory in that the various factors he cites are known to affect hypothalamic activity. Much recent evidence, however, indicates that the hypothalamus is motivationally important mainly because neutral pathways funnel compactly through it as they cross the brain. Electrical excitation or destruction of hypothalamic areas are indeed motivationally dramatic, but the same effects can be produced elsewhere. Again, however, Stellar was basing his theory on the evidence available at the time, and his integration of the evidence provided an important rallying point for a great amount of research.

### Bindra

More recently, Dalbir Bindra (e.g., 1969) has expanded the CMS concept along the lines we previously discussed in Chapter Seven. He argues strenuously that rewards produce motivational excitement rather than "reinforcing" particular responses. The so-called reinforced response is of special importance in any particular situation because it is the only one the experimenter (or teacher or parent) rewards. In many ways, Bindra's theory is a quasineurological theory, more dependent on behavioral than physiological data.[1] Thus, the Bindra and Palfai experiment (1967), showing that an incentive-related stimulus would arouse gross motor activity in deprived rats but not in nondeprived ones, is of this genre. Like its predecessors, Bindra's theory is "correct," insofar as central neural mechanisms are demonstrably important in motivation. At the same time, as we shall repeatedly see, peripheral physiological events (outside the central nervous system and even outside the nervous system entirely) are very important. The brain should not be looked upon *exclusively* as the organ of motivation.

### HUNGER

#### The Dual Hypothalamic Theory of Hunger

A convenient starting point in the study of physiological mechanisms underlying hunger and food preference is the dual hypothalamic theory of hunger. This theory says that the *lateral hypothalamus* is an *excitatory* area

---

[1]This is not new. Pavlov's theory of excitatory and inhibitory brain processes in conditioning was based on behavioral data (such conditioned responses as salivation), rather than on direct neurological experiments. This is not necessarily a bad strategy because it is possible to make many speculations about behavior on the basis of proposed neurological mechanisms. We must remember, however, that these "mechanisms" are often models (conceptual nervous systems, to use Hebb's phrase) and subject to change.

for feeding behavior and the *ventromedial nucleus* of the hypothalamus, just adjacent and medial to the lateral area, is an *inhibitory* area. These areas are shown in Figure 15.1. The proof of the theory lies in demonstrations

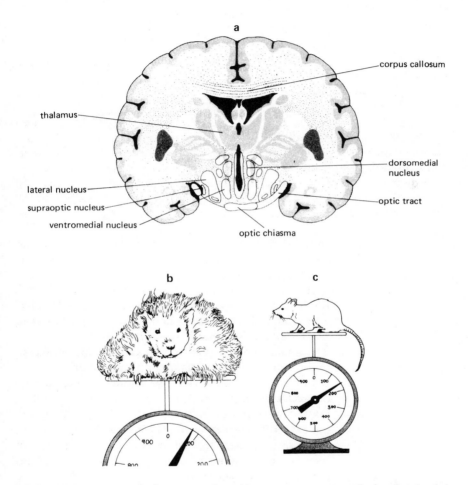

**Figure 15.1** *Hypothalamic nuclei. The cross-section of the brain (a) shows several of the hypothalamic nuclei. The obese rat (b) has lesions in the ventromedial nuclei. A normal rat (c) is shown for comparison. A rat with lesions in the lateral nuclei starves itself. (From Schneider & Tarshis, 1975, p. 278.)*

that stimulation of the lateral area leads to feeding behavior and destruction of the lateral area leads to *aphagia* (no eating). Conversely, stimulation of the ventromedial area leads to cessation of eating, while destruction leads to *hyperphagia* (extreme overeating.) These effects are summarized in Table 15-1.

**Table 15-1**    *Effects of Stimulation and Ablation of the Lateral Hypothalamic and Ventromedial Hypothalamic Areas on Feeding ( — = inhibitory and + = excitatory for feeding).*

|            | *Ablation* | *Stimulation* |
|------------|:----------:|:-------------:|
| Lateral    | −          | +             |
| Medial     | +          | −             |

### Lateral Hypothalamic Lesions

Teitelbaum and A.N. Epstein (1962), A.N. Epstein (1971) and Teitelbaum (1971) describe the effects of extensive bilateral lesions[2] of the lateral hypothalamic areas, followed by careful observation of the animals' patterns of eating and drinking. The *lateral hypothalamic syndrome* involves four discrete stages of recovery from the lesions. The amount of time required to pass through these stages may take days or months, depending on the exact size and location of lesions.

> *Stage 1.* In the first days after lesioning the animals neither eat nor drink. The animal must be tube fed with nutrients or it dies.
>
> *Stage 2.* The animal begins to eat, but only wet and palatable foods, such as chocolate chip cookies soaked in milk. The animal does not eat enough to survive, however, and requires additional tube feeding.
>
> *Stage 3.* The animal now begins to *regulate* its food intake so that it can survive by eating, but it will not drink water. It will, however, drink sweet solutions, such as sucrose or saccharin, in sufficient amount to survive.
>
> *Stage 4.* Stage 4 is the most complicated stage in that things are not exactly what they seem. The animal begins to drink water and appears to have recovered because it can regulate food and water intake adequately to maintain normal body weight.

The "recovered lateral" animal still has permanent deficits, however. It does not drink normally after water deprivation or saline injections and, in fact, maintains water intake by drinking as it eats, called *prandial drinking.* The animals are severely affected by slight changes in the taste of

---

[2]Bilateral lesions are necessary to demonstrate an effect of lesions because each brain area is typically represented in both hemispheres and animals seem to function quite well with only one area intact. On the other hand, stimulation on only one side is sufficient to show stimulation effects.

the water. The addition of an amount of quinine so minute that it hardly affects normal animals stops the lesioned animals from drinking.

The recovered lateral does not salivate nearly as much as a normal rat (Kissileff, 1973), and the eating and drinking of a recovered lateral can be mimicked by tying off the salivary glands of a normal rat. The recovered lateral apparently drinks only to wet its mouth when eating. It survives by accident!

Teitelbaum and Cytawa (1965) also reported that depression of cortical activity by application of potassium chloride[3] to the cortex of the recovered lateral reinstated feeding and drinking deficits for several days, but had only a very brief effect (hours) on normal animals. Teitelbaum (1971) argues that the lateral hypothalamic tissue remaining after lesioning is facilitated by the cortex and cortical depression therefore causes the animal to behave like a newly lesioned animal. Interestingly, lateral hypothalamic recovery parallels the *development* of eating and drinking in the infant rat. A newborn rat ingests milk but refuses water. A little older, it eats dry food and drinks water but does not drink normally in response to water deprivation.

### Lateral Hypothalamic Stimulation

***Electrical Stimulation.*** Electrical stimulation of the lateral hypothalamus produces stimulus-bound eating, drinking, or other motivational effects, persisting only when stimulation is applied. This is more than excitation of specific consummatory activity, however, because lever pressing for food is also aroused. Hoebel (1971) has an excellent review of this literature.

Valenstein, Cox, and Kakolewski (1970) report, however, that electrical stimulation with the *same* electrode may arouse eating one day, drinking the next, and gnawing at a block of wood on the third. This raises the intriguing possibility that brain areas are not entirely fixed and immutable in their function, perhaps changing daily.

***Chemical Stimulation.*** Grossman (1962) placed minute amounts of various crystaline chemicals directly into the lateral hypothalamus by means of permanently implanted hypodermic needles. Noradrenaline, a neural transmitter, produced eating in satiated animals, but depressed drinking. Conversely, carbacol (which is like acetylcholine, another neurotransmitter) stimulated drinking but inhibited eating. These chemicals also influenced bar pressing for food and water in the same manner. Control chemicals had no effects, showing that the eating and drinking were not due to simple irri-

---

[3]Applied to the rat cortex at about twenty percent concentration, potassium chloride temporarily depresses neural activity. The phenomenon is known as *spreading depression* and has been a useful experimental technique because it produces a reversible depressive effect.

tation of the stimulation sites. These effects were, overall, very much like those with normal hunger and thirst.

Chemical stimulation is effective in many brain areas, however. Fisher (1964) suggests that the whole limbic system is important to many motivational systems because chemical stimulation throughout it influences eating and drinking, reproductive and aggressive behaviors.

The experiments of Valenstein et al. are intriguing, but it does appear that the feeding and drinking areas of the brain are both anatomically and chemically separated. Chemical stimulation seems specific to the chemicals used, since different chemicals in the same location have different effects. Chemicals may spread from one location to another, but this spreading is minimized by using minute crystals. The existence of different kinds of adrenaline-sensitive neurons in the hypothalamus is also well documented.

### Role of Nonhypothalamic Areas in Hunger

The evidence now strongly indicates that the hypothalamus is primarily a way station where fiber tracts from many widely separated areas of the brain funnel together very compactly, then spread out again. Lesions in such a compact area can disrupt many different pathways and hence are highly dramatic in their effects. The same devastating effects found with hypothalamic lesions can be duplicated with lesions at other locations along the pathways winding through the hypothalamus (Grossman, 1975). Implicated areas range from the frontal lobes to the brainstem, the entire length of the brain. Many areas are serially connected, like extension cords strung together, so that a disconnection (lesion) at any point along the line will interfere with the function. As an example, Gold (1967) showed that if the hypothalamus was lesioned on *one* side of the brain and the brainstem tegmentum (roof) was damaged on the *other* side, the effects on feeding were the same as with *bilateral* hypothalamic lesions. The brainstem lesion apparently cut into the same system as the hypothalamic lesion, indicating that the two areas are "wired" in series.

An important new technique is the use of a very fine wire knife to make precise cuts (rather than destruction by electrolytic burning) deep in the brain. This technique produces minimal damage other than the cut itself. Such a cut between the lateral and ventromedial hypothalamic areas does not produce overeating and obesity. The ventromedial area, then, is not a "brake" which inhibits the activity of a lateral feeding area. Grossman (1975, p. 206) concludes that "surgical transections of all fibers that enter or leave the hypothalamus laterally . . . reproduce the effects of lateral hypothalamic lesions in every respect." We can again invoke the same caution that Karl Lashley (1950) made with regard to the location of memory: Motivation is not to be found in any single little niche in the brain. Rather, it is to be found in complex interrelated—and redundant—systems all over the brain.

### Sensorimotor Versus Motivational Deficits

One lateral hypothalamic pathway originates in the *globus pallidus* of the forebrain, an area involved in the control of movement and posture. Morgane (e.g., 1964) showed that globus pallidus lesions were more severe than lateral hypothalamic lesions. Whether lateral hypothalamic effects are due to motor deficits or motivational loss is still controversial. The motivational argument is supported by the facts that (1) animals *can* eat palatable foods even when they *will not* eat lab chow, and (2) there is a deficit in bar pressing, an arbitrary and noningestional response, which nevertheless recovers along with eating (Rodgers, Epstein, & Teitelbaum, 1965).

Considerable evidence indicates a motor deficit, however (Grossman, 1975). Thus, rats with lateral hypothalamic lesions are very inactive, fail to groom themselves, and do not respond well to sensory stimuli. Such gross symptoms may diminish, but subtle deficits in the rather fine movements needed to chew, bite, lick, and swallow may discourage the animals from eating all but the most palatable foods. Very likely there are both motor and motivational deficits.

### Ventromedial Hypothalamic Effects

Ventromedial hypothalamic lesions produce extensive overeating (hypothalamic hyperphagia) and very fat rats or cats. Rats may gain as much as 10 grams a day, as compared to 1 to 3 for normal animals, and may double or triple their adult body weights (e.g., from 400–500 to 1,000–1,200 grams). Figure 15.2 shows weight changes and food intake of lesioned and control rats. There are two stages of hyperphagia. In the first (*dynamic* hyperphagia), there is much eating and rapid weight gain. In the second (*static* hyperphagia), there is a leveling off of weight at a very high level.

The ventromedial-lesioned animal is typically, although not always, characterized by a finickiness of eating (Graff and Stellar, 1962). It tends to overeat highly palatable foods and undereat unpalatable ones. The animals do not eat more frequently but eat larger meals than normal. This suggests that they are not hungrier but are slower to stop because the "stop mechanism" for feeding is defective. Electrical stimulation of the ventromedial area will stop eating in progress, and simultaneous stimulation of lateral and ventromedial areas results in no eating (Wyrwicka & Dobrzecka, 1960). Neural activity in the two areas is also reciprocal; when one is increased, the other is decreased (Oomura, Kimura, Ooyama, Maeno, Iki, & Kuniyoshi, 1964). This kind of evidence has been the support for the satiety

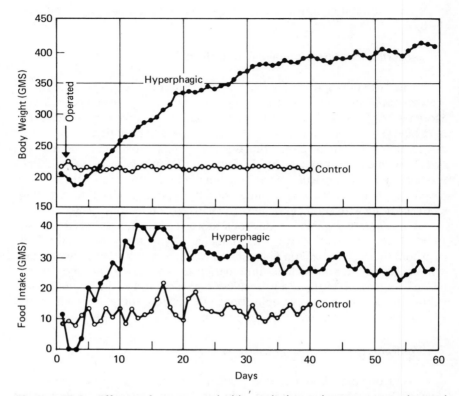

**Figure 15.2**  *Effects of ventromedial hypothalamic lesions on intake and weight changes in the rat. (From Teitelbaum, 1961, p. 41.)*

center hypothesis, but we already have seen the story is not this simple. Surgical separation of medial and lateral areas does not produce hyperphagia, and electrical stimulation of the medial area will stop many kinds of ongoing activities. Grossman (1966) proposed that the ventromedial area is a "center" for a range of affective responses. (Ventromedial-lesioned animals are also vicious, and their escape and avoidance behavior is enhanced.)

Powley and Keesey (1970) suggested that there is a *set point* for body weight that is established by a balance of activities represented by the ventromedial and lateral areas. If the ventromedial area is damaged, the set point goes up, and animals eat more readily; if the lateral area is damaged, the set point goes down, and they eat less readily. The animal tries to maintain whatever body weight its set point is adjusted for. They showed that lateral hypothalamic animals reduced to 80 percent of their normal body weight *before* lesioning did not show severe disruption of feeding and drinking after lesioning. As already noted, ventromedial animals eventually do level off their body weight and intake in the static phase, just as normal animals eventually stop growing. Two very recent reviews (Friedman & Stricker, 1976; Powley, 1977) have suggested some new ways of viewing hunger mechanisms.

### Start Cues For Eating

***Set Point Theory.*** Nisbett (1972), arguing in support of the set point theory, says the fat person is probably not gluttonous, probably not emotionally disturbed, and probably not out of order physiologically. He probably has a set point that is different than that of the average person and is eating because he is, in fact, hungry. The degree of fat one can attain is determined by the number of fat cells (adipocytes) a person has. This number, if not hereditary, is established very early in life and is supposedly constant thereafter. The size of these cells can vary, however. A person with a lot of fat cells has a higher set point than a person with few fat cells. It is easier for him to get below his set point, so he eats more readily.

Studies of starved people (or animals) show they eat more, eat faster, prefer more palatable foods, are less active, and have less interest in sex. The same is true of hypothalamic hyperphagic rats and of many fat people. But why should a fat person act like a starving person? Because, says Nisbett, society pushes him to keep his weight down and therefore he is continually below his set point even though above average weight. Left to his or her own devices, the "normally fat" person eats more and does not necessarily show the characteristics of a hungry person.

***Glucostatic Theory.*** The glucostatic theory says that feeding is initiated by a drop in blood sugar level and is stopped by an increase. Direct measures of blood sugar level do not correlate well with amount of food consumed, however. The most compelling evidence comes from the facts that (1) insulin injections increase glucose intake; (2) injections of glucose into the blood reduce lateral hypothalamic neural activity; and (3) glucose injections increase ventromedial activity (e.g., Anand, Chhina, & Singh, et al., 1962 Oomura et al. 1964).

### Stop Cues for Eating

***Satiation Hormone.*** A perennial problem in accounting for satiation is that feeding seems to stop before anything metabolically very important can happen. This suggests that some quickly-acting effect produced by food in the stomach temporarily cuts off feeding until a slower-acting metabolic effect has time to occur. A "satiation hormone" could do this. Tests of this hypothesis (by feeding hungry animals blood from nondeprived animals, for example) were negative until John Davis worked out the more elegant technique of switching the blood of hungry and nonhungry rats. A cannula implanted near the heart leads to a syringe. Blood is withdrawn simultaneously from two animals and is immediately transferred from one to the other by reversing the syringes. Davis, Gallagher, and Ladlove (1967) found that blood from a satiated rat inhibits eating by a deprived rat, but "hungry" blood does not stimulate eating in a satiated rat. Something in the satiated blood (not yet identified) inhibits feeding. Rosen, Davis, and Ladlove (1971) have also reported that blood from satiated donors decreases EEG activation in deprived animals.

*Stomach Distention.* Sharma and his associates (e.g., Sharma, Anand, Dua, & Singh, 1961) report that distention of the stomach with a water-filled balloon increases neural activity in the ventromedial area, but not in the lateral hypothalamic area. This provides another possibility for a fast-acting stop mechanism.

*Osmotic Dehydration.* Solid food is more concentrated than body fluids (is hypertonic) and hence pulls fluid from surrounding tissue into the stomach by osmosis. This dilutes the stomach and intestinal contents, but also reduces the water supply in the rest of the body. McCleary (1953) suggested that an animal stops taking in hypertonic food (or drink) when it begins to make him thirsty. If rats have fistulas put in them so that they drink one fluid but get something else put into the stomach, they respond to the osmotic properties of the fluid in the stomach (Mook, 1963). Osmotically equal concentrations of saline or sucrose tubed directly into the stomach equally inhibited drinking saline or sucrose, but water had a much smaller effect on the intake of either substance. Beck (1967) measured fluid volume in rats' gastrointestinal tracts after they drank different concentrations of sucrose. They drank less 37 percent sucrose than 18.5 percent (9.3 percent is body fluid concentration), but the actual dehydration produced by the two solutions was very similar. There was considerable variation among animals, but it seems at least plausible that dehydration influenced the termination of drinking. Any dehydrating solution ought to induce drinking (Jacobs, 1964b), but hypertonic glucose is very ineffective compared to saline. Possibly a glucoreceptor signals animals to stop consuming sugar and dehydration is the cue to stop drinking saline. Other receptors have also been posited, e.g., for amino acids. Pureto, Deutsch, Molina, and Roll (1976) give evidence for upper intestinal tract sensitivity to specific nutrients.

*Intestinal Volume.* Davis, Collins, and Levine (1975) have reported data indicating that gastrointestinal filling provides a negative feedback signal to curb ingestion. They also indicate that the site of the feedback is in the upper part of the small intestine rather than the stomach.

### Specific Hungers

By the term *specific hunger*, we mean that deprivation of a particular food substance leads to an increased preference for that substance. The best researched example is sodium appetite.

*Sodium appetite.* Rats whose adrenal glands have been removed show a sharp increase in intake of sodium chloride solution (Richter, 1936). Adrenal hormones are necessary for the regulation of the body's salt content, and without them too much salt is lost and has to be replaced. There is an inverted-U function for saline preference in normal animals, peaking at just about body concentrations of saline (0.9 percent) and dropping off to zero preference at about 3 percent. Compared to normal, the salt-depleted rat drinks more saline, shows a preference threshold at a lower concentration, and shows preference for higher concentrations.

Richter suggested that the sensory detection threshold for saline was lower for adrenalectomized animals. Indeed, an animal should survive better if it were more sensitive to a needed substance. Pfaffmann and Bare (1950) showed, however, that the threshold concentration of NaCl necessary to produce neural firing from the tongue was the same for both adrenalectomized and control rats. Williams and Teitelbaum (1956) then showed that a normal rat punished for failing to discriminate between water and saline could discriminate as well as the adrenalectomized rat. It is now generally accepted that the effect of salt depletion is not on detection, but on preference. Humans with severe salt depletion report that salt tastes better, and apparently the same is true for the rat. This change in preference is apparently not learned, either. Animals that have never previously experienced salt deficiency nor tasted saline solutions show the preference change immediately after being made salt deficient (Krieckhaus & Wolf, 1968; A.N. Epstein, 1967; Falk, 1961). Salt deficiency can be produced literally overnight so that there is no question of the animal learning about salt deficiency and recovery prior to an experiment.

*Other specific hungers.* There are a number of known specific hungers. After removal of the parathyroid glands, which regulate calcium content, rats consume large amounts of calcium. Rats without pancreases reduce sugar intake and thus avoid diabetes. Deprivation of some vitamins, fat, protein, carbohydrate, water, and other substances commonly leads to compensatory intake of the deprived substance. (see Cofer & Appley, 1964, p. 230, for additional specific examples).

There are certain problems of method that cloud the results of specific hunger research. A common procedure is to give animals a number of different substances, freely available cafeteria style. The question is: Will the animals indeed select foods in proper balance to keep themselves in good health? In order to test the hypothesis, one has to provide everything the animal needs, which may bias results in favor of proper dietary selection and the evidence from this procedure is not conclusive (Lát, 1967). There are two definite and opposing schools of thought on the question. One says that "nature knows best" and that the organism will "naturally" select a diet that is at least adequate. The other says that "nature is fickle" and it is not really safe to leave diet to chance, that some more rational approach to nutrition should be taken.

Harriman (1955) provided a striking example of the nature-is-fickle theory. He found adrenalectomized rats preferred 8 percent sucrose to 1.2 percent NaCl and died if these two alternatives had been provided prior to operation, as well as after. If the first preference test was postoperative, however, they at least consumed enough saline to survive. Young and Chaplin (1945) also found that rats made protein deficient after showing a preference for sucrose over casein continued to show the sucrose preference. If given the postdeficiency tests in a different apparatus, however, they preferred casein. More recent experiments (e.g., Cullen & Scarborough, 1969) have challenged Harriman's findings. Is it even reasonable, however, to suspect that every dietary deficiency has a mechanism to make some substance more preferred? Or is there a more generalized mechanism?

***The learning of specific hungers.*** Recent research indicates that when an animal is on a deficient diet it becomes ill, and the foods it is eating become aversive through association with the illness. The animal then chooses novel foods because they have not been associated with illness. A new food that eliminates the deficiency makes the animal feel better and becomes more preferred because its taste is associated with well-being. This hypothesis hardly accounts for the rapid preference changes that occur with salt depletion, but may well handle preferences that take more time to develop. The learning hypothesis mainly requires that the animal be able to discriminate between the "good" food and the "bad" in order to show a preference. Harris, Clay, Hargreaves, and Ward (1933) indeed found that vitamin B deficiency was corrected by dietary choice if the vitamin were tagged with a distinctive flavor (licorice) so the animal could discriminate it, but not otherwise.

Many studies (see reviews by Rozin & Kalat, 1971; Revusky & Garcia, 1970) now show that rats avoid foods associated with illness produced by X-rays or drugs (e.g., apomorphine). Furthermore, the food (conditioned stimulus) is presented several *hours* before the radiation or drug (unconditioned stimulus). This upsets any simple notions about the necessity of close contiguity between conditioned and unconditioned stimuli. It has been proposed that the aftertaste of food in the mouth when animals are made ill is the actual CS, and hence there really is a short CS-UCS interval. This is pretty clearly disproven by the fact that animals can differentiate between dry lab chow (paired with illness) and wet mash made from lab chow (not paired with illness). After several hours, there should be no difference in aftertaste, but the animals show avoidance of the appropriate food modes. Apparently the animals remember what they ate.

There are two competing theories to account for such data. The *interference theory* (Revusky & Garcia, 1970) is that the CS-UCS interval can span hours because there are no *interfering* taste stimuli between CS and UCS. This is experimentally necessary because a taste stimulus closer to the UCS would be the one conditioned. With external stimuli, however, many new stimuli inevitably come between CS and UCS if the interval is long. Such later stimuli would interfere with the intended CS-UCS association.

There may be different laws of learning (due to different types of neural connections) for taste in relation to illness than for the typical classical conditioning experiment. Garcia and Ervin (1968), in fact, did not get differential aversion to one of two external stimulus characteristics of food (two sizes of food pellet) with X-rays as a UCS. There was a discrimination if electric shock followed one size but not the other. They hypothesized that it is easy to develop external-(size)-external-(shock) associations or internal-(taste)-internal-(illness) pairings, but difficult to get external-internal pairings. This has led to a new line of research on the specificity of learning.

The second major alternative is the *learned safety theory* (e.g., Rozin & Kalat, 1971). Rats taste new stimuli very tentatively. (Wild rats are very "neophobic"—fearful of any new stimuli.) But, after a while, if nothing happens, the new stimulus (including food) is considered safe and the animal returns to it.

A new food associated with illness is avoided, however. The theory, then, is that animals avoid foods that are associated with illness and tentatively try out new foods until they "find" one that is safe (associated with well-being). The great advantage of this kind of mechanism is that it allows for "specific hunger" for practically anything.

A rather different line of research also indicates wide possibilities for specific taste preferences. Young rats just weaning prefer foods that their mothers eat and, even further back, prefer foods their mothers ate while pregnant. In the latter instance, we presume that the food taste worked its way into the amniotic fluid of the pregnant female. In either case, the young rats become familiar with particular "safe" tastes and show a preference for them (Galef, 1971; Galef & Henderson, 1972).

In summary, then, two different mechanisms seem related to specific hungers. The first involves an automatic change in taste preference due to deprivation, as with saline. This may also be true for sugars in those species that have a sugar preference. Sweet substances are consumed in greater quantity and preferred at higher concentrations by animals that are food deprived (e.g., Collier & Myers, 1961; Beck & Ellis, 1966; Jacobs & Sharma, 1969). An alteration in the mechanism underlying normal preferences may in part account for the finickiness of hypothalamically lesioned animals.

The second factor is a change in preference due to learning, particular flavors being avoided or approached depending on whether they are associated with danger (illness) or safety (well-being).

### Hunger and Obesity in Humans

Human obesity is a widely recognized health problem, but until very recently there has been little solid psychological research devoted to it. Stanley Schachter and his associates have recently compared eating by obese humans as closely as possible with that of the hypothalamic hyperphagic rat (e.g., Schachter, 1971a, b). The two species are remarkably similar. Both eat faster, are more finicky, are influenced to eat more in the presence of food than are normal weight subjects, but will not work more for food. One particularly ingenious experiment is described by Schachter (1971b, p. 135) as follows: "When a subject arrived he was asked simply to sit at the experimenter's desk and fill out a variety of personality tests and questionnaires. Besides the usual student litter, there was a bag of almonds on the desk. The experimenter helped herself to a nut, invited the subject to do the same, and then left him alone with his questionnaires and nuts for fifteen minutes. There were two sets of conditions. In one, the nuts had shells on them; in the other the nuts had no shells. I assume we agree that eating nuts with shells is considerably more work than eating nuts with no shells."

The striking result was that ten of twenty normal weight subjects ate nuts with shells and eleven of twenty ate them without shells. Of the overweight subjects, however, only one of twenty ate them with shells, while nineteen of twenty ate them without shells. Similarly, 22 percent of normal-weight patrons of Chinese and Japanese restaurants were observed to engage in eating with chopsticks, which is presumably more work (for Americans) than using a knife and fork. Only about 5 percent of obese patrons used chopsticks, however.

Schachter relates the eating behavior of obese subjects to emotionality, arguing that the obese subject is more reactive to external stimuli than the normal weight person, who is more reactive to internal cues for eating. An extensive series of experiments supports this hypothesis.

### Collier's Ecological Approach to Feeding Behavior

It has generally been implicit in our discussions to now that a *depletion-repletion* model accounts for much feeding behavior. A reduction of energy supplies (depletion) sets various mechanisms into operation to trigger feeding until there is a recovery of the lost energy supplies (repletion). We also noted counterexamples, however—palatability and social factors in particular.

George Collier, of Rutgers University, and his associates (e.g., Collier, Kanarek, Hirsch, & Marwine, 1976; Collier, Hirsch, & Hamlin, 1972) have taken the opposite tack. They argue that either animals or people *rarely* eat because they are depleted. Rather, they eat to *prevent* depletion. We can readily show that laboratory eating or drinking increases with deprivation but we seldom see or hear of this in nature. In fact, laboratory animals in their home cages are not normally food depleted when they initiate eating. The depletion-repletion model predicts that feeding should be correlated with amount of time since the last meal (or until the next one), but such correlations are rarely found. Laboratory animals do not starve themselves to the extent that we usually deprive them to get them to press levers or run mazes. Each kind of animal in its own particular ecological niche comes to know (whether by nature, nurture, or a combination) what to do to keep itself from getting overly hungry most of the time.

*Feeding Strategies.* Food supplies can be categorized in terms of three characteristics: *availability, caloric density,* and *nutritional quality.* Correspondingly, there are three kinds of animals, *herbivores, carnivores,* and *omnivores.* Collier suggests that each kind of animal has evolved in such a way as to take advantage of one or more of the food characteristics. Herbivores consume a readily available diet of low caloric density and nutritional quality (such as grass). The carnivore, however, eats food that keeps trying to escape (i.e., prey) and the diet is therefore less readily available. When obtained however, the diet has high nutritional value and relatively constant caloric density. Its composition is so much like that of the carnivore itself that it is also relatively easy to utilize. The omnivore gets meals that vary widely with reference to all these properties.

At a given time, three obvious (and perhaps other not so obvious) strategies determine the amount of food eaten: (1) *frequency* of eating, (2) *duration* of eating, and (3) *rate* of eating. Depending on their environmental circumstances, different species have available a variety of strategies to arrive at their necessary energy balances. Collier et al. (1972, 1976) studied three common laboratory animals: cats (carnivores), rats (omnivores), and guinea pigs (herbivores), in both free feeding and work situations.

*Free Feeding.* The cats ate nine to ten meals a day, mostly at night. If their diet were diluted so that more food was required to get the same amount of nutrients, they did *not* compensate by increasing their intake. They acted as if all diets were equivalent, which in nature they typically are, and steadily lost weight. Rats ate twelve to fifteen meals per day, also mostly at night. When their diet was diluted, however, they increased their intake and held weight constant. They were more flexible in their feeding behavior. Guinea pigs ate twenty-two to twenty-five meals a day and showed no diurnal cycle. When their diet was diluted with celluflour they did not show a compensatory increase in intake but neither did they lose weight. Apparently they just made more efficient use of what they had and ate more or less continuously regardless of what they were eating.

*Working for Food.* The usual level-pressing situations permits the animal a small and fixed amount of food as reward when it meets the requirements of the reinforcement schedule. Collier's animals had unlimited access to food when they lever-pressed the required number of times but food was automatically removed if they stopped eating for ten minutes. They then had to meet the response requirement again for more food.

With rats, as the number of responses per meal was increased, the animals ate fewer but larger meals. When, 5,120 responses per meal were required, the rats were reduced to one very large meal per day. They spent two to three hours continuously pressing the lever to get their meal. Compared to the usual lever-pressing schedules, with heavily deprived animals, the 5,120 response requirement is staggering.

The guinea pigs would also make the 5,120 responses per meal, but pressed faster and ate faster as the number of required responses increased. They seemed more eager to get more food quickly, as we would expect from animals that normally eat continuously.

Finally, the cats were able to get up to 12,240 responses per meal, eating only every three to four days. They still maintained their average body weight, however. This seems counterintuitive to anyone familiar with housecats. Most of us, however, probably reward their meowing too frequently by feeding, and they learn atypical eating habits.

Collier et al. (1976) conclude then that there are two different sets of factors important for feeding. The first is that a particular kind of animal in a particular environmental niche adjusts its particular feeding capabilities to the situation. This is an interaction between species and situation. The various strategies tend to keep animals from getting depleted. The second set of factors is based on body weight loss and is an emergency system that comes into play when the preventive mechanisms do not work. A third set of factors about which Collier has also importantly increased our understanding over the years, is taste and palatability of foods. These factors also operate to induce eating or drinking in nondeprived animals or people.

## THIRST

It is possible to survive without food for days, even weeks, with relatively little subjective discomfort. Thirst, however, is extremely unpleasant and in a hot, dry environment without water we may die within hours.[4] Death

---

[4] We refer to water from any source, including wine or foods with a high percentage of water, such as lettuce. Even such "dry foods" as soda crackers are about 10 percent water.

is inevitable within a few days at best because there is a continual output of water from the body for normal functioning (urine, perspiration, and respiratory evaporation).

Two very different classes of mechanisms control drinking. *Regulatory drinking* is done to offset a water deficit. As we shall see, this deficit can take two forms. *Nonregulatory drinking* is done for reasons other than or in addition to water deficit. We may drink coffee to be sociable, beer for its taste, and something else for medicinal reasons. In sufficient amount, of course, nonregulatory drinking alone would compensate for water loss. Since no animal, including the camel, actually stores water in the way that food can be stored as fat, regulatory drinking is necessary for most mammals unless they get enough fluid from nonregulatory drinking.[5]

### Regulatory Drinking

***The Stimulus to Water Drinking.*** Several laboratory procedures have been used to induce drinking or responding for water reinforcement. These include water deprivation, eating dry food, working in hot environments, stomach loads or injections of saline, and reduction of blood volume. Each of these operations could define thirst. As with hunger, however, it would seem that there must be some smaller number of internal mechanisms activated by these procedures.

***Dry Mouth.*** Walter Cannon thought the stimulus to drinking was a dry mouth, but this is clearly disproved as a necessary condition for regulatory drinking because artifically producing a dry mouth does not lead to more drinking. Atropine, for example, inhibits salivation but does not increase total fluid intake (the animal may drink somewhat more often, but does not drink a greater total amount). Tying off the salivary glands has the same effect, as does making large hypothalamic lesions. Steggerda (1941) described a man born without salivary glands who nevertheless drank normal amounts. A dry mouth may stimulate drinking to relieve the discomfort, or may be a learned cue to drinking, but it is not the critical stimulus for offsetting a water deficit.

***The Double Depletion Hypothesis.*** There are now two well-defined physiological systems known to control regulatory drinking: (1) an *osmotic gradient between intracellular and extracellular fluid spaces,* and (2) a *reduction of fluid volume* (Epstein, Kissileff, & Stellar, 1973). These represent *intracellular* and *extracellular* mechanisms, respectively.

---

[5]Some desert residents, such as the kangeroo rat, can metabolize all their water from such food as seeds. They can be made to drink, however, if put on a diet very high in protein. They will also drink Pepsi Cola when not thirsty (Robert Higgins, personal communication).

*The Osmotic Gradient: An Intracellular Mechanism.* Water depriva-tion reduces fluid volume but it also produces a more concentrated intracel-lular body fluid, especially with reference to sodium and chloride. Saline injections more concentrated than the normal 0.9 percent also induce drinking without altering total fluid volume. When concentrated saline, which does not readily cross cell membranes, is injected into an animal, two things happen. First, extracellular fluids become more concentrated. Second, water is pulled by osmosis from the inside of the cell to the outside.[6] To determine whether concentration per se was the major factor, Gilman (1937) injected dogs with urea. This substance readily crosses the cell membrane, so there is an equal increase in osmotic pressure on both sides. In contrast to saline injections, urea injections produced very little drinking. It was concluded that the *difference* in osmotic pressure on the two sides of the cell membrane (the osmotic gradient) was more important than an overall increase in osmotic pressure.[7] Specialized cells called *osmoreceptors* send appropriate signals to the rest of the brain to initiate activity.

Cell *distortion* may in fact be the critical element. If salts are *removed* from extracellular space, there is an *increase* in cell size (the osmosis work-ing in the other direction). This may lead to excessive drinking. It also leads to the paradoxical effect that a saline injection may *reduce* rather than increase drinking. The reason, of course, is that water now leaves the cells and they return to their normal size.

*The Site of the Osmoreceptor.* Hypothalamic areas are crucial to water regulation, although not exclusively so. One of the first clues to the importance of this area came from the study of *diabetes insipidus,* a disorder characterized by excessive drinking and urination. It can be produced by lesions of the *supraoptic nucleus* of the hypothalamus. When a normal animal has a water deficit, *antidiuretic hormone* (ADH, which is manu-factured in the supraoptic nucleus and stored in the underlying pituitary gland) is released. This hormone increases the rate of reabsorption of water from fluid being filtered through the kidneys so the animal does not lose as much by excretion. If the source of the ADH supply is destroyed, the animal urinates excessively and has to drink excessively to make up the loss (Ranson, Fischer, & Ingram, 1938). Injection of saline into the carotid artery, which supplies the hypothalamus with blood, both increases drinking and decreases urine output. It was then found (Stevenson, Welt, & Orloff, 1950)

[6]If two water compartments are separated by a semipermeable membrane (one that selectively lets things through), the water may move freely across the membrane in either direction. If salt is added to one compartment, however, the water moves from the nonsalt side to the salt side, tending to equalize the salt concentration on the two sides. The salt does not cross the membrane. The membrane then has different osmotic pressures on the two sides, an osmotic gradient.

[7]Grossman (1967a) points out that Gilman's animals often did drink after urea injec-tions, suggesting that simple osmotic increase might be a factor.

that lesions in the lateral hypothalamus produce *adipsia* (no drinking). Finally, Andersson (1952) reported that .1 cc injections of hypertonic saline into the goat hypothalamus produced *polydipsia* (copious drinking). Even with such small injections, the animals would start drinking within thirty to ninety seconds and consume a gallon of water, and then do the whole thing again after another injection. We now know that drinking can be elicited by electrical stimulation in a number of hypothalamic regions and in the limbic system and by various drugs placed into the limbic system (e.g., Fisher, 1964).

*Fluid Volume: The Extracellular Mechanism.* It has been long known that thirst in man often follows hemorrhaging, which does not alter osmotic pressure (Wolf, 1958). Although the reason was not understood until recently, it was generally believed that some kind of volume receptors were located within the vascular system rather than specialized cells in the hypothalamus. The mechanism of this "extracellular thirst" has now been elucidated, but is more complicated than the osmotic "intracellular thirst" mechanism.

The critical receptors for detecting changes in blood volume are pressure receptors in the veins. If major veins are tied off so that venous pressure decreases, there is an increase in drinking. Signals from the venous pressure receptors can be sent directly to the brain, but a more important mechanism operates through the kidney. When venous pressure drops, the kidney releases into the bloodstream a substance called *renin,* which is, in effect, a "thirst hormone." The renin acts on a normal substance in the bloodstream, called *angiotensinogen,* to form *angiotensin II.* Angiotensin II acts directly on the receptors in the hypothalamic region of the brain to produce thirst and drinking. A variety of substances injected directly into the brain can produce drinking, as indicated previously, but angiotensin II appears to be the most effective. This extracellular fluid level monitoring system seems also more sensitive than the intracellular osmotic system. Both systems influence ADH output and induce drinking but their "primary" areas of influence are in different parts of the hypothalamus (osmotic in the lateral area, extracellular in the anterior region Thompson [1975]).

**Cues for the Termination of Drinking.** Water intake appears to be "metered" by several methods: (1) "counting" or "metering" of the stimuli involved in actual drinking and swallowing; (2) stomach distention; and (3) absorption of ingested water and a reversal of the event(s) that led to drinking in the first place. There is at present no known specific brain area identified as a "satiety" area for drinking alone.

*Mouth Metering.* If a dog is fistulated (a tube leading from the esophagous is inserted, so that ingested fluid does not reach the stomach), it will drink an amount that is *proportional* to the number of hours without water. In absolute amount, it may drink twice as much as it would need, but intake is still proportionate to what it needs (Bellows, 1939). Since a normal dog offsets its deficits with nearly 100 percent accuracy, mouth metering cannot be the sole mechanism, but it does seem a useful one.

*Stomach Distention.* Towbin (1949) put balloons into the stomachs of thirsty dogs and showed that as more air was pumped into the balloon the dogs drank less. This suggested that stomach distention (from the balloon) was a cue to cut off or reduce drinking.

Distention cannot be the only cue, however. If a dog has a particular water deficit and enough water to offset the deficit is tubed into its stomach, it will immediately thereafter drink the same amount of water. It is as if the dog did not know the tubed water had been put in. If there is a delay of some fifteen minutes between tubing and allowing the animal to drink, however, the dog does not drink. This is presumably because there has been some time for the absorption of the tubed water into the body. The tubed water may be an ineffective cue because it clears the stomach very quickly and there really is not much distention from it. Substances with more bulk (e.g., solid foods) or with greater concentration (such as sucrose, glucose, or saline), which do not clear the stomach so quickly, may provide better stomach or intestinal distention cues and serve to terminate drinking.

*Reversal of the Initiating Stimulus.* As with food, water ingestion has often been thought to cease before there has been time to terminate the stimulus that started drinking in the first place. In fact, however, water is well on the way to absorption within fifteen minutes (e.g., O'Kelley & Beck, 1960; O'Kelly, Falk, & Flint, 1958). About 25 percent of a stomach load of water is absorbed within fifteen minutes. Novin (1962) measured the electrical resistance of fluids in the hypothalamic region of the rat brain during water deprivation and subsequent drinking. Resistance is lower after deprivation because the concentration of sodium and chloride ions is greater. Within less than ten minutes of the initiation of drinking, the electrical resistance of the brain fluid began to increase, showing that water was getting to the hypothalamus. It is also possible that *incomplete* water replenishment would inhibit drinking temporarily. If there were no further absorption because the animal had not drunk enough, it would drink more. If there were further absorption, it would not drink more.

Osmometric theories of thirst (e.g., Wolf, 1958) are based on the assumption that animals drink sufficient amounts of water to return body fluids to their normal osmotic values. The amount of water necessary to do this following any given injection of sodium chloride can readily be calculated. Corbit (1969) has produced rather impressive evidence and arguments that this is indeed what the rat does. This makes more sense for the rat, which drinks relatively slowly, however, than it does for the dog, which drinks in a few gulps. The net effect is the same, but the animals may not be metering the same things to reach the same osmotic endpoint. Blass and Hall (1976) have recently proposed a greater emphasis on peripheral factors in the cut-off for drinking.

### Nonregulatory Factors in Drinking

*Taste.* The normal rat *can* regulate its water balance without smelling or tasting water (Teitelbaum & Epstein, 1963). The animal has a tube permanently anchored to its skull, passed through its nose and into the esophagous so it can "eat" or "drink" without the normal activities of ingestion. Pressing a lever produces a squirt of water or liquid food directly into the stomach. With this procedure, rats can adequately regulate food and water balance. If food is diluted, they just press the lever more often and keep total nutrient intake nearly constant.

The normal animal, however, *does* have such sensory cues as taste and smell to guide it, and behavioral studies indicate these are important in normal water-regulatory behavior. Thus, while nondeprived or hungry rats strongly prefer sucrose solutions, thirsty rats are often indifferent in working for water or different sucrose solutions (e.g., Beck & Ellis, 1966; Beck & Bidwell, 1974). Water deprivation may alter some hedonic state so that water tastes better (Beck & Nash, 1969; Beck, Nash, Viernstein, & Gordon, 1972). Nondeprived rats, as well as those with lateral hypothalamic lesions, reject water as if it were aversive. They may lap at a water tube to avoid electric shock, but they are not really consuming the water (Williams & Teitelbaum, 1956). This suggests that hypothalamic lesions (or lesions in related areas) impair a mechanism by which water becomes more palatable when the animal is water deprived or salt injected. The rat then has to fall back on substances that are normally very palatable during nondeprivation, such as sucrose or saccharin solutions.

Animals with lesions in the lateral hypothalamic area also salivate less. This may influence drinking because (1) the mouth is uncomfortable unless wetted, and/or (2) lack of salivation may change water taste. The taste receptors may adapt to the more concentrated saliva when the normal animal is water deprived, and water then tastes different. With humans, water tastes sweeter after the tongue is adapted to sodium chloride (Bartoshuk, McBurney, & Pfaffman, 1964).

Fluid taste is not generally considered a regulatory factor in drinking, but given the importance of taste in salt depletion there is no reason to eliminate taste as a factor in water depletion. Just as salt depletion changes the acceptability of salt, so might water deprivation change the acceptability of water. This, of course, would place the burden of "thirst" phenomena on the incentive.

*Schedule-Induced Polydipsia.* Rats can be induced to drink water voraciously entirely by behavioral procedures. Falk (e.g., 1961) first described this phenomenon. Hungry rats were bar pressing for 45-mg food pellets delivered an average of once a minute. After three hours, Falk discovered the animals had consumed an average of about 92 ml of water, as compared to about 27 ml intake in their home cages in the previous twenty four hours. Falk's initial reaction was to think that the drinking tube was leaking, but he quickly discovered that the animals really were drinking three to four times their normal daily intake.

Various explanations have been proposed. For example, the drinking is "superstitious" behavior; the animal associates drinking with getting food pellets, which are assumed to reinforce drinking. In fact, however, drinking *follows* food pellet delivery rather than preceding it. Also, delivery of pellets without bar pressing leads to the same degree of overdrinking. A dry mouth interpretation has also been proposed: Every time the animal eats a dry pellet, it drinks to wet its mouth. In the process of getting a couple hundred pellets, the animal takes a couple hundred drinks. A *liquid* monkey diet, one-third water and having no unusual thirst-provoking agents (Falk, 1969), produces as big a drinking effect as do dry pellets, however, so the dry mouth theory does not work.

Falk (1969) suggests that this unusual drinking behavior might be considered "adjunctive behavior," in the same way that the displacement activities described by the ethologists are adjunctive to a thwarted behavior. Necessary conditions for showing schedule-induced polydipsia are that the animal be hungry and that the food pellets be small and widely spaced in delivery time. When food comes only infrequently, drinking becomes more probable, possibly because the stimuli controlling eating have also come to control drinking. Eating and drinking normally occur closely together, and when eating is momentarily thwarted the animals respond to the stimuli by drinking.

### Learning of Hunger or Thirst?

There is almost no evidence that hunger or thirst can be directly conditioned to external stimuli, although two experiments (Wright, 1965; Enscore, et al., 1976) have produced intriguing results. A somewhat different problem is whether animals have to learn to be hungry or thirsty in the first place. Ghent (1957), following Hebb (1949), argued that they do. For example, if an animal is fed only one hour a day, on the first few days of this deprivation schedule intake is lower than the usual twenty four-hour intake but gradually increases. Ghent argued that animals are learning to be hungry (or thirsty) on such a schedule. Her arguments are still sometimes taken to be conclusive (e.g., Wong, 1976).

Beck (1962), however, argued that deprivation schedule effects are due to a cumulating physiological deficit and showed that animals on repeated water-deprivation and recovery cycles drank the same amount each cycle. R. Williams (1967) showed the same for food deprivation and recovery cycles. Both of these experiments are contrary to the learning hypothesis. Kutscher (1964) also showed that amount of food or water consumed when an animal is returned to ad lib feeding and drinking is a function of the number of prior days on a deprivation schedule, positive evidence that such schedules produce an increasing physiological deficit. Tang and Collier (1971) obtained results similar to those of Beck and Williams in a lever-pressing experiment.

There is, however, a shorter latency to begin eating or drinking after prior experience on a deprivation schedule (e.g., Hatton and Almli, 1967; Schmidt, Stewart, & Perez, 1967; Bolles, 1962b). This may be viewed as an instrumental learning effect, an incentive motivational effect, or even the result of fewer competing responses because of familiarity with the feeding or drinking situation the second time around (Beck, 1964.) Such latency changes are not, however, evidence for learning of hunger or thirst per se.

## TASTE

As a physiological model for incentive motivation, the taste system is nearly ideal. First, it obviously is important. Second, many taste stimuli can be manipulated quantitatively, allowing the development of precise stimulus-response relations of both sensory and motivational interest. Third, some of the neurological correlates of taste are now becoming clear, both in terms of the manner in which taste stimuli are coded into the nervous system and in terms of their relation to food and water regulation. Finally, there are many cross-species comparisons that help elucidate taste mechanisms. There is a great deal of man in the rat (and vice versa).

### Taste Qualities and Their Stimuli

In man, there are four commonly accepted taste qualities: sweet, bitter, salty, and sour.[8] The corresponding prototype stimuli are sucrose, quinine, sodium chloride, and hydrocloric acid. Chemically, salty taste is produced

---

[8]Schiffman & Engelhard (1976) have recently presented evidence for several more taste qualities, based on rather sophisticated statistical techniques. The additional qualities have not yet worked their way into the motivation literature, however.

by water-soluble salts, with both positive and negative ions contributing to the salt taste. With sour, the degree of acid taste is correlated with the concentration of the hydrogen (H+) ions, a number of different acids having the same taste. Sweet taste is produced by a variety of organic compounds, including sugars, glycols, and alcohols, with no specific chemical similarities among them yet known. Similarly, there is no known specific chemical structure for all stimuli having a bitter taste.

It is generally believed that all other taste qualities are some combination of the activity of the neural systems underlying these four qualities. This sounds like an impoverished range of taste possibilities, but as is commonly known, much of what we attribute to taste is the result of olfaction as well.

### Neural Coding of Taste

***Recording Procedures.*** There are two basic techniques for recording neural responses to taste stimuli. One involves recording from individual nerve fibers, and the data are in the form of discrete neural "spikes" (i.e., individual firings of a nerve), which are counted before and after application of taste stimuli. The second method is to record from a fiber tract, where there are many nerve fibers. The output is a change in voltage level, recorded on an oscilloscope or pen writer. The voltage changes represent differences in the numbers of fibers firing. Peripheral recording (outside the central nervous system) is from one of three sources. The first is the *chorda tympani* branch of the *lingual* nerve. The front of the tongue is served by the lingual, which also, however, transmits impulses for touch, temperature, and pain sensitivity. The chorda tympani branch transmits only taste and gets its name from the fact that it passes near the eardrum to join the seventh cranial nerve (the facial). Taste fibers from the back of the tongue follow the ninth cranial nerve, the *glossopharyngeal.* Taste fibers from other parts of the mouth follow the tenth cranial nerve, the *vagus.* The taste fibers from these three sources combine to form the *tractus solitarius* in the brain stem, then proceed to the *arcuate nucleus* of the *thalamus,* and finally to the *somatosensory cortical areas* (precentral gyrus).

The taste receptors themselves are groups of elongated cells that together form *taste buds,* found mainly in the papillae of the tongue. The buds are mostly on the top of the tongue except in the middle portion, which lacks them. The front of the tongue is especially sensitive to sweet and salt, the sides to sour, and the back to bitter. This implies specific connections of these areas to the nervous system, but all taste receptors seem to be sensitive to a range of different taste stimuli. The actual life of a given taste cell is only a few days, raising the interesting question of how the ever-new cells manage to get connected to the right places in the nervous system (a question as yet unanswered).

The problem of neural coding is the problem of how chemical stimuli are translated into neural impulses in such a way that the brain is able to discriminate among the original stimuli. (The same problem holds, of course, for other sensory modalities). Due to the nature of nerve impulses themselves, there are certain limits to the possibilities for coding. Thus, according to the all-or-none law of nerve firing, a given nerve cell always fires at the same intensity. This means that intensity coding cannot be accounted for by intensity differences in individual nerve cells. There are also limits to the rate at which individual neurons can fire and there seem to be no qualitative differences in neurons that would discriminate those serving one sensory system (or subsystem) from those serving another system.

***Intensity Coding.*** It is generally believed that intensity coding is graded by the summated activity of many neurons. At low levels of stimulation (e.g., weak taste stimuli) a few neurons with low thresholds are stimulated. As intensity increases, other neurons with higher thresholds are "recruited." Figure 15.3 (Pfaffmann, 1960) shows the firing rates for increasing concentrations of the four standard taste stimuli. There is a rather close correlation between firing rates produced by sugars and their sweetness as judged by human observers (Halpern, 1967, p. 230).

***Quality Coding.*** Summated neural responses do not tell the whole story, however. The upper part of Figure 15.3 compares preference behavior for the four standard taste stimuli at different concentrations. We see that preference and aversion across these stimuli are virtually unrelated to intensity of nerve responses. Quinine, for example, is avoided at virtually any concentration high enough to be discriminated but NaCl shows the inverted-U for preference with low-magnitude neural responses. The *quality* of taste stimuli (e.g., difference between sweet and bitter) must be coded in some manner other than summated rate of neural firing.

A basic fact of taste sensitivity is that, although different parts of the tongue are relatively more sensitive to some stimuli than others, many taste buds are sensitive to several different qualities of taste stimuli. Pfaffmann (1955) first pointed this out clearly and then suggested how different taste qualities might be coded. His argument was that different stimuli would excite different *patterns* of receptors, the coding of a particular taste being determined by the *relative* amounts of firing by different fibers. A particular neuron in the taste system would be like a single piano string. A taste would be like a chord or melody. Thus a particular neuron could participate in many different tastes and the particular taste would be determined by the

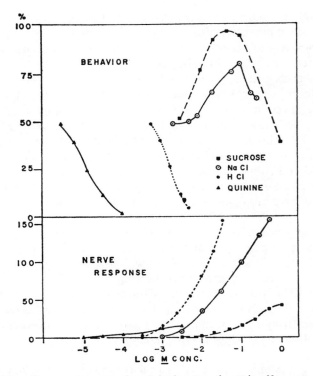

**Figure 15.3** *Composite graph of behavioral and afferent neural responses in the rat. Upper figure shows the preference-aversion responses as percentage intake as a function of stimulus concentration. Lower figure shows neural responses in arbitrary units. (From Pfaffmann, 1960, p. 257. Copyright © 1960 by the American Psychological Association. Reprinted by permission.)*

relationships among units active at the same time. Table 15-2 (Zotterman, 1961) shows a simple scheme for this. Erickson (e.g., 1963, 1967) has supported this pattern concept by showing that animals are "confused" by different chemical stimuli that produce similar firing patterns. Different patterns, however, are discriminated quite readily.

**Table 15-2** *Fiber-type Response In the Cat. (From Zotterman, Y., 1961, p. 207.)*

| Stimulus | "Water" fiber | "Salt" fiber | "Acid" fiber | "Quinine" fiber | Sensation evoked |
|---|---|---|---|---|---|
| H₂O (0.03 M Salt) | + | 0 | 0 | 0 | water |
| N_aCl (0.05 M) | 0 | + | 0 | 0 | salt |
| HCL (pH 2.5) | + | + | + | 0 | sour |
| Quinine | + | 0 | 0 | + | bitter |

***Sensory Coding and Motivation.*** How is all this related to motivation? The details of the perceptual-motivational linkage are not yet known, but most certainly involve nonsensory pathways. At some point, the taste pathways must branch off into the limbic system and hypothalamus. The effects of both lateral and ventromedial hypothalamic lesions would indicate this. Furthermore, Poschel (1968) found that electrical stimulation of positively rewarding brain areas increased sucrose preference. The sensory code, then, not only identifies a taste stimulus, but also feeds into motivational brain systems and partially determines approach and avoidance. Such behaviors are attenuated or exaggerated by the internal state of the animal, as well as its past experience with particular taste stimuli.

### Species Similarities and Differences

For many species, including dog, man, and rat, preferences for various taste stimuli are very similar; e.g., sweets are accepted and bitters are rejected. Some species also have a water-taste receptor not found in man. Where a cross-species commonality exists, it often extends even to specific threshold values for detection of the substance.

We have to be cautious about applying such terms as *sweet* and *bitter* to any particular stimulus, however, for these terms are based on human report and may not be applicable to other species. For example, the chick shows no preference for dextrose, maltose, or sucrose over water, but does show an active aversion to xylose (Kare & Ficken, 1963). The calf, on the other hand, shows a preference for both sucrose and xylose. The blowfly is sensitive to the tastes of water, salt, and sucrose in much the same way that man is (Dethier, 1966, 1967). It is safest to operationally describe the taste stimulus being used (e.g., the chemical involved, concentration, method of presentation, temperature, and method of response measurement) and to be perfectly clear among ourselves that subjective descriptions are nothing but that.

### Taste Adaptation, Cross-Adaptation, and Mixtures

***Adaptation.*** If the taste receptors are given continuous exposure to a particular taste stimulus they adapt to the stimulus, so that it tastes different. For example, the threshold concentration of NaCl increases as the concentration of an adapting NaCl solution is higher. Adaptation also changes the reported taste qualities of other concentrations of the same stimulus. For example, NaCl concentrations *higher* than the adapting solution are reported as *salty,* those at the adapting concentration are *tasteless,* and those *below* the adapting concentration are *bitter* (Bartoshuk, McBurney, & Pfaffmann, 1964). One such adapting solution is the saliva itself, which has interesting implications for hunger and thirst. For example, if an organism is water deprived, we would expect the saliva to be more concentrated and slightly saltier, and this would in turn affect taste, perhaps improving the taste of water.

*Cross-Adaptation.* Definitely specifiable stimuli are necessary for the study of taste mechanisms but are not necessary for survival; most natural taste stimuli are compounds. The simplest way to study compounds is to have one stimulus already on the tongue when a qualitatively different stimulus is applied. The initial stimulus is the adapting stimulus, the second is the test stimulus. This procedure is called *cross-adaptation.*

Some evidence has indicated that different salty stimuli do not cross-adapt with human subjects (Hahn, 1949). That is, the test solution was not changed in taste by the adapting solution. This is intriguing because we would expect that if there were a "salt receptor" there shoud be cross-adaptation with two salts. Beidler (1953, 1961), recording from the rat chorda tympani, seemed to confirm Hahn's results. McBurney and Lucas (1966), however, reported cross-adaptation effects with different salts on human magnitude estimations of test stimulus intensity. The discrepancy between the rat chorda tympani data and human estimations may be due to different parts of the nervous system being tapped. Thus, there *are* cross-adaptation effects in rat recordings from the tractus solitarius. There are probably changes in coding as impulses are carried through the nervous system to higher levels. Such changes are well documented for vision.

*Mixtures.* In general, the combination of two substances produces a less intense effect than the sum of the two substances, but the sum is usually more intense than either component alone. One apparent exception to this generalization (possibly an artifact of laboratory procedure and not found in nature) is the mixture of proper concentrations of glucose and saccharin. The resulting solution is consumed in far greater quantity than the sum of the two concentrations individually (Valenstein, Cox, & Kakolewski, 1970).

Two particular chemicals, *gymnemic acid* and extract of *miracle fruit,* have especially interesting and unique properties. The local application of gymnemic acid to the tongue reduces sensitivity to sucrose, saccharin, glycerine, and perhaps quinine, but citric acid, hydrochloric acid, solium chloride, ammonium chloride, and potassium chloride are not affected. The acid works on the peripheral taste system to selectively depress the effects of sweet-tasting stimuli.

If miracle fruit, indigenous to Nigeria and Ghana, is chewed prior to eating a normally sour substance, the sour substance tastes sweet. The berries are chewed by the natives prior to eating their sour maize bread or sour palm wine and beer. The active ingredient is a tasteless protein that must be held in the mouth for at least three minutes to be effective but the effect then lasts for several hours. It does not alter thresholds for any taste quality and does not depress the sour taste of acids. Rather, it brings about a sweet taste in addition to the normal sour taste of acid, like putting sugar in lemonade. Since gymnemic acid eliminates the effect, we know that miracle fruit operates on sweet receptors rather than sour (Kurihara, Kurihara, & Beidler, 1969).

## ELECTRICAL STIMULATION OF THE BRAIN (ESB): REWARD AND PUNISHMENT

Few experiments have generated as much intense interest as Olds and Milner's (1954) report that electrical stimulation of areas deep in the rat brain is a powerful reward. Simultaneously, other investigators (Delgado, Roberts, & Miller, 1954) found that electrical stimulation of the brain (ESB) could also be punishing. Virtually overnight, a new field of research was born.

Olds and Milner first noticed that the animals in their experiment continually returned to a part of an open field apparatus where they happened to have been when briefly shocked by a tiny electrical current through brain electrodes. It was as if they found the shocks pleasant. Guessing that the effect was rewarding, they tested rats in a T-maze and found the animals would go to the side where the stimulation was obtained. Finally, they reasoned that if the current were rewarding the animals would turn it on repeatedly by pressing a lever in a Skinner box arrangement like that diagrammed in Figure 15.4.

Figure 15.5 shows a cumulative lever-pressing curve for a single animal tested over thirteen hours. The animal pressed steadily when rewarded by brain stimulation, but stopped pressing when the current was eliminated. Olds (1958) shows data from an animal that responded about 2,000 times an hour for twenty-four consecutive hours before collapsing from fatigue. Since such animals were neither deprived nor in any apparent pain, it seemed they were seeking the stimulation and the phrase "pleasure centers" therefore came into use. This phrase, of course, says only that brain stimulation is a strong reward, but it does capture the flavor of the phenomenon. An immediate implication of these results was that they were incompatible with a drive reduction theory of reinforcement and many further questions are raised. What parts of the brain are involved in reward and what parts in punishment? Do conventional reinforcers have their effects via these same brain areas? Does brain stimulation function like conventional reinforcers such as food or electric shock?

### Loci of Positive and Negative Effects

To determine effective stimulation sites, the first step is to put an electrode into some specific brain area which is located by reference to a brain atlas. The electrode is constructed of fine wire insulated everywhere but at

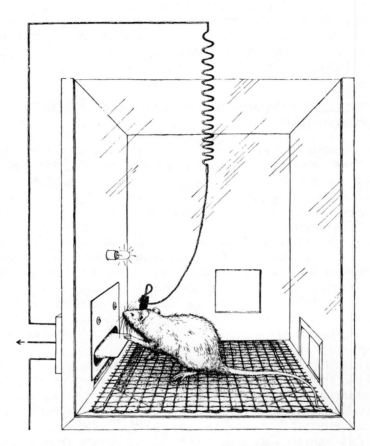

**Figure 15.4** A self-stimulation circuit is diagrammed here. When the rat presses on treadle it triggers an electric stimulus to its brain and simultaneously records action via wire at left. *(From Olds, "Pleasure Centers in the Brain," p. 108. Copyright © October 1965 by Scientific American, Inc. All rights reserved.)*

the tip. An anesthetized animal is fixed rigidly into a *stereotaxic instrument* so that its head cannot accidentally be moved, and, on the basis of standard "landmarks" on the skull, the stereotaxic instrument is used to lower the electrode into the brain very precisely. After placement, the electrode is permanently attached to the skull with screws and cement, exposed leads sticking through the scalp for attachement of wires from the source of stimulation.

This source can be 60 cycle house current, appropriately reduced in amperage and controlled in duration by a timer that is turned on either by

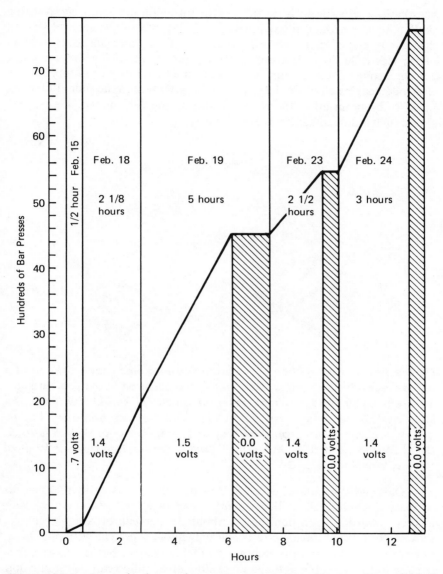

**Figure 15.5** *Smoothed cumulative response curve for rat. (From Olds & Milner, 1954, p. 424. Copyright © 1954 by the American Psychological Association. Reprinted by permission.)*

the experimenter or by the animal pressing a lever. The animal suffers no ill effects from the procedure and lives normally in its home cage.

The exact electrode placement must be verified post mortem. On completion of the experiment, the animal is sacrificed by an overdose of anesthesia and its brain is perfused with formalin and removed from the skull. The area around the electrode site is cut into thin slices and stained slices are mounted on microscope slides. From these slides, the exact location of the electrode tip is determined. Just prior to sacrificing the animal, a current strong enough to burn an area around the tip is passed through the electrode, leaving a hole in the brain that is easily seen in the slide. Referring back to the brain atlas, the electrode site is then determined. Figure 15.6 shows such a slide, magnified several times.

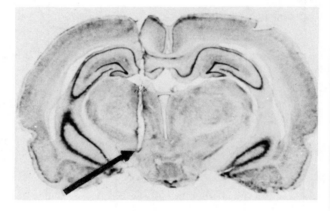

**Figure 15.6**   *Cross-section of rat brain showing electrode track. The tip of the electrode (dark arrow) had been in the posterolateral hypothalamus, an area which produces high rates of electrical self-stimulation. The slide was stained with cresyl echt violet, which shows nerve cell bodies in a dark color. (Photograph courtesy of Drs. G. F. Koob, G. R. Sessions, G. E. Martin, and S. L. Meyerhoff of the Walter Reed Army Medical Center, Washington, D.C.)*

Olds (1961) examined over 200 electrode placements. About 60 percent of these, including all of the neocortex and most of the thalamus, were neither rewarding nor punishing. About 35 percent of the placements showed positive reinforcing effects and only about 5 percent were punishing. Reward sites are found throughout the limbic system, but the most effective are in the lateral hypothalamic feeding area, followed by preoptic and septal areas, just in front of the hypothalamus. Pure negative reinforcement areas are scattered through the thalamus, dorsal tegmentum, and periventricular areas of the brain, generally closer to the midline of the brain than are the positive areas. These aversive areas do *not* correspond to the sensory pathways for pain. In several different mammalian species, equivalent brain areas are rewarding and punishing.

Positive and negative areas are often very close to each other, accounting at least in part for the fact that with some electrode sites there are "mixed" positive and negative effects (e.g., Delgado, Roberts, & Miller, 1954). The animal may press one lever to turn on stimulation and then another lever to turn it off, alternating between the two levers. One interpretation is that the electrode is simultaneously stimulating positive and negative areas but it takes a little more time for the aversive effect to build up than for the positive effect. The positive stimulation is initially more dominant, then the negative.

There are, of course, some species differences in effective electrode sites but the overall similarity across species is remarkable (Milner, 1970). In man, however, behavior for positive reinforcing effects is far less "urgent" than the all-powerful effect observed with lower animals. For obvious reasons, the amount of human research is slight and such as has been done has primarily been with clinical cases for whom electrodes were inserted for other reasons, or with psychotic patients for whom other treatments had failed.

### Similarities of ESB and Conventional Rewards and Drives

*Aversive Brain Stimulation.* In terms of drive theory, the criteria for judging whether aversive brain stimulation has drive properties are the same as for any other antecedent: It energizes many responses, an increase is punishing, and a decrease is reinforcing. Miller (1958) has shown by these criteria that such aversive stimulation is indeed functionally similar to such peripherally induced pain as foot shock. Animals would make the same response (turning a wheel) with aversive brain stimulation as they had previously learned for escape from foot shock. Cats also learned new responses reinforced by termination of aversive ESB and avoided stimuli paired with aversive ESB (Miller, 1961). It is concluded that aversive ESB and peripheral pain are highly similar. We must again raise an old precautionary note, however. To say that aversive brain stimulation is like peripheral pain is not the same as saying that such stimulation produces a drive, since both may be treated as negative incentives.

*Positive Brain Stimulation.* Is self-stimulation due to forced responding? Since the effective sites for electrical self-stimulation of the brain (ESSB) are frequently the same brain areas that lead to "stimulus-bound" eating and drinking, the question has been raised whether ESSB might be producing a similar stimulus-bound behavior. Could ESSB automatically elicit bar pressing, which in turn produces stimulation and more bar pressing? Olds (1956) answered this question negatively by comparing the course of maze learning by food-reinforced and ESB-reinforced rats. There was no difference in performance, indicating that ESB functions like food reinforcement when there is no question about the response (maze running) being "locked in" to the stimulation. The running cannot be locked, since it precedes the stimulation.

*Other Similarities.* Olds has also reported that the higher the intensity of positive ESB, the higher the grid shock rats will withstand to get it, just as hungry rats will cross an electrified grid for food. Furthermore, under all but the most extreme food deprivation rats actually prefer ESB to food. This is true, of course, only for the "best" electrode sites.

Hoebel (1969) argues that the lateral hypothalamus is involved in both reward and aversion, but these shift according to the animal's homeostatic balance. Various procedures for satiating animals (e.g., loading the stomach with food or forced feeding) *reduce* responding to get ESB and *increase* responding to turn it off. Similarly, if animals are forced to overeat until obese there is an increased *escape* from ESB and a decrement in responding to produce it. This reverses itself as body weights are allowed to return to normal. Food deprivation facilitates self-stimulation. (Margules & Olds, 1962; Hoebel & Teitelbaum, 1962). Ventromedial lesions, which lead to hyperphagia, also facilitate self-stimulation (Hoebel, 1969). In sum, these experiments show that responding for ESB fluctuates the way we would expect it to if it represented a neurological base for conventional appetitive rewards. Olds (1961) argued that in such experiments one is tapping directly into generalized systems underlying all positive and negative reinforcers.

The question may be raised: Is there any necessary connection between "specific drives" and particular electrode sites? This problem has been considered important for distinguishing between a drive interpretation of ESSB (different electrode sites have specific motivational effects) and an hedonic interpretation (generalized reward effects). Olds (1958) reported that ESSB with some electrodes was facilitated by hunger, but inhibited by male sex hormones. Conversely, other sites were facilitated by hormones and inhibited by hunger. Hoebel (1969) concludes, however, that responding at some electrode sites is indeed facilitated only by specific operations (e.g., food deprivation), and other sites are facilitated by many different procedures. The initial question no longer appears very crucial to the problem of drive versus incentive interpretations.

At various times, it has also been suggested, both facetiously and seriously, that the whole ESSB phenomenon might be just one big sex kick. A number of investigators have indeed reported that electrode sites that produce ejaculation in the rat are very effective self-stimulation sites. This is obviously not even a large part of the story, however, since stimulation of many of the most powerful reinforcing sites evokes feeding and drinking, not ejaculation.

### Differences Between ESB and Conventional Rewards

The primary differences between ESB and conventional reward effects are what Lenzer (1972) calls "behavioral lability." With ESB reward, animals often extinguish more rapidly, do not maintain responding well with partial reinforcement, do not perform as well in the straight runway, and have to be "primed" with free stimulations to get responding started at the beginning of a session. For each of these deficits, however, it has now been shown that proper training procedures are corrective. The "corrective" procedures are in fact those which make ESB training situations more like those used with food and water. For example, if the animal is food deprived both during training with ESB and extinction, it performs better under both conditions. Or, if a partial reinforcement schedule is gradually built up, the animal performs better on it (Lenzer, 1972; Trowill, Panksepp, & Gandelman, 1969).

Since ESB reward does in fact lead to erratic performance under some conditions, however, this has to be accounted for. The theoretical accounts of ESB effects, not surprisingly, can be classified as drive, drive stimulus, incentive, and response evocation theories.

### Theoretical Accounts of Electrical Self-Stimulation of the Brain

***Deutsch's Drive Decay Theory.*** Deutsch (1960), Deutsch and Howarth (1963), and Gallistell (1964) follow what is essentially a traditional drive-reinforcement theory. Deutsch assumes that drive and reinforcement effects follow different neural pathways but that the relatively large ESB electrode simultaneously stimulates both sets of pathways. Stimulation of the motivational pathway starts and maintains a response that stimulation along the reinforcement pathway can then reinforce. When the current is turned off, the neural activity in the motivational pathway declines very quickly and extinction is therefore rapid.

In one test of this theory, Deutsch and Howarth (1963) trained rats to bar press for ESB on a 100 percent reinforcement schedule. The lever was then immediately removed from the box for 0, 2.5, 5.0, 7.5, or 10 seconds for different groups of animals. It was then reinserted for extinction testing. If nonreinforced responding is necessary for extinction, we should expect no differences among these groups, since the amount of delay should be irrelevant, especially over such a small time range. The drive decay theory, on the other hand, says that if stimulation is kept from the animal for *any* reason (removing the lever in this instance) there will be reduced activity in the motivational pathway. The longer the delay, the lower the drive and hence fewer responses in extinction. The results supported the theory; there was an orderly decline in number of extinction responses with increasing delay.

In another experiment, Deutsch and Howarth showed that higher voltage ESB was followed by greater resistance to extinction. Their argument was that stronger stimulation produces a higher level of drive, which takes longer to decay when the current is no longer presented. Other, more subtle, experiments involving variations in stimulus parameters also supported the idea of two different kinds of pathways.

The drive decay theory is not without difficulty, however. Pliskoff and Hawkins (1963) supported the theory in one part of their research by showing that a few "free" stimulations *during the delay* between training and extinction did retard extinction. This is presumably because the interim stimulations kept the drive level up. The same authors also found, however, that if animals were given partial reinforcement during training they made many more responses during extinction. Such a partial reinforcement effect does not follow from the drive decay hypothesis. Even more importantly, Stutz, Lewin, and Rocklin (1965) found that animals could perform well with twenty minutes time out between short sessions of self-stimulation and Kornblith and Olds (1968) reported that animals could be trained successfully with just one trial a day. In Kornblith and Olds' experiment, there is no possibility of a drive carryover from one stimulation to the next response twenty four hours later and the results are completely contradictory to the Deutsch-Howarth hypothesis.

***Brain Stimulation as a Drive Stimulus.*** Lenzer (1972) suggests that with ESB reinforcement for each response the stimulation itself becomes a cue for further responding. The animal responding at a high rate is always reinforced while the aftereffect of the previous stimulation is still flowing through the neural circuitry. In extinction, this cue would not be present and hence responding would drop off rapidly. This is a stimulus generalization decrement account of extinction.

***Brain Stimulation as an Incentive.*** Trowill, Panksepp, and Gandelman (1969) argued that with satiated animals ESB is a pure incentive, much like saccharin. Similarly, just as saccharin is a more powerful incentive with deprived animals, so is brain stimulation. In partial support of their incentive interpretation, Trowill et al., cite a Crespi-shift type experiment in which the intensity of ESB was changed in the middle of a thirty minute session. Not only were there appropriate up and down shifts in response rates, but also there were both elation and depression effects. An incentive interpretation is supported in terms of both the suddeness of the behavioral changes following stimulus changes and the occurrence of overshooting and undershooting effects.

Mendelson (1966), using a T maze, also concluded that ESB reward in the goal box was an incentive variable. He found that if brain stimulation of nondeprived rats was withheld until after the animals entered the goal box they would still learn to select that side. The ESB in the goal box also produced stimulus-bound eating in the goal box. Stimulation in the start box, stem, or choice point of the maze were all ineffective without goal box stimulation. Mendelson argued that ESB in the goal box increased the incentive value of the food in much the same way that deprivation might. A drive interpretation was ruled out by the fact that the animals had already made their choice before stimulation was given. Mendelson (1967) has also reported that rats will press levers for ESB which produces stimulus-bound drinking. The argument, again, is that the ESB increases the incentive value of water. He discusses and rejects the proposition that it is just the stimulation itself which is rewarding in this situation.

The paradox for drive reduction theorists (see Chapters Four and Six) was that the same electrode that produces stimulus-bound eating is also a powerful reinforcer. From their point of view, how could stimulation that seems to increase drive also be reinforcing? This is no contradiction, however, for an incentive theorist because he *assumes* that incentives are arousing. When various techniques for increasing incentive motivation are added to brain stimulation, animals respond more for ESB (Hoebel, 1969). For example allowing animals to eat during self-stimulation, wafting odor of peppermint by them, or dripping sucrose randomly into the animal's mouth by tube while it is self-stimulating all increase the rate of responding. Evidence for an incentive interpretation of ESB effects does seem to be stronger than for a drive interpretation.

***Brain Stimulation as Response Evocation.*** Glickman and Schiff's (1967) response evocation theory of reinforcement (see Chapter Six) says that the sufficient condition for reinforcement is the arousal of response systems in the brain. With conventional reinforcers, the way we know if such systems have been aroused is if behavior is aroused. Since it is well known that the most powerful reinforcing sites for brain stimulation are the same ones that produce stimulus-bound eating and drinking, we know that the best brain locations for self-stimulation are at least related to responding.

Furthermore, other evidence indicates that stimulation at a given brain location does not always evoke the same kinds of responses. Rather, the particular response aroused (e.g., eating, drinking, or gnawing) may fluctuate from day to day (Valenstein, Cox, & Kakolewski, 1970). This allows for the possibility that much of the effectiveness of brain stimulation as an incentive is in evoking some kind of generalized approach behavior rather than necessarily evoking highly specific motor responses.

*A Note on Response Evocation.* Although brain stimulation is rewarding, it does not necessarily evoke further responses in the way that food and water do. We may diagram the typical sequence of events for food and brain stimulation reward as follows:

*Food:* Bar press ⟶ click ⟶ approach feeder ⟶ eat
*Brain Stimulation:* Bar press ⟶ stimulation

In the case of stimulation, there is no response intervening between bar press and reward. What would happen if conventional rewards were handled in this same way? Gibson, Reid, Sakai, and Porter (1965) trained rats to lick a dry dipper that then delivered sucrose. These animals were just as quick to stop licking the dry dipper when sucrose was omitted as were rats that licked the dipper for brain stimulation which was then suspended. In other words, when response requirements were made equivalent, the speed of extinction following either sucrose reward or brain stimulation reward was the same.

Gibson et al. then rearranged the situation so that pressing a lever produced the dipper. Licking the dipper produced brain stimulation for some animals and sucrose for others. Both groups then extinguished on bar pressing at the same rate, further supporting the idea that the two kinds of rewards are highly similar when response requirements are equated. Pliskoff, Wright, and Hawkins (1965) obtained similar results in an experiment where pressing one lever produced a second lever and pressing the second layer produced brain stimulation. Extinction on the first lever was typical of that for conventional rewards. The conclusion would seem to be that the effectiveness of conventional rewards can be downgraded if response requirements are reduced, and that of brain stimulation can be upgraded if response requirements are increased. Arousal of neural response systems is rewarding, but arousal of complete or multiple (sequential) response systems is even more rewarding.

### Brain Stimulation and Secondary Reinforcement

It has been difficult to show that brain stimulation can be used as the primary reinforcer for establishing a secondary reinforcer. This, again, may be due to using situations where brain stimulation does not involve a response. The simple Pavlovian pairing of a stimulus with food does not confer powerful reinforcing properties on that stimulus, so we might not expect it to happen with brain stimulation, either. The literature is contradictory (Kling & Riggs, 1971, p. 675), but a recent study by Bergquist and Holley (1974) appears to show a reliable demonstration that secondary reinforcement can be established using ESB as primary reinforcement.

## CONCLUSION

Since the mid-1950's there has been a literal explosion of research on the physiology of motivation. In this chapter we reviewed a small number of popular topics, but included discussion of physiology in previous chapters when it seemed appropriate. Physiological research has been greatly facilitated by technical developments, particularly those involving electrical stimulation and recording from the brain, as well as automated control of experiments and computerized data analysis. The new capabilities for studying awake and freely moving animals have drastically altered our ideas about the nervous system, with regard to the nature of rewards, for example. Finally, the simultaneous study of social and behavioral variables along with physiological variables has also begun to bear rich fruit. The work on hunger and obesity is a prime example of such multidisciplinary study, as is the research on aggression or on stress, discussed in earlier chapters.

chapter 16

# Epilogue

The introductory student of motivation is usually dismayed by the diversity and apparent disarray of motivational theories, concepts and data. To the advanced student such diversity is precisely what makes the field intriguing. I would hope that the reader has been caught up in some of this intrigue. From such a morass we cannot at this point draw any startling conclusions which will suddenly clarify and integrate the field, but from our study we can perhaps abstract some recurring problems and perhaps some trends.

1. The field of motivation, like psychology as a whole, is becoming more *cognitive* in its orientation. There are a number of indicators of this. The whole thrust of attribution theory is in this direction, not to speak of cognitive dissonance theory. The increasing concern with the motivational properties of stimulus information processing is another sign. A third indicator is research on cognitive factors in coping with stress and anxiety.

2. Motivation is becoming more *biological*. This may seem contradictory to the cognitive trend, but the two are nevertheless occurring simultaneously. The interest in biological aspects are spurred by the great progress achieved in research on such problems as hunger, thirst, maternal behavior, sex, aggression, behavior genetics and so on. The discovery that brain stimulation can be rewarding has in itself produced a revolution.

3. There is increasing interest in the interactions of cognitive, social and physiological determinants of behavior. In the areas of emotion and obesity, for example, it is clear that there are multiple causes (just as there are everywhere) and that understanding of these multiple factors is necessary. The simplistic views that obesity is due to emotional upset, on the one hand, or physiological disorder, on the other, are no longer tenable. The lip service historically paid to such interactions is now becoming a reality.

4. The problem of "motivational" vs. "associative" interpretations of behavior will continue to be a theoretical issue. The cue properties of drive stimuli, fear, incentive stimuli, frustration or achievement-arousal remain to be sorted out. In line with the increased interest in cognition, however, there may well be a greater emphasis on complex imagery and organization of internal stimuli than we have previously seen.[1] Thus, in considering the role of drive stimuli we may think of them as more complicated and structured than as just "internal stimuli to which responses are conditioned."

5. Approach and avoidance behaviors, and related concepts (e.g., desire and aversion, tendency to success and fear of failure, positive and negative incentives) are likely to remain at the core of motivation theory. There is no obvious reason to change the dimensions of behavior of concern to motivational theorists and motivational concepts will have to reflect

[1]There is already work along these lines. For example, Mischel (see Mischel, 1974, for a summary) has studied such factors in delay of gratification, research in which children can get an immediate small reward or a larger one if they are willing to wait.

these dimensions. New concepts may come into vogue but will probably still be concerned with the directional characteristics of behavior.

6. Finally, it may well be that there are behaviors which can be accounted for *without using motivational concepts*. Since the early part of this century most psychologists have postulated that all behavior is "motivated" in some sense. At the same time, however, there have been those (e.g., Skinner, Estes, and some personality theorists) who have not felt the need for motivational concepts. This is partly a definitional matter in the sense that we are talking about theory and syntax in addition to observed behaviors. Even with present conceptual schemes, however, it may be that some behaviors are indeed just responses to situations and no further motivational concepts are necessary to account for the occurrence of these behaviors.

# REFERENCES

Ad Hoc Committee on Ethical Standards in Psychological Research. *Ethical principles in the conduct of research with human participation.* Washington, D.C.: American Psychological Association, 1973.

ADAMETZ, J. H. Rate of recovery of functioning in cats with rostral reticular lesions. *Journal of Neurosurgery,* 1959, *16,* 85–98.

ADAMSON, R., HENKE, P., & O'DONOVAN, D. Avoidance conditioning following pre-adaptation to weak shock. *Psychonomic Science,* 1969, *14,* 119–121.

ALLPORT, G. W. Functional autonomy of motives. *American Journal of Psychology,* 1937, *50,* 141–156.

ALTMAN, J. *Organic foundations of animal behavior.* New York: Holt, Rinehart and Winston, 1966.

AMSEL, A. The role of frustrative nonreward in noncontinuous reward situations. *Psychological Bulletin,* 1958, *55,* 102–119.

AMSEL, A. Frustrative nonreward in partial reinforcement and discrimination learning: Some recent history and a theoretical extension. *Psychological Review,* 1962, *69,* 306–328.

AMSEL, A. Secondary reinforcement and frustration. *Psychological Bulletin.* 1968, *69,* 278.

AMSEL, A., & ROUSSEL, J. Motivational properties of frustration: I. Effect on a running response of the addition of frustration to the motivational complex. *Journal of Experimental Psychology,* 1952, *43,* 363–368.

ANAND, B. K., CHHINA, G. S., & SINGH, B. Effect of glucose on the activity of hypothalamic "feeding centers." *Science,* 1962, *138,* 597–598.

ANGER, D. The role of temporal discrimination in the reinforcement of Sidman avoidance behavior. *Journal of the Experimental Analysis of Behavior,* 1963, *6,* 477–506.

ANDERSON, R., MANOOGIAN, S., & REZNICK, S. The undermining and enhancing of intrinsic motivation in preschool children. *Journal of Personality and Social Psychology,* 1976, *34,* 915–922.

ANDERSSON, B. Polydipsia caused by intrahypothalamic injections of hypertonic NaCl solutions. *Experientia,* 1952, *8,* 157–158.

APPLEY, M. H., & TRUMBULL, R. *Psychological stress: Issues in research.* New York: Appleton-Century-Crofts, 1967.

ARDREY, R. *The territorial imperative.* New York: Dell, 1966.

ARONSON, E. Dissonance theory: Progress and problems. In R. P. Abelson, E. Aronson, W. J. McGuire, T. M. Newcomb, M. J. Rosenberg, & P. H. Tannenbaum (Eds.), *Theories of cognitive consistency: A sourcebook.* Chicago: Rand McNally, 1968.

ARONSON, E., & MILLS, J. The effect of severity of initiation on liking for a group. *Journal of Abnormal and Social Psychology,* 1959, *59,* 177–181.

ASCHOFF, J. Circadian rhythms in man. *Science,* 1965, *148,* 1427–1432.

ASERINSKY, E., & KLEITMAN, N. Regularly occurring periods of eye motility and concomitant phenomena during sleep. *Science,* 1953, *118,* 273.

ASHIDA, S. The effects of water and food deprivation in the heart rate of rats. *Psychonomic Science,* 1968, *11,* 245–246.

ASHIDA, S. The effects of deprivation and post-deprivation on the heart rate of rats. *Psychonomic Science,* 1969, *14,* 123–124.

ATKINSON, J. W. & RAYNOR, J. O. (Eds.), *Motivation and achievement.* Washington, D.C.: Winston, 1974.

ATKINSON, J. W. *An introduction to motivation.* New York: Van Nostrand, 1964.

ATKINSON, J. W. Introduction and overview. In J. W. Atkinson & J. O. Raynor (Eds.), *Motivation and achievement.* Washington, D.C.: Winston, 1974.

ATKINSON, J. W., & BIRCH, D. *The dynamics of action.* New York: Wiley, 1970.

ATKINSON, J. W., HEYNS, R. W., & VEROFF, J. The effect of experimental arousal of the affiliation motive on thematic apperception. *Journal of Abnormal and Social Psychology,* 1954, *49,* 405–410.

ATKINSON, J. W., & LITWIN, G. H. Achievement motive and test anxiety conceived as motive to approach success and motive to avoid failure. *Journal of Abnormal and Social Psychology,* 1960, *60,* 52–63.

ATKINSON, J. W. & RAYNOR, J. O. (Eds.) *Motivation and achievement.* Washington, D.C.: Winston, 1974.

ATKINSON, J. W., & WALKER, E. L. The affiliation motive and perceptual sensitivity to faces. *Journal of Abnormal and Social Psychology,* 1956, *53,* 38–41.

AUSUBEL, D. P. Introduction to a threshold concept of primary drives. *American Journal of Psychology,* 1956, *54,* 209–229.

AZRIN, N. H. Some effects of two intermittent schedules of immediate and non-immediate punishment. *Journal of Psychology,* 1956, *42,* 3–21.

AZRIN, N. H., & HOLZ, W. C. Punishment. In W. K. Honig (Ed.), *Operant behavior: Areas of research and application.* New York: Appleton-Century-Crofts, 1966.

BADIA, P., MCBANE, B., SUTER, S., & LEWIS, P. Preference behavior in an immediate versus variably delayed shock situation with and without a warning signal. *Journal of Experimental Psychology,* 1966, *72,* 847–852.

BAER, D. M. Laboratory control of thumbsucking by withdrawal and re-presentation of reinforcement. *Journal of the Experimental Analysis of Behavior,* 1962, *5,* 525–528.

BAILEY, C. J. The effectiveness of drives as cues. *Journal of Comparative and Physiological Psychology,* 1955, *48,* 183–187.

BANDURA, A. *Principles of behavior modification.* New York: Holt, Rinehart and Winston, 1969.

BANDURA, A. *Aggression: A social learning analysis.* Englewood Cliffs, N.J.: Prentice-Hall, 1973.

BANDURA, A., ROSS, D., & ROSS, S. A. A comparative test of the status envy, social power, and secondary reinforcement theories of identificatory learning. *Journal of Abnormal and Social Psychology,* 1963a, *67,* 527–534.

BANDURA, A., ROSS, D., & ROSS, S. A. Imitation of film-mediated aggressive models. *Journal of Abnormal and Social Psychology,* 1963b, *66,* 3–11.

BANDURA, A., & WALTERS, R. H. *Social learning and personality development.* New York: Holt, Rinehart, and Winston, 1963.

BARBER, T. X., DI CARA, L. V., KAMIYA, J., MILLER, N. E., SHAPIRO, D., & STOYVA, J. *Biofeedback and self-control,* 1975/76. Chicago: Aldine, 1976.

BAREFOOT, J. C., & STRAUB, R. B. Opportunity for information search and the effect of false heart rate feedback. *Journal of Personality and Social Psychology,* 1971, *17,* 154–157.

BARNETT, S. A. Experiments on "neophobia" in wild and laboratory rats. *British Journal of Psychology,* 1958, *49,* 195–201.

BARRY, H., III. Effects of strength of drive on learning and on extinction. *Journal of Experimental Psychology,* 1958, *55,* 473–481.

BARTOSHUK, L. M., MCBURNEY, D. H., & PFAFFMANN, C. Taste of sodium chloride solution after adaptation to sodium chloride: Implications for the "water taste." *Science,* 1964, *143,* 967–968.

BAUMEISTER, A., HAWKINS, W. F., & CROMWELL, R. L. Need state and activity level. *Psychological Bulletin,* 1964, *61,* 438–453.

BEACH, F. A. Analysis of factors involved in the arousal, maintenance, and manifestation of sexual excitement in male animals. *Psychosomatic Medicine,* 1942, *4,* 173–198.

BEACH, F. A. Ontogeny and living systems. In B. Schaffner (Ed.), *Group Processes,* New York: Macy Foundation, 1955.

BEACH, F. A. Locks and beagles. *American Psychologist,* 1969, *24,* 971–989.

BECHTEREV, V. M. *La psychologie objective.* Paris: Alcan, 1913.

BECK, R. C. On secondary reinforcement and shock termination. *Psychological Bulletin,* 1961, *58,* 28–45.

BECK, R. C. The rat's adaptation to a 33.5-hour water deprivation schedule. *Journal of Comparative and Physiological Psychology,* 1962, *55,* 646–648.

BECK, R. C. Effects of variations in water need and incentive concentration on barpressing. *Psychological Reports,* 1963, *13,* 31–37.

BECK, R. C. Some effects of restricted water intake on consummatory behavior in the rat. In M. J. Wayner (Ed.), *Thirst.* Oxford: Pergamon, 1964.

BECK, R. C. Drive shifting prior to extinction of bar pressing reinforced by different sucrose incentives. *Psychological Reports,* 1967, *21,* 417–421.

BECK, R. C. Clearance of ingested sucrose solutions from the stomach and intestine of the rat. *Journal of Comparative and Physiological Psychology,* 1967b, *64,* 243–249.

BECK, R. C. Human judgments of stimuli associated with shock termination: Thought experiments vs. real experiments. *Proceedings, 79th Annual Convention of the American Psychological Association,* 1971, Pp. 291–292, Washington, D.C.

BECK, R. C. Who volunteers for transcendental meditation research? Unpublished research, Department of Psychology, Wake Forest University, Winston-Salem, N.C. 27109, 1977.

BECK, R. C., & BIDWELL, L. D. Incentive properties of sucrose and saccharin under different deprivation conditions. *Learning and Motivation,* 1974, *5,* 328–335.

BECK, R. C., & BROOKS, C. I. Human judgments of stimuli associated with shock onset and termination. *Psychonomic Science,* 1967a, *8,* 327–328.

BECK, R. C., & BROOKS, C. I. A test of drive stimulus theory using saline stomach loads. *Psychological Reports,* 1967b, *20,* 1011–1014.

BECK, R. C., & DAVIS, J. V. Effects of real vs. pretend shock on semantic differential judgments and the GSR in some classical conditioning paradigms. *Journal of Research in Psychology,* 1974, *8,* 33–44.

BECK, R. C., & ELLIS, V. T. Sucrose reinforcement thresholds for hungry, thirsty, and non-deprived rats. *Psychonomic Science,* 1966, *4,* 199–200.

BECK, R. C., & GIBSON, C. F. False heart rate feedback and attractiveness ratings as an artifact of experimenter demand. Paper presented at Southeastern Psychological Association Meetings, Hollywood, Florida, May 1977.

BECK, R. C., & MCLEAN, J. F. Effect of schedule on reinforcement and stomach loads on bar pressing by thirsty rats. *Journal of Comparative and Physiological Psychology,* 1967, *63,* 530–533.

BECK, R. C., & NASH, R. Thirsty rats do prefer sucrose solutions. *Psychonomic Science,* 1969, *15,* 19–20.

BECK, R. C., NASH, R., VIERNSTEIN, L., & GORDON, L. Sucrose preferences of hungry and thirsty rats as a function of duration of presentation of test solutions. *Journal of Comparative and Physiological Psychology,* 1972, *78,* 40–50.

BECK, R. C., & OSBERG, A. G. Contrast effects in simulated classical aversive conditioning. Unpublished manuscript, Department of Psychology, Wake Forest University, Winston-Salem, N.C. 27109, 1977.

BEECROFT, R. S. Emotional Conditioning. *Psychonomic Monograph Supplements,* Vol. 2, No. 4 (Whole No. 20). Psychonomic Press. 1967.

BEIDLER, L. M. Properties of chemoreceptors of tongue of rat. *Journal of Neuro-physiology,* 1953, *16,* 595–607.

BEIDLER, L. M. Biophysical approaches to taste. *American Scientist,* 1961, *49,* 421–431.

BELANGER, D., & FELDMAN, S. N. Effects of water deprivation upon heart rate and instrumental activity in the rat. *Journal of Comparative and Physiological Psychology,* 1962, *55,* 220–225.

BELL, R. W., NOAH, J. C., & DAVIS, J. R., Jr. Interactive effects of shock intensity and delay of reinforcement on escape conditioning. *Psychonomic Science,* 1965, *3,* 505–506.

BELLOWS, R. T. Time factors in water drinking in dogs. *American Journal of Physiology,* 1939, *125,* 87–97.

BEM, D. J. An experimental analysis of self-persuasion. *Journal of Experimental Social Psychology,* 1965, *1,* 199–218.

BEM, D. J. Self-perception: An alternative interpretation of cognitive dissonance phenomena. *Psychological Review,* 1967, *74,* 183–200.

BEM, D. J. *Beliefs, attitudes, and human affairs.* Monterey, Calif.: Brooks/Cole, 1970.

BEM, D. J. Self-perception theory. In L. Berkowitz (Ed.), *Advances in experimental social psychology,* (Vol. 6). New York: Academic, 1972.

BENNETT, E. L., DIAMOND, M C., KRECH, D., & ROSENZWEIG, M. R. Chemical and anatomical plasticity of the brain. Science, 1964, *146,* 610–619.

BENSON, H. *Relaxation response.* New York: Morrow, 1975.

BENTHAM, J. *The principles of morals and legislation* [1789]. In E. A. Burtt (Ed.), *The English philosophers from Bacon to Mill.* New York: Modern Library, 1936.

BERGQUIST, E. H., & HOLLEY, J. R. Noncontingent brain stimulation enhancement of reward value of a conditioned stimulus associated with rewarding brain stimulation. *Journal of Comparative and Physiological Psychology,* 1974, *86,* 255–257.

BERKELEY, G. *Principles of human knowledge* (1710). In E. A. Burtt (Ed.), *The English philosophers from Bacon to Mill.* New York: Modern Library, 1939.

BERKOWITZ, L. Some aspects of observed aggression. *Journal of Personality and Social Psychology,* 1965, *2,* 359–369.

BERKOWITZ, L. The contagion of violence: An S-R mediational analysis of some effects of observed aggression. In W. J. Arnold and M. M. Page (Eds.), *Nebraska symposium on motivation, 1970.* Lincoln: University of Nebraska Press, 1970.

BERKOWITZ, L. Some determinants of impulsive aggression: Role of mediated associations with reinforcements for aggression. *Psychological Review,* 1974, *81,* 165–176.

BERKOWITZ, L., & GEEN, R. G. Film violence and the cue properties of available targets. *Journal of Personality and Social Psychology,* 1966, *3,* 525–530.

BERKOWITZ, L., & LE PAGE, A. Weapons as aggression-eliciting stimuli. *Journal of Personality and Social Psychology,* 1967, *7,* 202–207.

BERLEW, D. E. Interpersonal sensitivity and motive strength. *Journal of Abnormal and Social Psychology,* 1961, *63,* 390–394.

BERLYNE, D. E. *Conflict, arousal, and curiosity.* New York: McGraw-Hill, 1960.

BERLYNE, D. E. *Arousal and reinforcement.* In D. Levine (Ed.), *Nebraska symposium on motivation, 1967.* Lincoln: University of Nebraska Press, 1967.

BERLYNE, D. E. The reward value of indifferent stimulation. In J. T. Tapp (Ed.), *Reinforcement and behavior.* New York: Academic, 1969.

BERLYNE, D. E. *Aesthetics and psychobiology.* New York: Appleton-Century-Crofts, 1971.

BERMANT, G., & DAVIDSON, J. *Biological bases of sexual behavior.* New York: Harper & Row, 1974.

BERNARD, C. An introduction to the study of experimental medicine (1865). (H. C. Greene, Trans.) New York: Dover, 1957.

BERSCHEID, E., & WALSTER, E. H. *Interpersonal attraction.* Reading, Mass.: Addison-Wesley, 1969.

BERSCHEID, E., & WALSTER, E. A little bit about love. In T. L. Huston (Ed.), *Foundations of interpersonal attraction.* New York: Academic, 1974a.

BERSCHEID, E., & WALSTER, E. Physical attractiveness. In L. Berkowitz (Ed.), *Advances in experimental social psychology* (Vol. 7). New York: Academic, 1974b.

BERSH, P. J. The influence of two variables upon the establishment of a secondary reinforcer for operant responses. *Journal of Experimental Psychology,* 1951, *41,* 62–73.

BETTELHEIM, B. *The informed heart.* New York: Free Press, 1960.

BEVAN, W. The contextual basis of behavior. *American Psychologist,* 1968, *23,* 701–704.

BEXTON, W. H., HERON, W., & SCOTT, T. H. Effects of decreased variation in the sensory environment. *Canadian Journal of Psychology,* 1954, *8,* 70–76.

BINDRA, D. Neuropsychological interpretation of the effects of drive and incentive motivation on general activity and instrumental behavior. *Psychological Review,* 1968, *75,* 1–22.

BINDRA, D. The interrelated mechanisms of reinforcement and motivation, and the nature of their influence on response. In W. J. Arnold and D. Levine (Eds.), *Nebraska symposium on motivation.* Lincoln: University of Nebraska Press, 1969.

BINDRA, D., & BLOND, J. A time-sample method for measuring general activity and its components. *Canadian Journal of Psychology,* 1958, *12,* 74–76.

BINDRA, D., & PALFAI, T. Nature of positive and negative incentive-motivational effects on general activity. *Journal of Comparative and Physiological Psychology,* 1967, *69,* 288–297.

BIRCH, D., BURNSTEIN, E., & CLARK, R. A. Response strength as a function of hours of food deprivation under a controlled maintenance schedule. *Journal of Comparative and Physiological Psychology,* 1958, *51,* 350–354.

BIRK, L., CRIDER, A., SHAPIRO, D., & TURSKY, B. Operant electrodermal conditioning under partial curarization. *Journal of Comparative and Physiological Psychology,* 1966, *52,* 165–166.

BITTERMAN, M. E. Learning in animals. In H. Helson & W. Bevan (Eds.), *Contemporary approaches to psychology.* New York: Van Nostrand, 1967.

BITTERMAN, M. E., FEDDERSON, W. F., & TYLER, D. W. Secondary reinforcement and the discrimination hypothesis. *American Journal of Psychology,* 1953, *66,* 456–464.

BLACK, A. H. Autonomic aversive conditioning in infrahuman subjects. In F. R. Brush (Ed.), *Aversive conditioning and learning.* New York: Academic, 1971.

BLACK, A. H., CARLSON, N. J., & SOLOMON, R. L. Exploratory studies of the conditioning of autonomic responses on curarized dogs. *Psychological Monographs,* 1962, *76,* (Whole No. 548).

BLACK, R. W. On the combination of drive and incentive motivation. *Psychological Review,* 1965, *72,* 310–317.

BLACK, R. W. Incentive motivation and the parameters of reward in instrumental conditioning. In W. J. Arnold & D. Levine (Eds.), *Nebraska symposium on motivation.* Lincoln: University of Nebraska Press, 1969.

BLASS, E. M., & HALL, W. G. Drinking termination: Interactions among hydrational, orogastric, and behavioral control in rats. *Psychological Review,* 1976, *83,* 356–374.

BOBBITT, R. G., & BECK, R. C. Semantic differential judgments of single and multiple conditioned stimuli with an aversive delay conditioning paradigm. *Journal of Experimental Psychology,* 1971, *89,* 398–402.

BOLLES, R. C. A psychophysical study of hunger in the rat. *Journal of Experimental Psychology,* 1962a, *63,* 387–390.

BOLLES, R. C. The readiness to eat and drink: The effect of deprivation conditions. *Journal of Comparative and Physiological Psychology,* 1962b, *55,* 230–234.

BOLLES, R. C. A failure to find evidence of the estrus cycle in the rat's activity level. *Psychological Reports,* 1963, *12,* 530.

BOLLES, R. C. *Theory of motivation.* New York: Harper & Row, 1967.

BOLLES, R. C. Species-specific defense reactions and avoidance learning. *Psychological Review,* 1970, *71,* 32–48.

BOLLES, R. C. Species-specific defense reactions. In F. R. Brush (Ed.), *Aversive conditioning and learning.* New York: Academic, 1971.

BOLLES, R. C. Reinforcement, expectancy, and learning. *Psychological Review,* 1972, *79,* 394–409.

BOLLES, R. C. *Theory of motivation.* (2nd ed.) New York: Harper & Row, 1975.

BOLLES, R. C., GROSSEN, N. E., HARGRAVE, G. E., & DUNCAN, P. M. Effects of conditioned appetitive stimuli on the acquisition and extinction of a runway response. *Journal of Experimental Psychology,* 1970, *85,* 138–140.

BOLLES, R. C., & MOOT, S. A. Derived motives. *Annual Review of Psychology,* 1972, *23,* 51–72.

BOLLES, R. C., & MORLOCK, H. Some assymmetrical drive summation phenomena. *Psychological Reports,* 1960, *6,* 373–378.

BOLLES, R. C., & PETRINOVITCH, L. A technique for obtaining rapid drive discrimination in the rat. *Journal of Comparative and Physiological Psychology,* 1954, *47,* 378–380.

BONVALLET, M., & ALLEN, M. B. Prolonged spontaneous and evoked reticular activation following discrete bulbar lesions. *Electroencephalography and Clinical Neurophysiology,* 1963, *15,* 969–988.

BOOTZIN, R. R., HERMAN, C. P., & NICASSIO, P. The power of suggestion: Another examination of misattribution and insomnia. *Journal of Personality and Social Psychology,* 1976, *34,* 673–679.

BOWER, G. H., FOWLER, H., & TRAPOLD, M. A. Escape learning as a function of amount of shock reduction. *Journal of Experimental Psychology,* 1959, *58,* 482–484.

BOWER, G. H., McLEAN, J., & MEACHAM, J. Value of knowing when reinforcement is due. *Journal of Comparative and Physiological Psychology,* 1966, *62,* 183–192.

BOYATZIS, R. E. Affiliation motivation. In D. C. McClelland & R. S. Steel (Eds.), *Human motivation: A book of readings.* Morristown, N.J.: General Learning Press, 1973.

BRADY, J. V. Ulcers in "executive" monkeys. *Scientific American,* 1958, *199,* 95–100.

BREHM, J. W. Post-decision changes in the desirability of alternatives. *Journal of Abnormal and Social Psychology,* 1956, *52,* 384–389.

BREHM, J. W. Motivational effects of cognitive dissonance. *Nebraska symposium on motivation.* Lincoln: University of Nebraska Press, 1962.

BREHM, J. W., & COHEN, A. R. *Explorations in cognitive dissonance.* New York: Wiley, 1962.

BRELAND, K., & BRELAND, M. The misbehavior of organisms. *American Psychologist,* 1961, *16,* 681–684.

BRENNER, J., EISSENBERG, E., & MIDDAUGH, S. Respiratory and somatomotor factors associated with operant conditioning of cardiovascular responses in curarized rats. In P. A. Obrist, A. H. Black, J. Brener, & L. V. DiCara (Eds.), *Cardiovascular psychophysiology.* Chicago: Aldine, 1974.

BRIDGMAN, P. W. *The logic of modern physics.* New York: Macmillan, 1927.

BRILLHART, C. A. The relationship between heart rate, activity, and bar pressing with varying levels of sucrose incentive. Unpublished master's thesis, Wake Forest University, 1975.

BRILLHART, A. C., OSBERG, A. G., & BECK, R. C. Heart rates of hungry or thirsty rats during sucrose presentation. *Psychological Reports,* 1975, *36,* 907–910.

BROADHURST, P. L. Experiments in psychogenetics: Applications of biometrical genetics to behaviour. In H. J. Eysenck (Ed.), *Experiments in personality* (Vol. 1: *Psychogenetics and psychopharmacology).* London: Routledge & Kegan Paul, 1960.

BROCK, T. C. Effects of prior dishonesty on postdecision dissonance. *Journal of Abnormal and Social Psychology,* 1963, *66,* 325–331.

BROCK, T. C., & BUSS, A. H. Dissonance, aggression, and evaluation of pain. *Journal of Abnormal and Social Psychology,* 1962, *65,* 192–202.

BROCK, T. C., & BUSS, A. H. Effects of justification for aggression in communication with the victim on post-aggression dissonance. *Journal of Abnormal and Social Psychology,* 1964, *68,* 403–412.

BROGDEN, W. J., LIPMAN, E. A., & CULLER, E. The role of incentive in conditioning and learning. *American Journal of Psychology,* 1938, *51,* 109–117.

BROOKS, C. I. Frustration to nonreward following limited reward experience. *Journal of Experimental Psychology,* 1969, *81,* 403–405.

BROWN, F. A., Jr. Hypothesis of environmental timing of the clock. In J. D. Palmer (Ed.), *The biological clock: Two views.* New York: Academic, 1970.

BROWN, J. L. The effect of drive on learning with secondary reinforcement. *Journal of Comparative and Physiological Psychology,* 1956, *49,* 254–260.

BROWN, J. L. *The evolution of behavior.* New York: Norton, 1975.

BROWN, J. S. Gradients of approach and avoidance responses and their relation to level of motivation. *Journal of Comparative and Physiological Psychology,* 1948, *41,* 450–465.

BROWN, J. S. Pleasure seeking and the drive reduction hypothesis. *Psychological Review,* 1955, *62,* 169–179.

BROWN, J. S. *The motivation of behavior.* New York: McGraw-Hill, 1961.

BROWN, J. S. Factors affecting self-punitive locomotor behavior. In B. A. Campbell & R. M. Church (Eds.), *Punishment and aversive behavior.* New York: Appleton-Century-Crofts, 1969.

BROWN, J. S., & BELLONI, M. Performance as a function of deprivation time following periodic feeding in an isolated environment. *Journal of Comparative and Physiological Psychology,* 1963, *56,* 105–110.

BROWN, J. S., & FARBER, I. E. Emotions conceptualized as intervening variables—With suggestions toward a theory of frustration. *Psychological Bulletin,* 1951, *48,* 465–495.

BROWN, J. S., & JACOBS, A. Role of fear in motivation and acquisition of responses. *Journal of Experimental Psychology,* 1949, *39,* 747–759.

BROWN, J. S., KALISH, H. I., & FARBER, I. E. Conditioned fear as revealed by magnitude of startle response to an auditory stimulus. *Journal of Experimental Psychology,* 1951, *41,* 317–328.

BRUSH, F. R. (Ed.), *Aversive conditioning and learning.* New York: Academic, 1971.

BRUSH, F. R., MYER, J. S., & PALMER, M. E. Effects of kind of prior training and intersession interval upon subsequent avoidance learning. *Journal of Comparative and Physiological Psychology,* 1963, *56,* 539–545.

BUGELSKI, B. R. Extinction with and without sub-goal reinforcement. *Journal of Comparative Psychology,* 1938, *26,* 121–133.

BUGELSKI, B. R. *The psychology of learning.* New York: Holt, Rinehart, and Winston, 1956.

BURGESS, T. D. G., & SALES, S. M. Attitudinal effects of "mere exposure": A re-evaluation. *Journal of Experimental Social Psychology,* 1971, *7,* 461–472.

BUSS, A. H., BOOKER, A., & BUSS, E. Firing a weapon and aggression. *Journal of Personality and Social Psychology,* 1972, *22,* 296–302.

BUTLER, R. A., & HARLOW, H. F. Persistence of visual exploration in monkeys. *Journal of Comparative and Physiological Psychology,* 1954, *47,* 258–263.

BYKOV, K. M. *The cerebral cortex and the internal organs.* (W. H. Gantt, Trans. and Ed.) New York: Chemical Publishing, 1957.

BYRNE, D. *An introduction to personality.* (2nd ed.) Englewood Cliffs, N.J.: Prentice-Hall, 1974.

BYRNE, D., & NELSON, D. Attraction as a linear function of proportion of positive reinforcements. *Journal of Personality and Social Psychology,* 1965, *1,* 659–663.

CALDER, B. J., & STAW, B. M. The interaction of intrinsic and extrinsic motivation: Some methodological notes. *Journal of Personality and Social Psychology,* 1975, *31,* 76–80.

CAMP, D. S., RAYMOND, G. A., & CHURCH, R. M. Temporal relationship between response and punishment. *Journal of Experimental Psychology,* 1967, *74,* 114–123.

CAMPBELL, B. A. Theory and research on the effects of water deprivation on random activity in the rat. In M. J. Wayner (Ed.), *Thirst.* Oxford: Pergamon, 1964.

CAMPBELL, B. A., & CHURCH, R. M. *Punishment and aversive behavior.* New York: Appleton-Century-Crofts, 1969.

CAMPBELL, B. A., & CICALA, G. A. Studies of water deprivation in rats as a function of age. *Journal of Comparative and Physiological Psychology,* 1962, *55,* 763–768.

CAMPBELL, B. A., & KRAELING, D. Response strengths as a function of drive level and amount of drive reduction. *Journal of Experimental Psychology,* 1953, *45,* 97–101.

CAMPBELL, B.A., & KRAELING, D. Response strength as a function of drive level during training and extinction. *Journal of Comparative and Physiological Psychology,* 1954, *47,* 101–103.

CAMPBELL, B. A., & MASTERSON, F. A. Psychophysics of punishment. In B. A. Campbell & R. M. Church (Eds.), *Punishment and aversive behavior.* New York: Appleton-Century-Crofts, 1969.

CAMPBELL, B. A., & SHEFFIELD, F. D. Relation of random activity to food deprivation. *Journal of Comparative and Physiological Psychology,* 1953, *46,* 320–322.

CAMPBELL, B. A., SMITH, N. F., MISANIN, J. R., & JAYNES, J. Species differences in activity during hunger and thirst. *Journal of Comparative and Physiological Psychology,* 1966, *61,* 123–127.

CAMPBELL, D. T., & FISKE, D. Convergent and discriminant validation by the multitrait-multimethod matrix. *Psychological Bulletin,* 1959, *56,* 81–105.

CANNON, W. B. The James-Lange theory of emotions: A critical examination and an alternative theory. *American Journal of Psychology,* 1927, *39,* 106–124.

CANNON, W. B. Hunger and thirst. In C. Murchison (Ed.), *Handbook of general experimental psychology.* Worcester, Mass.: Clark University Press, 1934.

CANNON, W. B. *The wisdom of the body.* New York: Norton, 1939.

CANTOR, J. R., ZILLMANN, D., & BRYANT, J. Enhancement of experienced sexual arousal in response to erotic stimuli through misattribution of unrelated residual excitation. *Journal of Personality and Social Psychology,* 1975, *32,* 69–75.

CANTRIL, H., & HUNT, W. A. Emotional effects produced by the injection of adrenalin. *American Journal of Psychology,* 1932, *44,* 300–307.

CAPALDI, E. J. A sequential hypothesis of instrumental learning. In K. W. Spence & J. T. Spence (Eds.), *The psychology of learning and motivation* (Vol. 1). New York: Academic, 1967.

CARR, H. A. *Psychology, a study of mental activity.* New York: Longmans, 1925.

CASTANEDA, C. *The teachings of Don Juan: A Yaqui way of knowledge.* New York: Ballantine, 1968.

CHAPANIS, N. P., & CHAPANIS, A. Cognitive dissonance: Five years later. *Psychological Bulletin,* 1964, *61,* 1–22.

CHRISTIE, R. & GEIS, F. L. *Studies in Machiavellianism.* New York: Academic, 1970.

CHURCH, R. M. Response suppression. In B. A. Campbell & R. M. Church (Eds.), *Punishment and aversive behavior.* New York: Appleton-Century-Crofts, 1969.

COFER, C. N., & APPLEY, M. H. *Motivation: Theory and research.* New York: Wiley, 1964.

COHEN, A. R., BREHM, J. W., & FLEMING, W. H. Attitude change and justification for compliance. *Journal of Abnormal and Social Psychology,* 1958, *56,* 276–278.

COHEN, J. S., & OÖSTENDORP, A. Incentive preference under two levels of water deprivation in the rat. *Bulletin of the Psychonomic Society,* 1976, *8,* 381–384.

COHEN, P. S., & TOKIEDA, F. Sucrose-water preference reversal in the water-deprived rat. *Journal of Comparative and Physiological Psychology,* 1972, *79,* 254–258.

COLLIER, G. Some properties of saccharin as a reinforcer. *Journal of Experimental Psychology,* 1962, *64,* 184–191.

COLLIER, G. Thirst as a determinant of reinforcement. In M. J. Wayner (Ed.), *Thirst,* Oxford: Pergamon, 1964.

COLLIER, G., HIRSCH, E., & HAMLIN, P. The ecological determinants of reinforcement. *Physiology and Behavior,* 1972, *9,* 705–716.

COLLIER, G., KANAREK, R., HIRSCH, E., & MARWINE, A. Environmental determinants of feeding behavior or how to turn a rat into a tiger. In M. H. Siegel and H. P. Zeigler (Eds.), *Psychological research: The inside story.* New York: Harper & Row, 1976.

COLLIER, G., & KNARR, F. Defense of water balance in the rat. *Journal of Comparative and Physiological Psychology,* 1966, *61,* 5–10.

COLLIER, G., & MARX, M. Changes in performance as a function of shifts in the magnitude of reinforcement. *Journal of Experimental Psychology,* 1959, *57,* 305–309.

COLLIER, G., & MYERS, L. The loci of reinforcement. *Journal of Experimental Psychology,* 1961, *61,* 57–66.

COLLINS, B. E. Four components of the Rotter Internal-External Scale. *Journal of Personality and Social Psychology,* 1974, *29,* 381–391.

COMPTON-BURNETT, I. *Bullivant and the lambs.* New York: Knopf, 1949.

CONANT, J. B. *On understanding science: An historical approach.* New Haven: Yale University Press, 1947.

CORBIT, J. D. Osmotic thirst: Theoretical and experimental analysis. *Journal of Comparative and Physiological Psychology,* 1969, *67,* 3–14.

COUGHLIN, R. C. The aversive properties of withdrawing positive reinforcement: A review of the recent literature. *Psychological Record,* 1972, *22,* 333–354.

CRAIG, W. Appetites and aversions as constituents of instincts. *Biological Bulletin,* 1918, *34,* 91–107.

CRAVENS, R. W., & RENNER, K. E. Conditioned appetitive drive states: Empirical evidence and theoretical status. *Psychological Bulletin,* 1970, *73,* 212–220.

CRESPI, L. P. Quantitative variation of incentive and performance in the white rat. *American Journal of Psychology,* 1942, *55,* 467–517.

CRESPI, L. P. Amount of reinforcement and level of performance. *Psychological Review,* 1944, *51,* 341–357.

CROMWELL, R., ROSENTHAL, D., SHAKOW, D., & KAHN, T. Reaction time, locus of control, choice behavior, and descriptions of parental behavior in schizophrenic and normal subjects. *Journal of Personality,* 1961, *29,* 363–380.

CRONBACH, L. J. *Essentials of psychological testing.* New York: Harper & Row, 1970.

CRONBACH, L. J., & MEEHL, P. E. Construct validity in psychological tests. *Psychological Bulletin,* 1955, *52,* 281–302.

CROWDER, W. F., GAY, B. R., BRIGHT, M. G., & LEE, M. F. Secondary reinforcement or response facilitation? III. Reconditioning. *Journal of Psychology,* 1959, *48,* 307–310.

CROWDER, W. F., GAY, B. R., FLEMING, W. C., & HURST, R. W. Secondary reinforcement or response facilitation? IV. The retention method. *Journal of Psychology,* 1959, *48,* 311–314.

CROWDER, W. F., GILL, K., Jr., HODGE, C. C., & NASH, F. A., Jr. Secondary reinforcement or response facilitation? II. Response acquisition. *Journal of Psychology,* 1959, *48,* 303–306.

CROWDER, W. F., MORRIS, J. B., & MCDANIEL, M. H. Secondary reinforcement or response facilitation? I. Resistance to extinction. *Journal of Psychology,* 1959, *48,* 299–302.

CULLEN, J. W., & SCARBOROUGH, B. B. Effect of a preoperative sugar preference on bar pressing for salt by the adrenalectomized rat. *Journal of Comparative and Physiological Psychology,* 1969, *67,* 415–420.

DALTON, K. Menstruation and crime. *British Medical Journal,* 1961, *3,* 1752–1753.

DALY, H. B. Reinforcing properties of escape from frustration aroused in various learning situations. G. H. Bower (Ed.) *The psychology of learning and motivation* (Vol. 8). New York: Academic, 1974.

D'AMATO, M. R. Transfer of secondary reinforcement across the hunger and thirst drives. *Journal of Experimental Psychology,* 1955, *49,* 352–356.

D'AMATO, M. R. *Experimental psychology: Methodology, psychophysics, and learning.* New York: McGraw-Hill, 1970.

DANZIGER, K. The interaction of hunger and thirst in the rat. *Quarterly Journal of Experimental Psychology,* 1953, *5,* 10–21.

DARWIN, C. R. *The origin of the species.* [1859.] Modern Library, No. G 27. New York: Random House, 1936.

DASHIELL, J. F. A quantitative demonstration of animal drive. *Journal of Comparative and Physiological Psychology,* 1925, *5,* 205–208.

DAVIS, J. D. The reinforcing effect of weak-light onset as a function of amount of food deprivation. *Journal of Comparative and Physiological Psychology,* 1958, *51,* 496–498.

DAVIS, J. D., COLLINS, B. J., & LEVINE, M. W. Peripheral control of drinking: Gastrointestinal filling as a negative feedback signal, a theoretical and experimental analysis. *Journal of Comparative and Physiological Psychology,* 1975, *89,* 985–1002.

DAVIS, J. D., GALLAGHER, R. J., & LADLOVE, R. F. Food intake controlled by a blood factor. *Science,* 1967, *156,* 1247–1248.

DAVIS, J. D., & MILLER, N. E. Fear and pain: Their effect on self-injection of amobarbital sodium by rats. *Science,* 1963, *141,* 1286–1287.

DAVIS, K. E., & JONES, E. E. Changes in interpersonal perception as a means of reducing cognitive dissonance. *Journal of Abnormal and Social Psychology,* 1960, *61,* 402–410.

DAVITZ, J. R. Reinforcement of fear at the beginning and end of shock. *Journal of Comparative and Physiological Psychology,* 1955, *48,* 152–155.

DAVITZ, J. R., & MASON, D. J. Socially facilitated reduction of a fear response in rats. *Journal of Comparative and Physiological Psychology,* 1955, *48,* 149–151.

DAVITZ, J. R., MASON, D. J., MOWRER, O. H., & VIEK, P. Conditioning of fear: A function of the delay of reinforcement. *American Journal of Psychology,* 1957, *70,* 69–74.

DE CHARMS, R. Affiliation motivation and productivity in small groups. *Journal of Abnormal and Social Psychology,* 1957, *55,* 222–226.

DE CHARMS, R. *Personal causation: The internal affective determinants of behavior.* New York: Academic, 1968.

DE CHARMS, R., & MOELLER, G. H. Values expressed in children's readers: 1800–1950. *Journal of Abnormal and Social Psychology,* 1962, *64,* 136–142.

DECI, E. L. *Intrinsic motivation.* New York: Plenum, 1975.

DELGADO, J. Cerebral heterostimulation in a monkey colony. *Science,* 1963, *141,* 161–163.

DELGADO, J. M. R., ROBERTS, W. W., & MILLER, N. E. Learning motivated by electrical stimulation of the brain. *American Journal of Physiology,* 1954, *179,* 587–593.

DEMBER, W. N. *The psychology of perception.* New York: Holt, Rinehart and Winston, 1960.

DEMBER, W. N. The new look in motivation. *American Scientist,* 1965, *53,* 409–427.

DEMBER, W. N., & EARL, R. W. Analysis of exploratory, manipulatory, and curiosity behaviors. *Psychological Review,* 1957, *64,* 91–96.

DEMENT, W. The effect of dream deprivation. *Science,* 1960, *131,* 1705–1707.

DEMENT, W. The biological role of REM sleep (circa 1968). In W. B. Webb (Ed.), *Sleep: An active process.* Glenview, Ill.: Scott, Foresman, 1973.

DEMENT, W., & KLEITMAN, N. Cyclic variations in EEG during sleep and their relation to eye movements, body motility, and dreaming. *Electroencephalography and Clinical Neurophysiology,* 1957, *9,* 673–690.

DENENBERG, V. H. Early experience and emotional development. *Scientific American,* 1963, *208,* 138–146.

DENNY, M. R. Relaxation theory and experiments. In F. R. Brush (Ed.), *Aversive conditioning and learning.* New York: Academic, 1971.

DENNY, M. R., & ADELMAN, H. M. Elicitation theory: I. An analysis of two typical learning situations. *Psychological Review,* 1955, *62,* 290–296.

DESCARTES, R. Les passions l'ame [1650]. In H. A. P. Torrey (Tr.), *The philosophy of Descartes in extracts from his writings.* New York: Holt, 1892.

DETHIER, V. G. Insects and the concept of motivation. In D. Levine (Ed.), *Nebraska symposium on motivation.* Lincoln: University of Nebraska Press, 1966.

DETHIER, V. G. The hungry fly. *Psychology Today,* 1967, *1,* 64–73.

DEUTSCH, J. A. *The structural basis of behavior.* Chicago: University of Chicago Press, 1960.

DEUTSCH, J. A., & HOWARTH, C. I. Some tests of a theory of intracranial self-stimulation. *Psychological Review,* 1963, *70,* 444–460.

DICARA, L. V., & MILLER, N. E. Changes in heart rate instrumentally learned by curarized rats as avoidance responses. *Journal of Comparative and Physiological Psychology,* 1968, *65,* 8–12.

DINSMOOR, J. A. A quantitative comparison of the discriminative and reinforcing functions of a stimulus. *Journal of Experimental Psychology,* 1950, *40,* 458–472.

DINSMOOR, J. A. Punishment: I. The avoidance hypothesis. *Psychological Review,* 1954, *61,* 34–46.

DOLLAR, B. *Humanizing classroom discipline: A behavioral approach.* New York: Harper & Row, 1972.

DOLLARD, J., DOOB, L., MILLER, N. E., MOWRER, O. H., & SEARS, R. *Frustration and aggression.* New Haven, Conn.: Yale University Press, 1939.

DOLLARD, J., & MILLER, N. E. *Social learning and imitation.* New Haven, Conn.: Yale University Press, 1941.

DOUGLAS, R. J. Cues for spontaneous alternation. *Journal of Comparative and Physiological Psychology,* 1966, *62,* 171–183.

DUCHARME, R. Physical activity and deactivation: Abatement of cardiac rhythm during the course of instrumental activity. *Canadian Journal of Psychology,* 1966, *20,* 445–454.

DUFFY, E. Emotion: An example of the need for reorientation in psychology. *Psychological Review,* 1934, *41,* 184–198.

DUFFY, E. *Activation and behavior.* New York: Wiley, 1962.

DUNCAN, G. M. (Tr.), *The philosophical works of Leibnitz.* New Haven: Yale, 1890.

DUNHAM, P. J. Contrasted conditions of reinforcement: A selective critique. *Psychological Bulletin,* 1968, *69,* 295–315.

DUNHAM, P. J. Punishment: Method and theory. *Psychological Review,* 1971, *78,* 58–70.

DUNLAP, K. Are there any instincts? *Journal of Abnormal Psychology,* 1919, *14,* 307–311.

DYAL, J. On the combination of drive and incentive motivation: A critical comment. *Psychological Reports,* 1967, *20,* 543–550.

EBBINGHAUS, H. *Memory* [1885]. H. Ruger & C. Bussenius (Tr.), New York: Dover Publications, 1964.

EGBERT, L., BATTIT, G., WELCH, C., & BARTLETT, M. Reduction of postoperative pain by encouragement and instruction of patients. *New England Journal of Medicine,* 1964, *270,* 825–827.

EGGER, M. D., & MILLER, N. E. Secondary reinforcement in rats as a function of information value and reliability of the stimulus, *Journal of Experimental Psychology,* 1962, *64,* 97–104.

EGGER, M. D., & MILLER, N. E. When is a reward reinforcing? An experimental study of the information hypothesis. *Journal of Comparative and Physiological Psychology,* 1963, *56,* 132–137.

EIBL-EIBESFELDT, I. *Ethology: The biology of behavior.* (2nd ed., E. Klinghammer, Trans.) New York: Holt, Rinehart and Winston, 1975.

EISENBERGER, R. Explanation of rewards that do not reduce tissue needs. *Psychological Bulletin,* 1972, *77,* 319–339.

EISMAN, E. Effects of deprivation and consummatory activity on heart rate. *Journal of Comparative and Physiological Psychology,* 1966, *62,* 71–75.

EISMAN, E., THEIOS, J., & LINTON, M. Habit strength as a function of drive in a bar-pressing situation. *Psychological Report,* 1961, *9,* 583–590.

ELDER, T., NOBLIN, C. D., & MAHER, B. A. The extinction of fear as a function of distance versus dissimilarity from the original conflict situation. *Journal of Abnormal and Social Psychology,* 1961, *64,* 97–112.

ELLIOTT, R. Heart rate, activity, and activation in rats. *Psychophysiology,* 1975, *12,* 298–305.

ELLIS, V. Reinforcing effects of paired sucrose solutions as a function of food deprivation. Unpublished master's thesis, Wake Forest University, 1968.

ENDLER, N. S., & HUNT, J. McV. Sources of behavioral variance as measured by the S-R inventory of anxiousness. *Psychological Bulletin,* 1966, *65,* 336-346.

ENDLER, N. S., HUNT, J. McV., & ROSENSTEIN, A. J. An S-R inventory of anxiousness. *Psychological Monographs,* 1962, *76,* (Whole No. 536).

ENSCORE, S. D., MONK, D. L., KOZUB, F. J., & BLICK, K. A. Establishment of a secondary drive based on thirst: A replication. *Journal of General Psychology,* 1976, *94,* 193-197.

ENTWISLE, D. R. To dispel fantasies about fantasy-based measures of achievement motivation. *Psychological Bulletin,* 1972, *77,* 377-391.

EPLEY, S. W. Reduction of the behavioral effects of aversive stimulation by the presence of companions. *Psychological Bulletin,* 1974, *81,* 271-283.

EPSTEIN, A. N. Oropharyngeal factors in feeding and drinking. In C. F. Code (Ed.), *Handbook of physiology* (Section 6. Alimentary canal. Vol. 1). Washington, D.C.: American Physiological Society, 1967.

EPSTEIN, A. N. The lateral hypothalamic syndrome: Its implications for the physiological psychology of hunger and thirst. In E. Stellar and J. M. Sprague (Eds.), *Progress in physiological psychology.* New York: Academic, 1971.

EPSTEIN, A. N., KISSILEFF, H. R., & STELLAR, E. *The neuropsychology of thirst: New findings and advances in concepts.* Washington, D.C.: Winston, 1973.

EPSTEIN, A. N., & TEITELBAUM, P. Regulation of food intake in the absence of taste, smell, and other oropharyngeal sensations. *Journal of Comparative and Physiological Psychology,* 1962, *55,* 753-759.

EPSTEIN, S. Toward a unified theory of anxiety. In B. Maher (Ed.), *Progress in experimental personality research.* New York: Academic, 1967.

EPSTEIN, S., & FENZ, W. D. Steepness of approach and avoidance gradients in humans as a function of experience: Theory and experiment. *Journal of Experimental Psychology,* 1965, *70,* 1-12.

ERICKSON, R. P. Sensory neural patterns and gustation. In Y. Zotterman (Ed.), *Olfaction and taste.* New York: Macmillan, 1963.

ERICKSON, R. P. Neural coding of taste quality. In M. Kare & O. Maller (Eds.), *The chemical senses and nutrition.* Baltimore, Md.: The Johns Hopkins Press, 1967.

ERON, L. D., LEFKOWITZ, M. M., HUESMANN, L. R., & WALDER, L. Q. Does television violence cause aggression? *American Psychologist,* 1972, *27,* 253-263.

ESTES, W. K. An experimental study of punishment. *Psychological Monographs,* 1944, *57* (Whole No. 263).

ESTES, W. K. Stimulus-response theory of drive. In M. R. Jones (Ed.), *Nebraska symposium on motivation.* Lincoln: University of Nebraska Press, 1958.

ESTES, W. K. Reinforcement in human learning. In J. T. Tapp (Ed.), *Reinforcement and behavior.* New York: Academic, 1969.

ESTES, W. K., & SKINNER, B. F. Some quantitative properties of anxiety. *Journal of Experimental Psychology,* 1941, *29,* 390-400.

EVANS, S. Failure of the interaction paradigm as a test of Hull vs. Spence. *Psychological Reports,* 1967, *20,* 551-554.

FABRICIUS, E. Some experiments on imprinting phenomena in ducks. *Proceedings of the 10th International Ornithological Congress,* 1951, 375-379.

FALBO, T., & BECK, R. C. Naive psychology and the attributional model of achievement. Unpublished manuscript, Department of Psychology, Wake Forest University, Winston-Salem, N.C. 27109, 1977.

FALK, J. L. The behavior regulation of water-electrolyte balance. In M. R. Jones (Ed.), *Nebraska symposium on motivation.* Lincoln: University of Nebraska Press, 1961.

FALK, J. L. Conditions producing psychogenic polydispia in animals. *Annals of the New York Academy of Sciences,* 1969, *157,* 569–593.

FANTZ, R. L. The origin of form perception. *Scientific American,* 1961, *204,* 66–72.

FENZ, W. D., & EPSTEIN, S., Gradients of physiological arousal of experienced and novice parachutists as a function of approaching a jump. *Psychosomatic Medicine,* 1967, *29,* 33–51.

FESHBACH, S., & SINGER, R. D. *Television and aggression: An experimental field study.* San Francisco: Jossey-Bass, 1971.

FESTINGER, L. A theory of social comparison processes. *Human Relations,* 1954, *7,* 117–140.

FESTINGER, L. *A theory of cognitive dissonance.* Evanston, Ill.: Row, Peterson, 1957.

FESTINGER, L., & CARLSMITH, J. M. Cognitive consequences of forced compliance. *Journal of Abnormal and Social Psychology,* 1959, *58,* 203–210.

FINGER, F. W. Effect of food deprivation on running-wheel activity in naive rats. *Psychological Reports,* 1965, *16,* 753–757.

FINGER, F. L., REID, L. S., & WEASNER, M. H. The effect of reinforcement upon activity during cyclic food deprivation. *Journal of Comparative and Physiological Psychology,* 1957, *50,* 495–498.

FINK, J. B., & PATTON, R. M. Decrement of a learned drinking response accompanying changes in several stimulus characteristics. *Journal of Comparative and Physiological Psychology,* 1953, *46,* 23–27.

FISHER, A. E. Chemical stimulation of the brain. *Scientific American,* 1964, *210,* 60–68.

FISKE, D. W., & MADDI, S. R. A conceptual framework. In D. W. Fiske & S. R. Maddi (Eds.), *Functions of varied experience.* Homewood, Ill.: Dorsey, 1961a.

FISKE, D. W., & MADDI, S. R. (Eds.), *Functions of varied experience.* Homewood, Ill.: Dorsey, 1961b.

FLAHERTY, C. F., & AVDZEJ, A. Transituational negative contrast. *Animal Learning and Behavior,* 1976, *4,* 49–52.

FLAHERTY, C. F., & LARGEN, J. Within-subjects positive and negative contrast effects in rats. *Journal of Comparative and Physiological Psychology,* 1975, *88,* 653–664.

FOLK, G. E., Jr. *Textbook of environmental physiology.* Philadelphia: Lea and Febiger, 1974.

FORGUS, R. H., & MELAMED, L. E. *Perception: A cognitive-stage approach.* (2nd ed.) New York: McGraw-Hill, 1976.

FOWLER, H. Exploratory motivation and animal handling: The effect on runway performance of start-box exposure time. *Journal of Comparative and Physiological Psychology,* 1963, *56,* 866–871.

FOWLER, H. *Curiosity and exploratory behavior.* New York: Macmillan, 1965.

FOWLER, H. Suppression and facilitation by response-contingent shock. In F. R. Brush (Ed.), *Aversive conditioning and learning.* New York: Academic, 1971.

FOWLER, R. L., & KIMMEL, H. D. Operant conditioning of the GSR. *Journal of Experimental Psychology,* 1962, *63,* 563–567.

FOWLER, H., & MILLER, N. E. Facilitation and inhibition of runway performance by hind- and forepaw shock of various intensities. *Journal of Comparative and Physiological Psychology,* 1963, *56,* 801–805.

FOWLER, H., & TRAPOLD, M. A. Escape performance as a function of delay of reinforcement. *Journal of Experimental Psychology,* 1962, *63,* 464–467.

FOX, S. S. Self-maintained sensory input and sensory deprivation in monkeys: A behavioral and neuropharmacological study. *Journal of Comparative and Physiological Psychology,* 1962, *55,* 438–444.

FRACZEK, A., & MACAULAY, J. R. Some personality factors in reaction to aggressive stimuli. *Journal of Personality,* 1971, *39,* 163–177.

FRANCHINA, J. J. Escape behavior and shock intensity: Within-subject versus between-groups comparisons. *Journal of Comparative and Physiological Psychology,* 1969, *69,* 241–245.

FRENCH, E. G. Development of a measure of complex motivation. In J. W. Atkinson (Ed.), *Motives in fantasy, action and society.* New York: Van Nostrand, 1958.

FREUD, S. *A general introduction to psycho-analysis.* New York: Liveright, 1935. Originally published 1920.

FRIEDMAN, M., & ROSENMAN, R. H. *Type A behavior and your heart.* New York: Knopf, 1974.

FRIEDMAN, M. I., & STRICKER, E. M. The physiological psychology of hunger: A physiological perspective. *Psychological Review,* 1976, *83,* 409–431.

FRODI, A. The effects of exposure to aggression-eliciting and aggression-inhibiting stimuli on subsequent aggression. *Göteborg Psychological Reports,* 1973, *3* (Whole No. 8).

GALEF, B. G., Jr. Social effects in the weaning of domestic rat pups. *Journal of Comparative and Physiological Psychology,* 1971, *75,* 358–362.

GALEF, B. G., Jr., & HENDERSON, P. W. Mother's milk: A determinant of the feeding preferences of weaning rat pups. *Journal of Comparative and Physiological Psychology,* 1972, *78,* 213–219.

GALLISTEL, C. R. Electrical self-stimulation and its theoretical implications. *Psychological Bulletin,* 1964, *61,* 23–34.

GARCIA, J., & ERVIN, R. R. Gustatory visceral and telereceptor cutaneous conditioning—Adaptation in external and internal milieus. *Communications in Behavioral Biology,* 1968 (Part A), *1,* 389–415.

GARNER, W. R., HAKE, H. W., & ERIKSEN, C. W. Operationalism and the concept of perception. *Psychological Review,* 1956, *63,* 149–159.

GAZZANIGA, M. S. The split brain in man. *Scientific American,* 1967, *217,* 24–29.

GEEN, R. G. *Personality: The skein of behavior.* St. Louis: Mosby, 1976.

GEEN, R. G., & BERKOWITZ, L. Some conditions facilitating the occurrence of aggression after the observation of violence. *Journal of Personality,* 1967, *35,* 666–667.

GEEN, R. G., & O'NEAL, E. C. Activation of cue-elicited aggression by general arousal. *Journal of Personality and Social Psychology,* 1969, *11,* 289–292.

GEEN, R. G., & PIGG, R. Acquisition of an aggressive response and its generalization to verbal behavior. *Journal of Personality and Social Psychology,* 1970, *15,* 165–170.

GERARD, H. B., & MATTHEWSON, G. C. The effects of severity of initiation on liking for a group: A replication. *Journal of Experimental Social Psychology,* 1966, *2,* 278–287.

GHENT, L. Some effects of deprivation on eating and drinking behavior. *Journal of Comparative and Physiological Psychology,* 1957, *50,* 172–176.

GIBSON, C. F. An experimenter demand interpretation of the bogus-feedback effect. Unpublished master's thesis. Wake Forest University, 1977.

GIBSON, W. E., REID, L. D., SAKAI, M., & PORTER, P. B. Intracranial reinforcement compared with sugar-water reinforcement. *Science,* 1965, *148,* 1357–1359.

GILMAN, A. The relation between blood osmotic pressure, fluid distribution, and voluntary water intake. *American Journal of Physiology,* 1937, *120,* 323–328.

GIULIAN, D., & SCHMALTZ, L. W. Enhanced discriminated bar-press avoidance in the rat through appetitive preconditioning. *Journal of Comparative and Physiological Psychology,* 1973, *83,* 106–112.

GLANZER, M. Curiosity, exploratory drive, and stimulus satiation. *Psychological Bulletin,* 1958, *55,* 302–315.

GLASS, D. C. Changes in liking as a means of reducing cognitive discrepancies between self-esteem and aggression. *Journal of Personality,* 1964, *32,* 531–549.

GLICKMAN, S. E., & SCHIFF, B. B. A biological theory of reinforcement. *Psychological Review,* 1967, *74,* 81–109.

GOESLING, W., GOMES, M., LAVOND, D., & CARREIRA, C. Heart rate and avoidance conditioned activity in rats. *Journal of General Psychology,* 1976, *94,* 113–123.

GOLD, R. M. Aphagia and adipsia following unilateral and bilaterally asymmetrical lesions in rats. *Physiology and Behavior,* 1967, *2,* 211–220.

GOLDIAMOND, I., & HAWKINS, W. F. Vexierversuch: The log relationship between word frequency and recogniticn obtained in the absence of stimulus words. *Journal of Experimental Psychology,* 1958, *56,* 457–463.

GOLDSTEIN, D., FINK, D., & METTEE, D. R. Cognition of arousal and actual arousal as determinants of emotion. *Journal Personality and Social Psychology,* 1972, *21,* 41–51.

GOLDSTEIN, M. J. A test of the response probability theory of perceptual defense. *Journal of Experimental Psychology,* 1962, *63,* 23–28.

GOLDSTEIN, R., BEIDEMAN, L., & STERN, J. Effect of water deprivation and saline-induced thirst on the conditioned heart rate response of the rat. *Physiology and Behavior,* 1970, *5,* 583–587.

GOLDSTEIN, R., STERN, J., & ROUTHENBERG, S. Effect of water deprivation and cues associated with water on the heart rate of the rat. *Physiology and Behavior,* 1966, *1,* 199–203.

GOLDSTEIN, R., STERN, J., & STURMFELS, L. Heart rate as a function of water deprivation and conditioning: Some additional controls. *Psychonomic Science,* 1969, *17,* 280–281.

GOODENOUGH, F. L. *Mental testing.* New York: Rinehart & Company, 1949.

GORMEZANO, I., & MOORE, J. W. Classical conditioning. In M. H. Marx (Ed.), *Learning processes.* Toronto: Macmillan, 1969.

GOUGH, H., & HEILBRUN, A. B. *Adjective Check List manual.* Palo Alto, Calif.: Consulting Psychologists Press, 1965.

GRAFF, H., & STELLAR, E. Hyperphagia, obesity, and finickiness. *Journal of Comparative and Physiological Psychology,* 1962, *55,* 418–424.

GRAY, J. *The psychology of fear and stress.* New York: McGraw-Hill, 1971.

GREENE, J. E. Magnitude of reward and acquisition of a black-white discrimination habit. *Journal of Experimental Psychology,* 1953, *46,* 113–119.

GRICE, G. R. The relation of secondary reinforcement to delayed reward in visual discrimination learning. *Journal of Experimental Psychology,* 1948, *38,* 1–16.

GRICE, G. R., & DAVIS, J. D. Effect of irrelevant thirst motivation on a response learned with food reward. *Journal of Experimental Psychology,* 1957, *53,* 347–352.

GRIMSLEY, D. L. Effect of water deprivation and injections of hypertonic saline on the activity of rats. *Psychological Reports,* 1965, *16,* 1081–1085.

GROSSMAN, S. P. Direct adrenergic and cholinergic stimulation of hypothalamic mechanisms. *American Journal of Physiology,* 1962, *202,* 872–882.

GROSSMAN, S. P. The VMH: A center for affective reactions, satiety, or both? *Physiology and Behavior,* 1966, *1,* 1–10.

GROSSMAN, S. P. Neuropharmacology of central mechanisms contributing to control of food and water intake. In C. F. Code (Ed.), *Handbook of physiology* (Section 6. *Alimentary canal.* Vol. 1). Washington, D.C.: American Physiological Society, 1967a.

GROSSMAN, S. P. *A textbook of physiological psychology,* New York: Wiley, 1967b.

GROSSMAN, S. P. Role of the hypothalamus in the regulation of food and water intake. *Psychological Review,* 1975, *82,* 200–224.

GUTHRIE, E. R. *The psychology of learning.* (Rev. ed.) New York: Harper & Row, 1952.

GUTTMAN, N. Operant conditioning, extinction, and periodic reinforcement in relation to concentration of sucrose used as reinforcing agent. *Journal of Experimental Psychology*, 1953, *46*, 213–224.

GUTTMAN, N. Equal-reinforcement values for sucrose and glucose solutions compared with equal-sweetness values. *Journal of Comparative and Physiological Psychology*, 1954, *47*, 358–361.

GWINN, G. T. Effect of punishment on acts motivated by fear. *Journal of Experimental Psychology*, 1949, *39*, 260–269.

HABER, R. N. Discrepancy from adaptation level as a source of affect. *Journal of Experimental Psychology*, 1958, *56*, 370–375.

HAHN, H. *Beiträge zur Reizphysiologie*. Heidelberg: Scherer, 1949.

HAHN, W. W., STERN, J., & FEHR, F. Generalizability of heart rate as a measure of drive state. *Journal of Comparative and Physiological Psychology*, 1964, *58*, 305–309.

HAHN, W. W., STERN, J., & McDONALD, D. Effects of water deprivation and bar pressing activity on heart rate of the male albino rat. *Journal of Comparative and Physiological Psychology*, 1962, *55*, 786–790.

HALL, J. F. The relationship between external stimulation, food deprivation, and activity. *Journal of Comparative and Physiological Psychology*, 1956, *49*, 339–341.

HALL, J. F. The influence of learning in activity wheel behavior. *Journal of Genetic Psychology*, 1958, *92*, 121–125.

HALPERN, B. P. Some relationships between electrophysiology and behavior in taste. In M. R. Kare & O. Maller (Eds.), *The chemical senses and nutrition*. Baltimore, Md.: The Johns Hopkins University Press, 1967.

HARLOW, H. F. Mice, monkeys, men, and motives. *Psychological Review*, 1953, *60*, 23–32.

HARLOW, H. F. *Learning to love*. San Francisco: Albion, 1971.

HARRIMAN, A. E. The effect of a preoperative preference for sugar over salt upon compensatory salt selection by adrenalectomized rats. *Journal of Nutrition*, 1955, *57*, 271–276.

HARRIS, C. S. Perceptual adaptation to inverted, reversed, and displaced vision. *Psychological Review*, 1965, *72*, 419–444.

HARRIS, L. J., CLAY, J., HARGREAVES, F. J., & WARD, A. Appetite and choice of diet: The ability of the vitamin B deficient rat to discriminate between diets containing and lacking the vitamin. *Proceedings of the Royal Society, London*, 1933 (Serial B), *113*, 161–190.

HARRIS, V. A., & KATKIN, E. S. Primary and secondary emotional behavior: An analysis of the role of autonomic feedback on affect, arousal, and attribution. *Psychological Bulletin*, 1975, *82*, 904–916.

HARRISON, A. A. *Individuals and groups*. Monterey, Calif.: Brooks/Cole, 1976.

HART, M. *Act one*. New York: Random House, 1959.

HARVEY, J. H., & HARRIS, B. Determinants of perceived choice and the relationship between perceived choice and expectancy about feelings of internal control. *Journal of Personality and Social Psychology*, 1975, *31*, 101–106.

HATTON, G. I. Drive shifts during extinction: Effects of extinction and spontaneous recovery of bar-pressing behavior. *Journal of Comparative and Physiological Psychology*, 1965, *59*, 385–391.

HATTON, G. I., & ALMLI, C. R. Learned and unlearned components of the rat's adaptation to water deprivation. *Psychonomic Science*, 1967, *9*, 583–584.

HEARST, E. Aversive conditioning and the external stimulus. In B. A. Campbell & R. M. Church (Eds.), *Punishment and aversive behavior*. New York: Appleton-Century-Crofts, 1969.

HEBB, D. O. On the nature of fear. *Psychological Review,* 1946, *53,* 259–276.

HEBB, D. O. *The organization of behavior.* New York: Wiley, 1949.

HEBB, D. O. Drives and the CNS (conceptual nervous system). *Psychological Review,* 1955, *62,* 243–254.

HEBB, D. O. *Textbook of psychology.* (3rd ed.) Philadelphia: Saunders, 1972.

HEIDER, F. *The psychology of interpersonal relations.* New York: Wiley, 1958.

HEINROTH, O. Beiträge zur Biologie, nämentlich Ethologie und Physiologie der Anatiden. *Verhandlungen der V Internationalen Ornithologischen Kongress,* 1910, 589–702.

HELD, R. Plasticity in sensory-motor systems. *Scientific American,* 1965, *213,* 84–94.

HENDRICK, C., & BROWN, S. R. Introversion, extraversion, and interpersonal attraction. *Journal of Personality and Social Psychology,* 1971, *20,* 31–36.

HENDRY, D. P. (Ed.), *Conditioned reinforcement.* Homewood, Ill.: Dorsey, 1969.

HERRNSTEIN, R. J. Method and theory in the study of avoidance. *Psychological Review,* 1969, *76,* 49–69.

HESS, E. H. Ethology: An approach toward the complete analysis of behavior. In R. Brown, E. Galanter, E. H. Hess, & G. Mandler (Eds.), *New directions in psychology.* New York: Holt, Rinehart and Winston, 1962.

HILGARD, E. R. *Theories of learning* (2nd ed.). New York: Appleton-Century-Crofts, 1956.

HINDE, R. A. *Animal behavior: A synthesis of ethology and comparative psychology.* (2nd ed.). New York: McGraw-Hill, 1970.

HINDE, R. A., THORPE, W. H., & VINCE, M. A. The following response in young coots and moorhens. *Behaviour,* 1956, *9,* 214–242.

HIRSCHMAN, R. D. Cross-modal effects of anticipatory bogus heart rate feedback in a negative emotional context. *Journal of Personality and Social Psychology,* 1975, *31,* 13–19.

HOCKMAN, C. H. EEG and behavioral effects of food deprivation in the albino rat. *Electroencephalography and Clinical Neurophysiology,* 1964, *17,* 420–427.

HOEBEL, B. G. Feeding and self-stimulation. *Neural regulation of food and water intake. Annals of the New York Academy of Sciences,* 1969, *157,* 758–778.

HOEBEL, B. G. Feeding: Neural control of intake. In V. E. Hall, A. C. Giese, & R. Sonnenschein (Eds.), *Annual review of physiology* (Vol. 33). Palo Alto, Calif.: Annual Reviews, 1971.

HOEBEL, B. G., & TEITELBAUM, P. Hypothalamic control of feeding and self-stimulation. *Science,* 1962, *135,* 375–377.

HOFFMAN, H. S., & FLESHLER, M. The course of emotionality in the development of avoidance. *Journal of Experimental Psychology,* 1962, *64,* 288–294.

HOKANSON, J. E. Psychophysiological evaluation of the catharsis hypothesis. In E. I. Megargee & J. E. Hokanson (Eds.), *The dynamics of aggression.* New York: Harper & Row, 1970.

HOLMAN, G. L. Intragastric reinforcement effect. *Journal of Comparative and Physiological Psychology,* 1969, *69,* 432–441.

HOLZ, W. C., & AZRIN, N. H. Discriminative properties of punishment. *Journal of the Experimental Analysis of Behavior,* 1961, *4,* 225–232.

HORENSTEIN, B. R. Performance of conditioned responses as a function of strength of hunger drive. *Journal of Comparative and Physiological Psychology,* 1951, *44,* 210–224.

HORNER, M. Sex differences in achievement motivation and performance in competitive and noncompetitive situations. Unpublished doctoral dissertation, University of Michigan, 1968.

HULL, C. L. Goal attraction and directing ideas conceived as habit phenomena. *Psychological Review,* 1931, *38,* 487–506.

HULL, C. L. Differential habituation to internal stimuli in the albino rat. *Journal of Comparative Psychology*, 1933(a), *16*, 255–273.

HULL, C. L. *Hypnosis and suggestibility: An experimental approach.* New York: Appleton-Century-Crofts, 1933(b).

HULL, C. L. *Principles of behavior.* New York: Appleton-Century-Crofts, 1943.

HULL, C. L. *A behavior system.* New Haven, Conn.: Yale University Press, 1952.

HULL, C. L., HOVLAND, C. I., ROSS, R. T., HALL, M., PERKINS, D. T., & FITCH, F. B. *Mathematico-deductive theory of rote learning.* New Haven, Conn.: Yale University Press, 1940.

HUME, D. An enquiry concerning human understanding [1748.] In E. A. Burtt (Ed.), *The English philosophers from Bacon to Mill.* New York: Random House (Modern Library), 1939.

HUNT, H. F., & BRADY, J. V. Some effects of punishment and intercurrent "anxiety" on a simple operant. *Journal of Comparative and Physiological Psychology,* 1955, *48*, 305–310.

HUNT, J. McV. Motivation inherent in information processing and action. In O.J. Harvey (Ed.), *Motivation and social interaction: Cognitive determinants.* New York: Ronald Press, 1963.

HUNT, J. McV. Intrinsic motivation and its role in psychological development. In D. Levine (Ed.), *Nebraska symposium on motivation.* Lincoln: University of Nebraska Press, 1965.

HURVICH, L. M., & JAMESON, D. Opponent processes as a model of neural organization. *American Psychologist,* 1974, *29*, 88–102.

HUTCHINSON, R. R. The environmental causes of aggression. In J. K. Cole & D. D. Jensen (Eds.), *Nebraska symposium on motivation.* Lincoln: University of Nebraska Press, 1972.

HUXLEY, A. *The doors of perception.* New York: Harper & Brothers, 1954.

INSKO, C. A., & SCHOPLER, J. *Experimental Social Psychology.* New York: Academic, 1972.

IRWIN, F. W. *Intentional behavior and motivation: A cognitive theory.* Philadelphia: Lippincott, 1971.

ISRAEL, N. R. Leveling-sharpening and anticipatory cardiac response. *Psychosomatic Medicine,* 1969, *31*, 499–509.

ISTEL, J. Statistical report. *Parachutist,* 1961, *3*, 11–12. Cited in I. Janis, G. F. Mahl, J. Kagan, & R. F. Holt, *Personality.* New York: Harcourt Brace Jovanovich, 1969.

JACKAWAY, R., & TEEVAN, R. Fear of failure and fear of success: Two dimensions of the same motive. *Sex Roles,* 1976, *2*, 283–294.

JACKSON, D. N., AHMED, S. A., & HEAPY, N. A. Is achievement a unitary construct? *Journal of Research in Personality,* 1976, *10*, 1–21.

JACOBS, H. L. Evaluation of the osmotic effects of glucose loads in food satiation. *Journal of Comparative and Physiological Psychology,* 1964a, *57*, 309–310.

JACOBS, H. L. Observations on the ontogeny of saccharin preference in the neonate rat. *Psychonomic Science,* 1964b, *1*, 105–106.

JACOBS, H. L., & SHARMA, K. N. Taste versus calories: Sensory and metabolic signals in the control of food intake. *Neural regulation of food and water intake. Annals of the New York Academy of Sciences,* 1969, *157*, 1084–1125.

JACOBSEN, C. F. Functions of the frontal association area in primates. *Archives of Neurology and Psychiatry,* 1935, *33*, 558–569.

JAMES, W. What is an emotion? *Mind,* 1884, *9*, 188–205.

JAMES, W. *Principles of psychology.* New York: Holt, 1890.

JANIS, I., MAHL, G. F., KAGAN, J., & HOLT, R. R. *Personality*. New York: Harcourt Brace Jovanovich, 1969.

JENKINS, J. J., & HANRATTY, J. A. Drive intensity discrimination in the white rat. *Journal of Comparative and Physiological Psychology*, 1949, *42*, 228–232.

JENKINS, W. O. A temporal gradient of derived reinforcement. *American Journal of Psychology*, 1950, *63*, 237–243.

JOHNSON, D. M. *Systematic introduction to the psychology of thinking*. New York: Harper & Row, 1972.

JOHNSON, R. J. *Aggression in man and animals*. Philadelphia: Saunders, 1972.

JONES, E. E., ROCK, L., SHAVER, K. G., GOETHALS, G. R., & WARD, L. M. Pattern performance and ability attribution: An unexpected primacy effect. *Journal of Personality and Social Psychology*, 1968, *10*, 317–341.

JONES, H. E., & JONES, M. C. A study of fear. *Childhood Education*, 1928, *5*, 136–143.

JONES, M. C. The elimination of children's fears. *Journal of Experimental Psychology*, 1924, *7*, 382–390.

JONES, S. C. Some determinants of interpersonal evaluating behavior. *Journal of Personality and Social Psychology*, 1966, *3*, 397–403.

JOUVET, M. The states of sleep. *Scientific American*, 1967, *216*, 62–72.

JOUVET, M., & MICHEL, F. Recherches sur l'activité électrique cérébrale au cours du sommeil. *Comptes Rendus Société Biologie*, 1958, *152*, 1167–1170.

KALISH, H. I. Strength of fear as a function of the number of acquisition and extinction trails. *Journal of Experimental Psychology*, 1954, *47*, 1–9.

KALISH, H. I. Stimulus generalization. In M. Marx (Ed.), *Learning: Processes*. New York: Macmillan, 1969.

KALLMANN, F. J. The genetic theory of schizophrenia. *American Journal of Psychiatry*, 1946, *103*, 309–322.

KAMIN, L. J. The effects of termination of the CS and avoidance of the US on avoidance learning. *Journal of Comparative and Physiological Psychology*, 1956, *49*, 420–424.

KAMIN, L. J. The retention of an incompletely learned avoidance response. *Journal of Comparative and Physiological Psychology*, 1957, *50*, 457–460.

KAMMANN, R. Cognitive complexity and preferences in poetry. Unpublished doctoral dissertation, University of Cincinnati, 1964.

KANE, T. R., DOERGE, P., & TEDESCHI, J. T. When is intentional harm-doing perceived as aggressive? A naive reappraisal of the Berkowitz aggression paradigm. *Proceedings of the 81st Annual Convention of the American Psychological Association*, Montreal, Canada, 1973, *8*, 113–114. American Psychological Association: Washington, D.C.

KARE, M. R., & FICKEN, M. S. Comparative studies on the sense of taste. In Y. Zotterman (Ed.), *Olfaction and taste*. New York: Macmillan, 1963.

KATKIN, E. S. *Instrumental autonomic conditioning*. New York: General Learning Press, 1971.

KAUFMAN, E. L., & MILLER, N. E. Effect of number of reinforcements on strength of approach in an approach-avoidance conflict. *Journal of Comparative and Physiological Psychology*, 1949, *42*, 65–74.

KAUFMANN, H. *Aggression and altruism*. New York: Holt, Rinehart and Winston, 1970.

KELLER, F. S., & SCHOENFELD, W. N. *Principles of psychology*, New York: Appleton-Century-Crofts, 1950.

KELLEY, H. H. Attribution theory in social psychology. In D. Levine (Ed.), *Nebraska symposium on motivation*. Lincoln: University of Nebraska Press, 1967.

KELLOG, R., & BARON, R. S. Attribution theory, insomnia, and the reverse placebo effect: A reversal of Storms and Nisbett's findings. *Journal of Personality and Social Psychology,* 1975, *32,* 231–236.

KENDLER, H. H. Drive interaction: II. Experimental analysis of the role of drive in learning theory. *Journal of Experimental Psychology,* 1945, *35,* 188–198.

KESEY, K. *One flew over the cuckoo's nest.* New York: Viking Press, 1962.

KIESLER, C. A., & PALLAK, M. S. Arousal properties of dissonance manipulations. *Psychological Bulletin,* 1976, *83,* 1014–1025.

KIMBLE, G. A. Behavior strength as a function of the intensity of the hunger drive. *Journal of Experimental Psychology,* 1951, *41,* 341–348.

KIMMEL, E., & KIMMEL, H. D. A replication of operant conditioning of the GSR. *Journal of Experimental Psychology,* 1963, *65,* 212–213.

KIMMEL, H. D., & HILL, F. A. Operant conditioning of the GSR. *Psychological Reports,* 1960, *7,* 555–562.

KINSEY, A. C., POMEROY, W. B., & MARTIN, C. E. *Sexual behavior in the human male.* Philadelphia: Saunders, 1948.

KINSEY, A. C., POMEROY, W. B., MARTIN, C. E., & GEBHARD, P. H. *Sexual behavior in the human female.* Philadelphia: Saunders, 1953.

KINTSCH, W. Runway performances as a function of drive strength and magnitude of reinforcement. *Journal of Comparative and Physiological Psychology,* 1962, *55,* 882–887.

KISSILEFF, H. R. Nonhomeostatic controls of drinking. In A. N. Epstein, H. R. Kissileff, & E. Stellar (Eds.), *The neuropsychology of thirst: New findings and advances in concepts.* Washington, D.C.: Winston, 1973.

KLEITMAN, N. *Sleep and wakefulness.* Chicago: University of Chicago Press, 1963.

KLING, J. W. Speed of running as a function of goal-box behavior. *Journal of Comparative and Physiological Psychology,* 1956, *49,* 474–476.

KLING, J. W., & RIGGS, L. A. *Woodworth and Schlosberg's experimental psychology.* (3rd ed.) New York: Holt, Rinehart and Winston, 1971.

KLINGER, E. Fantasy need achievement. *Psychological Bulletin,* 1966, *66,* 291–306.

KLINGER, E. Consequences of commitment to and disengagement from incentives. *Psychological Review,* 1975, *82,* 1–25.

KLOPFER, P. H. *An introduction to animal behavior: Ethology's first century.* Englewood Cliffs, N.J.: Prentice-Hall, 1974.

KLUVER, H., & BUCY, P. C. Psychic blindness and other symptoms following bilateral temporal lobectomy in rhesus monkeys. *American Journal of Physiology,* 1937, *119,* 352–353.

KOCH, S., & DANIEL, W. J. The effect of satiation on the behavior mediated by a habit of maximum strength. *Journal of Experimental Psychology,* 1945, *35,* 167–187.

KOFFKA, K. *Principles of gestalt psychology.* New York: Harcourt, Brace, 1935.

KORNBLITH, C., & OLDS, J. T-maze learning with one trial per day using brain stimulation reinforcement. *Journal of Comparative and Physiological Psychology,* 1968, *66,* 488–491.

KRAELING, D. Analysis of amount of reward as a variable in learning. *Journal of Comparative and Physiological Psychology,* 1961, *54,* 560–564.

KRIECKHAUS, E. E., & WOLF, G. Acquisition of sodium by rats: Interaction of innate mechanisms and latent learning. *Journal of Comparative and Physiological Psychology,* 1968, *65,* 197–201.

KROGH, A. The language of the bees. *Scientific American,* 1948, *179,* 18–21.

KUO, Z. Y. How are our instincts acquired? *Psychological Review,* 1922, *29,* 244–365.

KUO, Z. Y. The genesis of the cat's response to the rat. *Journal of Comparative Psychology,* 1930, *11,* 1–30.

Kuo, Z. Y. Ontogeny of embryonic behavior in aves. *Journal of Experimental Biology,* 1932, *61,* 395–430, 453–489.

Kurihara, K., Kurihara, Y., & Beidler, L. M. Isolation and mechanism of taste modifiers: Taste-modifying protein and gymnemic acids. In C. Pfaffmann (Ed.), *Olfaction and taste.* (Vol. 3) New York: Rockefeller University Press, 1969.

Kurtz, K. H., & Siegal, A. Conditioned fear and magnitude of startle response: A replication and extension. *Journal of Comparative and Physiological Psychology,* 1966, *62,* 8–14.

Kutscher, C. Some physiological correlates of adaptation to a water deprivation schedule. In M. J. Wayner (Ed.), *Thirst.* Oxford: Pergamon, 1964.

Lacey, J. I. Somatic response patterning and stress: Some revisions of activation theory. In M. H. Appley & R. Trumbull (Eds.), *Psychological stress: Issues in research.* Englewood Cliffs, N.J.: Prentice-Hall, 1962.

Lacey, J. I., Kagan, J., Lacey, B. C., & Moss, H. A. The visceral level: Situational determinants and behavioral correlates of autonomic response. In P. Knapp (Ed.), *Expression of the emotions in man.* New York: International Universities Press, 1963.

Lacey, J. I., & Lacey, B. C. Some autonomic-central nervous system interrelationships. In P. Black (Ed.), *Physiological correlates of emotion.* New York: Academic, 1970.

Landis, C., & Hunt, W. A. Adrenalin and emotion. *Psychological Review,* 1932, *39,* 467–485.

Langer, E. J., & Roth, J. Heads I win, tails it's chance: The illusion of control as a function of the sequence of outcomes in a purely chance task. *Journal of Personality and Social Psychology,* 1975, *32,* 951–955.

Lashley, K. S. Experimental analysis of instinctive behavior. *Psychological Review,* 1938, *45,* 445–471.

Lashley, K. In search of the engram. *Symposium of the society of experimental biology.* 1950, *4,* 454–482.

Lát, J. Self-selection of dietary components. In C. F. Code (Ed.), *Handbook of physiology* (Section 6. *Alimentary canal.* Vol. 1). Washington, D.C.: American Physiological Society, 1967.

Lawler, J. Bar pressing by the albino rat as a function of concentration of sucrose incentive and hours of food deprivation. Unpublished master's thesis, Wake Forest University, 1970.

Lawson, R. *Frustration: The development of a scientific concept.* New York: Macmillan, 1965.

Lazarus, A. Psychiatric problems precipitated by Transcendental Meditation. *Psychological Reports,* 1976, *39,* 601–602.

Lazarus, R. S. Emotions and adaptation: Conceptual and empirical relations. In E. J. Arnold (Ed.), *Nebraska symposium on motivation.* Lincoln: University of Nebraska Press, 1968.

Lazarus, R. S. A cognitively oriented psychologist looks at biofeedback. *American Psychologist,* 1975, *30,* 553–561.

Leaf, R. C. Avoidance response evocation as a function of prior discriminative fear conditioning under curare. *Journal of Comparative and Physiological Psychology,* 1964, *58,* 446–449.

Leeper, R. The role of motivation in learning: A study of the phenomenon of differential motivational control of the utilization of habits. *Journal of Genetic Psychology,* 1935, *46,* 3–40.

Lefcourt, H. M. Internal versus external control of reinforcement: A review. *Psychological Bulletin,* 1966, *65,* 206–220.

LEITENBERG, H. Is time out from positive reinforcement an aversive event? A review of the experimental literature. *Psychological Review,* 1965, *64,* 428–441.

LENZER, I. I. Differences between behavior reinforced by electrical stimulation of the brain and conventionally reinforced behavior. *Psychological Bulletin,* 1972, *78,* 103–118.

LERNER, M. J., & MATTHEWS, G. Reactions to suffering of others under conditions of indirect responsibility. *Journal of Personality and Social Psychology,* 1967, *5,* 319–325.

LERNER, M. J., & SIMMONS, C. H. Observer's reaction to the "innocent victim": Compassion or rejection? *Journal of Personality and Social Psychology,* 1966, *4,* 203–210.

LEVINE, S. Stimulation in infancy. *Scientific American,* 1960, *202,* 80–86.

LEWIN, K., DEMBO, T., FESTINGER, L., & SEARS, P. S. Level of aspiration. In J. McV. Hunt (Ed.), *Personality and the behavior disorders.* New York: Ronald Press, 1944.

LICHTENSTEIN, P. E. Studies of anxiety: I. The production of feeding inhibition in dogs. *Journal of Comparative and Physiological Psychology,* 1950, *43,* 16–29.

LIDDELL, H. S. Conditioned reflex method and experimental neurosis. In J. M. Hunt (Ed.), *Personality and the behavior disorders.* New York: Ronald Press, 1944.

LINDSLEY, D. B. Emotions and the electroencephalogram. In M. L. Reymert (Ed.), *Feelings and emotions: The Mooseheart symposium.* New York: McGraw-Hill, 1950.

LINDSLEY, D. B. Emotion. In S. S. Stevens (Ed.), *Handbook of experimental psychology.* New York: Wiley, 1951.

LINDSLEY, D. B., SCHREINER, L. H., KNOWLES, W. B., & MAGOUN, H. W. Behavioral and EEG changes following chronic brain stem lesions in the cat. *Electroencephalography and Clinical Neurophysiology,* 1950, *2,* 483–498.

LITTMAN, R. A. Motives, history, and causes. In M. R. Jones (Ed.), *Nebraska symposium on motivation.* Lincoln: University of Nebraska Press, 1958.

LIVERANT, S., & SCODEL, A. Internal and external control as determinants of decision-making under conditions of risk. *Psychological Reports,* 1960, *7,* 59–67.

LOEW, C. A. Acquisition of a hostile attitude and its relationship to aggressive behavior. *Journal of Personality and Social Psychology,* 1967, *5,* 335–341.

LOGAN, F. A. *Incentive.* New Haven, Conn.: Yale University Press, 1960.

LOGAN, F. A. Decision making by rats: Delay versus amount of reward. *Journal of Comparative and Physiological Psychology,* 1965, *59,* 1–12.

LOGAN, F. A. Incentive theory and changes in reward. In G. H. Bower (Ed.), *The psychology of learning and motivation* (Vol. 2). New York: Academic, 1968.

LoLORDO, V. M. Positive conditioned reinforcement from aversive situations. *Psychological Bulletin,* 1969, *72,* 193–203.

LORENZ, K. Morphology and behavior patterns in closely allied species. In B. Schaffner (Ed.), *Group Processes.* New York: Josiah Macy Foundation, 1955.

LORENZ, K. Z. *King Solomon's ring.* New York: Crowell, 1952.

LORENZ, K. Z. *Evolution and modification of behavior.* Chicago: University of Chicago Press, 1965.

LORENZ, K. Z. *On Aggression.* New York: Harcourt Brace Jovanovich, 1966.

LOTT, D. F. Secondary reinforcement and frustration: A conceptual paradox. *Psychological Bulletin,* 1967, *67,* 197–198.

LOVAAS, O. I. Effect of exposure to symbolic aggression on aggressive behavior. *Child Development,* 1961, *32,* 37–44.

LOVAAS, O. I., & SIMMONS, J. Q. Manipulation of self-destruction in three retarded children. *Journal of Applied Behavioral Analysis,* 1969, *2,* 143–157.

MacCorquodale, K., & Meehl, P. E., Edward C. Tolman. In Estes, W., Koch, S. MacCorquodale, K., Meehl, P. E., Mueller, C. G., Schoenfeld, W. N., and Verplanck, W. S. *Modern learning theory.* New York: Appleton-Century-Crofts, 1954.

Mackintosh, N. J. *The psychology of animal learning.* New York: Academic, 1974.

Magoun, H. W. The ascending reticular system and wakefulness. In J. F. Delafresnaye (Ed.), *Brain mechanisms and consciousness.* Blackwell: Oxford, 1954.

MacLean, P. D. Psychosomatic disease and the "visceral brain": Recent developments bearing on the Papez theory of emotion. *Psychosomatic Medicine,* 1949, *11,* 338–353.

Maher, B. *Principles of psychopathology.* New York: McGraw-Hill, 1966.

Maier, S. F., Seligman, M. E. P., & Solomon, R. L. Pavlovian fear conditioning and learned helplessness: Effects on escape and avoidance behavior of (a) the CS-US contingency and (b) the independence of the US and voluntary responding. In B. A. Campbell & R. M. Church (Eds.), *Punishment and aversive behavior.* New York: Appleton-Century-Crofts, 1969.

Makosky, V. P. Fear of success, sex role orientation of the task, and competitive condition as variables affecting women's performance in achievement-oriented situations. Paper presented at the 44th annual meeting of the Midwestern Psychological Association, Cleveland, Ohio, May, 1972.

Malmo, R. B. Activation: A neuropsychological dimension. *Psychological Review,* *1959, 66,* 367–386.

Malmo, R. B. *On emotions, needs, and our archaic brain.* New York: Holt, Rinehart and Winston, 1975.

Mandler, G. Emotions. In T. M. Newcomb (Ed.), *New directions in psychology.* New York: Holt, Rinehart and Winston, 1962.

Mandler, G. *Mind and emotion.* New York: Wiley, 1975.

Mansson, H. H. The cognitive control of thirst motivation: A dissonance approach. Unpublished doctoral dissertation, New York University, 1965. Cited in P. G. Zimbardo. The cognitive control of motivation. *Transactions of the New York Academy of Sciences,* 1966, Series II, *28,* 902–922.

Marañon, G. Contribution à l'étude de l'action émotive de l'adrénaline. *Revue française d'Endocrinologie,* 1924, *2,* 301–325.

Margules, D. L., & Olds, J. Identical "feeding" and "rewarding" systems in the lateral hypothalamus of rats. *Science,* 1962, *135,* 374–375.

Mark, V. H., & Ervin, F. R. *Violence and the brain.* New York: Harper & Row, 1970.

Marler, P. On animal aggression: The roles of strangeness and familiarity. *American Psychologist,* 1976, *31,* 239–246.

Marler, P., & Hamilton, W. J., III. *Mechanisms of animal behavior.* New York: Wiley, 1966.

Maslow, A. H. Deficiency motivation and growth motivation. In M. R. Jones (Ed.), *Nebraska symposium on motivation.* Lincoln: University of Nebraska Press, 1955.

Masserman, J. H. *Behavior and neurosis.* Chicago: University of Chicago Press, 1943.

Masters, W. H., & Johnson, V. *Human sexual response.* Boston: Little, Brown, 1966.

Masters, W. H., & Johnson, V. *Human sexual inadequacy.* Boston: Little Brown, 1970.

Mathieu, M. Effects of overtraining and high activation on bar pressing of rats tested under water deprivation. *Journal of Comparative and Physiological Psychology,* 1973, *85,* 353–360.

May, M. A. Experimentally acquired drives. *Journal of Experimental Psychology,* 1948, *38,* 66–77.

May, R. *The meaning of anxiety.* New York: Ronald Press, 1950.

McAllister, W. R., & McAllister, D. E. Behavioral measurement of conditioned fear. In F. R. Brush, (Ed.), *Aversive conditioning and learning.* New York: Academic, 1971.

McBurney, D. H., & Lucas, J. A. Gustatory cross-adaptation between salts. *Psychonomic Science,* 1966, *4,* 301–302.

McCain, G. Partial reinforcement effects following a small number of acquisition trials. *Psychonomic Monograph Supplements,* 1966, *1,* 251–270.

McCall, R. B. Initial-consequent-change surface in light-contingent bar pressing. *Journal of Comparative and Physiological Psychology,* 1966, *62,* 35–42.

McCary, J. L. *Human sexuality.* New York: Van Nostrand, 1967.

McCary, J. L., & Copeland, D. R. (Eds.) *Modern views of human sexual behavior.* Chicago: Science Research Associates, 1976.

McCleary, R. A. Taste and postingestion factors in specific-hunger behavior. *Journal of Comparative and Physiological Psychology,* 1953, *46,* 411–421.

McClelland, D. C. Some social consequences of achievement motivation. In M. R. Jones (Ed.), *Nebraska symposium on motivation.* Lincoln: University of Nebraska Press, 1955.

McClelland, D. C. Risk-taking in children with high and low need for achievement. In J. W. Atkinson (Ed.), *Motives in fantasy, action, and society.* Princeton: Van Nostrand, 1958.

McClelland, D. C. *The achieving society.* Princeton: Van Nostrand, 1961.

McClelland, D. C. N Achievement and entrepreneurship: A longitudinal study. *Journal of Personality and Social Psychology,* 1965, *1,* 389–392.

McClelland, D. C., & Atkinson, J. W. The projective expression of needs. I. The effect of different intensities of the hunger drive on perception. *Journal of Psychology,* 1948, *25,* 205–232.

McClelland, D. C., Atkinson, J. W., Clark, R. A., & Lowell, E. L. *The achievement motive.* New York: Appleton-Century-Crofts, 1953.

McClelland, D. C., Rindlisbacher, A., & de Charms, R. C. Religious and other sources of parental attitudes toward independence training. In D. C. McClelland (Ed.), *Studies in motivation.* New York: Appleton-Century-Crofts, 1955.

McConnell, J. V. *Understanding human behavior: An introduction to psychology.* New York: Holt, Rinehart and Winston, 1974.

McGrath, J. E. *Social and psychological factors in stress.* New York: Holt, Rinehart and Winston, 1970.

McHose, J. H., & Moore, J. N. Expectancy, salience, and habit: A noncontextual interpretation of the effects of changes in the conditions of reinforcement on simple instrumental responses. *Psychological Review,* 1976, *83,* 292–307.

McKeachie, W. J., Lin, Y., Milholland, J., & Issacson, R. Student affiliation motives, teacher warmth, and academic achievement. *Journal of Personality and Social Psychology,* 1966, *4,* 457–461.

McKusick, V. A. *Human Genetics.* (2nd ed.) Englewood Cliffs, N.J.: Prentice-Hall, 1969.

Mednick, S. A. The associative basis of the creative process. *Psychological Review,* 1962, *69,* 220–232.

Meehl, P. E. On the circularity of the law of effect. *Psychological Bulletin,* 1950, *47,* 52–75.

Meinrath, A., & Beck, R. C. Heart rate and activity changes during bar pressing and consummatory responding for sucrose incentives in the rat. Paper presented at the 48th annual meeting of the Eastern Psychological Association, Boston, Mass., April, 1977.

Mellgren, R. L. Positive and negative contrast effects using delayed reinforcement. *Learning and Motivation,* 1972, *3,* 185–193.

MENDELSON, J. The role of hunger in T-maze learning for food by rats. *Journal of Comparative and Physiological Psychology,* 1966, *62,* 341–353.

MENDELSON, J. Lateral hypothalamic stimulation in satiated rats: The rewarding effects of self-induced drinking. *Science,* 1967, *157,* 1077–1079.

MENDELSON, J., & CHILLAG, D. Tongue cooling: A new reward for thirsty rodents. *Science,* 1970, *170,* 1418–1421.

MERYMAN, J. J. Magnitude of startle response as a function of hunger and fear. Unpublished master's thesis, State University of Iowa. Cited by Brown, 1961.

MEYER, D. R. Access to engrams. *American Psychologist.* 1972, *27,* 124–133.

MEYER, D. R., CHO, C., & WESEMANN, A. F. On problems of conditioned discriminated lever-press avoidance responses. *Psychological Review,* 1960, *67,* 224–228.

MICHAELS, R. R., HUBER, M. J., & McCANN, D. S. Evaluation of Transcendental Meditation as a method of reducing stress. *Science,* 1976, *192,* 1242–1244.

MILES, R. C. The relative effectiveness of secondary reinforcers throughout deprivation and habit-strength parameters. *Journal of Comparative and Physiological Psychology,* 1956, *49,* 126–130.

MILGRAM, S. *Obedience to authority: An experimental view.* New York: Harper & Row, 1974.

MILLER, G. A., GALANTER, E., & PRIBRAM, K. H. *Plans and the structure of behavior.* New York: Holt, Rinehart and Winston, 1960.

MILLER, N. E. The frustration-aggression hypothesis. *Psychological Review,* 1941, *48,* 337–342.

MILLER, N. E. Studies of fear as an acquirable drive: I. Fear as motivation and fear-reduction as reinforcement in the learning of new responses. *Journal of Experimental Psychology,* 1948, *38,* 89–101.

MILLER, N. E. Comments on multi-process conceptions of learning. *Psychological Review,* 1951a, *58,* 375–381.

MILLER, N. E. Learnable drives and rewards. In S. S. Stevens (Ed.), *Handbook of experimental psychology.* New York: Wiley, 1951b.

MILLER, N. E. Experiments on motivation: Studies combining psychological, physiological, and pharmacological techniques. *Science,* 1957, *126,* 1271–1278.

MILLER, N. E. Central stimulation and other new approaches to motivation and reward. *American Psychologist,* 1958, *13,* 100–107.

MILLER, N. E. Liberalization of basic S-R concepts: Extensions to conflict behavior, motivation and social learning. In S. Koch (Ed.), *Psychology: A study of a science* (Vol. 2). New York: McGraw-Hill, 1959.

MILLER, N. E. Learning resistance to pain and fear: Effects of overlearning, exposure, and rewarded exposure in context. *Journal of Experimental Psychology,* 1960, *60,* 137–145.

MILLER, N. E. Learning and performance motivated by direct stimulation of the brain. In D. E. Sheer (Ed.), *Electrical stimulation of the brain.* Austin: University of Texas Press, 1961.

MILLER, N. E. Some reflections on the law of effect produce a new alternative to drive reduction. In M. R. Jones (Ed.), *Nebraska symposium on motivation.* Lincoln: University of Nebraska Press, 1963.

MILLER, N. E., & BANUAZIZI, A. Instrumental learning by curarized rats of a specific visceral response, intestinal or cardiac. *Journal of Comparative and Physiological Psychology,* 1968, *65,* 1–7.

MILLER, N. E., & DWORKIN, B. R. Visceral learning: Recent difficulties with curarized rats and significant problems for human research. In P. A. Obrist, A. H. Black, J. Brener, & L. V. DiCara (Eds.), *Cardiovascular psychophysiology.* Chicago: Aldine, 1974.

MILLER, N. E., & KESSEN, M. L. Reward effects of food via stomach fistula compared with those of food via mouth. *Journal of Comparative and Physiological Psychology,* 1952, *45,* 555–564.

MILLER, N. E., & KRAELING, D. Displacement: Greater generalization of approach than avoidance in a generalized approach-avoidance conflict. *Journal of Experimental Psychology,* 1952, *43,* 217–221.

MILLS, J., & MINTZ, P. M. Effect of unexplained arousal on affiliation. *Journal of Personality and Social Psychology,* 1972, *24,* 11–13.

MILNER, P. M. *Physiological psychology.* New York: Holt, Rinehart and Winston, 1970.

MISCHEL, W. M. Cognitive appraisals and transformations in self-control. In B. Weiner (Ed.), *Cognitive views of human motivation.* New York: Academic, 1974.

MISCHEL, W. M. Introduction to personality. (2nd ed.) New York: Holt, Rinehart and Winston, 1976.

MOLTZ, H. Imprinting: Empirical basis and theoretical significance. *Psychological Bulletin,* 1960, *57,* 291–314.

MONTGOMERY, K. C. The effect of hunger and thirst drives upon exploratory behavior. *Journal of Comparative and Physiological Psychology,* 1953, *46,* 315–319.

MONTGOMERY, K. C. The relation between fear induced by novel stimulation and exploratory behavior. *Journal of Comparative and Physiological Psychology,* 1955, *48,* 254–260.

MONTI, P. M. Consummatory behavior as a function of deprivation level of the rat. *Psychonomic Science,* 1971, *25,* 23–25.

MOOK, D. G. Oral and post-ingestinal determinants of the intake of various solutions in rats with esophageal fistulas. *Journal of Comparative and Physiological Psychology,* 1963, *56,* 645–659.

MOOK, D. G. Saccharin preference in the rat: Some unpalatable findings. *Psychological Review,* 1974, *81,* 475–490.

MORGAN, C. T. *Physiological psychology.* New York: McGraw-Hill, 1943.

MORGAN, C. T. Physiological theory of drive. In S. Koch (Ed.), *Psychology: A study of science.* (Vol. 1). New York: McGraw-Hill, 1959.

MORGANE, P. J. Limbic-hypothalamic-midbrain interaction in thirst and thirst motivated behavior. In M. J. Wayner (Ed.), *Thirst.* Oxford: Pergamon, 1964.

MORRIS, C.W. Foundations of the theory of signs. In O. Neurath, R. Carnap, & C. Morris (Eds.), *International encyclopedia of unified science.* (Vol. 1). Chicago: University of Chicago Press, 1938.

MORRIS, D. The naked ape. New York: Dell, 1967.

MORUZZI, G., & MAGOUN, H. W. Brain stem and reticular formation and activation of the EEG. *Electroencephalography and Clinical Neurophysiology,* 1949, *1,* 455–473.

MOSKOWITZ, M. J. Running-wheel activity in the white rat as a function of combined food and water deprivation. *Journal of Comparative and Physiological Psychology,* 1959, *52,* 621–625.

MOSCOVITCH, A., & LoLORDO, V. M. Role of safety in the Pavlovian backward fear conditioning procedure. *Journal of Comparative and Physiological Psychology,* 1968, *66,* 673–678.

MOULTON, R. W. Effects of success and failure on level of aspiration as related to achievement motives. *Journal of Personality and Social Psychology,* 1965, *1,* 399, 406.

MOWRER, O. H. Preparatory set (expectancy)—A determinant in motivation and learning. *Psychological Review,* 1938, *45,* 61–91.

MOWRER, O. H. A stimulus-response analysis of anxiety and its role as a reinforcing agent. *Psychological Review,* 1939, *46,* 553–564.

Mowrer, O. H. On the dual nature of learning: A reinterpretation of "conditioning" and "problem solving." *Harvard Educational Review,* 1947, *17,* 102–148.

Mowrer, O. H. *Learning theory and behavior.* New York: Wiley, 1960a.

Mowrer, O. H. *Learning theory and the symbolic processes.* New York: Wiley, 1960b.

Mowrer, O. H., & Aiken, E. G. Contiguity vs. drive-reduction in conditioned fear: Temporal variations in conditioned and unconditioned stimulus. *American Journal of Psychology,* 1954, *67,* 26–38.

Mowrer, O. H., & Lamoreaux, R. R. Fear as an intervening variable in avoidance conditioning. *Journal of Comparative Psychology,* 1946, *39,* 29–50.

Mowrer, O. H., & Solomon, L. N. Contiguity vs. drive-reduction in conditioned fear: The proximity and abruptness of drive-reduction. *American Journal of Psychology,* 1954, *67,* 15–25.

Mowrer, O. H., & Viek, P. An experimental analogue of fear from a sense of helplessness. *Journal of Abnormal and Social Psychology,* 1948, *83,* 193–200.

Moyer, K. E. The physiology of aggression and the implications for aggression control. In J. L. Singer (Ed.), *The control of aggression and violence: Cognitive and physiological factors.* New York: Academic, 1971.

Muenzinger, K. F. Motivation in learning: I. Electric shock for correct response in the visual discrimination habit. *Journal of Comparative Psychology,* 1934, *17,* 267–277.

Muenzinger, K. F., & Fletcher, F. M. Motivation in learning: VII. The effect of an enforced delay at the point of choice in the visual discrimination habit. *Journal of Comparative Psychology,* 1937, *23,* 383–392.

Murray, E. J., & Berkun, M. M. Displacement as a function of conflict. *Journal of Abnormal and Social Psychology,* 1955, *51,* 47–56.

Murray, H. A. *Explorations in personality.* New York: Oxford University Press, 1938.

Myer, J. S. Punishment of instinctive behavior: Suppression of mouse-killing by rats. *Psychonomic Science,* 1966, *4,* 385–386.

Myer, J. S. Some effects of noncontingent aversive stimulation. In F. R. Brush (Ed.), *Aversive conditioning and learning.* New York: Academic, 1971.

Myer, J. S., & Ricci, D. Delay of punishment gradients for the goldfish. *Journal of Comparative and Physiological Psychology,* 1968, *66,* 417–421.

Myers, A. K., & Miller, N. E. Failure to find a learned drive based on hunger: Evidence for learning motivated by "exploration." *Journal of Comparative and Physiological Psychology,* 1954, *47,* 428–436.

National Institute of Mental Health, Center for Studies of Crime and Delinquency. *Report on the XYY chromosomal abnormality* (Public Health Service Publication No. 2103). Chevy Chase, Md.: National Institute of Mental Health, 1970.

Newcomb, T. M. The acquaintance process. New York: Holt, Rinehart and Winston, 1961.

Newcomb, T. M. Interpersonal balance. In R. P. Abelson, E. Aronson, W. J. McGuire, T. M. Newcomb, M. J. Rosenberg, & P. H. Tannenbaum (Eds.), *Theories of cognitive consistency: A sourcebook.* Chicago: Rand McNally, 1968.

Nisbett, R. E. Hunger, obesity, and the ventromedial hypothalamus. *Psychological Review,* 1972, *79,* 433–453.

Nisbett, R. E., & Borgida, E. Attribution and the psychology of prediction. *Journal of Personality and Social Psychology,* 1975, *32,* 932–943.

Nissen, H. W. Phylogenetic comparison. In. S. S. Stevens (Ed.), *Handbook of experimental psychology.* New York: Wiley, 1951.

Notz, W. W. Work motivation and the negative effects of extrinsic rewards: A review with implications for theory and practice. *American Psychologist,* 1975, *9,* 884–891.

Novin, D. The relation between electrical conductivity of brain tissue and thirst in the rat. *Journal of Comparative and Physiological Psychology*, 1962, *55*, 145–154.

Obrist, P. A. The cardiovascular-behavioral interaction—As it appears today. *Psychophysiology*, 1976, *13*, 95–107.

O'Kelly, L. I., & Beck, R. C. Water regulation in the rat: III. The artificial control of thirst with stomach loads of water and sodium chloride. *Psychological Monographs*, 1960, *74* (13, Whole No. 500).

O'Kelly, L. I., Falk, J. L., & Flint, D. Water regulation in the rat: I. Gastrointestinal exchange rates of water and sodium chloride in thirsty animals. *Journal of Comparative and Physiological Psychology*, 1958, *51*, 16–21.

O'Kelly, L. I., Hatton, G., Tucker, L., & Westall, D. Water regulation in the rat: Heart rate as a function of hydration, anesthesia, and association with reinforcement. *Journal of Comparative and Physiological Psychology*, 1965, *59*, 159–165.

O'Kelly, L. I., & Steckle, L. C. A note on long-enduring emotional responses in the rat. *Journal of Psychology*, 1939, *8*, 125–131.

Olds, J. Runway and maze behavior controlled by baso-medial forebrain stimulation in the rat. *Journal of Comparative and Physiological Psychology*, 1956a, *49*, 507–512.

Olds, J. Pleasure centers in the brain. *Scientific American*, 1956b, *195*, 105–116.

Olds, J. Differential effects of drive and drugs on self-stimulation at different brain sites. In D. E. Sheer (Ed.), *Electrical stimulation of the brain*. Austin: University of Texas Press, 1961.

Olds, J. Hypothalamic substrates of reward. *Physiological Review*, 1962, *42*, 554–604.

Olds, J., & Milner, P. Positive reinforcement produced by electrical stimulation of the septal area and other regions of the rat brain. *Journal of Comparative and Physiological Psychology*, 1954, *47*, 419–427.

O'Leary, C. J., Willis, F. N., & Tomich, E. Conformity under deceptive and non-deceptive techniques. *Sociological Quarterly*, 1969, Winter, 87–93.

Olton, D. S. Shock-motivated avoidance and the analysis of behavior. *Psychological Bulletin*, 1973, *79*, 243–251.

Ominsky, M., & Kimble, G. A. Anxiety and eyelid conditioning. *Journal of Experimental Psychology*, 1966, *71*, 471–472.

Oomura, Y., Kimura, K., Ooyama, H., Maeno, T., Iki, M., & Kuniyoshi, M. Reciprocal activities of the ventromedial and lateral hypothalamic areas of cats. *Science*, 1964, *143*, 484–485.

Orne, M. T., & Holland, C. C. On the ecological validity of laboratory deceptions. *International Journal of Psychiatry*, 1968, *6*, 282–293.

Orne, M. T., & Scheibe, K. E. The contribution of nondeprivation factors in the production of sensory deprivation effects: The psychology of the panic button. *Journal of Abnormal and Social Psychology*, 1964, *68*, 3–12.

Ornstein, R. *The psychology of consciousness*. San Francisco: Freeman, 1972.

Ornstein, R. E. *The nature of human consciousness: A book of readings*. San Francisco: Freeman, 1973.

Osgood, C. E. Can Tolman's theory of learning handle avoidance training? *Psychological Review*, 1950, *57*, 133–137.

Overmier, J. B., & Seligman, M. E. P. Effects of inescapable shock upon subsequent escape and avoidance responding. *Journal of Comparative and Physiological Psychology*, 1967, *63*, 28–33.

Owen, D. R. The 47,XYY male: A review. *Psychological Bulletin*. 1972, *78*, 209–233.

PAGANO, R. R., ROSE, R. M., STIVERS, R. M., & WARRENBURG, S. Sleep during transcendential meditation. *Science,* 1976, *191,* 308–310.

PAGE, H. A. The facilitation of experimental extinction by response prevention as a function of the acquisition of a new response. *Journal of Comparative and Physiological Psychology,* 1955, *48,* 14–16.

PAGE, M. M., & SCHEIDT, R. J. The elusive weapons effect: Demand awareness, evaluation apprehension, and slightly sophisticated subjects. *Journal of Personality and Social Psychology,* 1971, *20,* 304–318.

PALMER, J., & BYRNE, D. Attraction toward dominant and submissive strangers: Similarity versus complementarity. *Journal of Experimental Research in Psychology,* 1970, *4,* 108–115.

PAPEZ, J. W. A proposed mechanism of emotion. *Archives of Neurology and Psychiatry,* 1937, *38,* 725–743.

PATTERSON, M. L. An arousal model for interpersonal intimacy. *Psychological Review,* 1976, *83,* 235–245.

PATTY, R. A. Motive to avoid success and instructional set. *Sex Roles,* 1976, *2,* 81–83.

PATTY, R. A., & SAFFORD, S. F. Motive to avoid success, motive to avoid failure, state-trait anxiety, and performance. In C. D. Spielberger & I. G. Sarason (Eds.), *Stress and Anxiety* (Vol. 4). New York: Academic, 1976.

PENFIELD, W., & JASPER, H. H. *Epilepsy and the functional anatomy of the brain.* Boston: Little Brown, 1954.

PEPPER, S. A neural-identity theory of mind. In S. Hook (Ed.), *Dimensions of mind.* New York: Collier, 1959.

PERIN, C. T. Behavioral potentiality as a joint function of the amount of training and the degree of hunger at the time of extinction. *Journal of Experimental Psychology,* 1942, *30,* 93–113.

PFAFFMANN, C. Gustatory nerve impulses in rat, cat, and rabbit. *Journal of Neurophysiology,* 1955, *18,* 429–440.

PFAFFMANN, C. The pleasures of sensation. *Psychological Review,* 1960, *67,* 253–268.

PFAFFMANN, C., & BARE, J. K. Gustatory nerve discharges in normal and adrenalectomized rats. *Journal of Comparative and Physiological Psychology,* 1950, *43,* 320–324.

PIERSON, E. C., & D'ANTONIO, W. V. *Female and male: Dimensions of human sexuality.* Philadelphia: Lippincott, 1974.

PITTS, F. N. The biochemistry of anxiety. *Scientific American,* 1969, *220,* 69–75.

PLATT, J. R. Beauty: Pattern and change. In D. W. Fiske & S. R. Maddi (Eds.), *Functions of varied experience.* Homewood, Ill.: Dorsey, 1961.

PLISKOFF, S. S., & HAWKINS, T. D. Test of Deutsch's drive-decay theory of rewarding self-stimulation of the brain. *Science,* 1963, *141,* 823–824.

PLISKOFF, S. S., WRIGHT, J. E., & HAWKINS, T. D. Brain stimulation as a reinforcer: Intermittent schedules. *Journal of the Experimental Analysis of Behavior,* 1965, *8,* 75–88.

POPPER, K. R. *The logic of scientific discovery.* New York: Harper & Row, 1959.

POSCHEL, B. P. H. Do biological reinforcers act via the self-stimulation areas of the brain? *Physiology and Behavior,* 1968, *3,* 53–60.

POSTMAN, L. The history and present status of the law of effect. *Psychological Bulletin,* 1947, *44,* 489–563.

POSTMAN, L., BRONSON, W., & GROPPER, G. L. Is there a mechanism of perceptual defense? *Journal of Abnormal and Social Psychology,* 1953, *48,* 215–224.

POWLEY, T. L. The ventromedial hypothalamic syndrome, satiety, and a cephalic phase hypothesis. *Psychological Review,* 1977, *84,* 89–126.

Powley, T. L., & Keesey, R. E. Relationship of body weight to the lateral hypothalamic feeding syndrome. *Journal of Comparative and Physiological Psychology,* 1970, *70,* 25–36.

Premack, D. Toward empirical behavioral laws: I. Positive reinforcement. *Psychological Review,* 1959, *66,* 219–233.

Premack, D. Predicting instrumental performance from the independent rate of the contingent response. *Journal of Experimental Psychology,* 1961, *61,* 163–171.

Premack, D. Reinforcement theory. In D. Levine (Ed.), *Nebraska symposium on motivation.* Lincoln: University of Nebraska Press, 1965.

Premack, D. Catching up with common sense or two sides of a generalization: Reinforcement and punishment. In R. Glaser (Ed.), *The nature of reinforcement.* New York: Academic, 1971.

Pribram, K. H. Interrelations of psychology and the neurological disciplines. In S. Koch (Ed.), *Psychology: A study of a science* (Vol. 4). New York: McGraw-Hill, 1962.

Priest, R. F., & Sawyer, J. Proximity and peership: Bases of balance in interpersonal attraction. *American Journal of Sociology,* 1967, *7,* 21–27.

Pritchard, R. M. Stabilized images on the retina. *Scientific American,* 1961, *204,* 72–78.

Prokasy, W. F. The acquisition of observing responses in the absence of differential external reinforcement. *Journal of Comparative and Physiological Psychology,* 1956, *49,* 131–134.

Pureto, A., Deutsch, J. A., Mólina, F., & Roll, P. L. Rapid discrimination of rewarding nutrient by the upper gastrointestinal tract. *Science,* 1976, *192,* 485–486.

Quinsey, V. L. Some applications of adaptation-level theory to aversive behavior. *Psychological Bulletin,* 1970, *73,* 441–450.

Ramirez, I., & Fuller, J. L. Genetic influence on water and sweetened water consumption in mice. *Physiology and Behavior,* 1976, *16,* 163–168.

Ranson, S. W., Fischer, C., & Ingram, W. R. The hypothalamico-hypophyseal mechanism in diabetes insipidus. Paper read before Association for Research in Nervous and Mental Diseases, December 1936. In *The pituitary gland.* Baltimore, Md.: Williams and Wilkins, 1938.

Razran, G. The observable unconscious and the inferable conscious in current Soviet psychophysiology: Interoceptive conditioning, semantic conditioning, and the orienting reflex. *Psychological Review,* 1961, *68,* 81–147.

Reisen, A. H. Stimulation as a requirement for growth and function in behavioral development. In D. W. Fiske & S. R. Maddi (Eds.), *Functions of varied experience.* Homewood, Ill.: Dorsey, 1961.

Rescorla, R. A. Pavlovian conditioning and its proper control procedure. *Psychological Review,* 1967, *74,* 71–80.

Rescorla, R. A. Establishment of a positive reinforcer through contrast with shock. *Journal of Comparative and Physiological Psychology,* 1969, *67,* 260–263.

Rescorla, R. A., & LoLordo, V. M. Inhibition of avoidance behavior. *Journal of Comparative and Physiological Psychology,* 1965, *59,* 406–412.

Rescorla, R. A., & Solomon, R. L. Two-process learning theory: Relationships between Pavlovian conditioning and instrumental learning. *Psychological Review,* 1967, *74,* 151–182.

Reynolds, W. F., & Pavlik, W. B. Running speed as a function of drive, reward, and habit strength. *American Journal of Psychology,* 1960, *73,* 448–453.

Revusky, S. H. Hunger level during food consumption: Effects on subsequent preferences. *Psychonomic Science,* 1967, *7,* 109–110.

REVUSKY, S. H. Effects of thirst level during consumption of flavored water on subsequent preference. *Journal of Comparative and Physiological Psychology,* 1968, *66,* 777–779.

REVUSKY, S. H., & GARCIA, J. Learned associations over long delays. In C. H. Bower and J. T. Spence (Eds.), *The psychology of learning and motivation: Advances in research and theory* (Vol. 4). New York: Academic, 1970.

RICHMAN, C. L., GARDNER, J. T., Jr., MONTGOMERY, M. D., & BENEWICZ, K. L. Effects of body weight loss on position and brightness discrimination tasks. *Learning and Motivation,* 1970, *1,* 218–225.

RICHTER, C. P. Animal behavior and internal drives. *Quarterly Review of Biology,* 1927, *2,* 307–343.

RICHTER, C. P. Increased salt appetite in adrenalectomized rats. *American Journal of Physiology,* 1936, *115,* 155–161.

RICHTER, C. P. On the phenomenon of sudden death in animals and man. *Psychosomatic Medicine,* 1957, *19,* 191–198.

ROBERTS, L. E. Comparative psychophysiology of the electrodermal and cardiac control systems. In P. A. Obrist, A. H. Black, J. Brener, & L. V. DiCara (Eds.), *Cardiovascular psychophysiology.* Chicago: Aldine, 1974.

ROBERTS, L. E., LACROIX, J. M., & WRIGHT, M. Comparative studies of operant electrodermal and heart rate conditioning in curarized rats. In P. A. Obrist, A. H. Black, J. Brener, & L. V. DiCara (Eds.), *Cardiovascular psychophysiology.* Chicago: Aldine, 1974.

ROBBINS, D. Effect of duration of water reinforcement on running behavior and consummatory activity. *Journal of Comparative and Physiological Psychology,* 1969, *69,* 311–316.

ROBBINS, D. Partial reinforcement: A selective review of the alleyway literature since 1960. *Psychological Bulletin,* 1971, *76,* 415–431.

RODGERS, W. L., EPSTEIN, A. N., & TEITELBAUM, P. Lateral hypothalamic aphagia: Motor failure or motivational deficit? *American Journal of Physiology,* 1965, *208,* 334–342.

ROSEN, A. J., DAVIS, J. D., & LADLOVE, R. F. Electrocortical activity: Modification by food ingestion and a humoral satiety factor. *Communications in Behavioral Biology,* 1971, *6,* 323–327.

ROSENTHAL, R., & ROSNOW, R. L. (Eds.) *Artifact in behavioral research.* New York: Academic, 1969.

ROSVOLD, H. E., MIRSKY, A. F., & PRIBRAM, K. H. Influence of amygdalectomy on social behavior in monkeys. *Journal of Comparative and Physiological Psychology,* 1954, *47,* 173–178.

ROTTER, J. B. *Social learning and clinical psychology.* Englewood Cliffs, N.J.: Prentice-Hall, 1954.

ROTTER, J. B. Generalized expectancies for internal versus external control of reinforcement. *Psychological Monographs,* 1966, *80* (Whole No. 609).

ROUSSEL, J. S. Frustration effect as a function of repeated non-reinforcements and as a function of the consistency of reinforcement prior to the introduction of non-reinforcement. Unpublished master's thesis, Tulane University, 1952. Cited in Amsel, A. The role of frustrative nonreward in noncontinuous reward situations. *Psychological Bulletin,* 1958, *55,* 102–119.

ROUTTENBERG, A. The two-arousal hypothesis: Reticular formation and limbic system. *Psychological Review,* 1968, *75,* 51–80.

ROZIN, P., & KALAT, J. W. Specific hungers and poison avoidance as adaptive specializations of learning. *Psychological Review,* 1971, *78,* 459–486.

Rubin, Z. Measurement of romantic love. *Journal of Personality and Social Psychology,* 1970, *16,* 265–273.

Rubin, Z. *Liking and loving.* New York: Holt, Rinehart and Winston, 1973.

Ryle, G. *The concept of mind.* New York: Barnes & Noble, 1949.

Sales, S. Need for stimulation as a factor in social behavior. *Journal of Personality and Social Psychology,* 1971, *19,* 124–134.

Saltzman, I. J. Maze learning in the absence of primary reinforcement: A study of secondary reinforcement. *Journal of Comparative and Physiological Psychology,* 1949, *42,* 161–173.

Saltzman, I. J., & Koch, S. The effect of low intensities of hunger on the behavior mediated by a habit of maximum strength. *Journal of Experimental Psychology,* 1948, *38,* 347–370.

Schachter, S. *Emotion, obesity, and crime.* New York: Academic, 1971a.

Schachter, S. Some extraordinary facts about obese humans and rats. *American Psychologist,* 1971b, *26,* 129–144.

Schachter, S., & Singer, J. E. Cognitive, social, and physiological determinants of emotional state. *Psychological Review,* 1962, *69,* 379–399.

Schachter, S., & Wheeler, L. Epinephrine, chlorpromazine, and amusement. *Journal of Abnormal and Social Psychology,* 1962, *65,* 121–128.

Schachter, S. *The psychology of affiliation.* Palo Alto, Calif.: Stanford University Press, 1959.

Schaller, G. B. *The Serengeti lion.* Chicago: University of Chicago Press, 1972.

Schiffman, S. S., & Engelhard, H. H., III. Taste of dipeptides. *Physiology and Behavior,* 1976, *17,* 523–535.

Schlosberg, H. The relationship between success and the laws of conditioning. *Psychological Review,* 1937, *44,* 379–394.

Schmidt, H., Jr., Stewart, A. L., & Perez, V. J. Learned reduction of drinking latency. *Journal of Genetic Psychology,* 1967, *111,* 219–225.

Schneider, A. M., & Tarshis, B. *An introduction to physiological psychology.* New York: Random House, 1975.

Schneider, D. J. *Social psychology.* Reading, Mass.: Addison-Wesley, 1976.

Schoenfeld, W. N. An experimental approach to anxiety, escape, and avoidance behavior. In P. H. Hoch & J. Zubin (Eds.), *Anxiety.* New York: Grune & Stratton, 1950.

Schoenfeld, W. N., Antonitis, J. J., & Bersh, P. J. A preliminary study of training conditions necessary for secondary reinforcement. *Journal of Experimental Psychology,* 1950, *40,* 40–45.

Schopler, J., & Compere, J. S. Effects of being kind or harsh to another on liking. *Journal of Personality and Social Psychology,* 1971, *20,* 155–159.

Scott, J. P. *Aggression.* Chicago: University of Chicago Press, 1958.

Scott, J. P. Critical periods in behavioral development. *Science,* 1962, *138,* 949–958.

Scott, J. P. Theoretical issues concerning the origin and causes of fighting. In B. E. Eleftheriou & J. P. Scott (Eds.), *The physiology of aggression and defeat.* New York: Plenum, 1971.

Segal, M. W. Alphabet and attraction: An unobtrusive measure of the effect of propinquity in a field setting. *Journal of Personality and Social Psychology.* 1974, *30,* 654–657.

Seligman, M. E. P. On the generality of the laws of learning. *Psychological Review,* 1970, *77,* 406–418.

Seligman, M. E. P., Ives, C. E., Ames, H., & Mineka, S. Conditioned drinking and its failure to extinguish: Avoidance, preparedness, or functional autonomy? *Journal of Comparative and Physiological Psychology,* 1970, *71,* 411–419.

SELIGMAN, M. E. P., & JOHNSTON, J. C. In F. J. McGuigan & D. B. Lumsden (Eds.), *Contemporary approaches to conditioning and learning.* Washington, D.C.: Winston-Wiley, 1973.

SELIGMAN, M. E. P., & MAIER, S. F. Failure to escape traumatic shock. *Journal of Experimental Psychology,* 1967, *74,* 1–9.

SELIGMAN, M. E. P., MINEKA, S., & FILLIT, H. Conditioned drinking produced by procaine, NaCl, and angiotensin. *Journal of Comparative and Physiological Psychology,* 1971, *77,* 110–121.

SELYE, H. *The stress of life.* New York: McGraw-Hill, 1956.

SELYE, H. *Stress without distress.* Philadelphia: Lippincott, 1974.

SEWARD, J. P., SHEA, R. A., & ELKIND, D. Evidence for the interaction of drive and reward. *American Journal of Psychology,* 1958, *71,* 404–407.

SHANAB, M. E., & BILLER, J. D. Positive contrast in the runway obtained following a shift in both delay and magnitude of reward. *Learning and Motivation,* 1972, *3,* 179–184.

SHARMA, K. N., ANAND, B. K., DUA, S., & SINGH, B. Role of stomach in regulation of activities of hypothalamic feeding centers. *American Journal of Physiology,* 1961, *201,* 593–598.

SHEFFIELD, F. D. Avoidance training and the contiguity principle. *Journal of Comparative and Physiological Psychology,* 1948, *41,* 165–177.

SHEFFIELD, F. D. New evidence on the drive-induction theory of reinforcement. In R. N. Haber (Ed.), *Current research in motivation.* New York: Holt, Rinehart and Winston, 1966.

SHEFFIELD, F. D., & CAMPBELL, B. A. The role of experience in the "spontaneous" activity of hungry rats. *Journal of Comparative and Physiological Psychology,* 1954, *47,* 97–100.

SHEFFIELD, F. D., & ROBY, T. B. Reward value of a non-nutritive sweet taste. *Journal of Comparative and Physiological Psychology,* 1950, *43,* 471–481.

SHEFFIELD, F. D., WULFF, J. J., & BACKER, R. Reward value of copulation without sex drive reduction. *Journal of Comparative and Physiological Psychology,* 1951, *44,* 3–8.

SHERIDAN, C. L., & KING, R. G. Obedience to authority with an authentic victim. *Proceedings, Eightieth Annual Convention, American Psychological Association,* Honolulu, 1972, 165–166. Washington, D.D.: American Psychological Association.

SHIPLEY, T. E., & VEROFF, J. A projective measure of need for affiliation. *Journal of Experimental Psychology,* 1952, *43,* 349–356.

SIDMAN, M. Reduction of shock frequency as reinforcement for avoidance behavior. *Journal of the Experimental Analysis of Behavior,* 1962, *5,* 247–257.

SIDMAN, M. Avoidance behavior. In W. K. Honig (Ed.), *Operant behavior: Areas of research and application.* New York: Appleton-Century-Crofts, 1966.

SIEGEL, P. S., & MILBY, J. B. Secondary reinforcement in relation to shock termination. *Psychological Bulletin,* 1969, *72,* 146–156.

SIGALL, H., & LANDY, D. Radiating beauty: Effects of having a physically attractive partner on person perception. *Journal of Personality and Social Psychology,* 1973, *28,* 218–224.

SIMMONS, R. The relative effectiveness of certain incentives in animal learning. *Comparative Psychology Monographs,* 1924, *2* (Serial No. 7).

SKINNER, B. F. *The behavior of organisms.* New York: Appleton-Century-Crofts, 1938.

SKINNER, B. F. *Beyond freedom and dignity.* New York: Knopf, 1971.

SLUCKIN, W. *Imprinting and early learning.* Chicago: Aldine, 1965.

SMITH, K. A note on the possibility of a reinforcement theory of cognitive learning. *Bulletin of the Psychonomic Society,* 1974, *4,* 161–163.

SOKOLOV, E. N. Neuronal models of the orienting reflex. In M. A. B. Brazier (Ed.), *The central nervous system and behavior: Transaction of the third conference.* New York: Josiah Macy, Jr., Foundation, 1960.

SOLOMON, R. L. An extension of control group design. *Psychological Bulletin,* 1949, *46,* 137–150.

SOLOMON, R. L. Punishment. *American Psychologist,* 1964, *19,* 239–253.

SOLOMON, R. L., & BRUSH, E. S. Experimentally derived conceptions of anxiety and aversion. In M. R. Jones (Ed.), *Nebraska symposium on motivation.* Lincoln: University of Nebraska Press, 1956.

SOLOMON, R. L., & CORBIT, J. D. An opponent-process theory of motivation: I. Temporal dynamics of affect. *Psychological Review,* 1974, *81,* 119–145.

SOLOMON, R. L., & TURNER, L. H. Discriminative classical conditioning in dogs paralyzed by curare can later control discriminative avoidance responses in the normal state. *Psychological Review,* 1962, *69,* 202–219.

SOLOMON, R. L., & WYNNE, L. C. Avoidance conditioning in normal dogs and in dogs deprived of normal autonomic functioning. *American Psychologist,* 1950, *5,* 264.

SOLOMON, R. L., & WYNNE, L. C. Traumatic avoidance learning: The principles of anxiety conservation and partial irreversibility. *Psychological Review,* 1954, *61,* 353–385.

SOSA, J. N. Vascular effects of frustration on passive and aggressive members of a clinical population. Unpublished master's thesis, Florida State University, 1968.

SPENCE, K. W. The nature of theory construction in contemporary psychology. *Psychological Review,* 1944, *51,* 47–68.

SPENCE, K. W. Theoretical interpretations of learning. In S. S. Stevens (Ed.), *Handbook of Experimental Psychology.* New York: Wiley, 1951.

SPENCE, K. W. *Behavior theory and conditioning.* New Haven, Conn.: Yale University Press, 1956.

SPENCE, K. W. A theory of emotionally based drive (D) and its relation to performance in simple learning situations. *American Psychologist,* 1958, *13,* 131–141.

SPIELBERGER, C. D. Theory and research on anxiety. In C. D. Spielberger (Ed.), *Anxiety and behavior.* New York: Academic, 1966.

SPIELBERGER, C. D., & DeNIKE, L. D. Descriptive behaviorism versus cognitive theory in verbal operant conditioning. *Psychological Review,* 1966, *73,* 306–326.

SPRAGUE, J. M., CHAMBERS, W. W., & STELLAR, E. Attentive, affective, and adaptive behavior in the cat. *Science,* 1961, *133,* 165–173.

STAATS, A. W., STAATS, C. K., & CRAWFORD, H. First-order conditioning of meaning and parallel conditioning of GSR. *Journal of General Psychology,* 1962, *67,* 159–167.

STADDON, J. E. R. Temporal control, attention, and memory. *Psychological Review,* 1974, *81,* 375–391.

STAVELY, H. E., Jr. Effect of escape duration and shock intensity on the acquisition and extinction of an escape response. *Journal of Experimental Psychology,* 1966, *72,* 698–703.

STEGGERDA, F. R. Observations on the water intake in an adult man with dysfunctioning salivary glands. *American Journal of Physiology,* 1941, *132,* 517–521.

STEINER, W. G. Electrical activity of rat brain as a correlate of primary drive. *Electroencephalography and Clinical Neurophysiology,* 1962, *14,* 233–243.

STELLAR, E. The physiology of motivation. *Psychological Review,* 1954, *61,* 5–22.

STERN, R. M., BOTTO, R. W., & HERRICK, C. D. Behavioral and physiological effects of false heart rate feedback: A replication and extension. *Psychophysiology,* 1972, *9,* 21–29.

STERRITT, G. M., & SMITH, M. P. Reinforcement effects of specific components of feeding in young leghorn chicks. *Journal of Comparative and Physiological Psychology,* 1965, *59,* 171–175.

STEVENS, S. S. Psychology and the science of science. *Psychological Bulletin,* 1939, *36,* 221–263.

STEVENSON, J. A. F., WELT, L. G., & ORLOFF, J. Abnormalities of water and electrolyte metabolism in rats with hypothalamic lesions. *American Journal of Physiology,* 1950, *161,* 35–39.

STORMS, L. H., & BROEN, W. E., Jr. Drive theories and stimulus generalization. *Psychological Review,* 1966, *73,* 113–127.

STORMS, M. D., & NISBETT, R. E. Insomnia and the attribution process. *Journal of Personality and Social Psychology,* 1970, *16,* 319–328.

STROEBE, W. C., INSKO, A., THOMPSON, V. D., & LAYTON, B. D. Effects of physical attractiveness, attitude similarity, and sex on various aspects of interpersonal attraction. *Journal of Personality and Social Psychology,* 1971, *18,* 79–91.

STRONG, P. N., Jr. Activity in the white rat as a function of apparatus and hunger. *Journal of Comparative and Physiological Psychology,* 1957, *50,* 596–600.

STUTZ, R. M., LEWIN, I., & ROCKLIN, K. W. Generality of "drive-decay" as an explanatory concept. *Psychonomic Science,* 1965, *2,* 127–128.

SUTTERER, J. R., & BECK, R. C. Human responses to stimuli associated with shock onset and termination. *Journal of Experimental Research in Personality,* 1970, *4,* 163–170.

TANG, M., & COLLIER, G. Effect of successive deprivations and recoveries on the level of instrumental performance in the rat. *Journal of Comparative and Physiological Psychology,* 1971, *74,* 108–114.

TANNENBAUM, P. H., & ZILLMANN, D. Emotional arousal in the facilitation of aggression through communication. In L. Berkowitz (Ed.), *Advances in experimental social psychology* (Vol. 8). New York: Academic, 1975.

TAPP, J. T. Activity, reactivity, and the behavior-directing properties of stimuli. In J. T. Tapp (Ed.), *Reinforcement and behavior.* New York: Academic, 1969.

TARPY, R. M. Reinforcement difference limen (RDL) for delay in shock escape. *Journal of Experimental Psychology,* 1969, *79,* 116–121.

TART, C. T. *Altered states of consciousness: A book of readings.* New York: Wiley, 1969.

TAUB, E., & BERMAN, A. J. Movement and learning in the absence of sensory feedback. In S. J. Freedman (Ed.), *The neuropsychology of spatially oriented behavior.* Homewood, Ill.: Dorsey, 1968.

TAYLOR, J. A. A personality scale of manifest anxiety. *Journal of Abnormal and Social Psychology,* 1953, *48,* 285–290.

TEDESCHI, J. T., SMITH, R. B., III, & BROWN, R. C., Jr. A reinterpretation of research on aggression. *Psychological Bulletin,* 1974, *81,* 540–562.

TEITELBAUM, P. Disturbances in feeding and drinking behavior after hypothalamic lesions. In M. R. Jones (Ed.), *Nebraska symposium on motivation.* Lincoln: University of Nebraska Press, 1961.

TEITELBAUM, P. The encephalization of hunger. In E. Stellar & J. M. Sprague (Eds.), *Progress in physiological psychology,* New York: Academic, 1971.

TEITELBAUM, P., & CYTAWA, J. Spreading depression and recovery from lateral hypothalamic damage. *Science,* 1965, *147,* 61–63.

Teitelbaum, P., & Epstein, A. N. The lateral hypothalamic syndrome: Recovery of feeding and drinking after lateral hypothalamic lesions. *Psychological Review,* 1962, *69,* 74–90.

Teitelbaum, P., & Epstein, A. N. The role of taste and smell in the regulation of food and water intake. In Y. Zottermam (Ed.), *Olfaction and taste.* New York: Macmillan, 1963.

Theios, J. Drive stimulus generalization increments. *Journal of Comparative and Physiological Psychology,* 1963, *56,* 691–695.

Thistlethwaite, D. A critical review of latent learning and related experiments. *Psychological Bulletin,* 1951, *48,* 97–129.

Thompson, R. F. *Introduction to physiological psychology.* New York: Harper & Row, 1975.

Thompson, T. I., & Sturm, T. Visual reinforcer color and operant behavior in the Siamese fighting fish. *Journal of the Experimental Analysis of Behavior,* 1965, *8,* 341–344.

Thorndike, E. L. *Educational psychology.* Vol. 2. *The psychology of learning.* New York: Columbia University Press, 1913.

Thorndike, E. L. *The fundamentals of learning.* New York: Columbia University Press, 1932.

Thorpe, W. H. *Learning and instinct in animals.* (2nd ed.) London: Methuen, 1963.

Tinklepaugh, O. L. An experimental study of representative factors in monkeys. *Journal of Comparative Psychology,* 1928, *8,* 197–236.

Tinbergen, N. *The study of instinct.* Oxford: Clarendon, 1951.

Tinbergen, N. The curious behavior of the stickleback. *Scientific American,* 1952, *187,* 22–60.

Titchener, E. B. An historical note on the James-Lange theory of emotion. *American Journal of Psychology,* 1914, *25,* 425–447.

Toch, H. The social psychology of violence. Division 8 invited address, American Psychological Association Meeting, New York, September 1966. Reprinted in E. I. Megargee & J. E. Hokanson (Eds.), *The dynamics of aggression: Individual, group and international analyses.* New York: Harper & Row, 1970.

Tolman, E. C. Purposive behavior in animals and men. New York: Appleton-Century-Crofts, 1932.

Tolman, E. C. The determiners of behavior at a choice point. *Psychological Review,* 1938, *45,* 1–41.

Tolman, E. C. Cognitive maps in rats and men. *Psychological Review,* 1948, *55,* 189–208.

Tolman, E. C. Principles of purposive behavior. In S. Koch (Ed.), *Psychology: A study of a science.* (Vol. 2) New York: McGraw-Hill, 1959.

Tolman, E. C., & Honzik, C. H. Degrees of hunger; reward and nonreward; and maze learning in rats. *University of California Publications in Psychology,* 1930, *4,* 241–256.

Toulmin, S. *The philosophy of science—An introduction.* London: Hutchinson, 1953.

Towbin, E. J. Gastric distention as a factor in the satiation of thirst in esophagustomized dogs. *American Journal of Physiology,* 1949, *159,* 533–541.

Trapold, M. A., & Overmier, J. B. The second learning process in instrumental learning. In A. H. Black & W. F. Prokasy (Eds.), *Classical conditioning.* II. *Current theory and research.* New York: Appleton-Century-Crofts, 1972.

Trapold, M. A., & Winokur, S. Transfer from classical conditioning and extinction to acquisition, extinction, and stimulus generalization of a positively reinforced instrumental response. *Journal of Experimental Psychology,* 1967, *73,* 517–525.

TREICHLER, F. R., & HALL, J. F. The relationship between deprivation weight loss and several measures of activity. *Journal of Comparative and Physiological Psychology,* 1962, *55,* 346–349.

TRIPPLET, N. The dynamogenic factors in pacemaking and competition. *American Journal of Psychology,* 1897, *9,* 507–533.

TROWILL, J. A., PANKSEPP, J., & GANDELMAN, R. An incentive model of rewarding brain stimulation. *Psychological Review,* 1969, *76,* 264–281.

TRYON, R. C. Genetic differences in maze learning in rats. In National Society for the Study of Education, *The thirty-ninth yearbook.* Bloomington, Ill.: Public School Publishing, 1940.

TURNER, M. B. *Philosophy and the science of behavior.* New York: Appleton-Century-Crofts, 1967.

ULEMAN, J. S. The need for influence: Development and validation of a measure, and comparison with the need for power. *Genetic Psychological Monographs,* 1972, *85,* 157–214.

ULRICH, R. E., & AZRIN, N. H. Reflexive fighting in response to aversive stimulation. *Journal of the Experimental Analysis of Behavior,* 1962, *5,* 511–520.

ULRICH, R. E., & CRAINE, W. H. Behavior: Persistence of shock-induced aggression. *Science,* 1964, *143,* 971–973.

UNDERWOOD, B. J. *Psychological research.* New York: Appleton-Century-Crofts, 1957.

VALENSTEIN, E. *Brain control: A critical examination of brain stimulation and psychosurgery.* New York: Wiley, 1973.

VALENSTEIN, E. S., COX, V. C., & KAKOLEWSKI, J. W. Re-examination of the role of the hypothalamus in motivation. *Psychological Review,* 1970, *77,* 16–31.

VALENSTEIN, E. S., KAKOLEWSKI, J. W., & COX, V. C. Sex differences in taste preference for glucose and saccharin solutions. *Science,* 1967, *156,* 942–943.

VALENTINE, C. W. The innate bases of fear. *Journal of Genetic Psychology,* 1930, *37,* 394–419.

VALINS, S. Cognitive effects of false heart-rate feedback. *Journal of Personality and Social Psychology,* 1966, *4,* 400–408.

VALINS, S. The perception and labeling of bodily changes as determinants of emotional behavior. In P. Black (Ed.), *Physiological correlates of emotion.* New York: Academic, 1970.

VAN DE CASTLE, R. L. *The psychology of dreaming.* Morristown, N.J.: General Learning Press, 1971.

VERNON, W. Animal aggression: Review of research. *Genetic Psychology Monographs,* 1969, *80,* 3–28.

VERNON, W. M., & ULRICH, R. E. Classical conditioning of pain-elicited aggression. *Science,* 1966, *152,* 668–669.

VEROFF, J. Development and validation of a projective measure of power motivation. *Journal of Abnormal and Social Psychology,* 1957, *54,* 1–8.

VERPLANCK, W. S., & HAYES, J. R. Eating and drinking as a function of maintenance schedule. *Journal of Comparative and Physiological Psychology,* 1953, *46,* 327–333.

VON FRISCH, K. *The dance language and orientation of bees.* Cambridge, Mass.: Harvard University Press, 1967.

VON FRISCH, K. *Bees: Their vision, chemical senses, and language.* (2nd ed.) Ithaca, N.Y.: Cornell University Press, 1971.

VON HOLST, E., & VON ST. PAUL, U. Electrically controlled behavior. *Scientific American,* 1962, *206,* 50–59.

VORSTEG, R. H. Operant reinforcement theory and determinism. *Behaviorism,* 1974, *2,* 108–119.

WAGNER, A. R. Conditioned frustration as a learned drive. *Journal of Experimental Psychology*, 1963, *66*, 142–148.

WALKER, E. L. Reinforcement—"The one ring." In J. T. Tapp (Ed.), *Reinforcement and behavior*. New York: Academic, 1969.

WALLACE, R. K., & BENSON, H. The physiology of meditation. *Scientific American*, 1972, *226*, 84–90.

WALSTER, E. Passionate love. In B. Murstein (Ed.), *Theories of attraction and love*. New York: Springer, 1971.

WALSTER, E., ARONSON, E., ABRAHAMS, D., & ROTTMAN, L. Importance of physical attractiveness in dating behavior. *Journal of Personality and Social Psychology*, 1966, *4*, 508–516.

WARREN, R. M., & PFAFFMANN, C. Early experience and taste aversion. *Journal of Comparative and Physiological Psychology*, 1958, *52*, 263–266.

WATSON, J. B. *Psychology from the standpoint of a behaviorist*. Philadelphia: Lippincott, 1924.

WATSON, J. B., & RAYNER, R. Conditioned emotional reactions. *Journal of Experimental Psychology*, 1920, *3*, 1–14.

WAYNER, W. J., Jr., & REIMANIS, G. Drinking in the rat induced by hypertonic saline. *Journal of Comparative and Physiological Psychology*, 1958, *51*, 11–15.

WEBB, W. B. The motivational aspect of an irrelevant drive in the behavior of the white rat. *Journal of Experimental Psychology*, 1949, *39*, 1–14.

WEBB, W. B. Drive stimuli as cues. *Psychological Reports*, 1955, *1*, 287–298.

WEBB, W. B. *Sleep: An experimental approach*. New York: Macmillan, 1968.

WEBB, W. B. (Ed.), *Sleep: An active process*. Glenview, Ill.: Scott, Foresman, 1973.

WEBER, M. *The Protestant ethic and the spirit of capitalism*. (T. Parsons, Trans.) New York: Scribner, 1930. Originally published 1904.

WEINER, B. *Theories of motivation: From mechanism to cognition*. Chicago: Markham, 1972.

WEINER, B. An attributional interpretation of expectancy-value theory. In B. Weiner (Ed.), *Cognitive views of motivation*. New York: Academic, 1974.

WEINER, B., and KUKLA, A. An attributional analysis of achievement motivation. *Journal of Personality and Social Psychology*, 1970, *15*, 1–20.

WEISS, J. M. Psychological factors in stress and disease. *Scientific American*, 1972, *226*, 104–113.

WEISS, J. M., POHORECKY, L. A., SALMAN, S., & GRUENTHAL, M. Attenuation of gastric lesions by psychological aspects of aggression in rats. *Journal of Comparative and Physiological Psychology*, 1976, *90*, 252–259.

WEISS, R. F., & MILLER, F. G. The drive theory of social facilitation. *Psychological Review*, 1971, *78*, 44–57.

WHITE, T. H. *The bestiary: A book of beasts*. New York: Putnam, 1954.

WICKENS, D. D., & MILES, R. C. Extinction changes during a series of reinforcement-extinction sessions. *Journal of Comparative and Physiological Psychology*, 1954, *47*, 315–317.

WIKE, E. L. *Secondary reinforcement: Selected experiments*. New York: Harper & Row, 1966.

WIKE, E. L., & CASEY, A. The secondary reward value of food for satiated animals. *Journal of Comparative and Physiological Psychology*, 1954, *47*, 441–443.

WILCOXIN, H. C., DRAGOIN, W. B., & KRAL, P. A. Illness-induced aversions in rat and quail: Relative salience of visual and gustatory cues. *Science*, 1971, *171*, 826–828.

WILLIAMS, D. R., & TEITELBAUM, P. Control of drinking by means of an operant conditioning technique. *Science*, 1956, *124*, 1294–1296.

WILLIAMS, J. E., & BENNETT, S. M. The definition of sex stereotypes via the Adjective Check List. *Sex Roles,* 1975, *1,* 327–337.

WILLIAMS, J. E., & MORLAND, J. K. *Race, color, and the young child.* Chapel Hill, N.C.: University of North Carolina Press, 1976.

WILLIAMS, R. A. Effects of repeated food deprivations and repeated feeding tests on feeding behavior. *Journal of Comparative and Physiological Psychology,* 1968, *65,* 222–226.

WILLIAMS, S. B. Resistance to extinction as a function of the number of reinforcements. *Journal of Experimental Psychology,* 1938, *23,* 506–521.

WILSON, E. O. *Sociobiology, the new synthesis.* Cambridge, Mass.: Belknap Press of Harvard University Press, 1975.

WINCH, R. F. *Mate selection: A study of complementary needs.* New York: Harper & Row, 1958.

WINTER, D. G. *The power motive.* New York: Free Press, 1973.

WITKIN, H. A., MEDNICK, S. A., SCHULSINGER, F., BAKKESTRØM, E., CHRISTIANSEN, K. O., GOODENOUGH, D. R., HIRSCHHORN, K., LUNDSTEEN, C., OWEN, D. R., PHILIP, J., RUBIN, D. B., & STOCKING, M. Criminality in XYY and XXY men. *Science,* 1976, *193,* 547–555.

WOLF, A. V. *Thirst: Physiology of the urge to drink and problems of water lack.* Springfield, Ill.: Thomas, 1958.

WOLFE, J. B., & KAPLON, M. D. Effect of amount of reward and consummative activity on learning in chickens. *Journal of Comparative Psychology,* 1941, *31,* 353–361.

WOLFGANG, M. E. Victim-precipitated criminal homicide. *Journal of Criminal Law, Criminology, and Police Science,* 1957, *48,* 1–11.

WONG, R. *Motivation: A biobehavioral analysis of consummatory activities.* New York: Macmillan, 1976.

WOODS, P. J. Performance changes in escape conditioning following shifts in the magnitude of reinforcement. *Journal of Experimental Psychology,* 1967, *75,* 487–491.

WOODS, P. J., DAVIDSON, E. H., & PETERS, R. J., Jr. Instrumental escape conditioning in a water tank: Effects of variations in drive stimulus intensity and reinforcement magnitude. *Journal of Comparative and Physiological Psychology,* 1964, *57,* 466–470.

WOODWORTH, R. S. *Dynamic psychology.* New York: Columbia University Press, 1918.

WOODWORTH, R. S., & SCHLOSBERG, H. *Experimental psychology.* (rev. ed.) New York: Holt, Rinehart and Winston, 1954.

World Plan Executive Council. *Fundamentals of progress: Scientific research on Transcendental Meditation program.* Los Angeles: Maharishi International University Press, 1974.

WRIGHT, J. H. Test for a learned drive based on the hunger drive. *Journal of Experimental Psychology,* 1965, *70,* 580–584.

WRIGHTSMAN, L. S., Jr. Effects of waiting with others on changes in level of felt anxiety. *Journal of Abnormal and Social Psychology,* 1960, *61,* 216–222.

WYCKOFF, L. B. The role of observing responses in discrimination learning, Part 1. *Psychological Review,* 1952, *59,* 431–442.

WYCKOFF, L. B., SIDOWSKI, J., & CHAMBLISS, D. J. An experimental study of the relationship between secondary reinforcing and cue effects of a stimulus. *Journal of Comparative and Physiological Psychology,* 1958, *51,* 103–109.

WYNNE-EDWARDS, V. C. *Animal dispersion in relation to social behavior.* New York: Hafner, 1962.

WYRWICKA, W., & DOBRZECKA, C. Relationship between feeding and satiation centers of the hypothalamus. *Science,* 1960, *132,* 805–806.

YAMAGUCHI, H. G. Gradients of drive stimulus ($S_d$) intensity generalization. *Journal of Experimental Psychology,* 1952, *43,* 298–304.

YATES, A. J. *Frustration and conflict.* New York: Wiley, 1962.

YERKES, R. M., & DODSON, J. D. The relation of strength of stimulus to rapidity of habit-formation. *Journal of Comparative and Neurological Psychology,* 1908, *18,* 459–482.

YOUNG, P. T. The role of affective processes in learning and motivation. *Psychological Review,* 1959, *66,* 104–125.

YOUNG, P. T. *Motivation and emotion: A survey of the determinants of human and animal activity.* New York: Wiley, 1961.

YOUNG, P. T. Hedonic organization and regulation of behavior. *Psychological Review,* 1966, *73,* 59–86.

YOUNG, P. T. Evaluation and preferences in behavioral development. *Psychological Review,* 1968, *75,* 222–241.

YOUNG, P. T., & CHAPLIN, J. P. Studies of food preference, appetite, and dietary habit. III. Palatability and appetite in relation to bodily need. *Comparative Psychology Monographs,* 1945, *18,* (3, Whole No. 95).

ZAJONC, R. B. Social facilitation. *Science,* 1965, *149,* 269–274.

ZAJONC, R. B. Attitudinal effects of mere exposure. *Journal of Personality and Social Psychology Monograph Supplements,* 1968, *9,* (2, Pt. 2), 1–27.

ZAJONC, R. B., & SALES, S. M. Social facilitation of dominant and subordinate responses. *Journal of Experimental Social Psychology,* 1966, *2,* 160–168.

ZEAMAN, D. Response latency as a function of the amount of reinforcement. *Journal of Experimental Psychology,* 1949, *39,* 466–483.

ZEIGLER, H. P. Displacement activity and motivational theory: A case study in the history of ethology. *Psychological Bulletin,* 1964, *61,* 362–376.

ZIMBARDO, P. G. The cognitive control of motivation. *Transactions of the New York Academy of Sciences,* 1966, Series II, *28,* 902–922.

ZIMBARDO, P. The human choice: Individuation, reason, and order versus deindividuation, impulse, and chaos. In W. Arnold & M. Levine (Eds.), *Nebraska symposium on motivation.* Lincoln: University of Nebraska Press, 1969.

ZIMMERMAN, D. W. Durable secondary reinforcement: Method and theory. *Psychological Review,* 1957, *64,* 373–383.

ZIMMERMAN, D. W. Sustained performance in rats based on secondary reinforcement. *Journal of Comparative and Physiological Psychology,* 1959, *52,* 353–358.

ZOTTERMAN, YNGVE. Studies in the neural mechanisms of taste. In W. A. Rosenblith (Ed.), *Sensory communication.* New York: M.I.T. Press and John Wiley & Sons, 1961.

# Name Index

# Subject Index